REAI   'E EASTERN MEDITERRANEAN

Fi   e Cyprus Crisis to Carter and
                              urkish Arms Embargo

Realpolitik in the Eastern Mediterranean

From Kissinger and the Cyprus Crisis
to Carter and the Lifting of the
Turkish Arms Embargo

Chris P. Ioannides

PELLA

PELLA PUBLISHING COMPANY, INC.

New York, NY 10018-6401

2001

48460659   10-21-02

This book was published for The Center for Byzantine and Modern Greek Studies, Queens College of the City University of New York, which bears full editorial responsibility for its contents.

MODERN GREEK RESEARCH SERIES, X, SEPTEMBER 2001

REALPOLITIK IN THE EASTERN MEDITERRANEAN

From Kissinger and the Cyprus Crisis to Carter and

the Lifting of the Turkish Arms Embargo

© Copyright 2001
by
Chris P. Ioannides

Library of Congress Control Number 01-132435

ISBN 0-918618-81-9

ACKNOWLEDGMENTS
This publication was made possible, in part, by grants from the Alexander S. Onassis Public Benefit Foundation and from the City Council of New York, and its speaker, Peter F. Vallone, to the Queens College Center for Byzantine and Modern Greek Studies.

PRINTED IN THE UNITED STATES OF AMERICA
BY
ATHENS PRINTING COMPANY
337 West 36th Street
New York, NY 10018-6401

To Angelo K. Tsakopoulos
The Man from Rizes

MODERN GREEK RESEARCH SERIES

The purpose of this monograph series is to promote and disseminate scholarly works on the history, institutions, and the culture of the Greek people. It is sponsored and edited by the Center for Byzantine and Modern Greek Studies, Queens College of the City University of New York (formerly jointly with the Greek Seminar of the Center for Mediterranean Studies of the American University). This is the tenth publication within the framework of the Modern Greek Research Project—Harry J. Psomiades, Professor of Political Science, Queens College of the City University of New York, Director.

MODERN GREEK RESEARCH SERIES

Table of Contents

Introduction

Memoirs Without Memories of the Embargo

On October 3, 1974, the U.S. Congress took an almost unprecedented step in the annals of American foreign policy. It imposed an arms embargo against a NATO ally, Turkey, and did so over the strong objections of the executive branch, in this case President Gerald Ford and Secretary of State Henry Kissinger. The congressional embargo against Turkey was imposed in the aftermath of the Turkish invasion of the island republic in July and August 1974. The embargo was implemented because Congress reasoned that Turkey, a close American ally, had used U.S. arms for offensive purposes—the invasion of Cyprus—in violation of American law. The first phase of the invasion took place on July 20. On July 15, a military coup had overthrown the democratically elected president of Cyprus, Archbishop Makarios. The coup was engineered by the Greek military junta in Athens, which had been backed by the United States.

The Cyprus crisis in the summer of 1974 had a lasting effect on relations between the United States and two of its NATO allies, Greece and Turkey. Moreover, the Cyprus-Greece-Turkey triangle had important implications for American politics. Congress and the president found themselves in antagonistic camps as they vied for preeminence in foreign policy. The seed of discord was the embargo on arms sales to Turkey because it was through the embargo that Congress sought to assert its role in foreign policy.

Since that time, a plethora of books, articles, papers, and newspaper reports have been written on the imposition of the embargo, the assertiveness of Congress in foreign policy, and the role the "Greek lobby" has played in influencing Congress to make such an important decision. During the 1970s, the Greek lobby assumed mythical proportions. Indeed, it came to be considered the most powerful and effective lobby, second only to the Jewish lobby, even though its influence gradually diminished following the lifting of the embargo.

Nearly four years after the imposition of the embargo, President Jimmy Carter, who succeeded Gerald Ford, led a successful drive for its repeal. He did so despite pledges to the contrary made to the Greek American community during the campaign for the presidential election of 1976. Carter's repeal of the embargo represented a classic battle between the executive branch and Congress. In addition, the lifting of the embargo had serious effects in the Eastern Mediterranean because of its bearing on American interests in the area. In contrast to the wealth of material on the imposition of the embargo, however, relatively little has been written about its repeal. It was for this reason that I embarked upon writing a book on the political dynamics of the process that led to the lifting of the embargo. The repeal of the embargo represents an important but quite neglected subject of the Carter presidency.

There can be no meaningful understanding of the Carter administration's decision to lift the embargo without background on the Cyprus crisis in the summer of 1974, the crisis that led to the imposition of the embargo. The two core events of the Cyprus crisis, the military coup d'etat against Makarios and the Turkish invasion of Cyprus, occurred in July and August 1974 as the Watergate scandal was reaching its climax and presidential decision-making had become paralyzed. At the same time, the military dictatorship that had ruled Greece since April 1967 collapsed under the weight of the Cyprus crisis. The year 1974 was a tumultuous one for the United States. People remember it as the year when one of the most acute political crises in the history of the American republic occurred. The U.S. constitution calls for the impeachment of a president only if he has committed "treason or high crimes and misdemeanors." President Richard Nixon found himself close to being charged with an impeachable offense since he had abused the power of his office. Because of the Watergate scandal, Nixon was forced to resign on August 8, 1974. He was the only president to do so in the history of the republic.

When the purpose of a study is to throw light on the foreign policy of certain presidents, it is important to examine the memoirs of those presidents and their foreign policy teams. In order to gain a better understanding of decision-making during this period, I read the memoirs of a number of U.S. officials, including Nixon and Ford and the secretary of state under both of them, Henry Kissinger. By the time the embargo was imposed, in October 1974, President Nixon had already resigned and, in his memoirs, he did not have much to say about the embargo. He did refer, however, to the Cyprus crisis and the coup against Makarios.[1] President Ford referred mostly to the embargo in his memoirs. His focus was on his efforts to persuade Congress to lift the embargo.[2]

More importantly, Kissinger, the key player during the Cyprus crisis and its aftermath, wrote extensively about the crisis and the imposition of the embargo, devoting a rather long chapter in the third and last volume of his memoirs to these topics.[3] He also discussed the crisis in the second volume of his memoirs.[4] In his writings, the former secretary of state provided his interpretation of the nature of ethnic conflict in Cyprus as background for the crisis. He presented the role played by American diplomacy during the crisis, starting with the coup against Makarios and culminating in the Turkish invasion and its immediate aftermath. Finally, Kissinger presented a highly critical view of the role of Congress in "micro-managing" foreign policy. He offered the imposition of the arms embargo against Turkey as an example of congressional encroachment on the president's authority to conduct foreign policy.

The Cyprus crisis and its handling by Kissinger became a major controversy over which the secretary of state and Congress clashed. Kissinger already had a contentious relationship with the Congress, which was controlled by Democrats. Throughout his tenure in the Nixon administration, both as national security adviser and secretary of state, Kissinger clashed repeatedly with Congress over foreign policy. Kissinger's view of Congress was rather paternalistic. He resented congressional scrutiny of a number of controversial decisions the Nixon administration had made. These included the escalation of the Vietnam War, the secret bombing of Cambodia, the mishandling of the India-Pakistan War in 1971, the overthrow of Chile's president, Salvador Allende, and the sudden cut-off of aid to Kurdish rebels in Iraq.

---

[1]Richard Nixon, *The Memoirs of Richard Nixon* (New York: A Touchstone Book, The Richard Nixon Library Edition, 1990), p. 1047.

[2]Gerald Ford, *A Time to Heal* (New York: Harper and Row, 1979), pp. 137–138.

[3]Henry Kissinger, *Years of Renewal* (New York: Simon and Schuster, 1999). See esp. chapter 7, "Cyprus, a Case Study in Ethnic Conflict," pp. 192–239.

[4]Henry Kissinger, *Years of Upheaval* (Boston, Toronto: Little Brown and Co., 1982), pp. 1187–1193.

Domestic opposition to the Vietnam War was the main reason that Nixon manufactured an "enemies list," which, in turn, led to a series of illegal activities and abuse of power. The logical consequence was the Watergate scandal and the resignation of Nixon in disgrace. While Kissinger had managed to survive the Watergate scandal and was retained as secretary of state by Ford, in the final analysis, Kissinger was part and parcel of the Nixon era. During that era, he had been the most important political actor in the United States after Nixon. In fact, for a few months in the spring and summer of 1974, when the Nixon presidency was paralyzed due to Watergate, Kissinger, for all practical purposes, exercised the powers of the president. In the end, Kissinger served Nixon well. He was an essential part of the Nixon era that created the mentality that led to the abuse of power and the Watergate scandal.[5]

Under these circumstances, at a time when Congress had become the defender of the constitution and the rule of law against the abuses of the Nixon administration, Kissinger, Nixon's right hand, could not but have had an antagonistic relationship with Capitol Hill. The secretary of state certainly had many admirers for his successes in foreign policy. The Nixon-Kissinger opening to China and Kissinger's legendary shuttle diplomacy in the Middle East were remarkable achievements indeed. Still, Kissinger could not disassociate himself morally or politically from the abuses of the Nixon era. As a consequence, Kissinger's relations with Congress, especially after 1973, were carried out under a cloud of mistrust for the secretary of state.

The Cyprus crisis in the summer of 1974 precipitated an open clash not only regarding the decisions made by Kissinger during the crisis, but also regarding earlier policies of the Nixon administration, especially its support for the Greek military junta. This support is well documented. There is convincing evidence that the Nixon adminis-

---

[5]For a critical and thoroughly documented study on Kissinger, his role in the Nixon White House, and his role in foreign policy decision-making and in the abuse of power during that era, see Seymour Hersch, *The Price of Power: Kissinger in the Nixon White House* (New York: Summit Books, 1983). For a somewhat more favorable study on Kissinger but one that is still critical of several of his policies, see Walter Isaacson, *Kissinger: A Biography* (New York: A Touchstone Book, 1992). For a favorable study on Kissinger, see Marvin Kalb and Bernard Kalb, *Kissinger: The Virtuoso of Diplomacy, the Legend, the Dazzle, the Man Within* (New York: Dell Publishing, 1975).

tration condoned the July 15, 1974 coup against Makarios, which was engineered by the U.S.-backed Greek junta. As for the Turkish invasion of Cyprus, which ensued on July 20, 1974, the record is becoming increasingly clear that Secretary of State Kissinger condoned the first phase of the invasion, resulting in the occupation of about 8 percent of Cypriot territory. More importantly, a series of American actions, as well as a failure to act, facilitated the second phase of the invasion on August 14, which led to the occupation of an additional 30 percent of the Republic of Cyprus.

In his memoirs, Kissinger focused on the decisions he had to make during the Turkish invasion of Cyprus in an effort to avert a general Greek-Turkish conflagration in the Eastern Mediterranean. These decisions were made as the Watergate scandal was reaching its climax, with Nixon's resignation occurring on August 8, 1974. The former secretary of state offered a dramatic picture of the paralysis at the White House and how it affected the decision-making process during the Cyprus crisis. In the absence of presidential authority due to the Watergate paralysis, Kissinger assumed, de facto, the responsibilities of the president when it came to making critical foreign policy decisions during that period. In the end, the ultimate responsibility for managing or mismanaging the Cyprus crisis of July and August 1974 fell on the shoulders of Secretary of State Henry Kissinger.

In November 1976, the Nixon-Kissinger era ended formally with the victory of Georgia Governor Jimmy Carter over President Gerald Ford. It is generally accepted that Carter was a man of integrity who came to office in order to restore the faith of the American public in the institutions of government. The Carter administration was to be one of truthfulness and transparency. There was to be no place in this administration for misleading Congress, in contrast to the Nixon presidency, which had betrayed public trust. Indeed, Carter's election campaign in 1975 and 1976 emphasized character, integrity, trustworthiness, and ethical values.

Trust, morality, and competence became the focus of Carter's successful campaign strategy.[6] It appeared that Carter and his campaign team tended to equate moral leadership with moral character.[7]

---

[6]See Kenneth Morris, *Jimmy Carter: American Moralist* (Athens, Georgia: University of Georgia Press, 1996), pp. 210–213.

[7]On this subject, see ibid., pp. 212–214.

In the campaign, Carter allowed his moral character to be contrasted with that of Nixon and Vice President Spiro Agnew. While avoiding direct attacks on Nixon and Agnew for being dishonest, Carter attacked them indirectly and successfully.[8] Privately, however, Carter could not hide his contempt for Nixon.[9]

Throughout the campaign for the White House, Carter's "contract" with the American people revolved around the promise: "I will never lie to you." This was not just a response to the need of the times, but it was also a reflection of Carter's promotion of his own moral character.[10] Political observers still believe that Carter won the election primarily because the American people saw him as trustworthy. Writing in 1998 in the midst of the Monica Lewinsky affair, a scandal revolving around morality and truthfulness, which threatened to unseat President Bill Clinton, David Broder, one of the most respected American journalists, observed: "[Jimmy Carter] won [the nomination] over a field of more credentialed Democrats and then defeated Ford essentially by repeating a six-word incantation: I will never lie to you."[11] Carter's mission was to restore the public's trust in its government. As he put it, "There is a simple and effective way for public officials to regain public trust—be trustworthy."[12]

The country deserved to have a more ethical government, Carter argued, precisely because Americans deserved to have a government that reflected "the goodness of the American people." Candidate Jimmy Carter conveyed his message against cynicism and in favor of a moral renewal in America as follows:

> It is obvious that domestic and foreign affairs are directly interrelated.... Recently, we have discovered that *our trust has been betrayed*. The *veils of secrecy* have seemed to thicken around Washington.... Our people are understandably concerned about this lack of competence and *integrity*.... Our

---

[8]Ibid., p. 214.

[9]See Kandy Strout, *How Jimmy Won: The Victory Campaign from Plains to the White House* (New York: Morrow, 1977), p. 16.

[10]Morris, *Jimmy Carter*, p. 16.

[11]David Broder, "Halos and Hardball from the White House: Carter is an Example of Good Character, but Bad Political Skills," *Washington Post*, September 23, 1998.

[12]See Jimmy Carter, *Why Not the Best? Jimmy Carter, the First Fifty Years* (Fayetteville: The University of Arkansas Press, 1996), p. 148.

political leaders have simply underestimated the *innate quality and character of our people.* It is time to reaffirm and strengthen *our ethical and spiritual* and political beliefs.[13] (Emphasis added.)

It was unmistakable that Carter was referring to Nixon when he spoke of "betrayed trust" and to both Nixon and Kissinger when he referred to the "veil of secrecy in Washington." Under Carter, the morality emanating from the deeply held values of the American people was to be reflected in foreign affairs. Carter's foreign policy was meant to be a departure from the realpolitik of Henry Kissinger. The secretary of state was indeed the master of realpolitik, which he defined as follows:

Realpolitik—Foreign policy based on calculations of power and the national interest.[14]

Thus, Kissinger followed a foreign policy that was power-oriented. He placed the "national interest," which revolved around American geopolitical and economic interests, above ethical values and tended to sidestep the rule of law.[15] The congressional embargo on arms sales to Turkey revolved precisely around the rule of law, with Congress championing the supremacy of law, while Kissinger invoked the "national interest" to evade the rule of law.

When Jimmy Carter became the Democratic presidential candidate, the image he projected was that of a leader who was determined to reverse the domination of realpolitik impulses in American foreign

---

[13]Ibid., pp. 155–157. Carter's book was first published in October 1975, five months prior to the New Hampshire primary. It was meant to be a campaign autobiography. It served a dual purpose: to make the obscure governor of Georgia known to the media and the broader American public and to convey Carter's message of moral renewal to the American people. The Carter campaign distributed complementary copies of the book throughout the country, while other copies were sold for $5 at political rallies. Carter's *Why Not the Best?* became instrumental in helping him capture the White House. See Doug Brinkley's introduction to the 1996 edition of the book, pp. xi, xxvii-xviii.

[14]Henry Kissinger, *Diplomacy* (New York: Simon and Schuster, 1994), p. 137.

[15]On Kissinger's belief in and practice of realpolitik, see Isaacson, *Kissinger: A Biography*, esp. chapter 29, "Morality in Foreign Policy: Kissinger's Realpolitik and How It was Challenged," pp. 651–672.

policy. The ethical values of the American people were to become a guiding principle in Carter's foreign policy. Realpolitik was to be replaced by an emphasis on human rights. Carter's opponents criticized him, saying that this was not a realistic prescription for the foreign policy of a superpower with global interests and responsibilities, but Carter projected an image of a leader who was guided, above all, by moral principles.

Like other Americans, Greek Americans put their trust in Carter. His presidency was to signal a new dawn in American politics, a radical departure from Nixon's deceptions and Kissinger's cynicism and realpolitik. It was in this vein that candidate Carter told the Greek American community, in September 1976, that he would follow a different policy than Kissinger had when it came to the Cyprus issue. The solemn pledge by Carter to the Greek Americans was that, as president, he was going to "pursue a foreign policy based on principle and in accordance with the rule of law."

When Carter entered the White House in January 1977, he had to deal with the aftermath of the Cyprus crisis. It was necessary for the Carter presidency to find ways to work with a Congress that was still inclined to assert itself in foreign affairs. The congressionally imposed embargo on arms sales to Turkey was the most evident act demonstrating congressional ascendancy in foreign policy. This ascendancy came about as a reaction to the abuses of power by the Nixon-Kissinger administration.

Statements about this in the memoirs of Carter administration decision-makers constitute an important source on the Carter presidency and the lifting of the embargo. The fact that the Carter administration lifted the embargo after long preparation and a fierce political battle with Congress led me to the initial conclusion that Carter and his key foreign policy aides had discussed the embargo affair to one degree or another. What I discovered while reading several of these memoirs was not what I had anticipated.

Since he left office in January 1981, Jimmy Carter has written his memoirs, in which he discussed his presidency.[16] In his writings, he paid a great deal of attention to foreign policy issues around the globe. The Middle East received special attention. For reasons that have

---

[16]Jimmy Carter, *Keeping Faith: Memoirs of a President* (Toronto, New York: Bantam Books, 1982).

never been explained, Carter left the embargo affair, Cyprus, and Greek-Turkish relations completely out of his memoirs. Yet, the lifting of the embargo was characterized repeatedly by Carter and top officials in his administration as the "number one foreign policy priority" in Congress. The president, therefore, dedicated considerable time and effort in 1977 and during the first eight months of 1978 dealing with the Cyprus issue, Greek-Turkish relations, and the drive to repeal the embargo.

As part of his personal involvement with the Cyprus issue and Greek-Turkish relations, President Carter met with Turkish Prime Minister Süleyman Demirel and Greek Prime Minister Constantine Karamanlis in May 1977. In late May and early June 1978, Carter met again with Karamanlis and Turkish Prime Minister Bülent Ecevit. The former president made no reference to these meetings in his memoirs.

Carter also appointed Clark Clifford as his special envoy to Greece, Turkey, and Cyprus, and he spent considerable time discussing issues concerning these countries with Clifford, especially the strategy to lift the embargo. Again, the former president made no reference to the discussions he had with Clifford on the embargo and the Cyprus issue in his memoirs. Carter did mention Clifford in his memoirs but not because of Clifford's role as his personal diplomatic envoy or because of the substantial assistance he gave the administration in the effort to lift the embargo. Carter mentioned Clifford's role as Burt Lance's private lawyer in the Lance affair.[17] It is noteworthy that the former president remembered Clifford's role as Lance's lawyer and omitted his role as a public servant and special diplomatic emissary who was appointed by Carter.

Furthermore, President Carter discussed the embargo affair at length with his national security adviser, Zbigniew Brzezinski; his secretaries of state and defense, Cyrus Vance and Harold Brown, respectively; and his chiefs of staff. In addition, from May until the end of July 1978, the president invited over 100 members of Congress, including the leadership of both parties and the chairmen of congressional committees dealing with foreign and defense policy, to the White House and lobbied them concerning the lifting of the embargo. Carter also read and acted upon a number of memoranda concerning the effect of the embargo on Turkey and the southeastern flank of

---

[17]Ibid., pp. 135–136.

NATO. Some of these memoranda have the personal comments of the former president in the margins.

This deep involvement of Carter in the effort to repeal the embargo was consistent with his working style. It was the style of an activist president, who was intimately involved in policy formulation, paid great attention to detail, and acted as the "gatekeeper of all information for decision-making."[18] Being a president with such a style, Carter tended to screen large amounts of information and read numerous documents daily. This was one of the ways Carter sought to be on top of foreign policy and control it from the White House.[19] As he put it, "I like to be personally involved so that I can know the thought processes that go into final decisions."[20] In other words, it was President Carter, himself, who made the decision to lift the embargo, having discussed the matter with his close advisers and having read a large number of documents about the issue. In the final analysis, Carter was the architect of the lifting of the embargo and, without such presidential leadership, it is doubtful that his administration would have succeeded in lifting the embargo in the Democratic Congress. Under these circumstances, it is quite remarkable that the embargo affair is totally missing from Carter's memoirs.

Equally remarkable is the fact that the other protagonists of the embargo issue and its repeal, National Security Adviser Zbigniew Brzezinski, Secretary of State Cyrus Vance, and Clark Clifford, also failed to discuss the embargo affair or said very little about it in their memoirs. In his memoirs, Brzezinski's only reference to the embargo and the fight with Congress to repeal it is a 21-word statement toward the end of his book asserting that the lifting of the embargo was among the foremost foreign policy accomplishments of President Carter.[21] Vance, in his memoirs, made no mention of the

---

[18]On Carter's presidential style and his attention to detail, see Alexander Moens, *Foreign Policy Under Carter: Testing Multiple Advocacy Decision Making* (Boulder, Colorado: Westview Press, 1990), pp. 34–36.

[19]On Carter's determination to be his own "secretary of state," see Zbigniew Brzezinski, *Power and Principle: Memoirs of the National Security Adviser, 1977–1981* (New York: Farrar, Straus, Giroux, 1983), p. 5; Robert Hunter, *Presidential Control of Foreign Policy* (New York: Praeger, 1980), p. 37; Hendley Donovan, *Roosevelt to Reagan* (New York: Harper and Row, 1985), pp. 162–163.

[20]Quoted in an interview by Neil Pierce in Thomas Cronin and Rexford Turgwell, eds., *The Presidency Reappraised* (New York: Praeger, 2nd ed., 1977), pp. 44–45.

[21]Brzezinski, *Power and Principle*, p. 529. Brzezinski made a very brief reference

embargo.[22] Clifford devoted three pages to Cyprus in his memoirs. He barely referred to the embargo, however, even though he had played a critical role in its repeal. In just 32 words, Clifford mentioned that the embargo was imposed in 1974 and that "Congress eventually agreed to the lifting of the arms embargo."[23]

It can be argued that, in the larger scheme of things, Cyprus is marginal with regard to American foreign policy and that decision-makers who have dealt with the Cyprus issue have considered it to be secondary and not worth mentioning in their memoirs. This might as well be the case. The issue here, however, is not Cyprus per se, but congressional assertiveness in foreign policy manifested through the congressional embargo on arms sales to Turkey. As such, the embargo and the effort of the Carter administration to repeal it involved, by necessity, the Congress of the United States, its role in foreign policy, and its interaction with the executive branch and the foreign policy agencies of the government. In this vein, the personal and intense involvement of Carter and his foreign policy team in the effort to lift the embargo, the congressional hearings, the public debate, and the media attention to the matter all elevated the embargo affair to a level that made it a salient foreign policy issue.

This was the case for at least half of the Carter presidency, 1977 and especially 1978. The congressional fight over the embargo was as intense as the debate over the Panama Canal Treaties. The Panama Canal Treaties received considerable attention in the memoirs of Jimmy Carter as well as in the memoirs of his top foreign policy advisers. They all went into great detail in describing the administration's tactics on how to prevail over a reluctant Congress and win the Panama Canal vote.[24] It is, therefore, even more remarkable that the

---

to Cyprus in his book. He wrote that a Presidential Review Memorandum on Cyprus and the Aegean was to be completed by January 31, 1977, and that Vance proposed that a special envoy be sent to the region. Cyprus and the Aegean were to be part of the issues that the Carter administration was to try to settle peacefully in 1977–1978. See ibid., pp. 51, 53.

[22]Cyrus Vance, *Hard Choices: Critical Years in America's Foreign Policy* (New York: Simon and Schuster, 1983).

[23]Clark Clifford with Richard Holbrooke, *Counsel to the President: A Memoir* (New York: Random House, 1991), pp. 625–628.

[24]For a discussion of the Panama Canal Treaties and the debate in Congress, see Carter, *Keeping Faith*, pp. 152–185; Brzezinski, *Power and Principle*, pp. 134–139, 144–145, 201–202, 521–522, 526–528; Vance, *Hard Choices*, pp. 140–152.

administration's monumental effort to prevail over Congress regarding the embargo has been totally ignored in the memoirs of key players in the episode.

It was not only key foreign policy-makers in the Carter administration that left the embargo episode out of their memoirs. For some reason, the embargo issue was also left out of serious conferences on Carter's foreign policy, which took place years later. The most important of these conferences, perhaps, took place at Hofstra University in 1990.[25] Over a decade had elapsed since the end of the Carter presidency. Fifty former Carter administration officials and scholars came together to assess foreign policy under Carter and to look into Carter's post-presidency era. All of these former policy-makers and scholars presented papers and took part in panel discussions that examined the multifaceted aspects of foreign policy in the Carter era. Among the issues examined were Soviet-U.S. relations, the Arab-Israeli conflict and the Camp David accords, the Iranian hostage crisis, the Panama Canal Treaties, Indo-American relations, relations with Africa, and relations with Cambodia. Special attention was given to the human rights policies under the Carter presidency.

It was quite remarkable that the embargo episode was left out of the conference. On the other hand, a paper dealing with U.S.-Romanian relations was given at the conference.[26] The Carter administration and Congress spent considerably more time and energy debating the embargo issue, Greek-Turkish relations, and Cyprus than they did discussing relations between the United States and Romania.[27] In other words, there is little doubt that the issues of the embargo and relations between the United States and Turkey were far more salient foreign policy issues than U.S.-Romanian relations. Yet, these issues reflecting the role of the United States in the Eastern Mediterranean

---

[25]For the proceedings of this conference, prepared under the auspices of Hofstra University, see Herbert D. Rosenbaum and Alexej Ugrinsky, eds., *Jimmy Carter: Foreign Policy and Post Presidential Years* (Westport, Connecticut: Greenwood Press, 1994).

[26]See Joseph F. Harrington "American-Romanian Relations: A Case Study in Carter's Human Rights Policy," in ibid., pp. 89–101.

[27]This is reflected in the press coverage of the embargo issue and of Romania. There is a plethora of reports, articles, and editorials on the embargo and Carter's drive to repeal it, while it is hard to find a report on the Carter administration's dealings with Romania.

were not included in the conference on Carter's foreign policy. The word "Turkey" was mentioned once during the conference, but it was in the context of German economic aid to Ankara.[28]

The Hofstra University conference proceedings also included two addresses by Carter on the foreign policy of his administration, which had been given at a town meeting and a high school colloquium that had also taken place at Hofstra University. As was the case with his memoirs, Carter made no mention of the embargo affair, the unresolved Cyprus issue, or U.S. relations with Turkey or Greece in these addresses. The failure of key foreign policy-makers of the Carter administration to address the embargo issue in their memoirs and the omission of this issue from a major conference on Carter's foreign policy might lead one to think that the embargo episode was so insignificant that it deserves to be forgotten. This is not necessarily the case, however, if only for the sake of historical accuracy. The embargo on arms sales to Turkey and its repeal do constitute an integral part of the Carter presidency and its interaction with Congress. Furthermore, the consequences of lifting the embargo were quite serious for American interests and policies in the Eastern Mediterranean. As such, the lifting of the embargo deserves to be examined instead of being condemned to oblivion.

A careful study of the Carter administration's successful effort to repeal the arms embargo against Turkey brings to the surface a dimension of the administration that has not been examined. Nineteen months passed between the time Carter took office in January 1977 and August 1978, when the embargo was repealed. By any standards, the embargo issue was a critical one during the first two years of the Carter presidency.

During his post-presidential years, through the Carter Center in Atlanta, former president Jimmy Carter has remained actively involved in world affairs. The Carter Center has been promoting human rights and the peaceful resolution of conflicts around the globe. In this respect, Carter's post-presidency has been remarkable. Indeed, the former president has won universal praise for his activist role in defense of the human, social, and economic rights of the dispossessed around the world.

Compared to his interest in other areas of the world, however,

---

[28]Rosenbaum and Ugrinsky, eds., *Jimmy Carter*, p. 24.

Carter has shown little interest in becoming actively involved in conflict resolution concerning Cyprus.[29] The best indication of this is Carter's book on conflict resolution, *Talking Peace: A Vision for the Next Generation*, written in 1993.[30] In the book, the former president wrote about ethnic and sectarian conflicts around the globe, from the Middle East, to Africa, to Asia, to Latin America. There is no mention of the Cyprus dispute. In fact, in the Eastern Mediterranean section of a map that appears in the book, all the countries shown are identified with one exception: Cyprus. The island appears on the map without a name.[31]

In the pages that follow, the basic hypothesis of my study is that Carter was to be a president whose foreign policy would be guided by human rights. Pragmatism had to be balanced by ethical principles in the formulation and exercise of American foreign policy. In fact, ethical considerations and the principle of human rights were to prevail over the cynical realpolitik policies of Nixon and Kissinger. As far as relations with Congress were concerned, again, Carter was to depart from the Nixon-Kissinger line of deception and antagonism, and work closely with Capitol Hill in foreign affairs. A good case study to prove or disprove this hypothesis revolves around the way in which Carter dealt with the Cyprus crisis and, especially, the question of the congressionally-imposed embargo on arms sales to Turkey.

In this respect, some of the basic questions that have to be addressed include: (a) Did Carter really practice what he preached and abandon Kissinger's realpolitik, or did he, despite his rhetoric, follow the logic of this realpolitik? (b) Did the Carter administration present to Congress an accurate picture of the situation in occupied Cyprus and the conditions in Turkey, or did the White House submit misleading reports to Congress regarding these issues? (c) What was the strategy adopted by the Carter administration in order to persuade a reluctant Congress to lift the embargo? (d) What were the dynamics in Congress that allowed Carter to succeed? Did the "southern" factor play a role in this regard? (e) How did the administration

---

[29]Based on the thorough account of Carter's post-presidential years by Douglas Brinkley, *The Unfinished Presidency: Jimmy Carter's Journey Beyond the White House* (New York: Viking Penguin, 1998).

[30]Jimmy Carter, *Talking Peace: A Vision for a New Generation* (New York: Puffin Books, 1993).

[31]Ibid., p. 6.

view the role of the Soviet Union in the Eastern Mediterranean at the time? Was Soviet threat assessment realistic or exaggerated? (d) How did the Carter administration's view of the Israeli-occupied territories and Turkish-occupied Cyprus compare? (f) Did President Carter adopt conflict resolution principles in the case of the Cyprus dispute that were similar to those he espoused in Egyptian-Israeli peace talks at Camp David? If not, what were the reasons for adopting a different approach to the Cyprus conflict?

The objective of this work, therefore, is to answer these kinds of questions and provide documented evidence to support my answers. In the process, my hope and expectation is to fill the existing gap concerning the repeal of the embargo on arms sales to Turkey in the accounts on the Carter presidency, its relations with Congress, and its policies toward the Eastern Mediterranean.

In researching and writing this book, I was assisted by several institutions and individuals. I wish to express my great appreciation to the Carter Library in Atlanta for the support it gave me in my research. The Carter Library made important documents covering the Carter presidency and pertaining to the embargo issue available to me. I also wish to thank the Karamanlis Foundation in Athens, especially its director, Professor Constantine Svolopoulos, for giving me permission to translate several documents from the Karamanlis archive. They include minutes of meetings between then Prime Minister Constantine Karamanlis and top officials of the Carter administration, including President Carter.

An early draft of the manuscript and a later one were read by Professor Stanley Kyriakides of William Patterson College in New Jersey. Over the years, I have been the beneficiary of Dr. Kyriakides' unique insights on the Cyprus dispute and his profound understanding of the workings of the American government. His critique of the manuscript and comments have been enormously helpful to me in writing the final draft of my book. I owe Dr. Kyriakides my deepest gratitude. Jack Prattas, Esquire, of Toronto, also read an earlier draft of the manuscript. His intimate understanding of legal matters and international law, as well as his perspective on American foreign policy from a Canadian vantage point, enabled him to make a very constructive critique of the manuscript and offer extremely useful comments. I wish to express my heartfelt appreciation for Mr. Prattas's valuable assistance. Finally, I would like to thank Professor Van Coufoudakis of

Indiana University and Professor Harry J. Psomiades of Queens College, CUNY. I have been greatly benefited from their support over the years and they also gave me their encouragement and unique insights as I worked on this book. Above all, I cherish their friendship. Needless to say, of course, any errors of omission or commission in this book are mine alone.

Chris P. Ioannides
Sacramento, California
April, 2001

CHAPTER 1

The Nixon-Kissinger Years: Watergate, the Greek Junta, and the Cyprus Crisis

Crisis in the Midst of a Crisis

During the final days of his presidency, as the Watergate scandal was reaching its climax, Richard Nixon and his foreign policy team were confronted with a serious international crisis in the Eastern Mediterranean. This crisis lasted one month, from July 15 to August 15, 1974. On July 15, the military junta in Athens engineered a coup d'etat against the democratically elected president of Cyprus, Archbishop Makarios. Five days later, on July 20, Turkey invaded Cyprus. On July 23, the Greek junta collapsed and veteran Greek leader Constantine Karamanlis returned from exile to restore democratic rule in Greece. On August 14, Turkey launched the second phase of the invasion, which resulted in the occupation of 38 percent of the territory of the Republic of Cyprus.

By any standards, these were extraordinary developments characterized by all the elements that constitute an international crisis. They were violent events, taking place over a very short period of time in a strategic region where the United States had vital interests. As a result of these events, the threat of a general Greek-Turkish conflagration emerged, which had profound implications for the stability of NATO's southeastern flank and the high-priority interests of the United States in the area. As Secretary of State Henry Kissinger put it, the overwhelming concern of policy-makers in Washington "was to prevent a war between two NATO allies that would destroy the Alliance's southeastern flank and open the way to Soviet penetration of the Mediterranean."[1]

---

[1]Kissinger, *Years of Renewal*, p. 207–208.

The Cyprus crisis, therefore, was a major international crisis that required the immediate attention of American policy-makers, from the president to the secretaries of state and defense to other top foreign policy officials.

In his memoirs, Nixon described the events of July 1974 in Cyprus:

> On July 15, 1974, there was a violent coup on the strife-torn island of Cyprus. Fighting between the Greek and Turkish Cypriot factions seemed imminent. I suggested to Kissinger that he send Assistant Secretary of State Joseph Sisco over to monitor the situation at the scene. I noted in my diary, "The Cyprus thing brought home the fact that with the world in the situation it is in, with the peace as fragile as it is in various parts of the world, a shake-up in the American presidency or a change would have a traumatic effect abroad and a traumatic effect at home."[2]

It is obvious that in the middle of July 1974, Nixon was totally preoccupied with his own survival because of the Watergate scandal. He saw the events in Cyprus in the context of his agonizing effort to stay in power because, as he put it, "with peace as fragile as it is," his resignation would have been "traumatic" for the world and for America. Nixon did not last long; he resigned three weeks later on August 8, 1974.

When the July 15 coup against Makarios and the subsequent Turkish invasion of Cyprus took place, President Nixon was in his residence in San Clemente, California. The preoccupation with Watergate had led to a virtual White House paralysis, and this had had a debilitating effect on the conducting of foreign policy.

It was under these dramatic circumstances in Washington, where the American republic was undergoing its deepest political crisis in a century, that the Cyprus crisis erupted. Given the absence of presidential leadership and authority due to Watergate, the burden of making critical decisions on how to handle the Cyprus crisis fell upon the shoulders of Secretary of State Henry Kissinger. Part of this burden was shared by Under Secretary of State Joseph Sisco. It was Sisco

---

[2]Nixon, *The Memoirs of Richard Nixon*, p. 1047.

who traveled to the Eastern Mediterranean during those critical days in order to carry out Kissinger's policies.

The events in the Eastern Mediterranean in July and August 1974 and a series of decisions made in Washington that shaped some of these events had an effect on the fate of three countries, Cyprus, Greece, and Turkey. The Republic of Cyprus was the most profoundly affected. Following its invasion, Turkey occupied the northern part of Cyprus where 74 percent of the island's economic resources were located. The indigenous Greek population was forced to leave, finding refuge in the southern part of the island.[3] A policy of colonization began, as the Turkish government sent tens of thousands of settlers to the occupied territory. The Turkish invasion of Cyprus brought about the de facto partition of the country, which is still in effect.

The Cyprus crisis also had a direct effect on relations between the United States and two of its allies in NATO, Greece and Turkey. While Greece and Turkey avoided war over Cyprus, a period of protracted tension between them ensued. At the same time, the two countries went through periodic crises in their relations with Washington. In Greece, the national unity government of Prime Minister Constantine Karamanlis was confronted with a wave of anti-American sentiment. Greece's interests and the country's national honor suffered a serious blow as a result of the Turkish invasion and occupation of Cyprus. During the first phase of the invasion, Turkey occupied only about 8 percent of Cypriot territory. When Turkey launched the second phase of its invasion on August 14 and captured an additional 30 percent of the country, the Karamanlis government had to do something. The strong anti-Turkish sentiment in Greece was combined with an even stronger anti-Americanism. Turkey was the traditional enemy that had invaded Cyprus. It was the United States, however, that had supported the seven-year junta that had oppressed the Greek people. In Greek eyes, it was this U.S.-backed junta that, through the coup against Makarios, had opened the gate for the Turkish invasion of Cyprus. The policy-makers in Washington failed to comprehend

---

[3]The Greek Cypriots left behind in the territory occupied by Turkey and the Turkish Cypriots that remained in the government-controlled area in the south were eventually exchanged. By the fall of 1974, Cyprus was, de facto, divided into two areas, one in the south with an overwhelmingly Greek population and one in the occupied north with an overwhelmingly Turkish population.

the depth of Greek anguish, which was threatening to undo the U.S.-Greek alliance.

The Greek government had to take some steps to defuse an explosive domestic situation that could have led to uncontrollable developments. After all, the dictatorship had just ended and, as more details of the magnitude of the junta's human rights violations became public, the bitterness against the United States grew over its support for the colonels. Thus, Karamanlis was confronted with the dilemma of either going to war with Turkey in order to save the honor of the nation or facing the public's rage against the United States at an extremely delicate moment. Another coup in Greece had not been ruled out, and the first thing he had to do was control the armed forces, establish law and order, and bring stability to the country. The position of Greece in the Western alliance system, especially the alliance with the United States, was at stake. Had Karamanlis decided to permanently sever Greece's ties with NATO, and by extension the United States, the decision would have been met with overwhelming popular approval. Such was the intensity of anti-American sentiment at the time.

Faced with this dilemma, Karamanlis performed a balancing act. He decided that the only way to avoid war with Turkey was to pull Greece out of NATO's military command structure, a decision he announced on August 16, 1974, as Turkey completed its conquest of 38 percent of Cypriot territory. At the same time, he declared that Greece would remain a member of NATO. The Greek prime minister's decision was meant to be a protest against NATO and the United States for watching passively as a powerful NATO ally conquered a small country.

By walking a tightrope and utilizing his enormous prestige, Karamanlis was able to avoid a rupture with the United States and keep Greece in the Western camp. His actions went a long way in defusing the explosive situation in Greece and allowed him to concentrate on consolidating democratic rule in the country. Karamanlis's decision to withdraw Greece from NATO's military command structure did affect NATO's strategy in the Eastern Mediterranean, and this meant that policy-makers in Washington had to deal with new dynamics in the region.

The Cyprus crisis also had a serious effect on U.S. relations with Turkey. The handling of the crisis by the Nixon and Ford administrations, and especially by Secretary of State Kissinger, ushered in a chain reaction in Washington that culminated in the imposition of an embargo on arms sales to Turkey on October 3, 1974. A combination of factors, including congressional assertiveness in foreign policy and Greek American mobilization, led to the imposition of the embargo. In turn, the embargo brought about a serious crisis in U.S.-Turkish relations. Reacting to the embargo, Turkey closed down six American military bases on Turkish soil in the summer of 1975. Ankara also intensified its rapprochement with Moscow and facilitated the passage of Soviet warships, including an aircraft carrier, through the Dardanelles. The Cyprus crisis of the summer of 1974 and its repercussions in Greece and Turkey had caused the most serious turmoil in the southeastern flank of NATO since the two countries joined the alliance in 1952.

In Washington, the Cyprus crisis and its aftermath, especially the embargo, embroiled two presidents, Gerald Ford and Jimmy Carter, in a political fight with Congress. However, it was the Carter presidency that had to engage in the most serious fight with Congress, a classic, albeit bitter, fight between the executive and legislative powers, which was not new to American politics. The way the fight was resolved, through the eventual lifting of the embargo by President Carter, left a mark on his presidency. It also left the Cyprus issue unresolved, while relations between Greece and Turkey continued to go through periodic tension that brought the two countries close to war on several occasions. For over two decades since the Turkish invasion, the unresolved Cyprus dispute has continued to poison relations between Greece and Turkey and affect the domestic politics of both countries.

It is quite obvious that the preoccupation of the United States with the Watergate scandal as it was approaching its conclusion seriously affected Washington's handling of the Cyprus crisis and the manner in which it dealt with two key allies on the verge of war, Greece and Turkey. The Watergate scandal, however, had another dimension that linked it to the tumultuous events in the Eastern Mediterranean in the summer of 1974. This had to do with the support the Greek military junta had received from the Nixon administration over the years. The Turkish invasion of Cyprus was precipitated, after all, by the coup against Makarios staged by the U.S.-backed Greek junta.

In retrospect, it is the Greek junta that provides the thread linking the Watergate scandal to crisis decision-making in Washington during the climax of this scandal. Consequently, a brief examination of the Nixon administration's ties to the junta becomes necessary in order to shed some light on an important aspect of the most acute crisis in the American presidency in the twentieth century. In turn, this can lead to a better understanding of decisions made in Washington during the 1974 Cyprus crisis.

The Takeover by the Greek Military Junta

On April 21, 1967, military officers staged a coup that overthrew the democratically elected government of Greece under Prime Minister Panayiotis Kanellopoulos. He was a conservative politician known for his integrity and dedication to democracy. The junta ruled Greece with an iron hand for seven years. Initially, many sectors of Greek society either welcomed or condoned the junta because they thought it would rid the country of corrupt politicians and put an end to the political and social turmoil that had plagued the nation from 1964 to 1967.

The rising star of Greek politics at the time of the coup was Andreas Papandreou, whose father, George Papandreou, had been prime minister in 1964 and 1965. Andreas Papandreou, known to Greeks simply as "Andreas," had gone to live in the United States in 1939. He graduated from Harvard, taught economics at the University of Minnesota, and later became chairman of the Economics Department at the University of California, Berkeley. He was well connected with influential circles of the Democratic Party, including Illinois Senator Adlai Stevenson, California Governor Pat Brown, and Harvard Economics Professor John Kenneth Galbraith. In 1951, Andreas married Margaret Chant in Minnesota. It was the second marriage for both.[4]

Andreas Papandreou returned to Greece in 1961. He became involved in politics and eventually came to represent the left wing of

---

[4]Andreas and Margaret had four children together, all born in the United States. In 1989, the 70-year-old Andreas divorced Margaret following a tumultuous affair with a 34-year-old stewardess, Dimitra Liani, whom he married the same year.

the Center Union Party, his father's party. In 1964, Andreas served as deputy minister of coordination in the Center Union government. He became the arch villain in the eyes of many conservatives as well as a number of officers in the military. They saw him as a leader who was going to deliver Greece to communism. To a substantial degree, many policy-makers in Washington, who had developed a strong antipathy to the younger Papandreou, shared this alarmist view with the Greek colonels.[5] Andreas Papandreou was arrested in the early morning hours of April 21, 1967, when the military coup occurred, and was detained for eight months. On January 15, 1968, he was released and sent into exile in France. He then based his activities against the Greek junta in Stockholm, Sweden, and Toronto, Canada.

In September 1968 in the midst of the U.S. presidential campaign, Spiro Agnew, the Republican vice-presidential candidate who was of Greek descent on his father's side, launched an open attack against Andreas Papandreou. During a press conference on September 27, Agnew, who was to be elected vice president five weeks later, was asked a question about the Greek military regime. He first praised the junta and then charged that "the communist forces [were] under Andreas Papandreou."[6]

The military men who staged the coup came from the ranks of the middle and junior officers, mostly colonels and majors. They attributed Greece's ills to communist subversion and corrupt politicians, above all the "arch demagogue Andreas Papandreou." Ostensibly, the colonels came to power to "save Greece" from communism and restore democratic rule. They proclaimed that they would do so after they cleansed the "anti-national and corrupt elements of the past" from the political system, which they said resembled the "Augean Stables." Although Greece was going through a period of serious political turmoil at the time, it was in no danger of being taken over by communists.

Immediately after the coup occurred, the junta strongman,

[5]On the antipathy of many Washington officials toward Andreas Papandreou, see Lawrence Stern, *The Wrong Horse: The Politics of Intervention and the Failure of American Policy* (New York: New York Times Books, 1977), esp. chapter 3, "The Andreas Fixation," pp. 25–34.

[6]See Maurice Goldbloom, "United States Policy in Post-War Greece," in *Greece Under Military Rule*, ed. Richard Clogg and George Yannopoulos (New York: Basic Books, 1972), pp. 245–246.

Colonel George Papadopoulos, assured the Greek people that the country had been placed "in a temporary cast," which would be removed soon, and that the armed forces would return to their barracks in the near future. By and large, the initial reaction of the Greek people to the coup fluctuated between numbness and a degree of relief, reflecting the feelings of ambivalence toward the colonels.

The military takeover did not cause popular opposition. Along with Andreas Papandreou and the cadres around him, the colonels quickly neutralized the other sources of organized opposition, such as the leaders of all major parties, especially the prominent figures of the Communist Party of Greece (KKE) and its labor unions. All political leaders were taken into custody. Cadres from all the political parties that might resist the coup, 6,138 in all, were also arrested and sent into internal exile. Thus, in a matter of hours, the leaders of any potential popular opposition were behind bars and, in effect, the Greek people found themselves without political guidance for a while.

A large number of Greeks were tired of the country's virulent partisan politics, the flagrant intervention of the Royal Palace in politics, the social turmoil, the strikes, the demonstrations, the virtual shutdown of universities, and the acute polarization and malaise that prevailed in the country at the time of the coup. The junta's promise that it had come to clean house and would return to the barracks soon— two years were thought to be the maximum—carried a certain appeal for many Greeks. For a limited period, between April 1967 and the end of 1968, the junta took advantage of the public's ambivalent attitude toward it in order to consolidate its rule and, in fact, was able to generate a respectable amount of popular support.[7] The colonels had imposed censorship so it is difficult to gauge the degree of popular support for the junta with precision.

---

[7]On the initial condoning or support of the junta by the majority of Greeks, see Orestis Vidalis, *Istoriko Imerologio: Chronia Ekpatrismou, 1968–1975* (A Historical Diary: Years of Exile, 1968–1975), vol. II, Athens: Libro, 1977), pp. 993–994. In 1968, Vidalis found refuge in the United States, where he dedicated his time and effort to rallying opposition forces within the U.S. against the junta. His two-volume book offers the most detailed account of opposition to the junta in the United States. On the initial reaction of the Greek people to the military junta, Vidalis wrote: "The great majority of the Greek people, influenced by the success of the coup and especially by the political turmoil that preceded the military takeover, not only accepted the coup at the beginning, but was relieved by the coup in the hope that the abolition of democracy was temporary." Vidalis, ibid., vol. II, pp. 993–994.

There were, however, several manifestations of support for the colonels. The appearance of several of the junta's key figures at public functions, such as events commemorating national anniversaries and soccer matches or other athletic events, where tens of thousands of people were gathered, elicited applause, cheers, and even enthusiasm. Certainly, there were informants among the crowds, but they could not force tens of thousands of people in open stadiums to cheer the colonels enthusiastically. In the countryside, the colonels received a warm welcome in most of the areas they visited. This welcome was not unrelated to the populist economic measures of the government. The junta raided the public treasury in order to distribute money to social classes such as farmers and retirees, with the purpose of winning public support.

The situation began to change in 1969 and, by 1970, popular support for the junta had almost evaporated, while the legitimacy of its rule was being challenged by all political forces, be it conservative, centrist, or leftist. There was little cheering or enthusiastic applause for the colonels at their public appearances, despite the fact that there were more informants in the crowds than there had been in 1967 or 1968. As the junta entrenched itself and repression increased so did opposition to the regime. It is not surprising that the Greek people want to forget the fact that many of them condoned the junta and some of them even supported it at the beginning. A Greek joke points out the public's denial of its support for the junta:

QUESTION: How many of the eight million Greeks supported the junta?

ANSWER: Eight million supported the junta, and eight million opposed it.

Like other dictators, the three colonels leading the junta takeover, George Papadopoulos, Stylianos Pattakos, and Nicholaos Makarezos, believed that they had a sacred mission to "save the nation" from all sorts of enemies, real and imaginary. Papadopoulos, in particular, combined cunning and a conspiratorial mind with elements of Puritanism and paranoia.

One of the first objectives of the junta was to gain legitimacy by advancing a new ideology that presumably would appeal to the Greek people. Soon after he came to power, Colonel Papadopoulos embarked on a campaign to introduce and explain the junta's ideology.[8] He did so in the style of a father figure teaching and scolding his "children," the Greek people. Papadopoulos's speeches presented convoluted, nonsensical arguments under the rhetoric of Greek nationalism and the Christian Orthodox ethic, as the dictator understood them. The junta published his speeches in an eight-volume series entitled *To Pistevo Mas* (Our Creed). They conveyed a messianic vision of a "Greece of Greek Christians," or *Ellas Ellinon Christianon.*[9] Nothing is more telling of the absurdity of this vision than the fact that one of the first actions of the colonels was to ban the performance of a number of classical Greek plays, both tragedies and comedies. The junta considered the masterpieces of Sophocles and Aristophanes to be subversive. Classical Greece was a threat to the colonels, although they had come to power to build an authentic Greece by glorifying the past.

In the process of building this "New Greece," the colonels established a regime of repression and systematically violated human rights. Their rule was marked by concentration camps for political prisoners, the torture of political opponents and dissident army officers, the killing of student protesters at the Athens Polytechnic University, and foreign policy disasters. The culmination of the junta's follies was the coup against the president of Cyprus, Archbishop Makarios, on July 15, 1974, which precipitated the Turkish invasion of the country five days later.

American Ties to the Greek Junta

The overwhelming majority of Greeks maintain that the United States engineered the military coup of April 21, 1967. Whether this can be proved with hard evidence is still a matter of controversy. A more relevant question that evokes less speculative answers is what the nature of the relationship between the United States and the Greek military dictatorship was during its seven-year rule.

---

[8]On the junta's ideology and its efforts to gain legitimacy, see Constantine Danopoulos, *Warriors and Politicians in Modern Greece* (Chapel Hill: Documentary Publications, 1984), pp. 56–84.

[9]See George Papadopoulos, *To Pistevo Mas: Logoi ke Synentevxeis* (Our Creed: Speeches and Interviews), (Athens: Press General Directorate, 1968–1972), 8 vols.

There has been a long history of foreign interference in Greek politics. From the establishment of the modern Greek state in 1821 until the pronouncement of the Truman doctrine on April 12, 1947, foreign powers, primarily Britain, France, and Russia, were directly involved in Greek affairs.[10] After the Truman Doctrine was implemented, the United States found itself actively involved in the Greek civil war (1945–1949). The Truman Doctrine represented a turning point in American foreign policy. Greece and Turkey, although it was primarily Greece, became the places where the United States, under President Harry Truman, drew the line in the fight against Soviet-led communism.[11] In Greece, the United States supported the nationalist, royalist, and anti-communist forces against the communist guerrillas, whose goal was to take over and transform Greece into a "Peoples' Republic." The generous, multifaceted American aid enabled the Greek armed forces to defeat the communists. In addition, starting in 1948 through the Marshall Plan, Greece entered a period of sustained economic reconstruction and growth.[12]

Beginning in 1947 and throughout the 1950s, the United States emerged as the "protector" of Greece. In the process, American interference in Greek affairs was extensive and often quite overt.[13] During this period, and generally speaking, the Royal Palace and the armed forces followed the American *desiderata*. The ruling conservative party, the National Radical Union Party (ERE), accommodated, more or less, these American desires. Several of Washington's policies, however, especially when it came to relations with Turkey, did not neces-

---

[10]See Theodore Coloumbis, John Petropoulos, and Harry Psomiades, eds., *Foreign Interference in Greek Politics: An Historical Perspective* (New York: Pella Publishing Co., 1976), pp. 15–99.

[11]For reflections on the Truman Doctrine 50 years later, see Eugene Rossides, ed., *The Truman Doctrine of Aid to Greece: A Fifty-Year Retrospective* (New York and Washington, D.C.: The Academy of Political Science and the American Hellenic Institute, 1998).

[12]On the enormous benefits of the Marshall Plan for the Greek economy, see the account by James Warren, Jr., "Origins of the 'Greek Economic Miracle:' The Truman Doctrine and the Marshall Plan Development and Stabilization Program," in Rossides, ed., *The Truman Doctrine*, pp. 77–105. Warren served with the Marshall Plan Mission to Greece. He was chief of the Import Program Office of the Mission (1950–1954).

[13]See Couloumbis, Petropoulos, and Psomiades, eds., *Foreign Interference*, pp. 113–145.

sarily serve Greece's national interests. Still, on balance, it can be pointed out that the greatest salutary effect of the Truman Doctrine was that it prevented Greece from becoming a communist totalitarian state. This, however, was not accomplished without a price.[14] Therefore, a study of the military takeover of April 21, 1967, should take into account, among other factors, the history of U.S. intervention in Greece in the post-Second World War period.

It is instructive to examine the ties between key junta figures and the United States during this period. In the 1950s and early 1960s, George Papadopoulos was serving as a lieutenant colonel in the State Information Agency (KYP), the Greek equivalent of the CIA. In this capacity, he developed close ties with the CIA. Andreas Papandreou, the leader who was to become prime minister and rule Greece for eight consecutive years, from 1981 to 1989, and then from 1993 to 1996, was convinced that the April 21, 1967 coup d'etat was engineered by the United States. At the time of the coup, the administration of President Lyndon Johnson was in power in Washington. Papandreou believed firmly that the colonels came to power and retained this power only because they had American support. He openly charged that the leader of the coup, Colonel Papadopoulos, had "specialized in conspiratorial techniques in America under the auspices of the CIA and became the CIA's leading agent in Greece."[15]

The question of the ties between the junta leaders and the CIA has been more or less settled. It is generally accepted that Papadopoulos and the top leadership of the junta had developed, over time, multi-

---

[14]Despite the inevitable negative side effects of the Truman Doctrine on Greek society and politics, on balance, Greece was better off with the Truman Doctrine than without it. In retrospect, following the collapse of the Soviet Union and the communist regimes in the Balkans, the Truman Doctrine acquires an even greater significance. Without it, Greece would have shared the fate of neighboring Albania, Yugoslavia, and Bulgaria. Their communist regimes failed miserably and collapsed. All three former communist countries, Yugoslavia and Albania especially, underwent violent convulsions in the 1990s. Greece, on the other hand, continued to prosper as a democracy and was in a position to provide economic and humanitarian assistance to its former communist neighbors and the suffering peoples of the Balkans. See Christos P. Ioannides, "Has the Truman Doctrine Benefited Greece?," *The Greek American*, March 15, 1997, p. 8.

[15]Andreas Papandreou, *Democracy at Gunpoint* (New York: Doubleday and Co., 1970), pp. 221–222. Papandreou described the April 21, 1967 coup as essentially an operation carried out by officers linked to the CIA. This appears in the part of the book entitled, "The Coup," pp. 221–236.

faceted ties with the CIA. Papadopoulos's ties with the CIA were especially close.[16] However, there is no clear-cut answer to the question of whether the United States engineered the military coup.

The role of the CIA in the colonels' coup is still being debated. For one thing, the Greek military had intervened in politics on several occasions during the first half of the twentieth century,[17] before the United States became involved in Greece in 1947 through the Truman Doctrine. As for an American role in the coup, retired British officer Christopher Woodhouse, who was a strong opponent of the junta, maintained that "almost certainly there was no CIA plot either, though Greek mythology still insists that there was."[18]

On the other hand, Christopher Hitchens, a British author who lives in Washington and is a prolific writer on Cyprus, argued the opposite. The essence of Hitchens' argument is that the United States and the CIA had a long history of involvement in the politics of Greece and Cyprus, and they played an active role in the 1967 coup in Greece and an even more active role in the 1974 coup against Makarios, which brought about the Turkish invasion of the country.[19]

---

[16]The complex ties between the CIA and key leaders of the junta, especially Papadopoulos, are described by Alexis Papachelas, *O Viasmos tes Demokratias: O Amerikanikos Paragon, 1947–1967* (The Rape of Democracy: The American Factor, 1947–1967) (Athens: Estia, 1977). Papachelas presented a very complicated relationship between American Embassy officials and CIA officers in Greece, on the one hand, and the Greek military officers who staged the coup, on the other. Papachelas documented the development of multifaceted ties between Papadopoulos and the CIA over the years. These ties did not necessarily mean that the coup was executed on orders from the United States. On Papadopoulos's ties with the CIA see ibid., pp. 24, 82–83, 115, 145, 272–273. On the intimate ties between the CIA and Papadopoulos and the other colonels, see also Theodore Couloumbis, *The United States, Greece, and Turkey: The Troubled Triangle* (New York: Praeger, 1983), pp. 50–51. There are those who argue that Papadopoulos went on the CIA payroll in 1952. See Brendan O'Malley and Ian Craig, *The Cyprus Conspiracy: America, Espionage, and the Turkish Invasion* (London: I.B. Tauris Publishers, 1999), p. 126.

[17]Thanos Veremis, *The Military in Greek Politics: From Independence to Democracy* (Montreal: Black Rose Books, 1977).

[18]See C.M. Woodhouse, *The Rise and Fall of the Colonels* (New York: Franklin Watts, 1985), pp. 20, 27–28. Woodhouse became famous through his exploits during the German occupation of Greece where, as a British officer, he fought the Nazis along with the Greek resistance.

[19]Christopher Hitchens, *Hostage to History: Cyprus, From the Ottomans to Kissinger*, 3rd ed. (London, New York: Verso, 1977), pp. 61–166.

In his book, Lawrence Stern, the award-winning national editor of the *Washington Post*, argued, as Hitchens did, that the CIA began playing an active role in Greek politics with the implementation of the Truman Doctrine. Still, the CIA role in the 1967 coup is not clear. Stern suggested that there are serious discrepancies in CIA accounts preceding and following the coup and that, among the CIA agents stationed in Greece, there were some who sympathized with the colonels. According to Stern, the CIA operatives who were most sympathetic to the military takeover were Greek American agents stationed in Athens.[20]

In between the Woodhouse thesis and the more popular—in Greece and Cyprus—Hitchens thesis, there is the argument that the CIA did intervene in Greek politics in the 1950s and 1960s, and this included the undermining of the government of Prime Minister George Papandreou in 1964 and 1965. At the time, Washington was obsessed with Andreas Papandreou, who was seen as the leader of a Marxist-oriented popular front. As such, he was perceived as extremely dangerous to American interests. In this way, the CIA contributed to the political crisis in Greece from 1965 to 1967 by working behind the scenes and supporting the Royal Palace in its effort to prevent a victory for George Papandreou and his son Andreas in the parliamentary elections, expected to take place in the spring of 1967.[21] Andreas was slated to play an important role in his father's administration. It was this dynamic, the interplay of internal and external factors, that precipitated the April 1967 military coup. This, however, does not mean that the United States and the CIA engineered the colonels' coup.[22] Constantine Karamanlis, the leader who restored democracy in Greece in 1974, following the collapse of the military junta, also cast doubt on the theory that it was the United States that engineered the coup.

Karamanlis, who passed away in 1998, emerges as a towering figure in post-Second World War Greek politics, despite his mistakes and his many detractors. He became the leader of the conservative

---

[20]Laurence Stern, *The Wrong Horse*, pp. 11–19, 41–46.

[21]Ibid., pp. 35–40; O'Malley and Craig, *The Cyprus Conspiracy*, pp. 125–126.

[22]This thesis is advocated in a book by a strong critic of the junta, who argued that the popular view of a direct CIA role in the coup is not supported by credible evidence. See Solon Gregoriades, *Istoria tes Diktatorias* (*History of the Dictatorship*) (Athens: K. Kapopoulos Publications, 1975), pp. 29–35, 45–46.

National Radical Union Party (ERE) and ruled Greece for eight years (1955–1963). Following a dispute with the Royal Palace, Karamanlis left Greece for Paris in November 1963. He lived there in self-exile until July 24, 1974, when he returned triumphantly to Greece to restore democratic rule. During his nearly 11 years in exile, Karamanlis came under the intense pressure of several of his associates to speak up with regard to the role of the United States in the imposition of military dictatorship in Greece and, especially, the American support for the junta. Karamanlis had denounced the junta repeatedly but refused to openly criticize the United States as the instigator of the coup. Instead, on several occasions, he stated that the primary reasons for the imposition of the military dictatorship in Greece had been domestic.[23]

This placed Karamanlis squarely at odds with Andreas Papandreou, who attributed most of Greece's travails, including the April 1967 military coup, to American intervention. By doing so, Papandreou absolved himself of any responsibility for the political turmoil of the mid-1960s. In addition, the apportioning of exclusive blame for the coup to the United States reinforced the Greek tendency to blame foreign powers, the U.S. especially, for everything that went wrong in the country. A substantial part of the public, especially the left, tended to see an "American conspiracy" behind all the failures and blunders of Greek foreign policy.

One could make a reasonable argument that, initially, the new administration of President Richard Nixon needed some time to formulate and carry out its policies toward the Eastern Mediterranean. After all, the military takeover of Greece had occurred during the Johnson administration. One year, the period between January and December 1969, was more than enough for Nixon's foreign policy

---

[23]The information on Karamanlis's position regarding the role of the United States in the April 21, 1967 military coup and American support for the junta is found in the voluminous history of Karamanlis's political life, Constantinos Svolopoulos, ed., *Archeio, Gegonota, Keimena: Konstantinos Karamanlis, 50 Chronia Politikis Istorias* (*Archive, Events, Records: Constantine Karamanlis, 50 Years of Political History*, 11 vols. (Athens: Ekdotiki Athinon, 1992–1996), hereafter cited as *The Karamanlis Archive.* See *The Karamanlis Archive*, vol. 7, 1963–1974, Second Period, April 21, 1967-July 24, 1974, pp. 25–26, 34–37, 97–98, 122–124, 130–136, 141–145, 212–213, 256–257, 272–274, 283–284, 333–337; vol. 9, 1974 -1977, Second Period, September 4, 1975-October 21, 1977, p. 389.

team to study the situation in Greece and arrive at certain conclusions. During this period, however, the Nixon White House took steps
indicating that it was inclined to support the Greek junta. This
became apparent in March 1969.

When former U.S. president Dwight Eisenhower died on March
28, 1969, a score of foreign dignitaries came to Washington for his
funeral. Colonel Stylianos Pattakos, who was vice premier of Greece
and a member of the junta triumvirate that had carried out the coup,
represented Greece. King Constantine of Greece also came to Washington for the funeral. He had fled Greece in December 1967, following a failed half-hearted attempt to overthrow the junta. Nixon
refused to see the king in order not to offend the junta. He did meet,
however, with Pattakos at the White House in an atmosphere of cor-
diality.[24] This was indicative of Washington's friendly attitude toward
the Greek junta. Before the coup, the Royal Palace—King Constantine; his father, the former King Paul; and his mother, the former
Queen Frederica—had been so staunchly pro-American that they
were considered subservient to the United States. Now, the young
king was in exile, Greece was ruled by a dictatorship, and the king was
not an especially welcome guest in Washington.

During the junta, the Nixon administration paid occasional lip
service to the restoration of democracy in Greece. The junta regime
might have been deplorable, but it was the only viable alternative for
Greece, the administration's argument went. The administration's
actual policy, however, was one of support for the junta, despite several voices of skepticism in the State Department. In fact, a number
of State Department officials made an attempt to keep a certain distance from the junta and maintain an embargo on heavy weapons to
Greece, which was imposed in May 1967, the month after the takeover
by the colonels, by the administration of Lyndon Johnson.

At the White House, however, President Nixon and his National
Security Adviser Henry Kissinger decided that the colonels should be
supported and that the arms embargo against Greece should be lifted
because "of overriding U.S. security interests."[25] This embargo was

---

[24]Woodhouse, *The Rise and Fall*, p. 63.

[25]Seymour Hersch, *The Price of Power*, p. 140. Hersch documented Nixon's decision to support the Greek junta by citing the National Security Decision Memorandum, No. 34, November 14, 1969.

gradually lifted by the summer of 1970. By that time, however, it was becoming clear that the junta was politically and morally bankrupt, that the Greek people were increasingly becoming opposed to the oppressive military regime, and that Western European democracies were distancing themselves from the Greek dictatorship.

The Nixon administration took a further step to solidify its support for the colonels. In the summer of 1972, the junta and the United States government reached an agreement concerning the homeporting of the Sixth Fleet at the port of Piraeus. By September 1, 1972, American naval units, including an aircraft carrier, were anchored in the "friendly" waters of the colonels' Greece.[26] Piraeus became the largest homeporting facility for the Sixth Fleet in the Eastern Mediterranean. The Nixon administration argued that the homeporting of the Sixth Fleet would have a "moderating effect" on the Greek junta and would encourage it to move toward democratization. Following the homeporting agreement, the junta felt quite secure since it appeared that the United States was undoubtedly on its side.

In November 1972, Nixon won a landslide victory over George McGovern, while Kissinger was as influential as ever. With the continued support of the Nixon administration, the colonels felt that their future was guaranteed.[27] Twelve months later, instead of the democratization that the Nixon administration had been trumpeting, the junta resorted to brute force to quell student protests at the Athens Polytechnic University. The junta's security forces killed scores of pro-democracy protesters. The Nixon-Kissinger policy of "constructive engagement" with the Greek dictatorship was in shambles.

The Nixon administration was the only Western ally that became a de facto apologist of the junta. Washington provided generous military aid to the junta and assisted it in obtaining much-needed loans. Moreover, high administration officials, from the Pentagon and civilian agencies, kept arriving in Athens to pay tribute to the junta. Most memorable and graphic was the visit of Vice President Spiro Agnew in October 1971. Other American dignitaries who visited Greece included Defense Secretary Melvin Laird, Commerce Secretary Mau-

---

[26]On the agreement between the Nixon administration and the Greek dictators for the homeporting of the Sixth Fleet in Piraeus, see Stern, *The Wrong Horse*, pp. 71–73. See also Woodhouse, *The Rise and Fall*, pp. 100–111.

[27]See Woodhouse, ibid., p.111.

rice Stans, and Donald Nixon, the president's brother, who was vice president of the Marriott Corporation.[28] Stans, who visited Greece in 1971, read a message from President Nixon to the Greek people in which the president praised the economic achievements of the military regime. Stans stated that he had been asked by Nixon to "convey to the Government of Greece and the Greek people his warmth and confidence."[29] The junta leaders made maximum use of these visits by playing them up in the government-controlled media, which included the print media, radio, and television, in order to demonstrate the commitment of the U.S. to supporting the regime.

Another very important dimension of American support for the junta was Washington's policy of protecting it from a series of measures taken against it by the European Economic Community and the Council of Europe. Several European democracies, such as Italy, the Netherlands, West Germany, and, especially, Denmark, Norway, and Sweden were critical of the junta. Overall, most European democracies kept a certain distance from the dictatorship, especially after 1969. The opposite occurred in the United States as the Nixon administration increased its support for the junta after 1969.[30] The American relationship with the junta turned out to be one of "comfortable and occasionally paternalistic symbiosis."[31]

In the final analysis, there is little doubt that the Nixon administration decided to throw its weight behind the junta. The logic of realpolitik, strategic considerations, and "U.S. national security concerns" overrode concerns regarding the abolition of democratic rule, the violation of human rights, and press censorship. The American

---

[28]Maurice Goldbloom, "United States Policy in Post-War Greece," pp. 249–250. On visits by high-ranking American officials to the colonels' Greece, see also Couloumbis, *The United States, Greece, and Turkey*, p. 52, and Stern, *The Wrong Horse*, pp. 63–64.

[29]Stern, ibid., p. 64.

[30]This account of the Nixon administration's support for the junta draws upon Couloumbis's *The United States, Greece, and Turkey*, pp. 51–53. On this topic, see also Woodhouse, *The Rise and Fall*, esp. chapter 7, "The American Commitment," and chapter 8, " Towards a Home Port, " pp. 87–111.

[31]This description belongs to Theodore Couloumbis, *The United States, Greece, and Turkey*, p. 84. Couloumbis, a junta critic, has first-hand knowledge of events in Washington where he was a professor of international relations at American University. He also testified before congressional committees both during the junta era and in the aftermath of the Cyprus crisis.

government's actions contributed to the prolongation of the junta's rule. In turn, the junta carried out the coup against Makarios that precipitated the Turkish invasion of Cyprus.

Greek American Support for the Colonels

The Greek military regime took maximum advantage of the visits to Greece of many prominent Greek Americans, such as Agnew and Boston-based businessman Tom (Thomas) Pappas, who befriended the colonels.

The most prominent Greek American apologist of the junta was, no doubt, Agnew. During his visit to Greece from October 16 to 23, 1971, he clearly demonstrated his support for the Greek dictators and had ample opportunity to meet with the leadership of the regime. He met repeatedly with the junta leader, Prime Minister George Papadopoulos, and held extensive discussions with him. He also met and deliberated with the other top leaders of the junta, vice premiers Stylianos Pattakos and Nicholaos Makarezos. In other words, Agnew had enough time to formulate his own opinion about the military rulers of Greece.

During the fourth day of his stay, on Tuesday, October 19, 1971, Agnew and his family visited Gargalianoi, his father's village, in the Peloponnese. Papadopoulos, who called Agnew "brother," accompanied him. Agnew told the villagers of Gargalianoi that President Nixon had sent his warm wishes to them along with those of "2 million Americans of Greek descent."

Overall, throughout his stay in Greece, Agnew appeared quite comfortable with the colonels and had high praise for their achievements. The theme of Papadopoulos's speeches in honor of Agnew was that the junta leader and his regime were defenders of Western civilization and champions of the U.S.-Greek alliance. Agnew made it clear that he agreed with Papadopoulos's assessment of relations between the United States and Greece under the junta. Even though Papadopoulos's speeches were, in many respects, nonsensical, Agnew had high praise for the colonel, calling him "the distinguished prime minister of Greece." The U.S. vice president also declared that, having visited the Greek countryside and "being someone who has been active on issues of local administration, I recognized and appreciated the achievements of the present Greek government."[32] In the minds of Greeks, both those who supported and those who opposed the military regime, Agnew's embrace of the junta leaders was an unmistakable sign that the United States was supportive of the junta.

Agnew's visit to Greece was not just a personal visit in order to become re-acquainted with his roots. Agnew's ties with Greek matters did exist, but they were not particularly strong. His father, Theofrastos Anagnostopoulos, a Greek Orthodox, had married a woman from Virginia, Margaret Akers Pollard, an Episcopalian. Their only child, Spiro, born in 1918, was raised an Episcopalian and never learned Greek.[33]

Thus, while there was a personal aspect to Agnew's visit to the land and village of his father, he was also visiting the country as vice president of the United States. In this official capacity, he represented the Nixon administration's friendly attitude toward the Greek junta. At the same time, Agnew's praise for the colonels reflected the prevailing attitude among the Greek American community.[34] Consequently, when Agnew boasted that he was bringing with him the warm wishes of 2 million Greek Americans, he was not far from the truth.

It is well documented that only a small minority in the Greek American community opposed the junta. The attitude of the great majority fluctuated between sympathy for the junta and condoning its rule, and apathy concerning developments in Greece.[35] The most important Greek American institution, the Greek Orthodox Church,

[32]Information on Agnew's visit and all his speeches, as well as the speeches by junta leaders in his honor, are found in a pro-junta magazine, *April-Greece, A Monthly Illustrated National Review* (October 1971): pp. 6–23. The word "April" in the title commemorated the takeover by the junta on April 21, 1967.

[33]For a sympathetic biography of Spiro Agnew, which includes the origins of his parents and his upbringing, see Joseph Albright, *What Makes Spiro Run: The Life and Times of Spiro Agnew* (New York: Dodd, Mead, and Co., 1972), esp. pp. 1–42.

[34]For a critique of Agnew and the majority of Greek Americans who supported the junta, see Peter Pappas, "The Junta in America," *The Greek American* (April 18, 1987): pp. 20–21.

[35]The author was a student at the University of Pennsylvania in the early 1970s. Philadelphia had a substantial Greek community. In this community, opposition to the junta was quite limited and revolved around some Greek American academics and a small number of Greek students at universities and colleges in the Philadelphia area. Most Greeks in the area were either sympathetic to the junta or were apathetic to developments in Greece.

was rather sympathetic to the junta during most of its rule, while the oldest and largest Greek American organization, the American Hellenic Educational Progressive Association (AHEPA), was also sympathetic or tolerated the colonels.[36]

This widespread support for the Greek junta or the condoning of it by the Greek American community served as an added rationalization in the minds of administration officials for maintaining their support for the dictators. In fact, the State Department invoked the Greek American community's support for the junta in order to justify its own support for the colonels.[37]

It is highly unlikely that the Nixon administration would have changed its policy toward Greece had the majority of Greek Americans opposed the junta. Still, Greek American support for the colonels was utilized by the administration to fend off criticism of the dictatorship in Congress and the media. National Security Adviser and, later, Secretary of State Henry Kissinger did not appear to mind that Greek Americans, acting as an ethnically-based pressure group, supported his policies toward the junta. Kissinger, however, was highly critical of Greek Americans when they mobilized against his policies during the Cyprus crisis and its aftermath in the summer of 1974. With regard to the Greek American response to the Cyprus crisis, Kissinger was indignant that narrow ethnic politics were at work and were affecting negatively the "national interests" of the United States in the Eastern Mediterranean. Kissinger adopted a similar attitude toward the Jewish community. He welcomed Jewish American support for his Middle Eastern policies but became indignant when Congress adopted positions advocated by Jewish American groups,

---

[36]On Greek American support for the junta, see Van Coufoudakis, "The Reverse Influence Phenomenon: The Impact of the Greek-American Lobby on the Foreign Policy of Greece," in *Diasporas in World Politics: The Greeks in Comparative Perspective,* ed. Dimitris Constas and Athanasios Platias (London: The Macmillan Press, 1993), p. 53. See also James Pyrros, "PASOK and the Greek Americans: Origins and Development," in *Greece Under Socialism: A NATO Ally Adrift,* ed. Nicolaos Stavrou (New Rochelle, NY: Aristide D. Caratzas, 1988), pp. 321–333. A detailed account of the activities of those who opposed the junta in the United States is found in Vidalis, *Istoriko Imerologio* (A Historical Diary), passim.

[37]See Clifford Hackett, "The Role of Congress and Greek-American Relations," in *Greek-American Relations: A Critical Review,* ed. Theodore Couloumbis and John Iatrides (New York: Pella Publishing Co., 1980), p. 143. Vidalis, *Istoriko Imerologio* (A Historical Diary), pp. 863, 996.

positions that were not necessarily consistent with what Kissinger perceived as the "national interest."[38]

This dynamic, involving the Nixon administration in Washington, the Greek American community, and the Greek regime, can be termed the "reverse influence" of the Greek lobby. The Greek lobby was born in August 1974 in the immediate aftermath of the Turkish invasion of Cyprus. Like other ethnic lobbies, the Greek lobby's efforts were directed at influencing the foreign policy of the United States. Strictly speaking, therefore, one cannot refer to a Greek lobby as such during the junta period. Still, many Greek Americans, acting as a pressure group, were active in promoting American interests in the colonels' Greece. This Greek American activism corresponded to the phenomenon of "reverse influence" by an ethnic group. Even after 1974, there were several occasions when the Greek lobby directed its efforts toward influencing the Greek government to adopt policies that were more desirable to the United States.[39]

Opposition to the Colonels in the U.S.

The Nixon administration's support for the Greek junta did not represent nationwide approval of the colonels in the United States. The American attitude toward the colonels was by no means monolithic. In the State Department, there were several officials who were rather unsympathetic to the Greek junta. Under Secretary of State Joseph Sisco was willing to meet with several of the junta's opponents. During those meetings, Sisco and some of his associates did not appear to be sympathetic to the junta.[40] This attitude, however, was never translated into diplomatic action, and the United States continued to follow a policy of support for the junta.

---

[38]On Kissinger's criticism of Greek American and Jewish American groups, see Kissinger, *Years of Renewal*, pp. 131, 192, 232–233, 236.

[39]For a thorough analysis of the "reverse influence" phenomenon, see Van Coufoudakis, "The Reverse Influence," pp. 51–75. Coufoudakis, a professor of international relations at Indiana-Purdue University, was a junta critic who also observed the activities of the Greek lobby in Washington closely and testified on Cyprus before congressional committees.

[40]Several of these meetings between junta opponents and State Department officials, including Joseph Sisco, are described in Vidalis, *Years of Exile*, vol. I., pp. 344–349, 399–400.

In Congress, which was controlled by the Democrats, there was considerable opposition to the junta but not enough to stop the flow of arms to Athens. During a series of hearings in Congress on the situation in Greece, officials from the defense and state departments downplayed the violation of human rights in the country and lent credibility to the colonels' promises that they were committed to restoring democratic rule.[41] These officials were sharply criticized by members of Congress, especially during hearings before the European Affairs Subcommittee of the House Foreign Affairs Committee in 1972. Democratic Congressman Benjamin Rosenthal, elected in Queens, New York, chaired this subcommittee. This congressional criticism of the colonels, while it failed to change the Nixon administration's policies, did encourage the junta's opponents in the U.S. and Canada.[42]

Regarding the American media, the most influential newspapers, including the *Washington Post* and the *New York Times*, took a clear stand against the Greek colonels. Among literary circles, condemnation of the junta was loud and clear. On American campuses, liberal professors, many of whom were Jewish, took a strong stand against the colonels. Several retired U.S. military officers disagreed with the Nixon administration and the Pentagon on the matter. Several of them were former high-ranking officers who became critics of the Greek junta and supported several opposition efforts against it around the United States. The most notable critics of the junta were retired General Lauris Norstad, former Supreme Allied Commander Europe, and retired Colonel James Webel, who had served in Greece as NATO's liaison to the Greek General Staff from 1960 to 1964. Also critical of the junta was retired General H.J. Vander Heide, who had served as the head of the American Military Mission for aid to Greece from 1959 to 1961.[43]

---

[41]U.S. Congress, House. Subcommittee on Europe and Subcommittee on the Near East. *The Decision to Homeport in Greece. Report.* Washington, D.C.: December 31, 1972, U.S. Government Printing Office, 1972. See also Couloumbis, *The United States, Greece, and Turkey*, p. 52.

[42]On congressional opposition to the Greek junta, see Clifford Hackett, "The Role of Congress and Greek-American Relations," pp. 132–134.

[43]On opposition to the junta by several retired American officers, including Generals Norstad and Heide, and Colonel Webel, see Vidalis, *Istoriko Imerologio* (A Historical Diary), pp. 65–75, 78–79, 85–94 passim, 158, 166, 433- 440, 503–504.

Among Greek Americans, there was a small group that fought the junta tenaciously. It consisted primarily of academics in several American universities and exiles that were able to leave Greece after the military takeover. Their voices were not unimportant because they were able to form a loose coalition with other opponents of the junta in academia, the literary world, and the press. It was this group of Greek Americans, through its ties to Greece, that was able to provide crucial information to the media and to Congress on the repressive policies of the military regime.

Indeed, a significant number of the members of the U.S. Congress, a large number of academics, most of the press, prominent intellectuals, and several retired army officers all expressed clear opposition to the junta. In the final analysis, however, what counted in the eyes of the Greek people were the policies of the administration in Washington, which supported the junta until it ended. The Greek people, from the left, center, and right, resented U.S. support for the dictatorship. In the end, this American support for the junta was the main cause, but not the only one, behind the anti-American sentiment that prevailed in Greece in the 1970s and 1980s. Andreas Papandreou was not the prime generator of anti-Americanism in Greece. He did fan the flames of anti-Americanism that already existed, however, in order to gain popular support. It was only a matter of time until Papandreou would come to power riding the wave of anti-Americanism.

George Rallis: A Friend's Plea to America

As the Nixon administration's support for the Greek military dictatorship became entrenched in the national security bureaucracy, it led to two interrelated consequences. First, the administration succeeded in defeating all attempts in Congress and all efforts of the junta critics to change Nixon's policies toward Greece and put distance between Washington and the colonels. Second, the Nixon administration failed to heed the warnings of those who saw a storm coming in the Eastern Mediterranean, especially in relations between Greece and the United States, on the one hand, and between Greece and Turkey, on the other. A major cause for the brewing storm was American support for the junta and its ramifications for Greece and the region.

One of the most characteristic episodes in this respect took place in Washington on March 9, 1972, during the hearings before the European Affairs Subcommittee of the House Foreign Affairs Committee, chaired by Congressman Rosenthal, one of the most persistent critics of the junta. Following the Turkish invasion of Cyprus, Rosenthal emerged as a leading figure in the fight to impose the embargo on arms sales to Turkey.

Testifying before the subcommittee was a prominent Greek leader, George Rallis. Rallis came from a patrician family with long involvement in politics. Ideologically, he was anti-communist, genuinely pro-American, and a middle-of-the-road conservative. Throughout his political career, he behaved with moderation and avoided excesses. Rallis's credentials as a conservative, a true democrat, and a loyal friend of the United States were impeccable. He was also a cultured man and, overall, he represented what Americans believed the model for European political leaders should be.

Rallis was a leading figure in the conservative National Radical Union Party (ERE), which ruled Greece from 1955 to 1963 under the premiership of Constantine Karamanlis. Rallis served in the Karamanlis cabinet during that period. He also served in several ministerial positions, including that of foreign minister in the New Democracy government of Karamanlis from 1974 to 1980. From May 1980 to October 1981, Rallis was prime minister of Greece.

When the junta came to power, Rallis was initially jailed and then sent into internal exile. He was freed in 1969. He traveled to the United States in the spring of 1972 in order to meet members of Congress in Washington and inform them of the situation in Greece. Accompanying Rallis was Demetrios Papaspyrou, a leading figure of the Center Union Party and a former speaker of parliament. Rallis's testimony before Congress was in English, while Papaspyrou testified in Greek, which was translated into English.[44]

On March 9, 1972, Rallis opened his testimony before the European Affairs Subcommittee by declaring that the support of the United States for the Greek military dictatorship was a grave error. He cited specific examples of American support, such as Washington's 1972 agreement with the junta for the use of Piraeus by the U.S. Sixth

---

[44]Professor Nicolaos Stavrou of Howard University, who was a well-known opponent of the junta, assisted Papaspyrou in his testimony.

Fleet as a homeport. He also pointed to the October 1971 visit to Greece by Vice President Spiro Agnew, who had high praise for the colonels. He told the subcommittee that contemporary alliances were not just agreements among rulers, as had been the case in the eighteenth and nineteenth centuries, but they also took the sentiments of the people seriously into account. The overwhelming majority of the Greek people, Rallis declared, did not entertain friendly sentiments for the United States, precisely because Washington was supporting an oppressive military dictatorship, which was terrorizing the Greek people. Rallis estimated that 90 percent of the Greek people believed "that the American government closes its eyes and condones the Greek dictatorship because [Washington] receives strategic benefits, such as the naval base in Piraeus." U.S. support for the Greek dictators constituted a contradiction and hypocrisy on the part of the United States, a nation that wanted to appear to be the leader of the free, democratic world, Rallis proclaimed.

Then, the Greek leader gave Washington a sober warning. A climate of anti-Americanism was widespread in Greece. This anti-Americanism was not only hurting U.S. interests in Greece, but it was also bound to poison relations between Athens and Washington in the future and would have a negative effect on Greek foreign policy, Rallis concluded.[45]

Rallis's plea to Washington to change its policy of support for the junta fell on deaf ears at the Nixon-Agnew White House. Following Rallis's testimony before the House subcommittee, Vice President Spiro Agnew stated that, during his trip to Greece six months earlier, he had found that the Greek people were supporting the regime. Those who opposed it were either communists or idiots, Agnew declared with sarcasm. Rallis responded with a sense of humor: "I suppose that I belong to the last category [of idiots]."[46] Following his testimony before Congress, Rallis met with Under Secretary of State Joseph Sisco at the State Department. He received a friendly welcome

---

[45]Based on Rallis's account of his testimony to the European Affairs Subcommittee of the House International Relations Committee. See George Rallis, *Politikes Ekmystirevseis, 1950–1989: Apokalyptikes Martyries gia Krisimes Stigmes tes Sychronis Ellinikis Politikis Zoes* (Political Confessions, 1950–1989: Anecdotal Evidence Concerning Critical Moments in Contemporary Greek Political Life) (Athens: Proskenio Publishing, 1990), pp. 199–200.

[46]Ibid., pp. 198–199.

and had the opportunity to provide the higher echelons of the Department with first-hand information on the situation in Greece.[47] Rallis's visit, however, had no effect on U.S. policy toward Greece, as it continued to be firmly pro-junta.

Rallis's testimony before the House European Affairs Subcommittee constituted a prophetic warning to Washington by a genuine friend of the United States. He attributed a major part of the responsibility for the rising tide of anti-Americanism in Greece to Washington's actions. Rallis's warnings regarding increasing anti-Americanism in Greece and its implications did not take long to materialize. Following the collapse of the junta in July 1974 in the midst of the Cyprus disaster precipitated by the colonels, the overwhelming majority of Greeks were bitter toward the American support that had been given to the military dictatorship. Seven years later, the Greek people elected Andreas Papandreou prime minister, a man who had made anti-Americanism the centerpiece of his electoral campaign.

Clinton's Near Apology

As the years have passed, upon serious reflection, several American officials have expressed regrets that the U.S. role in Greece and Cyprus from 1967 to 1974 was not positive. On a visit to Cyprus in November 1997, Richard Holbrooke, President Clinton's special Cyprus envoy, admitted that the United States shared part of the responsibility for the tragic events of the 1960s in the region and, especially, the 1974 Cyprus crisis.[48] After he became U.S. ambassador to the United Nations in 1997, Holbrooke also expressed regret over U.S. policy during the Cyprus crisis at a meeting with Democratic Congresswoman Carolyn Maloney of New York and several Greek American leaders on January 11, 2000, in New York City. The purpose of the meeting, held at the initiative of Maloney, was to allow Ambassador Holbrooke to discuss the Cyprus issue. According to Maloney, Holbrooke strongly condemned the Turkish invasion and stated that U.S. foreign policy under the Nixon administration at the time of the

---

[47]Vidalis, *Istoriko Imerologio* (A Historical Diary), p. 589.

[48]*Cyprus News Agency,* November 12, 1997.

crisis constituted a terrible mistake that Washington had to work to correct.[49]

Nicholas Burns, the U.S. ambassador to Greece, who replaced Thomas Niles, spoke in a similar vein. Before arriving in Athens in September 1997, Burns had served in the high-visibility position of State Department spokesman. His criticism revolved around the role the United States had played in Greece during the junta era. Ambassador Burns stated:

> On the other hand, I think with the benefit of hindsight, it was a very great mistake for the United States to have supported the military dictatorship between 1967 and 1974. I mean, after all, this was the birthplace of democracy.... *We supported the military dictators* who robbed the Greek people of their democracy, who suspended the rule of law, and who jailed people. I think it was a very great mistake for the leading democratic nation in the world, the United States, to have supported an anti-democratic regime. I said this publicly on the day I was sworn into office by [Secretary of State] Madeleine Albright with her standing beside me . . .[50] (Emphasis added.)

The statements by Holbrooke and Burns acknowledging these errors and injustices were meant to heal wounds of the past. The fact that they were made by U.S. officials of such stature gave weight to the expressions of regret. The statements were well received both in Greece and Cyprus, where the wave of anti-Americanism had already receded by the early 1990s.

The anti-American climate resurfaced in the spring of 1999 when the United States led the NATO alliance in the war over Kosovo. The overwhelming majority of Greeks, more than 95 percent, opposed the American-led attack on Serbia. Performing a balancing act, the PASOK (Panhellenic Socialist Movement) government of Prime Minister Costas Simitis supported NATO, but Greece did not participate directly in the bombing. Simitis had succeeded Andreas Papandreou in January 1996.

---

[49]See interview with Congresswoman Maloney in *Proini*, January 12, 2000.

[50]See Ambassador Burns' interview in the magazine *Greek America*, vol. 4, issue 6 (September 1998): p. 24.

When President Bill Clinton paid a brief visit to Greece on November 19 and 20, 1999, left-wing demonstrators protested violently and went on a rampage in the center of Athens. Their protests revolved around two issues. The first was that Clinton's visit almost coincided with events commemorating the student uprising at Athens Polytechnic University on November 17, 1973. The second issue was the NATO bombing of Yugoslavia over Kosovo. The president acknowledged the protests and made a point to refer to a painful chapter of relations between the United States and Greece, the junta period. Speaking to top Greek government officials and business and community leaders, President Clinton proclaimed:

> I have been thinking about that history today again in both its painful as well as its proud aspects. When the junta took over in 1967 here, the United States allowed its interests in prosecuting the Cold War to prevail over its interests—I should say, its obligation—to support democracy, which was, after all, the cause for which we fought the Cold War. It is important to acknowledge that.[51]

This was tantamount or very close to an apology for the support the United States had provided for the junta. The president of the United States extended this apology himself directly to the Greek people in Athens. This act was perhaps one of the most important symbolic gestures an American president has made to Greece since the collapse of the junta in 1974. As such, Clinton's apology was also an indirect acknowledgement of shared American responsibility for the Cyprus crisis in 1974. After all, it was the U.S.-backed junta that staged the coup against Archbishop Makarios, the president of Cyprus, which, in turn, precipitated the Turkish invasion. Clinton's acknowledgement of American support for the Greek junta added further credence to the existing body of evidence on the American role in the junta's coup against Makarios and the ensuing Turkish invasion of Cyprus.

Three decades after the imposition of the junta in Greece, the question of whether the United States engineered the April 21, 1967

---

[51]See "Remarks by the President and Prime Minister Simitis of Greece to the Government of Greece, Business and Community Leaders," The White House, Office of the Press Secretary, November 20, 1999.

coup becomes secondary because the framing of the U.S. role in Greece in conspiratorial terms leads to endless speculation with no conclusive answer. What appears to be of more serious consequence is the acknowledgement by Clinton in Athens in 1999 that the United States supported the junta even though it had the opportunity to distance itself from the dictatorial regime.

By supporting the Greek dictatorship, the United States exercised substantial influence over the course of events that culminated in the junta's coup against Makarios and the Turkish invasion of Cyprus, triggered by the coup. Perhaps the most appropriate description of the American role in the junta is found in statements by retired Lieutenant General Orestis Vidalis to his American interlocutors. Vidalis, a decorated Greek army officer, was trained in the United States. He fought the Germans, who invaded Greece in 1941, and, in 1948 and 1949 during the Greek civil war, he fought the communist guerrillas. Vidalis, who was also loyal to King Constantine, supported the king in his failed attempt to overthrow the colonels in December 1967. Vidalis left Greece for the United States in the fall of 1968. From that time until the collapse of the junta in July 1974, he traveled around the United States in order to solicit support for the restoration of democracy in Greece. Vidalis met with many members of Congress and several officials in the Nixon administration. In his meetings with American officials, including Under Secretary of State Joseph Sisco, Vidalis presented the following basic argument:

> We Greeks are responsible for the creation of the existing situation [the military dictatorship]. But we are not responsible for the prolongation of the junta rule and, certainly, we will not be responsible for the epilogue, if you do not listen to us. *Since you are cooperating closely with the military regime on strategic grounds, you are also sharing the responsibility for extending its rule.* Most important is *how this episode will end.* Depending how the junta rule will end, this will determine the future of Greece and its relations with the West."[52] (Emphasis added.)

This was an ample and prescient warning on how the junta would

---

[52]Vidalis, *Istoriko Imerologio (Historical Diary)*, pp. 5, 346.

end. Orestis Vidalis, a sincere friend of the United States who had also fought the communists on the battlefield, gave the warning in person to numerous officials in Washington and around the country. Several other true friends and admirers of the United States, including George Rallis, gave a similar warning to Washington when they testified before Congress in March 1972. They warned the United States that it was becoming the co-author of the epilogue that would follow the end of the junta's rule. The epilogue for which the United States would be held responsible was a real disaster, and it has determined the course of Greek politics for over two decades. It was an epilogue that brought misery to Cyprus. It also affected, profoundly and negatively, for a long period of time not only Greece's relations with NATO, but also Turkey's relations with the Western alliance, especially the United States. The United States bears heavy responsibility for the writing of this epilogue.

Tom Pappas, the Junta, and Watergate

While Vice President Spiro Agnew was the most prominent Greek American supporting the Athens junta, another well-known Greek American, Boston-based businessman Tom Pappas, gave multifaceted support to the junta. He received preferential treatment by the junta because of the investments he already had in Greece. In the early 1960s, he was granted the right to build a $125 million steel, petrochemical, and oil refinery complex in Greece.[53] As part of the deal, Pappas was awarded the gasoline distribution concession for Esso (later Exxon), which was appropriately named Esso Pappas. In this way, Pappas became a household name in Greece, as a chain of Esso Pappas gas stations emerged throughout the country. Overall, Pappas became one of the main economic beneficiaries of the junta's favoritism.[54] This occurred while it was widely rumored that he maintained ties with the CIA, something that Pappas did not disavow.[55]

It also happened that Tom Pappas was a friend of President

---

[53]Hersch, *The Price of Power*, p. 137.

[54]Woodhouse, *The Rise and Fall*, p. 164.

[55]On reports about Pappas's ties with the CIA, see Hersch, *The Price of Power*, pp. 138–139; Stern, *The Wrong Horse*, p. 65; O' Malley and Craig, *The Cyprus Conspiracy*, p.132.

Nixon's. He had known Nixon since 1947 and had been a major contributor and fund-raiser for his election campaigns. It was also
believed that Pappas had influenced Nixon in his decision to pick
Spiro Agnew as his vice-presidential running mate in 1968.[56] However, it appears that, deep down, Nixon entertained a low view of
Agnew. When the matter of his own resignation came up on April 30,
1973, Nixon exclaimed ". . . [Resigning] . . . might not be a bad idea.
. . . The only problem is, I mean, you get Agnew. You want Agnew?"[57]

During the junta years, Pappas commuted between Boston,
Athens, and Washington. He had an office in Athens and had easy
access to the junta leaders. In fact, as soon as the colonels took over,
they appointed Paul Totomis to the position of minister of public
order. This was an extremely important ministry since it was responsible for security, a paramount concern of the junta. It was the responsibility of this ministry to maintain law and order and seek, identify,
and detain the "enemies of the nation." Totomis was a Pappas associ-
ate. He had spent time in the United States and, after he returned to
Greece, he became a top manager in the Pappas enterprises.[58] During
the junta years, Pappas also maintained ties with the Greek intelligence service KYP (*Kratike Yperesia Pleroforion,* or State Information
Agency), the equivalent of the American CIA.[59]

When Spiro Agnew visited Greece in October 1971, his friend
Tom Pappas was there and hosted a lunch in honor of the vice president. American dignitaries visiting Athens during the junta era also
met with Pappas. He usually hosted lunches or receptions for the dignitaries, which were attended by top junta officials.

---

[56]On Tom Pappas's close ties to Nixon, see Stanley I. Kutler, *The Wars of Watergate: The Last Crisis of Richard Nixon* (New York: W.W. Norton and Co., 1992), pp.
205–208, 276, 387, 491; Stern, *The Wrong Horse,* p. 63; Hersch, *The Price of Power,* pp.
137–139.

[57]This conversation took place between President Nixon and his speechwriter
Ray Price and is found in the Nixon tapes. A transcript of the Nixon tapes, with com-
mentary, was published in the book by Stanley I. Kutler, *Abuse of Power: The New
Nixon Tapes* (New York: The Free Press, 1997), p. 380.

[58]On Pappas's close ties to the junta, see Woodhouse, *The Rise and Fall,* pp. 31,
63, 77, 89, 94, 164; Hitchens, *Hostage to History,* 122, 127–129, 130; Hersch, *The Price
of Power,* pp. 137–138.

[59]See Petros Arapakis, *To Telos tes Siopis* (The End of Silence) (Athens: Nea Synora, 2000), p. 147–148. At the time of the Cyprus crisis in 1974, Arapakis had the rank
of admiral and was serving as chief of the Greek Navy.

When Nixon confided in Tom Pappas during the Watergate scandal, it was quite clear to the White House that Pappas had extremely close ties, both political and financial, to the Greek junta. As revealed in the Nixon tapes, the White House wanted Tom Pappas to play a key role in the effort to raise $1 million in hush money to cover up the Watergate scandal. The idea was that Pappas would work closely with John Mitchell, the attorney general and chairman of the Committee to Re-Elect the President. Pappas was the vice president of the Finance Committee to Re-Elect the President. In this vein, John Dean, counsel to the president, who first played a major role in the Watergate cover-up and then repented, referred to Pappas as the "Greek bearing gifts."[60] During the Watergate congressional investigation, Pappas denied that he had raised any payoff funds.

The Nixon tapes indicate that H.R. (Bob) Haldeman, Nixon's chief of staff, told the president on March 2, 1973, that ". . . [Pappas] is the best source we've got for that kind of thing [finding hush money]." Haldeman then praised Pappas for his ability to raise money. Stanley I. Kutler, one of the most authoritative students of the Nixon presidency, published a transcript of these tapes and also provided commentary. The transcript of the Nixon-Haldeman conversation is preceded by the following commentary by Kutler:

> This conversation [March 2, 1973] reveals Nixon's knowledge of the cover-up details. He and Haldeman discuss Thomas Pappas' role as principal funder of the hush money to the burglars—"this other activity," the President put it. Pappas, a prominent Nixon fund-raiser, had important ties to the fascist regime of the Greek colonels in Athens. Without hesitation, Nixon approves Pappas' request that the American Ambassador [Henry Tasca], who supported the colonels, be retained at his post. But Pappas' most important asset is that, as Haldeman succinctly states, he dealt "in cash."[61]

The following is the transcript of the Nixon-Haldeman conversation:

---

[60]John Dean, *Blind Ambition: The White House Years* (New York: Simon and Schuster, 1976), p. 197; see also the transcript of the Nixon tapes in Kutler, *Abuse of Power*, p. 256.

[61]Kutler, *Abuse of Power*, pp. 217–218.

HALDEMAN: . . . One of the major problems John [Dean] is working on is the question of financial, continuing financial activity in order to keep those people [Watergate burglars] in place. And the way he is working on that is via Mitchell to Tom Pappas.

NIXON: Yeah

HALDEMAN: Which is the best source we've got for this kind of thing. Pappas is extremely anxious that [Ambassador Henry Tasca] stay in Greece. . . . On our plan was, you know, to remove him and put someone else in Greece, but Mitchell says it would be a very useful thing to just not disrupt that.

NIXON: Good. I understand. No problem. Pappas has raised the money for this other activity or whatever it is. How's he doing?

HALDEMAN: I think it's just—you know, he is (unintelligible) raise money. . . . He put a thing together over there [Greece] and he just—sold his company out or something and picked up something else and parlayed that into something, and apparently he is sort of one of the unknown J. Paul Gettys of the world right now. . . . And he is able to deal in cash."[62]

This exchange and Haldeman's statements that discussed Pappas's ability to "deal in cash" and raise hush money, along with his business ventures in Greece, are of particular interest. These ventures were the preferential concessions granted to Pappas by the Greek junta. Haldeman's comments indicated clearly that the Nixon White House was well aware of the fact that Pappas had major business ventures in the colonels' Greece and was making money from those ventures. This did not appear to be a matter of concern to the Nixon White House. On the contrary, Pappas was admired for his ability to succeed financially in Greece at that time.[63]

On March 7, 1973, Nixon invited Pappas to the White House.

---

[62]Ibid., p. 218.

[63]The Watergate Special Prosecutor's staff named Pappas as a subject of its investigation. Pappas, however, was not criminally implicated. When he testified before the Watergate grand jury, he denied contributing any Watergate payoff funds. See Stern, *The Wrong Horse*, pp. 63–64; Hersch, *The Price of Power*, p. 139.

They met in the Oval Office, and the following conversation took place:

> NIXON: Let me say one thing. I want you to know I was mentioning last night. I am aware of what you're doing to help out some of these things that Maury's [Maurice Stans'] people and others are involved in. I won't say anything further, but it's very seldom you find a friend like that, believe me.
>
> PAPPAS: Thank you.
>
> NIXON : Frankly, let me say Maury's clean as he can be.
>
> PAPPAS: Sure.
>
> NIXON : But it's down the line. Down the line they are guilty. You know that. . . . But nobody in the White House was involved. It's just stupid.
>
> PAPPAS: I spent eight months, did you know that.
>
> NIXON : Eight months?
>
> PAPPAS: Yes. . . . Every day at the office I made 12 trips back and forth from the time I started in January.
>
> NIXON : How did you do it?
>
> PAPPAS: Well, I did it because—well (unintelligible).
>
> NIXON : And basically, as you say, we were so shocked—I was so shocked to hear such a stupid thing, mainly if you were going to bug somebody, for Christ's sake, first, you shouldn't bug them. But, second, if you are going to do it, [why] the National Committee? They don't know a goddam thing.
>
> PAPPAS: That's right.
>
> NIXON : I thought it was the most [stupid?] thing. But, you know, amateurs. That's what it is. Amateurs. Believe me.[64]

What stands out in this conversation is three-fold. First, Nixon was not known to be a person to show his emotions. Thus, his praise

---

[64]Kutler, *Abuse of Power*, p. 226.

for Pappas indicated that they were close friends. Second, Nixon's reference to the Watergate break-in was quite intriguing. As Nixon put it to Pappas, it was "stupid" to break into the Democratic National Committee (DNC) office because they didn't "know a goddam thing." Pappas responded, "That's right." Third, Pappas's reference to the 12 trips he made "back and forth" raises the question of whether his trips included visits to the colonels' Greece in order to find ways to raise money for Nixon.

This cryptic conversation raises the question of whether Nixon, who was conspiratorial by nature, was referring to activities that would be embarrassing if made public. Such activities might have been financial, considering that Pappas's main role was to raise money for Nixon's political needs.

Watergate and the "Greek Connection"

Tom Pappas's close ties to the Greek junta and the fact that the Nixon White House wanted him to play a key role in the efforts to raise hush money during the Watergate scandal bring to the surface once more the theory that there was a "Greek connection" to the break-in at the DNC office in the Watergate complex on June 17, 1972. A team of White House "burglars" carried out the break-in. There had been an earlier break-in at the DNC office on May 28, 1972, but its results were considered unsatisfactory because some of the bugging devices planted were not working well. Therefore, a second break-in was carried out in the early morning hours of June 17.[65]

It was the June 17 break-in and the arrest of the burglars that triggered the Watergate scandal. If the theory concerning the Greek connection to the Watergate break-in is correct, Tom Pappas was at the epicenter of it. According to this theory, the objective of the break-in was to find out whether Larry O' Brien, the DNC chairman, had information regarding allegations that illegal foreign funds had been channeled to the Nixon campaign. These illegal funds revolved around allegations of a sizable contribution from the Greek junta to the Nixon campaign fund in 1968. If, indeed, the colonels had made such

---

[65]G. Gordon Liddy, *Will: The Autobiography of G. Gordon Liddy*, 3rd ed. (New York: St. Martin's Press, January 1977), pp. 234–246.

a contribution to the campaign and if such information had been made public, it would have destroyed Nixon's bid to be elected president. In a sense, allegations of an illegal contribution by the junta to the Nixon campaign fund in 1968 constituted old information by 1972, when the Watergate break-in occurred. Still, if they had been true, these charges would have been so explosive that the Democrats would have made prompt use of them in the 1972 campaign. This could have caused very serious political damage to Nixon considering that he never shook the image of "tricky Dick."

The planner of the Watergate break-in, G. Gordon Liddy, wrote in his memoirs that "the purpose of the second break-in was to find out what O'Brien had *of a derogatory nature about us,* not for us to get something on him or the Democrats."[66] (Emphasis added.) It was this contention—that the purpose of the break-in was to find out what damaging information the Democrats had about Nixon—that fueled speculation on the "Greek connection."

The source of the information concerning allegations of a contribution by the Greek dictators to the Nixon campaign originated with Greek journalist Elias Demetrakopoulos. He left Greece for the United States following the military coup of April 21, 1967. He subsequently lived in Washington, where he engaged in multifaceted activities against the Greek dictatorship. He became well known in Congress for these activities and especially for his criticism of Kissinger's policies toward the colonels. Demetrakopoulos found a strong ally is his fight against the junta in Senator George McGovern.[67] The Greek journalist was also an open critic of Nixon's friend Tom Pappas and his close ties to the junta.[68] According to Demetrakopoulos, he, himself, told O'Brien that the Greek junta had transferred $549,000 to the Nixon campaign fund in three installments in 1968. Several reports indicated that the conduit for these payments was none other than Nixon's confidant and the colonels' friend, Tom Pappas, who transported the junta's cash payments from Athens to the United States.[69] According to Kutler, four years later, Pappas's role

---

[66]Ibid., 237.

[67]Hitchens, *Hostage to History,* pp. 124–129.

[68]Ibid., pp. 87–88, 126–28.

[69]Based on the accounts of Anthony Summers, Hersch, Kutler, and Hitchens. See Anthony Summers, *The Arrogance of Power: The Secret World of Richard Nixon* (New

as fund-raiser for Nixon's re-election was even more important than it had been in 1968. Kutler wrote:

> He [Pappas] solicited hundreds of thousands of dollars from businessmen. He also raised illegal funds from foreign sources. (Receiving foreign money apparently was not unusual for a Nixon campaign: Philippine President Ferdinand Marcos reportedly contributed in both 1968 and 1972.)[70]

As far as the 1968 presidential campaign was concerned, the information regarding allegations of an illegal contribution by the Greek junta to the Nixon election campaign fund was obviously explosive. For a variety of reasons, the Democrats, including President Lyndon Johnson, who was presumably told about the contribution to the Nixon campaign fund for the forthcoming elections, did not wish to make this information public at the time. Thus, the secret ended up locked in O'Brien's Watergate office. It was precisely this information on the Greek junta's contribution to the Nixon campaign fund that the Watergate burglars were looking for when they broke into the DNC office.

The "Greek connection" theory has long been around and is mentioned in most books dealing with the Watergate scandal. The logical question is that, if indeed the Democrats were in possession of such explosive information, which would have sunk the Nixon campaign in 1968, why didn't they use it? In a highly acclaimed book published in 1998 on the Johnson presidency, there is an explanation for Johnson's decision not to make use of the information regarding the money funneled by the Greek junta into the Nixon campaign fund. According to the author of the book, Robert Dallek, Elias Demetrakopoulos, who furnished Larry O'Brien with this information, urged O'Brien to pass the information on to Johnson and tell him that CIA Director Richard Helms could confirm the story. Indeed, O'Brien gave Johnson the information, but the president refused to act upon it.[71]

According to Dallek, Johnson did not take action regarding this

---

York: Viking, 2000), pp. 285–286. See also Hersch, *The Price of Power*, pp. 137–139; Kutler, *The Wars of Watergate*, pp. 206–208; Hitchens, *Hostage to History*, pp. 126–130.

[70]Kutler, ibid., p. 207.

[71]Robert Dallek, *Flawed Giant: Lyndon Johnson and his Times* (New York: Oxford University Press, 1998), pp. 579–580.

highly damaging information against Nixon for three reasons. First, the Johnson administration viewed the Greek junta positively, while it considered Demetrakopoulos a troublemaker. Second, Johnson did not want to act in a way that might help Vice President Hubert Humphrey, who was running for president at the time. Third, Johnson had a visceral mistrust of Nixon and was concerned that, if Nixon became president, he would "indict all of us."[72] For these reasons, Johnson did not want to use the "Greek connection" story at that time but wanted to keep it as back up to be used against Nixon in the future.[73] Another reason for Johnson's inaction might have been that he was so preoccupied with the Vietnam War that he was not able to pay attention to the Tom Pappas affair.[74] Thus, the Democrats made no use of the information, explosive as it was, regarding the funneling of Greek junta money into the Nixon campaign fund.

There is no smoking gun to prove the "Greek connection" theory. It would be more appropriate to call it "the Greek junta connection," theory. It is one of several theories regarding the reason behind the second Watergate break-in, the cover-up of which led to Nixon's resignation.[75] Whatever the truth might be, there is little doubt that the Nixon administration had a close connection with the Greek junta. One channel for the multifaceted American support for the junta ran through Tom Pappas, the intimate friend of the colonels with financial interests in Greece, who was also a good friend of President Nixon's and a fund-raiser for him. Recognizing the depth of the Nixon administration's support for the junta is essential if one wishes to understand the complex dynamics that led to the overthrow of Makarios by the junta and the ensuing Turkish invasion of Cyprus, events that both took place, ironically, during the climax of the Watergate scandal.

Greek Blunders and the Cyprus Crisis

The Turkish invasion of Cyprus caused a mass mobilization of the Greek American community. What transpired in the summer of 1974

---

[72]Ibid., p. 580.

[73]Ibid.

[74]Summers, *The Arrogance of Power*, p. 287.

[75]For other Watergate theories, in addition to the "Greek connection," see Kutler, *Wars of Watergate*, pp. 198–205.

was phenomenal. The Greek American community suddenly exploded. Greek Americans had not been known to actively oppose the policies of the U.S. government by holding mass rallies in Washington and other cities around the nation. In fact, the opposite had been true, as the great majority of Greek Americans had tended to condone or support U.S. policies in the Eastern Mediterranean. This had been clearly manifested by Greek American support, with few exceptions, for the policies of Nixon and Kissinger toward the Greek junta. In the aftermath of the invasion, however, Greek Americans began an intense lobbying effort that, combined with other factors such as congressional assertiveness in foreign policy, led to the imposition of an embargo on arms sales to Turkey. Greek American anger was primarily directed against Secretary of State Henry Kissinger, who had made the critical decisions during the Cyprus crisis.

Since 1974, the prevailing view among Greeks in Greece and Cyprus has been, and still is, that the United States, the Nixon administration, and Kissinger, to be exact, played an instrumental role in the coup against Makarios as well as the Turkish invasion that followed. In other words, among these Greeks, the single factor explanation, known as the "American role," tends to dominate the analysis of the Cyprus crisis of the summer of 1974.

Washington's actions and omissions did have a critical bearing on the outcome of events leading to the 1974 Cyprus crisis.[76] In addition to the American role, however, one has to consider other factors and look at the broader picture in order to provide a satisfactory explanation for the dramatic developments of that period. In this respect, one also has to acknowledge the Greek, Turkish, and British roles as essential factors that shaped the tumultuous developments of that summer in the Eastern Mediterranean. It was the interplay of all these forces that led to the forced division of Cyprus in July and August 1974.

Over the years, since the late 1950s, the policies of the governments of Greece and Cyprus have been characterized by a series of foreign policy blunders. They include the Zurich-London agreements, which granted Cyprus a semi-independent status through a

---

[76]For a comprehensive analysis of the American role in Cyprus throughout the junta years, see Van Coufoudakis, "To Kypriako, he Ellino-Tourkikes Scheseis ke he Yperdynameis" (The Cyprus Issue, Greek-Turkish Relations and the Superpowers), in *He Ellino-Tourkikes Scheseis, 1923–1987* (Greek-Turkish Relations, 1923–1987), ed. Alexis Alexandris et. al. (Athens: Gnose, 1988), pp. 227–238.

bizarre constitution that gave veto power to the minority community, the Turkish Cypriots.[77] This was combined with a system of guarantor powers—Britain, Greece, and Turkey—which had the right of unilateral intervention. Britain secured its interests on the island through two major sovereign military bases. Certainly, the Greek and Cypriot leadership at the time came under intense western presure to sign the agreements. Still, Greek Prime Minister Constantine Karamanlis and Archbishop Makarios, shared responsibility for accepting the Zurich-London agreements, which were defunct from the outset.

Less than three years after Cyprus became independent, the new island republic found itself at a constitutional impasse. This was hardly surprising, considering that there was almost a consensus that the constitution of Cyprus was unworkable. In 1959, the State Department's Bureau of Intelligence and Research prepared a report that cast serious doubt on the viability of the Cypriot constitution.[78]

The president of the Republic of Cyprus, Archbishop Makarios, had legitimate reasons for seeking to amend a dysfunctional constitution. At the end of November 1963, therefore, he proposed 13 amendments to the constitution, and it appeared that Britain had no real objection to these proposals. Archbishop Makarios officially announced the 13 amendments on November 30, 1963. Upon hearing this announcement, Sir Arthur Clark, the British High Commissioner, told Makarios: "Your Beatitude, what you are doing today is an act of great statesmanship."[79]

However, Makarios's timing with regard to the amendments was quite inopportune. His proposals were made at a time when Greece was undergoing a political crisis and was ruled by a caretaker government. Consequently, Athens was quite skeptical of Makarios's initia-

---

[77]On the unique constitution of Cyprus and its dysfunction and contribution to the Cyprus crisis of 1963, see the study by Stanley Kyriakides, *Constitutionalism and Crisis Government* (Philadelphia: University of Pennsylvania Press, 1968). On the subject of the dysfunctional constitution, see also T.W. Adams, "The First Republic of Cyprus: A Review of an Unworkable Constitution," *Western Political Science Quarterly*, vol. 19, no. 3 (September 1966): pp. 475–490.

[78]See Elias Vlanton and Diana Alicia, "The 1959 Cyprus Agreement: Oracle of Disaster," *The Journal of the Hellenic Diaspora*, vol. xi, no. 4 (Winter 1984): p. 5–31. The authors analyze the 1959 declassified State Department report on the Cyprus constitution.

[79]Quoted in Dimitrios Bitsios, *Cyprus: The Vulnerable Republic* (Thessaloniki: Institute for Balkan Studies, 1975), p. 123.

tive.[80] The Turkish government had made it clear that it opposed any unilateral action to change the status quo in Cyprus.[81] Certainly, Makarios never intended to act unilaterally. The Turkish side had always been suspicious of him because he was a Greek nationalist and, above all, because he was a priest and the head of the Greek Orthodox Church of Cyprus.

Equally important was the fact that, when Makarios submitted his amendment proposals at the end of November 1963, the United States was experiencing the shock of the assassination of President John F. Kennedy. Makarios's decision to propose the amendments at such an inopportune time precipitated the Cyprus crisis of 1963 and 1964, which ushered Cyprus into a protracted period of conflict. Thus, while he did not intend to impose the amendments unilaterally, his decision to propose them at that time constituted yet another Cypriot blunder.

Four years later, the military junta that had come to power in Greece committed yet another blunder. It started with intercommunal fighting in Cyprus in mid-November 1967. Turkey threatened to invade Cyprus unless Greece withdrew its military division from the island. President Johnson sent Cyrus Vance to the region as his special envoy in order to defuse the crisis. The junta in Athens quickly capitulated to all Turkish demands and withdrew the Greek division from the island.

Greek Prime Minister George Papandreou had dispatched this infantry division to Cyprus in the summer and fall of 1964. It was a reinforced infantry division with elite forces and special anti-tank support. Its mission was to deter a Turkish invasion. The United States did not appear to object to the presence of the Greek division in Cyprus. Viewed from a local perspective, the Greek division, consisting of a regular army, was a stabilizing factor on the island. It was preferable to have a disciplined army commanded by NATO-trained officers, the Greek officers in Cyprus, than to deal with Greek Cypriot irregulars. Indeed, most of the bloodshed on the island occurred when fighting took place between Greek Cypriot and Turkish Cypriot irregulars. This happened between December 1963 and April 1964. Thereafter, with the exception of a flare-up in August 1964, there was

---

[80]Ibid., pp. 122–123.
[81]Ibid.

little fighting on the island until the November 1967 crisis. From a regional perspective, the Greek division was also a stabilizing factor because it restored the balance of power between the Greek and Turkish forces in the Eastern Mediterranean.

Under the prevailing military conditions on the island from 1964 to 1967, a Turkish invasion was unlikely to succeed for two main reasons. First, considering the rather poor performance of the Turkish invasion forces in July 1974, it was not likely that Turkey could have launched a successful invasion of Cyprus between 1964 and 1967 given the fact that the country was defended by a Greek division. Second, even if Turkey had entertained the idea of invading Cyprus then, the presence of the Greek division would have served as a tripwire. If Turkey had attacked Cyprus, it would have automatically triggered a Greek-Turkish war. The prospect of a war between NATO allies Greece and Turkey was extremely undesirable to the United States. That was precisely the reason behind President Johnson's letter to Turkish Prime Minister Ismet Inonu on June 4, 1964. Johnson gave a stern warning to Turkey, which abandoned the idea of invading Cyprus. The Greek division in Cyprus had, indeed, served as a deterrent against a Turkish invasion.

This situation changed when the November 1967 crisis erupted on the island. The junta's capitulation to Turkey during the crisis was a prelude to what followed seven years later. The withdrawal of the Greek division from Cyprus by the junta undermined the existing balance of power. It left Cyprus extremely weak militarily and increased the likelihood of a Turkish invasion. The military coup engineered by the Athens junta against Makarios in July 1974 did precipitate a Turkish invasion. In the final analysis, this invasion was facilitated by the Greek military junta through the withdrawal of the Greek division from the island in November 1967 and, seven years later, through the coup against Makarios.

From Blunders to Folly

These were serious blunders on the part of the Greek side.[82] More

---

[82]Some of the blunders of the governments of Greece and Cyprus are discussed by Theodore Couloumbis, *Kypriako: Lathi, Didagmata, Prooptikes* (The Cyprus Issue: Mistakes, Lessons, Prospects) (Athens: Sideris Publishing, 1996), pp. 80–86.

than anything, they were self-inflicted wounds that did not heal with the passage of time. On the contrary, these mistakes were compounded by even greater ones. The July 1974 coup against Makarios represented the culmination of the Greek blunders. Indeed, the history of policies followed by the Cypriot leadership and the Greek government since the 1950s has constituted a series of blunders. Still, the coup staged against Makarios by the Greek junta stands out as a folly.[83] It is extremely unlikely that a democratic government in Greece would have overthrown a democratically-elected president of Cyprus, especially the charismatic Makarios, who enjoyed overwhelming popular support in Cyprus and considerable political support in Greece. Makarios was also a well-known leader of the non-aligned movement.

The 1974 Cyprus crisis was directly linked to the internal politics of Cyprus and Greece. Since the early 1970s, the island republic had been experiencing political turmoil as violent cycles of infighting occurred among Greek Cypriots, both supporters and opponents of President Makarios. The Greek junta had played a key role in fomenting the upheaval in Cyprus aimed at subverting the rule of Makarios, who was perceived as leftist-oriented.[84] Compounding the problem was the return to Cyprus of the leader of EOKA, General George Grivas.[85] Upon his return in 1971, he established EOKA-B, whose objective was to bring about *enosis*, or the union of Cyprus with Greece. To

---

[83]Barbara Tuchman, *March of Folly: From Troy to Vietnam* (New York: Ballantine Books, 1984). Tuchman defines "folly" as "the pursuit of policy contrary to the self-interest of the constituency or state involved. Self-interest is whatever conduces to the welfare or the advantage of the body being governed; folly is a policy that in these terms is counter-productive." (p. 5) Tuchman examines four conflicts through the ages and how the follies of leaders and governments led to disaster. These follies were the Trojan War and the Trojan Horse, the Protestant secession from the Holy See, the American Revolution and the colonial policies of Britain, and, finally, the Vietnam War. Tuchman argues that "folly is a child of power. . . . The power to command frequently causes failure to think that the responsibility of power often fades as its exercise augments." (p. 32) This appears to be quite applicable to the decisions of the Greek junta concerning Cyprus.

[84]Marios Evryviades, "The Problem of Cyprus," *Current History*, vol. 70, no. 412 (January 1976): pp. 20–21, 38–40; Coufoudakis, "To Kypriako" (The Cyprus Issue), pp. 232–237.

[85]EOKA stands for the acronym *Ethniki Organosi Kyprion Agoniston* (National Organization of Cypriot Fighters). It carried out a guerrilla campaign against the British from 1955 to 1959.

achieve this, EOKA-B began a campaign against Makarios, who was seen as abandoning the cause of *enosis*. Motivated by the dream of *enosis*, those who opposed Makarios, with few exceptions, fell behind Grivas.

Complicating the situation was the fact that Grivas and Makarios had a love-hate relationship, while Grivas's view of the Greek junta was ambivalent. However, the end result of the Grivas-led EOKA-B movement was the subversion of Makarios's rule. EOKA-B was assisted by Greek officers in the Cypriot National Guard, who were doing the bidding of the Athens junta. Overall, EOKA-B's and Grivas's role at the time was highly destabilizing and led to a disaster. Grivas died in January 1973, leaving behind confusion among the cadres and followers of EOKA-B. Following Grivas's death, events moved quickly. In the end, the EOKA-B episode constituted yet another Greek blunder, one committed by Makarios's opponents.

The fiercely anti-communist and paranoid junta in Athens viewed Makarios as an instrument of the Cypriot communist party (AKEL) and, by extension, of Moscow, a sort of "Castro of the Mediterranean." It was a view that was not inconsistent with the attitude of the Nixon administration toward Makarios. At the same time, the junta had reached a dead end. This became clear following the uprising at the Athens Polytechnic University in mid-November 1973. On November 17, the junta crushed a student rebellion at the university, killing over 30 protesters in the process. The uprising had the overwhelming support of the Greek people. Manifestations of this support were obvious as hundreds of thousands of Athenians expressed solidarity with the students in one way or another.

The killing of the students at the Polytechnic had a profound effect on the Greek public. The only analogous event in the United States was the killing of four students who were protesting the Vietnam War at Kent State University on May 4, 1970. The shock to the American public caused by the killing of these students became one of the turning points in the opposition against the war. One could multiply the impact of the Kent State incident many times over in order to comprehend the impact of the killing of students at the Polytechnic by the Greek junta. These killings left the vast majority of the Greek people embittered not just against the junta, but also against the United States, which had been supporting the colonels.

An incident involving several American students, who happened

to be in Athens at the time of the uprising at the Polytechnic, demonstrated the validity of the Greek sentiment. As the uprising was reaching its climax and the junta was beginning its crackdown on the
participants on November 17, 1973, a group of American students
engaged in archaeological excavations were staying at the American
School of Classical Studies in the Greek capital. This school was a
walking distance of half an hour from the Polytechnic. Late in the
afternoon of November 17, the students decided to walk toward the
Polytechnic. As they approached a side street in the vicinity of the
Polytechnic, they heard the chanting of thousands of people. "Down
With the Junta. Bread, Education, Freedom." (*Kato e hunta. Psomi,
paedia, eleftheria*). The area around the Polytechnic swarmed with
policemen. Suddenly, a Greek student coming from the direction of
the Polytechnic ran toward the American students. As he approached
them, eight policemen jumped on the student, pulled him down, and
began beating and kicking him with visceral hatred. The student bled
profusely as he was taken away. The American students were shaken
and utterly disgusted by the spectacle, while one of them observed:
"This is the regime that our government is supporting. This is where
our tax dollars are going."[86]

What happened at the Athens Polytechnic University in November 1973 demonstrated beyond a doubt that the regime Washington
had been sustaining for years was an oppressive dictatorship hated by
the Greek people. Faced with the prospect of the regime's demise in
the aftermath of the crackdown at the Polytechnic, a group of officers
thought that a way out was to oust the junta strongman, George
Papadopoulos. Earlier, he had abolished the monarchy and declared
himself the "president of the republic." At the time of the Polytechnic
uprising, Papadopoulos was attempting to create a political system
that would allow limited political freedom. It was to be a system of
"guided democracy" with the armed forces being the permanent
guardians of the country's political and social order. It was a system
not unlike the one that existed and still exists in Turkey. The Polytechnic uprising buried Papadopoulos's effort to imitate the Turkish
model of a democracy guided by the army.

On November 25, 1973, a new junta overthrew Papadopoulos and

---

[86]This eyewitness account was described to the author in February 2000 by an
American who had been one of these students.

his associates, appointing a new puppet government. The strongman of the new regime was Brigadier Demetrios Ioannides. He was the head of the military police, which had been engaged in the torturing of the junta's opponents. Ioannides remained an enigmatic figure who shunned publicity.

Given the impasse at which the junta found itself, it needed some kind of national success to shore up its shaky rule. It was primarily for this reason that the junta in Athens proceeded with the military coup against Makarios.[87] The Cypriot National Guard carried out the July 15, 1974 coup on orders from Athens. It was led by Greek army officers loyal to the junta in Athens. The coup against Makarios, a charismatic leader and popular president since being elected to office in 1960, was seen by the junta as an opportunity to achieve such a national success. Cyprus was to be the place where Greek nationalism would triumph, the junta believed. The coup was a disastrous move that led instead to national humiliation. There was fierce resistance to the coup and its puppet regime headed by Nikos Sampson, who was appointed by Ioannides as "president" of Cyprus. Sampson was a controversial figure. He was a veteran EOKA fighter and one of several local chieftains who had taken part in the intercommunal fighting in 1963 and 1964. Britain and Turkey had a deep disdain for Sampson.

With the Athens-instigated coup against Makarios and the installation of the highly controversial Sampson as president of Cyprus, it was as if the Greek junta were presenting a gift to Turkey. For some time, Ankara had been looking for an opportunity to invade Cyprus. That is precisely what transpired five days after Makarios was overthrown. From the outset, the Turkish objective of the invasion was to capture 34 to 38 percent of Cypriot territory. Without the coup against Makarios, it is very doubtful whether Turkey could have found such a unique opportunity to invade Cyprus and occupy 38 percent of its territory. While the Greek and Greek Cypriot leadership have committed a series of blunders over time, none of them compares to the junta's coup against Makarios. The junta's coup in Cyprus ranks among the greatest Greek follies of the twentieth century.

---

[87]The key figures of the Greek military regime at the time were President Phaedon Gizikis, Prime Minister Adamandios Androutsopoulos, and Foreign Minister Constantinos Kypraios. The chief of the armed forces was General Gregorios Bonanos. The real ruler of the country, however, was Brigadier Demetrios Ioannides, who wielded power behind the scenes.

For his part, Makarios seemed to have underestimated the junta in Athens and openly challenged it by demanding on July 2, 1974, that it withdraw its military officers from the Cypriot National Guard. Makarios was certainly justified to be alarmed by the junta's subversive policies in Cyprus. The Cypriot President, however, was dealing with a paranoid regime in Athens that was desperately seeking ways to hang on to power. Thus, the junta used the Makarios letter as an excuse, a poor one, to justify the coup against the Cyprus president. In fact, the idea of a coup had been seriously considered before Makarios's letter to the junta dated July 2. There were, therefore, a series of interrelated events, some being the product of deliberate decisions and others being the unintended consequence of shortsighted or self-defeating policies.

Whatever responsibility the United States might have had with respect to the Cyprus crisis, there were a number of decisions for which Washington could not be assigned blame. In this vein, one should point out Makarios's appearance before the U.N. Security Council on July 19, 1974. Following his overthrow, which almost killed him, and his escape from Cyprus, a justifiably bitter Makarios addressed the Security Council, calling the coup against him an "invasion." Makarios stated:

> [The coup] is clearly an invasion from outside, in flagrant violation of the independence and sovereignty of the Cyprus Republic. . . . the events of Cyprus do not constitute an internal matter of the Greeks of Cyprus. *The Turks of Cyprus are also affected. The coup of the Greek junta is an invasion,* and from its consequences the whole people of Cyprus suffers, both Greeks and Turks.[88] (Emphasis added.)

This address by Makarios came to haunt him. Less than 12 hours after the speech, Turkey invaded Cyprus. The basic justification for the Turkish action was that the coup staged by the Greek junta against Makarios had been an invasion, and Turkey had to intervene to restore the status quo ante and protect the Turkish Cypriots who were faced with a serious threat. Undoubtedly, Makarios's speech had nothing to do with the Turkish invasion. By the time Makarios spoke

---

[88] *Security Council Official Records,* July 19, 1974, S/PV 1780.

in New York, the Turkish National Security Council and Prime Minister Ecevit had already ordered the invasion and the Turkish armada had left the port of Iskenderun (Alexandretta) on its way to Cyprus. Still, the fact that Makarios stated that the coup against him constituted an invasion, which had also affected the Turkish Cypriots, was used as an argument to reinforce Ankara's thesis that its invasion was based on treaty obligations and was, therefore, justified.[89]

The overthrow of Makarios by the Greek junta and the ensuing Turkish invasion, therefore, should be placed in the context of a series of blunders in Greece and Cyprus, divisive Greek politics, the strong ideological left-right polarization in both Greece and Cyprus, and above all the catastrophic policies of the Greek junta. Entering this mixture was the support for the Greek dictatorship by the U.S. government, a factor that places considerable blame on the United States for the Cyprus crisis in the summer of 1974.

Cyprus and the Turkish Construct of "Greek Encirclement"

When Turkey invaded Cyprus on July 20, 1974, Ankara's official argument was that it was intervening in order to fulfill its treaty obligations and to restore the status quo ante. There were other motivations and objectives, however, behind the Turkish action. The July 15, 1974 coup against Makarios provided Turkey with the long-sought opportunity it was seeking to place Cyprus under its strategic control.

Since 1955, the Turkish elite has held the view that Cyprus would be a serious security threat to Turkey if the island republic came under "Greek control." In the Turkish nationalist discourse, the term "Greek control" has referred to two interrelated matters.

First, although the Greek Cypriots constitute an 80 percent majority in Cyprus, they do not have—in Turkish thinking—the right to self-determination because this could result in their rule over Cyprus. This is viewed as tantamount to the "Hellenization" of the island republic and is unacceptable to Turkey. This notion of Hell-

---

[89]See Rauf Denktash, *The Cyprus Triangle* (London: K. Rustem and Brother, 1988), pp. 65–66; Necati Ertekün, *The Cyprus Dispute and the Birth of the Turkish Republic of Northern Cyprus*, 2nd ed. (Nicosia: K. Rustem and Brother, 1984), p. 32; Zaim Necatigil, *The Cyprus Question and the Turkish Position in International Law* (Oxford: Oxford University Press, 1989), p. 77.

enization has been a constant theme of statements by Turkish Cypriot leader Rauf Denktash.[90]

Second, in the Turkish mind, Greece still has a grandiose plan to revive Byzantium, the Great Idea (*Megali Idea*). Veteran Turkish leader Bülent Ecevit has firmly believed that this is the case. In 1998, while he was serving as deputy premier, he stated:

> Greece had always had designs on Turkey.... The Greeks have a rather unrealistic approach to international relations. They still nurture the idea of irredentism, the ideals of *Megali Idea* and Panhellenism.[91]

These combined factors, the internal Hellenization of Cyprus and the strategic control of Cyprus by Greece, an external power hostile to Turkey, have created a scenario, an imaginary threat, for Turkey. That scenario is that Turkey is about to be surrounded by Greece and deprived of access to its southern sea lanes. In this way, Greece, still driven by the *Megali Idea*, could create a "noose around Turkey," leading to the "asphyxiation" of the country in case of conflict. All of this has been encapsulated in the notion of "Greek encirclement." This notion has been a construct that has been invoked by Turkish leaders in order to explain and justify their policies toward Greece and Cyprus. In the Turkish political discourse, the construct of Greek encirclement has been expressed through the terms *Yunan çemberi* or *Yunan çevrelemesi. Yunan kuşatması* (Greek siege) is another term that has been used.[92]

The fear of Greek encirclement has two main sources. The first is

---

[90]See İlnur Çevik's interview with Denktash in the *Turkish Daily News*, September 17, 1999. In the interview, Denktash was critical of the Cyprus government's negotiating positions because they were "leading to the transformation of Cyprus into a Hellenic republic."

[91]See İlnur Çevik's interview in the *Turkish Daily News*, May 12, 1998.

[92]For more recent uses of the "Greek encirclement" construct in Turkish discourse, see Suat İlhan, *Türk Askeri Kültürünün Tarihi Gelişmesi: Kutsal Ocak* (The Historical Evolution of Turkish Military Culture: Sacred Hearth) (İstanbul: Ötüken, 1999), pp. 267–269, 278–279. See also Metin Erksan, *Mare Nostrum* (İstanbul: Hil Yayın, 1997), pp. 52–55; Mustafa Ergun Olgun, "Turkey's Tough Neighborhood: Security Dimensions of the Cyprus Conflict," in *Cyprus: The Need for New Perspectives*, ed. Clement Dodd (Huntington, Cambridgeshire: Eothen Press, 1999), pp. 232–233.

tied to historical memory, the Greek attempt in 1921 to conquer a substantial part of Turkey and reach Ankara. This represented Greece's Great Idea, and the pursuit of it led to the greatest Greek folly of the twentieth century. The Great Idea was buried in 1922 with the monumental Greek defeat at the hands of Kemal Atatürk, who waged the war of Turkish independence. The role that the great powers—Britain, France, and Russia—were playing in Asia Minor at the time contributed to the Greek defeat.

This defeat, known as the Asia Minor Catastrophe (*Mikrasiatiki Catastrophe*), put an end to the historic presence of a large Greek population in Asia Minor, estimated at the time at 1.8 million.[93] It also gave rise to the modern Turkish state, born out of the ashes of the Ottoman Empire.

Despite this Greek defeat, the fear of Greek encirclement remained alive in Turkey, though it was in a dormant state primarily for two reasons. Turkey felt that Greece wanted to control the Aegean Sea and render it a "Greek lake" if the opportunity arose. The Dodecanese Islands, which had been under Italian rule, were ceded to Greece by the allies in 1948, following the defeat of the Italians in the Second World War. Turkey felt that these islands were unjustly ceded to Greece. Up until today, Turkish leaders, including Prime Minister Ecevit, do not hesitate to remind Greece that it was awarded the Dodecanese Islands unjustly. It was only because of Turkish magnanimity that the Dodecanese were ceded to Greece by the allies, Ecevit suggested.[94]

These islands, however, had Greek populations, had been culturally Greek for many centuries, and had been awarded to Greece as part

---

[93]On the Asia Minor Catastrophe, see Harry J. Psomiades, *The Eastern Question, the Last Phase: A Study in Greek-Turkish Diplomacy* (Thessaloniki: Institute for Balkan Studies, 1968); Michael Llewellyn-Smith, *Ionian Vision: Greece in Asia Minor, 1919–1922* (London: Allen Lane, 1973); Alexandros Pallis, *Greece's Anatolian Venture and After: 1915–1922* (London: Methuen and Co. Ltd., 1937); Xenofontos Strategou, *He Ellada sten Mikra Asia: Istoriki Episkopese* (Greece in Asia Minor: A Historical Overview) (Athens: Demiourgia Publishers, Fifth Edition, 1994, First Edition, 1925).

[94]Ecevit stated: "If Turkey intended, to say, annex the Dodecanese Islands, it had repeated opportunities to do so during World War II. Had Turkey joined the war, as a gesture, a few months before the end of the war, that would have been enough for us to take the islands. Turkey did not even attempt to [do] that." See Ecevit's interview with *TRT Television Network*, 18:15 hours, July 17, 1997, in *PIO, Turkish Press and Other Media*, Nicosia, July 22, 1997.

of the Second World War peace settlement. Greece fought on the side of the allies and suffered enormous losses during the war.[95] Turkey, on the other hand, remained neutral throughout the war. Still, Ankara's attitude was that the allies should have rewarded neutral Turkey with the Dodecanese Islands because, in the past, they had belonged to the Ottoman Empire.

With the Dodecanese Islands under Greek control, Ankara feared that Greece would create all sorts of navigational problems for Turkey in both the northern and the southern Aegean Sea and transform the Aegean into a "Greek lake." Greece, however, has never created any navigational problems in the Aegean. It has abided by the Law of the Sea Convention to the letter and has strictly adhered to international maritime law and international agreements it signed with regard to the passage of military vessels in the Aegean. Foreign commercial shipping in the Aegean sea lanes has enjoyed freedom of navigation as stipulated by international maritime law. It has been in the interest of Greece, being one of the great merchant marine powers, to abide by international rules in regulating commercial shipping. Thus, the Turkish belief that Greece would treat the Aegean as a "Greek Lake" by impeding freedom of navigation has been unfounded altogether.

Adding to worry in Turkey that Greece would turn the Aegean into a "Greek lake," the Cyprus issue burst onto the scene in the 1950s. The Greek Cypriot nationalist movement of the 1950s, calling for self-determination and *enosis*, the union of Cyprus with Greece, began to revive Turkish fears of Greek encirclement. By 1955, when the EOKA campaign began, Turkey had adjusted its foreign policy regarding Cyprus. If Cyprus came under Greece's control, it would be a "dagger directed at the soft underbelly of Turkey," Ankara's argument went. Beginning in 1955, the notion of Greek encirclement became a steady undercurrent in Turkey's policy toward Cyprus.[96] The combination

---

[95]Out of a population of 6 million, close to 800,000 Greeks perished during the German occupation of Greece (1941–1945).

[96]See Turkey, Ministry of Foreign Affairs, *Turkey and Cyprus: A Survey of the Cyprus Question with Official Statements of the Turkish Viewpoint* (London: Embassy of Turkey, 1956), pp. 12–21, 24, 54–55; Suat Bilge, "The Cyprus Conflict and Turkey," in *Turkish Foreign Policy in Transition: 1950–1974*, ed. Kemal Karpat (Leiden: E.J. Brill, 1975), p. 142. For a Turkish map illustrating the "Greek encirclement" of Turkey, see Derviş Manizade, *Kıbrıs: Dün, Bugün, Yarın* (Cyprus: Yesterday, Today, Tomorrow) (Istanbul: Kıbrıs Türk Kültür Derneği, Yaylacık Matbaası, 1975), p. 200.

of an Aegean transformed into a Greek lake and a Cyprus serving as a Greek military base became the standard argument in Turkey in its quest to confront the Greek encirclement. In 1997, former Turkish ambassador to Washington, Şükrü Elekdağ, one of the most respected Turkish diplomats, wrote the following:

> *Greece will encircle Turkey* with a strategic control belt by means of the Crete-Rhodes-Cyprus chain of islands stretching from the Ionian Sea to the Iskenderun Bay, and it will possess the possibility of blocking all the sea access routes to Anatolia."[97] (Emphasis added.)

Turkish Cypriot leader Rauf Denktash views Cyprus as a strategic threat to Anatolia if Turkey does not control the island. He stated:

> The Ottomans had occupied the island because Cyprus was either protecting or threatening the southern shores of Anatolia. One who rules Anatolia cannot give up Cyprus.[98]

The notion of Greek encirclement has been closely linked to the ideology of Pan-Turkism.[99] This was the ideology of Turkish irredentist nationalism, which originated during the final decades of the Ottoman Empire. The overall objective of Pan-Turkism, utopian as it may appear, was to bring under one national roof the *Dış Türkler,* or Outside Turks. These Outside Turks included a wide range of groups with Turkic origins, covering an area from the Adriatic coast of Yugoslavia to the rest of the Balkans, to Greece and Cyprus, to Iraq and Central Asia. During the Second World War, while Turkey remained neutral, the Pan-Turkish groups in the country, who were quite influential, favored Nazi Germany. Through its neutrality, Turkey hoped that a German victory would lead to Turkish control of Cyprus since Britain would be defeated.[100]

---

[97]See Şükrü Elekdağ„ "The Greek Base in Paphos and the S-300s," *Milliyet,* September 22, 1997.

[98]See *Kıbrıs,* June 21, 2000.

[99]The discussion on Pan-Turkism is primarily based on the important work of Jacob Landau, *Pan-Turkism in Turkey: A Study of Irredentism* (Hamden, Connecticut: Archon Books, 1981).

[100]On Turkish neutrality during the Second World War and Ankara's expectations in the event Germany won, see Frank Weber, *The Evasive Neutral: Germany,*

Pan-Turkish ideology in Turkey has experienced highs and lows. Over the last three decades, it has been in the mainstream of Turkish politics, even though it has not been the dominant component.[101] The political and social philosophy of Kemal Atatürk became the basic source of legitimacy and the dominant ideology of the new nation. Kemalism purportedly put an end to Turkish irredentist claims against all neighboring countries. In this sense, advocates of Pan-Turkism had to accommodate their message to the ideology of the state without abandoning the basic Pan-Turkish irredentist tenets.

Since the late 1960s, Pan-Turkish nationalism has been represented by the Nationalist Movement Party, or MHP (*Milliyetçi Hareket Partisi*). This party was founded in 1969 by a retired colonel, Alparslan Türkeş.[102] The MHP under Türkeş became synonymous with extreme right-wing politics. The main symbol of the MHP was, appropriately, the legendary *Bozkurt,* or Grey Wolf. Therefore, the MHP developed highly organized youth groups called *bozkurtlar* (grey wolves). The *bozkurtlar* were paramilitary operatives also known as "commandos." They carried out their activities, including acts of political violence through organizations known as "Idealist" (*Ülkücü*). Türkeş's MHP was intimately linked to the Idealist groups. The most important of these groups was the *Ülkü Ocakları Derneği* (Association for the Hearths of Ideals). The groups were responsible for most of the extreme right-wing violence that plagued Turkey in the 1970s. They were fiercely nationalistic, were believers in Pan-Turkism, and were vehemently anticommunist. They were able to penetrate the state apparatus and maintained close ties with a variety of officials in police and intelligence agencies.[103]

Britain, and the Quest for a Turkish Alliance in the Second World War (Columbia, Missouri, and London: University of Missouri Press, 1979). The chapter "Turkey and the Russian Campaign: Cyprus and Caucasus" presents Turkish thinking about the Eastern Mediterranean in a post-war settlement. See pp. 107–141.

[101]See "Pan-Turkism in the Republic of Turkey: Back into the Mainstream," in Landau, *Pan-Turkism in Turkey,* pp. 144–175, 185.

[102]On the establishment of the MHP by Türkeş, see Hakkı Öznur, *Ülkücü Hareket* (The Idealist Movement), vol. 1 (Ankara: Alternatif Yayınları, 1999), pp. 163–230. On the ideology and domestic program of the MHP, see E. Burhan Arıkan, "The Programme of the Nationalist Action Party: An Iron Hand in a Velvet Glove?" in *Turkey Before and After Atatürk: Internal and External Affairs,* ed. Sylvia Kedourie (London: Frank Cass, 1999), pp. 120–134.

[103]On the ties of right-wing paramilitary groups, including the *Bozkurtlar* and

Throughout the 1970s, Türkeş's MHP became notorious for its ties to the violence of the right-wing paramilitary groups. Among the paramilitary groups tied to the Idealist organizations of the MHP was the Anti-Communist Front, an organization engaged in political assassinations. One of the leading figures of the Anti-Communist Front was Mehmet Ali Ağca, a self-confessed sympathizer of the Association for the Hearths of Ideals.[104] On February 1, 1979, the Anti-Communist Front assassinated Abdi İpekci. As editor of the *Milliyet* newspaper, İpckci, who advocated liberal-leftist positions, had emerged as one of the most respected Turkish journalists. Mehmet Ali Ağca was arrested for İpekci's murder but was able to escape under mysterious circumstances from the maximum security Maltepe military prison in Turkey. Ağca was found guilty for İpekci's assassination and was condemned to death in absentia. Later, his sentence was commuted to ten years in jail. Ağca reappeared on May 14, 1981, at Vatican Square in Rome. On that day, he shot and gravely wounded Pope John Paul II.[105]

One of the most critical reasons behind the MHP's durability and vitality has been its founder and leader, Alparslan Türkeş. As was the case with other fascist and neo-fascist parties, Türkeş emerged as the personification of the movement as it developed into a personality cult revolving around him. As he performed the role of supreme leader of the MHP, the party's followers attributed extraordinary

the Idealists, with state agencies, see Birand, *The Generals' Coup in Turkey: An Inside Story of 12 September 1980* (London: Brassey's Defense Publishers, 1987), pp. 48–50; Mehmet Ali Birand, "Agca Foresaw His Return," *Turkish Daily News*, June 15, 2000; Stephen Kinzer, "Will Turk Tell Secrets on Shooting of the Pope?" *New York Times*, June 15, 2000.

[104]Birand, *The Generals' Coup*, pp. 48, 244.

[105]Mehmet Ali Ağca was tried and convicted in Italy for the shooting of the Pope and was sentenced to life in prison. Subsequently, he was forgiven by the Pope and, in June 2000, the Italian government granted a pardon to Ağca. He was sent back to Turkey, where he was jailed again in order to serve 10 years for İpekçi's murder. Ağca's pardon and return to Turkey reignited speculation as to who was really behind the attempt to assassinate the Pope. The focus was on former communist intelligence agencies in Eastern Europe. At the same time, Ağca's return to Turkey generated new interest in his ties with Idealist groups and the role of the MHP in the political violence of the 1970s. See İlnur Çevik, "Ağca Back Home, Eyes on MHP," *Turkish Daily News*, June 15, 2000; Birand, "Ağca Foresaw His Return," *Turkish Daily News*, June 15, 2000; Kinzer, "Will Turk Tell Secrets on Shooting of the Pope?" *New York Times*, June 15, 2000.

qualities to him, and he became known as *Baş buğ*, the Turkish equivalent of "Fuhrer."

Türkeş, who was born in Cyprus in 1917, had a remarkable career in Turkish politics. In May 1960, he was among the leaders of the coup that overthrew the regime of Turkish Prime Minister Adnan Menderes. From that time until his death in 1997, Türkeş was able to bring Pan-Turkish ideology back into the mainstream of Turkish politics. While Pan-Turkism did not replace Kemalism as the dominant ideology, Türkeş and his party were taken seriously in Turkish political discourse.

Cyprus was at the top of Türkeş's agenda. His nationalist party saw Cyprus as a Turkish island that was vital to Turkish interests.[106] It believed that Turkish policy toward Cyprus should aim at preventing the island from coming under Greek control. In other words, the Greek encirclement of Turkey via Cyprus should be prevented at all costs. To provide the best guarantee against this Greek threat, Turkey should conquer Cyprus and place it under its strategic control. The 1974 Turkish invasion accomplished this goal to a considerable degree. Türkeş, however, considered it a grave error that Turkey did not continue its advance to place the whole of Cyprus under its control.

After Türkeş's death, a power struggle ensued in the MHP. Eventually, following a bitter power struggle within the party, Devlet Bahçeli succeeded Türkeş. He strove to give the MHP a more moderate image than that of the extremist Grey Wolves. This strategy by Bahçeli appeared to enhance the party's popular appeal.[107] In the parliamentary elections on April 18, 1999, Bahçeli's MHP scored significant political gains and came in a close second to the Democratic Socialist Party (DSP) of Bülent Ecevit. In the 550-seat National Assembly, the DSP won 136 seats while the MHP secured 130 seats.

In the past, Ecevit had considered the MHP, the party of the extremist Grey Wolves, to be a fascist-oriented party and had condemned its political violence. Following the 1999 elections, however, Ecevit formed a coalition government with the MHP, even though

---

[106]For a comprehensive view of Türkeş's positions concerning Cyprus, see Alparslan Türkeş, *Dış Politikamız ve Kıbrıs* (Our Foreign Policy and Cyprus) (İstanbul: Kıbrıs Türk Kültür Derneği, 1966).

[107]On the MHP under the leadership of Devlet Bahçeli, see the special section entitled "All About the MHP," in *Turkish Daily News*, April 27, 1999.

Ecevit's wife had expressed serious misgivings regarding such a possibility because of the MHP's violent past.[108] In the end, despite the serious differences between Ecevit's DSP and Bahçeli's MHP, the parties came together and formed a coalition government for two main reasons. First, a DSP-MHP coalition was the only way out of yet another political impasse that would have been acceptable to the armed forces. Second, Ecevit's DSP and Bahçeli's MHP were linked through the umbilical cord of Turkish nationalism and shared the belief that Turkey was still confronted with the threat of Greek encirclement.

When Turkish Prime Minister Bülent Ecevit ordered the invasion of Cyprus in 1974, the protection of the rights of the Turkish minority in the country played an important role in his decision. At the same time, the notion of Greek encirclement provided the underpinning behind his action. Ecevit was a true believer in this notion. He carried this belief with him up until the late 1990s, when he staged a political comeback, first as deputy prime minister and then as prime minister of Turkey.

The years 1998 and 1999 were a time when the question of Cyprus's accession to the European Union was high on the agenda of Greek-Turkish relations. Ecevit's fundamental objection to Cyprus's potential accession to the EU rested on the fear that Cyprus would become "Greek" surreptitiously by joining the EU. Ecevit saw Cyprus's accession as an indirect way for Greece to control the Republic of Cyprus through the European Union. Thus, Prime Minister Ecevit stated on July 18, 1999:

> Furthermore [if a federal Cyprus became an EU member] Turkey would face serious dangers as well. Greece, which has *encircled* Turkey to the west by means of the islands, would have *surrounded* Turkey from the south as well because it would have been connected to south Cyprus in a de facto

---

[108]On May 15, 1999, Bülent Ecevit's wife, Rahşan, expressed misgivings about a DSP-MHP coalition under the premiership of her husband. Rahşan Ecevit was the DSP Deputy Chairwoman and reminded the Turkish public that violent attacks by the Grey Wolves against leftist supporters of her husband had taken place in the 1970s. See "Insulted, Far-Right Party Snubs Coalition Talks in Turkey," *Associated Press,* May 16, 1999.

if not official manner. This would constitute a serious threat
to Turkey.[109]

In other words, Ecevit saw the accession of Cyprus to the EU as a Trojan Horse facilitating Greece's control of Cyprus and "encirclement of
Turkey."[110]

Turkish Cypriot leader Rauf Denktash shared Ecevit's view.
Denktash's longstanding belief has been that "Greek control" of
Cyprus threatens the vital interests of Turkey because Greece is a hostile power. In fact, from the ideological point of view, Denktash
belongs to the advocates of Pan-Turkism. Like Ecevit, Denktash saw
Cyprus's bid for accession to the European Union as a Greek ploy to
encircle Turkey. The Turkish Cypriot leader advanced this thesis even
after the Greek government of Prime Minister Costas Simitis lifted its
veto on Turkey's EU candidacy during the bloc's summit in Helsinki
on December 10 and 11, 1999, and allowed Turkey to become a candidate, a significant concession to Ankara. Greek-Turkish relations
improved dramatically after the Helsinki summit. Two earthquakes in
1999 gave impetus to these improved relations. When a devastating
earthquake hit northeastern Turkey on August 17, 1999, Greece
responded swiftly and aided the suffering people in the earthquake
zone. When a strong earthquake hit the Athens area three weeks later,
on September 6, Turkey reciprocated. This demonstration of solidarity between the two peoples set in motion a process between Athens
and Ankara that has been called "seismic diplomacy," which has contributed to the improvement in bilateral relations.

Still, Denktash persisted in viewing Greece in hostile terms. In
February 2000, speaking at the Turkish Military Academy in Ankara,
an elite school of the army, Denktash proclaimed:

Greece's tactic is to make Cyprus an EU issue without making Turkey a member of the EU. Greece plays the game of
claiming ownership over Cyprus and urges Turkey to with-

---

[109]See the interview with Ecevit on the program "Political Pulse," *TRT Television
Network*, 18:30 hours, July 18, 1999. Ecevit had expressed similar views as deputy
prime minister. See the interview with Ecevit in the *Turkish Daily News*, May 12, 1998.

[110]For the Turkish view that perceives Greece as manipulating the EU in order
to "control all Cyprus" and avoid dealing with disputes in the Aegean, see "Critics Say
Greece Gaining Time not to Solve Major Issues," *Turkish Daily News*, April 6, 2001.

draw it soldiers from the TRNC, alleging that there is no need for her guarantees.[111]

Two months later, as if to leave no doubt that Greece and Hellenism were still enemies, Denktash repeated his belief that Turkey is in Cyprus to stay because of Ankara's strategic interests. The Turkish Cypriot leader proclaimed:

> Turkey, because of Turkey's strategic interests, will not level the island *to its enemies and Hellenism.* Therefore, in the 21st century, Cyprus will be important for Turkey as much as it was in the past.[112] (Emphasis added.)

Denktash made this statement following his "re-election as president of the TRNC" on April 20, 2000. The government of Turkish Prime Minister Ecevit gave its full support to Denktash in his bid for "re-election," prompting other candidates to protest this open support.[113] In addition, on April 13, 2000, just prior to the "presidential elections" in the "TRNC," the Turkish government announced that it was giving Denktash the most prestigious Turkish award, the International Atatürk Peace Prize. In this way, Ankara reasserted its support for Denktash and his stand on Cyprus, including the position that Turkey should control Cyprus in order to defend itself against the "threat of Hellenism," which meant Greek encirclement.

On June 8, 2000, Ecevit returned to the question of the Aegean as if to leave no doubt that Greece was still pursuing a policy aimed at encircling Turkey. Speaking at the Aksaz naval base in the Aegean, Ecevit stated:

> It would be sufficient to look at the map to understand the

---

[111]On Denktash's speech, see "Cyprus: Denktash Addresses Academy on Greek-Turkish Peace," *Anatolia News Agency,* in *FBIS,* February 14, 2000.

[112]*Anatolia News Agency,* "Denktash Says Confederation Only Solution," April 26, 2000.

[113]On April 22, 2000, the Republican Turkish Party (RTP) of Mehmet Ali Talat asked the "High Election Council" to cancel the "presidential elections." Among the reasons cited in the petition was the Turkish government's open support for Denktash. See Bayrak Radio, "RTP Applies for Cancellation of the April 15 Elections," 15:30 hours, April 22, 2000, in *PIO, Turkish Cypriot Press and Other Media,* April 24, 2000.

mess that the Aegean issue is. Turkey appeared to be *imprisoned* by its own coastline. We do have the right for a *just correction* [of the map], which considers the economy and security of the country.[114] (Emphasis added.)

Then, the Turkish prime minister proceeded to reject Greece's position that any bilateral dispute in the Aegean should be submitted to the International Court of Justice in The Hague, in accordance with the decisions of the European Council at the Helsinki summit on December 10 and 11, 1999. Instead, Ecevit insisted that Greece should enter into a direct dialogue with Turkey to discuss differences over the Aegean. In this way, Ecevit was challenging one of the European Council's conclusions in Helsinki, which stated that candidates for EU membership should resolve any border disputes in accordance with the provisions of the U.N. Charter and, failing this, should resort to the International Court of Justice. This was stipulated in Paragraph 4 of the European Council's conclusions and was aimed primarily at the settlement of Greek-Turkish differences in the Aegean.[115] It was Ankara's acceptance of these European Council conclusions in their entirety that led the EU to grant Turkey candidate status at its Helsinki summit.

In other words, the Turkish prime minister continued to argue that the existing status quo in the Aegean should be revised in order to satisfy Turkish demands, irrespective of any EU directives, such as those at the Helsinki summit. The rationale behind this Turkish revisionist policy is that Greece has "imprisoned" Turkey in the Aegean and is aiming at its "encirclement."

---

[114]See *Turkish Daily News*, June 9, 2000.

[115]Paragraph 4 of the European Council conclusions at the Helsinki summit provided: "[Candidate States] must share the values and objectives of the European Union as set out in the Treaties. In this respect, the European Council stresses the principle of peaceful settlement of disputes in accordance with the United Nations Charter and urges candidate States to make every effort to resolve any outstanding border dispute and other related issues. Failing this, they should within a reasonable time bring the dispute to the International Court of Justice. The European Council will review the situation relating to any outstanding disputes, in particular concerning the repercussions on the accession process and in order to promote their settlement through the International Court of Justice, at the latest by the end of 2004. See "Helsinki European Council, December 10–11, 1999, Presidency Conclusions," *EU Summit Communiqué*, Helsinki, December 11, 1999.

Ecevit's belief that Greece still aims at encircling Turkey has been echoed in his government. Turkish State Minister Abdulhanuk Mehmet Çay proclaimed in July 2000 that Turkey invaded Cyprus not only to protect the Turkish Cypriots, but also to safeguard its own security. Turkey should be an intervening party in Cyprus "even if there was not a single Turk on the island," Çay stated. He added:

> With the transfer of the Dodecanese Islands to Greece, Turkey has been placed under siege and cannot even breathe.[116]

Çay was reaffirming that the encirclement belief is still deeply held among the country's ruling elite.

The Turkish leaders who advance the encirclement construct invoke Atatürk in order to give credence to their thesis. Thus, during his February 2000 speech at the Turkish Military Academy in Ankara, Rauf Denktash reminded his audience that Cyprus has a very important geopolitical position because Atatürk stated in 1936 that, "if Cyprus is in the hands of an enemy, it means that the supplies of Turkey are blocked."[117] In this vein, Ecevit has also cited Atatürk. In explaining the Greek plan to encircle Turkey through the control of Cyprus, Ecevit proclaimed in July 1999:

> As you know, during military exercises in the 1930s, Ataturk advised Turkish officers not to neglect Cyprus, saying that Cyprus's control by a hostile state will create a very serious threat to Turkey.[118]

The "hostile state" Ecevit was referring to was Greece. These views of Turkey's civilian leaders corresponded to those of the military leadership. As in the case of Ecevit, Turkey's military commanders continued to use Atatürk's dicta in order to justify their policies towards Cyprus. On January 12, 2001 a symposium took place at the Turkish

---

[116]See "Turkish Minister: In 1974, Turkey Arrived in Cyprus to Safeguard its Own Security as Well," *Anatolia News Agency,* Ankara, July 28, 2000.

[117]See "Cyprus: Denktash Addresses Academy," *Anatolia News Agency,* in *FBIS,* February 14, 2000.

[118]Interview with Ecevit on the program "Political Pulse," *TRT Television Network,* 18:30 hours, July 18, 1999.

Military Academy in Ankara. The subject was about Turkey's security and the Europan Union. One of the main speakers was the commander of the Academy, General Nahit Senoğul. He expressed doubts about the EU's sincerity towards Turkey and then proceeded to discuss the Cyprus issue. First, General Senoğul invoked Atatürk to justify the Turkish position on Cyprus and then proclaimed:

> North Cyprus is the breathing pipe of Turkey to the Mediterranean. Turkey, even if it stays alone in the world, will not allow to be strangulated.[119]

General Senoğul was repeating the Turkish axiom of "Greek encirclement" that presumably aims at "asphyxiating" Turkey via Greek control of Cyprus.

The invocation of Atatürk by Turkish leaders in order to justify their policies founded on the construct of "Greek encirclement" demonstrates how deeply ingrained is this belief among the Turkish elite. Kemal Atatürk and his ideas and pronouncements remain the basic source of legitimacy for the Turkish political and military elite.

However, the question remains: Was the Turkish fear of *Yunan Çemberi* (Greek encirclement) based on reality or was it an artificial construct aimed at justifying Turkey's aggressive posture toward Greece and the Aegean and, especially, toward Cyprus? Greek foreign policy from the end of the Second World War to the end of the twentieth century never had a strategic objective to "encircle Turkey." A combination of geographical, demographic, ideological, economic, and strategic factors dictated an approach that was against any notion that Greece should adopt a policy promoting the strategic encirclement of Turkey.

---

[119]General Senoğul's statement in Turkish was as follows: "Kuzey Kıbrıs, Türkiye'nin Akdeniz'deki nefes borusudur. Türkiye dünyada tek başına kalsa dahi, nefes borusunum sıkılmasına müsaade etmeyecektir." See *Milliyet*, İstanbul, January 13, 2001. For a critical view of the thesis that Cyprus represents a "breathing pipe" for Turkey to the Mediterranean, see the article of Murat Belge, "Niçin Kıbrıs?" (Why Cyprus), *Radikal*, Istanbul, January 26, 2001. Murat Belge is a well known Turkish historian and wrote this article partially in response to General Senoğul's statements.

Greek National Priorities and the
Dictates Against an "Encirclement" Policy

The Turkish construct of Greek encirclement, which has guided Ankara's policies in the Eastern Mediterranean for almost five decades, has extremely serious flaws. A factor mitigating against a grand Greek policy aimed at encircling Turkey has to do with the geographical and demographic disparities between Turkey and Greece. In terms of territory, Turkey is about six times the size of Greece, and the population of Turkey is six times larger than that of Greece.[120] In these terms, Turkey is a huge country compared to Greece. Precisely because Turkey is such a large country and had the potential to become a powerful regional actor, it was able to build the second-largest army in NATO and project an image of a regional superpower. It would be a monumental, if not impossible, task for a small country such as Greece to conceive and carry out a policy that aimed at encircling Turkey, a neighboring giant.

In addition to Greece's enormous territorial and demographic disadvantages, the social, economic, and political conditions in the country could not possibly support a policy of territorial aggrandizement through the encirclement of Turkey. Greece experienced the devastation brought about by the Nazis during the German occupation from 1940 to 1944. The destruction of the country was all but completed during the civil war that followed from 1945 to 1948. In the aftermath of these twin catastrophes, the Greeks were literally starving. They were a people exhausted by war and deprivation, and had neither the desire nor the means to "encircle Turkey."

Under these circumstances, the ruling establishment of the impoverished nation had two overall objectives. The first was reconstruction, and the second was securing the country against the communist threat. These objectives were, in fact, complementary since their implementation and success depended on U.S. diplomatic and military support and multifaceted material aid.

Securing the country against the communist threat had a domes-

---

[120]Turkey covers 780,580 sq. km., while Greece covers 131,940 sq. km. The Turkish population in 1996 was 62.5 million, while the Greek population was 10.5 million. The population disparity is growing due to the fact that the Turkish population growth rate is four times that of Greece: 1.67 percent for Turkey and 0.42 percent for Greece. See Central Intelligence Agency, *The World Fact Book: 1997–98*, pp. 192, 497.

tic as well as an external component. Domestically, communism was confronted primarily through the repressive mechanisms of the state. A nationwide security apparatus was established to suppress communist activities. The armed forces were part of this apparatus. The Greek Army forged extremely close ties with the United States and, from 1947 on, the Greek armed forces were rebuilt through the Truman Doctrine. In addition to domestic communism, Greece had to face international communism. On the external front, Greece's northern neighbors, Albania, Yugoslavia and Bulgaria, succumbed to communist rule. The Truman Doctrine provided Greece with security against both domestic and international communism. When Greece joined NATO in 1952, its northern borders were guaranteed by the formidable Western alliance led by the United States. Turkey joined NATO the same year.

Under the circumstances prevailing in the 1940s and 1950s, Greece simply did not have the resources or the capability to pursue any Great Idea in order to encircle Turkey. Greece's national ideology and the country's priorities were defined by the needs of domestic reconstruction and the fight against communism. They were also subordinate to the logic of the cold war. Greece and Turkey were NATO allies, and their foreign policy priorities fell, by definition, within the parameters of the Western alliance. It would have been unthinkable for Greece to advance a policy that aimed at the encirclement of another ally, Turkey.

There was, of course, support in Cyprus and Greece for the EOKA struggle in the 1950s. This support was linked to Greek nationalism and the belief that the "unredeemed" Greeks of Cyprus had the right to determine their own future, which was translated into *enosis,* or the union of Cyprus with Greece. In the aftermath of the Second World War, the Greeks of Cyprus comprised 80.2 percent of the population, while the Turkish Cypriots represented 17.9 percent.[121] Like other peoples, whether in Africa or Asia, Greek Cypriots demanded the right of self-determination. In an era when de-colonization had

---

[121]These demographic figures are based on the census conducted by the British Colonial Administration in 1946. In addition to Greek Cypriots and Turkish Cypriots, the census indicated that Armenians constituted 0.8 percent of the population, Maronites represented 0.4 percent, and "others" were 0.6 percent. See Great Britain, Colonial Office, *Census Reports,* 1881, 1946, 1960; Great Britain, *Cyprus Annual Reports* (under varying titles), Colonial Office, 1879–1959.

reached its height, the Cypriot demand to get rid of British colonial rule was seen as quite legitimate and reasonable by the Greeks. Self-determination for Cyprus was not only a just cause, but it was also consistent with the prevailing international trend of the time. Moreover, the Greeks believed that the West, Britain especially, had a moral obligation to Greece and Cyprus considering that both Greeks and Greek Cypriots had fought the Nazi forces side-by-side with the British at the Greek front and in North Africa. The Greeks contrasted their own role and sacrifices during the war to the role Turkey played by remaining neutral. In turn, this contrast reinforced the Greek belief that, if there were post-war claims in the Eastern Mediterranean, Britain would side with the Greeks out of gratitude.

Given this British "debt" to the Greeks and considering the perspective of de-colonization and the right to self-determination, Greek support for Cyprus did not necessarily represent part of a grandiose plan to "encircle Turkey" for the purpose of reviving the Byzantine Empire. Greek popular sentiments of solidarity with the "Cypriot brethren" reflected the ethnic and cultural bond among Greeks and, in this sense, the idea of *enosis* did represent Greek irredentist nationalism. This, however, was not tantamount to the pursuit of a Great Idea and was never translated into a government policy or into a strategic dogma of encircling Turkey. As it turned out, it was Greece, under Prime Minister Constantine Karamanlis, that played a pivotal role in reaching a compromise agreement on Cyprus through the Zurich-London agreements of 1959. These agreements were not favorable to the Greek Cypriot majority, and they certainly removed any prospect of Greek encirclement of Turkey via Cyprus.

When the Greek armed forces staged a coup in April 1967, they saw themselves as representing the epitome of patriotism and the embodiment of Greek national values. By definition, any policy aimed at the Greek encirclement of Turkey would require the armed forces to be the main instrument in the process of carrying it out. Without the military muscle to implement such a policy, the concept of a Greek encirclement of Turkey would be meaningless.

When the junta took over in Greece in 1967 and was in a position to chart its own foreign policy, the army officers did not embark on a crusade aimed at the encirclement of Turkey. Quite the opposite was true. The colonels were obsessed with communism and saw Turkey as a partner in the fight against the "common enemy." In fact, the junta strongman, Colonel George Papadopoulos, entertained the idea of a "Graeco-Turkish federation." He declared:

> We should unite the two shores of the Aegean. . . . I want to underscore my belief in the need to bring about a federation [between Greece and Turkey]. If I had some magic power, I would do everything to make this federation a reality, and I would lead our people in this direction.[122]

The mindset that Greece and Turkey could move toward establishing a "federation," was demonstrated shortly after the colonels came to power. First, the junta naïvely thought that it could strike a deal with Turkey over Cyprus and agreed to a summit meeting with the Turkish leadership on September 9 and 10, 1967, in Kesan, Turkey, and Alexandroupolis, Greece. The meeting ended in utter failure.

When a new crisis erupted in Cyprus two months later in mid-November 1967, the Greek junta capitulated hastily to all of Turkey's demands and withdrew the Greek division that had been on the island since the summer of 1964. From 1968 on, the Greek officers that were commanding the Cypriot National Guard made the fight against communism in Cyprus one of their primary objectives. The prevailing attitude of many, but by no means all, of these officers was that "our main enemy in Cyprus is not the Turks; our enemy is the communists."[123] This policy of the junta, which contained the incipient elements of subversion of the Cyprus government, brought it into a direct confrontation with Makarios and led to the disaster of July 1974.

Thus, the junta's coup against Makarios had little to do with any grandiose plan of the colonels to "encircle Turkey." Indeed, if the junta's real objective had been to promote *enosis* in order to encircle Turkey, the colonels would have taken elementary precautions to defend Cyprus against the certainty of a Turkish invasion. Not only did they fail to do so, but the junta also abandoned Cyprus in panic. In the end, the junta's actions demonstrated, beyond any doubt, that throughout its rule, from April 21, 1967, to July 23, 1974, Greece never

---

[122]See the interview with Papadopoulos in the Turkish newspaper *Milliyet*, June 28, 1968.

[123]This is based on the author's personal observations while in Cyprus in 1970.

followed a policy aimed at encircling Turkey, even when it staged the July 15, 1974 coup against Makarios, which triggered the Turkish invasion of Cyprus.

Greece's decision during the EU Helsinki summit in December 1999 to lift its veto on allowing Turkey to become a candidate for EU membership was an additional indication that Athens did not aim at the encirclement of Turkey. It is illogical to maintain that Greece desires to encircle Turkey through the control of the Aegean or Cyprus while Athens is supporting Ankara's membership in the EU and assisting Turkey in preparations for joining the European family of nations. Furthermore, given the fact that Cyprus is on track in its preparations for becoming a member of the EU, it is inconceivable that Greece and Cyprus would pose a military threat to Turkey, which is a candidate for membership in the EU.[124] Still, Turkish Prime Minister Bülent Ecevit and Turkish Foreign Minister Ismail Cem continue to view Cyprus as a potential threat to Turkey. In this respect, they insist that the Turkish invasion of 1974 was an "act of liberation" and that the Turkish occupation army is a "military force that has brought freedom."[125] As a consequence, Turkey argues that there can be no Cyprus settlement before the Greek Cypriots recognize the Denktash regime, the "Turkish Republic of Northern Cyprus," as an independent sovereign state.

For these reasons, despite the improvement in Greek-Turkish relations that began in 1999, Turkey has been steadfastly opposing Cyprus's future accession to the EU by viewing this development as a kind of Trojan Horse to facilitate the "Hellenization" of Cyprus through the EU. The construct of Greek encirclement is still in the back of the Turkish mind. The Greek side's hope and expectation is that, since Turkey aspires to become a member of the European Union, it will move away from the threat of superior military power as the arbiter in Greek-Turkish relations and efforts to find a Cyprus settlement. For Greece, as well as the other EU members, it is inconceivable that EU member and candidate states could use the threat of force to settle differences.

---

[124]On this point, see Gregory R. Copley, "Turkey Falters on the Edge of Ataturk's Dream," *Defense and Foreign Affairs Strategic Policy,* vol. xxviii, no. 3, March 2000, p. 8.

[125]See the April 11, 2000 interview with Turkish Foreign Minister Ismail Cem on the *TRT Television Network* in *PIO: Turkish Cypriot Press and other Media,* Nicosia, April 11, 2000.

The combination of these geographical, demographic, economic, ideological, and military factors, as well as the dictates of the cold war and EU dynamics, demonstrates convincingly that Greece has had no desire and has not been in a position to follow a policy aiming at the encirclement of Turkey. Over the last five decades, no Greek government has adopted such a policy. It simply has not been part of Greece's national priorities and has been far beyond Greek capabilities. As a result, the Turkish construct of Greek encirclement has been an artificial construct that has generated an imaginary fear of such encirclement. This construct has served the purpose of rationalizing Turkey's demands in the Aegean and Ankara's policies concerning Cyprus, especially the 1974 invasion and continuing occupation of the northern part of the island republic. Indeed, without the advancement of the Turkish thesis of "Greek encirclement," it would have been problematic for Ankara to justify its aggressive posture in the Eastern Mediterranean.

Whether the "Greek encirclement" thesis will continue to exert decisive influence on Turkish foreign policy remains an open question given the prospects for Turkey to join the European Union. A Turkey that is integrated into the European Union will have an extremely difficult task in justifying its position that is threatened to be "encircled" by another European Union member, Greece. In fact, if Turkey is to become full member of the European Union, it will have to abandon its "Greek encirclement" thesis because it contradicts the raison d' etre of European integration.

The Question of the Legality of the Turkish Invasion

The 1959 Zurich-London agreements, which granted Cyprus its semi-independent status, did stipulate that Cyprus could not come under Greek domination. Domestically, the principle of majority rule was circumvented to such a degree that the political rights of the great majority of the population were neutralized. In other words, the Turkish Cypriot minority of 18 percent was granted privileges and veto rights that prevented the Greek Cypriot majority of 80 percent from exercising real power. The Turkish Cypriot minority community saw the rights granted to it through the agreements as vital to its security and its very survival in the newly established republic. The

Greek Cypriot majority community, on the other hand, regarded the privileges granted to the minority community as excessive and as a violation of the fundamental democratic rights of the majority.

Certainly, the legitimate rights of the Turkish Cypriot minority had to be respected and guaranteed in the new republic. But, in the case of Cyprus, minority rights were supposed to be protected by undermining the fundamental rights of the majority. The end result was that politics in the new Cypriot republic became a zero-sum game. This prevented the emergence of a consociational political system in which antagonistic groups and subcultures manage to find a modus vivendi and establish mechanisms of conflict resolution in multireligious or multiethnic societies.[126] Inevitably, this led to the collapse of the constitution and to ethnic conflict barely three years after the declaration of Cypriot independence.

Two treaties, the Treaty of Alliance and the Treaty of Guarantee complemented the domestic constitutional arrangement. They both granted special rights to three external powers, Britain, Greece, and Turkey. All three had the right to intervene in Cyprus's internal affairs in order to "restore the status quo ante" if it was threatened or disturbed. This was an unprecedented arrangement in the post-colonial period precisely because it sought to perpetuate a semi-colonial status for Cyprus. Indeed, no other colony in the world that won its independence agreed to be placed under the permanent tutelage of external powers.

The most important aim behind all of these peculiar agreements and conditions governing Cyprus's "independence" was to secure British and, by extension, Western interests on the island. These interests were also well served through the two sovereign British bases. Among all the colonies that the British gave up, it was only in Cyprus that they insisted on such a peculiar and quasi-democratic constitution and on maintaining military bases in perpetuity. Still, Turkey was the primary beneficiary of the Zurich-London agreements because the British bases did not pose a military threat to Cyprus. While the bases represented a remnant of British colonialism, their presence was not seen as undermining the vital interests of Cyprus. In fact, the vast

---

[126]See Kyriacos Markides, *The Rise and Fall of the Cyprus Republic* (New Haven: Yale University Press, 1977), pp. 44–47. On the theory of consociational democracy, see also Brian Barry, "Political Accommodation and Consociational Democracy," *British Journal of Political Science* 5 (October 1975): pp. 477–505.

majority of the Greek Cypriots, even those that were communists, condoned the presence of the British bases. The pro-Moscow communist party, AKEL, paid lip service to anti-imperialism but did not adopt a policy that called for the removal of the British bases. In addition, the bureaucracy of the new Cypriot republic was British-oriented, while the economy relied, to a great extent, on Britain. Turkey posed the major problem with regard to Cyprus's national security precisely because the Zurich-London agreements granted Ankara the role of "protector" of Cyprus. Britain was also a protector, but most Greek Cypriots did not feel threatened if Britain played the role of the "big brother." It was quite a different story with Turkey, however.

The Treaty of Guarantee gave Turkey, along with Britain and Greece, the right of intervention in Cyprus. This treaty reinforced the dormant territorial ambitions of Turkey regarding Cyprus and increased the temptation for Ankara to invade the island republic if certain conditions arose. This temptation or proclivity was quite strong because Ankara had a dogma and a policy stipulating that it should possess strategic control of Cyprus. Behind this dogma was the fear of "Greek encirclement."

Ostensibly, Turkey invaded Cyprus to restore the status quo ante, protect the Turkish Cypriots, and prevent the union of Cyprus with Greece. In other words, the political objective of the invasion was to restore the constitutional order abolished by the colonels in Greece through the overthrow of the legitimate president of the Republic of Cyprus, Archbishop Makarios. Ankara cited Article 4 of the Treaty of Guarantee as justification for its right to intervene in Cyprus.[127] Assuming that the Turkish interpretation of this article had some merit—an interpretation of dubious validity under international law—the Turkish occupation army should then have withdrawn as

---

[127] *Treaty of Guarantee*, Article 4: "In the event of a breach of the provisions of the present Treaty, Greece, Turkey, and the United Kingdom undertake to consult together with respect to the representations or measures necessary to ensure observance of those provisions. In so far as common or concerted action may not prove possible, each of the three guaranteeing Powers reserves the right to take action with the *sole aim of re-establishing the state of affairs* created by the present Treaty." (Emphasis added.) The Treaty of Guarantee is found in *Great Britain, Colonial Office, Cyprus*, Cmnd. 1093, London: Her Majesty's Stationery Office, 1960, pp. 86–87. For the Turkish viewpoint regarding Ankara's "right" to intervene in Cyprus according to the Treaty of Guarantee, see Necatigil, *The Cyprus Question*, pp. 101–124.

soon as the status quo ante was restored. Indeed, the Treaty of Guarantee, Article 4, states specifically that a guarantor power can intervene in Cyprus for only one purpose, namely, to restore the status quo ante or, as the treaty puts it, "with the sole aim of re-establishing the state of affairs created by the present Treaty."[128]

The status quo ante and legitimacy in Cyprus were restored when, according to the constitution, the president (speaker) of the House of Representatives became acting president in the absence of the president of the republic, Archbishop Makarios. This happened on July 23, 1974, when the Sampson regime collapsed and President of the House of Representatives Glafcos Clerides became acting president of Cyprus.[129] One might dispute, as Turkey did, the claim that legitimacy was restored when Clerides became president because, the Turkish argument went, Clerides did not follow strict constitutional procedures in assuming the office of president.[130]

Even if one accepts this line of reasoning, the constitutional status quo ante and legitimacy in Cyprus were fully restored five months later. On December 7, 1974, the legitimate president of Cyprus, Archbishop Makarios, who had been elected democratically, returned to Nicosia and assumed his duties in accordance with the constitution. Turkey rejected outright the Cyprus government's plea that it withdraw its occupation army and refused to recognize Makarios and his government as the legitimate authority in Cyprus, calling his presidency "illegitimate."[131] Ironically, following the overthrow of Makarios by the junta in Athens, Turkish Prime Minister Ecevit, who had ordered the invasion of Cyprus for the purpose of restoring the status quo ante, appeared to be very upset by the archbishop's overthrow. While in London for consultations with the British government on July 17, 1974, barely 48 hours after the overthrow of Makarios, Ecevit told British Foreign Secretary James Callaghan that he was "almost

---

[128]*Treaty of Guarantee*, Article 4.

[129]According to Part (a), Article 4, of the Cypriot constitution, "The President and the Vice-President shall be elected for a period of five years. In the event of absence, impediment, or vacancy of their posts, the President and the Vice-President shall be replaced by the President and Vice-President of the House of Representatives, respectively.

[130]For the Turkish viewpoint concerning the legality of Clerides' presidency, see Necatigil, *The Cyprus Question*, p. 87.

[131]See Denktash, *The Cyprus Triangle*, pp. 76–77.

weeping over the departure of the Archbishop, and he hoped that one day a dialogue with him might create a sense of nationhood on the island."[132]

No other government in the world accepted the Turkish argument that the rule of Makarios was "illegitimate," and the archbishop remained the universally recognized president of the Republic of Cyprus. The United Nations not only continued to recognize Makarios and his government as the sole legitimate authority in Cyprus but, over the years, the U.N. Security Council and the U.N. General Assembly also issued numerous resolutions to that effect. U.N. Security Council resolutions have called for the "restoration of the independence, sovereignty, and territorial integrity of Cyprus" and for the "withdrawal of all foreign forces" from the republic's territory.[133] In this way, the United Nations has deprived Turkey of any residual legal justification for the continued occupation of Cyprus. From the legal point of view, the Turkish invasion and occupation have constituted a breach of international law.[134]

While there still might be disagreements concerning the exact interpretation of the international treaties concerning Cyprus, the policies followed on the ground, which resulted in the Turkish invasion and occupation of the country, have not corresponded to the restoration of constitutional order. From the very first day of the inva-

---

[132]Quoted by James Callaghan, *Time and Chance* (London: Collins, 1987) p. 341.

[133]Among the numerous U.N. resolutions regarding Cyprus, see *U.N. Security Council Resolution 353*, July 20, 1974; *U.N. Security Council Resolution 360*, August 16, 1974; *U.N. Security Council Resolution 367*, March 12, 1975; *U.N. Security Council Resolution 541*, November 18, 1983; *U.N. Security Council Resolution 550*, May 11, 1984; *U.N. Security Council Resolution 750*, April 10, 1992.

[134]For a persuasive argument asserting that the Turkish invasion constituted a violation of the Zurich-London agreements, the U.N. Charter, and international law in general, see the article by a British legal authority, Sir David Hunt, "The Use of Force in the Middle East: The Case of Cyprus," *Mediterranean Quarterly*, vol. 2, no. 1 (Winter 1991): pp. 66–70. Sir David Hunt, KCMG, OBE, was a former private secretary to prime ministers Clement Attlee and Winston Churchill. He had also served as British High Commissioner in Uganda, Cyprus, and Nigeria, and had been British Ambassador to Brazil. Another preeminent authority on international law, Robert McDonald, a Canadian, also argued that the Turkish invasion constituted a violation of international law and the U.N. Charter. See R. St. J. McDonald, "International Law and the Conflict in Cyprus," *The Canadian Yearbook of International Law*, vol. 19 (1981): pp. 3–49. For the Turkish viewpoint justifying the invasion under international law, see Necatigil, *The Cyprus Question*, pp. 75–124.

sion, the Turkish Army engaged in the systematic expulsion of the indigenous Greek Cypriot population from their homes. By the fall of 1974, Turkey had also initiated a policy of colonization of occupied Cyprus. Thousands of Turkish settlers began arriving in northern Cyprus to live in the abandoned Greek towns and villages. Less than three years after the invasion, Turkey had succeeded in expelling 98 percent of the Greek population from the occupied territory. By 1990, there were only 593 Greek Cypriots left in the occupied territory, in the Karpasia peninsula, while the number of settlers from Turkey had reached 74,000.[135] In other words, 16 years after the invasion, 99.8 percent of the Greek inhabitants of occupied Cyprus had been forced to leave, while the colonization of Cyprus continued. The forceful removal of the Greek population and the massive colonization were hardly compatible with the letter or spirit of Article 4 of the Treaty of Guarantee, which stipulated that the sole aim of any intervention would be to restore the status quo ante.

In addition, these Turkish policies culminated in a move that violated yet another basic agreement that formed the foundation on which the Republic of Cyprus was established. On November 15, 1983, the Denktash regime proclaimed the unilateral independence of the occupied territory under the name "Turkish Republic of Northern Cyprus." This was an act of separatism that partitioned Cyprus. Such an act is explicitly prohibited by Article 22 of the Treaty of Establishment, which provided for the "Basic Structure of the Republic of Cyprus." In this respect, Article 22 stipulated:

It shall be recognized that the total or partial union of Cyprus with any other State, or a *separatist independence* of Cyprus (i.e., the *partition* of Cyprus into two independent States) shall be excluded.[136] (Emphasis added.)

The spirit of Article 22 of the Treaty of Establishment is echoed in Article 1 and Article 2 of the Treaty of Guarantee. Both articles explicitly prohibit "either union or partition of the Island."[137] Cer-

---

[135]The policies of the changing demography of Cyprus are discussed in more detail in chapter 11.

[136]See *Treaty on Cyprus, Related Treaties*, Article 22.

[137]Specifically, Article 1 of the Treaty of Guarantee stated: ". . . The Republic of Cyprus undertakes not to participate, in whole or in part, in any political or economic

tainly, there was the manifested desire of Turkey to protect the rights of the Turkish Cypriots. These rights, however, were prescribed in the Treaty of Establishment and the Treaty of Guarantee and clearly precluded any action by the guarantor powers that could result in the partition of Cyprus.

This was precisely the American position in 1964, when President Lyndon Johnson sent a stern warning to Turkey when Ankara was planning to invade Cyprus. Following a thorough study of the Treaty of Establishment and the Treaty of Guarantee, the legal experts of the State Department concluded that these treaties did not allow intervention by the guarantor powers if such intervention resulted in the partition of Cyprus. Based on the State Department's finding, Johnson sent a letter to Turkish Prime Minister İsmet İnönü on June 5, 1964, which included the following:

> It is my impression that you believe that such intervention by Turkey is permissible under the provisions of the Treaty of Guarantee of 1960. I must call to your attention, however, our understanding that the proposed intervention by Turkey would be for the purpose *of effecting a form of partition of the Island, a solution that is specifically excluded by the Treaty of Guarantee.*[138]

In this way, the U.S. president made it quite clear to Ankara that any intervention by Turkey that resulted in the partition of Cyprus was illegal under international law.

The policies followed by the Turkish occupation army over the years have made it clear that the objective of the invasion was not to restore the status quo ante or simply prevent the union of Cyprus with Greece. Rather, the Turkish objective was to create a new status quo on the island, that of a partitioned Cyprus whose northern region is

---

union with any State whatsoever. With this intent, it prohibits all activity tending to promote directly or indirectly either the union or partition of the Island." Article 2 of the Treaty of Guarantee stipulated: "[Greece, Britain, and Turkey] undertake to prohibit, as far as lies within their power, all activity having the object to promote directly or indirectly either the union of the Republic of Cyprus with any other state, or the partition of the Island."

[138]See "President Johnson's Letter to Prime Minister İnönü," June 5, 1964, *Middle East Journal*, vol. 20, no. 3 (Summer 1966): p. 386.

part of Turkey, while the whole island fell under the strategic control of Ankara. In this way, the prospect of the imaginary "Greek encirclement" would be put to rest once and for all.

CHAPTER 2

Anglo-American Antagonism: London Opposes Coup and Invasion, Washington Condones Both

Cyprus in Crisis: Divergent Perspectives in London and Washington

Greek and Turkish actions during the July 1974 Cyprus crisis had a critical bearing on developments in the Eastern Mediterranean between July 15 and August 15, 1974. The picture is not complete, however, if one does not take into account the important role played by the United States and Britain during this period. Their decisions had a profound influence on the course of events that ultimately determined the fate of Cyprus. At the time, foreign policy decision-making in Washington was in disarray because of presidential paralysis due to the Watergate scandal. In the absence of a functioning presidency, foreign policy decision-making was concentrated in the hands of Henry Kissinger, who was secretary of state and national security adviser at the same time. It was Kissinger, not Nixon, who made the critical decisions during the Cyprus crisis of July and August 1974. Few, therefore, blame Nixon for the Cyprus debacle. The main criticism has been directed against Kissinger. He has been widely blamed for condoning the coup against Makarios and the ensuing Turkish invasion.

At the time of the Cyprus crisis, the Labor government of Prime Minister Harold Wilson ruled Britain. The British Foreign Office under James Callaghan, the British Defense Ministry, and the British military bases in Cyprus mobilized instantly, and they monitored the unfolding dramatic events extremely closely. In fact, given the paralysis in Washington and the vantage point that Britain enjoyed in Cyprus, the British foreign policy agencies were in a better position than Washington was to observe and evaluate developments on the island.

Viewed 25 years later, without the passions that prevailed at the time, U.S. policies under Kissinger strongly indicated that, at first, the United States condoned the coup against Makarios. Then, when Turkey invaded Cyprus, Washington condoned the invasion and subsequently accommodated the Turkish conquest of more than one-third of Cyprus. As it turned out, the United States was not a mere passive observer of developments in and around Cyprus at the time. Through Secretary of State Kissinger, Washington played a determinant role in shaping events on the ground in Cyprus. The other major player in the crisis, besides Turkey and Greece, was Britain. With respect to the coup against Makarios and the Turkish invasion that followed, the British government took a different approach than the one adopted by the United States. If Kissinger had followed British advice, the fate of Cyprus would have been different.

In his memoirs, Kissinger attempted to demonstrate that he had a better understanding of the Cyprus crisis and the situation unfolding on the ground than the British. He did this by concentrating on the personality of British Foreign Secretary James Callaghan and ignoring altogether the British Foreign Office as an institution. In this vein, Kissinger argued that Callaghan had little "experience in crisis diplomacy, and Cyprus was about as maddening a problem as could be wished for any diplomat."[1] In addition, Kissinger added that the British foreign secretary was an experienced political operator whose "principal experience had been in ministries concerned with domestic British problems." As a consequence, Kissinger concluded, " . . . there are ethical limits in British politics not generally observed in ethnic conflicts, let alone between Greeks and Turks." The U.S. secretary of state proclaimed that "unlike Callaghan, my experience in mediation came from Middle East diplomacy . . ."[2]

Kissinger's View of the British in Cyprus

There are serious flaws in Kissinger's view of the British role during the Cyprus crisis and the British ability to comprehend and manage

---

[1] Kissinger, *Years of Renewal*, p. 209.
[2] Ibid.

ethnic conflicts. It is quite doubtful that Kissinger had a better understanding of the Cyprus conflict than Callaghan and the other British
decision-makers at the time. Even if one accepts Kissinger's assertion
that Callaghan's experience was in domestic British politics, the
colonial and post-colonial policies of Britain toward Cyprus were
interwoven into domestic British politics. Unlike most American
politicians, British politicians, in general, have had a good understanding of the situation in the Commonwealth, especially in Cyprus.

During the British colonial rule of Cyprus from 1878 to 1960,
Cyprus adopted the British administrative system, and its bureaucrats
were British-trained. The generation that ruled Cyprus from the time
of independence until 1974 was, by and large, British-educated.
Indeed, most of Makarios's ministers and the top bureaucrats of his
administration were British-educated. In general, the Cypriot governmental and administrative structure was geared toward Britain. As
a result, Britain maintained extremely close ties with Cyprus's
bureaucracy, society, and politics.

In the defense and security fields, no other former colonial possession of Britain acquired the importance that Cyprus did after its
independence in 1960. That is how important Cyprus was for Britain's
interests in the Middle East. In addition to the military role Britain was
entitled to play in Cyprus through its sovereign military bases, provided for in perpetuity in the Zurich-London agreements, there was
another factor that enhanced British military presence on the island.
Beginning in April 1964, a British military contingent provided the
backbone of the U.N. Peacekeeping Force in Cyprus (UNFICYP). This
force was present in the region where the invasion occurred, and it
monitored Turkish military actions closely. Thus, British soldiers in
the force were eyewitnesses to Turkish actions in Cyprus in the critical
months of July and August 1974. Overall, Britain not only had a special bond with Cyprus, but it also had human assets on the ground,
which gave it a unique, if not better, understanding of the situation
unfolding during the Cyprus crisis than the State Department.

Kissinger's tendency was to ignore the institutional aspect of
British foreign policy during the Cyprus crisis. Yet, the British foreign
and colonial offices had had a long history of dealing with Cyprus.
Unlike the State Department, which became involved in Cyprus in
1964, Britain ruled Cyprus from 1878 until the island became independent in 1960. During the last phase of British rule, the period after

the Second World War, Britain was confronted with the nationalist demands of the Greek Cypriots, who constituted the great majority of the island's population. They demanded self-determination, which would have led to *enosis,* or the union of Cyprus with Greece, ending British colonial rule. In April 1955, the nationalist movement in Cyprus took a violent turn. An underground organization known as EOKA, the National Organization of Cypriot Fighters, launched a guerrilla campaign against the British.[3] The leader of EOKA was a Cypriot-born retired colonel of the Greek army, George Grivas, who assumed the nom de guerre *Digenis.* The political leader of the Greek Cypriots was Archbishop Makarios, the ethnarch. EOKA, Grivas-Digenis, and Makarios enjoyed the overwhelming support of the Greek Cypriot population.

Britain resorted to the policy of "divide and rule" and, through a series of actions, London encouraged Turkey and the Turkish Cypriots to become directly involved in the dispute. A calculated British policy, especially after 1955, encouraged Turkey to demand *taksim,* or partition. British Colonial Secretary Alan Lennox-Boyd played an instrumental role in this regard. He adopted the position that, if EOKA kept up its campaign and the Greek Cypriots and Makarios insisted on self-determination, then Britain should view the Turkish demand of partition favorably. Lennox-Boyd's position eventually prevailed in London as the government of Prime Minister Harold Macmillan followed a policy of using partition as a threat in order to pressure the Greek Cypriots and Greece.[4] The inevitable result of this

---

[3]On the EOKA campaign, see the memoirs of its leader George Grivas-Digenis, *Apomnimonevmata Agonos EOKA, 1955–1959* (Memoirs of the EOKA Struggle, 1955–1959 (Athens: 1961). Several British authors have written extensively on the EOKA campaign. Among others, see Charles Foley, *Legacy of Strife: Cyprus from Rebellion to Civil War* (Baltimore: Penguin, 1964); Nancy Cranshaw, *The Cyprus Revolt: An Account of the Struggle for Union with Greece* (London: George Allen, 1978); Robert Holland, *Britain and the Revolt in Cyprus, 1954–1959* (Oxford: Oxford University Press, 1998).

[4]An authoritative account of Britain's policy of using partition as a means to preserve its position in Cyprus is found in Holland, *Britain and the Revolt in Cyprus*, pp. 100, 163–167, 202–203, 255–257, 263–265, 285. On Britain's divisive policies, see also Van Coufoudakis, "The Dynamics of Political Partition and Division in Multiethnic and Multireligious Societies—The Cyprus Case," in *Essays on the Cyprus Conflict*, ed. Van Coufoudakis (New York: Pella Publishing Company, 1976), pp. 33–34. Michael Attalides, *Cyprus: Nationalism and International Politics* (New York: St. Martin's Press, 1979), pp. 1–21, 46–49.

divisive British policy was ethnic polarization and cycles of Greek-Turkish ethnic violence on the island.

In this regard, Britain condoned and even encouraged the illegal activities of the TMT (Turkish Resistance Organization), a Turkish Cypriot underground organization. The TMT launched violent attacks against the Greek Cypriots, who reacted violently as well. By 1956, a full-fledged ethnic conflict was taking place in Cyprus. As a result of British policies, the Greek Cypriots had to fight on two fronts, one against the British and another against Turkish Cypriot nationalists who had been agitated by the British. At the diplomatic level, the Greek side also had to deal with an Anglo-Turkish front in NATO and other international fora.

The British objective was to exercise maximum pressure on Greece so that Athens would persuade Grivas and Makarios to give up the EOKA struggle. It was with this mindset and in this context that the British government condoned the pogrom against the Greek community of Istanbul (Constantinople), which took place on the evening of September 6, 1955. It occurred in an atmosphere of nationalist frenzy over Cyprus and, as a result, the Greek minority and its institutions in Turkey suffered a devastating blow.[5] The government of Turkish Prime Minister Adnan Menderes organized the pogrom. There are certain indications that some sectors of the British foreign policy apparatus might even have encouraged the anti-Greek riots in Turkey as a means to put pressure on Greece.[6] As for the United States, Secretary of State John Foster Dulles adopted a position that was tantamount to condoning the pogrom against the Greeks and their churches and institutions.[7]

---

[5]The anti-Greek pogrom in Istanbul (Constantinople) resulted in the destruction of 73 churches, 8 cemeteries, 26 schools, 1,004 homes, 4,212 shops and stores, 21 factories, 12 hotels, 97 restaurants, and 23 warehouses. These figures were taken from official State Department documents. See *American Embassy in Ankara to Department of State*. Subject: "The Istanbul-Izmir Disturbances of September 6, 1955." Dispatch No. 228, Confidential, 1 December 1955.

[6]Holland, *Britain and the Revolt in Cyprus,* pp. 76–77.

[7]Secretary of State John Foster Dulles received detailed accounts of the pogrom from the American Consulate in Istanbul and the American Embassy in Ankara. He remained silent for 12 days. Then, on September 18, 1955, Dulles sent identical notes to the Turkish and Greek prime ministers. In his notes, Dulles failed to condemn or even criticize the pogrom. He only referred obliquely to the "unhappy events of the last two weeks." On Dulles's notes to the Turkish and Greek governments, see Alexis Alexandris, *The Greek Minority in Istanbul and Greek-Turkish Relations, 1918–1974* (Athens: Center for Asia Minor Studies, 1983), p. 267.

Cyprus won its independence in 1960, but Britain had already sowed the seeds of ethnic conflict. It did not take long for ethnic violence to erupt anew in Cyprus. By Christmas 1963, large-scale clashes had begun, with the Greek Cypriots gaining the upper hand this time around. Greece and Turkey came close to war, and a series of events over the next decade culminated in the coup against Makarios and the Turkish invasion in July 1974. The point is that Britain had played a catalytic role in fomenting ethnic discord, which had plagued the island intermittently since 1955.

Given this British role of injecting ethnic strife into the volatile mixture of the Cyprus dispute in the post-Second World War period, Kissinger's statement that there were "ethical limits in British politics not generally observed in ethnic conflicts, let alone between Greeks and Turks," demonstrated that the secretary of state did not comprehend fully Britain's role in Cyprus over the years. Certainly, Kissinger's argument regarding British ethical constraints was meant to demonstrate that, at the time of the Cyprus crisis in 1974, London suffered from a lack of understanding of the nature and vicissitudes of ethnic conflict in Cyprus. In the end, however, Kissinger's interest in Cyprus was incidental and remained marginal compared to his global concerns. In reality, British policy-makers had a superior understanding of Cypriot political and ethnic dynamics, both before and during 1974, than Kissinger ever did.

In addition to all of this, and leaving the Watergate crisis aside, Kissinger had another handicap when he dealt with the Cyprus crisis in July and August 1974, one that the British did not have at the time. If one takes into account Kissinger's support for the Greek junta over the years and the fact that it was the junta that overthrew Makarios, it becomes clear that the U.S. secretary of state dealt with the Cyprus crisis with the burden of the junta on his shoulders. In his memoirs, Kissinger avoided any serious discussion of American support for the Greek junta as if this were an irrelevant matter with respect to influencing the course of events in the Eastern Mediterranean. Still, it was the American support for the junta that contributed to its longevity, and it was Washington's condoning of the junta's policies that also contributed to Athens' disastrous decisions regarding Cyprus.

Kissinger's view of the Greek junta in his memoirs is quite indicative of how he perceived the situation in the Eastern Mediterranean. In true realpolitik terms, Cyprus was a pawn on the regional cold war chessboard. Under the inherent logic of realpolitik, if the oppressive Greek military dictatorship was acceptable to the United States for the purpose of fighting the cold war so was Turkish control over part of Cyprus.

At the time of the Cyprus crisis in the summer of 1974, Britain not only felt a special responsibility for Cyprus, but it also recognized that Turkey had embarked on territorial expansion. Britain was unwilling to leave this unchallenged. Britain had treaty obligations concerning Cyprus, according to the Zurich-London agreements. Callaghan admitted that Britain had a duty to intervene militarily in Cyprus. As he put it, "I dare say legally we had [a duty to intervene]."[8] In addition, Britain had considerable interests to defend in Cyprus.

Following the Turkish invasion and occupation of 38 percent of Cypriot territory, Turkey proceeded to transform the occupied area into a huge military base. The British sovereign base in Dekelia is adjacent to territory occupied by the Turkish armed forces. The enormous Turkish military presence in Cyprus, which sought to place the entire island under Ankara's strategic control, was not necessarily consistent with Britain's interests on the island and in the Eastern Mediterranean region at the time. In the final analysis, Britain maintained extremely close ties with the island. These ties far exceeded those between the U.S. and Cyprus, which had developed only after independence. It can be argued that overall British interests on the island and, by extension, in the Middle East did not necessarily coincide with those of the United States. This, of course, did not negate the fact that, over time, Britain remained the United States' closest ally and allowed Washington to make use of the British military bases in Cyprus.

British Foreign Secretary James Callaghan explained Britain's feeling that it had a special responsibility for Cyprus during the summer of 1974:

> *Britain felt special responsibility to Cyprus* as a member of the Commonwealth, and to her people because of our past links, as well as our responsibility under the 1960 Treaty. The United States had neither a similar background of history nor a similar treaty relationship.[9] (Emphasis added.)

---

[8]Quoted in the book by O'Malley and Craig, *The Cyprus Conspiracy*, p. 159.
[9]Callaghan, *Time and Chance*, p. 339.

Kissinger's concern, on the other hand, was not so much the fate of Cyprus. Rather, his main concern was how to fight the cold war, prevent Soviet penetration into the region, and preserve the integrity of the southeastern flank of NATO.[10]

Under the circumstances of the summer of 1974, London felt strongly that British military action in Cyprus would be justified under international law and under Britain's treaty obligations to guarantee the sovereignty and territorial integrity of the island republic. In addition, Britain had another reason to support the legitimate government of President Makarios. The Greek military junta engineered the coup that overthrew him. The first Labor government of British Prime Minister Harold Wilson, from 1964 to 1970, had been quite unsympathetic to the junta in Athens, while Washington and Kissinger had supported it. This had been one of several areas of disagreement between the first Wilson government and the Nixon administration. In fact, when Wilson returned to power in February 1974, there was no joy in Washington. The British prime minister was seen as leaning too far to the left domestically and as being too open-minded to Soviet ideas on disarmament, while he appeared willing to make even deeper defense cutbacks in Britain. This created alarm among Wilson's conservative opponents, who found a willing ear in Washington.[11] When the Cyprus crisis erupted in July 1974, London and Washington viewed Cyprus and the Eastern Mediterranean through different lenses.

Kissinger, the Cyprus Crisis, and the Watergate Paralysis

A basic argument of U.S. Secretary of State Kissinger in his memoirs was that he was in a better position than Callaghan and the British to manage the Cyprus crisis because he had a superior understanding of the problem. This contention was not based on fact for it ignored the British role in Cyprus over the decades. This role had been tied to British colonial bureaucracy and the institutional memory of the British Foreign Office. Britain's profound understanding of Cyprus, its people, and its problems, combined with British military capabil-

---

[10]Ibid.

[11]On American suspicions of Wilson, see O'Malley and Craig, *The Cyprus Conspiracy*, pp.148–150.

ities on the ground at the time of the Turkish invasion, gave London an advantage over Washington in managing the crisis. This is particularly the case if one also considers Kissinger's preoccupation with the Watergate crisis.

More important than Callaghan's personality, therefore, was the fact that Britain was in a better position than the United States to follow developments on the ground in Cyprus. In July and August 1974, the British foreign policy decision-making system was operating smoothly in contrast to what was happening in the United States. The Watergate scandal had literally paralyzed the presidency and had profoundly affected foreign policy decision-making.

In his memoirs, Kissinger provided an eloquent description of the prevailing paralysis in presidential decision-making during the last two weeks of July and early August 1974, when the Cyprus crisis erupted. He referred to the "absence of a functioning presidency" during the last two weeks in July, precisely at the height of the crisis:

> Our system requires a strong President to establish coherence; as Presidential authority disintegrates, so does the ability to settle disputes.... Foreign countries were watching with awe and confusion the *growing paralysis* of one of the key supports of the international system ...
>
> Nixon was in San Clemente and, while I briefed him regularly [on Cyprus] he was in no position to concentrate or decide between my basic view and [Secretary of Defense James] Schlesinger's especially not in a rapidly changing situation. The preoccupation with Watergate had reached a point where we were losing even the ability to transmit papers bearing on vital foreign policy matters instantaneously between the President [in San Clemente] and the White House. So many documents relating to Watergate were being moved over the circuits to San Clemente that on July 19 I had to ask for special priority for cables bearing on *the Cyprus crisis*.[12] (Emphasis added.)

Thus, Kissinger confirmed that highly abnormal conditions were prevailing in Washington at the time of the Cyprus crisis.

---

[12]Kissinger, *Years of Upheaval,* pp. 1187, 1191–1192.

This view was reinforced by Kissinger's counterpart in London, James Callaghan. He wrote in his memoirs:

> The failure [of U.S.-British coordination during the crisis] was not merely caused by different perceptions. It was another malign consequence of the Watergate affair, which at that time was rapidly approaching its climax and engaged so much of Henry Kissinger's attention that on occasion *he and I lost contact during critical hours.* . . . His pre-occupation with the consequences of Richard Nixon's final days as President prevented us from having that continuous face-to-face personal contact that would have settled differences and enabled Britain and America to march together.[13]

In the final analysis, unlike the paralysis prevailing in Washington, the foreign policy decision-making process in London was orderly. It could operate more efficiently than the process in Washington could in a crisis situation, such as the one that erupted in Cyprus in July and August 1974. By the same token, Britain could not be effective in defusing the crisis without American support. Even though there was paralysis in Washington, the British plan to back its crisis diplomacy in Cyprus with the threat of the use of military force required American support. Such support, however, became highly problematic because Washington and London viewed the worsening crisis in Cyprus from divergent perspectives. The most glaring example was how differently London and Washington treated the president of Cyprus, Archbishop Makarios, following his overthrow by the Greek military junta on July 15, 1974.

Makarios Overthrown: British Dismay, American Condoning

Britain to the Rescue of Makarios

For some time, the national security bureaucracy in Washington, with some individual exceptions, had tended to view Makarios as the "Castro of the Mediterranean." In his memoirs, Kissinger disputed that

---

[13]Callaghan, *Time and Chance*, p. 339.

this was the case.[14] Still, the reactions of the State Department and the Pentagon during the Cyprus crisis cast serious doubt on Kissinger's assertions that Makarios was simply a nuisance and nothing more. The way London and Washington reacted to the news of Makarios's overthrow and the announcement of his death, later proved wrong, offered a good indication of how Britain's policies toward Cyprus diverged from those of the United States.

As it turned out, Makarios survived the July 15, 1974 coup. While the Presidential Palace was under heavy attack by the Cypriot National Guard, he managed to escape and find his way to Ktima, the capital of the Paphos district. Paphos is a mountainous area located in the southwestern part of the island. Makarios enjoyed the strongest support in this region, having been born in Panayia, a village in the area. The archbishop's loyal supporters in Paphos put up a fierce resistance to the National Guard. In Ktima, there was a small auxiliary radio station through which Makarios broadcast a message to the Greek people of Cyprus on the afternoon of the coup that had failed to kill him. The archbishop was overwhelmed with emotion but spoke in a steady voice as he addressed his people. He opened his address as follows:

> Greek people of Cyprus. The voice you are hearing is famil-
> iar to you. You know who is addressing this message to you. I
> am Makarios. I am the one you have elected to be your leader.
> I am not dead, as the junta of Athens and its local represen-
> tatives had wished. I am alive. I am with you as standard-
> bearer in the common struggle. . . . Resist the junta . . .[15]

Makarios's message and his urging of the people to resist the coup staged by the Greek junta caused the National Guard to intensify its attacks on the city of Ktima, and the archbishop was in immediate danger of being killed or apprehended. Through the UNFICYP contingent in Paphos, he contacted the British military base in Akrotiri. Makarios requested that the British pick him up with a helicopter,

---

[14]Kissinger, *Years of Renewal*, p. 199.

[15]Quoted from the book by Costas Tzortzis, *To Chroniko tes Kypriakes Tragodias: Dokumenta gia to Praxikopima ke ten Eisvoli* (The Chronicle of the Cyprus Tragedy: Documents on the Coup and the Invasion) (Nicosia: Lithopress, 1991), p. 43.

take him to the Akrotiri base, and then transport him to London.[16]

Makarios's request reached British Foreign Secretary James Callaghan in London. Before it was discovered that Makarios was still alive, the British government had decided that, even if he had been killed, Britain should not recognize the puppet regime of Nikos Sampson.[17] Following consultation with Prime Minister Harold Wilson, Callaghan instructed the British forces in Cyprus to rescue the archbishop. On Tuesday, July 16, 1974, a British Royal Air Force (RAF) helicopter rescued Makarios and took him safely to the Akrotiri base. That evening, the archbishop was flown to Malta and, from there, to London.

Washington Content to See Makarios Go

Upon the archbishop's arrival in London, the Wilson government received him as Cyprus's head of state. The mood in Washington, however, was quite different. Prior to the coup, Tom Pappas, Nixon's confidant and the junta's close friend, visited Lambros Stathopoulos, the head of the State Information Agency (KYP), the Greek equivalent of the CIA. Pappas told Stathopoulos that "the Americans don't like Makarios," that the situation in Cyprus had to be "cleaned up," and that circumstances were favorable to do so.[18]

On July 15, 1974, the day of the coup against Makarios, Cyprus

---

[16]Three years later, Makarios described in detail his escape from the Presidential Palace, his brief stay in Paphos, and his rescue by the British. He did so in an interview with the Greek newspaper *To Vima* 12 days before his death. See *To Vima*, July 23, 1977.

[17]Callaghan, *Time and Chance*, p. 337.

[18]Quoted by Arapakis, *To Telos tes Siopis*, p. 147. Admiral Petros Arapakis was a central figure in the Greek junta during the last few months of its rule. In his capacity as chief of the Greek Navy, he served in the Greek General Staff. He wrote this book in order to provide his version of the events surrounding the coup against Makarios, the subsequent Turkish invasion of Cyprus, and Athens' role in all of these events. Arapakis had intimate knowledge of developments taking place during the critical weeks and days leading up to the coup against Makarios. He had a highly negative view of Brigadier Demetrios Ioannides, the real ruler of Greece between November 1973 and July 23, 1974. It was Ioannides who made the decision to overthrow Makarios and, in this decision, he was supported by other key figures of the junta. Arapakis maintained that he was kept in the dark concerning the decision and that he was resolutely opposed to any move by Athens against Makarios. See Arapakis, *To Telos tes Siopis*, pp. 125–147.

Radio announced that the archbishop had died under the rubble of the Presidential Palace in Nicosia. There was elation at the Pentagon when the announcement was heard. The prevailing mood in the Pentagon corridors that afternoon was that "the s.o.b got what he deserved."[19] In the State Department, upon learning that Archbishop Makarios had survived, one official remarked, "How inconvenient."[20] On the day of the coup, Cypriot Ambassador to Washington, Dimis Dimitriou, visited Kissinger at the State Department. He was struck by the fact that the secretary of state "failed to express his condolences over the reported death of the Archbishop."[21]

Britain, from the very beginning, denounced the coup, rescued Makarios, gave him refuge, and recognized him as the legitimate president of Cyprus. Unlike Britain, Washington took no diplomatic action to indicate its opposition to the violent overthrow of the democratically elected government of Cyprus.[22] Washington's failure to take a clear stand and condemn the overthrow of Makarios was, in essence, implicit acceptance of the Greek junta's coup in Cyprus.[23] Following Kissinger's instructions, State Department spokesman Robert Anderson repeatedly refused to criticize the coup and, when asked, repeatedly avoided stating whether Makarios was still the legitimate president of Cyprus.

On July 18, it was announced that Makarios was proceeding from London to New York, where he was going to address the U.N. Security Council the next day. On July 22, the Cypriot leader was to meet with Secretary of State Henry Kissinger. At a press briefing on July 18,

---

[19]An individual who was serving at the Pentagon on July 15, 1974, spoke to the author in person, providing him with this information regarding the prevailing mood at the Pentagon the day Makarios was overthrown. This individual had served in the U.S. armed forces with distinction. He wishes to remain anonymous.

[20]Quoted by Stern, *The Wrong Horse*, p. 111.

[21]On the coup against Makarios and the reaction in Washington, see the perceptive analysis of Charles McCaskill, " The United States and Cyprus from 1974 to 1991," in *Cyprus: Domestic Dynamics, External Constraints*, ed. Christos P. Ioannides (New Rochelle, NY: Aristide D. Caratzas, Publisher, 1992), pp. 107–112, esp. p. 112. McCaskill, an American diplomat, served in Cyprus from 1960 to 1964 and was Cyprus Desk Officer at the State Department from 1965 to 1967.

[22]John Campbell, "The United States and the Cyprus Question, 1974 -75," in Coufoudakis, *Essays on the Cyprus Conflict*, p. 19.

[23]Couloumbis, *The United States, Greece, and Turkey*, pp. 88; Coufoudakis, "To Kypriako" (The Cyprus Issue), pp. 37–38.

the State Department spokesman was asked the following question:

Q: Was the Secretary meeting with Makarios on Monday, July 22, as a private citizen, *as Archbishop, or as President of Cyprus?*

A: He's meeting with *Archbishop* Makarios on Monday.[24] (Emphasis added.)

In this way, the United States appeared to be tilting toward the junta regime in Cyprus as it failed to acknowledge that Makarios was the legitimate president of the country and failed to condemn the Sampson regime.[25] Washington was to be the lonely voice in the international community that was rather understanding of the actions of the Greek junta in Cyprus. The rest of the world—the NATO allies in Europe, the non-aligned countries, Eastern Europe, and Moscow—all denounced the coup against Makarios.

A few days after the State Department spokesman implied that Makarios was not the legitimate president of Cyprus, Kissinger was asked whether Archbishop Makarios was the "legitimate ruler in Cyprus." The question was asked on July 25, 1978, during Kissinger's joint press conference with visiting German Foreign Minister Hans Dietrich Genscher. The secretary of state responded as follows:

The State Department posture is that we will go along with any solution that is acceptable to the parties. We do not have a candidate of our own in the Cyprus situation. . . . The U.S. position is that we will go along with any solution that is acceptable to Greece and Turkey and to the Cypriot people. We are not pushing a candidate of the United States.[26]

Kissinger was not asked about the settlement of the Cyprus dispute or whether he favored one candidate for president of Cyprus over another. He was simply asked whether the United States considered Makarios to be the legitimate president of Cyprus. The secretary

---

[24]Stern, *The Wrong Horse*, pp. 112–113.
[25]McCaskill, "The United States and Cyprus," p. 112.
[26]See *Department of State Bulletin*, vol. LXXXI, no. 1834, August 19, 1974, p. 283.

of state gave a highly convoluted answer and did not state that Makarios was still the legitimate president. In fact, his response left open the possibility that Makarios might not be the legitimate president. By stating that the U.S. was not "pushing a candidate" of its own, Kissinger was clearly implying that the legitimate president of Cyprus might be someone other than Makarios. When Makarios returned to Cyprus on December 7, 1974, and assumed his presidential duties in accordance with the constitution, Kissinger did not see this as the restoration of legitimacy. In this regard, Kissinger wrote:

> On December 7, 1974, Makarios returned to Cyprus, further restricting the freedom of action of all parties.[27]

In other words, Kissinger saw Makarios's return to Cyprus through the lens of pure realpolitik. What was important to the secretary of state was not whether Makarios was the democratically elected president of Cyprus. What was important to him was the avoidance of any action or step that could lead to the "destabilization" of the status quo. Following the invasion, the status quo clearly favored Turkey.

A month after the coup against Makarios and the failure of the State Department to condemn it, Assistant Secretary of State for European Affairs Arthur Hartman testified on August 19, 1974, before the Subcommittee on Europe of the House Committee on Foreign Affairs. He had just returned from Geneva where the foreign ministers of Greece, Turkey, and Britain had met in an attempt to reach a Cyprus settlement. The Geneva meeting failed because, on August 14, Turkey unleashed the second phase of its invasion and, in 24 hours, cut Cyprus in two, occupying 38 percent of its territory. Thus, Hartman's testimony came at a critical moment, a few days after Turkey completed its military objective in Cyprus.

During Hartman's testimony, the issue of the overthrow of Makarios by the Greek junta and the State Department's stand on the matter came under intense scrutiny. This was particularly the case with regard to Congressman Benjamin Rosenthal, the chairman of the subcommittee. The following exchange took place between Rosenthal and Hartman:

---

[27]Kissinger, *Years of Upheaval*, p. 237.

MR. ROSENTHAL: Let me deal with the role of the United States. When the military junta initiated the downfall of the Makarios government and installed Mr. Sampson, we said nothing. Isn't that correct?

MR. HARTMAN: We knew that that was a probable cause for intervention by Turkey.

MR. ROSENTHAL: We did not contest that intervention in Cyprus by the military junta, did we?

MR. HARTMAN: I think we did.

MR. ROSENTHAL: No, we did not. Do you have a statement that suggests that we did?

MR. HARTMAN: I know what actions we took and know what we did with the parties, and I know what we conveyed to them as our understanding of what that situation would produce.[28]

When challenged openly by Rosenthal, Hartman was at a loss and could not point to a State Department statement that criticized the coup against Makarios. Instead, like Kissinger, Hartman gave a convoluted answer concerning the extent to which the United States engaged in private diplomacy at a time when Cyprus was swept by violence. Evidently, Hartman believed that the Greek junta deserved to be treated with the niceties of private diplomacy while it was violating every rule of diplomacy, democracy, and human rights in Cyprus and Greece.

Britain and the Ghost of Suez

Following the July 15 coup against Makarios, the British Labor government of Harold Wilson anticipated the likelihood of Turkish military action against Cyprus and a major crisis in the Eastern Mediterranean. It, therefore, made an attempt to prevent such a disas-

---

[28]See *Hearings Before the Committee on Foreign Affairs and the Subcommittee on Europe, House of Representatives*, August 19 and 20, 1974, 93rd Congress, Washington, U.S. Government Printing Office, 1974, p. 9.

trous course of events. The British effort was two-pronged. It involved intense diplomacy, accompanied by a military contingency plan. Foreign Secretary James Callaghan, who was to become prime minister in April 1976, led the British team handling the Cyprus crisis.

On the diplomatic front, the British objective was to find ways to restrain Turkey. For this reason, Britain strongly opposed the coup against Makarios and called on the Greek military junta to withdraw its officers from the Cypriot National Guard. Developments moved fast, however, and diplomacy alone had little chance to succeed. This became evident following the urgent visit to London by Turkish Prime Minister Bülent Ecevit, who arrived the evening of July 17 and left the next day. During his visit, Prime Minister Wilson and Foreign Secretary Callaghan sought to assure Turkey that Britain was doing all it could to restore constitutional order in Cyprus. Not only had the Wilson government kept a certain distance from the Greek junta, but it had also had a visceral disdain for Nikos Sampson, the man who replaced Makarios.[29] The British government wanted Sampson removed as soon as possible so that the status quo ante could be restored. In order to placate Turkish fears, Callaghan made it clear to Ecevit that the restoration of the status quo ante did not mean that the status of the Turkish Cypriots before the coup was satisfactory to Britain. The Turkish Cypriots had legitimate grievances that needed to be addressed, the British foreign secretary added.[30]

Ecevit made it clear from the outset that nothing short of a Turkish military presence in Cyprus would be satisfactory to Ankara. Ecevit asked Wilson to allow Turkey to use the British military bases in Cyprus to land troops on the island, given the fact that both Britain and Turkey were guarantor powers. This was necessary, Ecevit argued, in order to protect the Turkish Cypriots. Britain rejected this Turkish request outright. Both Wilson and Callaghan told the Turkish prime minister that Cyprus needed fewer Greek troops, not more Turkish troops.[31] It was for this reason that Britain was pressuring the Greek

---

[29]British disdain for Sampson went back to EOKA's anti-British campaign from 1955 to 1959. He was the head of an execution squad and was arrested and sentenced to life imprisonment. The feeling was mutual, as Sampson had developed a sustained hatred for the British. One reason could be that he was severely tortured during his internment.

[30]Callaghan, *Time and Chance*, pp. 339–341.

[31]Ibid., p. 340.

military regime to withdraw its army officers from the Cypriot National Guard immediately. Ecevit left London without reaching an agreement for any concerted action. There were ominous signs that Turkey was about to invade Cyprus. Amazingly, Britain was more concerned about this possibility than the junta in Athens, where the Greek General Staff appeared to be impervious to the impending invasion. The junta and its strongman, Demetrios Ioannides, were, in fact, more concerned about the consolidation of the colonels' puppet regime in Nicosia.

Under the circumstances, the Wilson government decided to buttress its diplomacy with military preparations in and around Cyprus. Britain dispatched a naval task force to the area near Cyprus. It consisted of the aircraft carrier *Hermes*, the guided missile destroyer *Devonshire*, the frigates *Rhyl* and *Andromeda*, and the submarine *Onslaught*. These naval vessels were patrolling the waters around Cyprus by July 18. At the same time, Britain dispatched 3,300 troops and an elite unit of marines to its two sovereign military bases in the southern part of Cyprus, doubling the forces already there. In addition, British tanks and helicopters kept arriving at the bases. These forces were supported by warplanes at the British bases, which included Lightning fighters and two squadrons of Vulcan bombers.[32] These combined British forces were to perform a dual role. The first objective was to provide protection for the 17,000 British residents of Cyprus as well as British vacationers on the island. The second objective was to provide a deterrent against the imminent Turkish invasion. Still, under the circumstances, the military capabilities of Britain alone were not enough to guarantee success.

Britain needed U.S. diplomatic and military cover. This was the case because the implications of the British initiative were not strictly military. The initiative also had broader diplomatic and strategic implications since the cohesion of the NATO alliance was at stake. The United States, Britain, and Turkey were all NATO allies, and a military confrontation between Britain and Turkey in the Eastern Mediterranean was bound to have profound effects on NATO.

Furthermore, Britain was no longer the dominant power in the

---

[32]Information based on the book by O'Malley and Craig, *The Cyprus Conspiracy,* pp. 159–160, 171, 183. Callaghan confirmed the dispatch of British reinforcements to Cyprus during the Cyprus crisis. See Callaghan, *Time and Chance*, pp. 347, 351.

Eastern Mediterranean. The United States was the dominant power in the region, and Washington had more influence over Greece and Turkey. The Wilson government did not forget the lesson the United States taught to British Prime Minister Anthony Eden. Eden led Britain into the disastrous invasion of the Suez Canal in Egypt in October 1956.[33] One major reason for this British—and French— failure was that the United States opposed the invasion. Cyprus was one of the main bases from which this joint British-French invasion was launched. The British government was determined to avoid a repetition of the Suez disaster and, consequently, it decided that no British military action could be taken concerning Cyprus without American support. Callaghan made this very clear in his memoirs:

> I had no intention of exposing Britain to the kind of differences with the United States which existed at the time of the Suez invasion and which had resulted in a terrible setback for British arms and influence. During that contest, the radar of the American fleet had deliberately interfered with and confused the signals of the British and French ships. Further, American destroyers had moored themselves alongside Egyptian ships in harbour so that the Royal Navy could not fire. I was determined that if military force had to be used in Cyprus, *there must be a clear understanding with the United States, with their support fully guaranteed.*[34] (Emphasis added.)

Apparently, Wilson and Callaghan did not want to see the U.S. Sixth Fleet repeating the role it had played in Suez in 1956. After all, by 1974, the Sixth Fleet was much more powerful than it had been in 1956, and its electronic warfare capabilities, which could have jammed British communications, were far superior as well.

By the second week of July 1974, a carrier task force of the Sixth Fleet was sailing close to Cyprus. Throughout the crisis, from July 15 to mid-August, this task force sailed about 100 to 150 nautical miles southwest of Cyprus. A number of fighter jets taking off from a U.S.

---

[33]The Suez adventure is described in the memoirs of its main protagonist Anthony Eden, *The Memoirs of Anthony Eden: Full Circle* (Boston: Houghton Mifflin Co., 1960), esp. Book III, Suez, pp. 467–654.

[34]Callaghan, *Time and Chance*, p. 341.

aircraft carrier stayed in the air and monitored the situation on the ground in Cyprus. The flying time from the aircraft carrier to the theater of operations near the tiny port city of Kyrenia, where the Turkish troops landed on July 20, was only five to seven minutes. Likewise, on July 18, the Sixth Fleet began monitoring the activities of the British naval task force sailing around Cyprus. Britain had good reason to secure American cooperation for any military action concerning Cyprus. Suez had taught the British a bitter lesson, and the Wilson government remembered it very well.

Under these circumstances, Britain needed the support of the United States, which would involve the Sixth Fleet, before it would issue any threat of military action against the imminent Turkish invasion of Cyprus. Repeatedly, just prior to the invasion, British Foreign Secretary Callaghan asked Washington for support in a joint British-American military action. The primary burden of such an action was to be carried by Britain but, still, the Wilson government needed American cover. Kissinger denied this cover and refused to support Britain.[35] Early on the morning of July 20, 1974, the Turkish invasion of Cyprus began.

The Turkish Invasion

The Turkish invasion of Cyprus, under the code name "Attila," began at 4:45 a.m. on July 20. At that time, Turkish F-4 Phantom jets began attacking a variety of military targets. An hour later, Turkish paratroopers were dropped on the outskirts of Nicosia, the capital, while helicopters unloaded commandos in the Turkish Cypriot enclave in the same area. Shortly thereafter, amphibious crafts began landing troops and materiel at a location known as Five Mile Beach, five miles west of Kyrenia. It took several hours for the Cypriot National Guard to mobilize in order to resist the invasion. While Cyprus was already under a combined Turkish air and naval bombardment, the Greek General Staff in Athens did not want the Cypriot National Guard to react and wanted it to show restraint. In fact, the Greek General Staff, under orders from its chief, General Gregorios Bonanos, ordered the Cypriot National Guard command to refrain from any action against

---

[35]Ibid., pp. 351–352.

the approaching invading Turkish armada because the Turks "were conducting naval exercises."[36]

The Cypriot National Guard Command, therefore, instructed its military units near the area of the invasion not to be concerned because the Turkish armada approaching Cyprus was conducting military maneuvers.[37] As a result, during the first few hours of the invasion, the most critical time for the success or failure of such an operation, the invading Turkish forces met no resistance. The Greek junta had neutralized the Cypriot National Guard and, in this way, had facilitated the Turkish invasion. It was only at 9 a.m. on July 20, four hours after the invasion had commenced, that the Greek General Staff gave orders to the Cypriot National Guard Command to take military action against the invading forces.[38]

There was no government in Cyprus and no organized fighting force to oppose the invasion. Politically speaking, the Sampson regime installed by the Greek junta had no popular support and no legitimacy. Militarily, the Cypriot National Guard, which had been created in 1964 precisely for the purpose of thwarting a Turkish invasion, was in total disarray. The existing plan, which the National Guard had been practicing for years, called for a lightning response to an invading force. Each military unit had a prescribed assignment that, through a high degree of coordination, would have resulted in an attack on the invading forces even before they attempted to land. Following the orders from Athens to the National Guard, this plan was not implemented. In fact, the attention of the National Guard was not on Kyrenia, where the invasion was taking place. Rather, the officers who had carried out the coup were preoccupied with the consolidation of their shaky rule, while the National Guard was still hunting Makarios's supporters, who had opposed the coup.

The Turkish invasion, therefore, took place while the Greek Cypriots were engaged in a fratricidal civil war and were paying very little attention to Turkey. The National Guard and its ally, EOKA-B,

---

[36]This critical information was documented by the chief of the Greek Navy at the time, Admiral Petros Arapakis, in his *Telos tes Siopis*, pp. 165–193.

[37]See the account of George Sergis, *E Mache tes Kyprou: Ioulios-Avgoustos 1974* (The Battle of Cyprus: July-August 1974) (Athens: Vlassis Bros., 1996), pp. 291. Sergis, a retired brigadier of the Greek army, provided an hour-by-hour military analysis of the Turkish invasion.

[38]Arapakis, *Telos tes Siopis*, p. 168.

were fighting Makarios's loyal forces and other supporters of the archbishop. Most of those killed during the coup were supporters of
Makarios. Greek Cypriots were killing each other as Turkish troops
landed near Kyrenia. The Turkish Cypriots and Turkey pointed to this
civil war among Greeks, which was very real, as one of the main jus-
tifications for the invasion. The internecine killing among Greeks in
Cyprus was hardly reassuring to the Turkish Cypriots, who had been
the underdogs since the intercommunal fighting of 1963 and 1964. In
Turkey's eyes, the civil war among Greek Cypriots made it inconceivable that the Turkish Cypriots would accept a settlement based on the
pre-1963 status quo.

Equally important was the fact that Greece, the military power
that logically could have deterred the invasion, was in no position to
do so. The junta that ruled Greece had precipitated the invasion by
overthrowing Makarios, a reckless action, and, after doing so, it had left
Cyprus defenseless. For the Greeks, this was the worst kind of betrayal
of Cyprus. For the Turks, the Greek junta offered the long-sought
opportunity to invade Cyprus. In the final analysis, the timing of the
invasion was ideal for Turkey because its invading army had no credible military opponent to overcome, while, at the same time, Ankara
could point to the civil war raging among the Greeks on the island.

Even under these circumstances, the Turkish objective of gaining
rapid control over a large part of Cypriot territory did not come about
as easily as Ankara had expected. In fact, even though the Cypriot
National Guard was in utter disarray and Cyprus had no navy or air
force to challenge the invading Turkish forces, the first phase of the
Turkish invasion could not be considered a military success. As it
turned out, if the Cypriot National Guard had not been in disarray
because of the coup against Makarios and had had elementary air and
naval support, the battle of Cyprus waged in the third week of July
1974 might have had a different outcome.

Greek Cypriot military units, acting on the initiative of individual officers rather than on the basis of a coordinated plan, began a
fierce counter-attack late in the evening of July 20, which lasted until
the early morning hours of July 21. The invading forces were tested to
the limit and, for a few hours, the success or failure of the invasion
hung in the balance.[39] The Turkish armed forces, however, the sec-

---

[39]Mehmet Ali Birand, *Thirty Hot Days* (London: K. Rustem and Brother, 1985),
pp. 30–32. Birand had access to top Turkish decision-makers at the time of the inva-

ond-largest army in NATO, had absolute air and naval superiority over the Greek Cypriots, and they were able to withstand the counter-attack. But it took three days for the Turkish Army to establish a secure bridgehead near Kyrenia and prevail over the fragments of the Cypriot National Guard that were resisting the invasion.

Despite the fact that the Turkish Air Force had free reign over and around Cyprus and the Turkish Navy did not have to confront the Greek Navy, coordination and command and control were rather poor among the three branches of the Turkish armed forces. This was amply demonstrated on July 21, when Turkish fighter planes attacked a Turkish naval unit, sinking one of the ships near the southwestern coast of Cyprus. Turkish Prime Minister Bülent Ecevit, who had ordered the invasion, made an attempt to blame the "devious" Greeks for sabotaging efforts to conclude a cease-fire. With bitter humor, Kissinger described the discussion he had with Ecevit on July 21, when the Turkish prime minister accused the Greeks of putting Turkish flags on their warships and impersonating Turkish pilots. This was an attempt by Ecevit to blame the Greeks for attacking Turkish naval units sailing toward Cyprus. The following farcical conversation took place over the telephone between Kissinger and Ecevit:

ECEVIT: We have a problem. We doubt the reliability of Greece. [Greek junta strongman] Ioannides' word of honor is a joke. We have now figured out what the joke is behind his words. He said we could fire on any ships bearing Greek flags. His ships are drawing Turkish flags!

KISSINGER: Well, no one can blame you if you sink your own ships.

---

sion and gave a vivid description of the ferocious battle that was waged on the first night of the invasion. On the great difficulty confronted by the Turkish invading army and the prospect of failure during the night of July 20, see also Neoklis Sarris, *E Alli Plevra: Politiki Chronographia tes Tourkikes Eisvolis sten Kypro me Vasi Tourkikes Piges* (The Other Side: A Political Chronicle of the Turkish Invasion of Cyprus Based on Turkish Sources) (Athens: Grammi, 1977), pp. 200–214. Sarris is a Greek academic who was born and educated in Turkey before he left for Greece in the mid-1960s. He was involved in Turkish politics and was active in leftist circles, where he met Bülent Ecevit, a socialist deputy at the time. Sarris's analysis of the Turkish invasion is based on Turkish sources.

ECEVIT: No, Dr. Kissinger, they are not our ships. They are Greek ships drawing Turkish flags.

KISSINGER: Yes, Mr. Prime Minister, but you can sink them if they are not your ships but are flying Turkish flags.

ECEVIT: They are using two tricks. We are NATO Allies, and the Turkish [meaning Greek] pilots know our codes. They speak Turkish. They call our pilots in Turkish using our code words. We can no longer rely on the words of Greece.

KISSINGER: What exactly is it that you want? I know you are an intelligent man. I know you from the days of Harvard. With all due respect, I cannot take this . . .[40]

Even Kissinger appeared, for a moment, to be losing patience with Ecevit due to his unsubstantiated accusations that the Greeks were attacking Turkish warships. The Greek military junta was collapsing at that time, and no Greek Air Force fighter planes or naval units had been sent to the theater of operations in Cyprus. As it turned out and due to poor coordination, it was the Turks themselves who attacked one of their own warships.[41] In the afternoon of July 21, 1974 Turkish fighter planes attacked a Turkish naval unit consisted of one frigate and two destroyers that were sailing off the shore of Paphos in northwestern Cyprus. As a result, the Turkish airforce sunk one of of its own destroyers, the Kocatepe, killing 54 of its crew.[42]

At 5 p.m. on the afternoon of July 22, the Turkish government, the Greek government, the Turkish commanders who had carried out the invasion, and the commanders of the Cypriot National Guard agreed to a U.N.-sponsored cease-fire. It came about through the combined efforts of the U.N. Peacekeeping Force in Cyprus (UNFICYP), Secretary of State Henry Kissinger, and Under Secretary of State Joseph Sisco. Sisco had been dispatched to Greece and Turkey by Kissinger. He had visited Athens and Ankara, where he exerted a great deal of effort to avert a Greek-Turkish war. British Foreign Secretary James Callaghan also played a key role in arranging and implementing the cease-fire because, through the British troops serving in UNFICYP,

---

[40]Kissinger, *Years of Renewal,* pp. 221–222.
[41]Ibid., p. 222.
[42]Birand, *Thirty Hot Days,* pp. 40–43.

the British government had a better grasp of the situation on the ground than any other third party. For the next three weeks, the focus of diplomatic attention was Geneva. In this Swiss city, with its long tradition of hosting diplomatic meetings, Britain undertook to defuse the Cyprus crisis.

Failure in Geneva: The U.S. Veto of the British Intervention Plan

Britain took the initiative, with American support, to bring together the two other guarantors powers, Turkey and Greece, in Geneva. The Geneva conference took place in two phases, July 25 to 30 and August 9 to 14, 1974. The conference was presided over by British Foreign Secretary James Callaghan. Turkey was represented by Foreign Minister Turan Güneş. Veteran Greek politician George Mavros represented Greece. At the time, he was serving as foreign minister in the newly established government of national unity under Prime Minister Constantine Karamanlis. Mavros's task was not to be envied. Not only did he have to deal with the extremely grave situation in Cyprus, but he was also concerned about the situation in Greece, which was still extremely volatile. The military junta had collapsed, but the armed forces were still in great turmoil and the risk of a military confrontation with Turkey was quite real.

The foreign ministers were joined on August 9 by Acting President of Cyprus Glafcos Clerides and Turkish Cypriot leader Rauf Denktash. The United States also had a representative in Geneva, Under Secretary of State for European Affairs Arthur Hartman. He was sent to Geneva by Henry Kissinger as his personal representative.

Turkey's frequent violations of the July 22 cease-fire, the continuous advancement of Turkish forces, the forcing of thousands of Greek Cypriots to flee their homes, and the pouring of reinforcements into Cyprus from the Turkish mainland convinced Britain that Ankara's objective was to launch a second phase of the invasion and cut Cyprus in two.[43] The British government had direct, accurate information regarding the military situation on the ground since British forces were serving under the UNFICYP umbrella. These British soldiers found themselves in the theater of operations in the

---

[43]Callaghan, *Time and Chance*, pp. 350, 352–353.

Kyrenia region. They did not take part in the fighting but served in a humanitarian capacity. They were able to help many Greek Cypriots come under U.N. protection in designated areas. The main U.N.-controlled location was the Dome Hotel in Kyrenia, where British blue helmets helped about 1,000 Greek Cypriots find refuge.

At the same time, these British forces witnessed first-hand the Turkish violations of the cease-fire and the advancement of the Turkish forces. They were taking place while the first round of the Geneva negotiations was underway from July 25 to July 30. From July 22, 1974, when the cease-fire was declared, until July 30, the invading Turkish forces advanced and occupied an additional four percent of Cypriot territory. The Turks, therefore, doubled the territory they had placed under their control between July 20 and July 22. As eyewitnesses, the British UNFICYP forces had been providing continuous, first-hand information to the British foreign secretary in Geneva. It did not take long for Callaghan to realize that the Turkish objective was to keep advancing until Ankara had control over the territory it had planned to occupy all along.

When the Geneva conference began, the British objective was not to push back the Turkish forces, which had already occupied about eight percent of the northern part of Cyprus by the end of July. Rather, Britain wanted Turkey to honor the cease-fire and wanted to prevent a new Turkish offensive that would split the island in two. This was a limited military objective, which could have been achieved if the United States had supported Britain.

During the course of the Geneva negotiations, Britain exerted all effort to defuse the situation and bring about an agreement stipulating that the opposing parties would honor the cease-fire and proceed toward seeking a peaceful settlement of the conflict. There were two main stumbling blocks to this British effort. First, Turkey was in no mood to compromise and demanded that the Greek side agree that 34 percent of Cypriot territory should come under Turkish control. Second, Britain needed American backing for its plan to threaten to use military force to deter a further Turkish advance in Cyprus.

From the outset, the Turkish foreign minister adopted an uncompromising position. In his memoirs, Callaghan described the Turkish attitude in Geneva:

Turan Gunes, the Turkish Foreign Minister, was a dark,

loquacious character who looked somewhat like Groucho Marx but without the humor. He was capable of repeating the same interminable argument time after time until words lost their meaning. He was moved neither by passion nor patience. He was an expert at obstruction, once holding up one of our meetings for several hours as he elaborated his objections to name-plates that identified us at the table. He sometimes disappeared without a trace at critical moments and was said to be visiting a casino.[44]

Considering these Turkish tactics, aimed at giving more time to Turkey to transfer additional troops and tanks to the area under its control in Cyprus, it was inevitable that the Geneva negotiations would have little chance of success.

The only realistic hope for a successful outcome in Geneva was a combined Anglo-American threat of military action in the event that Ankara attempted to expand its territorial gains. Callaghan repeatedly attempted to convince Secretary of State Kissinger to support Britain in sending a clear message to Turkey that further territorial advancement would be met by force.[45]

Callaghan told Kissinger's representative in Geneva, Arthur Hartman, that Britain was afraid Turkey was preparing to launch a second offensive in Cyprus. On instructions from Washington, Hartman attempted to convince the British foreign secretary that Turkey had no intention of conquering more land. Hartman argued that, taking into account the situation on the ground in Cyprus and the fact that Greece had a new democratic government, it would be rational for Turkey to show restraint and avoid further military action in Cyprus.[46] Callaghan, who had a very accurate picture of the situation on the ground in Cyprus doubted Hartman's assessment of the situation and told him so. The turn of events proved Callaghan right. The British foreign secretary repeated his warning that the United States and Britain had to be prepared for all eventualities, including a further Turkish advance in Cyprus.[47]

---

[44]Ibid., p. 348.
[45]Ibid., pp. 352–353.
[46]Ibid., p. 351.
[47]Ibid., p. 351; O'Malley and Craig, *The Cyprus Conspiracy*, p. 210.

On August 11, while the negotiations were still deadlocked, Hartman gave the American response to Callaghan's request that there should be Anglo-American military preparations to meet the eventuality of a renewed Turkish offensive in Cyprus. The encounter between Hartman and Callaghan was described by Callaghan in his memoirs:

> At noon on Sunday 11 August 1974, he [Hartman] returned with the Administration's reply. Hartman is an able career diplomat, a European and Soviet affairs expert, courteous, quiet but firm in manner, and an excellent analyst. On this occasion, he abandoned the relaxed informality we had become accustomed to as *he informed me stiffly that the United States was not happy with Her Majesty's Government's approach.*[48]

Then, Hartman explained to Callaghan that Kissinger had spoken with Ecevit on the phone and had impressed upon him the fact that any further military action in Cyprus would have serious consequences. Kissinger was satisfied that the Turkish prime minister understood his message, Hartman told Callaghan. Hartman then gave Callaghan a warning:

> The Secretary of State *would react very strongly* against any further announcement of British military activities, because it would have an adverse effect on his tactics with Ecevit.[49]

It was remarkable that the United States, through Hartman and upon instructions from Secretary of State Kissinger, was using rather un-diplomatic language toward its best ally, Britain. This was quite indicative of the deep disagreement between Washington and London over Cyprus. Callaghan asked Hartman to inform Kissinger of his anxiety over the fact that the Turks were not being handled effectively and that Britain and the United States were not preparing their response in the event of further Turkish military action. Then Callaghan gave his warning to Kissinger:

---

[48]Callaghan, *Time and Chance*, p. 352.
[49]Ibid.

I believed the *worst interpretation should be put on Turkish future intentions* and there *were sufficient pointers in this direction to prepare contingency plans. What was the United States going to do if the Turks enlarged their bridgehead?* . . . Britain was ready to strengthen a static defense against possible lines of Turkish advance by moving more reinforcements and flying in further Phantoms. . . . But I must be assured of American support if I were to do so, and in light of our conversation this would apparently not be forthcoming.[50] (Emphasis added.)

The British foreign secretary was quite frustrated with the American opposition to supporting diplomacy with threats of the use of force. After all, Cyprus was in the midst of a war, a broader Greek-Turkish war was looming, and it made sense for Britain and the United States not to remove the military option from the picture. If there was a diplomat who understood this basic principle of diplomacy during military crises better than anybody, it was Henry Kissinger. For this reason, Callaghan sent another stern warning to Kissinger:

As soon as Hartman had left, I fired off a telegram to Henry Kissinger, saying that these important differences were impairing our mutual confidence. I reiterated that it was not sufficient to approach the Turks through the medium of diplomacy. The correct policy was to tackle them on parallel lines, namely, convince them that we were in earnest on *both diplomatic and military levels.* This was the most likely way to achieve results.[51] (Emphasis added.)

Kissinger responded by reiterating his opposition to threats of military action. According to Tom McNally, Callaghan's chief political adviser at the time, "Kissinger was the key not to give Britain any military support, or even support British military action."[52]

Kissinger did not dispute the fact that he opposed Callaghan's

---

[50]Ibid., pp. 352–353.

[51]Ibid., p. 353.

[52]O'Malley and Craig, *The Cyprus Conspiracy*, p. 210.

persistent request for U.S. support for the flexing of Britain's considerable military muscle during the 1974 Cyprus crisis. This opposition
was described in Kissinger's memoirs:

> . . . *We therefore rejected Callaghan's request to support the*
> *threat of a British air strike against Turkish cease-fire violations.*
> I cabled to Hartman: . . . It is out of the question to be asking
> a president [Gerald Ford] in the first 48 hours of his admin-
> istration to consider supporting military action. . . . We will
> do everything we can to assist in keeping the talks going, but
> we will have little room for maneuver if he [Callaghan] *con-*
> *tinues to rattle the saber.*[53] (Emphasis added.)

Taking into account the memoirs of Kissinger and Callaghan, it is
beyond dispute that the United States opposed British military action
during the Turkish invasion of Cyprus. Deprived of American support in this regard, the British foreign secretary was unable to keep the
Geneva conference going. The Turkish foreign minister had assured
Callaghan twice that Turkey had "no intention of her troops advancing nor of them remaining on the island."[54] Callaghan knew better,
however, since British military forces in the theater of operations in
the Kyrenia region and British naval units around Cyprus had confirmed that Turkey was preparing for the second phase of its invasion.

The Geneva conference collapsed less than 48 hours after
Kissinger had reasserted his opposition to any British threat of military action in Cyprus. Late Tuesday evening, August 13, Turkish Foreign Minister Güneş presented his ultimatum. Turkey was making a
final proposal that had to be responded to that evening. Ankara proposed the establishment of six cantons in Cyprus, which would come
under Turkish control. They would cover 34 percent of the island. The
response of Greek Foreign Minister George Mavros and Acting
Cyprus President Glafcos Clerides was that it was impossible to negotiate such a proposal, especially since it was made in the form of an
ultimatum. They both asked for 36 hours to give them time to travel
to Athens and Nicosia, respectively, for consultations and return with
a response. Güneş rejected the request and, at 2:25 a.m. on August 14,

---

[53]Kissinger, *Years of Renewal,* pp. 228.
[54]Callaghan, *Time and Chance,* p. 350.

the Geneva conference collapsed. Immediately thereafter, a dejected Callaghan began a press conference. As he was conducting the press conference, the Turkish General Staff gave the order to launch the second phase of the attack on Cyprus.

While Britain was asking for American support for military action and Kissinger was denying it, British Royal Air Force (RAF) strike aircraft stationed at the British bases in Cyprus were ready for action. They could have reached the theater of operations in the Kyrenia region in three minutes. In addition, Britain had already dispatched a carrier task force to the vicinity of the island. It is quite likely that, given the military inefficiency of the invading Turkish forces, a British threat to use force could have compelled Turkey to honor the cease-fire rather than face a direct British-Turkish military confrontation. If the United States had supported Britain, Turkey would have been even more likely to honor the cease-fire and avoid a confrontation with Britain.

One should also consider that Turkey would have been at a disadvantage in a naval confrontation with Britain. The British Navy remained one of the best in the world. This was demonstrated eight years later, when a British armada crossed the Atlantic and fought and won a war with Argentina over the Falkland Islands, 8,000 miles away.

Cyprus was closer to Britain, by far, than the Falklands, and Britain maintained two major bases on the island. The Turkish invasion of Cyprus was to a great extent a naval operation, and the invading Turkish armada would have had to stand up to the formidable British Royal Navy. There would certainly have been the threat of the Turkish Air Force. Still, there is little doubt that the RAF and its pilots, with the tradition of winning the battle of Britain against the Luftwaffe, would have been superior to the Turks. In addition, Turkey would have had to be concerned with Greece. Ankara would not have been able to dedicate all of its forces to Cyprus and leave Thrace and the Aegean region exposed to a Greek attack. Overall, compared to the Falklands War, the circumstances in and around Cyprus in 1974 would not have been worse for the British armed forces. The unknown factor, however, would have been the role of the U.S. Sixth Fleet sailing in the vicinity of Cyprus. The ghost of Suez was hanging over British decisions during that critical time in Cyprus. Without American support or, at least, American assurance that the Sixth Fleet would not intervene in any form or fashion, Britain would not have acted in Cyprus.

During the last week of July 1974, Turkey had backed down when confronted with a credible threat of British military force. During that week, Turkish troops and tanks amassed near the Nicosia airport, which was defended by 500 British and Canadian troops serving in the U.N. peacekeeping force in Cyprus. Turkish Prime Minister Bülent Ecevit made clear threats that these Turkish forces, supported by strike aircraft, would attack the airport and its defenders. When Britain protested to Turkey, Ecevit proposed to an aghast Harold Wilson, the British prime minister, that Turkish fighter jets would avoid hitting the British forces but would attack the Canadian troops. Wilson told Ecevit that, if the British or Canadian forces serving in the peacekeeping force came under attack, he would order British Phantom fighter jets to take off from the British bases in Cyprus and shoot down any Turkish fighter that participated in the attack. Ninety minutes later, Turkey backed down. Ecevit called Wilson and withdrew his threat.[55] Given this Turkish retreat when faced by British military might, the likelihood that Turkey would have launched the second phase of its invasion on August 14 seems remote if Britain's military threat had been supported by the United States during the second round of the Geneva conference.

In his memoirs, Kissinger failed to mention the Nicosia airport incident.[56] In all likelihood, the former secretary of state avoided the subject because it demonstrated that diplomacy backed by the threat of force, by Britain, proved effective and restrained the Turks at this particular instance during the Cyprus crisis. Ironically, the backing of diplomacy by military force constituted one of Kissinger's cardinal beliefs.

Not surprisingly, the British perspective of the coup against Makarios and the Turkish invasion that followed was different than that of the Americans. Kissinger underscored this in his memoirs. In the instructions he gave to Assistant Secretary of State for International Organizations William Buffum, who was going to Geneva to attend the Greek-Turkish negotiations, Kissinger included the following:

---

[55]O'Malley and Craig, *The Cyprus Conspiracy*, p. 198. See also Callaghan, *Time and Chance*, p. 347. The Nicosia airport incident and the Turkish retreat are also examined at length by Francis Henn, "The Nicosia Airport Incident of 1974—A Peacekeeping Gamble," *International Peacekeeping*, vol. I, no. 1 (Spring 1994): pp. 80–98.

[56]Kissinger, *Years of Renewal*, pp. 193–239.

> Be cooperative with Callaghan but, on those things that affect
> our interests, we must make the decisions ourselves . . .[57]

British Foreign Secretary Callaghan made it clear in his memoirs that
there was a serious disagreement with the United States during the
Cyprus crisis.[58] It was one of the rare occasions that Britain had a serious disagreement with the United States.

At the time, Turkey had good reason to be displeased with the
British and to be pleased with Kissinger. Mehmet Ali Birand, the well-
known Turkish journalist and author, who covered the Geneva negotiations and was privy to the thinking of the Turkish leadership,
described Kissinger's role during July and August 1974:

> In the United States, Kissinger's intention was to wait for the
> Sampson regime to settle down, meanwhile giving it support
> behind the scenes. He had realized that nothing but harm
> would be done to American interests by strong opposition to
> the Turkish intervention, and had consequently refrained
> from sending any letter [to the Turkish government] similar
> to the one written by President Johnson on a previous occa-
> sion. He preferred to see Turkey on the island before resort-
> ing to "power politics." This was a realistic policy from which
> he stood to lose nothing. Washington was happy to see
> Clerides replace Makarios, who was considered dangerous.[59]

It was under these circumstances that Kissinger prevented the
British from threatening to take military action in order to contain the
Turkish invasion forces in Cyprus. When Turkey launched the second
phase of its invasion, the United States watched passively, without any
sincere discontent, as Turkish tanks rolled through the hills into the
central valley of Cyprus. The operation started early in the morning
on Wednesday, August 14. Within 24 hours, about 30,000 Turkish soldiers, supported by about 160 tanks and under the cover of the Turkish Air Force, cut Cyprus in two. The Turkish Army advanced easily
and captured 30 percent of Cypriot territory beyond the eight percent
it had already captured during the first phase of the invasion. The old

---

[57]Ibid., p. 210.
[58]Callaghan, *Time and Chance*, pp. 338–339, 341, 351–353.
[59]Birand, *Thirty Hot Days*, p. 58.

Turkish dream of *taksim,* or partition, was coming true. Thirty-eight percent of Cypriot territory, the part where 73 percent of the island's economic resources were found, came under Turkish control.

The American public hardly noticed the dismembering of the island republic. All attention was still on Washington. President Nixon had just resigned in disgrace because of the Watergate scandal. The new president, Gerald Ford, was in the process of learning the ropes of power. His first objective was to reassure an uneasy nation that it was in steady hands. The fate of Cyprus was hardly on the mind of the average American at the time. Still, Congress had a role to play in the matter. There was no love lost between Kissinger and Congress, and the Cyprus crisis became one more issue in their contentious relations.

Kissinger Under Fire

On August 15, 1974, as the Turkish Army was completing its conquest of more than one-third of Cypriot territory, House Majority Whip John Brademas and several other representatives visited Kissinger at the State Department in order to protest the second phase of the Turkish invasion and the passive response of the United States. Kissinger attempted to explain that he had had to deal with other major crises, the most important of which was the resignation of President Nixon a week earlier. He had also been dealing with the Geneva negotiations, and he did not hesitate to criticize Britain for contributing to the failure of these negotiations.[60]

The members of Congress did not know the real reason behind Kissinger's displeasure with the British. British Foreign Minister Callaghan had tried to salvage the Geneva negotiations. As a last resort, he had proposed to Kissinger that Britain, with American support, make it clear to Turkey that a further military advance in Cyprus would be met with military force, primarily British. During the August 15 meeting in Washington, the secretary of state did not tell this to the members of Congress who were protesting U.S. inaction during the second phase of the Turkish invasion, which had just taken place. Little did they know that the problem was not just U.S. inac-

---

[60]Stern, *The Wrong Horse,* pp. 140–141.

tion, but it was also a deliberate U.S. decision to prevent British action to deter further Turkish advances in Cyprus.

Whether U.S. decision-making at the time was guided or motivated by the desire to see Cyprus partitioned remains an open question. Strong arguments have been made either way. In his memoirs, Kissinger strongly denied such motives.[61] Others disagreed and pointed to an active American role in the coup in Cyprus and to Washington's condoning or facilitating of the Turkish invasion.[62]

One of the strongest critics of Kissinger's role in the Cyprus crisis, and other crises as well, was the late George Ball. He was under secretary of state in the administrations of John F. Kennedy and Lyndon Johnson, and he was a widely respected figure in the foreign policy establishment.[63] He also advised the administration of Jimmy Carter on the Iranian crisis. President Johnson assigned Ball the unenviable task of handling the 1964 Cyprus military crisis, which involved widespread fighting between Greek Cypriots and Turkish Cypriots, as well as a Turkish threat to invade the island republic. Ball traveled to the region and gained first-hand knowledge of the Cyprus issue. In the process, he placed major blame for the 1964 crisis on the Greek side. In fact, Ball developed a strong antipathy, close to hatred, for Makarios.[64] Still, Ball became a vocal critic of Kissinger's handling of the 1974 Cyprus crisis. Ball wrote:

> Trying to run the State Department single-handedly from an airplane, Secretary Kissinger knew nothing about Cyprus and did not bother to inform himself. As a result, he absentmindedly let the Greek junta mount a coup in Cyprus that incited a Turkish invasion.[65]

---

[61] Kissinger, *Years of Renewal*, pp. 194, 199, 204–205.

[62] See Stern, *The Wrong Horse*. Lawrence Stern, who died in 1979, was a renowned journalist for the *Washington Post*. He placed major blame for the 1974 Cyprus crisis on the shoulders of Kissinger. See also Hitchens, *Hostage to History*, pp. 75–100; O' Malley and Craig, *The Cyprus Conspiracy*, esp. pp. 151–237.

[63] For a highly laudatory account of Ball's lifelong role in U.S. foreign policy, see James A. Bill, *George Ball: Behind the Scenes in U.S. Foreign Policy* (New Haven: Yale University Press, 1997). Ball died in 1994.

[64] On Ball's role in handling the Cyprus crisis of 1964 and his strong antipathy toward Makarios, see George Ball, *The Past Has Another Pattern* (New York: W.W. Norton and Co., 1982), pp. 337–359.

[65] Ibid. p. 359.

At critical moments during the last two weeks of July and the first two weeks of August 1974, the United States was in a position to restrain Turkey. The military action proposed by Britain against Turkish cease-fire violations would have changed the course of history in the Eastern Mediterranean. One might argue, as Kissinger did, that the United States could not have prevented the Turkish invasion of July 20, 1974. One could also put the blame on the Greek junta for precipitating the invasion. For the sake of argument, one might ignore the fact that the United States and Kissinger had supported the Greek junta over the years.

Still, the second phase of the invasion on August 14, 1974, was preventable. In Greece, the junta had collapsed and democracy was being restored. As for Cyprus, Turkey had made its point. It had invaded the island, established a bridgehead, and made sure that the interests of the Turkish Cypriots would be safeguarded. Evidently, these were not the Turkish objectives when the invasion was launched. A second phase was necessary in order to occupy the 38 to 40 percent of Cypriot territory that Turkey had targeted from the outset.

The second phase of the Turkish attack came precisely at a time when Washington was going through the most dramatic phase of the Watergate scandal, Nixon's resignation and the transition to the new Ford administration. Kissinger was in the midst of all of this and seemed to acknowledge that the crisis situation in Washington contributed to the Turkish decision to renew the attack. Kissinger wrote:

> Turkey was determined not to become enmeshed in endless negotiations [in Geneva], which would keep it from taking advantage of the unique opportunity afforded by the American presidential transition. At 7:00 a.m. local time on August 14, Turkey cut the Gordian knot by seizing the territory it had been demanding.[66]

There is little doubt that Turkey took advantage of the paralysis in Washington. Yet, specific decisions made by policy-makers in Washington accommodated the second phase of Turkey's invasion. Cyprus found itself partitioned through the force of Turkish arms and through American actions that condoned the first phase of the inva-

---

[66]Kissinger, *Years of Renewal*, p. 231.

sion and facilitated the second phase, which led to the conquest of one-third of Cypriot territory.

Overall, Kissinger's explanations of his handling of the Cyprus crisis suffered from a fundamental contradiction. The essence of his argument to the members of Congress, and as stated in his memoirs, was that he had to operate in a highly abnormal situation in Washington. The absence of presidential leadership had a serious bearing on foreign policy decision-making, Kissinger argued. That was precisely the reason the former secretary of state gave to justify why he did not go to Geneva to take part in the critical negotiations:

> . . . During the crucial four days of the political negotiations [in Geneva] my days and—to an even greater degree—my emotions were focused on the easing of Nixon's travail and preparing for the transition to Ford. . . . The presidential transition constrained our options even further because it *prevented* some such dramatic move as *my joining the negotiations* [in Geneva], which would, at a minimum, *have slowed down the rush toward military action.*[67] (Emphasis added.)

In this way, Kissinger confirmed that the United States was not in a position to apply the full weight of its influence at the Geneva negotiations, in particular, and in the Cyprus crisis, in general, due to the political crisis in Washington.

On the other hand, British foreign policy decision-making was operating smoothly, and Britain was willing and ready to step in and play a leading role in managing the Cyprus crisis, given the vacuum in Washington described by Kissinger. Yet, it was the same Kissinger who prevented the British from filling the vacuum and who presented the United States as a power that had sufficient influence to persuade Britain, a close ally, not to take military action in Cyprus. At the same time, Kissinger made the United States appear impotent and without any influence to persuade another close ally, Turkey, to respect the cease-fire and refrain from further military action in Cyprus after July 23, 1974. The secretary of state relied solely on diplomacy in his attempt to restrain Turkey from launching a second offensive in Cyprus. By ruling out the threat of force, he deprived the United States

---

[67]Ibid., pp. 227, 228.

of the full leverage it possessed as a superpower. Not surprisingly, the Turks ignored Kissinger's admonitions not to resort to further military action in Cyprus for they realized that U.S. diplomacy was handicapped as it was not backed by the formidable military might of the United States.

What transpired during the Cyprus crisis was remarkable when it came to U.S. diplomacy. It was indeed unprecedented for Kissinger to be brushed aside by foreign leaders. The Soviets respected him and listened carefully to his views, the Chinese did the same, and the Arabs and Israelis placed their faith in his skills. Hence, the secretary of state acquired the reputation of being a global "Magus" and was given the nickname "Super K." Therefore, it was quite extraordinary that, during the 1974 Cyprus crisis, the diplomatic overtures of the "Magus," or "Super K," were ignored altogether by the Turkish leadership. The reason was simple. The Turkish government recognized at the beginning of the crisis, starting with Kissinger's condoning of the coup against Makarios, that the United States was unwilling to use its full diplomatic leverage, supported by its enormous military assets in the region, to preserve the independence and territorial integrity of Cyprus.

Turkish author Mehmet Ali Birand put it differently when he wrote that "[Kissinger] preferred to see Turkey on the island in force before resorting to power politics."[68] This view was not very different from the one expressed by Leslie Gelb, known both as a journalist and as a State Department official in the Carter administration. He served as director of politico-military affairs under Secretary of State Cyrus Vance. Writing on the 1974 Cyprus crisis, Gelb concluded:

> Among other estimates of the Cyprus situation that emerge, it appears that once the Turkish troops had landed on the island in force, *the impartial American position* enabled them to overrun Greek Cypriot forces and provided no time for diplomacy to work.[69] (Emphasis added.)

As a consequence, this American "impartiality" favored Turkey, the

---

[68]Birand, *Thirty Hot Days*, p. 58.

[69]See Leslie Gelb, "Inside the Cyprus Crisis: How U.S. Policy Appeared to Change Course," *New York Times*, September 9, 1974.

power that was stronger militarily and had the upper hand against a very weak opponent, the tiny Republic of Cyprus.

In the end, Kissinger, during an acute military crisis in the Eastern Mediterranean, opted for depriving American diplomacy of an indispensable tool, the supportive weight of the U.S. military. It is the ultimate irony that the master of realpolitik, Kissinger, chose to violate the cardinal rule of realpolitik, namely, that diplomacy, in crisis situations especially, should be supported by military might and the threat of force.[70]

In the final analysis, the antagonism between Britain and the United States during the Cyprus crisis only confirmed that Washington could not walk away from the developments that had led to the coup against Makarios, the Turkish invasion that followed, and the forceful division of Cyprus in the summer of 1974. That is precisely the reason why Kissinger felt compelled to devote a rather lengthy chapter in his memoirs to this crisis a quarter of a century later.[71]

The Rule of Law

It was under these dramatic circumstances in Cyprus, Athens, Ankara, Washington, London, and Geneva in the months of July and August 1974 that the Greek American mobilization took place against the Turkish invasion and U.S. policies toward Cyprus. This mobilization came about as congressional opposition to the "imperial presidency" of Richard Nixon was reaching a climax.

In the fall of 1974, Congress invoked the rule of law and, following several votes, it imposed an arms embargo against Turkey on October 3, 1974. In imposing the embargo, Congress cited the violation of the Foreign Assistance Act of 1961, Section 505 (d); the Foreign Military Sales Act, Section 3 (c); and U.S.-Turkish bilateral agreements under these acts. These acts provide that American arms furnished to other countries can be used for defensive purposes only.[72] According to the congressional resolution imposing the

---

[70]On Kissinger's belief in the rule that diplomacy should be supported by military might, see Isaacson, *Kissinger*, pp. 653–656.

[71]Kissinger, *Years of Renewal*, pp. 192–239.

[72]Section 503 (d) of the Foreign Assistance Act of 1961, as amended, provided: "Any country which hereafter uses defense articles furnished such a country under

embargo, Turkey violated these laws by using U.S.-supplied military equipment for aggressive purposes, the invasion and occupation of northern Cyprus.

The arms used by the Turkish armed forces during the invasion of Cyprus and during the consolidation of the military occupation were indeed American. The invading fleet consisted of U.S.-made vessels. The air strikes against the Greek Cypriots were carried out by F-4 Phantoms. The tanks used to advance into Greek villages, towns, and cities were M-48s. The armored personnel carriers were M-133s. The 105 mm. towed howitzers and the 106 mm. recoilless anti-tank rifles were also manufactured in the United States, as were the general purpose military vehicles, mines, and communication gear.

The law that imposed the arms embargo against Turkey became operational on February 5, 1975. The embargo was imposed over the strong objections of President Gerald Ford, Secretary of State Henry Kissinger, the Pentagon, and the national security bureaucracy in general.

When Jimmy Carter assumed the presidency, he found the embargo in place. In dealing with the explosive situation in the Eastern Mediterranean, Carter had to balance realism and morality. In foreign affairs, his moral message was to be carried out through the support of human rights. The embargo became a test case for the Carter presidency on how realism and morality could be balanced. As it turned out, the Carter administration and President Carter, personally, became advocates of realpolitik and fought Congress tenaciously over the embargo.[73]

---

this Act, the Mutual Security Act of 1954, as amended, or any predecessor foreign assistance Act, in substantial violation of the provisions of this chapter (22 U.S.G. 2311 et seq.) or any agreements entered into pursuant to any such Acts shall be immediately ineligible for further assistance."

[73]There were other areas where Carter's human rights philosophy prevailed over realpolitik. Such was the case, for instance, with regard to Chile, where the Carter administration pursued an aggressive human rights policy and kept a certain distance from the regime of General Augusto Pinochet. See Vernon Vavrina, "The Carter Human Rights Policy: Political Idealism and Realpolitik," in *Jimmy Carter*, ed. Rosenbaum and Ugrinsky, pp. 104–105.

CHAPTER 3

Carter: Trust, Morality, Human Rights, and Promises to Greek Americans

Toward a New Foreign Policy

With the election of Jimmy Carter to the presidency in November 1976, a significant part of the American public expected a new dawn in U.S. foreign policy. Throughout the presidential campaign, Carter proclaimed that the general principles that were to guide his foreign policy would reflect the moral values of the American people. In a Carter White House, ethical considerations and human rights were to play a pivotal role in foreign policy, in contrast to the realpolitik that had been the hallmark of the Nixon administration and, especially, Henry Kissinger. The sale of American arms to undemocratic regimes around the world was linked to the human rights question. Carter vowed to re-examine U.S. policies regarding arms sales in order to take into account the degree of respect for human rights in the recipient countries.

Human rights were to become one of the most enduring legacies of the Carter presidency. As one of Carter's biographers put it:

> . . . With his Baptist background emphasizing individuality and his years of involvement with the civil rights struggle in Georgia, a globalization of his personal concern was natural. For Carter, being a devout Christian, a Baptist, and an American was inseparable from being committed to human rights.[1]

In the aftermath of the Vietnam War, which divided America, and

---

[1]Peter G. Burne, *Jimmy Carter: A Comprehensive Biography from Plains to Post-presidency* (New York: Scribner, 1997), p. 383.

the Watergate scandal, which shook the institution of the presidency to its foundations, Carter represented a welcome change. He appeared genuine, simple, and, above all, honest. He meant to offer what the United States needed the most, at the time: a president with a moral compass and integrity, who could be trusted and could restore confidence in government.

Under these circumstances, when Carter promised during the election campaign to elevate human rights to the top of his foreign policy agenda, it resonated well among the American public. When Carter gave his inaugural address on January 20, 1977, he declared solemnly: "Our commitment to human rights must be absolute. . . . Our moral sense dictates a clear preference for those societies which share with us an abiding respect for individual human rights."[2] Indeed, above all, the Carter era was characterized by a president who was engaged in a moral crusade to correct, to the extent possible, both the domestic and foreign ills.

The emphasis on human rights by Carter was a reflection of his worldview and the vision the new president had for a new foreign policy, one that was to be called post-cold war foreign policy. As such, this policy was to replace the policy of anti-Sovietism, containment, and realpolitik with a policy of preventive diplomacy, international interdependence, and human rights.[3] This new approach to foreign policy did not last long, however, for a variety of reasons. They had to do with developments in the international environment, primarily the Iranian revolution and the Soviet invasion of Afghanistan. In addition, Carter's new approach met with resistance within the national security bureaucracy. A contributing factor was that Carter's national security adviser, Zbigniew Brzezinski, was ambivalent concerning whether Carter's post-cold war policies could work. By 1978, Brzezinski argued that a policy of containment was necessary to counter Soviet expansionism.

This advice was reflected in a series of memoranda Brzezinski addressed to the president. In a memorandum to the president dated April 7, 1978, Brzezinski wrote:

---

[2]"Inaugural Address of President Jimmy Carter," January 20, 1977, *Public Papers of the Presidents of the United States: Jimmy Carter, 1977* (Washington: U.S. Government Printing Office, Book I, January 20 to June 24, 1977), pp. 2–3.

[3]See Jerel Rosati, "The Rise and Fall of America's First Post-Cold War Foreign Policy," in Rosenbaum and Ugrinsky, ed., *Jimmy Carter*, pp. 37–38.

I think it is not unfair to summarize the Soviet strategy as involving the following elements:

. . . To prevent a rapid resolution of the Middle Eastern problem and to increase U.S. difficulties, in the hope of radicalizing the Arabs and of gaining greater leverage.

To exploit any opportunities in Africa, or elsewhere, to advance Soviet interests, either directly or indirectly.

To intimidate the U.S. and its allies by massive propaganda campaigns . . . ,

Our response. . . . We should, in view of the above, tell the Soviets very frankly that their behavior in Africa is *intolerable*. If Soviet/Cuban forces are intruded into the Southern African conflict, *this will jeopardize détente as a whole and we will react strongly. This should be stated directly, unambiguously, and forcefully.*[4] (Emphasis added.)

Two months after this memorandum was written, Brzezinski wrote another memorandum to the president expressing similar views with regard to Soviet policies. In a May 5, 1978 memorandum, Brzezinski wrote:

I think it is fair to say that the Soviets are now engaged in a process which could *undermine our influence in the Middle East,* isolate and surround such friends as Iran and Saudi Arabia, and out-flank both the Middle East and perhaps our West European friends through both the radicalization of Africa and through more direct intrusion of Soviet/Cuban military presence. If successful, this could produce far-reaching consequences for the political orientation of Western Europe ("Finlandization") and or our friends in the Middle East.[5] (Emphasis added.)

It was clear that, in these memoranda to the president, Brzezinski was calling attention to the fact that the Soviets were actively pursuing a policy of undermining American interests and influence around

---

[4]The White House, Memorandum to the President, from Zbigniew Brzezinski—Subject: NSC Weekly Report # 53, April 7, 1978.

[5]The White House, Memorandum to the President, from Zbigniew Brzezinski—Subject: *NSC Weekly Report # 57,* May 5, 1978.

the globe and were penetrating the Middle East and Africa. Brzezinski advised the president that the United States should stand up and contain Moscow.

While Carter was under pressure from within his administration to stand up to the Soviets, a strong conservative movement that called for a tougher policy toward the Soviet Union was on the rise. These factors, combined with Carter's image as a weak leader, contributed to the president's inability to sustain his post-cold war foreign policy. By 1978, after barely a year in office, Carter's new foreign policy approach was more or less abandoned.[6]

Carter's post-cold war foreign policy was tested soon after he entered the White House. The new president was confronted on several fronts with the challenge of whether to follow realism in foreign policy or promote ethical principles and human rights.[7] The deteriorating situation in Iran presented Carter with the dilemma of whether to press the Shah for drastic political reform, which included respect for human rights, or whether to continue Washington's previous policies based on realism and the containment doctrine. While Carter received contradictory advice, in the end, he failed to pressure the Shah to institute quick, radical reforms. After vacillating for a while, Carter reluctantly followed Brzezinski's advice to stand by the Shah. At the same time, however, the president did not adopt Brzezinski's view that the Shah should use his army to put down the revolution by force.[8] Certainly, one can argue that, by the time Carter came to power in January 1977, it was too late to "save" the Shah because the country was already in a deep crisis leading to revolutionary conditions.[9]

---

[6]These points were made by Rosati, "The Rise and Fall of America's First Post-Cold War Foreign Policy," pp. 44–47.

[7]On this subject, see Vernon Vavrina, "The Carter Human Rights Policy: Political Idealism and Realpolitik," in Rosenbaum and Ugrinsky, ed., *Jimmy Carter,* pp. 103–117.

[8]On Brzezinski's role in influencing President Carter's decisions on Iran, and on the dispute between Brzezinski and Vance, see the critical views in James Bill, *The Eagle and the Lion: The Tragedy of American-Iranian Relations* (New Haven and London: Yale University Press, 1988), pp. 243–260, 331–333, 409–410. See also the comments of William B. Quandt, discussant in Kenneth Thompson's "Negotiations at Home and Abroad: Carter's Alternatives to Conflict and War," in Rosenbaum and Ugrinsky, eds., *Jimmy Carter,* pp. 73–74.

[9]On the crisis already faced by Iran at the beginning of 1977, see Christos P. Ioannides, *America's Iran: Injury and Catharsis* (University Press of America: Lanham,

On January 16, 1979, the Shah fled Iran. On February 1, 1979, Ayatollah Khomeini returned triumphantly to his homeland after 16 years in exile. American interests in Iran had received a fatal blow. Less than a year later, the U.S. Embassy in Tehran was taken over by Iranian militants, who took 52 American diplomats hostage. The diplomats were held hostage for 14 months, and what became known as the "hostage crisis" contributed heavily to Carter's defeat by Ronald Reagan in the November 1980 presidential election.[10] Carter paid a heavy price for America's failure in Iran.

The other area where human rights collided with realpolitik was the Eastern Mediterranean. The previous administrations of Nixon and Ford had followed a policy of realpolitik toward Greece, Cyprus, and Turkey. Realpolitik provided the rationale behind the decision by Nixon and Kissinger to sidestep democracy and human rights and, instead, support the Greek military junta. Realpolitik also led Kissinger to make a series of fateful decisions in July and August 1974, decisions that contributed to the coup against Makarios and the Turkish invasion of Cyprus. Under Carter, Kissinger's policies were to come to an end. Candidate Jimmy Carter promised the Greek American community that he was determined to put an end to American realpolitik in the Eastern Mediterranean.

The Promises Made by Carter and Mondale: Keep the Embargo

For Carter, the U.S. failure in Cyprus was yet another example of what happens when foreign policy is guided by realpolitik, which violates the rule of law and is devoid of ethical considerations. Throughout the presidential campaign, Jimmy Carter and his vice-presidential running mate, Senator Walter Mondale of Minnesota, made several promises to Greek Americans concerning Cyprus, which the Greek Americans took seriously.

On September 16, 1976, candidate Jimmy Carter met in Wash-

New York, London, 1984), pp. 35–36. See also Amin Saikal, *The Rise and Fall of the Shah* (Princeton: Princeton University Press, 1980), pp. 187–192; Bill, ibid., pp. 216–243.

[10]The dynamics leading to the hostage crisis were examined by the author in a book based on first-hand experience and field research in Tehran during the crisis, February-March 1980. See Ioannides, *America's Iran*, esp. pp. 69–135.

ington with the leadership of the American Hellenic Educational Progressive Association (AHEPA), including its president Xenofon Microutsicos. AHEPA was the largest Greek American organization, and it had played an important role in mobilizing Greek Americans in the summer and fall of 1974, which, in turn, contributed to the imposition of the congressional arms embargo against Turkey. The ground for this meeting had been prepared by a warm message that candidate Carter had sent to AHEPA on the occasion of its fifty-fourth national convention at the end of August 1977.[11]

After the meeting with the AHEPA leadership, Carter addressed a group of prominent Greek Americans, including the AHEPA leadership, and presented a policy statement on the issues of special concern to Greek Americans, with Cyprus being the paramount subject. Subsequently, on September 17, 1976, the Carter-Mondale campaign issued a policy statement, which included the following points made by candidate Carter:

> The policy of the Ford Administration of tilting away from Greece and Cyprus has proved a disaster for NATO and for American security interests in the Eastern Mediterranean.
>
> Despite repeated warnings, the *Administration failed to prevent the 1974 coup against President Makarios* engineered by the former military dictatorship in Athens. The *Administration failed to prevent or even limit the Turkish invasion* that followed. The *Administration failed to uphold even the principle or the rule of law* in the conduct of our foreign policy. American law requires that arms supplied by the United States be used solely for defensive purposes.
>
> Today, more than two years later, no progress toward a negotiated solution on Cyprus has been made.
>
> The lack of progress is disappointing and dangerous. Peace must be based upon the United Nations General Assembly Resolution 3212 of 1 November 1974 endorsed by Cyprus, Greece, and Turkey, calling among other things for *the removal of all foreign military forces* from Cyprus. The widely reported *increase of colonization of Cyprus* by Turkish

---

[11]Carter's message to AHEPA resembled his policy statement of September 16, 1977. See *National Herald* (Ethnikos Kyrex), August 29, 1976.

military and civilians should cease. *Greek-Cypriot refugees should be allowed to return to their homes.* Both Greek and Turkish Cypriots should be assured of their rights, both during and after *the withdrawal of all foreign troops from Cyprus.*

The United States must pursue a foreign policy based on principle and in accordance with the *rule of law.*[12] (Emphasis added.)

As if to emphasize the seriousness of his pledges to the Greek Americans, candidate Carter repeated these points in October 1976, just prior to the election. In a telegram to Archbishop Iakovos, the head of the Greek Orthodox Church of North and South America, honoring his name day and sixty-fifth birthday, Carter repeated his criticism of the Ford administration and stated:

These have been trying years for the Greek Americans. . . . They have seen the U.S. government tilting away from Greek democracy and away from a principled policy concerning the tragic events in Cyprus. They have seen *our government ignore the rule of law* and pursue a course on Cyprus that has failed. It has failed to bring about the end of the division of the island, it *has failed to remove foreign troops from the island* and to make possible *the return of the refugees to their homes . . .*[13] (Emphasis added.)

In a message to AHEPA at its fifty-fourth convention in August 1977, Mondale stated:

I want you to know that I share your profound concern over the tension and tragedy that exists today in the Eastern Mediterranean. . . . *I am proud of my record in the Senate on*

---

[12]See, Jimmy Carter-Walter Mondale, Press Release, *Presidential Candidate Jimmy Carter Meets with Order of AHEPA Leaders. Releases Policy Statement on Issues Affecting the United States, Greece, and Cyprus,* Washington, D.C., September 17, 1977. The complete text of Carter's electoral statement appears in the Appendix, Document A. Carter's electoral promises were also presented in the AHEPA News Release, Washington, September 17, 1976. See also the Greek American newspaper *National Herald* (Ethnikos Kyrex), New York, September 29, 1978.

[13]*Hellenic Times,* New York, October 21, 1976.

Cyprus. I opposed the Turkish invasion; *I supported efforts to cut off U.S. Military Aid to Turkey* until progress had been made toward ending through negotiation the bitter division of that island in the *illegal presence of Turkish troops.* With you, I am still waiting for the first sign of movement toward a lasting and just peace.[14] (Emphasis added.)

The pledges made by Carter and Mondale to Greek Americans received wide publicity in the Greek American press and the press in Greece and Cyprus. A wave of optimism, indeed enthusiasm, swept over Greeks in the United States and around the world. At last, they thought, an American president would demand an end to the Turkish occupation of the northern part of Cyprus and would uphold the rule of law according to which the arms embargo had been imposed against Turkey. It was not just Greek Americans who saw in the promises of Carter and Mondale a clear commitment to uphold the embargo until Turkey committed itself to withdrawing its occupation army from Cyprus. When Carter proposed the lifting of the embargo, the *New York Times* reminded him of this in an editorial:

> ... When Jimmy Carter was a candidate for President, he held that the restriction of arms sales should stand until Ankara withdrew the force that enables Turkish Cypriots, with 20 percent of the island's population, to occupy roughly 40 percent of its territory."[15]

There was yet another important reason for Greek Americans to place their trust in Jimmy Carter. Cyrus Vance was a key foreign policy adviser to Carter during his campaign. Vance was a strong supporter of the embargo and had unique experience in Cypriot and Greek-Turkish affairs. President Lyndon Johnson had appointed Vance as his special envoy on Cyprus, whose task it was to defuse yet another military crisis on the island. Violent clashes erupted between Greek Cypriots and Turkish Cypriots in mid-November 1967 in the Kofinou area and threatened to trigger the outbreak of a general Greek-Turkish war. Vance was able to accomplish his task through visits to Cyprus, Greece, and Turkey.

---

[14]*National Herald* (Ethnikos Kyrex), August 29, 1976.
[15]*New York Times*, July 22, 1978.

Given the fact that Vance belonged to the elite of the eastern Democratic foreign policy establishment and had experience in foreign affairs, Carter was widely expected to appoint him to a major foreign policy post, most likely that of secretary of state. With such credentials, Vance's support for maintaining the embargo could not be taken lightly. This was especially the case because other prestigious members of the Democratic foreign policy establishment shared Vance's views.

This became quite clear when Vance testified before the House International Relations Committee on July 10, 1975. He made a joint appearance with former under secretary of state George Ball, another influential member of the eastern Democratic establishment. The matter at hand before the committee was the proposed legislation to restore certain military assistance to Turkey. Vance and Ball made a joint statement in which they opposed the lifting of the embargo.

In his testimony, Vance asserted that Turkey had violated American law when it used American arms to invade Cyprus. He also said that the embargo was justifiably imposed in order to uphold the rule of law. If the embargo were to be lifted, Vance asserted, it would send Turkey the message that its previous actions, i.e., the invasion, were justified. It would also remove any pressure on Turkey for substantial concessions in the effort to settle the Cyprus dispute. Both Vance and Ball argued that the lifting of the embargo would send the wrong message internationally because:

> . . . It would create a widespread impression that no nation that has acquired arms from the United States need any longer pay attention to the conditions on which those arms were made available, but would be free to use them in pursuit of its own interests in local conflicts.[16]

In this way, through their testimony, two distinguished Democrats, the most respected, perhaps, in the field of foreign policy, echoed the basic argument of those in Congress who supported the embargo. Lifting it would remove any incentive for Turkey to show goodwill in Cyprus.

---

[16]See "Statement by George W. Ball and Cyrus R. Vance," July 10, 1975, House of Representatives, Extension of Remarks, *Congressional Record*, 94th Congress, 1st Session, vol. 121, part 17, July 8, 1975-July 14, 1975, pp. 22258–22259.

Given these factors, Carter's promises to the Greek American community did not appear to be made in a vacuum. In fact, they reflected to a considerable degree the view of some of the most influential members of the Democratic foreign policy elite. As such, Carter's electoral promises acquired additional credibility among Greek Americans.

As if to underscore the appreciation of the Greek American community for the Carter-Mondale ticket, prominent leaders of the community met at the Waldorf-Astoria Hotel in New York City on October 18, 1976, and announced the formation of the National American Hellenic Committee to Elect Carter/Mondale. Well-known Greek American Democrats and Republicans joined the committee. Massachusetts Governor Michael Dukakis, a Democrat, and the former mayor of San Francisco, George Christopher, a Republican, became the honorary chairmen of the committee. Charles Maliotis, a Democrat from Boston, and Andrew Athens, a Republican from Chicago, were named chairmen. The committee sent telegrams of support to Carter and Mondale and initiated a campaign in the Greek American press urging Greek Americans to vote for the Carter-Mondale ticket.[17]

In addition to the enthusiasm of Greek Americans, there was satisfaction in Congress regarding Carter's pledge to uphold the embargo. All of the members of Congress who had fought hard and prevailed over the campaign orchestrated by the Ford administration to repeal the embargo were pleased to hear Carter's pledges on Cyprus. If Carter became president, they thought, they would not have to wage any more bitter fights against the administration in order to uphold the embargo. Congressional supporters of the embargo were soon to be bitterly disappointed.

Carter Wins, Greeks Celebrate

The election of Jimmy Carter to the presidency on November 2, 1976, was greeted with great enthusiasm in the Greek American community. Carter's victory was seen, justifiably at the time, as a defeat for Kissinger's cynicism and realpolitik. Considering that morality had

---

[17] *Hellenic Times*, October 21, 1976.

been a central theme of Carter's campaign and that he, himself, appeared to be a paragon of morality, Greek Americans saw in Carter and his foreign policy the exact opposite of Kissinger's philosophy and policies. In addition, Carter had made specific promises regarding Cyprus, and he had pledged, personally, to abandon the "disastrous Ford-Kissinger policies in the Eastern Mediterranean." Candidate Jimmy Carter was quoted as having characterized Kissinger as a "cowboy."[18] Greek Americans, like most Americans, had no reason to doubt Carter's sincerity because he was seen as a different kind of politician, one who was honest and kept his promises. With Carter in power, Greek Americans expected the Kissinger era in foreign affairs to be over.

Even greater was the enthusiasm in Cyprus as Greek Cypriots looked at Carter as their savior, sort of a messiah. The day after Carter's victory resembled a national holiday all over free Cyprus. Church bells rang, schools were closed, and public servants took the day off. The president of the Republic of Cyprus, Archbishop Makarios, called heads of government agencies asking them to close their offices for a day of celebration. The director of the public information service and government spokesman, Miltiades Christodoulou, received a call from Makarios who asked him, "Are you still working?" Christodoulou responded, "Why the question? Is it a holiday?" Makarios then exclaimed, "Carter won!"[19] In Greece, there was elation as well. Not only had Carter promised to address Greek grievances regarding Cyprus but, in his electoral promises, he had also been critical of the support given to the Greek military junta by Nixon's Republican administration, including Secretary of State Kissinger.

The opposite mood prevailed in Turkey. The government of Prime Minister Süleyman Demirel had hoped that Gerald Ford would be elected and that Kissinger would remain the secretary of state in a Ford administration. When Carter won, there was great disappointment and anxiety in Turkey. Carter's promise to elevate human rights as the guiding principle of his foreign policy made the Turkish government nervous because the Turkish record on human rights had

---

[18]See Burne, *Jimmy Carter: A Comprehensive Biography*, p. 383.

[19]Miltiades Christodoulou, *He Poreia ton Ellino-Tourkikon Scheseon ke e Kypros* (The Course of Greek-Turkish Relations and Cyprus), vol. II (Nicosia: Proodos Publishers, 1995), p. 495.

been poor. More importantly, the Demirel government believed that Carter's promise to the Greek Americans to maintain the embargo until Turkey agreed to withdraw its occupation army from Cyprus was a bad omen for things to come. Under a Carter administration, the Turks feared that they were going to be pressured to make concessions on Cyprus that would be unacceptable to them. Thus, when Carter was elected, "it came as a cold shower to Ankara" with Prime Minister Demirel and Foreign Minister İhsan Sabri Çağlayangil appearing quite upset.[20]

---

[20]See Mehmet Ali Birand, *Pazaremata* (Bargaining), a Greek translation of Birand's book *Diyet* (Athens: Floros Publishers, 1985), p. 272.

CHAPTER 4

The Carter Team: How to Deal with Greek Americans and the Eastern Mediterranean

The National Security Adviser: Zbigniew Brzezinski

As soon as Carter assumed power in January 1977, he had to deal with the demands of the national security bureaucracy to lift the arms embargo against Turkey. General Alexander Haig, the Supreme Allied Commander Europe who later became secretary of state under Ronald Reagan, was the Pentagon's primary advocate of lifting the embargo. Ideologically speaking, Haig was much more to the right than President Carter and his secretary of defense, Harold Brown. Haig had fought along with Kissinger against the imposition of the embargo. Since Haig was the commander of NATO, his word carried weight under Carter. Turkish journalist Mehmet Ali Birand, who has been close to the Turkish foreign policy elite, claimed that Haig appeared to be one of the staunchest supporters of lifting the embargo in his meetings with Turkish leaders.[1]

The embargo, the Pentagon's argument went, was causing serious damage to American national security interests in the Eastern Mediterranean. The embargo had had a devastating effect on Turkey militarily, and it was alienating Ankara and pushing this strategically positioned ally of the United States closer to the Soviet Union. At the same time, it was argued, the embargo was not achieving its stated objective, which was to pressure Turkey to enter into a negotiated Cyprus settlement, one that would lead to the withdrawal of the Turkish occupation army and the return of refugees to their homes. These arguments were echoed at the National Security Council and the State Department.

---

[1] Birand, *Pazaremata* (Bargaining), pp. 401–402, 421.

Upon assuming power, President Carter appointed Zbigniew Brzezinski as his national security adviser. Brzezinski was to emerge as the most controversial personality on the Carter team. Carter, himself, acknowledged this.[2]

In his capacity as head of the National Security Council (NSC), Brzezinski's role was to provide the president with foreign policy options and the rationale and justification for specific policies, in this case toward the Eastern Mediterranean. Every morning, Brzezinski met the president to discuss foreign policy. Carter described a typical day at the White House:

> My first scheduled meeting at the Oval Office each day was with National Security Adviser Zbigniew Brzezinski, when he brought me the Presidential Daily Briefing (known as PDB) from the intelligence community. I would see him several times during the day at different hours, and in times of crisis he was either at my side or coordinating meetings with my Cabinet and other leaders in the Situation room . . .[3]

There is little doubt that Brzezinski had a decisive influence on Carter's foreign policy even though his influence was balanced by that of Secretary of State Cyrus Vance.[4] Brzezinski played a crucial role in the debate over the embargo because of his institutional role of adviser to the president on national security and because of his worldview. In his memoirs, Brzezinski did not discuss the internal White House debate on lifting the embargo, the role of the NSC in the matter, or Carter's decision to lift the embargo. This decision was based to a substantial degree on Brzezinski's advice.

Massachusetts Democratic Congressman Paul Tsongas, who was generally supportive of Carter and who was running for a seat in the U.S. Senate at the time, considered Brzezinski to be the architect of Carter's policy concerning the lifting of the embargo.[5] Given Brzezinski's Soviet-centric worldview[6] and the fact that the Soviet threat was

---

[2]Carter, *Keeping Faith*, p.51.
[3]Ibid.
[4]Carter, *Keeping Faith*, pp. 51–55.
[5]See the interview with Tsongas in *Proini*, June 19, 1978.
[6]The term Soviet-centric to describe Brzezinski's view of the world was used by Bill, *The Eagle and the Lion*, p. 257.

the main argument in support of lifting the embargo, Tsongas's view that Brzezinski played a key role in the embargo issue made sense.

Brzezinski, who was born in Poland, had a deep sense of the history of his native land and the relationship between Poland and Russia. After graduating from Harvard, he became an eminent scholar on the Soviet Union and Eastern Europe at Columbia University. The Polish people admired Brzezinski for his great accomplishments in the United States.

Under both imperial and communist Russia, Poland felt the oppressive weight of its mighty neighbor to the east. To the west, Poland shared a border with Germany, and the Polish people had also experienced the might of Germany. During the Second World War, Poland was invaded by the Nazis. Brzezinski and his family fled Poland at the outset of the war. Following the country's liberation by the Red Army, it fell under communist rule and Soviet domination.

Brzezinski was quite familiar with the travails of his native Poland under imperial and communist Russia. Brzezinski's knowledge, however, went far beyond the conventional familiarity of the average Polish citizen with Russian affairs. He became a renowned Sovietologist.[7] Moreover, he had a profound understanding of Poland's relations with Germany, especially during the Second World War. At the same time, like Kissinger, who was also European-born—he was born in Bavaria, Germany—Brzezinski had a deep understanding of European history and the encounter between Europe and the Ottoman Empire. The Russian-Turkish rivalry had played an especially important role in the history of eastern and southern Europe over the centuries, and Brzezinski had exhibited great familiarity with this historic rivalry.[8] Brzezinski emerged as an admirer of Kemal Atatürk and considered Turkey to be a pivotal state in the region and a key American ally.[9] A logical conclusion of this was that a weakened Turkey, as a

---

[7]On Poland under communist rule and Soviet domination, see Zbigniew Brzezinski, *The Soviet Bloc: Unity and Conflict* (Cambridge: Harvard University Press, 1967), esp. pp. 230–268, 338–366.

[8]See Zbigniew Brzezinski, *The Grand Chessboard: American Primacy and Its Geostrategic Imperatives* (New York: Basic Books, 1997), pp. 235–237.

[9]On Brzezinski's admiration for Atatürk, see the forward he wrote for the book by Paul Henze, *Turkey and Ataturk's Legacy: Turkey's Political Evolution, Turkish-U.S. Relations, and Prospects for the 21st Century* (Haarlem, Netherlands: Research Center for Turkestan and Azerbaijan, Turquoise Series, no. 2, 1998), p. 5. On Turkey's pivotal role in the region, see Brzezinski, *The Grand Chessboard*, pp. 53, 133–138, 204.

result of the embargo in this case, could only benefit Russia. A strong Turkey, on the other hand, could continue to be a "thorn" in Russia's underbelly. The lifting of the embargo would strengthen Turkey and allow it to continue playing the role of the "thorn."

NSC Officer Paul Henze:
An Insider's Account of the Embargo Issue

At the National Security Council, one of Brzezinski's assistants was Paul Henze, an expert on Turkey. Serving as the NSC staff officer responsible for Greece, Turkey, and Cyprus, he played an important role in charting the Carter administration's Turkish policy, especially in the turbulent years preceding the Turkish military coup of September 12, 1980.[10] He was also a key player in President Carter's successful drive to repeal the arms embargo.

Henze had served in the American Embassy in Ankara twice, once as the CIA station chief.[11] In Henze's words, he had "traveled and lived in the country for more than 40 years."[12] He was fluent in Turkish, had worked closely with the Institute for Turkish Studies in Washington, had been a trustee of the American Turkish Foundation, and had generally been considered a longstanding friend of Turkey. Henze's admiration for Kemal Atatürk, for the system he introduced in Turkey, and for the modern Turkish state, in general, is well established. This admiration is reflected in his 1998 book entitled *Turkey and Ataturk's Legacy: Turkey's Political Evolution, Turkish-U.S. Relations, and Prospects for the 21st Century.*

Henze was not simply a dispassionate expert on Turkey. He had the greatest admiration for the Turkish world and for Turkey, itself. Brzezinski gave Henze the responsibility of providing his expert advice on Turkey's historical rival, Greece. Equally important was the fact that Henze was Brzezinski's adviser on Cyprus. When Carter came to power, Greek-Turkish relations revolved around Cyprus, and

---

[10]On Henze's important policy-making role regarding Turkey, see Birand, *The Generals' Coup in Turkey,* pp. 124, 172, 185–186.

[11]On Henze's serving as CIA station chief in Turkey, see Philip Taubman and Leslie Gelb, "U.S. Aides Cautious in Pope Shooting," *New York Times,* January 27, 1983, p. A12.

[12]Henze, *Turkey and Ataturk's Legacy,* p. 9.

it was over the Turkish invasion of Cyprus and the Turkish occupation of part of the island republic that Congress chose to challenge the executive branch and impose an embargo on arms sales to Turkey.

Henze's account of the embargo, his attitude toward Greek Americans, and his views on Cyprus acquire special significance since he was both the NSC staff officer in charge of Greece, Turkey, and Cyprus, and the key adviser to Brzezinski for these countries. In turn, in his capacity as national security adviser, Brzezinski advised President Carter on matters concerning these countries. Henze took part in meetings between Carter and the prime ministers of Greece and Turkey, Constantine Karamanlis and Süleyman Demirel, respectively.

Henze was one of the key White House officials who planned and carried out the decision to lift the embargo. He described his role as follows:

> The process [of lifting the embargo] took eight months and a great investment of effort by the State Department, the Pentagon and the White House, including *the continuous personal involvement of the President himself*... (Footnote 107): The day-to-day effort was overseen by a group consisting of State Department Counselor Matthew Nimetz, Deputy Assistant Secretary of Defense James Siena, Madeleine Albright, then Brzezinski's Assistant for Congressional Relations, and myself as NSC Staff Officer responsible for Greece, Turkey and Cyprus... (Footnote 121): I was the NSC staff officer in charge of Turkish affairs during the entire Carter Administration and involved in all decisions and actions relating to Turkey, Greece and Cyprus.[13] (Emphasis added.)

Given that Brzezinski wrote the forward to Henze's book and praised his NSC assistant in his own memoirs, there is no reason to doubt that Henze was, indeed, a key White House player in the embargo affair.[14] Henze reciprocated by praising Brzezinski in his book:

> I am especially grateful to *my good friend*, Zbigniew Brzezinski, for giving me the opportunity to bring my experience and

---

[13]Ibid., pp. 88, 104.
[14]On Brzezinski's praise for Henze, see Brzezinski, *Power and Principle*, p. 300.

knowledge of Turkey to bear on the U.S. national security process during the critical years that reached a climax in the fall of 1980.[15] (Emphasis added.)

There is little doubt that Carter's national security adviser took Henze's advice on Turkey, Greece, and Cyprus very seriously.

Another factor that renders Henze's views significant is historical. Among the several officials in the Carter administration who played a direct and important role in the effort to lift the embargo, Henze emerges as a rare voice that gives an account of the whole affair. The other major players in the drive to lift the embargo, from Brzezinski to Cyrus Vance to Clark Clifford, the president's special envoy to Greece, Turkey, and Cyprus, to President Carter, have failed to discuss the embargo issue in their memoirs.

In view of the silence of the main actors behind the drive to lift the embargo, Henze's account of the matter acquires special significance. Partially, at least, his account reflects the National Security Council mindset on the embargo issue and how the NSC perceived Greek American lobbying.

"It's All the Greeks' Fault"

In his book, Henze disputed the fact that Carter made specific promises to the Greek American community during his election campaign. He wrote:

> Candidate Jimmy Carter, needing the support of as many minority groups as possible to win the election, had Greek business friends and tilted toward Greek interests during his campaign. *Nothing specific was promised*, but the impression was created that new pressures would be brought to bear on Turkey as soon as the Democrats took office.[16] (Emphasis added.)

The assertion that candidate Carter promised nothing specific to Greek Americans is contradicted by the facts. It is a matter of record

---

[15]Henze, *Turkey and Ataturk's Legacy*, p.10.
[16]Ibid., p. 87.

that Georgia Governor Jimmy Carter made specific promises to AHEPA on September 16, 1976. Contrary to Henze's assertion, Carter's promises to the Greek American community were quite specific as well as emphatic.[17]

Regarding the Cyprus issue, Henze espoused the Turkish position. He wrote in 1987:

> Thus, a pattern has emerged that has persisted for thirty years [since the mid 1950s]: it has invariably been the Greeks on the island or politicians in Greece who have changed *whatever status quo* has existed in Cyprus, while Turkey has always been reactive.[18] (Emphasis added.)

Considering that Henze blamed the Greek side for provoking the Cyprus dispute while asserting that the Turkish side was just reacting, it is not surprising that he stated in his 1998 book that "Greek Cypriots were more prone [to violence] than Turkish Cypriots." Henze, however, provided no evidence to justify such an unqualified and condemnatory claim pertaining to an entire ethnic group.[19]

In addition, the right of the Greek Cypriot majority, representing 80 percent of the population of Cyprus, to oppose British colonialism and seek self-determination in the mid-1950s was disputed by Henze since this constituted a "change in the status quo." That was precisely the Turkish position at the time.[20] This line of reasoning places all the blame for Cyprus's misfortunes squarely on the Greek side, including the 1974 Turkish invasion and the consequences of the invasion. Certainly, the Greek side did share responsibility for the misfortunes through its series of misguided policies and blunders concerning Cyprus. Turkey, however, as well as Britain and the United States have also been heavily involved in the affairs of Cyprus and share responsibility.

---

[17]See Carter's promises as they appear in the Appendix, Document A.

[18]See Paul Henze, "Out of Kilter—Greeks, Turks, and U.S. Policy," *The National Interest*, no. 8 (Summer 1987): p.76.

[19]Henze, *Turkey and Ataturk's Legacy*, p. 65.

[20]On the Turkish government's position on Cyprus in the mid-1950s, see Turkey, Ministry of Foreign Affairs, *Turkey and Cyprus: A Survey of the Cyprus Question with Official Statements of the Turkish Viewpoint* (London: Embassy of Turkey, 1956).

In the end, the essence of Henze's argument was that the violence inflicted upon the Greeks by the Turkish side over the years was justifiable and constituted legitimate defense because all of the blame rested with the Greek side. Such a view of the Cyprus conflict, however, is not supported by factual evidence and reflects one side of the conflict, the Turkish side. Espousing a one-sided view of the conflict, Henze provided advice to Brzezinski on how to deal with the intractable Cyprus dispute.

The "Irrational Greeks" and the "Rational Turks"

Henze's solid pro-Turkish sentiment was combined with an apparent antipathy toward Greece and Greek Americans. This became apparent in his book on Turkey, especially in the section that covers the embargo. Henze wrote the following referring to Greece's withdrawal from NATO's integrated military structure immediately after the second phase of the Turkish invasion, which occurred on August 14, 1974:

> *Illogically, in a fit of pique* Greece had withdrawn from military participation in NATO in the aftermath of the Cyprus crisis.[21] (Emphasis added.)

The decision to leave NATO's integrated military structure, but still remain a member of NATO, was made personally by Greek Prime Minister Constantine Karamanlis. Repeatedly, Karamanlis explained to American officials, including Cyrus Vance, Clark Clifford, and President Carter the reason behind this decision. Karamanlis explained that he had decided to withdraw from the alliance's military command structure in order to protest NATO's inaction and condoning of the invasion of a small island republic by a NATO member, Turkey. The alternative, Karamanlis pointed out, was to go to war with Turkey. The second phase of the Turkish invasion and the specter of tens of thousands of Greek Cypriots forced to leave their homes, while thousands were missing, had created enormous pressure on Karamanlis to go to war with Turkey. Simultaneously, anti-American fever

---

[21]Henze, *Turkey and Ataturk's Legacy*, p. 84.

was reaching a climax and pressure was building on the Greek prime minister to close down the American bases in Greece.

Given the tumultuous circumstances in Greece in the summer of 1974, Karamanlis decided that the most prudent way out was for Greece to leave NATO's military command structure. No one else could have taken the responsibility for such a decision. Karamanlis was the sole embodiment of legitimacy at the time, and only he could have convinced the Greek people that, instead of going to war, withdrawing from NATO's military command structure would be a less painful alternative. At the time, many Greeks were so angry at the United States that they advocated Greece's complete withdrawal from NATO and a rupture of relations with the United States. Karamanlis prevailed over these passions. Using his enormous prestige, he was able to avert a war with Turkey and a permanent rift with the United States.

Because of Karamanlis's leadership, the American bases in Greece remained open, were fully operational, and served American strategic interests in the region throughout the period during which Greece stayed away from NATO's integrated military structure. Karamanlis's decisive step of withdrawing from NATO's military structure while keeping the American bases intact spared Greece and Turkey a catastrophic war. By 1980, with Karamanlis's strong backing, Greece had returned to NATO's military command structure. To have taken these steps orderly and peacefully, to have prevented a permanent rupture with the Western alliance, and to have averted a war with Turkey were all extraordinary achievements by Constantine Karamanlis.

The British foreign secretary at the time, James Callaghan, found Karamanlis's decision to withdraw from NATO's military structure quite understandable under the circumstances. Callaghan paid tribute to the Greek prime minister's leadership because, by withdrawing from the military structure, Karamanlis "saved his country from a war that would have been disastrous for the future of the new democracy."[22] Likewise, George Ball, former under secretary of state under Johnson, had high praise for Karamanlis's leadership at the time. Testifying at a congressional hearing on Cyprus, barely six days after Karamanlis's decision to take Greece out of NATO's integrated military structure, Ball stated:

---

[22]Callaghan, *Time and Chance*, pp. 355–356.

[Karamanlis and his colleagues] are men who historically have had great bonds of friendship with the United States and the Western Allies, but they are under enormous pressures to take some actions which respond to the public will if they are to survive as a democratic government. The public will right now is highly emotional, particularly when there are new sources of agitation, such as Mr. Papandreou just returning to Greece. While I deeply regret the action of the Greek Government [the withdrawal from NATO's integrated military structure], I can very well understand why they felt compelled to take it.[23]

These were the circumstances under which Karamanlis decided to take Greece out of NATO's integrated military structure after he restored democracy in the country. It did not take long for Karamanlis to be recognized as a reasonable, responsible leader who became highly respected by his peers in Europe. It was the decisions of this leader that Henze characterized as "illogical" and a result of a "fit of pique."

In contrast to viewing Karamanlis's decision to pull Greece out of NATO's military structure as an act based on emotionalism and lack of reason, Henze viewed Ankara's decision to close down five American bases as a rational and more or less justifiable action in response to the imposition of the U.S. arms embargo against Turkey. According to the U.S. Defense Department, the closure of these bases hampered the U.S.'s ability to monitor Soviet strategic nuclear activities.

Henze explained that the Turks were "shocked and offended by the arms embargo." When they realized that "the U.S. Executive Branch lacked the strength to overcome congressional obstinacy" with respect to the imposition of the embargo, they decided to take "countermeasures" by closing down five American bases as a protest against the embargo.[24] In July 1975, the government of Prime Minister Süleyman Demirel shut down the bases. Thus, during the embargo years, Henze viewed the Greeks, personified by Karamanlis, as emo-

---

[23]See *Cyprus-1974: Statement of Honorable George Ball, Former Under Secretary of State.* Hearings before the Committee on Foreign Affairs, Subcommittee on Europe, House of Representatives, August 19 and 20, 1974, 93rd Congress, 2nd Session, Washington, D.C., U.S. Government Printing Office, 1974, p. 51.

[24]Henze, *Turkey and Ataturk's Legacy*, p. 84.

tional and irrational, while he saw the Turks, personified by Demirel, as reasonable people for whom the United States should exhibit understanding and empathy in reaction to their anger.

Kinship and Political Action in Washington: Greek, Polish, and Czech Americans

In his book, Henze also regarded the role of Greek Americans in the embargo affair as highly negative and stated:

> In its inception, the congressional arms embargo against Turkey to punish her for using U.S. supplied arms in what was generally called an invasion of Cyprus was not as much an initiative of Greeks in Greece as of their *kinsmen* in America. They were suffering from a *collective neurosis* caused by *years of disappointment over the failure of democracy in Greece and the colonels' excesses*, resentment of the colonels' betrayal of Greek interests in Cyprus, and even *embarrassment over the fall of the U.S. vice presidency of Spiro Agnew*. Agnew had both supported the colonels strongly and disgraced the highest office to which a Greek American had ever risen. The Greek Americans were ripe for exploitation by *ethnically oriented politicians* for whom political opportunism was a higher priority than the national interest.[25] (Emphasis added.)

This analysis of the causes behind the mobilization of the Greek American community in the aftermath of the Turkish invasion of Cyprus merits attention, considering the important role Henze played as the main adviser to Brzezinski on Greek-Turkish relations and on Cyprus.

Henze's position was that the embargo "was not as much an initiative of Greeks in Greece as of their *kinsmen* in America." (Emphasis added.) This brings up the role of ethnic politics in America and the ties of a variety of ethnic groups to their countries of origin. The feeling of kinship with Greeks in Cyprus constituted a very strong motivational force that drove Greek American political activism in

---

[25]Ibid., pp. 82–83.

the aftermath of the Turkish invasion of Cyprus. Feelings of kinship, however, play a similar role for other ethnic groups—Albanian Americans, Armenian Americans, Chinese Americans, Cuban Americans, Hispanic Americans, Irish Americans, Jewish Americans, and Polish Americans, for example—as they attempt to influence their elected representatives in Washington.

A certain sense of affinity and pride on the part of ethnic groups in America with respect to the countries and cultures they or their ancestors came from is normal and expected, and is an integral part of ethnic politics, which have a long tradition in the United States. Even top officials in the foreign policy establishment who happen to be foreign-born do not hide their feelings of kinship with the lands they came from. These feelings have become more pronounced and publicized over the last 30 years, as the United States has begun moving away from the "melting pot" model and has adopted the "mosaic" concept. Under the "beautiful mosaic" model, Americans can be proud of their ethnic heritage and still be "good patriotic Americans." As a consequence of a combination of demographic, social, political, and cultural trends, the U.S. is more tolerant of other races, ethnicities, religions, and cultures than it was 30 years ago. Being a "hyphenated" American is not only accepted, but it is also celebrated, as ethnic groups publicly display their cultures and roots across the land. The sense of kinship with other lands has been integrated into the new American mosaic paradigm

In the Carter administration, Henze worked under National Security Adviser Zbigniew Brzezinski, who shared a certain feeling of kinship with his native Poland and its people. He was proud of his Polish roots, and it was quite natural and understandable that he felt some affinity and empathy for the country of his origin. The feeling was mutual and, following the collapse of communism and the emancipation of Poland from Soviet tutelage, Brzezinski, being a popular figure in his native land, was mentioned as a potential presidential candidate in 1998.

President Carter happened to be an admirer of Poland. At a White House reception in February 1978 honoring Polish American leaders, Carter paid tribute to Poland and its people, and he referred to the warm welcome he had received a few months earlier when he visited the country. The president then paid tribute to Brzezinski. He stated:

We are tied together [with Poland] culturally, and I think perhaps, most important of all, we are tied together through blood kinship. There are millions of Polish Americans here. … During the campaign, I was permitted to visit many communities in our Nation, which have a heavy concentration of Americans of Polish descent. Dr. Brzezinski, who was on the receiving line, is very close to me, and the man who's had the most effect on my life, other than my own father, Admiral Hyman Rickover, as you know, is also from Poland.[26]

Indeed, President Carter admired the Polish people and was proud to have Polish-born Brzezinski as his top foreign policy adviser.

Another member of the National Security Council who, like Brzezinski, was born in Eastern Europe, was Madeleine Albright. She was a Brzezinski protégé and worked along with Henze in the drive to lift the embargo. Albright did so in her capacity as congressional relations officer at the National Security Council.[27] Up until today, Albright has said little regarding her exact role in the Carter White House drive to lift the embargo.

Albright was born in Czechoslovakia. Both the kinship she felt for the Czech people and the traumatic experiences of these people, first under the Nazis and then under the Soviets, left a lasting impression on Albright. The Hitler-Chamberlain Munich accord in September 1938 sealed the fate of Czechoslovakia, as it became the first victim of Nazi Germany. Albright internalized the West's surrender in Munich and, like most Czechs, she considered it, rightly so, a symbol of appeasement and capitulation to Hitler and to dictators in general. In fact, Munich and her sense of kinship with Czechoslovakia had a profound effect on her worldview and "shaped her foreign policy thinking for life."[28]

The Munich appeasement guided her policies when she became secretary of state in 1997 in President Bill Clinton's administration. It was Munich that contributed decisively to her opposition to Yugoslav dictator Slobodan Milosevic and her determination to use military

---

[26]Presidential Papers, Carter, 1978, vol. I, "Reception Honoring Polish Americans: Remarks at White House Reception," February 6, 1978, pp. 283.

[27]Brzezinski, *Power and Principle*, p. 571.

[28]See the biography of Albright by Michael Dobbs, *Madeleine Albright: A Twentieth-Century Odyssey* (Henry Holt and Co.: New York, 1999), p. 34.

force against Serbia. As secretary of state, Albright was the strongest advocate of NATO's war against Milosevic, from April to June 1999, as a way of reversing his policy of "ethnic cleansing" against the ethnic Albanians of Kosovo. In fact, the alliance's air campaign against Serbia became known as "Madeleine's war."[29]

Albright's closeness to her native land was also manifested when she was mentioned as a possible presidential candidate in the Czech Republic. None other than the popular Czech president, Vaclav Havel, made it known that he favored Albright as his successor. Havel told Albright this in August 1998 when she was serving as U.S. secretary of state.[30] However, she ruled out the possibility that she would seek the presidency of the Czech Republic. "My heart is in two places, but America is where I belong," Albright stated.[31]

Like Brzezinski and Albright, who felt a sense of kinship with the people and lands of their birth, Greek Americans felt a sense of kinship toward the Greeks of Cyprus and were deeply moved by their suffering in the summer of 1974. The ensuing political mobilization of the Greek American community, the majority of which was American-born, had a lot to do with this sense of kinship. The loyalty of these Greek Americans to the United States was never in doubt.

With regard to the Cyprus issue, Greek Americans employed moral and legal arguments centering on the "rule of law," which played a critical role in persuading Congress to impose the arms

---

[29]See, "Albright at War: Behind the Scenes with Secretary of State as She Pushes for Victory in Kosovo," *Time*, May 17, 1999. This was a special issue of *Time* magazine with Albright on its cover. It was devoted to the Kosovo crisis and NATO's air campaign against Serbia. This campaign was, to an overwhelming degree, an American affair, as the U.S. contributed close to three-quarters of the airplanes, personnel, and logistics in the air war. *Time* described the following scene, which captures Albright's thinking: "When the Italian and French ministers proposed a softening in the language they would use to threaten Milosevic, Albright's close aide Jamie Rubin whispered to her that she could probably accept it. She snapped back, "Where do you think we are, Munich?" *Time*, May 17, 1999, p. 29. *Newsweek* magazine characterized Albright as "hard-line Munich baby." See "Victory at a Price," *Newsweek*, June 14, 1999, pp. 27–29.

[30]See "Is Albright Launching Her Listening Tour?" *Time Daily*, February 27, 2000; "Albright Eyes Czech Presidency," *BBC World News*, February 28, 2000; "Albright Faces Quiz Over Czech Presidency," *BBC World News*, March 5, 2000.

[31]See "Albright Again Rules Out Seeking Czech Presidency," *Associated Press*, March 8, 2000.

embargo against Turkey. The year 1974, when the embargo was debated and imposed by Congress, was also a year of moral and political crisis in America, a crisis associated with the Vietnam War and the Watergate scandal. The rule of law became the epicenter of the political debate in the United States as Congress challenged Nixon's "imperial presidency." To a considerable degree, Greek American lobbying was successful because it rode the wave of the rule of law that swept Washington at the time in the unique and propitious political environment associated with the post-Vietnam era and the Watergate scandal. If a different atmosphere had prevailed in Washington, it is quite doubtful that Greek American mobilization alone would have succeeded in bringing about the congressional arms embargo against Turkey.

On the "Collective Neurosis" of Greek Americans

In his book, Henze attempted to psychoanalyze Greek Americans. His diagnosis was that they "were suffering from a collective neurosis."[32] The use of this psychological term indicated that Henze saw Greek Americans as a group suffering from a certain disorder.[33]

This diagnosis constituted a sweeping generalization that referred to all Greek Americans without exception. Henze inferred that the "neurotic" behavior exhibited by Greek Americans could not be patri-

---

[32]Henze, *Turkey and Ataturk's Legacy*, p. 82.

[33]For the definition of "neurosis" and the different categories of "neurosis" see American Psychiatric Association, *Diagnostic and Statistical Manual of Mental Disorders*, Second Edition (DSM-II), (Washington, DC: APA, 1968), pp. 39–41. Twelve yearls later, in 1980, the American Psychatric Association (APA) published the third edition of its *Diagnostic and Statistical Manual of Mental Disorders,* referred to as DSM-III. This third edition adopted a different approach on how to define "neurosis." Accordingly, DSM-III states in the part 'Neurotic Disorders': "At the present time, however, there is no consensus in our field as to how to define 'neurosis.' Some clinicians limit the term to its descriptive meaning whereas others also include the concept of a specific etiological process. To avoid ambiguity, the term *neurotic disorder* should be used only descriptively. The tern *neurotic process*, on the other hand, should be used when the clinician wishes to indicate the concept of a specific etiological process involving the following sequence . . . Thus, the term *neurotic disorder* is used in DSM-III without any implication of a special etiological process." See American Psychatric Association, *Diagnostic and Statistical Manual of Mental Disorders*, Third Edition (DSM-III), (Washington, DC: APA, 1980), pp. 9–10.

otic because, as a result of their "neurosis," they could not engage in rational thinking that would serve the national interest. Henze argued that the Greek lobby and those influenced by it "harmed high priority interests of the United States."[34]

Greek Americans, the Junta, and Spiro Agnew

In order to explain the "collective neurosis" of the Greek American community, Henze dwelled on the motivational dynamics of this community. He attributed this neurosis to "years of disappointment over the failure of democracy in Greece and the colonels' excesses." It is beyond dispute, however, that the great majority of Greek Americans either condoned or supported the junta. To state, therefore, that the Greek American community as a whole was disappointed because Greece was ruled by the junta ran contrary to the facts. Yet, Henze cited this "disappointment" as a major reason behind this collective neurosis of Greek Americans.

Henze cited another reason for the Greek American neurosis, one concerning Spiro Agnew's resignation from the office of vice president in October 1973. Greek Americans, Henze argued, were embarrassed by Agnew's resignation. "Agnew had both supported the colonels strongly and disgraced the highest office to which a Greek-American had ever risen," Henze added. In other words, Agnew embarrassed Greek Americans because he was forced to resign and because he was a supporter of the Greek junta. However, Agnew's support for the junta could hardly have been a source of embarrassment for Greek Americans. Furthermore, this support had little to do with Agnew's ethnic origins. Traditionally and institutionally, the vice president follows the policies of the president. Agnew supported the Greek junta because it was the policy of the Nixon administration. If Nixon had opposed the junta, Agnew would also have been a champion of democracy in Greece. In fact, before he became Nixon's running mate, Agnew appeared rather unsympathetic to the Greek junta.

There is some truth to Henze's assertion that Greek Americans were embarrassed by Agnew's resignation since many in the Greek American community were proud of the vice president's Greek ori-

---

[34]Henze, *Turkey and Ataturk*, p. 83.

gins. Still, the attitude of the Greek American community toward Agnew's resignation can be understood only if placed in the context of Agnew's relationship to this community. Sociologist Charles Moskos has examined this relationship, which he presented as complex and problematic.[35]

Overall, Agnew's relationship with the Greek American community was tenuous and circumstantial, even divisive. Thus, while many Greek Americans felt proud that the vice president of the United States was of Greek origin, many others did not consider him a true Greek.[36] His demise was a cause of embarrassment, but there is no evidence to support the thesis that it had a lingering effect on the psyche of the Greek American community. In fact, following the initial embarrassment over Agnew's resignation, the Greek American community quickly forgot him.[37] The collapse of the junta and the restoration of democracy in Greece amidst the Turkish invasion of Cyprus brought Greek Americans together in support of the new democratic government of Greece and in opposition to the invasion. The "Agnew syndrome" was hardly on the minds of Greek Americans when they mobilized and demonstrated by the tens of thousands in New York and Washington against U.S. policy toward Cyprus in July and August 1974.

By the same token, if one accepts Henze's argument that Agnew's resignation was an embarrassment to a whole ethnic group, the Greek American community, then the individuals and groups that had supported and admired Nixon over the years should have felt much greater embarrassment and shame when Nixon resigned. After all, Nixon was the only president to resign in the history of the American republic. Moreover, the resignation of a president in disgrace had such a profound effect on the United States that the effects of the resignation and the Watergate scandal still reverberate today. On the other hand, Agnew and his resignation from the vice-presidency are all but forgotten. In fact, it is rare for a vice president to be remem-

---

[35]See Charles Moskos, *Greek Americans: Struggle and Success* (New Brunswick: Transaction, 1989), 2nd ed., pp. 118–120.

[36]Peter Maroudas, "Greek American Involvement in Contemporary Politics," in *The Greek American Community in Transition,* ed. Harry Psomiades and Alice Scourby (New York: Pella Publishing Company, 1982), pp. 101, 103–105; Moskos, *Greek Americans,* pp. 118–120.

[37]Moskos, pp. 119–120.

bered even if he has accomplished something while in office. Henze, however, did not see a reason why President Nixon's friends, supporters, and admirers should have "suffered from a collective neurosis" due to any embarrassment over his resignation in utter disgrace.

Thus, the major causes Henze cited as being behind the collective neurosis of Greek Americans are not supported by evidence. In fact, the existing evidence tends to support the opposite of what Henze maintained regarding Greek American opposition to the junta, while Henze tended to greatly oversimplify Agnew's ties with the Greek American community.

Henze's conclusion that the Greek American community suffered from a collective neurosis amounted to stereotyping a whole community. Such stereotyping failed to explain the causes behind the remarkable political mobilization of this ethnic group from 1974 onward.

Henze was also highly critical of the members of Congress who supported the imposition of the arms embargo. He labeled them "ethnically oriented" and "political opportunists who put ethnic interests above the national interest." Henze failed to identify any of these "opportunist politicians" by name. Since the majority of senators and representatives voted for the imposition of the embargo, the majority of the 93rd Congress of the United States, in Henze's logic, followed the path of "political opportunism" and placed ethnic interests, Greek interests, above the national interest. Such logic cast doubt on the patriotism of the Congress of the United States. The 93rd Congress was the Congress, however, that rose to the occasion during the Watergate scandal. The whole Watergate episode demonstrated that it was this Congress, the one that later imposed the embargo, that placed the constitution and the national interest above everything else.

Moreover, if one looked at the individual members of Congress who supported the embargo, it would be difficult to make the argument that they were political opportunists who placed ethnic interests above the national interest. Supporters of the embargo included several Second World War veterans and heroes such as Republican Senator Bob Dole of Kansas. Another strong supporter of the embargo was Republican Senator Paul Laxalt of Nevada. Laxalt was a staunch supporter of a strong national defense and a close friend of Ronald Reagan's. The number of Greek Americans living in Nevada did not exceed 0.5 percent of the state's population, and the "Greek vote" was so negligible that it could hardly have had any political effect in the state. The same held true for Montana. Both of its congressmen, Max Baucus, a Democrat, and Ron Marlenee, a Republican, voted against lifting the embargo. The number of Greeks in Montana is negligible, barely 0.2 percent of the population. The votes of these senators and representatives in favor of upholding the embargo could not be explained by "political opportunism" and catering to "ethnic interests." Still, Henze indicted all the members of Congress who supported the embargo on grounds that were totally unfounded, revealing his intolerance for members of Congress who happened to disagree with the Carter administration on the embargo issue.

The view, therefore, that emerges out of Henze's book was a highly negative stereotype of an ethnic group, Greek Americans. It created a caricature of an ethnic community, one that was abnormal, out of the mainstream, and untrustworthy, one that had too much influence, and one that exercised a corruptive influence on Congress, the media, and government officials.[38] Henze's logic led to the inescapable conclusion that Greek Americans were disloyal and that their political role was harmful to the U.S. Furthermore, Henze did not hide his utter contempt for Congress because it supported the embargo. Under the circumstances, there is little doubt that the advice Henze gave to Brzezinski favored one of the parties of the Cyprus dispute, Turkey. In the end, when it came to Greek-Turkish relations and to Cyprus, Brzezinski's friend and closest aide, Paul Henze, was not just pro-Turkish, but he was also driven by an obvious antipathy toward the Greeks. It is not surprising, therefore, that Carter's national security adviser became such a passionate advocate of lifting the arms embargo against Turkey.

The Scene at the State Department

When President Carter appointed Cyrus Vance as his secretary of state, Congress and the media viewed it quite favorably. Vance combined a reputation of integrity with solid credentials in foreign and defense affairs. He had been secretary of the army under President Kennedy and deputy secretary of defense under President Johnson.

---

[38]See Henze, *Turkey: Ataturk's Legacy*, pp. 83–84.

Vance was seen as a contrast to Kissinger. The latter was flamboy-ant, loved publicity, and thrived on controversy. Vance was low-key and soft-spoken, and he did not seek publicity. In addition, Kissinger was associated with Nixon and the abuse of power, and he was the architect of realpolitik. Vance, on the other hand, was a man who be-lieved in due process and who would inject into American foreign policy a sense of being guided by a moral compass and higher princi-ples such as human rights. That was what Carter wanted of Vance. He was also to serve as a balance to the controversial Brzezinski.

Prior to becoming secretary of state, Vance had been one of the primary supporters of the arms embargo against Turkey. During a July 10, 1975 hearing before the House International Relations Committee, he gave a lengthy testimony in support of the embargo. Furthermore, he had served as President Johnson's special envoy for Cyprus during the November 1967 military crisis in the island republic.

As secretary of state, however, after initial reluctance, Vance changed course. The bureaucratic paradigm prevailed in the case of Vance, as was the case with other secretaries of state who came to the State Department with the ambition to change the world. The State Department was an enormous bureaucratic structure with a value system and modus operandi that had taken shape and solidified over three decades of the cold war. Change could only be brought about incrementally, unless the United States was confronted with extraor-dinary emergencies such as the revolutionary turmoil in Iran. Under such circumstances, the State Department was capable of re-adjust-ing its policies to meet the challenge, even though, in the case of Iran, the National Security Council and Brzezinski seemed to win the upper hand.

The State Department bureaucracy tended to view the embargo affair from two perspectives that reinforced each other. First, the cold war perspective dictated a policy of containment. Carter and Vance did make an effort to bring about change by adopting a post-cold war foreign policy, but this effort was short-lived, lasting for about a year.

Second, the State Department had to protect its own turf, which was another reason to oppose the embargo from the very beginning. Along with the White House, the State Department saw the embargo as a serious encroachment by Congress on what was considered to be a privilege of the executive branch, the conducting of foreign policy. The embargo had to be repealed in order to restore the proper balance between the executive branch and Congress. Vance succumbed to this logic and led the charge to lift the embargo. In doing so, not only did he serve his president well, but he was also fighting to reclaim the authority that rightfully—in the view of the executive branch—belonged to the State Department and not to Congress.

Vance's endorsement of the policy of lifting the embargo was critical. Carter would have been much more reluctant to go along with Brzezinski, a fervent advocate of lifting the embargo, if Vance had disagreed. Brzezinski, who had a more aggressive style than Vance, met the president daily and exercised a great deal of influence on him. Still, the president valued Vance's opinion and would often side with his secretary of state when he had to choose between the advice of Vance and Brzezinski.[39]

Deputy Secretary of State Warren Christopher was also deeply involved in the decision to lift the embargo. It was Christopher who flew to Ankara to inform Turkish Prime Minister Bülent Ecevit of the administration's decision. When Bill Clinton became president in January 1993, he appointed Christopher secretary of state. Assistant Secretary of State for European Affairs George Vest worked with Christopher in the drive to lift the embargo. Working closely with them was Matthew Nimetz, who served as counsel at the State Department and was a general troubleshooter, with emphasis on the Eastern Mediterranean. It also happened that Nimetz was a law partner of Vance's. At the State Department, Nimetz also worked with Nelson Ledsky, who was serving as head of the Turkish desk. Later, under the administration of President George Bush, Ledsky served as the State Department's special Cyprus coordinator.

The Legendary Clark Clifford Joins the Team

In order to deal with the Eastern Mediterranean, Carter added Clark Clifford, a legendary figure in foreign affairs, to his foreign policy team. On February 3, 1977, the White House announced the appointment of Clifford as the "president's personal emissary to Greece,

---

[39]This view was shared by several of Carter's advisers including Hamilton Jordan, his chief of staff. See Hamilton Jordan, *Crises* (New York: G.P. Putman's and Sons, 1982), p. 48. See also Robert Strauss, *Washington Post*, December 20, 1979.

Turkey, and Cyprus." Clifford was the quintessential Washington insider and was highly respected in the foreign policy and defense communities. He was a good Democrat who served under several Democratic presidents. Like President Harry Truman, he was Missouri-born. He had been a close adviser to Truman and had been highly influential in the formulation of the Truman Doctrine. Clifford rode the train along with President Truman and British Prime Minister Winston Churchill to Fulton, Missouri, where Churchill made his famous "iron curtain" speech. As presidential historian Michael Beschloss put it, ". . . By 1963, Clifford was the premier Washington amalgam of lawyer, lobbyist, and behind-the-scenes adviser to myriad Democratic politicians, starting with John Kennedy and Lyndon Johnson."[40]

Given his credentials, it was not surprising that Clifford had been a foreign policy adviser to President Kennedy and a confidant of President Johnson, who had appointed him secretary of defense in 1968. Indeed, few in Washington could match the credentials of Clark Clifford in foreign affairs. It was to Clifford, the lawyer, that Bert Lance turned for assistance in his defense against allegations of wrongdoing. Lance was a trusted friend of Carter's and was appointed director of the Office of Management and Budget by him. The allegations, though never proved, forced Lance to resign in September 1977.[41]

Carter's appointment of Clark Clifford as his special envoy to Greece, Turkey, and Cyprus indicated that the new president was serious about resolving the Cyprus dispute. Clifford became Carter's close adviser in the president's drive to lift the embargo.

Clifford's role was key in the drive to lift the embargo. He had enormous prestige in the foreign policy community and was also close to Secretary of State Vance. He spearheaded the effort to lift the embargo by focusing on the Soviet threat, the critical role of Turkey in the NATO alliance, and the fear that Turkey might leave the alliance and move closer to the Soviet Union if the embargo remained in place. This view was shared, among others, by Henze and Brzezinski at the National Security Council, Secretary of Defense Harold Brown,

---

[40]See Michael R. Beschloss, *Taking Charge: The White House Tapes, 1963–1964* (New York: Touchstone, Simon and Schuster, 1997), p. 90.

[41]The Lance affair was described in Carter, *Keeping Faith*, pp. 125–137. It was also described by Clifford in Clark Clifford, with Richard Holbrooke, *Counsel to the President: A Memoir* (New York: Random House, 1991), pp. 628–632.

the Joint Chiefs of Staff, and General Alexander Haig, Supreme Allied Commander Europe. After a year in office, President Carter, himself, came to espouse the same alarmist view.

In addition to the official team that Carter had at his disposal, the White House succeeded in mobilizing a supportive network of retired generals, veterans groups, academics, and media personalities that favored the lifting of the embargo.

Overall, Carter was able to put together a first-class foreign policy team in order to prepare the ground for the fight with Congress over the embargo. It included old hands in foreign affairs, such as Vance and Clifford, and new dynamic players, such as Brzezinski, Brown, and Haig.

In the end, President Carter relied on the recommendations of the national security bureaucracy in formulating his policies on Greece, Turkey, and Cyprus, and in reaching his decision to lift the embargo. Within this bureaucracy, certain players were more important than others. To a considerable degree, Carter relied on the advice of Brzezinski who, in turn, relied on Paul Henze's expert advice, which, nonetheless, clearly favored the Turkish side of the dispute. The fact that Vance eventually agreed with Brzezinski and Clifford on the need to lift the embargo made it easier for Carter to go along with his national security adviser and to rationalize and justify his own decision to repeal it.

The Carter administration's drive to lift the embargo and its efforts toward a Cyprus settlement rested on a strategic rationale revolving around the Soviet threat. However, the question of the Soviet threat against Turkey and the Eastern Mediterranean can be addressed only if one takes Turkish-Soviet relations into serious consideration. This is especially the case for the period preceding the imposition of the embargo as well as the embargo years, 1974 to 1978. A closer look at the evolution of Turkish-Soviet relations would indicate that the Soviet threat against Turkey began to decrease in the 1970s.

CHAPTER 5

The Clifford Mission in Cyprus

The Meeting with Karamanlis

Shortly after Clark Clifford was appointed President Carter's special envoy to Greece, Turkey, and Cyprus in early February 1977, he was dispatched to the region. During the second half of the same month, Clifford embarked on a mission to bring about a negotiated Cyprus settlement, which, in turn, would facilitate the lifting of the embargo. For this purpose, Clifford visited Athens, Ankara, and Nicosia, and he attempted to bring all sides of the dispute to the negotiating table. He was accompanied by State Department counsel Matthew Nimetz and Nelson Ledsky, the head of the State Department's Turkish desk.

Clifford's first stop was Athens, where he had extensive talks with Prime Minister Constantine Karamanlis. The U.S. envoy met with the Greek leader on February 18, 1977. Karamanlis presented his views to Clifford in a spirit of friendship, and the Greek leader made it abundantly clear that he was a friend of the West and the United States and that he would continue a policy of close alliance and friendship with America. At the same time, Karamanlis told Clifford that, while the Greek people entertained no animosity toward the United States, they were bitterly disappointed about a number of American decisions and policies regarding Cyprus and Greek-Turkish relations.[1]

The Greek leader explained to Clifford that several U.S. decisions regarding Cyprus and Greek-Turkish relations had been misguided and counterproductive. Karamanlis's basic argument was that the

---

[1]The minutes of the February 18, 1977 Clifford-Karamanlis meeting are found in *The Karamanlis Archive*, vol. 9, pp. 389–395. A transcript of this meeting appears in the Appendix, Document B. In his memoirs, Clifford barely mentioned his meeting with Karamanlis. He described it in 42 words. See Clifford, *Counsel to the President*, p. 626.

problems in the Eastern Mediterranean, Cyprus, and the Aegean had been caused by Turkish expansionism. Karamanlis pointed to Turkey's aggressive actions in Cyprus, especially the second phase of its invasion on August 14, 1974. Karamanlis pointedly told Clifford that the United States and Britain had done nothing to stop this Turkish aggression, which was totally unjustified. As a consequence, the Greek prime minister had been under enormous pressure to go to war with Turkey. The only way to avoid war had been to express Greece's protest against the inaction of NATO and the United States by leaving the integrated military structure of the alliance.

Karamanlis reminded Clifford that the president of Cyprus, Archbishop Makarios, had already made painful concessions to Turkey by accepting the idea of a bizonal, bicommunal federal system and agreeing to the control of 18 to 22 percent of Cypriot territory by Turkish Cypriots. The Greek prime minister added that Makarios could negotiate an adjustment of up to 25 percent of Cypriot territory for the Turkish Cypriots, even though the Turkish Cypriot population represented only 18 percent of the total population of Cyprus. But Makarios could not go beyond 25 percent because the Greek Cypriots would never accept further concessions to Turkey. Despite Makarios's moderation, Turkey had remained adamant and had refused to negotiate a fair settlement, as it continued its occupation of Cyprus, Karamanlis indicated. This was a clear sign that Turkish objectives in Cyprus were expansionist, Karamanlis told Clifford.[2]

With regard to Greek-Turkish relations, the Greek leader told Clifford that the tension between the two NATO allies was due to the expansionist policies of Turkey. In a dispassionate way, Karamanlis told Clifford:

I ask you Mr. Clifford to believe me, that I did prevent the outbreak of war on two occasions, both of which were the consequences of Turkish provocation. The first one was during the second round of the Turkish invasion of Cyprus [August 1974]. The second one was in the Aegean when Turkey provocatively sent into the Aegean the "Sismic" boat [August 1976]. It was with great difficulty that I managed to restrain the situation from blowing up. But neither the Greek

---

[2] *Karamanlis Archive*, p. 390.

people nor I would be able to tolerate a third round of tension. Yet, the Turks are provoking me daily.[3]

Karamanlis outlined Turkey's demands to revise the status quo in the Aegean. If Greece accepted Turkey's demands concerning the Aegean continental shelf and airspace, this would mean that Turkey would draw a dividing line in the middle of the Aegean "east of which line there are 500 Greek islands with a Greek population of 320,000," Karamanlis stated. Karamanlis added that there was a territorial status quo in the Aegean, which had been determined by the Treaty of Lausanne in 1923, and Greece honored this treaty and all of its international obligations. Yet, Greece, in a gesture of goodwill, would agree to submit the issue of the continental shelf to the International Court of Justice in The Hague. Furthermore, Karamanlis reminded Clifford that, on April 17, 1976, Greece had proposed to Turkey that Athens and Ankara sign a non-aggression pact. Turkey initially accepted the proposal but later rejected it.

The Greek leader also dealt with another issue raised by Turkey, the defense of Greek islands in the Aegean. Turkey had been threatening these islands, Karamanlis explained. Given the experience of Cyprus, Greece had a responsibility to defend them against Turkey's landing fleet, the largest in the Mediterranean, and a special Turkish military force, the Third Army of the Aegean, consisting of 120,000 men. This force, stationed on the Turkish mainland, almost equaled the total strength of the Greek armed forces, Karamanlis told Clifford.

Karamanlis also referred to Turkish complaints concerning the Muslim minority in Thrace and the minority question. He presented Clifford with the following facts:

When the Lausanne Treaty was signed in 1923, there were 111,000 Greeks in Turkey and 106,000 Muslims in Thrace. Today, there are only 15,000 Greeks left in Turkey while the Muslims of Thrace have increased to 120,000. If there is a minority question, it is Greece that is entitled to raise such a question and demand the restoration of the population balance provided by the Lausanne Treaty.[4]

---

[3]Ibid., p. 391.

[4]Ibid., p. 392. Two decades later, by 1997, as a result of continuous pressure, the number of Greeks in Turkey diminished to about 2,000.

Karamanlis then dealt with the U.S.-Greek alliance and NATO. "Greece is not against NATO," he stated, but the Turkish invasion and occupation of Cyprus in 1974 and NATO's inaction had forced Greece to take certain actions. Greece's withdrawal from the integrated military structure of NATO in August 1974 had not meant that Greece was also withdrawing from the alliance, but it was seeking a special relationship with NATO. This special relationship meant the following:

First, during peacetime in Europe, the Greek armed forces would be under Greek command because of the need to confront the Turkish threat. Second, in time of war between East and West, Greece would be an integral part of the NATO alliance and would place all of its forces under NATO command. Third, in Greek defense planning that had been communicated to NATO, the country's special relationship with NATO would become operational when needed. Fourth, Greece would re-examine its position in NATO and, when the reasons that forced Athens to withdraw from NATO's integrated military structure had been removed, Greece would return to the military structure.[5]

On the question of the American bases in Greece, Karamanlis reaffirmed the Greek position that these bases would remain in Greece because they served the common defense of the alliance. What remained to be negotiated between Athens and Washington was the status of the bases, which had to be adjusted to conform to present conditions. The conditions under which the bases agreement had been signed in 1952 had changed, and the agreement needed to be renegotiated to serve the interests of the parties, Greece and the United States. Overwhelming domestic pressure to close down the bases came from main opposition leader Andreas Papandreou and the left. Yet, Karamanlis resisted this pressure even though his popularity would have soared if he had closed them.

Finally the Greek prime minister put forward the Greek position on the arms embargo against Turkey. On three occasions during his talks with Clifford, Karamanlis stated categorically that Greece opposed the lifting of the embargo. Under the prevailing circumstances, with Greece showing moderation and Turkey continuing its intransigent and provocative policies, the lifting of the embargo would lead to a dangerous situation, Karamanlis noted. He told Clifford:

---

[5]Ibid., p. 389.

If the embargo is to be lifted before there is substantial progress on Cyprus and on Greek-Turkish relations, we will all regret it. This is so because the lifting of the embargo will lead to the deterioration of the situation in the Aegean especially, which is becoming an even more dangerous issue than Cyprus. Lifting the embargo will remove any means of pressuring Turkey.[6]

Karamanlis asked Clifford to convey the positions of the Greek government, along with his own suggestions as prime minister, to President Carter.

Clifford thanked the prime minister for presenting the Greek views with such clarity and honesty. He assured Karamanlis that he had taken note of all the views and suggestions and that the Carter administration would take them into account when it embarked on formulating its new policies toward the region. The policy review by the Carter administration might take some time, Clifford stated, adding that the new administration was not tied to the policies of the previous administration.

Clifford told Karamanlis that the objective of his visit to the region was to examine the situation and report back to President Carter, who wanted to resolve the existing differences between two allies, Greece and Turkey. The way to deal with these problems was two-fold, the American envoy argued. First, the United States sought to strengthen its relations with Greece. Second, at the same time, American responsibilities in NATO required that a similar relationship exist between the U.S. and Turkey. The development of the "right relationship" between the United States and Turkey constituted additional protection for Greece. If, for instance, the United States cut off its ties with Turkey, its ability to assist in the resolution of Greek-Turkish differences would evaporate, Clifford asserted.[7]

Then Clifford raised the issue that, a year later, was to become the Carter administration's central argument for lifting the embargo. The Soviet Union was increasing its military capabilities, and this dictated the settlement of any disputes that might exist among NATO allies. The Soviet threat would be emphasized in Ankara because it was very important to the Turks, Clifford told Karamanlis.

---

[6]Ibid., p. 390.
[7]Ibid., p. 391.

At this point, the Greek prime minister commented on the question of the Soviet threat and the role of Turkey in the alliance by pointing out that it had been a mistake for the previous U.S. administrations, those of Nixon and Ford, to overrate the strategic role of Turkey. A consequence of this had been that the U.S. had succumbed to Turkish blackmail and had treated Greece unfairly. Karamanlis added:

> However, when one succumbs once to blackmail, this blackmail never ends. Turkey behaves with arrogance and audacity. Ankara threatens to leave NATO. The fact is that even if Turkey is asked to leave NATO, it won't. It would have been easier for Greece to leave NATO or become neutral if another government had been in power. In this case, the United States would find itself between two kinds of blackmail. The moderation and prudence of the Greek government has to be appreciated. If Turkish expansionism is not confronted effectively, war could be unavoidable . . .[8]

Karamanlis's statements that Greece might have left NATO altogether if "another government had been in power" and that "the moderation and prudence of the Greek government has to be appreciated" were implicit references to the rising popularity of Panhellenic Socialist Movement (PASOK) leader Andreas Papandreou. He was running for the office of prime minister in the November 1977 parliamentary elections on an anti-American platform as he had done in the November 1974 elections. One of PASOK's main slogans in the election campaigns was "Out With NATO. Out With the American Bases."

Clark Clifford asked whether his aides, Matthew Nimetz and Nelson Ledsky, and U.S. Ambassador to Greece Jack Kubisch, who were present during the envoy's talks with Karamanlis, had any comments. Ambassador Kubisch stated that the views expressed by Karamanlis reflected the steady policy that the Greek prime minister had been following. Nimetz asked how the United States, Europe, and the United Nations could promote the bicommunal talks in Cyprus. Karamanlis told Nimetz that the Turks needed to be convinced that they should behave more reasonably since the Greek Cypriot proposals were so

---

[8]Ibid., p. 392.

moderate. The United States should not succumb to Turkish black-mail, he reasoned. He said that it was important to remember that the Aegean issue was even more dangerous than the Cyprus problem because Turkish provocations might lead to war. The risk of war in the Aegean was a recurrent theme in the prime minister's presentation of his views.

The meeting ended on a positive note as Clifford thanked Kara-manlis and expressed the conviction that the United States would reciprocate by extending similar hospitality to the Greek leader when he visited Washington. This meeting was especially significant with respect to relations between the United States and Greece. For the first time, the Greek prime minister had the opportunity to present the official Greek positions on a broad spectrum of issues to the new administration in Washington. They included the Cyprus dispute and the reasons for Greece's withdrawal from the military wing of NATO in August 1974. The meeting also covered the Aegean issue, the Greek minority in Turkey, relations with NATO, and the American bases in Greece. The fact that the Greek positions were presented to a diplo-mat of Clark Clifford's stature, who was also the president's special envoy, gave added significance to the meeting on February 18, 1977. Moreover, the presence of Matthew Nimetz and Nelson Ledsky at the meeting meant that the State Department would have a very clear pic-ture of the Greek viewpoint. Karamanlis's assertion that the lifting of the embargo was bound to have highly negative consequences domes-tically and regionally was of extreme importance. The prime minister made it crystal clear to Clifford and his aides that Greece was against the repeal of the embargo before the achievement of substantial progress on Cyprus and on Greek-Turkish relations. Before leaving Athens, Clifford visited the Acropolis and posed for photographs next to a young boy dressed in the Greek national costume. The Greeks were quite pleased with Clifford's symbolic gesture.

Sequel in Ankara

Clifford's next stop was Ankara. Mehmet Ali Birand, the Turkish chronicler of the embargo period, provided a vivid description of the envoy's visit to the Turkish capital from February 20 to 22, 1977. Clif-ford discussed the embargo question with Turkish Prime Minister

Süleyman Demirel. According to Birand, Demirel emphasized two issues: the prospect of congressional approval of a new Defense Cooperation Agreement between the United States and Turkey, and the lifting of the embargo. The two issues were inextricably linked for, as long as an arms embargo was in place against Turkey, Congress would not approve any new agreement authorizing military aid to Turkey.

Demirel's attitude toward Clifford was aggressive and defiant. He protested the imposition of the embargo in the strongest possible way and accused the United States of undermining U.S.-Turkish relations. According to Birand, Demirel told Clifford:

> The embargo has to be repealed by May [1977]. Our [U.S.-Turkish] relations have to be restored to their previous status. However, since you have disturbed them, you have the responsibility to put them back on the right track. You give too much attention to Greece, but Turkey is the only country that is developing according to democratic standards. If some day Turkey is lost and you witness *Russia descending into the Persian Gulf,* what are you going to do?[9] (Emphasis added.)

Demirel was masterfully playing the Soviet threat card since he realized that he was dealing with one of the architects of the Truman Doctrine. The Turkish leader knew that one of the major U.S. concerns was Soviet penetration into the Eastern Mediterranean and the Middle East. That is why he raised the specter of a Russian descent into the Middle East. Then Demirel told Clifford in an accusatory fashion:

> You have sold weapons to communist Yugoslavia but you have locked the arms we have bought with our own money in your warehouses. Have you forgotten that the West supports our common defense?[10]

Clifford responded, always according to Birand:

---

[9]Birand, *Pazaremata* (Bargaining), p. 300. In his memoirs, Clifford makes a very brief reference, seven lines in all, to his meeting with Demirel in Ankara. See Clifford, *Counsel to the President,* p. 626.

[10]Birand, *Pazaremata* (Bargaining), p. 300.

What you are saying is right. You know me better than anyone else. I am the one who initiated the Truman Doctrine.
The Soviet threat exists now as it did before. We must, under
any circumstances, heal the wound of NATO [the embargo].
In reality, *Cyprus is an insignificant matter.* What is important
is for Turkey and NATO to regain their old power.[11] (Emphasis added.)

Then, Clifford explained to Demirel that the Carter administration had to persuade Congress to lift the embargo because, in the
United States, Congress could not be ignored. Congress understood
the reasons for the first phase of the Turkish invasion of Cyprus, he
said, but it could not understand the reasons for the second phase of
the invasion. Clifford said it was time for Turkey to make some goodwill gestures in order to help Washington lift the embargo. Turkey
might take some steps so that the Cyprus talks could resume, the
American envoy concluded.[12]

Subsequent to the meeting with Demirel, Clifford met with Turkish Foreign Minister İhsan Sabri Çağlayangil in order to work out a
formula for the resumption of the intercommunal negotiations in
Cyprus. Çağlayangil rejected the idea that Turkey should come up
with territorial proposals. "Territory is important for them [the Greek
Cypriots] so let them come up with such a proposal," he said. Clifford
responded: "Will you be able to come up with proposals on the constitutional aspect of the Cyprus issue?" The Turkish foreign minister
responded: "Certainly."[13]

When talking to Turkish officials during a reception at the American Embassy in Ankara, Matthew Nimetz floated the following idea:
Makarios would submit a map designating the proposed territory
under Greek Cypriot and Turkish Cypriot control, and the Turkish
side would present proposals on the constitutional aspect of the
Cyprus issue. In this way, substantial negotiations on the Cyprus issue
would begin, and this would enable Carter to ask Congress for increased military aid to Turkey, leading to the lifting of the embargo.[14]

Prior to his departure from Turkey, Clifford met once more with

---

[11]Ibid.
[12]Ibid.
[13]Ibid., p. 301.
[14]Ibid., pp. 301–302.

Çağlayangil and proposed the idea that Nimetz had floated the night before. It sounded reasonable, and Çağlayangil told Clifford: "It's not a bad idea as a transitional formula. This way we can pressure the priest [Makarios]." Clifford concluded from his meetings in Ankara that, first, Makarios would present his constitutional and territorial proposals, accompanied by a map. Then, the Turks would present their own constitutional proposals to be followed by their territorial proposals, accompanied by a map.[15] Clifford left Ankara with the expectation that the Turkish side would reciprocate with its own territorial proposals if Makarios presented a map. The next and most critical test was to secure the cooperation of the "priest," Archbishop Makarios, the president of Cyprus.

Winning the Archbishop's Trust: Makarios Gives Way and a Map is Provided

The most critical of Clifford's meetings took place in the Cypriot capital, Nicosia, from February 23 to 25, 1977. The U.S. envoy and his aides met with Makarios twice. They also visited the occupied part of Nicosia and met with Turkish Cypriot leader Rauf Denktash.

Clifford described his meetings with Makarios in his memoirs. Following the customary pleasantries between the Americans and Cypriots, the aides of both men left the room and Makarios and Clifford continued the discussion on a one-on-one basis. They talked about their careers and about John F. Kennedy, who had been greatly admired by Makarios. It was a hot day, according to Clifford, who described the meeting:

> As we talked, Makarios gradually stripped down, taking off first his religious robes, then his impressive religious hat, finally even his white shirt. The result was a dramatic downscaling of the Archbishop. Minus the full religious garb which made him recognizable throughout the world, he became a fairly short, balding man in an undershirt; but the partial disrobing also had the effect of humanizing him and gave our talks a more informal air.[16]

---

[15]Ibid.
[16]Clifford, *Counsel to the President*, pp. 626–627.

It is debatable whether Clifford's description of the archbishop's disrobing is fully accurate. It is extremely unlikely that the head of the Greek Orthodox Church of Cyprus would have taken off his white shirt and sat in his undershirt in front of a foreign guest. Patroklos Stavrou was under secretary to President Makarios, something like a chief of staff, throughout Makarios's tenure. Moreover, Stavrou had been a Makarios protégé since the mid-1950s. He was a very close and trusted aide of Makarios until the archbishop died in August 1977. Stavrou, who was well acquainted with Makarios's daily routine, his modus operandi, and mannerisms, strongly disputed the assertion that Makarios took off his shirt in front of Clifford. "On occasion, Makarios could take off his religious garment, but never his shirt. It is impossible," Stavrou maintained.[17] It is conceivable that Clifford, unfamiliar with Greek Orthodox ecclesiastical garments, was confused as to exactly what the archbishop took off. Greek Orthodox clergymen wear several layers of garments. They might take one layer off, but there is still another one under it.

Clifford appeared to form a positive impression of Makarios, and the archbishop viewed the American envoy sympathetically. As Patroklos Stavrou put it, "Clifford appeared to speak with sincerity and a deep desire to promote a Cyprus settlement."[18] It was an auspicious beginning for the talks between them.

During his second meeting with Makarios, on February 25, Clifford was able to persuade the Cypriot leader to accept the idea of a package deal for a Cyprus settlement. At the side of Makarios during this meeting with Clifford was Tassos Papadopoulos. He was a most trusted aide of Makarios since the mid-1950s and a well-known political leader and experienced negotiator. Papadopoulos was the official representative of the Greek Cypriots at the intercommunal talks.

Clifford explained to Makarios and Papadopoulos his package deal as follows: During the forthcoming meetings of the two sides in Vienna under the auspices of U.N. Secretary General Kurt Waldheim, the Greek Cypriots would agree to present a comprehensive proposal for a permanent settlement. This proposal would consist of two parts. The first part would cover constitutional issues in the framework of a bizonal, bicommunal federal system, and the jurisdictions of the cen-

---

[17]Interview with Patroklos Stavrou, April 25, 1999. Heretofore, Stavrou, *Interview*.

[18]Ibid.

tral government. The second part would consist of concrete, written proposals for a territorial settlement, accompanied by a map indicating the percentage of territory that would come under the jurisdiction of the Turkish side in the bizonal, bicommunal federal system.

In essence, Clifford's package deal revolved around the formula of "land for settlement." The Greek Cypriots would get back a respectable amount of land, but they would have to accept a bizonal, bicommunal federal system, which meant that the Turkish side would have control over the land to be placed under Turkish Cypriot jurisdiction. It was a prescription that was reminiscent of the "land for peace" formula in the Arab-Israeli negotiations.

Makarios was extremely reluctant to accept a deal that included a map. The Cypriot leader feared two developments. First, placing dividing lines on a map of Cypriot territory carried the danger that the partition of Cyprus would be accepted. As Stavrou put it, Makarios was torn apart by the idea that he would have to submit a map because he felt "as if he, himself, [were] dividing with a knife the already bloodied body of Cyprus."[19] Another close aide to the Cyprus president, Miltiades Christodoulou, confirmed Makarios's anxiety when he agreed to Clifford's proposal that he submit a map at the Vienna meeting. Christodoulou was present when Makarios said good-bye to Clifford after agreeing to submit the map. As Christodoulou described it, "Makarios was very skeptical, and he was wondering aloud, 'Have I done the right thing?' (*Kala ekana?*)"[20]

Second, Makarios feared that Turkey might not reciprocate and might refuse to come forward with constructive proposals on the territorial issue. In this case, the Cypriot side would appear to have made painful concessions concerning both constitutional and territorial issues without any reciprocity on the part of Turkey. Makarios conveyed his deep apprehension concerning this possibility to Clifford.

Using his diplomatic expertise and persuasion skills that had served several U.S. presidents so well over the years, along with the weight of his role as President Carter's personal envoy, Clifford was able to convince Makarios that his fears were unjustified. After all, Clifford had just been to Ankara and, while he was in Cyprus, he had

---

[19]Stavrou, *Interview.*

[20]Christodoulou, *He Poreia ton Ellino-Tourkikon Scheseon* (The Course of Greek-Turkish Relations), p. 506.

also held meetings with Turkish Cypriot leader Rauf Denktash, in which he pressed his idea of a package deal. The American envoy was able to win over Makarios by using his power of persuasion. According to Tassos Papadopoulos who took part at Clifford-Makarios meeting, the American envoy told the Archbishop: "I will do my best to persuade the Turks to respond to both your contitutional and territorial proposals."[21] This was not tantamount to a promise by Clifford that the Turkish side would reciprocate. Still, even though Clifford made no such promise to the Archbishop, Makarios saw good faith in the presidential emissary and thought that an American envoy of his stature would be able to deliver by convincing the Turks to reciprocate.[22]

By the time the U.S. envoy left Cyprus, it was clear that Makarios had accepted his proposal regarding the submission of a map with extreme apprehension. From then on, the demeanor of the Cypriot leader was characterized by great agony that he had made an enormous concession.[23]

The Cypriot delegation to the Vienna negotiations that were about to commence on March 31, 1977, was headed by Tassos Papadopoulos. Just prior to his departure for the Austrian capital Papadopoulos received a early morning call from Makarios. The Cypriot President wanted to see Papadopoulos on his way to the airport. Papadopoulos arrived in a hurry at the Archbishopric. Makarios offered him coffee and proceeded to discuss several matters irrelevant to the impending negotiations. Papadopoulos respectfully reminded the Archbishop that he had a plane to catch. Makarios went on with his conversation. Finally the Archbishop got up and said good by to his representative at the Vienna talks. Papadopoulos kissed the Archbishop's hand and said farewell. As Papadopoulos hurried to the door, Makarios, as in an afterthought, told him. "Do you think I did the right think to submit a map." Papadopoulos realized that the Archbishop was agonizing over the whole affair.[24]

The concept of an exchange of maps in Vienna appeared to be

---

[21]Based on the account of Tassos Papadopoulos in a conversation with the author, Nicosia, March 10, 2001. Heretofore, Papadopoulos, *Interview*.

[22]Ibid.

[23]Papadopoulos, *Interview*; Stavrou, *Interview*; Christodoulou, *He Poreia ton Ellino-Tourkikon Scheseon* (The Course of Greek-Turkish Relations), pp. 505–508.

[24]This episode was described to the author by Papadopoulos, *Interview*.

quite consistent with the American philosophy of how the negotiations would proceed. First, the Greek Cypriots would submit a map designating that the Turkish zone was to be about 20 percent of Cypriot territory. This figure would certainly be far below Turkish expectations and, therefore, unacceptable to Ankara. Then, the Turkish side would present its own map designating that the territory under its control was to be from 32 to 34 percent, which would be unacceptable to the Greek Cypriots. Then, Clifford would offer a compromise that would return 12 to 13 percent of the Turkish-occupied territory to the Greek Cypriots, while placing 25 to 26 percent under Turkish Cypriot administration. According to American thinking, this would be a reasonable, equitable proposal, as both sides would have to scale down their initial territorial demands. The United States was working as an honest broker and, as such, it would have won the acceptance of both sides.

Given the fact that the Greek Cypriots could be persuaded to accept a proposal that placed 25 percent of Cypriot territory under Turkish Cypriot control, as Karamanlis had told Clifford on February 18, there was real potential for a Cyprus accord in Vienna. It all depended on the Turkish ability to demonstrate some degree of reciprocity in return for the enormous concessions made by the Greek Cypriots. That was what Clifford expected would take place in Vienna. Then, a giant step forward would be taken, which would settle the Cyprus dispute once and for all. Clifford left Cyprus with this mindset, which justified his optimism.

The bottom line was that, if all went well in Vienna, the Carter administration could persuade Congress to repeal the arms embargo against Turkey. Clifford's optimism was echoed when he appeared before the House Committee on International Relations on March 10, 1977, and stated that "with good faith on both sides, a settlement is definitely possible before the end of the year."[25]

Great Expectations and Failure in Vienna

The meetings in Vienna took place from March 31 to April 7, 1978, under the auspices of U.N. Secretary General Kurt Waldheim and his

[25] *New York Times*, March 11, 1977.

special Cyprus representative, Xavier Perez de Cuellar, who later succeeded Waldheim as secretary general. The presence of the U.N. secretary general was a clear sign of the importance of the meetings and
the high expectations of the international community. The Greek
Cypriot delegation was headed by Tassos Papadopoulos.[26] Michael
Triantafillides and Stella Souliotou, who assisted him, were both eminent legal figures in Cyprus. Umit Süleyman Onan, a renowned Turkish Cypriot lawyer, headed the Turkish Cypriot delegation.

In his opening statement at the talks, Papadopoulos clarified the
position of the Greek Cypriot side:

> The Greek Cypriot side has come to Vienna prepared to dis-
> cuss in adequate depth all aspects of the Cyprus problem. It
> will not be helpful and would in our view be premature to
> enter upon a prolonged discussion of the constitutional
> aspect before real progress has been made on *the territorial
> issue,* which we consider to be vitally linked to all aspects of
> the Cyprus problem. That is why it is essential that there
> should emerge during these negotiations a clear and concrete
> picture of what the *Turkish side proposes on the territorial
> aspect.*[27] (Emphasis added.)

Fulfilling Makarios's promise to Clifford, Papadopoulos submitted constitutional and territorial proposals at the negotiating table. A
map designating the area to come under Turkish Cypriot administration in the new federal state accompanied the territorial proposals.
This area was clearly marked on the map and represented 20 percent
of the Republic of Cyprus.[28]

The Turkish Cypriot side was to take the next step. First, it was
expected to submit constitutional proposals. Second, it was expected
to respond to the Greek Cypriot territorial proposals by submitting

---

[26]Papadopoulos described the Vienna negotiations during an address to the
International Symposium of Journalists on the Cyprus Problem, Nicosia, July 18–20,
1977 (Nicosia: Cyprus Journalists Union, 1978), pp. 125–128.

[27]See "Opening Statement by Mr. Tassos Papadopoulos Made on 31 March 1977
at the First Meeting of the Second Phase of the Cyprus Inter-communal Talks," in
Necati Ertekün, *The Cyprus Dispute and the Birth of the Turkish Republic of Northern
Cyprus* (Nicosia: K. Rustem and Brother, 1984), pp. 290–292.

[28]See Christodoulou, *He Poreia ton Ellino-Tourkikon Scheseon* (The Course of
Greek-Turkish Relations), pp. 507–512.

its own proposals on this issue along with a map. This was the meaning of reciprocity as it was understood by Makarios, Clifford, and Waldheim.

In his opening statement, Waldheim echoed the Greek Cypriot side's expectation that the unfolding negotiations were going to tackle the crucial territorial question and that there was going to be a *quid pro quo* by the two sides. Waldheim stated:

> These guidelines [agreed to earlier by the two sides] cover the principal aspects of an agreed, peaceful, durable, and just solution of the Cyprus problem. They include, as we all know, *the territorial and constitutional issues.* It is my understanding that *both sides have agreed to discuss all of these aspects* during the forthcoming meeting. It is further agreed by all concerned that a solution of these very complex problems must of necessity result in a package deal and that, therefore, an agreement on any item would become final in the framework of agreement on all.[29] (Emphasis added.)

The U.N. secretary general left little doubt that the territorial aspect of the Cyprus dispute could not be separated from the constitutional aspect in the negotiations that were about to begin. He confirmed that Clifford's approach to the negotiations would be in the form of a package deal, which had been accepted by Makarios. A statement by Waldheim also confirmed Clifford's expectation that the Turkish side would reciprocate and present its own territorial proposals: "It is my understanding that both sides have agreed to discuss all of these aspects [territorial and constitutional] . . . that will result in a package deal."

The international community had good reason to expect that the Turkish side would abide by its commitment and submit both constitutional and territorial proposals. Instead, Turkish Cypriot representative Onan dashed these expectations at the outset of the negotiations. In his opening statement, he referred to "the political, legal, constitutional, human, and security" aspects of the Cyprus problem. He failed, however, to respond to the Greek Cypriot territorial proposals. It was an indication of things to come.

---

[29]See "U.N. Secretary-General's Opening Statement at the Cyprus Talks in Vienna 31 March 1977," in Ertekün, *The Cyprus Dispute*, pp. 286–287.

Following the submission of the Greek Cypriot territorial proposals, along with a map, Onan refused to reciprocate. He indicated that
the Turkish Cypriot side was not going to present a map and insisted
that the territorial issues were separate from the constitutional questions. At the Vienna talks, the Turkish side took the position that "the
Greek Cypriot side would be expected to make proposals on the territorial aspect and the Turkish Cypriot side would not be expected to
submit any proposals or a map on the territorial aspect."[30] Here lay
Clifford's grave miscalculation. He was able to persuade Makarios to
submit territorial proposals, accompanied by a map, by telling that he
would do his utmost to persuade the Turks to reciprocate. The Turkish side however, was unwilling to reciprocate precisely because it had
no intention of giving up any territory. Reciprocating meant that the
Turkish side would have to come up with a map designating less than
38 percent of Cypriot territory under Turkish control. Even if 34 percent were designated, for instance, which would still be unacceptable
to the Greek Cypriots, it would show some good faith and a desire to
compromise. That was the logic behind Clifford's drive to have both
sides agree to submit a map. Turkey, however, was in no mood to give
up even 1 percent of its conquest in Cyprus.

The Greek Cypriot representative, Tassos Papadopoulos, challenged the Turkish Cypriot representative, Umit Süleyman Onan, five
times to respond to the Cyprus government's territorial proposals.
Papadopoulos told Onan point-blank:

> From all you have said all these days on the territorial aspect,
> am I right in thinking that either you have said nothing on
> the territorial aspect or that your intention is to keep every
> inch of territory that you now occupy?[31]

Onan responded:

> I have not come here to tell you either whether we give any-
> thing back or what we want.[32]

---

[30]For a Turkish Cypriot perspective of the Vienna talks, see Ertekun, *The Cyprus Dispute*, pp. 49–51.

[31]Papadopoulos's account of the Vienna negotiations and his exchange with Onan is found in *International Symposium*, pp. 125–128.

[32]Ibid., p. 126.

This statement made it abundantly clear that Turkey was in no mood to engage in a discussion on a territorial compromise. By adopting this stance at the Vienna talks, the Turkish side left Clifford exposed. Nelson Ledsky, an aide of Clifford, was present at the Vienna negotiations. He made every effort to salvage the situation by trying to convince the Greek Cypriot delegation that the Turkish Cypriots had been forthcoming and that there was adequate ground to continue the negotiations. Ledsky made a special effort to persuade the head of the Greek Cypriot delegation, Tassos Papadopoulos, that there were positive elements in the Turkish Cypriot proposals to keep the negotiations going.

One of the meetings between Ledsky and Papadopoulos in Vienna took place early in the morning and prior to a meeting between the Greek Cypriot and Turkish Cypriot delegations. At this meeting, Ledsky told Papadopoulos that the Turkish Cypriot proposals covered all substantial matters and constituted ground for progress in the negotiations.[33] Papadopoulos told Ledsky that contrary to expectations, the Turkish Cypriot side did not submit any territorial proposals. Papadopoulos reminded Ledsky of what Clifford told Makarios in Nicosia on February 25th. Makarios was persuaded then by Clifford to submit both constitutional and territorial proposals along with a map. The Greek Cypriot side kept its promise, Papadopoulos told Ledsky. On his part, Ledsky kept insisting that the Turkish Cypriots have responded to the Greek Cypriot proposals and that their responses met the criteria set by Clifford. Papadopoulos reminded Ledsky again that Clifford told Makarios that he will do his best to persuade the Turks to submit territorial proposals but they failed to do so. The expectation of the UN Secretary General was also that the Turkish Cypriots would submit territorial proposals. Ledsky appeared to dispute the understanding between Makarios and Clifford. The Cypriot negotiator had with him the minutes of the meeting between Makarios and Clifford which confirmed what the U.S. envoy told Makarios on February 25th. "Here are the minutes of the meeting Mr. Ledsky. You can see yourself," Papadopoulos told Ledsky and pushed the minutes on the table at Ledsky's direction.[34] It was an ignominious end of the meeting as Ledsky could not dispute the min-

---

[33]Papadopoulos, *Interview.*
[34]Based on the account of Papadopoulos, Ibid.

utes of the Clifford-Makarios meeting. It was a sign of things to come in Washigton, because Ledsky's unappreciative attitude toward major Greek Cypriot concessions, represented in reality the overall attitude of the Carter White House towards the Cyprus government's conciliatory policies.

To make matters worse, back in Nicosia, Turkish Cypriot leader Rauf Denktash immediately rejected the Greek Cypriot territorial proposals. He characterized them as unrealistic and called the map designating 20 percent of Cypriot territory under Turkish Cypriot control "a map with imaginary borders." Onan argued that the Greek Cypriot territorial proposals and the map were "not consistent with realities."[35] The realities Onan was referring to concerned the existing territorial status quo whereby 38 percent of Cyprus was under Turkish military occupation.

The Vienna meetings ended in failure as it became clear that the Turkish side was not willing to discuss territorial questions, let alone make territorial concessions. Clifford had created certain expectations not only on the part of the Greek Cypriots, but also at the United Nations. As a result of his miscalculation, the high hopes for a breakthrough in Vienna were dashed. Prompted by the U.N., as a face-saving device, both the Greek Cypriot and the Turkish Cypriot sides agreed to resume the negotiations in the summer of 1978. This allowed U.N. Secretary General Waldheim and the Carter administration to argue that the Vienna negotiations had not really collapsed.

---

[35]See the book by Turkish Cypriot leader Rauf Denktash, *The Cyprus Triangle* (London: K. Rustem and Brother, 1988), p. 84.

CHAPTER 6

The Politics of Deception

April 15, 1977: Carter's Misleading Report to Congress

On April 3, 1977, as the Vienna negotiations were reaching a dead-lock, Cyprus President Makarios suffered a heart attack. As soon the Vienna talks ended on April 7, 1977 the chief Greek Cypriot negotia-tor, Tassos Papadopoulos, rushed back to Nicosia and visited the ail-ing Archbishop at the hospital. Makarios's doctors told Papadopoulos not to engage in any conversation with the Archbishop that could cause him stress. Papadopoulos entered Makarios's room. His chest was tied to cardiac wires. The Archbishop saw his trusted aide and pulled up the sheet to cover his chest. Papadopoulos wished Makar-ios well and he responded: *"Kala ekana pou edosame charte stin Vienni?"*[1] (Have I done the right thing that we have submitted a map in Vienna?) The Archbishop, with his heart weakening, could not hide his great agony.

Makarios had a second heart attack on August 3, 1977, and died that day. Several of his closest associates attributed his first heart attack to the fact that the talks in Vienna were failing. Makarios felt that he had fallen into a trap by accepting Clark Clifford's framework for the negotiations.[2] From the failure at Vienna on, Makarios believed that Clifford and, by extension, President Jimmy Carter, had deceived him. Two episodes indicated clearly that Makarios was not unjustified in his belief that he had been deceived by the Carter administration. One had to do with a report that Carter submitted to Congress. The other concerned a discussion between Makarios and Clifford.

The law imposing the arms embargo against Turkey required that

---

[1]Papadopoulos, *Interview.*
[2]Stavrou, *Interview;* Christodoulou, *Greek-Turkish Relations,* p. 512.

201

the president submit a report to Congress every two months concerning "Progress Towards a Negotiated Settlement" (Public law 94–104). In his April 15, 1977 report to Congress on the issue, Carter explained the Clifford mission to Athens, Ankara, and Nicosia, and commented on the Vienna negotiations:

> *Both leaders* [Makarios and Denktash] recognized that what would be needed to move the Vienna talks forward were *specific discussions* of the *two central issues*: future *territorial arrangements* and the division of responsibility between central and regional governments.[3] (Emphasis added.)

Carter confirmed the essence of what Clifford had promised Makarios. The United States would support a package deal. The territorial aspect of the Cyprus dispute would be interwoven into the constitutional aspect. Both aspects would be discussed and settled at the Vienna negotiations. As far as territory was concerned, the understanding would be that the Turkish side would put forward its own specific territorial proposals once the Greek Cypriots had submitted theirs. Carter's report confirmed that the U.N. secretary general expected the Turkish side to fulfill its promise to submit territorial proposals in reciprocation for those submitted by the Greek Cypriots.

Carter explained what had transpired in Vienna at the beginning of April. He reported to Congress:

> We had not expected any dramatic breakthroughs at these meetings and none occurred. The two sides are still far apart in their views. But the meeting moved forward the process . . .[4]

Carter's official statement to Congress was quite misleading. First, he avoided telling Congress the reasons behind the failure of the Vienna talks. He did so by offering the explanation that no dramatic breakthrough had been expected at the talks. This was highly questionable, however, if two factors were taken into consideration.

First, following his February 1977 trip to Athens, Ankara, and

---

[3]See "The Cyprus Conflict: Message to the Congress Reporting on Progress Made Toward a Negotiated Settlement," April 15, 1977, *Presidential Papers, Carter, 1977,* Book I, pp. 638–639.

[4]Ibid.

Nicosia, Clark Clifford had reported to Washington that a Cyprus settlement was within reach. What Clifford had in mind was a breakthrough in Vienna. Second, the Greek Cypriot delegation had offered
the opportunity for such a breakthrough in Vienna by submitting territorial proposals as Makarios had promised Clifford on February 25,
1977. The map accompanying these proposals placed 20 percent of
Cypriot territory under Turkish jurisdiction in the framework of a
bizonal, bicommunal federation. This 20 percent could have been
increased to 25 percent if Turkey had demonstrated flexibility on constitutional matters. By any standards, these were enormous concessions on the part of the Greek Cypriot side. It had accepted, in essence,
a dividing line across the republic and the granting of a disproportionate share of territory and power to the Turkish Cypriots. The
main reason that Makarios had accepted the idea of a settlement
based on a bizonal, bicommunal federation was Turkey's superior
military power. The Cypriot leadership did make these concessions,
however, painful as they were, and expected some appreciation of its
goodwill by the Carter administration.

Carter's report to Congress, however, failed to acknowledge that
the Greek Cypriot side had made very significant concessions at the
negotiating table in Vienna, a clear demonstration of good faith. This
reflected the Carter administration's attitude toward the Greek Cypriots, which can be contrasted with its policy toward the Turkish side.

Carter adopted a tactic of exaggerating or even inventing Turkish
goodwill regarding Cyprus. This became clear in the Cyprus report
that Carter submitted to Congress on January 20, 1978. One-quarter
of the one-and-a-half-page report was dedicated to Turkish statements of good intentions. As evidence of these good intentions,
Carter lauded a statement made to the press by Turkish Foreign Minister İhsan Sabri Çağlayangil. He pointed out that Çağlayangil had
demonstrated "Turkish flexibility with respect to both the territorial
and constitutional aspects [of the Cyprus question] ... and reaffirmed
the Turkish government's intent to withdraw its troops from the
island once a settlement is in effect. This Administration has welcomed Foreign Minister Çağlayangil's statements as containing a
number of positive elements . . ."[5]

---

[5]See "The Cyprus Conflict: Message to the Congress Reporting Progress Made
Toward a Negotiated Settlement," January 20, 1978, *Presidential Papers, Carter, 1978*,
Book I, p. 127–128.

Çağlayangil's press statement concerning Cyprus was a public relations exercise. The Turkish foreign minister was a dedicated nationalist who espoused the same ideas on Cyprus as other Turkish nationalists, such as Bülent Ecevit. In the Turkish nationalist discourse, Cyprus belonged, in the final analysis, to Turkey, and the island was absolutely indispensable with regard to Turkey's vital interests in the Eastern Mediterranean. Writing in the Turkish newspaper *Güneş* in May 1988, Çağlayangil, who had retired by then, declared that Turkey would never withdraw its army from Cyprus. This was the case because the Turkish forces in Cyprus not only provided security for the Turkish Cypriots, but the island was also an inseparable part of Turkey's defense system, the former Turkish foreign minister argued.[6] This had been Çağlayangil's belief all along. His statement to the press as foreign minister a decade earlier concerning Turkey's intention to withdraw its army from Cyprus had merely been a tactical move in order to impress the U.S. Congress and facilitate Carter in his drive to repeal the arms embargo against Turkey.

Utilizing Çağlayangil's statement, President Carter conveyed to Congress the impression that Turkey had been exhibiting good faith toward a negotiated settlement. Exhibiting utter naïveté, Carter was sending the message that he trusted Turkish intentions concerning Cyprus. Otherwise, the president would not have presented a mere public relations exercise by Ankara to Congress as evidence that Turkey was demonstrating goodwill and the "intent to withdraw its troops from the island once a settlement is in effect." Such a statement was diplomatically meaningless.

Since the Turkish invasion of Cyprus in 1974, the Turkish position has been that it will withdraw its troops from Cyprus once a settlement is reached. Turkey's terms for a settlement, however, have been that it maintain its control of the occupied territory. Since the invasion, Turkey has insisted that its army in the occupied region was there to stay, and that was what Çağlayangil was reconfirming in his article in *Güneş* in May 1988. This condition for a settlement has not only been unacceptable to the Greek Cypriots, but it has also violated U.N. resolutions. The ongoing diplomatic impasse in Cyprus, along

---

[6]Excerpts from Çağlayangil's interview in *Güneş* were published in the Greek Cypriot newspaper *Simerini* und the title "Cyprus is part of Turkey's defense, Çağlayangil declares." See *Simerini*, Nicosia, May 20, 1988.

with the continuing Turkish military occupation, 23 years after Carter gave credence to Turkey's "intentions" to withdraw its army from the country, demonstrates the degree to which Carter misled Congress.

Carter's praise for the statements of Turkish officials, such as Çağlayangil, and the president's confirmation in Congress that this statement demonstrated Ankara's goodwill concerning Cyprus contrasted with the way he treated the Greek Cypriot side. The Makarios government did not merely make statements to the press about its goodwill concerning the negotiations. It submitted concrete proposals and made enormous concessions at the negotiating table in Vienna.

Carter's approach to lifting the arms embargo against Turkey was to downplay the actual concessions and good faith of the Greek Cypriot side as much as possible. On the other hand, Carter overplayed the nominal goodwill of the Turkish side, which was not translated into any reciprocal concessions at the negotiating table. That was exactly Nelson Ledsky's tactic in his encounter with Tassos Papadopoulos during the Vienna intercommunal talks of March 31-April 7, 1977. It was for this reason that Carter chose to leave out of his April 15 report to Congress the very important concessions made by the Greek Cypriot side at the negotiating table in Vienna.

Carter not only avoided mentioning the specific major concessions by the Cyprus government in Vienna, but he also omitted any reference to the Turkish side's refusal to submit its own territorial proposals. This refusal was the primary cause of the failure of the Vienna talks. One might argue that, for tactical reasons, President Carter did not want to assign blame for the failed talks to the Turkish side and thus jeopardize the prospects for future negotiations. The Turkish side maintained that Clifford had misunderstood Ankara's position concerning the timing for the submission of its own map.[7] In this context, Carter reported to Congress that no breakthrough had been expected in Vienna and that the two sides remained far apart. This assessment might have been unfair to the Greek Cypriots, but it might have been necessary as a tool of diplomacy.

However, Carter went far beyond this assessment and stated:

Most important, in my view, is the fact that for the first time

---

[7]Birand, *Pazaremata* (Bargaining), pp. 302–303.

since 1974 concrete, detailed proposals were *put forward by each side covering the two central* [territorial and constitutional] *issues.*[8] (Emphasis added.)

The president, therefore, informed Congress that "each side," both the Greek Cypriots and the Turkish Cypriots, had put forward "detailed proposals . . . covering the two central issues" of the Cyprus question, the territorial issue and the role of the central and regional governments. The question of which side had submitted territorial proposals in Vienna was stated in an official communiqué issued under the auspices of the United Nations after the talks. The communiqué stated the following:

Proposals were submitted on the territorial aspect by the representative of the Greek Cypriot side; and on the constitutional aspect by the representative of the Turkish Cypriot community.[9]

The official U.N. record stated, therefore, that the Greek Cypriot side had submitted detailed territorial proposals, accompanied by a map, and that the Turkish Cypriot side had not submitted any territorial proposals or a map. Given this fact, President Carter's report to Congress, asserting that the Turkish Cypriot side had submitted proposals on both the territorial and constitutional issues of the Cyprus question, was false. Carter deceived Congress by leading it to believe that both sides had submitted territorial proposals in Vienna and that both sides had exhibited good faith.

This misleading report to Congress was the first indication that Carter's administration was seeking ways to lift the embargo, even without any real progress on Cyprus. It was important to the Carter White House that it give Congress the impression that the Turkish side was negotiating in good faith and was not responsible for the continuing Cyprus impasse. The logic behind Carter's report to Congress was that, if there was an impasse, both sides were responsible for

---

[8]See "The Cyprus Conflict: Message to the Congress Reporting on Progress Made Toward a Negotiated Settlement," April 15, 1977, *Presidential Papers, Carter, 1977*, Book I, p. 639.

[9]The text of the Vienna communiqué is found in Ertekün, *The Cyprus Dispute*, p. 319.

it. In this way, through his April 15, 1977 report, Carter introduced the principle of "equal blame, equal distance" between the two sides in the Cyprus dispute. From then on, Carter's policy toward Cyprus became increasingly guided by the operational principle of "equal distance." In the final analysis, this meant that, for the Carter administration, the Greek and Turkish sides in Cyprus were politically and morally equivalent, and, if wrongs had been committed, both sides were equally wrong. Under this logic, the arms embargo against Turkey could not be justified because it assigned the role of the wrongdoer in Cyprus to only one side, the Turks.

Makarios and Clifford: Last Words

Makarios's agony and his feeling of being let down by the Carter administration and the president's personal envoy, Clark Clifford, became evident 10 weeks after the failure of the Vienna meetings. The Cyprus president was in London to attend the annual Commonwealth meeting from June 10 to 15, 1977. Makarios and his entourage were staying at the Grosvenor House Hotel. During his stay in London, on or about June 13, Clifford called Makarios at his hotel. Makarios's close aide, Patroklos Stavrou, described the event.

Stavrou said that he was at the hotel with Makarios when the telephone rang. Stavrou picked up the phone. The call was from Clifford, who recognized Stavrou's voice. The American envoy asked to speak to Makarios. Stavrou was not sure whether Makarios wanted to speak to Clifford, so he attempted a delaying tactic. He told Clifford that Makarios was resting in his suite and that he had to go and notify him personally about the call. Clifford responded that he would wait as long as was necessary.

Stavrou walked into Makarios's room and told him that Clifford was waiting on the line to talk to him. Makarios remained silent for a while and then burst out in anger:

> *Ton apateona! Tolma na mou telefona akomi? De tha tou miliso!* (The impostor. He has the audacity to call me? I am not going to talk to him!)

Stavrou told Makarios that what he said might be the case, but it would be a good idea to talk to Clifford anyway. Makarios responded:

> He fooled me (*me xegelase*). He let me believe that the Turks would be forthcoming in Vienna with their territorial proposals if we submitted a map, and they did not. Now, he has the audacity (*tolma*) to want to talk to me.

In the end, Makarios seemed to relent. Stavrou, still unsure whether Makarios would talk to Clifford, put the U.S. envoy's call through to the archbishop's extension and left the room. Back in his own room, Stavrou checked Makarios's telephone line and realized that it was busy. Makarios was talking to Clifford.

As soon as the conversation ended, Stavrou rushed into the archbishop's room. The Cyprus president told Stavrou that Clifford had invited him to travel to the United States for a thorough medical checkup, given his heart condition. Clifford told Makarios that President Carter cared about his condition and sent his best wishes. Makarios told Clifford that he would travel to the U.S. for a checkup, provided that he would also be able to meet with President Carter. Cyprus was more important than his heart, Makarios reasoned. Clifford told Makarios that he could not promise that such a meeting could be arranged. Makarios thought Clifford's answer was clearly an evasion of the question and was quite a hypocrisy (*ypokrisia*).[10] The Cypriot leader was already distressed over Clifford's failure to persuade the Turks to show flexibility at the Vienna negotiations. Now, Clifford was being evasive regarding whether he could arrange a Washington meeting between Carter and Makarios. This reinforced Makarios's belief that he was being deceived by the American envoy. In turn, this prompted Makarios to decline Clifford's offer to travel to the United States just for heart treatment. The Cypriot leader suffered a second heart attack seven weeks later and died on August 3, 1977.

It appeared that Clifford also felt deceived, not by Makarios, but by the Turkish side. According to Turkish author Mehmet Ali Birand, Clifford made his feelings known to Turkish Prime Minister Süleyman Demirel on May 9, 1977, in London, a month after the early April failure of the Vienna talks. Clifford had accompanied President Carter to London to take part in the annual summit of NATO leaders. As

---

[10]Stavrou, *Interview.*

Birand put it, Clifford discussed the Cyprus issue with Demirel and told him in an annoyed manner: "You have deceived me; you did not support me. Everything has been ruined because you were unable to take a step on the territorial issue and the constitutional question."[11] Clifford reminded Demirel of the problem Carter had with Congress regarding the embargo. According to Birand, Clifford told Demirel: "Don't you understand that, in Congress, we are counting heads?"[12] Despite Clifford's frustration with Ankara, he returned to Washington and continued his effort to lift the embargo, even though he realized that Turkey was in no mood to make concessions on Cyprus.

Years later, in 1991, when Clifford wrote his memoirs, he painted a very sympathetic picture of Makarios. He called Makarios "a legendary figure . . . a crafty but likable politician, tough and single-minded. . . . I developed a sincere affection for him. He had fought for his beliefs all his life and had vision."[13]

Clifford maintained that, had Makarios lived, the Cyprus dispute would have been settled. However, Clifford's account of his meetings with Makarios in February 1977 differed sharply from the accounts of Makarios's aides and those of Birand. For instance, Clifford claimed that Makarios "unexpectedly offered to make some concessions in order to get the talks started" in Vienna. Clifford failed to mention the concessions Makarios made, namely, that he agreed to submit a map at the Vienna talks. More importantly, the American envoy omitted the fact that Makarios took this painful step only after Clifford told him that he would do his best to persuade Turkey to reciprocate and submit territorial proposals as well. Furthermore, Clifford referred to the Vienna negotiations as follows: "As Makarios had promised, the intercommunal talks started in Vienna in April." Yet, he failed to mention what transpired at the talks. The Vienna negotiations failed primarily because the Turkish side refused to produce any territorial proposals.

Clifford's admiration for Makarios was rather puzzling. When Makarios died on August 3, 1977, Clifford was part of a large American delegation at the funeral. The delegation included Chief Justice Warren Burger, members of Congress, and President Carter's sister,

---

[11]Birand, Pazaremata (Bargaining), p. 310.
[12]Ibid.
[13]Clifford, *Counsel to the President*, pp. 626–627.

Ruth Stapleton. Clifford described the following scene at Makarios's funeral:

> One by one, the members of the American delegation approached the open coffin to pay final respects. Some impulse within me caused me to lay my hands upon those of the Archbishop for a brief moment, causing the crowd around the coffin suddenly to hush. Congressman Paul Simon, a member of the delegation, told me later that he felt the crowd was waiting for their leader to rise from his coffin.[14]

Clifford's fond memories of Makarios appeared to be sincere. Since Clifford died in January 1999, we will never know whether he painted a sympathetic portrait of Makarios with the knowledge that the archbishop had no reciprocal feelings toward him. Makarios, the man whom the American envoy admired as a "legendary figure," died with the belief that Clifford, the quintessential Washington insider, had deceived him. Clifford's posthumous respect for Makarios might have been his way of seeking redemption, considering that, wittingly or unwittingly, he had failed to fulfill the promises he made to the archbishop in February 1977. This respect might also have been Clifford's revenge toward the Turkish side, given the fact that he believed Ankara had deceived him in February 1977. Makarios was the Turks' nemesis and was hated by Turkish Cypriot leader Rauf Denktash. Bestowing high praise on Makarios might have been Clifford's way of getting even with the Turks. The laying of Clifford's hands upon those of the dead archbishop was an extraordinary gesture for Greeks and Turks to witness. It might also have been Clifford's way of saying to Makarios, "I am sorry."

Carter's Backpedaling in London: Meeting with Demirel and Karamanlis

Two weeks after the failure of the Cyprus negotiations in Vienna and one week after President Carter submitted his April 15 report on

---

[14]Ibid., p. 627.

Cyprus to Congress, key members of Congress met with Carter to discuss the impasse in the talks. On April 22, 1977, the president met at the White House with the four Democratic members of Congress who had led the campaign to impose the arms embargo against Turkey in 1974 and were considered to be the leading figures of the "Greek lobby." They were House Majority Whip John Brademas of Indiana, Representative Benjamin Rosenthal of New York, Senator Thomas Eagleton of Missouri, and Senator Paul Sarbanes of Maryland.

According to the account the four members of Congress gave to the *New York Times*, they had met with the president to express their concern "about the direction of emerging Administration policy towards Turkey." These congressional leaders wanted to hear from the president, himself, whether linkage between settling the Cyprus issue and supplying arms to Turkey was still the administration's policy. The president had made no mention of such linkage in his report to Congress a week earlier. During the meeting, "the President said that, in light of elections in Turkey, he could not declare publicly that there was a linkage between a settlement on Cyprus and arms for Turkey, but he assured them [the congressional leaders] that such a linkage did exist."[15]

About two weeks later, however, Carter backpedaled as to whether there was linkage between the embargo and the Cyprus issue. This occurred during the annual NATO summit meeting in London the second week of May 1977. On the sidelines of the summit, President Carter met Turkish Prime Minister Süleyman Demirel and Greek Prime Minister Constantine Karamanlis for the first time. Clark Clifford was present at Carter's meetings with the prime ministers.

Clifford first met with Demirel on May 9 to discuss the Cyprus issue. A second meeting between Carter and the Turkish prime minister occurred on May 10 at the Winfield House. Clifford was present at the meeting, along with Secretary of State Cyrus Vance and National Security Adviser Zbigniew Brzezinski. According to Birand, the discussion between Carter and Demirel focused on the embargo. Demirel complained strongly to Carter that the embargo was unjustified and that being treated in such a way by the United States deeply offended the Turkish people. Carter listened patiently to the Turkish complaint and then told Demirel that he had inherited the embargo

---

[15]*New York Times*, June 15, 1977.

and did not believe that it served a useful purpose.[16] At the same time, Carter explained to Demirel that he had to deal with Congress and that, unless there was progress on Cyprus, the embargo would be maintained and Congress would refuse to approve the U.S.-Turkish Defense Cooperation Agreement.

Following the meeting, Carter and Demirel gave a joint press conference. Demirel said very little. He stated that his meeting with Carter had been useful and that he had expressed his "deep concern" to the president. At the press conference, Carter answered four questions dealing with arms sales, the American bases in Turkey, and Cyprus. The final question was as follows:

QUESTION: Is there still a linkage, Mr. President, between the Cyprus question and arms supplies?

THE PRESIDENT: Well, *my own analysis is that the items should be separated,* that progress on Cyprus is very important to the Cypriots, to Turkey, to Greece, and to the rest of the world, certainly including the United States. And I'm sure that the Turkish leaders, the Greek leaders, and Turkish and Greek Cypriots, and we all will do what we can to bring about peace in Cyprus.

I also think that the military cooperation agreement is important. We have strongly recommended that the Congress approve it. An immediate approval is not likely at this point, but I think it is very likely in the future. *That should be a separate item.* And the *third separate item* is the sale of military equipment to Turkey. I think the Congress will very quickly approve the $175 million authorization. So although we all want all three to be realized, *in our minds they are separate,* and each one is unique in its difficulty . . .[17] (Emphasis added.)

Carter's statement in London was the first direct indication that he intended to repeal the arms embargo against Turkey. Certainly, his

---

[16]Birand, *Pazaremata* (Bargaining), pp. 313–314. In his memoirs, Carter made no mention of his London meeting with the prime minister of Turkey.

[17]"Meeting with Prime Minister Suleyman Demirel of Turkey: Remarks to Reporters Following the Meeting," *Presidential Papers, Carter, 1977,* Book I, May 10, 1977, pp. 847–848.

earlier report to Congress on April 15, 1977, had been a sign of things
to come. Yet, in this report, Carter had not dealt directly with the issue
of the embargo and the resumption of military aid to Turkey. In London, however, he stated unequivocally that, in his mind, there existed
no linkage between U.S. arms supplies to Turkey—prohibited by the
embargo—and a Cyprus settlement. In this way, Carter was decoupling the embargo from progress in Cyprus, which centered on the
withdrawal of the Turkish occupation army from the island. The message Carter sent to Turkey on May 10, 1977, was that the Turkish occupation of Cyprus was not an obstacle to improving U.S.-Turkish
relations and that the United States should provide arms to Turkey
even though there had been no progress toward a Cyprus settlement.
The purpose of the embargo, however, had been precisely to make the
resumption of American military aid to Turkey conditional on a
Cyprus settlement

Still, at the same time, Carter asserted that a Cyprus settlement
remained a high priority for him. This appeared to be a contradictory
objective but, in reality, it represented the beginning of the Carter
administration's dual track policy. On the one hand, an effort was
underway to insulate the Cyprus dispute from the issues of military
and economic aid to Turkey, in general, and the Defense Cooperation
Agreement with Turkey, in particular. Since Congress appeared reluctant to separate the embargo and the question of military aid to
Turkey from developments in Cyprus, Carter had adopted a parallel
policy aimed at achieving some progress on Cyprus in order to have
a stronger hand in dealing with the inevitable fight in Congress over
the repeal of the embargo.

On May 10, 1977, the same day President Carter met with Turkish Prime Minister Demirel, he held a meeting with Greek Prime
Minister Karamanlis. Vance, Brzezinski, and Clifford joined Carter for
the meeting. The new U.S. president was meeting the leader who had
restored democracy in Greece, following seven years of military dictatorship from 1967 to 1974, for the first time. The meeting did not
go well, and Clifford had a lot to do with it.

Karamanlis described his meeting with Carter:

> I had the opportunity to present to the American president
> our issues. As a new president, he appeared poorly informed.
> He had with him, however, Clark Clifford, an old hand in

diplomacy and an expert on NATO. Clifford kept interrupting us. Thus, while I was talking about the Cyprus issue, Clifford intervened and raised the question of Greece's return to NATO. I was forced to respond rather abruptly and told them, "You do know why I left NATO. *You are not without blame for this decision of mine.* If you really desire that I return to the alliance, you only have to contribute to settling the Cyprus dispute. After this, our meeting ended in a clearly cold climate.[18] (Emphasis added.)

Following the London meeting with Carter, Karamanlis was left with the impression that the U.S. president was seeking to decouple the embargo from the Cyprus dispute while stressing the need to achieve progress in Cyprus.[19]

In the final analysis, by the spring of 1977, Carter had embarked on an effort to redefine the embargo debate in Washington by taking the initiative away from Congress. To accomplish this, it was necessary for the president to begin changing his message concerning his commitment to the principle of linking the embargo and the Cyprus issue. The first step toward this goal was for Carter to sound ambivalent and send mixed signals to Congress on the issues of the embargo and Cyprus. In the April 15, 1977 report he submitted to Congress, he indicated that the Turks had exhibited good faith at the Vienna negotiations, while this had not been the case. On April 22, 1977, he met with congressional leaders and assured them that he stood by the linkage principle, that is, the lifting of the embargo was linked to tangible progress toward a Cyprus settlement. Less than three weeks later, on May 10, 1977, Carter, while in London, cast very serious doubt on whether the linkage principle was still applicable to Cyprus.

The Trusting Greek Americans

The mixed signals coming out of the Carter White House regarding the embargo began to cause concern among the Greek American community. As a consequence, Greek American leaders, led by Arch-

---

[18] *Karamanlis Archive*, vol. 10, pp. 246–247.
[19] Ibid., vol. 9, pp. 436–437.

bishop Iakovos, head of the Greek Orthodox Church of North and South America, sought to clarify the situation through meetings at the highest government level. On November 18, 1977, a meeting was arranged at the White House between Vice President Walter Mondale and Archbishop Iakovos and other Greek American leaders. Although, initially, Carter was not to be included in the meeting, he dropped by toward the end of the meeting.

In Archbishop Iakovos's account of this White House meeting,[20] he said that the vice president had been very cordial, and he emphasized the friendly, "trusting" atmosphere prevailing throughout the meeting. The archbishop and the Greek American leaders—American Hellenic Educational Progressive Association (AHEPA) Supreme President Peter Derzis, United Hellenic American Congress (UHAC) President Andrew Athens, and archdiocese counsel Peter Kourides—had expressed their frustration over the lack of progress on the Cyprus issue and the administration's silence concerning Turkey's continuing violation of human rights in the area of Cyprus it occupied. Archbishop Iakovos, being the leader of the Greek Orthodox Church in the United States, was especially sensitive to the issue of protecting the Christian Orthodox in Cyprus. He was alarmed at the persistent reports concerning the conversion of Christian churches into mosques in the Turkish-occupied territory, a practice that the Carter administration had failed to address.

Vice President Mondale acknowledged the "justified impatience [of Greek Americans] to see the pre-election promises" regarding Greece and Cyprus fulfilled. Archbishop Iakovos quoted Mondale:

> We recognize that in this period, during which we have been the ones responsible for running the country, we have not succeeded in making any significant progress in the direction you would want and which we would want. I assure you, however, that we are in constant contact with the appropriate officials here and elsewhere. Allow me to say that *under no condition do we renege on our promises* and that in a very short time we should be able to convey to you some good or en-

---

[20]See the interview with Archbishop Iakovos in *The Orthodox Observer*, New York, December 7, 1977. *The Orthodox Observer* is the official publication of the Greek Orthodox Archdiocese of North and South America. In his memoirs, Carter made no mention of this meeting with Archbishop Iakovos at the White House.

couraging news, something we owe to this cause and to you.[21] (Emphasis added.)

As the meeting was coming to an end, President Carter walked in and greeted the Greek American leaders very cordially. According to Archbishop Iakovos, Carter seemed to "echo approximately the same assurances given by the Vice President."[22] The president, who appeared troubled and worried, indicated to the White House guests that they should be disappointed over the lack of progress in resolving the Cyprus question. Carter asked the Greek American leaders for their understanding regarding the fact that he could not discuss his efforts concerning Cyprus publicly.[23]

Archbishop Iakovos and the other Greek American leaders at the meeting failed to pose a credible challenge to what the vice president and president were saying. There were clear signs in April and May 1977 that the president was moving in the direction of de-linking the embargo from the Cyprus issue. The Greek American leaders did not ask for any explanation with regard to the president's misleading report to Congress on Cyprus on April 15, 1977. They also failed to ask the president to clarify his May 10, 1977 statement in London asserting that there was no linkage between arms supplies to Turkey and the Cyprus issue.

Following the White House meeting, Archbishop Iakovos said that he and the other leaders had been more or less satisfied with the meeting for three reasons. First, Carter and Mondale had acknowledged that the disappointment of Greek Americans over the lack of progress on Cyprus was justified. Second, an atmosphere of "trust" had prevailed during the meeting. Carter's use of the words "trust me" had been the key to catapulting him into the White House. Like other Americans, Greek Americans, including Archbishop Iakovos and the other community leaders, trusted the president and vice president when they spoke about "trust."

The third reason for Greek American satisfaction was the reassurance that Carter's pre-election promises were far from forgotten and remained a continuous reminder of an unfulfilled moral obliga-

---

[21] See *The Orthodox Observer*, December 7, 1977.
[22] Ibid.
[23] Ibid.

tion of the administration.[24] In the minds of the Greek American leaders, the fulfilling of campaign promises had to do with trust. This was a rather naïve view of how important foreign policy matters are dealt with in Washington. It was also a reflection of the limitations of Greek American political influence in Washington. The image projected by the Greek American community at that time was that Archbishop Iakovos was its political leader. This was the case despite serious objections by some sectors of the community. One of the skeptics concerning the role of the archbishop as the community's political spokesman was Eugene Rossides, the founder of the American Hellenic Institute (AHI). Rossides had been instrumental in advancing the "rule of law" argument that led to the imposition of the embargo, while AHI became the first Greek American lobbying organization in Washington.

In the end, however, the archbishop's statement that he still trusted Carter carried considerable weight among Greek Americans. Archbishop Iakovos was a charismatic leader, but his political role in Washington was bound to be circumvented by the constitution and the realities of American politics. The separation of church and state constitutes a fundamental principle of U.S. politics.[25]

By the same token, however, the archbishop was dealing with a president whose religiosity was quite evident. President Carter spoke openly about his faith in Jesus Christ. He addressed fellow southern Baptists as "brothers and sisters in Christ." He professed his "commitment to serving God." He also proclaimed: "I have never detected nor experienced any conflict between God's will and my political duty. It's obvious that, when I violate one, at the same time I violate the other."[26]

As the spiritual leader of the Greek American community, Archbishop Iakovos would have uttered exactly the same words to his flock. In the end, the archbishop's trust in Carter and his promises had a lot to do with the fact that he saw a quality in the president that other

---

[24]Ibid.

[25]The principle of separation of religion and politics eroded somewhat in the late 1980s and in the 1990s, when the Christian Coalition became an important player in American politics and a major force in the Republican Party.

[26]See President Carter's "Remarks to Members of the Southern Baptist Brotherhood Commission," Atlanta, Georgia, June 16, 1978, *Presidential Papers, Carter, 1978*, Book I, pp. 1113–1117.

presidents had not had, at least not to the extent that Carter did. When Carter communicated with Iakovos, the archbishop tended to see that there was a bond between them, not so much a political bond because Iakovos was closer to the Republicans, but a spiritual bond, the bond of Christian faith.

Following the November 18, 1977 White House meeting, Archbishop Iakovos's statements were rather optimistic regarding progress on the Cyprus issue, which he envisioned would result in a U.S.-sponsored settlement leading to the end of the Turkish occupation. The archbishop's optimism was not rooted in fact but, rather, reflected his own expectations based on the trust he and most of the Greek Americans had in Carter.

Congressional Anxiety Over Carter's Mixed Signals

On February 3, 1978, the State Department submitted to Congress its annual report on the state of human rights around the globe, which included country reports on Turkey, Cyprus, and Israel and the occupied territories. These three reports made it clear that the Carter administration was about to change course with regard to its Cyprus policy. While Turkey was engulfed by political violence, the report on the state of human rights in the country was positive overall. The report on Cyprus did not treat the area under Turkish military control as "occupied territory." In contrast, in the report on Israel, the areas under Israeli military control were treated as "occupied territories" with all the international implications of this acknowledgement.[27]

Five days after the State Department report was submitted, the four members of Congress who had led the drive to impose the embargo, senators Eagleton and Sarbanes and congressmen Brademas and Rosenthal, sent a letter to President Carter. The letter was dated February 8, 1978.[28] This letter expressed the deep anxiety of these members of Congress, an anxiety shared by other supporters of

---

[27]The sections of the State Department human rights report on Turkey, Cyprus, and Israel are discussed in detail in chapter 11.

[28]See Congressional Record, Senate, 95th Congress, 2nd Session, vol. 124, Part 15, July 21, 1978 to July 31, 1978, p. 22547. The complete text of the letter appears in the Appendix, Document F.

the embargo, that the Carter administration was moving toward lifting the embargo.

These members of Congress reminded Carter of his campaign promises, which had established the principle of linkage between a just Cyprus settlement and U.S. military aid to Turkey. Under the linkage principle, the embargo could be lifted on the condition that Turkey agreed to a just Cyprus settlement leading to the withdrawal of the Turkish occupation army. More importantly, Carter was reminded that he had reaffirmed the linkage principle as president when he met these four members of Congress on April 22, 1977. The four stated in the letter:

> ... we recall and have reposed confidence in your direct assurances at the White House meeting with you that such linkage does indeed exist.[29]

In the letter, the leaders of the drive to impose the embargo also pointed to a pattern of action by the Carter administration that indicated a departure from the linkage principle. They cited five examples of this pattern.

First, for the year 1977, Turkey had received a 40 percent increase in U.S. military aid, from $125 million to $175 million. Carter was reminded that this significant increase was to serve as an inducement for Turkey to take positive action in Cyprus. Turkey refused to compromise in Cyprus and the administration's hope "proved empty," the letter stated.

Second, the Department of Defense had gone beyond the restrictions in U.S. law limiting the amount of military sales to Turkey by using NATO'S Maintenance and Supply Agency in Luxembourg to supply Ankara with weapons. This circumvention undermined efforts to pressure Turkey into working toward a Cyprus settlement.

Third, U.S. Ambassador to Turkey Ronald Spiers had stated in an interview in Ankara that "the embargo doesn't serve any American interest" and that "sanity will prevail and it [the embargo] will be removed." Other high-ranking U.S. military officials had made similar statements. In this way, the administration had encouraged Turkish intransigence concerning Cyprus.

---

[29]Ibid.

Fourth, in the fall of 1977, the United States had sided with very few other countries at the United Nations in order to weaken a General Assembly resolution calling for action in Cyprus. More recently, the February 3, 1978 State Department report on human rights in Cyprus had presented an "unfair and inaccurate report of the tragic events on that island."

Fifth, the State Department's military aid request for the next fiscal year had reduced aid to Cyprus but had maintained the same level of aid to Turkey. Moreover, press reports indicated that the administration was getting ready to request congressional approval of a four-year, $1 billion defense agreement with Turkey without any linkage to progress on Cyprus.

In addition to these five points, the four congressional leaders warned Carter that the approval of military sales to Turkey through a new Defense Cooperation Agreement, without linking arms transfers to that country to a Cyprus settlement, was bound to undermine the pro-Western government of Greece. The warning was an apparent reference to the increasing appeal of opposition leader Andreas Papandreou, the leader of the Panhellenic Socialist Movement (PASOK).

The actions by administration officials, cited by the four congressional leaders, were inconsistent with the linkage principle and pointed only in one direction: President Carter was moving toward the unconditional lifting of the arms embargo against Turkey. In order to illustrate their heightened anxiety and the urgency of the matter, these members of Congress pointed out the following to the president:

> *Our restrained comment* in the face of these developments has largely been due to *the assurance we have received from you* and your representatives that the Administration is committed to pursuing a policy of linkage.[30] (Emphasis added.)

This was a poignant reminder to President Carter that Eagleton, Sarbanes, Brademas and Rosenthal were really unsettled by the actions of his administration. They had shown restraint in their letter because they still had residual trust in Carter's word. Once more,

---

[30]Ibid.

Carter's morality and integrity had come into play. A president with Carter's ethical standing was supposed to be truthful and keep his word.

The February 8, 1978 letter from these important members of the president's party constituted a landmark in Carter's drive to lift the embargo. The five points raised in the letter led to an inescapable conclusion regarding the direction in which Carter administration officials were moving. Still, Carter was given the benefit of the doubt. It was unlikely that the actions of officials in his government had been taken without the approval of the White House and the State Department. It was possible, however, that some of the actions were not known to the president, either because of bureaucratic miscommunication or steps taken by overzealous officials who wanted to see the embargo lifted.

The letter made it known to the president that members of his administration were undermining the fundamental principle of his Cyprus policy, that of linkage. It was up to Carter to either reaffirm his policy of linkage or ignore the letter. Ignoring the letter would be confirmation that all five actions undermining the embargo had indeed taken place with the approval of the White House. Carter ignored the letter. Instead, he continued his quest for ways to convince Congress to lift the embargo. What remained was finding the appropriate way and time to break the news.

Breaking the Promise

The first clear sign that the Carter administration had already embarked on a drive to repeal the embargo came in March 1978. During a routine hearing of the Senate Appropriations Subcommittee on Foreign Operations, Secretary of State Cyrus Vance stated that the proposed Defense Cooperation Agreement with Turkey would be linked to developments in Cyprus. Since the imposition of the embargo in 1974, congressional supporters of the embargo had been arguing against the ratification of the 1976 Defense Cooperation Agreement with Turkey. They had insisted that any defense pact with Turkey should be linked to progress on Cyprus, including the withdrawal of the Turkish occupation army.

Following Vance's remark at the Senate hearing, there was a

strong protest from the government of Prime Minister Bülent Ecevit in Ankara. The Turkish Foreign Ministry informed the American Embassy that U.S. military aid to Turkey should not be linked to Cyprus since such linkage was bound to jeopardize the new Defense Cooperation Agreement between the United States and Turkey.

As a consequence, the State Department acted quickly and issued a clarification. State Department spokesman Hodding Carter III clarified that there was no linkage between the proposed defense pact with Turkey and "specific events in negotiation," meaning Cyprus.[31] This was consistent with President Carter's statements in 1977, when he began the process of de-linking the embargo from a Cyprus settlement. At the same time, Vance's remark at the Senate hearing linking military aid to Turkey and the Cyprus issue was indicative of the difficulty the secretary of state was having reversing his earlier views in support of the embargo. Vance needed a little more time to get used to the idea that, as secretary of state, he was to play a leading role in the fight to lift the embargo. In the end, the February 8, 1978 warning to President Carter by the four members of Congress was coming true. The administration was about to propose a new Defense Cooperation Agreement with Turkey without linking it to Cyprus.

The lifting of the embargo involved a two-pronged effort. First, the Carter administration had to persuade Congress to repeal the embargo. Second, the administration had to find ways to placate the Greek American community. After all, the president had given his word to this community concerning Cyprus.

President Carter and Vice President Mondale still enjoyed the residual trust of Greek Americans when, on March 24, 1978, the president invited a group of congressional leaders, including Greek American Congressman John Brademas, to the White House to inform them of his decision to propose the lifting of the embargo. Not much happened in Congress the week after the meeting because of the Easter break. The storm erupted after Congress returned from the break.

The president was on a visit to Nigeria when, on April 2, 1978, the *New York Times* reported in a front-page article that the Carter administration had decided to push for the repeal of the arms embargo against Turkey. The *New York Times* article was entitled

---

[31]*New York Times*, March 14, 1978.

"President, in Shift, to Seek End of Ban on Arms to Turkey; Carter is Acting Out of Concern that Ankara May Reduce Ties to Atlantic Alliance." The article said that "the Carter Administration, in *a major policy shift*, has decided to urge Congress to end a three-year-old arms embargo against Turkey without waiting first for concessions toward ending the Cyprus dispute, officials said today." (Emphasis added.)

The *New York Times* reported that the decision to lift the embargo had been made by President Carter, himself, just before he departed on an overseas trip. According to the newspaper, Turkey had not been asked to make any pledges to resolve the Cyprus dispute, but Carter administration officials said that the United States expected Turkey to move on the issue once Washington had taken the first step. The report also noted that Carter's decision would pit the administration against the organized Greek American community and supporters of Greece on Capitol Hill. Carter's decision had been made on the advice of Secretary of State Cyrus Vance, Secretary of Defense Harold Brown, and National Security Adviser Zbigniew Brzezinski.[32] In turn, Brzezinski had relied on the advice of Paul Henze, the National Security Council staff officer for Turkey, Greece, and Cyprus.

The *New York Times* report on Carter's about-face fell like a bombshell in the Greek American community as well as in Greece and Cyprus. Just a few months earlier, on November 18, 1977, Vice President Mondale had assured Archbishop Iakovos and other Greek American leaders that the administration would keep its promises concerning Cyprus. At that White House meeting, Mondale told the archbishop that, "in a very short time, we should be able to convey to you some good or encouraging news."[33] Now, with great determination, the Carter administration was calling for the lifting of the embargo. The *New York Times* called this decision a "major policy shift." The *Congressional Quarterly Almanac* wrote that Carter's decision represented "the reversing of his campaign position."[34] There was no doubt that President Carter had reneged on his campaign promises.

Greek Americans were in for a rude awakening on the morning of Saturday, April 2, 1978. "Betrayal" was the term most commonly

---

[32] *New York Times*, April 2, 1978.

[33] *The Orthodox Observer*, December 7, 1977.

[34] See "Military Aid Bill: Turkey Arms Ban Lifted," *1978 Congressional Quarterly Almanac* (95th Congress, 2nd Session, vol. xxxxiv, Washington, D.C., 1978), p. 416.

used by Greek Americans and political leaders in Greece and Cyprus upon receiving news of Carter's about-face.[35] A monthly newspaper published by AHEPA, the oldest and largest Greek American organization, reported the administration's decision to lift the embargo under the banner headline "President Carter Betrays the Greek-Americans and the People of Greece and Cyprus."[36] For weeks following the announcement on lifting the embargo, the Greek American media were full of daily editorials attacking Carter for deceiving the Greek American community to the point that the name "Carter" became synonymous with deception. Still, Greek American leaders expressed the hope that Carter would be unable to persuade Congress to repeal the embargo. One of the key Greek American leaders who maintained such hope was House Majority Whip John Brademas.[37]

The decision to pressure Congress to lift the embargo should not have come as a surprise to the Greek American community, especially the Greek American lobby. President Carter had been sending mixed signals concerning the embargo and the Cyprus question throughout 1977. It was to be a matter of time before he would challenge Congress over this issue. The Greek American lobby was unable to react effectively in April and May 1977, when it became clear that the president was wavering in his commitment to the principle of linking the embargo to progress on Cyprus.

The Greek American community was also unable to react in a meaningful way to the State Department human rights report on Cyprus, which was submitted to Congress on February 3, 1978. This report made it abundantly clear that the Carter administration's policy on the territories occupied by Israel differed from its policy on the area of Cyprus occupied by Turkey. While the former were treated as "Israeli-occupied territories," the latter was considered an area under "Turkish Cypriot Administration."[38] In other words, the Carter administration had moved closer to Ankara's position and had refused to consider the area under Turkish control in Cyprus as "occupied territory." This had profound legal and diplomatic implications for Cyprus and for the question of the embargo. The Greek American

[35]See the Greek American newspaper *Proini*, New York, April 3, 1978.

[36]*The AHEPA Messenger*, New York, April 1978, vol. 1, no. 2.

[37]*National Herald* (Ethnikos Kyrex), April 5, 1978.

[38]The State Department human rights report is discussed in detail in chapter 11.

lobby had failed to recognize the gravity of the situation and had adopted a rather complacent attitude such as the one expressed by Archbishop Iakovos following his White House meeting of November 18, 1977.[39]

As a result of this failure, the Greek American lobby did not initiate a massive, coordinated reaction to President Carter's wavering concerning the embargo throughout 1977 and early 1978. In turn, this Greek American complacency tended to encourage the administration to move gradually in the direction of lifting the embargo. Thus, when Greek Americans were informed on April 2, 1978, of the decision to lift the embargo, they were caught off-guard primarily because of their own complacency.

Reaction in Greece

In Greece and Cyprus, there was a storm of protest among political leaders, the media, and the public at large. The overwhelming feeling among the political leadership and the public was that President Carter had stabbed the Greeks in the back. George Mavros, leader of the centrist, pro-Western United Democratic Center Party (EDHK), stated that Carter's decision to push for the repeal of the embargo was incomprehensible, given his earlier pledges. Mavros warned that the lifting of the embargo would lead to a Greek-Turkish conflict. "The existing anti-American wave in Greece is bound to assume dangerous proportions," he warned.[40] Key leaders of the ruling New Democracy Party, including Prime Minister Constantine Karamanlis, warned that the repeal of the embargo would lead to a wave of anti-Americanism, providing a major boost to socialist leader Andreas Papandreou and bringing him closer to power.[41]

On March 31, 1978, the Carter administration notified the Greek government of its intention to seek the repeal of the embargo. This was done through the American Ambassador in Athens, Robert McCloskey, who informed Greek Deputy Foreign Minister Evangelos Averof of the administration's decision. At the time, Averof was the

---

[39]See Archbishop Iakovos's statement in *The Orthodox Observer*, December 7, 1977.

[40]*Proini*, April 3, 1978.

[41]*New York Times*, April 2, 1978; *National Herald* (Ethnikos Kyrex), April 3, 1978.

second-most important figure in the government and in the New Democracy Party after Karamanlis. Averof had many years of experience in Greek foreign affairs and was perhaps the staunchest pro-American leader in the ruling New Democracy Party. Upon receiving the news from Ambassador McCloskey, Averof informed him of the Greek public's overwhelming opposition to the lifting of the embargo. The foreign minister asked whether the United States had received any commitment from Turkey to be flexible on Cyprus. The ambassador, apparently responding with great discomfort, said that Turkey had made no promises to the United States with regard to Cyprus.

Realizing that the Carter administration had reneged on its pledges and was seeking to lift the embargo unconditionally, Averof told McCloskey:

> The damage is done. *Those who preach anti-Americanism in Greece now appear to be vindicated both morally and politically.* On the other hand, those who follow a pro-western policy are in retreat and find it difficult to defend their position in front of public opinion. . . . The influence and prestige of the pro-Western camp in Greece is still great, but it cannot sustain continuous blows. If this took place [if the pro-Western camp succumbed to the blows], then the consequences for the West and for the United States would be serious. Even the American bases in Greece would be gravely at risk and could be removed.[42] (Emphasis added.)

Averof asked the ambassador to convey the grave fears of the Greek government to Washington. Averof's concern regarding the impact of the lifting of the embargo on the Greek political scene was prescient. What the Greek foreign minister conveyed to the ambassador was the real prospect that Andreas Papandreou would come to power riding a wave of anti-Americanism.

On April 11, 1978, Prime Minister Karamanlis received Ambassador McCloskey, who gave him a personal letter from President Carter dated April 6, 1978. In the letter, Carter officially informed Karamanlis of his decision to seek repeal of the embargo. Upon receiving the letter, Karamanlis told McCloskey:

---

[42]*Karamanlis Archive*, vol. 10, p. 174.

The United States has succumbed to the Turkish policy of blackmail.... *The Greek Cypriots have made concessions which satisfy most of Turkish demands.* They accept a bizonal federation, a weak central government, and are willing to accept 25 percent of Cypriot territory to be under Turkish Cypriot control. It is impossible to understand the workings of the Turkish mind. The Turks are rejecting a favorable Cyprus settlement.... The Turks even refuse to submit any proposals on Cyprus. This decision [to seek the lifting of the embargo] is a mistake. Instead of making Turkey more reasonable, it will make Ankara more intransigent. As a result, *there is not going to be any progress on Cyprus,* and there will be no settlement of the Aegean issues.[43] (Emphasis added.)

Karamanlis repeated these positions in his April 18 written response to Carter's letter. In Karamanlis's letter, the Greek prime minister added the warning that the lifting of the embargo would make it more difficult for him to improve Greece's relations with NATO. It was an indirect warning that anti-Americanism was on the rise and so was the popularity of Andreas Papandreou. The warnings of the Greek government fell on deaf ears in Washington.

NATO Summit in Washington: Carter's Admiration for Ecevit

Thirteen months later, the Greek and Turkish prime ministers, Karamanlis and Ecevit, were in Washington to attend the annual NATO summit, which took place from May 28 to 31, 1978. By that time, Washington's relations with Ankara resembled a honeymoon due to Carter's public commitment to seek the lifting of the embargo. This honeymoon was quite evident during the summit meetings and during Carter's White House meeting with Ecevit on May 31.[44] During the meetings in Washington, Carter developed an affinity for Ecevit. What transpired at the NATO summit was indicative of Carter's admiration for Ecevit. The alliance names an honorary president

---

[43]Ibid., pp.188–189.

[44]See Mehmet Ali Birand, *The Generals' Coup in Turkey: An Inside Story of 12 September 1980* (London: Brassey's Defense Publishers, 1987), p. 70. In his memoirs, President Carter failed to mention his meetings with Ecevit.

every year, and this president is selected from among the leaders of the member states on a rotational basis. For the year 1979, the honorary president was Turkish Prime Minister Bülent Ecevit.

On May 29, 1978, all the leaders of NATO countries spoke at the Washington summit meeting. Following Ecevit's speech, the most enthusiastic applause came from President Carter. The European leaders were more restrained as they had a more realistic view of the situation in Turkey, which was deteriorating rapidly. Several of them had already dealt with Ecevit and were more conscious than Carter was that it had been Ecevit who ordered the invasion of Cyprus in 1974. This was particularly the case with the British, who were represented at the summit by Prime Minister James Callaghan. He had dealt directly with Ecevit during the 1974 Cyprus crisis and his experience with the Turkish leader had been negative. At the NATO summit, however, Carter could not hide his admiration for Ecevit. On May 30, 1978, Carter hosted an official dinner in honor of the leaders of NATO countries. During his toast at the dinner, Carter had this to say about Ecevit:

> I've enjoyed very much being with our President [sic] this evening, Prime Minister Ecevit. *I've learned a lot about politics from him.* We have very distinguished members here, and I called one over to meet him tonight, Senator Bob Morgan of North Carolina. And when he came over, Prime Minister Ecevit told him that he used to live in North Carolina and worked for the Winston-Salem newspaper, and he said. "I've even got Tar Heel cufflinks on." So he's [Ecevit's] taught me a great deal.[45]

The praise Carter gave Ecevit indicated that the two had established a good relationship. Carter's flattery also conveyed the impression that somehow the Turkish leader practiced politics the way it was practiced in the United States, especially given Ecevit's seeming familiarity with American culture. At that time, however, the political situation in Turkey was moving toward chaos as the country became

---

[45]"North Atlantic Summit: Toast of the President at the Dinner Honoring the Heads of Delegation, March 30, 1978," *Presidential Papers, Carter, 1978*, Book I, p. 1016.

engulfed by waves of political violence and terrorism. Furthermore, Ecevit's legacy in Turkish politics was that of a warrior, the leader who had invaded and occupied Cyprus. Above all, for Turks, Ecevit was the conqueror of Cyprus. After July 1974, the Turkish prime minister was referred to in Turkey as *Karaoğlan* Ecevit. In Turkish folklore, the name *Karaoğlan* refers to heroic warriors. It was this *Karaoğlan* Ecevit, the warrior, that Carter came to admire in the naïve belief that he was embracing a pacifist of the type found in the U.S. Democratic Party.

This view of Ecevit as a social democrat dedicated to social justice was not limited to the Carter White House. A number of other liberal Democrats saw Ecevit in a similar light. They included Senator George McGovern of South Dakota, who had led the effort in the Senate to lift the embargo. They also included journalists of the caliber of Lawrence Stern.[46] This was quite remarkable considering that Stern was one of the strongest critics of the Nixon administration and its policies toward the Greek junta. Stern had been especially harsh in his criticism of Secretary of State Henry Kissinger and his handling of the Cyprus crisis in the summer of 1974, a crisis revolving around the Turkish invasion of Cyprus, ordered by Turkish Prime Minister Bülent Ecevit.

Karamanlis to Carter: Keep the Embargo

On May 31, 1978, Greek Prime Minister Constantine Karamanlis met with President Carter for an extensive exchange of views. Present at the meeting on the American side, besides Carter, were Vice President Walter Mondale, Deputy Secretary of State Warren Christopher, Deputy National Security Adviser David Aaron, State Department Counsel Matthew Nimetz, Assistant Secretary for European Affairs George Vest, and Paul Henze, National Security Council staff officer for Turkey, Greece, and Cyprus. Henze's presence at a U.S.-Greek summit meeting was an indication of how deeply he was involved in the effort to lift the embargo and how trusted he was by Brzezinski.

During the meeting, the views presented by Karamanlis on Greek-Turkish relations, Cyprus, the Aegean, and NATO were almost

---

[46]Stern, *The Wrong Horse*, p. 157.

identical to the ones he had presented to Clark Clifford in Athens in February 1977. Meeting face-to-face with the U.S. president in the White House, Karamanlis gave Washington a warning:

> ... I adopt moderate positions *at the expense of my popularity* because I believe that the problems with Turkey should be solved for the mutual benefit as well as for the sake of the Alliance. . . . The lifting of the embargo might contribute to the improvement of American-Turkish relations. In Greece and Cyprus, however, there are bitter feelings and *the anti-American sentiment is bound to increase*. . . . When I arrived in Greece [in July 1974] I found a strong wave of anti-western and anti-American sentiment. I struggled to persuade this public that Greece belongs to the West, and *I paid a price.* In 1974, I won 74 percent of the vote. In the last elections [in 1977], I barely received 42 percent of the vote. If this bitterness of the Greek people continues, *I am not sure if I can control the situation.* I ask you Mr. President to take this point seriously.[47] (Emphasis added.)

In this way, Prime Minister Karamanlis made it clear that the lifting of the embargo would undermine his party's rule and lead to the election of the anti-American Panhellenic Socialist Movement (PASOK) and its leader, Andreas Papandreou. Washington was being warned at the highest level, in a friendly but direct way, that the lifting of the embargo would have very negative consequences in Greece. It would not facilitate a Cyprus settlement and would also harm U.S. interests in the region. This was a plea for understanding from inside the White House by Karamanlis, a towering figure in post-Second World War Greece and a sincere friend of the United States throughout his life.

Less than 48 hours after his meeting with President Carter, the Greek prime minister repeated his warning concerning the negative consequences of lifting the embargo to Congress. This took place on June 2, 1978, during a meeting between Karamanlis and members of the House International Relations Committee. The chairman of the committee was Clement Zablocki, Democrat of Wisconsin, who was

---

[47] *Karamanlis Archive*, vol. 10, pp. 242–243, 246.

an ardent supporter of lifting the embargo. Karamanlis answered about 30 questions from members of the committee. He was asked about the May 20, 1978 Turkish Cypriot proposals regarding Famagusta (Varosha), which the Carter administration had been promoting in Congress as a gesture of Turkish goodwill. Karamanlis left no doubt concerning his perception of these proposals. He told the committee members that "the Turkish Cypriot proposals on Cyprus are so poor that they constitute a great insult to common intelligence."[48]

Then Karamanlis was asked a question implying that he did not object to the lifting of the embargo. This rumor had been circulating in the House International Relations Committee during the last week of May 1978, and Karamanlis found the opportunity to put it to rest. He was asked to comment on a statement by someone in the Carter administration a week earlier. This official had asserted that, if the embargo were lifted, the Greek prime minister would not make it a domestic issue in Greece. Karamanlis's response was instant and blunt. He declared:

> First, no one in the American government has the authorization to speak in my name. Second, the question is not whether I would or would not make a domestic issue of the lifting of the embargo. It is the Greek people who are going to make it an issue. *The lifting of the embargo could even lead to the fall of my government and to my resignation.*[49] (Emphasis added.)

In this way, the Greek prime minister left no doubt that he regarded the lifting of the embargo as a threat to the survival of his pro-Western government. He had warned President Carter, in person, not to lift the embargo, and he was repeating his warning to Congress. Karamanlis's prescient warning was not taken seriously by the Carter administration. To a degree, this response reflected an old attitude in Washington of taking Greece for granted. Turkey, on the other hand, was a country that the U.S. national security bureaucracy rarely took for granted and always feared it might lose.

Above all, however, there was the Carter administration's inabil-

---

[48]Ibid., p. 252.
[49]Ibid.

ity to comprehend, let alone appreciate, the depth of feeling of the Greek people concerning Cyprus in the aftermath of the Turkish invasion of Cyprus. The invasion and subsequent Turkish occupation of Cyprus had left a deep scar in the Greek psyche and had wounded the honor of the nation. For the Greeks, this trauma was directly associated with U.S. policies in the region.

American policy-makers, however, tended to downplay Greek national pride. They saw the appeal of Andreas Papandreou more in terms of demagoguery and less in terms of tapping into historical memory and a deep sense of being wronged by Turkey, a close ally of the United States. Papandreou was a charismatic leader whose message to the Greek people was not devoid of demagoguery. Yet, it was not his demagoguery that generated the deep sense of being wounded among Greeks. Rather, it was the real tragedy that had befallen Cyprus and the role the United States had played in this tragedy.

On the other hand, while the Carter administration tended to dismiss the depth of Greek feeling concerning Cyprus, it was extremely sensitive to Turkish sentiments and took pains not to act in any way that might be interpreted as offensive to Turkish national pride. When it came to national issues, the feelings of the Turkish people were always uppermost in the minds of Washington policy-makers. This attitude of the Carter administration fit the long-held bureaucratic perception in Washington that the Turks were a proud people and tough to please, while the Greeks were presumed to be "preemptively accommodating."[50]

Successive administrations made a similar mistake when a rather dismissive attitude toward popular sentiment permeated their policies toward the Shah's Iran. In Iran, the consequences of an American attitude that dismissed the sentiments of the Iranian people and their discontent with the Shah were catastrophic. This attitude was a by-product of realpolitik. The Iranian revolution that took place on Carter's watch was a disaster for U.S. interests in the Gulf region. In Greece, there was no revolution. Instead, a charismatic leader, Papandreou, and his party, PASOK, came to power democratically by riding a wave of anti-Americanism and promising radical change in domestic and foreign policies.

Carter's decision to lift the arms embargo against Turkey pro-

---

[50]See Couloumbis, *The United States, Greece, and Turkey*, p. 69.

vided Papandreou with a powerful weapon against the pro-Western government of Karamanlis, a weapon that fanned the flames of anti-Americanism. After all, Papandreou held the United States responsible for the seven-year dictatorship, for the coup against the Cyprus president, Archbishop Makarios, and for the Turkish invasion of Cyprus. The main slogans of his socialist party, PASOK, established in September 1974, were "National Independence," "Greece for the Greeks," "Free Cyprus," and "Out With NATO and the American Bases." When Papandreou was informed of Carter's decision to lift the embargo, he proclaimed:

> ... it is worth commenting on the cynicism of an Administration [Carter's] that pretends to care about human rights. The Carter Administration does not hesitate to arm the country [Turkey] which in collaboration with the Nixon Administration launched in 1974 the brutal invasion against tiny Cyprus.... Lifting the embargo now constitutes a direct threat against Greece's territorial integrity...[51]

Then, Papandreou called for the closing of the American bases in Greece and Greece's withdrawal from NATO. The meteoric rise of PASOK to power had a lot to do with U.S. policies toward Greece, Cyprus, and Turkey and, especially, the lifting of the arms embargo against Turkey.

---

[51]See *Proini*, April 3, 1978.

CHAPTER 7

Persuading a Reluctant Congress

Restoring Presidential Preeminence in Foreign Policy

By the spring of 1978, after a little more than one year in office, the political standing of President Jimmy Carter was quite low. He was generally considered a weak president who tended to moralize, had great difficulty with his own party, the Democrats, in Congress, and had few domestic accomplishments.[1] This was reflected in opinion polls. By May 1978, Carter's approval rating had dropped to 30 percent.[2]

Foreign policy, a field in which the president traditionally enjoys an advantage over Congress, was an arena where Carter could shore up his weakened presidency. It is not uncommon for presidents to seek foreign policy successes when their public approval ratings are low. Congress appeared reluctant to cede the clout it had gained in foreign policy in the immediate aftermath of the Vietnam War and Watergate. This was a major reason for the Carter White House's complaints about congressional "veto power" in foreign affairs.[3] If Carter could achieve victories in foreign policy, an area in which Congress had been seen as encroaching on presidential authority, it would constitute a step toward restoring the president's authority in the conducting of foreign policy. It would also help improve Carter's domestic standing.

In the years following Watergate, the imposition of the embargo on arms sales to Turkey represented one of the boldest, if not the boldest, actions taken by Congress in the realm of foreign policy. The

---

[1] See, for instance, the *Time* magazine essay by Harry Grunwald, "Are We 'Destroying' Jimmy Carter?" *Time*, May 15, 1978, pp. 97–98; Hedrick Smith, "A Changed Man, A Changed Office, Not Yet in Step," *New York Times*, May 21, 1978.

[2] *Time*, ibid., p. 18.

[3] Smith, "A Changed Man," *New York Times*, May 21, 1978.

embargo legislation imposed conditions concerning the way the executive branch could conduct foreign policy. President Gerald Ford, the Pentagon, and the State Department under Secretary of State Henry Kissinger fought Congress with tenacity in order to regain the executive branch's prerogatives in foreign policy. In the end, they lost when Congress voted on October 3, 1974, to impose an arms embargo against Turkey.

President Ford clearly saw the embargo question as a matter concerning the president's ability to carry out his duties in the management of foreign policy. Before the imposition of the embargo, Ford met with the leaders of the embargo effort in the House and Senate. The House members were Democrats John Brademas, Paul Sarbanes, and Benjamin Rosenthal, while the effort in the Senate was led by Thomas Eagleton. As President Ford put it, " I tried to persuade them that if we stopped delivery of arms for which the Turks had paid already, they would probably respond by closing down vital intelligence facilities we have been using for years near the border with the Soviet Union. I tried to convince Rosenthal in particular that a weakening Turkey would imperil the future security of Israel." Then Ford stated the following:

> None of my arguments made any headway. *Congress was determined to interfere with the President's traditional right to manage foreign policy*, and if this interference had dire consequences for the country as a whole, well, that was just too bad.[4] (Emphasis added.)

Ford's description of the embargo question in these terms made it clear that he and Congress were locked in battle over the issue. Indeed, the embargo became a test of wills between the White House and Congress over the degree to which Congress can curtail presidential power in the conducting of foreign policy. The Eastern Mediterranean became a major arena where the president and Congress tested their wills.

Ford's Secretary of State, Henry Kissinger, viewed the embargo issue in a similar vein. Referring to the Cyprus crisis of July and August 1974 and the ensuing debate in Washington, Kissinger wrote:

---

[4]Ford, *A Time to Heal*, pp. 137–138.

Ford was not—nor could have been—sufficiently familiar with the details of the issues relating to Cyprus to reverse course—even if the latitude for it existed, which I doubt. Thus, for better or worse, I as the principal link to the previous administration must assume the major responsibility for the decisions.[5]

Thus, Kissinger's views on the subject of Cyprus and the embargo controversy in Washington assume added significance because, under the circumstances, he was the most important defender of ensuring that the management of foreign policy remained a presidential privilege. In his latest book, *Years of Renewal*, Kissinger dedicated a chapter to Cyprus, including his handling of the crisis of July and August 1974 and the debate in Washington over the congressional arms embargo against Turkey. Kissinger opened his chapter on Cyprus as follows:

The Cyprus crisis turned out to be a seminal event for Ford's presidency. . . . It also had the effect of launching the Ford Administration into an immediate and totally unanticipated *clash with Congress*. In the first four months of the Ford presidency, Congress cut off military aid to Turkey. . . . Once a pattern of *congressional micromanagement* was established, comparable measures followed in short order: the Jackson-Vanik and the Stevenson Amendments in December 1974, severely restricting trade and credits to the Soviet Union; the cutoff of aid to Indochina in March 1975; the prohibition against assistance to groups in Angola resisting a Cuban expeditionary force in December 1975; and a host of restrictions on various other activities. The trend *to limit presidential discretion* in foreign policy has continued—if not accelerated—in the interval.[6] (Emphasis added.)

In the end, as Kissinger confirmed, the embargo question was not just a matter concerning ethnic conflict on a small, distant island in the Eastern Mediterranean or the proper role of the United States in

---

[5]Kissinger, *Years of Renewal*, p.194.
[6]Ibid., p. 195.

this conflict. In fact, the embargo represented something much deeper. The embargo and the ensuing debate over it became the domain in which the presidency and Congress clashed over the executive branch's preeminence in foreign policy. Congress was in the process of curtailing presidential discretion in foreign affairs, while the president was fighting to re-establish his preeminence. The Cyprus crisis and the embargo debate set the stage for a longer-term struggle between the presidency and Congress. The October 1974 embargo on arms sales to Turkey became the harbinger of a series of congressional actions in foreign policy. Within 14 months of the imposition of the embargo, Congress took action affecting U.S. policy toward the Soviet Union, the Far East, and Africa.

In other words, the Cyprus crisis of the summer of 1974 and the involvement of Congress in the affair forced the retreat of the White House from foreign policy matters where, institutionally, the president had previously had the first word. Kissinger saw this as a clash between the presidency and Congress, with the latter attempting to take away from the president the right to execute the day-to-day tactics necessary to carry out U.S. foreign policy around the globe.[7]

The State Department and Pentagon bureaucracies obviously shared this view. In the end, by opposing the embargo, Kissinger was defending not only the president's privileges in foreign policy, but also the vested interests of the enormous national security bureaucracy.

The Cyprus crisis and the resultant congressional arms embargo against Turkey were setting a precedent whereby the president had to cede even more power to Congress in the conducting of foreign policy. This congressional assertiveness in foreign policy was hardly new. The Cyprus crisis and the embargo represented the fourth time the pendulum had swung toward Congress's side in American history.[8]

---

[7]Ibid., p. 233.

[8]The first time congressional assertiveness in foreign policy occurred was between 1837 and 1861, and it encompassed the presidencies of Martin Van Buren, William Harrison, John Tyler, James Polk, Zachary Taylor, Millard Fillmore, Franklin Pierce, and James Buchanan. The second time was between 1869 and 1897 and covered the terms of presidents Ulysses S. Grant, Rutherford B. Hayes, James Garfield, Chester Arthur, and Grover Cleveland. The third time was between 1917 and 1933 and covered the second term of President Woodrow Wilson as well as the terms of presidents Warren Harding, Calvin Coolidge, and Herbert Hoover. See Thomas Frank and Edward Weisband, *Foreign Policy by Congress* (New York: Oxford University Press, 1979), pp. 5–6.

The question was not only whether Congress had asserted itself in foreign affairs by imposing the embargo, but also how long such congressional predominance would last. Greek American mobilization and lobbying did influence Congress in its decision to impose the embargo. Still, this congressional initiative challenging the president's policies in the Eastern Mediterranean took place in a political environment in which relations between the executive branch and Congress were being redefined to favor Congress.[9]

Since President Ford and his secretary of state had failed to dissuade Congress from imposing the embargo, it was the Carter White House's turn to wrestle back the authority that the executive branch believed was being usurped by Congress. Consequently, the repeal of the embargo would serve to restore the proper balance between the president and Congress. As soon as he took office, Carter and his rather inexperienced team from Georgia ran into trouble with Congress, which was controlled by the president's own Democratic Party.

The Carter administration's primary argument in support of lifting the embargo was couched in national security considerations. As such, the argument could provide political cover for Carter's failure to keep his promises to Greek Americans concerning Cyprus. This could be done by explaining that promises made could not be kept because of changed circumstances and the intervening of international factors that could not have been anticipated. In the case of the embargo, the revolutionary turmoil in Iran was such a factor, which made Turkey's strategic position and regional role even more important than before. This would be a reasonable explanation for Carter's inability to keep his promises.

At the same time, the need to elevate the presidency to its appropriate standing, so that the president, who believed that he was a paragon of morality, could do more good, could have provided additional justification for Carter to shift policies and lift the embargo. A less self-righteous president might have found ways to justify policies that violated earlier pledges. Yet, Carter simply refused to acknowledge that he had not kept his promises, another indication of his moralizing attitude.

While Carter was able to attain some success in foreign affairs, especially regarding the Camp David accords, in the end, it was for-

---

[9]Ibid., p. 35.

eign policy, especially the hostage crisis in Iran, that undermined his presidency. The fact that American diplomats were held hostage inside the U.S. Embassy in Tehran throughout 1980 and Carter failed to secure their release confirmed to Americans that he was, indeed, a weak president who did not deserve another term. The Soviet invasion of Afghanistan in December 1979 posed another grave challenge to the Carter presidency. For Carter's domestic critics, this act of Soviet aggression was yet another sign of American weakness. Republican presidential candidate Ronald Reagan took full advantage of the perception that Carter was a weak president, and he rode to victory in the November 1980 election.

The year 1978 gave Carter a number of foreign policy successes, such as the Panama Canal Treaties and the sale of arms to Israel and friendly Arab countries such as Egypt and Saudi Arabia. His most important foreign policy accomplishment, however, was the signing of the Camp David accords in September 1978. From the perspective of the Carter White House, the lifting of the embargo on arms sales to Turkey was another important foreign policy success, especially since it was a sign that Congress's encroachment on foreign policy was diminishing.[10]

The White House Strategy to Repeal the Embargo

Throughout the cold war, the U.S. foreign policy agenda was dominated by relations with the Soviet Union, communist China, and the communist world in general, as well as the formulation of policies towards communism on a global level. Arguments over the Soviet communist threat were routinely employed by the White House in its effort to influence Congress when it appeared reluctant to follow the executive branch's foreign policy strategy. It was the communist threat and the fear of the "domino effect" that led to the "Gulf of Tonkin Resolution" and the subsequent involvement of the United States in the disastrous Vietnam War. According to the domino effect, if the United States had allowed Vietnam to fall into communist hands, the rest of Southeast Asia would have followed suit. This logic

---

[10]See *Washington Post*, August 3, 1978. Brzezinski considered the lifting of the embargo to be one of the major foreign policy successes of the Carter administration. See Brzezinski, *Power and Principle*, pp. 528–529.

led the United States into deeper military involvement in the Vietnam quagmire.

In a similar vein, President Ford used the standard cold war arguments when he made an unsuccessful effort to repeal the embargo in the summer of 1975. As Ford put it, the refusal by Congress to repeal the embargo represented "the most serious wrong decision since I have been in Washington, which is 27 years." Then President Ford explained why the congressional embargo was wrong:

First, they [the members of Congress] haven't solved the Cyprus problem. No. 2, [the embargo] weakened NATO. No. 3, because of the Turkish aid embargo, they [the Turks] have lessened our own national security capability by preventing us from using intelligence-gathering installations.[11]

Ford's statement that Congress's refusal to repeal the embargo represented the worst decision it had made since 1948 was an exaggeration *in extremis,* but exaggeration was a political necessity in order to prevail over a reluctant Congress.

Ford was partially successful in his efforts to persuade Congress to lift the embargo. On October 2, 1975, the House of Representatives, succumbing to heavy administration pressure, voted for a partial lifting of the embargo. Congress did not vote for the total lifting of the embargo at the time because it was still in a defiant and assertive mood in the wake of the Vietnam War and the Watergate scandal. The American public was still looking for an administration that would bring catharsis to the executive branch and restore the moral authority of the presidency. Despite Ford's personal integrity, this could not be accomplished with the remnants of the Nixon administration and with Kissinger, the master of realpolitik, still at the helm of foreign policy.

Where Ford failed, Carter was able to succeed by prevailing over Congress and repealing the embargo. Ironically, Carter employed the arguments Ford and Kissinger had used, which focused on national security. In addition to the forcefulness of these arguments, Carter had two significant advantages over the Ford administration. Carter had a reservoir of moral persuasion that Ford's secretary of state,

---

[11] *Washington Post,* August 7, 1975.

Henry Kissinger, could not employ effectively on Capitol Hill. Second, Carter was dealing with a Democratic Congress. These were the factors that made the difference and enabled Carter to persuade a highly skeptical Congress to repeal the embargo. It was an uphill struggle, however, and Carter had to use all the power and authority of the presidency and put his own personal prestige on the line in order to win the congressional battle to lift the embargo.

The White House strategy in dealing with Congress on the embargo issue was described in two White House memoranda. One was addressed to the president, and the other was directed by the president to members of Congress.

The first memorandum, dated May 17, 1978, was written to the president by Frank Moore, the White House congressional liaison. Moore was a good political friend of Carter's in Georgia, and the president wanted to assign the important job of relations between the White House and Congress to an entrusted individual.[12] The coauthor of the memorandum was Bob Beckel, an assistant to Moore.

The Moore-Beckel memorandum sketched the strategy to be followed on the embargo issue in the Senate and House of Representatives. This memorandum was written barely 48 hours after Carter had won a major congressional battle involving the sale of fighter planes to Israel, Egypt, and Saudi Arabia. The sale was opposed by the majority of the Democrats in the Senate, while the Jewish lobby worked hard to defeat it. In the end, Carter prevailed by relying on Republican votes.[13]

From the outset, the May 17, 1978 memorandum indicated to the president that winning the embargo vote was going to be an uphill battle. Majorities on Capitol Hill "may be put together with great difficulty... [and with] more than an ounce of luck," the memorandum stated. The situation in the House of Representatives was especially problematic. President Carter acknowledged this by writing in the margins of the first page of the memorandum: "Frank, against these odds it will take a lot of planning & work. Let's go."[14]

The memorandum was quite revealing because it set out the

---

[12]On Carter's high praise for Moore, see Carter, *Keeping Faith*, pp. 44–45.

[13]The sale of arms to the Middle East is discussed in chapter 12.

[14]The White House, Memorandum to the President—Subject: Turkish Arms Embargo, Status Report, from Frank Moore and Bob Beckel, May 17, 1978 (hereinafter referred to as *Memo*, May 17, 1978).

administration's basic argument in favor of lifting the embargo and the tactics to be followed on Capitol Hill. The political reality in Congress—in this case, the fact that the majority of Democrats opposed Carter's efforts to lift the embargo—dictated both the message and the tactics of the White House.[15] For Carter to win in Congress, he needed the majority of the conservative votes. According to the memorandum, Carter needed the support of 100 or more Republicans to win in the House and 25 or more to win in the Senate. In other words, he could not rely on his own party to win the embargo vote. Without the support of the great majority of Republicans in Congress, it was certain that he would lose the vote.

Traditionally, Republicans were somewhat more amenable to national security arguments stemming from the Soviet threat than Democrats were. Carter needed their votes desperately and, for this reason, the strategy he adopted in order to win in Congress focused precisely on the Soviet threat. The over-emphasis on the Soviet threat was likely to win more conservative votes in Congress. Carter's message to Congress concerning the embargo had to be tailored to suit conservative ears. Equally important was the fact that many southern Democrats were also amenable to the arguments that appealed to conservative Republicans. Liberal ideas and human rights had to give way to arguments on national security. These arguments represented the hard-nosed realpolitik of Henry Kissinger.

In this regard, the White House memorandum of May 17, 1978, was quite instructive. Discussing the need to win in the Senate, the memorandum stated:

> ... Senators Church and McGovern will help, but this issue clearly needs *bipartisan, conservative support*. Senator Bentsen has offered to help and we may pick up additional *conservative* support after the Armed Services committee holds hearings on the embargo next week. ... If we are to sell the lifting of the embargo on the Hill, it must be on U.S. and NATO security grounds, i.e., *the threat from Russia*." (Emphasis added.)

In other words, the Soviet threat was to become the fundamental

---

[15]Ibid.

argument in winning the embargo battle in Congress. The national security argument replaced human rights considerations, which Carter had intended to promote when he became president. At the same time, the reliance on Republicans to win yet another vote in the Democratic Congress was a "risky proposition in an election year," as the memorandum put it.

In the Senate, the memorandum said, the situation was somewhat less difficult for the administration. Unlike the House, the Senate leadership was not committed to maintaining the embargo. The Senate majority leader, Democratic Senator Robert Byrd of West Virginia, had opposed the embargo from the beginning and was known for his strong pro-Turkish views. The argument put forth by embargo supporters for the need to uphold the rule of law did not sound convincing to Senator Byrd. On the other side of the aisle, the Senate minority leader, Republican Senator Howard Baker of Tennessee, was rather sympathetic to the administration's request to lift the embargo. He was reluctant, however, to openly appear as if he were siding with the Carter White House in yet another congressional vote. On May 15, Baker had played a key role in securing Republican support for Carter's sale of arms to Israel, Egypt, and Saudi Arabia.[16]

In addition to the fortuitous circumstance of having the Senate leadership favorably disposed to the administration on the embargo issue, the White House counted on the support of the chairmen of two key committees, Senator John Sparkman of Alabama, chairman of the Senate Foreign Relations Committee, and Senator John Stennis of Mississippi, chairman of the Senate Armed Services Committee. The Senate Armed Services Committee offered the most promising venue for the embargo hearings because Senator Stennis and five key members of the committee, three Democrats and two Republicans, had already indicated that they would work with the White House to rally support in the Senate for the repeal of the embargo. The Democratic senators on the committee were Lloyd Bentsen of Texas, Frank Church of Idaho, and George McGovern of South Dakota. The Republican senators on the committee were John Tower of Texas, and John Chafee of Rhode Island. The three Democrats had earlier been supporters of the embargo, only to be persuaded by Carter to change their positions. This was a very good sign for the White House. The

---

[16] *Time*, May 29, 1978, pp. 14–15.

support of Church and McGovern, particularly the latter, was of special significance because they had broken with the liberal ranks and had sided with the administration. Tower's support was important, given the respect he enjoyed in the Senate on matters of national defense.

It was no accident that the key leaders in the Senate supporting the administration were mostly from the south. Senate Majority Leader Byrd was from West Virginia, Senate Minority Leader Baker was from Tennessee, Senator Sparkman, chairman of the Senate Foreign Relations Committee, was from Alabama, and Senator Stennis, chairman of the Senate Armed Services Committee, was from Mississippi, while senators Bentsen and Tower were both from Texas.

The situation in the House was more difficult than it was in the Senate because the House leadership opposed the lifting of the embargo. However, the May 17 memorandum pointed out that, among the three top House leaders, Speaker Tip O'Neill, Majority Leader Jim Wright, and Majority Whip John Brademas, Wright's opposition to lifting the embargo was not as strong as that of O'Neill or Brademas. The memorandum noted that Wright's opposition was related to his desire not to break with the position of the speaker or Brademas on the issue.

Still, there was a core of White House supporters in the House, which included Democratic congressmen Clement Zablocki of Wisconsin, Lee Hamilton of Indiana, and Steven Solarz of New York. On the Republican side, Republican congressmen Paul Findley and John Anderson of Illinois provided major support. These representatives were to be some of the strongest supporters of the White House's drive to lift the embargo. They worked with the White House to generate the material that was sent to all House members on the issue. Once a week, these representatives sent letters in support of the president's drive to lift the embargo to their House colleagues.

Since the circumstances in the Senate appeared to be more favorable, the May 17 memorandum to the president recommended that the embargo vote take place first in the Senate. Having won there, the White House could use the momentum generated by the victory to achieve victory in the House as well. According to the memorandum, the president had to meet with small groups of representatives and senators at the White House twice a week in order to win their votes. The president was also to take part in larger briefings of state delegations and special caucuses. In addition to the president's active involvement in the process, the memorandum called for Secretary of State Cyrus Vance, Under Secretary of State Warren Christopher, Assistant Secretary of State George Vest, and State Department Counsel Matthew Nimetz to meet regularly with members of Congress the following week. Clark Clifford, the president's special envoy to Greece, Turkey, and Cyprus, was to brief as many members of Congress as possible.

The memorandum also suggested to the president that the chances of winning in Congress would be enhanced if the administration's bill to repeal the embargo were accompanied by an amendment. This amendment was to contain language that would placate Greek Americans and the governments of Greece and Cyprus. The amendment, which later became known as the McGovern amendment, after the name of its sponsor, would state that the United States remained committed to a Cyprus settlement based on U.N. Security Council resolutions and on the 1977 guidelines for intercommunal talks. These guidelines had been agreed to by Cyprus President Makarios and Turkish Cypriot leader Rauf Denktash when they met in Nicosia in February 1977. The Makarios-Denktash agreement provided for the establishment of a bizonal, bicommunal federation that guaranteed the fundamental liberties of all Cypriots. In addition, the amendment would stipulate that the U.S. president was to submit a bimonthly report to Congress on the progress being made toward a Cyprus settlement. With such provisions in the amendment, the Carter administration expected that it would be easier for wavering members of Congress to support the lifting of the embargo.

In addition to the tactics to be followed in Congress, the May 17 memorandum proposed a series of actions to be taken in order to mobilize a network around the country to support the president's policy of lifting the embargo. Since victory in Congress depended on Republican support, the memorandum stressed the importance of the support of former president Gerald Ford and former secretary of state Henry Kissinger. At the request of the White House, both Ford and Kissinger had already begun lobbying Republican members of Congress to lift the embargo.

The memorandum also proposed encouraging the influential Atlantic Council of the United States and various veterans' organizations to contact members of Congress in support of the president's effort. The White House would coordinate the activities of this support network.

The network included the retired chairman of the Joint Chiefs of Staff, Admiral Thomas Moorer, who actively lobbied members of Congress to support the lifting of the embargo. Admiral Moorer was from Alabama and was very useful to Carter, a fellow southerner, in lobbying members of Congress from the south.[17] In addition to Admiral Moorer, four former allied commanders of NATO including Lyman Lemnitzer and Andrew Goodpaster wrote to members of Congress, using the standard national security arguments in urging them to lift the embargo.

Several veterans' organizations wrote letters to Congress and the press in support of the president as part of the network. In May 1978, Frank Rugiero, the national commander of the American Veterans of World War II, Korea, Vietnam (AMVETS), wrote a memo requesting the support of the organization's members for lifting the embargo.[18] On May 19, Administrator of Veterans' Affairs Max Leland, accompanied by leaders of several national veterans' organizations, visited the White House, where the president sought their support.

Academics also testified before congressional committees concerning the repeal of the embargo. One of them was Albert Wohlstetter of the University of Chicago, who testified on April 25, 1978, before the House International Relations Committee. He was an authority on arms control and employed national security arguments and the Soviet threat to justify the lifting of the embargo.

In addition, Carter sought the support of minority politicians such as Andrew Young, Carter's political ally who had been appointed U.S. ambassador to the United Nations, to mobilize black support for the administration's effort.[19] Congresswoman Barbara Jordan of Texas, a prominent black member of the House, was quite influential in the Black Caucus, and Carter sought her support.

The significant domestic political obstacles threatening to derail the president's effort to lift the embargo in the Senate and, particularly, in the House were compounded by the fact that, up until the spring of 1978, Turkey had not taken any steps indicating a willing-

---

[17] *New York Times*, May 4, 1978.

[18] On the AMVETS memo, see *Proini*, English Section, June 24, 1978.

[19] *Memo*, May 17, 1978.

ness to compromise on Cyprus. Without such steps by Ankara, the White House believed that it would be very difficult to win in Congress. For that reason, the May 17, 1978 memorandum pointed out the necessity of a goodwill gesture by the Turkish government. In this respect, the memorandum proposed the following:

> Winning in the two Houses will be infinitely easier if the Turkish government displays some new flexibility on Cyprus between now and mid-June. Secretary Vance made this point at a breakfast meeting with [Turkish] Ambassador [to the United States Melin] Esenbel on May 17. Our hope would be to get from Ecevit some promise of a further troop withdrawal and the return of Greek Cypriot refugees to new Famagusta. . . . *If Ecevit can project a conciliatory image and suggest that progress on Cyprus lies just around the corner,* our chances for a favorable House and Senate vote will be immediately enhanced. (Emphasis added.)

In the ensuing days and weeks, Turkey and Turkish Cypriot leader Rauf Denktash followed the prescription in the White House memorandum. On May 20, 1978, just three days after the May 17 memorandum was written, Denktash announced a "compromise" proposal revolving around Famagusta (Varosha). The proposal was based on the idea of returning about 35,000 Greek Cypriot refugees to their homes in Famagusta, under certain conditions. The Cyprus government rejected Denktash's proposal outright on the grounds that it would legitimize the occupation of the rest of Cyprus, while Famagusta would not come under the authority of the legitimate government of Cyprus.

Despite the fact that the other party to the dispute, the Greek Cypriots, opposed the Denktash proposal, Secretary of State Vance endorsed it as a positive step that could open the way to a negotiated settlement.[20] As the *New York Times* put it, "The United States has praised the declaration in an effort to build up support in Washington for ending the arms embargo against Turkey."[21] In the final analysis, the Denktash proposal on Famagusta was put forth primarily to

---

[20]*New York Times,* May 25, 1978.
[21]Ibid.

impress Congress. It was an effective tactic because, according to the *New York Times*, "Congressional advocates of lifting the embargo also have received the [Denktash] statement with enthusiasm."[22] The proposal concerning Famagusta was to be the selling point of the Carter administration's attempt to convince Congress to lift the embargo since it demonstrated that progress on the Cyprus issue was "just around the corner."

The May 17 memorandum was followed by another memorandum on the subject of the embargo. On June 1, 1978, the White House produced a presidential memorandum that was circulated among selected members of Congress. It was based on the May 17 memorandum by Moore and Beckel and consisted of an action plan for the weeks leading up to the embargo vote in Congress.[23] This plan included a series of meetings between the president and about 100 members of Congress during the second and third weeks of June. In addition, the presidential memorandum instructed Secretary of State Cyrus Vance, Secretary of Defense Harold Brown, Joint Chiefs of Staff Chairman General David Jones, and CIA Director Admiral Stansfield Turner to engage in a coordinated effort on Capitol Hill to sway uncommitted members of Congress. The president also requested the presence in Washington of General Alexander Haig, Supreme Allied Commander Europe, to assist in the lobbying effort. In addition, the presidential memorandum, following the suggestions of the May 17 memorandum, called for a public relations campaign to win grass roots support, primarily through major veterans' organizations.

In the final analysis, these two memoranda indicated, and subsequent action demonstrated, that the Carter White House was engaged in a systematic campaign to lift the embargo. This was done by mobilizing the foreign policy agencies of the government and a support network of non-governmental organizations and influential individuals to the maximum extent possible. Leading this mobilization and overseeing the execution of the plan described in these memoranda was the president of the United States, himself. Carter was the kind of president who paid close attention to detail in executing his decisions. He left nothing to chance. The effort to lift the arms embargo against

---

[22]Ibid.

[23]For the text of the June 1, 1978 memorandum, see *New York Times*, June 2, 1978.

Turkey became a test of Carter's leadership. Failure to win the embargo battle would have been more than a political setback for Carter. It would also have been a personal failure, given the amount of time and energy he had devoted to this test of wills between the president and Congress.

CHAPTER 8

Turkey: Playing the Soviet Card and Winning in Washington

The Fear of Losing Turkey

The months between the beginning of April and the end of July 1978 were crucial for the Carter administration as it sought to repeal the embargo. During this period, the Carter foreign policy team was also involved with the Panama Canal Treaties; problems in Rhodesia and South Africa; Soviet penetration into Africa, the Horn of Africa and Angola, especially; and the SALT II negotiations with Moscow.

The Middle East was also very high on the agenda. Carter's Middle East team was busy developing ideas and plans for a summit at Camp David between Egypt and Israel in September. In the spring of 1978, a fight also was imminent between the administration and Congress over a controversial package to sell fighter planes to Israel, Egypt, and Saudi Arabia. Moreover, the revolutionary turmoil in Iran was about to become the dominant issue among policy-makers in Washington by the end of the year. Looming in the background of any discussion of the Middle East was Turkey and the arms embargo.

Henry Kissinger was advising the Carter administration on several of these foreign policy issues.[1] In fact, Carter and his foreign policy team sought out Kissinger's advice throughout their tenure in office. Notwithstanding his election campaign denouncements of Kissinger's policies as "cynical," Carter evidently considered Kissinger's advice to be valuable. In addition, Kissinger still had his admirers in the foreign policy establishment and in the State Department. The White House considered it beneficial to have Kissinger's support on important foreign policy issues, especially with regard to U.S.-

---

[1]On seeking the advice of Kissinger, see Carter, *Keeping Faith*, 159, 171, 219.

Soviet relations. This was preferable to having the former secretary of state become a critic of Carter's policies.

Kissinger also had considerable influence on the Carter administration's policies toward revolutionary Iran. Kissinger, Nelson and David Rockefeller, and John McCoy were instrumental in pressuring President Carter and his advisers to allow the Shah to come to the United States in October 1979 for medical treatment for lymphoma. Kissinger exercised very strong pressure and personally asked Carter and Vice President Mondale to let the Iranian leader enter the country on humanitarian grounds.[2] The argument put forth by Kissinger and others who advocated the Shah's entry was couched in "ethical and humanitarian" terms. It was argued that the United States had a moral obligation to allow him to enter the country for treatment. The United States could not abandon an old ally and allow him to wander like a "flying Dutchman" around the world, Kissinger argued. At the National Security Council, Brzezinski became a passionate advocate of admitting the Shah. Carter succumbed to the ethical arguments and decided to allow the Shah to come to the United States on October 22, 1979.

Carter's decision to admit the Shah constituted a folly because it led to predictable consequences. The people of Iran remembered the CIA coup of August 16–19, 1953, very well. It overthrew the country's legitimate prime minister, Mohammed Mossadeq, and restored the Shah to power. The U.S. Embassy in Tehran had played a pivotal role in the CIA coup.[3] The Shah's admission to the United States was seen in Khomeini's Iran as the prelude to another coup, this time against

---

[2]On Kissinger's pressure to admit the Shah as well as pressure from other quarters, see Terence Smith, "Why Carter Admitted the Shah," *New York Times Magazine*, May 17, 1981, pp. 36–44; James Bill, *The Eagle and the Lion*, pp. 293–296, 328–340; Ioannides, *America's Iran*, pp. 76–89.

[3]It is beyond dispute that the CIA overthrew the legitimate government of Iran in August 1953. On April 16, 2000, the *New York Times* published the official history of the CIA coup in Iran as it was written by one of the actors behind the coup, Dr. Donald N. Wilber, a CIA agent. He was the chief planner of the coup and went to Iran for that purpose. Wilber wrote the history of the coup, code-named TPAJAX, for the CIA archives. The CIA document describing the coup and the important role played by the American Embassy in Tehran in carrying it out was written by Wilber in March 1954. The document is entitled "CIA Clandestine Service History: Overthrow of Premier Mossadeq of Iran, November 1952-August 1953." See James Risen, "Secrets of History: The CIA in Iran," *New York Times*, April 16, 2000.

the revolution. As a consequence, militant students attacked and took over the U.S. Embassy in Tehran on November 4, 1979, 13 days after the Shah was admitted to the United States. The embassy takeover and the hostage-taking of 52 American diplomats for 14 months marked Jimmy Carter's presidency and doomed his re-election chances.

Kissinger's advice in this regard was disastrous for the Carter presidency. One might argue that Carter was more amenable to ethical and humanitarian arguments than to the logic of realpolitik, and that was why he succumbed to pressure by Kissinger and others to admit the ailing Shah. Still, the support Kissinger gave to the White House in its drive to lift the arms embargo against Turkey was couched in the logic of realpolitik. The Carter White House appreciated Kissinger's support concerning the embargo issue, even though no moral considerations were invoked by the former secretary of state.

Thus, the logic of realpolitik drove the effort to repeal the embargo. Accordingly, the White House followed the strategy that was set out in the May 17 memorandum. First, Carter and his aides had to secure the necessary votes in Congress and, second, the president needed to placate the Greek American community.

The White House effort to persuade Congress to lift the embargo led to coordinated action on two fronts. The first involved the mobilization of the national security community in support of repealing the embargo. The second had to do with direct contacts with members of Congress and the use of the presidential power of persuasion and political cajoling to influence the votes of a selected number of legislators.

The mobilization of the national security community in support of lifting the embargo was essential for two interrelated reasons. First, the fundamental argument behind the need to lift the embargo invoked reasons of national security, specifically the Soviet threat. Second, historically, the White House has been more likely to win over congressional support when invoking the issue of national security and the vital foreign policy interests of the United States. In this vein, top Pentagon, State Department, and CIA officials have appeared before congressional committees.

President Carter and his advisers argued that the lifting of the embargo was essential in the context of the overall U.S. strategy toward the Soviet Union. Turkey played a critical role in the southeastern flank of NATO as a bulwark against the Soviets. The arms embargo, the argument went, had had a devastating effect on the Turkish armed forces, which, in turn, had undermined NATO's strategy in the Eastern Mediterranean and the Middle East. The embargo was pushing Turkey toward neutralism. It was a powerful national security argument.

In announcing Carter's shift in policy, which led him to ask Congress to lift the embargo, the New York Times reported that the president had reached this decision on the advice of his top foreign policy advisers. According to the newspaper, their recommendation was based on the fear that, unless the United States moved quickly, Turkey might reduce its ties to NATO and, perhaps, adopt a more neutral stance in the Eastern Mediterranean.[4]

On April 6, 1978, during testimony before the House International Relations Committee, Secretary of State Cyrus Vance made the official announcement to Congress concerning the administration's request to lift the embargo. If the United States does not lift the embargo, "there will be those in Turkey who will question the basis for its continued participation in the Western alliance," he warned Congress.[5]

In early May, a month after the White House decision to seek the lifting of the embargo, Secretary of Defense Harold Brown testified before the Senate Foreign Relations Committee. He stressed the strategic importance of Turkey for NATO and the alliance's need to have a strong defense against Soviet adventurism in the Eastern Mediterranean and the Middle East. Brown warned that, if the embargo were not lifted, NATO's defense against the Soviets would not be possible because Turkey might be forced to seek non-Western arms suppliers. The secretary of defense was referring to the Soviet Union.[6]

Three weeks later, in a New York Times interview on May 23, 1978, the Supreme Allied Commander in Europe, General Alexander Haig,

---

[4]New York Times, April 2, 1978.

[5]See Secretary of State Vance, Administration Policy in the Eastern Mediterranean, Statement before the House Committee on International Relations, the Department of State, Bureau of Public Affairs, Washington, D.C., April 6, 1978 (hereinafter referred to as Vance, Administration Policy). The complete text of Vance's testimony appears in the Appendix, Document J.

[6]Proini, May 3, 1978.

warned of the devastating consequences of the embargo on NATO's defenses and posed the following question in a most alarming fashion: "... Is it in Greece's interest to have a Turkey armed by the Soviet Union as a neighbor?"[7] A month later, General Haig repeated his dire warning to Congress. Testifying before the Senate Armed Services Committee, he urged Congress to lift the embargo and warned that, if it were not lifted, Turkey would be compelled to turn to the Soviet Union for aid.[8] In the final analysis, the Carter administration was raising the specter of a "who-lost-Turkey-to-the-Soviets" debate and was preemptively placing the responsibility at Congress's doorstep.

The fear of losing Turkey appeared quite real to the embargo's opponents because, in July 1975, the Turkish government had suspended operations at five U.S. military bases in the country in retaliation for the embargo. Four of the bases were used for intelligence gathering, and one was a naval base. According to the State Department, the loss of the four intelligence facilities hampered the ability of the United States to monitor Soviet space, missile, and military systems development and strategic nuclear activities.[9] Defense Secretary Brown argued that, as a consequence of the closing of the military bases, Washington's ability to verify Soviet compliance with strategic arms agreements had been damaged.[10] In the end, the basic argument of the Carter administration revolved around the Soviet threat. The embargo was hurting Turkey, a key NATO ally, and the Soviet Union was becoming the beneficiary.

The citing of the Soviet threat to rationalize the lifting of the embargo reflected traditional containment policies toward the Soviet Union. This appeared to be inconsistent with Carter's goal of ushering in a new era in American foreign policy, the post-cold war era. This new era, however, was short-lived. By 1978, the Carter foreign policy team, led by Brzezinski, was moving away from the post-cold war era foreign policy and was returning to containment, a policy that was traditional and familiar to the national security bureaucracy.

---

[7] *New York Times*, May 23, 1978.

[8] Ibid., June 29, 1978.

[9] Letter by Douglas J. Bennet, Assistant Secretary for Congressional Relations to Senator John Sparkman, Chairman of the Senate Foreign Relations Committee, June 28, 1978, *Congressional Record*, vol. 124, part 15, July 25, 1978, pp. 22511–22513. The text of Bennet's letter appears in the Appendix, Document O.

[10] *New York Times*, April 7, 1978.

Cyprus as a Catalyst for Turkish-Soviet Rapprochement

The alarm expressed by the Carter administration over the possibility that Turkey could fall into the arms of Russia was highly exaggerated. Since the 1960s, Turkey had been able to perform a balancing act in its relations with the Western alliance and the Soviet Union. It was in this context that Turkey embarked on improving its relations with Moscow.[11]

At the same time, whenever the opportunity arose, Turkey reminded the United States that it lived next to the Soviet menace and that it was a front-line country standing in the way of Russia's old dream. Historically, a major Russian objective had been to extend its territory to the warm waters of the Mediterranean and to the Middle East, even before oil was discovered in the region.

From 1964 onward, Turkey and the Soviet Union began high-level contacts and signed a series of economic and cultural agreements. By the end of the decade, their relations could be called cordial. Thus, Turkey followed the example of France and Germany in normalizing relations with the Soviets, engaging in fruitful economic cooperation with them and practicing what came to be known as the policy of détente. This Turkish policy of rapprochement with the Soviet Union was a by-product of the international dynamics of the 1960s. It was the result of broader trends in East-West relations. In this regard, Turkey was able to follow an autonomous foreign policy in the context of détente but always within the overall framework of the Atlantic alliance.[12]

Greece, on the other hand, was unable to develop an autonomous foreign policy in the 1960s and, unlike Turkey, failed to chart a policy of détente toward Russia. In fact, the notion of détente and closer ties with Russia advocated by the centrist government of Greek Prime Minister George Papandreou in 1964 and 1965 was seen by the Greek armed forces as serving the objectives of the communists. In the

---

[11]For a comprehensive view of Turkish-Soviet relations, see Kemal Karpat, "Turkish-Soviet Relations," in *Turkish Foreign Policy in Transition, 1950–1974*, ed. Kemal Karpat (Leiden: E.J. Brill, 1975), pp. 72–107.

[12]On the development of Turkish-Soviet détente, see the outstanding study of Alvin Rubinstein, *Soviet Policy Toward Turkey, Iran, and Afghanistan* (New York: Praeger, 1982). See esp. chapter 1, "Soviet-Turkish Relations: The Origins and Evolution of Coexistence," and chapter 2, "The Wary Détente," pp. 1–55.

1960s, the idea that the Greek prime minister would pay a visit to Moscow, as his Turkish counterpart had, was seen by the Greek army, the Royal Palace, and many conservatives as tantamount to treason. When the idea was floated that Prime Minister George Papandreou might visit the Soviet Union in 1964, he was warned publicly in the conservative press that he might go to Moscow as prime minister but would return to Athens as private citizen. Papandreou abandoned the idea. The fear of communism was the major reason behind the Greek military coup three years later, in April 1967.

The Cyprus dispute became a catalyst for Ankara's overtures toward Moscow.[13] In fact, American involvement in the Cyprus crisis during the first six months of 1964 precipitated Ankara's rapprochement with Moscow. The Johnson White House had been preoccupied by the Cyprus crisis since the eruption of intercommunal violence during the Christmas holidays of 1963. President Lyndon Johnson appeared determined not to allow this crisis to escalate and lead to a Greek-Turkish confrontation. The United States was keenly aware that such a confrontation would be a serious blow to NATO and could only benefit the Soviet Union. More importantly, Johnson did not want a crisis or complications in U.S.-Soviet relations at that stage. When the Cyprus crisis erupted during the 1963 Christmas holidays, the United States was still in deep shock over the assassination of President John F. Kennedy in Dallas on November 22, 1963. Under the circumstances, the new Johnson foreign policy team did not want an Eastern Mediterranean crisis on its hands, one that could potentially lead to the involvement of the Russians.

Johnson's Warning to Turkey

The potential of a Greek-Turkish confrontation over Cyprus was quite real at the time. While the intercommunal violence was occurring during the 1963 Christmas holidays and early January 1964, Turkish fighter planes flew over Nicosia, the Cypriot capital, as Turkey threatened to invade the island republic. In Greece, the government placed the armed forces on alert and warned Turkey against any military action in Cyprus. Greek-Turkish tension over Cyprus was

---

[13]Karpat, "Turkish-Soviet Relations," pp. 91–92.

extremely high during this period, while the Soviet Union was ready to exploit any rupture in the southeastern flank of NATO.

The Cyprus crisis preoccupied the Johnson White House from January to August 1964, as it sought to avert a Greek-Turkish confrontation and potential Soviet meddling in the situation. The American official who played a major role in handling the Cyprus crisis at the time was Under Secretary of State George Ball. He was highly respected among the foreign policy establishment and emerged as one of the closest advisers to President Johnson. An exchange between President Johnson and Ball at the White House on the afternoon of Tuesday, January 28, 1964, is quite revealing:

> BALL: Mr. President, we have been working all day on this Cyprus matter. We have a plan, which I think is a pretty good one ... which would involve our putting a small unit in, but in a manner where we would have an agreement in advance so we would not get in the middle ... and then there would be mediation machinery set up.

> PRESIDENT JOHNSON: ... I'd like to move you, or Harriman or somebody, Bobby Kennedy or Bob McNamara, somebody— I'd like to move them over there and let them make an all-out diplomatic effort. Maybe put an airplane carrier or two there ... and say to those people, "Now we are going to make preparations and we are ready for a quick entry and *we are not going to support you Turks* if you pull anything like this. ... *We are not going to give you aid and back you up to fight you in the next breadth and you just behave yourselves.*" Tell the Greeks the same thing and let somebody go there—you or Averell Harriman or some of these other fellows that may be traveling around now—and say to them, "Now we've got to work out an agreement here." ... And then have a couple of carriers off there, where you could move people in if you needed to, but *just not let these damned British run us in there.* They're just in a habit of doing this kind of stuff.[14] (Emphasis added.)

This exchange demonstrates that President Johnson was determined to prevent the situation in the Eastern Mediterranean from

---

[14]Beschloss, *Taking Charge*, p. 191.

deteriorating and was equally determined not to allow Turkey to invade Cyprus. Not only had he ordered two aircraft carriers to come into the region, but he had also made it clear, using very strong language, that the United States was ready to punish Turkey if it carried out any military action against Cyprus. In fact, Johnson threatened to impose an arms embargo against Turkey if it dared attack Cyprus. Certainly, Johnson delivered a similar warning to Greece, but what mattered was his warning to Turkey. The Cyprus government was concerned about the military threat coming from Turkey, not from Greece. The Greek government's position was that it would intervene in defense of Cyprus only if Turkey attacked the island republic. President Johnson demonstrated his mistrust for Britain's role in Cyprus, expressing concern that the British had a tendency to pursue their own objectives in the region. These objectives were not necessarily identical to those of the United States.

The Anglo-French invasion of Egypt, the Suez crisis, eight years earlier, in late October 1956, was a case in point. During the crisis, the United States openly opposed the invasion, which was carried out by Britain, France, and Israel. The administration of Dwight Eisenhower ordered the Sixth Fleet to maneuver in such a way as to thwart British attacks on Egyptian targets. This American opposition was a major reason behind the failure of the Anglo-French operation.

Eighteen years later, the July-August 1974 Cyprus crisis brought to the surface an intense disagreement between Britain and the United States over how to deal with Turkey. As in the case of the Suez crisis, the American position prevailed. This disagreement between the two allies, however, did confirm that American and British interests in the region were not necessarily identical. In the final analysis, President Johnson's position in January 1964 was unequivocally against any Turkish military action in Cyprus. Again, the American position prevailed, confirming the strategic dominance of the U.S. in the Eastern Mediterranean.

This was clearly demonstrated again in June 1964, following yet another crisis in Cyprus. At the time, the Turkish government of Prime Minister İsmet İnönü was making preparations to invade the island.[15] Ankara was determined to invade Cyprus, but President Johnson thwarted its plans following a clear warning.

---

[15]Harris, *Troubled Alliance*, p. 114.

In a blunt letter to İnönü, Johnson warned Ankara on June 5, 1964, that NATO's protective umbrella would not cover Turkey if it invaded Cyprus and the Soviets moved against Turkey as a result. Johnson also cautioned Ankara that it could not use American arms to invade Cyprus.[16] President Johnson warned Turkey:

> ... Furthermore, a military intervention in Cyprus by Turkey could lead to direct involvement of the Soviet Union. I hope you will understand that your NATO allies have not had a chance to consider whether they have an obligation to protect Turkey against the Soviet Union if Turkey takes a step which results in Soviet intervention without the full consent and understanding of its NATO allies. . . . I wish also, Mr. Prime Minister, to call your attention to the bilateral agreement between the United States and Turkey in the field of military assistance. Under Article IV of the Agreement with Turkey of July 1947, *your government is required to obtain United States consent for the use of military assistance for purposes other than those for which such assistance was furnished.*[17] (Emphasis added.)

President Johnson dealt with Turkey like no other president has since then. Unlike all the presidents who succeeded him, Johnson did not hesitate to tell the Turkish leadership what was really on his mind. This becomes clear by reading the June 5, 1964 letter to İnönü as well as the January 28, 1964 exchange between President Johnson and George Ball. Only Johnson dared utter the words "we are not going to support you Turks . . . and just behave yourselves," as he warned them against acting in a way that was detrimental to the broader interests of the Western alliance.

Since the Johnson presidency, the "what-if-we-lose-Turkey" syndrome has guided the policies of all other presidents, Nixon, Ford, Carter, Reagan, Bush, and Clinton. This syndrome has allowed the phenomenon of "reverse leverage" to permeate American policies toward Turkey and, to some extent, toward Iran. In other words, the

---

[16]The Johnson letter to İnönü was drafted by Secretary of State Dean Rusk, who was assisted by George Ball.

[17]President Johnson's letter to the Turkish prime minister is found in the *Middle East Journal*, vol. 20, number 3 (Summer 1966): pp. 386–388.

substantial American leverage over Ankara has remained unutilized, while the junior partner of the U.S.-Turkish alliance has been able to exert disproportionate leverage over the policies of the superpower, the United States, in order to serve Turkish national interests. Only Lyndon Johnson made use of American diplomatic and strategic leverage over Turkey, leverage that was quite effective. Turkey abandoned its plans to invade Cyprus.

Johnson's attitude toward Turkey was not meant to be a favor to Greece or the Greek Cypriots, for that matter.[18] In fact, when he invited Greek Prime Minister George Papandreou to Washington the last week of June 1964, Johnson and his aides were quite blunt with the Greek leader. Papandreou found himself under intense American pressure to agree to a summit meeting with Turkish Prime Minister İnönü in order to bring about a Cyprus settlement.[19] Moreover, George Ball, a key adviser to Johnson, was not only unsympathetic to the Greek Cypriots, but he had also developed a visceral dislike for the president of Cyprus, Archbishop Makarios. Following a meeting with Makarios in Nicosia on February 12 and 13, 1964, Ball described the archbishop in the most unfavorable terms. He characterized the policies of Makarios toward the Turkish Cypriots as "cruel and reckless . . . and bloody-minded."[20] Upon his return to Washington, Ball painted a dark picture of Makarios. He told President Johnson:

He [Makarios] must be cheating about his age; no one could acquire so much guile in only fifty-one years.[21]

---

[18]It has been argued that Greek American lobbying played a role in influencing President Johnson to write his letter to İnönü. Whatever role Greek Americans played at the time, there was no organized "Greek lobby" in the true sense of the word. On the subject of "Greek American lobbying" in 1964, see Jacob Landau, "Johnson's 1964 Letter to İnönü and the Greek Lobbying of the White House," *Jerusalem Papers on Peace Problems*, Jerusalem: Hebrew University, 1979.

[19]See Andreas Papandreou, *Democracy at Gunpoint* (New York: Doubleday and Co., 1970), pp. 132–136. Andreas Papandreou accompanied his father, Prime Minister George Papandreou, to Washington and took part in the talks with Johnson in his capacity as a member of his father's cabinet. On the Johnson administration's pressure on the Papandreou government, see Coufoudakis, "To Kypriako" (The Cyprus Issue), pp. 224–225.

[20]See George Ball, *The Past Has Another Pattern* (New York: W.W. Norton and Co., 1982), p. 345.

[21]Ibid., p. 344.

It is apparent that, in dealing with the Cyprus crisis of 1964, the Johnson administration did not act out of sympathy for the Greek Cypriots.[22] The American objective was to avert a broader conflict in the Eastern Mediterranean involving Greece and Turkey. In the process, President Johnson demonstrated that the United States had considerable leverage over Turkey. The asymmetry of power and the Turkish reliance on the United States for its defense and economic needs were the obvious sources of American leverage over Turkey. This leverage has also been a permanent instrument in Washington's diplomacy toward Greece. The difference has been that only President Johnson has used this leverage over Turkey, while all presidents, from Eisenhower to Clinton, have been more inclined to use American leverage as a means of exacting concessions from Greece and Cyprus, rather than from Turkey.

Johnson's letter to İnönü incensed the Turks. They felt insulted and came to the conclusion that the United States was taking the side of the Greeks on an issue that was vital to Turkey. Johnson's letter generated a wave of anti-American feeling in Turkey. More importantly, this letter became a catalyst for Turkey's rapprochement with the Soviet Union.[23] In carrying out a policy of rapprochement with Moscow, Ankara performed a delicate balancing act. While Turkey normalized relations with the Soviet Union and received multiple benefits as a result, it simultaneously remained dependent on the United States for its defense and continued to be anchored in NATO.

In November 1964, barely five months after Johnson sent his letter to İnönü, the Turkish prime minister sent his foreign minister, Feridun Erkin, to Moscow, and the process of Turkish-Soviet rapprochement was on track. The joint communiqué issued on November 6, 1964, at the end of Erkin's visit, dealt with Cyprus, among other issues, and called for "the respect of the legal rights of the two national communities."[24] Turkey was quite pleased because Moscow's accept-

---

[22]On American policies during this period, see Coufoudakis, "To Kypriako" (The Cyprus Issue), pp. 222–226.

[23]On the Johnson letter and Turkey's adverse reaction to it, see George Harris, *Troubled Alliance: Turkish-American Problems in Historical Perspective, 1945–1971* (Washington, D.C.: American Enterprise Institute and Hoover Institution, 1972), pp. 112–119; Feroz Ahmad, *The Making of Modern Turkey* (London: Routledge, 1993), p. 225: Tozun Bahcheli, *Greek-Turkish Relations Since 1955* (Boulder: Westview Press, 1990), pp. 62–63; Karpat, "Turkish Soviet Relations," pp. 91–92, 101–102.

[24]Rubinstein, *Soviet Policy Toward Turkey*, p.31.

ance of the principle of two national communities in Cyprus was close to the Turkish position. This position stipulated that the Turkish Cypriots were not a minority but a national community and that the Cyprus problem could not be defined in terms of majority-minority relations. Moscow's recognition of the existence of two national communities in Cyprus was also compatible with the idea of a federal settlement in Cyprus, an idea that Turkey increasingly supported in the mid-1960s. At the time, a federal settlement in Cyprus was anathema to the Greek Cypriots.

In early January 1965, Soviet President Nikolai Podgorny paid a visit to Turkey that was hailed as historic. In October 1967, Turkish Prime Minister Süleyman Demirel paid a highly publicized and successful visit to the Soviet Union. Demirel's visit to Russia was followed by a visit to Moscow of Turkish President General Cevdet Sunay in November 1969.[25] These visits confirmed that Turkish-Soviet relations had entered a new and constructive phase.

The Cyprus government of Archbishop Makarios persisted in following a policy of non-alignment with the support of the influential communist party of Cyprus, AKEL. In ideological terms, Makarios, the head of the Greek Orthodox Church of Cyprus, which also happened to be the largest landowner in Cyprus, was by no means pro-communist. In terms of East-West relations, however, Makarios's non-aligned policy facilitated the Soviet strategic objectives in the Eastern Mediterranean.[26]

The Cypriot leadership failed to realize that Soviet support for the "independence, territorial integrity, and non-alignment of the Republic of Cyprus" was not motivated by altruism but was, rather, a policy of expediency. In reality, Russian strategic objectives in the Middle East dictated that Moscow woo Turkey in order to expedite the descent of the Russian fleet into the Eastern Mediterranean. According to Soviet thinking, the Turkish straits had a paramount strategic signifi-

---

[25]Ferenc Vali, *Bridge Across the Bosporus: The Foreign Policy of Turkey* (Baltimore: The Johns Hopkins University Press, 1971), pp. 176–181; Bruce Kuniholm, "Turkey and the West Since World War II," in *Turkey Between East and West*, ed. Vojtech Mastny and R. Craig Nation (Boulder: Westview Press, 1996), pp. 55–60; Karpat, " Turkish Soviet Relations," pp. 87–107.

[26]For a comprehensive analysis of Cypriot-Soviet relations, Soviet-American rivalry over Cyprus, and Makarios's non-aligned policies, see Joseph S. Joseph, *Cyprus: Ethnic Conflict and International Politics* (New York: St. Martin's Press, 1997), pp. 57–78.

cance. Even if Cyprus were to provide naval facilities to the Soviets, their use would be rather limited if Turkey posed problems concerning the passage of Soviet naval units into the Mediterranean.

This did not mean that the Soviets were disinterested in Cyprus. Quite the opposite was true. Moscow did not want to see Cyprus come under NATO control. For this reason, the non-aligned policies of Cyprus pleased Russia. Moscow was also careful not to alienate AKEL, which enjoyed considerable popular support. Non-alignment, however, did not provide any security for Cyprus. The non-aligned countries, especially the Arab states, did little to help Cyprus during the Turkish invasion. Cyprus's only credible military ally that could have provided security to the island republic was Greece, a member of NATO.

A non-aligned Cyprus served Soviet regional interests and, for this reason, Moscow performed a balancing act. It gave lip service and occasional diplomatic support to Makarios while, at the same time, it cultivated its ties with Turkey and moved closer to the idea of federation and the existence of two national communities in Cyprus. This tended to favor Turkey.

The Makarios government entertained the futile, if not naïve, notion that Moscow would choose to support Nicosia against Ankara in the Cyprus dispute and that Soviet military power would work as a deterrent against any Turkish military move in Cyprus. However, when Turkey invaded Cyprus in July 1974, a critical moment, Russia stood by and watched, and it avoided any action that could have posed difficulties for Ankara. By sitting on the sidelines, the Russians facilitated Turkey's military attack on Cyprus, or made it less difficult.[27]

There is little doubt that the Soviet Union condoned the invasion, something that was deeply appreciated by Turkey at the time. Not unjustifiably, the Turks felt that Moscow was supportive of the Turkish military action against Cyprus.[28] In the final analysis, the Soviets considered Cyprus expendable, something that neither Makarios nor the left in Greece and Cyprus were able to comprehend. As a consequence, Makarios's diplomatic architecture, based on the axiom that non-alignment and Soviet sympathy would protect Cyprus against Turkey, suffered an irreparable blow when Turkey invaded the island republic on July 20, 1974.

---

[27]Ibid., 73.

[28]See Birand, *Thirty Hot Days*, p. 23; Karpat, "Turkish-Soviet Relations," p. 107.

Certainly, Makarios's non-aligned policies were not without diplomatic benefit. This was especially the case at the United Nations, where Cyprus won successive victories in the General Assembly, thanks to the support of the non-aligned countries in Africa and Asia. Still, this support at the U.N. was hardly enough to provide Cyprus with a credible military defense against Turkey, especially during a time of crisis such as July 1974.

Both sides benefited from the dramatic improvement in Turkish-Soviet relations in the 1960s. Ankara succeeded in having Moscow acknowledge that it had no territorial designs against Turkey and that bilateral ties could improve even though Turkey maintained its close ties with NATO. This was a great victory for Turkey because Ankara could proceed to establish close ties with Moscow, while it remained a close NATO ally with all the security, diplomatic, and economic benefits that this implied. Turkey reaped substantial economic and diplomatic benefits from its ties with Russia as well. In the late 1970s, Turkey used these ties as powerful leverage in pressuring the Carter administration to lift the arms embargo.

The Turkish Straits: Ankara, Master of the Game

The Turkish-Soviet rapprochement offered very substantial benefits to the Soviets as well. Moscow needed Turkish goodwill because, during the 1960s, the Eastern Mediterranean became the region where the projection of Soviet naval power received top priority in Russia. A new global strategy by the United States, combined with regional developments, rendered the Eastern Mediterranean region vital to Soviet interests. By 1963, the United States had introduced Polaris submarines carrying Sea Launched Ballistic Missiles (SLBM) into the Eastern Mediterranean. These missiles were capable of striking the Soviet Union, adding another nuclear threat to Moscow. One way of dealing with this new strategic threat to Russia was to have a powerful naval fleet in the Eastern Mediterranean.

As far as regional developments were concerned, several interrelated factors—Arab nationalism, the Arab-Israeli conflict, and the radicalization of Arab politics—converged in the 1960s to facilitate a Soviet military presence in Egypt and Syria. The Soviet naval presence in the Eastern Mediterranean became one of the logical consequences of Moscow's ties with Arab regimes in the area.

The Soviet strategic and regional objectives in the Eastern Mediterranean and the Middle East elevated the significance of the Dardanelles, also known as the Turkish straits, to new heights for Moscow. The straits have always been of critical importance in the long relationship between Russia and Turkey. Both under Czarist Russia and later under Stalin, control of the straits was at the epicenter of the ties between Russia and Ottoman Turkey and, later, Republican Turkey. Descending into the warm waters of the Eastern Mediterranean has always been a Russian objective, whether under the Czars or the Soviets. In the final analysis, Russia needed the Turkish straits to advance and protect its commercial and strategic interests in the Eastern Mediterranean and the Middle East.

Following Stalin's death in 1953, the Soviets opted to manage the question of the straits within the framework of the 1936 Montreux Convention and under an interpretation of the Convention that suited Moscow's interests. Beginning in the early 1960s, Turkish diplomacy accommodated Soviet needs regarding transit rights of warships through the straits. Alvin Rubinstein, one of the most seasoned American observers of Russia, put it this way:

> Turkey's interpretation of the key provisions [of the Montreux Convention] *accorded with Soviet interests.* Nowhere have the far-reaching advantages accruing to Moscow from Soviet-Turkish accommodation been more evident than in *the ease with which Soviet ships are permitted to transit the Straits.* . . . Even though the USSR's military capability has grown enormously, Turkey regarded its activities in the Eastern Mediterranean, including its permanent forward naval deployments and quest for military bases in the Arab world, with surprising equanimity.[29] (Emphasis added.)

Other strategic analysts in Washington shared the assessment that Turkey accommodated Russian interests in the Eastern Mediterranean by interpreting the Montreux Convention in a way that facilitated the passage of Soviet warships through the straits.[30]

---

[29]Rubinstein, *Soviet Policy Toward Turkey,* pp. 43, 35.
[30]Edward Luttwak, *The Political Uses of Sea Power* (Baltimore: The Johns Hopkins University Press, 1974), pp. 60–61.

The indispensability of the Turkish straits for Moscow was amply demonstrated during the Six Day Arab-Israeli War in June 1967 and its aftermath, and during the October 1973 Arab-Israeli War, the Yom Kippur War. During the Six Day War and its immediate aftermath, Soviet naval activity in the Eastern Mediterranean increased dramatically. The number of Soviet warships in the area reached 72.

The Six Day War ended disastrously for the Arabs. In six days, Israel destroyed the military might of Egypt and Syria. The armed forces of both countries had been trained and equipped by Moscow. Following the Arab defeat, the Soviet Union committed itself to rebuilding the devastated armies of Egypt and Syria. It was a strategic decision that required an enormous amount of Soviet investment, both in military and economic terms.[31] Soviet aid to Egypt and Syria resulted in a significant strategic benefit for Moscow. Both Arab countries provided port facilities for the Soviet fleet, while Egypt made available its airports to Soviet naval aircraft. This Soviet military foothold in Egypt and Syria depended to a considerable degree on the ability of Soviet warships and commercial vessels to pass through the Turkish straits with relative ease. Turkey facilitated the Soviets in their quest to build up and consolidate their military presence in the Eastern Mediterranean and the Middle East. Rubinstein described the Turkish policy of accommodating the Russians:

> After the 1967 June War, to avoid the [Montreux Convention] clause that requires "at least eight days' notification of the intention to pass" through the Straits, Moscow flooded the Turkish Foreign Ministry with stand-by applications for transit ... to obtain permissions whether they were effectively used or not. *The Turks did not object to this ploy.*[32] (Emphasis added.)

In other words, without the relatively free passage through the straits, the Soviet Union would have had grave difficulty maintaining a permanent fleet in the Mediterranean, and Moscow's objective of

---

[31]On Soviet policies in the Middle East in the 1950s, 1960s, and especially after the 1967 Arab-Israeli War, see Michael Confino and Shimon Shamir, eds., *The U.S.S.R. and the Middle East* (Jerusalem: Israel Universities Press, 1973).

[32]Rubinstein, Soviet Policy Toward Turkey, p. 44.

increasing its influence in Egypt and Syria would have become more problematic.

Several Russian war vessels could reach the Mediterranean through the Straits of Gibraltar. Many other ships, however, including cruisers, destroyers, frigates, and helicopter and aircraft carriers, sailed into the Mediterranean from the Black Sea through the Dardanelles. The Soviet Mediterranean fleet could not be sustained for long without the naval logistical support from Russia's Black Sea fleet. The Dardanelles, therefore, were essential for the projection of Soviet naval power in the Mediterranean.[33] Thus, within five years, between 1964 and 1969, the number of Soviet warships sailing through the Dardanelles more than tripled.

Just prior to the Yom Kippur War in October 1973, the Soviet Union had 52 naval vessels in its Mediterranean fleet. During the war, the Soviet fleet almost doubled to 95 war vessels. The power of this fleet almost matched that of the U.S. Sixth Fleet and limited its effectiveness.[34] Washington and Israel were displeased with Turkey's facilitation of the passage of Soviet warships through the straits, while also allowing the Soviet Air Force to use Turkish airspace to re-supply Egypt and Syria with military materiel.[35]

Writing shortly after the October 1973 Arab-Israeli War, Edward Luttwak, a strategic analyst in Washington, described how Turkey chose to accommodate Soviet interests in the Eastern Mediterranean and the Middle East in the face of increased Russian strategic and naval power. Luttwak wrote:

> . . . *the Turks have chosen to conciliate the Russians,* and have been able to do so at little or no direct cost to themselves. It is only in respect to strategic transit that Turkey is of primary importance to the Soviet Union, and this is the area where the

---

[33]On the significance of the Dardanelles in Turkish-Soviet relations, see Vali, *Turkish Foreign Policy,* 181–197; Karpat, "Turkish Soviet Relations," 73–74, 99; Rubinstein, *Soviet Policy Toward Turkey,* pp. 43–46.

[34]Keith Allen, "The Black Sea Fleet and Mediterranean Naval Operations," in *The Soviet Navy: Strengths and Liabilities,* ed. Bruce W. Watson and Susan M. Watson (Boulder: Westview Press, 1986), p. 220.

[35]On Washington's displeasure, see Rubinstein, *Soviet Policy Toward Turkey,* p. 44.

concessions have been made. Examples of such deflection where the Russians are conciliated *at the expense of western rather than specifically Turkish interests* include the overland traffic agreement (unimpeded Russian transit to Iraq and Syria by road), the generous Turkish interpretation of the Montreux Convention, which regulates ship movements in the Straits, and, above all, the over flight accorded to Russian civilian and military aircraft across Turkish airspace.[36] (Emphasis added.)

Thus, while Turkey was, technically speaking, neutral with regard to the October 1973 Arab-Israeli War, Ankara's speedy accommodation of Soviet naval and air needs in the Eastern Mediterranean during this war was not a favorable development for Israel.

It was only logical that Turkey's accommodation of Soviet naval and military needs in the Eastern Mediterranean would be extended to commercial shipping as well. Accordingly, the number of Soviet commercial ships passing through the straits increased dramatically in the 1960s. In 1955, Soviet commercial vessels going through the straits weighed 1.2 million tons, while, in 1969, they reached 26.3 million tons.[37] The improvement of Soviet-Turkish relations, therefore, should be viewed in the wider context of regional developments in the Eastern Mediterranean and the Middle East as well as in the broader climate of détente in Europe.

Relations between Turkey and Russia continued to improve in the 1970s. At the end of December 1975, Soviet Premier Alexei Kosygin paid an official visit to Turkey. In a joint Turkish-Soviet communiqué, Ankara and Moscow vowed to improve their political and economic relations and agreed to sign a document pledging continued friendly bilateral relations during upcoming top-level meetings. The Turkish invasion and occupation of the northern part of Cyprus in the summer of 1974 had not appeared to pose a problem for the Soviet Union as it continued to improve relations with Turkey. Yet, the left, both in Cyprus and Greece, still entertained the naïve notion that Moscow should become the anchor for the policies of these countries against the Turkish occupation of Cyprus. In reality, the Soviet Union had lit-

---

[36]Luttwak, *The Political Uses of Sea Power*, pp. 60–61.
[37]Karpat, "Turkish-Soviet Relations" pp. 73–74.

tle concern for the fate of Cyprus, as long as it did not become a forward base for NATO. This was prevented through the non-aligned policies of Makarios. The island republic was seen in Moscow through the cynical lenses of Russian strategic interests dictating Soviet accommodation with Turkey.

In March 1977, Turkish Foreign Minister İhsan Sabri Çağlayangil, who was serving in the coalition government of Prime Minister Süleyman Demirel, was in Moscow. There, he signed a long-range economic agreement with the Soviets, including the granting of $1.3 billion in credits for Turkey's heavy industry. Relations between Turkey and the Soviet Union continued to improve, especially in the economic field, with Turkey emerging as the clear beneficiary. By 1976, Turkey had emerged as the number-one recipient of Soviet economic assistance outside the Third World. By that year, Soviet economic aid to Turkey amounted to $1.18 billion dollars, rendering Ankara one of the largest recipients of Soviet aid.[38] This aid had an underlying strategic objective. By assisting Turkey and other Middle Eastern countries economically, Moscow hoped to undermine U.S. influence in the Mediterranean and facilitate its own drive to acquire a foothold in the region.[39] Moscow did not want to antagonize Turkey unnecessarily. For the sake of serving its broader strategic interests in the Eastern Mediterranean, especially its foothold in Egypt and Syria, the Soviets had to accept and acknowledge Turkey's position in NATO and its special ties with the United States.

The *Kiev* Sails into the Warm Seas

On July 18, 1976, the Soviet Union's naval capabilities in the Mediterranean were enhanced substantially with the addition of an aircraft carrier, the first to join the Soviet fleet in the Mediterranean. A 45,000-ton aircraft carrier, the *Kiev,* sailed through the Dardanelles with the permission of the Turkish government of Prime Minister Süleyman Demirel. Starting in 1968, in the aftermath of the 1967 Arab-Israeli War, the Soviets, with Turkish permission, sent two helicopter carriers, the *Moskva* and the *Leningrad,* through the straits. This was part

---

[38]Ibid.

[39]See Alvin Rubinstein, *The Foreign Policy of the Soviet Union* (New York: Random House, 1972), p. 420.

of Moscow's overall policy in the Middle East and was a strategic response to the deployment of the U.S. Sixth Fleet in the region.

The Montreux Convention sets limits on the types of war vessels that are allowed to pass through the Dardanelles and on their tonnage, restricting the passage of large war vessels. Goodwill visits by war vessels to Black Sea ports can be considered an exception to this rule.[40] Most Western observers agree that the Montreux Convention does not allow the passage of aircraft carriers, such as the *Kiev,* through the straits. The passage of the *Moskva* and the *Leningrad* were also questioned as possible violations of the convention.[41] Consequently, Turkey, with NATO's support, could have procrastinated and could have created complications for the Soviet Union and the navigation of its carriers through the straits.

With regard to the *Moskva* and *Leningrad* helicopter carriers, Turkey could make use of a more flexible interpretation of the Montreux Convention to justify their passage, but the *Kiev* was the first genuine aircraft carrier built by the Soviets. As Rubinstein put it:

> [The passage through the straits of the] *Kiev* was regarded by most western analysts as a *definite violation* [of the Montreux Convention] because, unlike *Moskva* and *Leningrad*, it mounts a large angled flight deck and carries not only helicopters but also 30 Yak-36 vertical/short take off and landing (V/STOL) jet aircraft.[42] (Emphasis added.)

Rubinstein characterized the fact that Turkey allowed a Soviet aircraft carrier to sail through the straits as a "de facto revision of the Montreux Convention" by Ankara.[43]

The Turkish justification for allowing the *Kiev* to sail through the

---

[40]The relevant articles of the Montreux Convention with regard to aircraft carriers are: Article 11, Article 14, Article 15, and Appendix II, B-2-a, b. The official text of the Montreux Convention in Greek and French can be found in the *Official Gazette of the Kingdom of Greece*, no. 333, August 7, 1936, pp. 1695–1710.

[41]See Allen, "The Black Sea Fleet and Mediterranean Naval Operations," p. 218; Christos Rozakis and Petros Stangos, *The Turkish Straits* (Dortrecht: Martinus Nijhoff, 1987), pp. 132–133.

[42]Rubinstein, *Soviet Policy Toward Turkey*, p. 45. See also Barry Buzan, "The Status and Future of the Montreux Convention," *Survival*, vol. 18, no. 6 (November-December 1976): p. 243.

[43]Rubinstein, *Soviet Policy Toward Turkey*, p. 45.

straits was that the Soviet warship could not be categorized as an air-craft carrier. Rather, the Turks argued, with apparent Soviet consent, that the *Kiev* was a "croisier lance-missiles de lutte anti-sous marine," or "an anti-submarine missile cruiser."[44] This definition of the vessel, which was beyond any reasonable doubt an aircraft carrier, consti-tuted legal acrobatics on the part of Ankara. Such acrobatics had rarely been practiced by any other NATO country when it came to military relations with the Soviet Union. In the final analysis, Turkey expedited Russia's descent into the warm waters of the Mediterranean by allowing an aircraft carrier to sail through the straits in violation of the Montreux Convention.

The Turkish government's flexibility in allowing a Soviet aircraft carrier to pass through the Dardanelles was deeply appreciated by Moscow, while it caused anxiety in NATO. Ankara allowed the vessel to sail through the straits 17 months after the imposition of the arms embargo against Turkey by the U.S. Congress, sending a message to Washington that it was capable of moving closer to the Soviet Union if the embargo continued. It was a pressure tactic that was deeply felt in the Ford White House. After all, the presence of a Soviet aircraft carrier in the Eastern Mediterranean strengthened Russian naval capabilities significantly in comparison to the U.S. Sixth Fleet. It also enhanced Soviet prestige in the Arab world, especially in Egypt and Syria. Indeed, the sailing of the *Kiev* into the Mediterranean repre-sented a Soviet coup when it came to the forward deployment of Russian strategic assets.

The Ford administration chose not to make a major issue of the *Kiev* episode. In fact, the Ford administration and Secretary of State Kissinger did not appear to take a determined stance concerning such an unorthodox, if not bizarre, interpretation of the Montreux Con-vention by Turkey, an interpretation that facilitated Soviet penetra-tion into the Eastern Mediterranean.[45]

---

[44]See the study by Ioannis Nikolaou, *O Diaplous ton Tourkikon Stenon kata teis Diethneis Synthykes kai Praktiki* (Passage Through the Turkish Straits According to International Treaties and Practice), Athens: Sideris Publishers, 1995, p. 90.

[45]There is little in the public record, memoirs, or declassified documents to demonstrate that the United States objected to the Turkish interpretation of the Montreux Convention, which favored the Soviets. There is also little to indicate that Washington made this an issue to be resolved by the NATO alliance in a way that involved Turkey being asked to abide by the Montreux Convention, which does not allow aircraft carriers such as the *Kiev* to pass through the Dardanelles.

A plausible explanation for their behavior is that Ford, Kissinger, and the Pentagon were fearful of antagonizing Turkey under the circumstances. The Demirel government had already closed down several U.S. military bases in Turkey to protest the embargo, and it was capable of closing down more. If Washington had challenged Turkey on the status of the straits, it might have created even more complications in U.S.-Turkish relations and Ankara might have moved even closer to Russia, the thinking went. This was a genuine fear since Washington was operating under the "what-if-we-lose-Turkey" syndrome. It can be argued that the Ford administration tolerated—with great, but unspoken, resentment—the Turkish decision to allow the passage of the *Kiev* through the straits. In this way, American strategic interests in the region became a captive to Turkish national interests and the threat that Ankara might move closer to Moscow if the embargo were not lifted.

Turkey's management of the Turkish-Soviet relationship, especially Ankara's facilitation of the passage of Russian warships through the straits, strengthened the Turkish hand in Washington. Ironically, the fact that the Soviet Union was looking toward Turkey for help in fulfilling its strategic needs in the Eastern Mediterranean, such as the presence of an aircraft carrier like the *Kiev,* enabled Turkey to use the Soviets as leverage to promote the lifting of the embargo. It is not unreasonable to suggest that Moscow was willing to see the embargo lifted even if this restored the American posture in Turkey. This was an acceptable price for the Soviets to pay if the side effect of the lifting of the embargo was the enhancement of Russia's strategic position in the Eastern Mediterranean.

This might have appeared inconsistent with Soviet strategic objectives but, in reality, it was not. The Soviets understood very well that Turkey was solidly anchored in NATO and was indispensable to the United States. They accepted it as fact and decided that they could live with it. Moscow could normalize and cultivate relations with Turkey to the maximum extent for the sake of Russia's strategic interests in the Eastern Mediterranean and the Middle East. Ankara's willingness to facilitate the passage of Russian warships and merchant vessels through the straits and into the warm waters of the Mediterranean was a Soviet gain. It was the fulfillment of an old Russian dream, which compensated for the gains the United States might have accrued through the lifting of the embargo.

In Greece and Cyprus, most Greeks, especially the left, being swept along by anti-Americanism, failed to recognize the essence, let alone the nuances, of the evolving Soviet-Turkish relationship. They were unable to realize that Soviet strategic interests in the Eastern Mediterranean and the Middle East took precedent over Moscow's ideological solidarity with fellow communists in Greece or Cyprus. Thus, the left in both countries, continued to view Moscow as the "savior against Turkish expansionism," which was, according to the leftist view, in the service of "American imperialism."

Socialist Greek opposition leader Andreas Papandreou viewed "Turkish expansionism as a by-product of American imperialism." Still, his views on the Soviet role in the Eastern Mediterranean diverged from those of the left. As early as 1976, he stated that, in the final analysis, Soviet policies in the Eastern Mediterranean favored Turkey. Asked specifically if the Soviet Union was neutral concerning Greek-Turkish differences in the Aegean, Papandreou responded:

> Regrettably, [the Soviet Union] is not even neutral. I would say it is pro-Turkish for a number of reasons.... Moscow has no reason to be neutral in the dispute between Greece and Turkey. It is beneficial for the Soviets to maintain better relations with Turkey than with Greece for reasons of [Soviet] national interests. . . . The Soviet Union would be disinterested if, for instance, Turkey occupied one of the Aegean islands or part of Greek Thrace . . .[46]

Two years later, when Washington embarked on the process of lifting the embargo, Papandreou declared, in April 1978, that Moscow's policy toward Turkey was facilitating the lifting of the embargo. This, however, did not cause Papandreou to moderate his anti-Americanism. On the contrary, the subsequent lifting of the embargo gave impetus to Papandreou's anti-American campaign.

Carter Meets Demirel

While Ankara was improving relations with Moscow and facilitating

---

[46]Andreas Papandreou, *He Ellada stous Ellines* (Greece for the Greeks), Athens: Karathanasi Publications, 1976, pp. 404–405.

the passage of Soviet warships through the straits, it was making sure that the United States had not forgotten the Soviet threat and the fact that Turkey was crucial to NATO's defense. This was apparent when President Carter met with Turkish Prime Minister Demirel on May 9, 1977, in London within the context of the annual NATO summit, two months after Turkish Foreign Minister Çağlayangil's visit to Moscow. During his meeting with Carter, Demirel advanced arguments that were similar to the ones he had presented to Clark Clifford in February 1977. "Turkey is the most faithful ally of the West," Demirel told the U.S. president, and he added in an accusatory tone:

> We have taken risks for the West's defense. But you rewarded us by imposing the embargo. While you are selling arms to 92 countries, you have imposed an embargo on Cuba and Turkey. You mixed up Cyprus with Turkish-American relations and turned [the Cyprus issue] into a dangerous direction. And now the common man [in Turkey] wonders, what have I done to America and I am confronted with such behavior? I cannot find an answer. You are partial [to the Greeks] and no problem can be solved this way.

Demirel complained to Carter for about 15 minutes and then came to the Soviet threat:

> Greece and ourselves, not tomorrow, but at some point, will resolve our differences. Leave us alone. But, under your policy, things will become more difficult and, one day, *if Russia moves across Turkey, it will reach the warm seas and the oil.*[47] (Emphasis added.)

As Birand put it, the Soviet threat and the prospect of Russia's descent into the "warm seas" of the Mediterranean appeared to be Carter's weak spot.[48] The Turkish prime minister, in addition to expressing his indignation over the embargo, brilliantly exploited Turkey's geopolitical position and America's fear of the Soviet Union. The Soviet threat began to weigh on Carter's mind as he listened to Demirel's statements on Turkey's importance to the United States in

---

[47]Birand, *Pazaremata* (Bargaining), pp. 312–313.
[48]Ibid.

thwarting Russia's ambition to descend into the "warm seas" of the Mediterranean. No one from the Carter team, including the president and National Security Adviser Zbigniew Brzezinski, gave the Turkish prime minister a polite diplomatic reminder concerning the *Kiev* incident. It had been just 10 months since Demirel had allowed the Soviet aircraft carrier to descend into the Mediterranean, in violation of the Montreux Convention, and, thus, strengthen substantially the Soviet naval presence in region.

What was especially remarkable was Brzezinski's silence.[49] After all, it had been Brzezinski, more than anyone else in the Carter administration, who had been skeptical about Carter's post-cold war foreign policy and had pushed for a return to the policy of containment. Soviet penetration into the Middle East and the Horn of Africa, and into Angola via Cuban proxies, had been paramount in Brzezinski's thinking when he called for standing up to Soviet expansionism. Yet, Brzezinski failed to ask for an explanation from Ankara concerning the expansion of the Soviet naval presence in the Eastern Mediterranean by sending the *Kiev* through the Turkish straits. In the end, however, it was the president of the United States who failed to exhibit leadership when challenged by the Turkish prime minister. The president's failure to stand up to Demirel and point out the fact that his government had facilitated the descent of the *Kiev* into the Mediterranean was an indication that Carter was not a particularly strong leader.

Ankara could draw only one conclusion: Turkey had done the right thing by allowing the *Kiev* to sail through the straits. This encouraged Turkey to play up the Soviet card in order to increase pressure on the Carter administration to lift the embargo. Unwittingly, the Carter administration was providing additional impetus to Turkey to make further use of the Soviet leverage to pressure Washington. In turn, the Carter White House cited Turkey's rapprochement with Moscow as the primary reason to lift the embargo. In the final analysis, the Carter administration had succumbed to a Turkish

---

[49]Brzezinski made no mention in his memoirs of the London meeting with Turkish Prime Minister Demirel. In his memoirs, he also failed to mention the descent of the aircraft carrier *Kiev* into the Mediterranean as an example of Soviet penetration into this critical geostrategic region. In addition, President Carter failed to mention the London meeting with Demirel in his memoirs.

policy of subtle blackmail as Ankara used the Soviet card to pressure Washington.

Only five months earlier, in February 1977, Greek Prime Minister Constantine Karamanlis had warned the Carter administration that it would be succumbing to Turkish blackmail if it took Ankara's overtures toward Moscow and its pressure on NATO at face value. Like Washington policy-makers, the Greek prime minister was also concerned about the Soviet threat, but he had a much better understanding of Turkish bargaining tactics than the Carter administration.

CHAPTER 9

Ecevit: American Misperceptions of a Nationalist Hawk

Bülent Ecevit: Pro-Russian?

The Turkish-Soviet rapprochement continued in 1978 under the government of Turkish Prime Minister Bülent Ecevit, which succeeded the Demirel administration. At the end of April 1978, when Carter had already embarked on pressuring Congress to lift the arms embargo against Turkey, Soviet Chief of General Staff General Nikolai Organov visited Ankara. He discussed ways of furthering Soviet-Turkish military cooperation with Ecevit. To underscore the importance of his visit, General Organov also met with Turkish President Fahri Korutürk.

Following Organov's visit to Turkey, Greek opposition leader Andreas Papandreou accused the Karamanlis government of leading Greece into isolation. Papandreou charged that the Greek government, by "being so subservient to America," had isolated Greece from the Eastern bloc. Turkey, on the other hand, was following a policy that promoted its own national interests. Papandreou pointed out that, in this respect, Organov's visit to Ankara coincided with the debate in Washington to repeal the embargo and was decisive in assisting the Carter administration in its drive to lift it. The Greek opposition leader concluded that the Soviet Union still had some explaining to do regarding Organov's visit to Turkey.[1]

The third week of June 1978, Ecevit paid an official visit to Moscow just as the Carter White House had begun to intensify its efforts in Congress to push for the repeal of the embargo and the congressional debate on the issue had begun. While he was in Moscow, Ecevit signed a non-aggression pact and several trade and cultural

---

[1] *Proini*, May 3, 1978.

agreements with the Soviet Union. Ecevit was not breaking new ground but was following the policy of détente that his conservative predecessors had begun.

The timing of the visit was quite effective as a pressure tactic. As if to underscore the fact that his visit was indeed related to the embargo issue, Ecevit made a shrewd statement in Moscow. At a press conference, he stated that he saw "hopeful signs in congressional circles in the United States that the embargo would soon be lifted."[2] The fact that Ecevit made this statement in Moscow was Turkey's way of sending a message to Washington that was quite threatening in the eyes of Washington policy-makers. His statement conveyed the subtle message that, he, as a socialist, could steer Turkey even closer to the Soviet Union if the embargo were not lifted.

Given the continuous improvement in Turkish-Soviet relations, culminating in Ecevit's visit to Moscow, the question arises whether Washington's alarmist view that Turkey might indeed leave the Western camp and move toward neutralism was justified. To those in Washington who saw, with anxiety, the improvement of Turkish-Soviet ties, Ankara could say that it fell within the context of the broader policies of Western European powers, which were seeking rapprochement with the Soviet Union. The prime example was West Germany under Chancellor Willy Brandt and his *Ostpolitik*. It was Brandt who led the Europeans in the direction of peaceful coexistence and détente with the Soviet Union.

Brandt's successor, Helmut Schmidt, carried on the policy of détente. He was also on very good terms with fellow socialist Bülent Ecevit. In fact, among the European allies, Schmidt emerged as the strongest supporter of lifting the embargo, even though he insisted that its repeal should be linked to progress on Cyprus. What worked in favor of Turkey was the fact that Schmidt had been in close contact with President Carter and had made it clear to the U.S. president that he favored the lifting of the embargo. The German chancellor was not oblivious to Greek concerns in this respect. On the contrary, he had developed a cordial relationship with Greek Prime Minister Constantine Karamanlis. Still, historically, Germany had had a special relationship with Turkey, and Schmidt continued the traditional German policy of support for Ankara.

---

[2] *New York Times*, June 24, 1978.

Russian Uneasiness with Ecevit

In Washington, there was fear that Ecevit would strike a deal with the Russians in order to move Turkey away from the Western alliance—a nightmarish scenario. Such a radical reorientation of Turkish foreign policy did not and could not have happened, however. There were several reasons why such a foreign policy change could not have taken place under Ecevit.

First, the agreements signed by Ecevit in Moscow were, according to Western diplomats, "bland and neutral" and did not change Turkey's strategic position in NATO.[3] When Ecevit went to Moscow, the ongoing embargo debate in the U.S. Congress was high on his mind.

Moscow looked at Ecevit with a certain amount of suspicion. The Russians preferred to deal with known quantities in Turkey's conservative governments, such as those of Demirel, rather than deal with Ecevit. It was under Demirel that Turkey became the largest recipient of Soviet economic aid outside the communist bloc.[4] Moreover, it was Demirel who allowed the aircraft carrier *Kiev* to sail through the Turkish straits in July 1976. As for Ecevit, Moscow viewed his domestic policies of "social democracy" as constituting a Western Trojan Horse that could become a paradigm for neighboring communist regimes in the Balkans.[5] Interestingly enough, the Soviets entertained a similar distrust of Greek socialist leader Andreas Papandreou when he came to power in 1981. Moscow suspected that Papandreou somehow represented an American ploy to reduce the influence of Greek communists and introduce a social democratic model in the Balkans. Such a model could "contaminate" the communist regimes in the region, primarily Bulgaria and Romania, but also Yugoslavia. Thus, the domestic orientations of Ecevit and Papandreou along the lines of the social democratic left were not necessarily welcome news for Soviet communism.

The Predominance of the Turkish Military

The second reason why Ecevit would not have effected any radical

---

[3]New York Times, June 24, 1978.
[4]Birand, *Pazaremata* (Bargaining), p. 76.
[5]Ibid.

change in Turkish foreign policy was the fact that he was a very weak prime minister. In 1978, Ecevit did not have the power base to reorient Turkey's foreign policy away from NATO. He could have taken such a radical step only with the approval of the powerful military establishment. The Turkish military, while approving of a policy of détente, had remained fiercely nationalistic and anti-communist, and it never would have tolerated a policy that led Turkey toward neutralism, let alone permit it to fall under the Soviet sphere of influence. The Turkish armed forces, the self-appointed guardians of the social and political order, considered the country's pro-Western orientation to be a sacred axiom. In reality, the attitude of the armed forces reflected the fact that the Turks remained "intensely suspicious of their colossal northern neighbor." This was the case despite the dramatic improvement of Turkish-Soviet relations from the 1960s onward.[6]

The predominance of the Turkish military in the country's political life was affirmed not long after Süleyman Demirel replaced Ecevit as prime minister in November 1979. Faced with increased domestic turmoil—fighting between the left and the right and sectarian violence on the campuses and in the streets of major cities—the Turkish military overthrew the civilian government of Prime Minister Demirel and assumed direct power on September 11, 1980. In this way, the Turkish armed forces reasserted their role as the most powerful, authoritative, and respected institution in society since the establishment of the Turkish republic in 1923. Even if one were to assume that there had been substantial popular support for a neutralist or more pro-Soviet foreign policy under Ecevit in 1978, the Turkish military would have had veto power over such matters and also would have had the will and power to withstand popular pressure. This was demonstrated time and again, and, even today, the Turkish military remains the ultimate arbiter in politics.

Ecevit: A Nationalist's Suspicion of Russia and "Orthodox Encirclement"

The third reason why a turn by Ankara toward the Soviets would have been extremely unlikely was the fact that Ecevit was a fierce national-

---

[6]See Frank Tachau, "Republic of Turkey," in *The Middle East: Its Government and Politics*, ed. Abdi Al-Marayati (Belmont, California: Duxbury Press, 1972), p. 397.

ist, despite his socialist orientation on domestic issues. Ecevit subscribed to the Kemalist ideology of secularism with a leftist bent, but he was a nationalist *par excellence.*

Being a dedicated nationalist, Ecevit was gravely suspicious of Russia and its ambitions in the Eastern Mediterranean. During his first term in office in 1973 and 1974, Ecevit continued the policy of détente with Russia. At the same time, he established closer relations with the United States and maintained a special relationship with Secretary of State Henry Kissinger, who was an architect of détente.[7] Ecevit followed a similar policy during his second term in office, which coincided with the tenure of the Carter administration. Ecevit continued the policy of détente with the Soviet Union, while he moved closer to the United States. The fear of Russia, however, had always been a major factor in Ecevit's *Weltanschauung.* This was reaffirmed in the 1990s, after the Soviet Union had collapsed and Russia was a much weaker and less threatening power than it had been in the past.

Ecevit's role and influence in Turkish politics diminished in the 1980s and early 1990s. However, by the second half of the 1990s, the veteran Turkish politician had staged a comeback. He became vice premier in July 1997 and then became prime minister in January 1999, heading a caretaker government that would carry out new elections on April 18, 1999.

These elections were won by Ecevit's party, the Democratic Socialist Party (DSP). It won the largest bloc of seats in parliament, 136, but fell far short of winning the majority in the 550-seat National Assembly. One of the reasons behind Ecevit's victory was that the elections were held in an environment of deep disillusionment with political parties. Most of the parties and their leaders were under a cloud of corruption. This was particularly the case with former prime minister Tansu Çiller and her New Path Party. Çiller's rule, from 1993 to 1996, had been characterized by a series of scandals. Among the traditional leaders, Ecevit emerged as the one with clean hands. Indeed, throughout his political career, which had spanned over a quarter of a century, Bülent Ecevit had maintained his personal integrity, which was reflected in the modest lifestyle he followed. This resonated well with a public that was fed up with political corruption.

---

[7]On the improvement of U.S.-Turkish relations under Ecevit, see Karpat, "Turkish-Soviet Relations," p. 106.

The ultra right-wing Nationalist Movement Party (*Milliyetçi Hareket Partisi*, or MHP) of Devlet Bahçeli came in a close second to Ecevit's DSP, securing 130 seats. Bahçeli had succeeded MHP leader Alparlsan Türkeş, who died in 1977. Türkeş and his party were passionate advocates of Pan-Turkism, which considered Cyprus to be a Turkish island. In fact, Türkeş believed that Turkey's failure to continue its military advance in 1974 to place all of Cyprus under Turkish control had been a grave error.

Ecevit's formation of a coalition government with the MHP, the party of the extreme nationalist Grey Wolves, reaffirmed the fact that the Turkish leader was a fierce nationalist, especially when it came to the question of Kurdish minority rights and foreign policy.[8] While there were very serious ideological differences between Ecevit's leftist-oriented DSP and the extreme right-wing MHP, both parties were linked through the umbilical cord of Turkish nationalism.

From 1997 onward, Ecevit had been, for all practical purposes, in charge of foreign policy under the watchful eye of the armed forces. His attitude toward the new post-communist Russia, however, was that of a cold warrior. He repeatedly attacked the "imperial ambitions" of Russia in the region as Ankara engaged in profitable economic deals with Moscow. Confirming their ambivalence toward non-communist Russia, Ecevit and other Turkish leaders advanced the thesis in 1997 and 1998 that Russia, under Boris Yeltsin, was leading an effort to form a coalition of Orthodox powers aiming at the encirclement of Turkey. The other members of this Orthodox coalition were, according to this thesis, Serbia, Greece, and Cyprus.

In this regard, Ecevit stated on January 21, 1997:

Turkey is being *surrounded by an Orthodox siege* that starts from Serbia, goes through Greece, Russia, the Caucasus, and ends in south Cyprus. . . . Should Cyprus fall into the hands of a country hostile to Turkey, it [Turkey] will be surrounded not only from the west from the Aegean, but to the south from the Mediterranean as well, and Russia will be involved in this siege for the first time.[9] (Emphasis added.)

---

[8]Steven Kinzer, "Results in Turkish Election Reflect Kurdish War's Fault Line: The Two Parties That Did Best [DSP and MHP] Insist There is No Kurdish Problem," *New York Times*, April 20, 1999.

[9]See Ecevit's interview with *TRT Television Network*, January 21, 1997.

In this way, Ecevit was linking the threat of "Orthodox encirclement" with the existing fear of "Greek encirclement," reinforcing the nightmare that Turkey could be surrounded by enemies.

In July 1997, Ecevit, having become vice premier, stated that ". . . Russia's initiatives to turn the Eastern Mediterranean into its sphere of influence are self-evident." Likewise, Turkish Foreign Minister Ismail Cem declared that "the Orthodox partnership led by Russia is dangerously spilling into Cyprus via the Balkans."[10]

The idea of an *Ortodoks ekseni,* or Orthodox axis, against Turkey, led by Russia in the wake of the collapse of communism, reflected an imaginary fear rather than a reality.[11] Above all, the notion of an Orthodox alliance against Turkey rested on the assumption that the bonds of Christian Orthodoxy among the Balkans, Eastern Europe, and Russia were strong enough to lay the foundation for a political and military alliance among Orthodox countries. This argument suffered from a fundamental flaw because, historically speaking, the Orthodox churches in the Balkans and Eastern Europe have been national churches *par excellence.* As such, they have spearheaded the nationalist movements in these regions. Bulgarian nationalism, for instance, has been interwoven with the Bulgarian Orthodox Church.[12] However, their common Orthodox faith did not prevent Greece and Bulgaria from engaging in a fierce clash for over three decades. Indeed, from the 1890s to the 1920s, Greek nationalism met Bulgarian nationalism in a bloody confrontation.

Likewise, in the aftermath of the collapse of communism in the Balkans, the common Orthodox faith did not bring together Greece and the newly established regime in Skopje known as the Former

---

[10]See the article "The Air Base in Paphos and the S-300," *Milliyet,* Istanbul, September 22, 1997.

[11]On the "anti-Turkish Orthodox axis," see Gülden Ayman and Nurşen Ateşoğlu Güney, "Değişen Uluslararası Koşullarda Strateji, Türkiye Ve Komsuları" (Turkey and its Neighbors, Strategy in a Changing International Environment), in Faruk Sönmezoğlu, Derleyen, *Türk Dış Politikasının Analizi* (Analysis of Turkish Foreign Policy) (Istanbul: Der Yayınları, 1994), p. 145.

[12]On the critical role that the Bulgarian Orthodox Church played in the development of Bulgarian nationalism, see Thomas Meininger, *The Formation of a Nationalist Bulgarian Intelligentsia, 1835–1878* (New York: Garland Publishing, 1987), pp. 60–119; Assen Nicoloff, *The Bulgarian Resurgence* (Cleveland, 1987), pp. 37–60; R.J. Compton, *A Concise History of Bulgaria* (Cambridge: Cambridge University Press, 1997), pp. 46–86.

Yugoslav Republic of Macedonia (FYROM). The most massive expression of Greek nationalist feeling over the last two decades has been over the "Macedonian issue." This outpouring of Greek national sentiment was directed against a fellow Orthodox country, FYROM, and its attempt to use the name "Macedonia" as the official name of the new country. The intensity of the nationalist mobilization in Greece over the Macedonian issue from 1991 to 1993 far exceeded any expression of nationalist sentiment against the "traditional enemy," Turkey. Even at the height of the 1974 Cyprus crisis and its aftermath, the expression of public support for Cyprus and against Turkey never reached the level of mass mobilization that occurred against the regime in Skopje, focusing on the Macedonian issue.

The Greek Orthodox Church led this mass mobilization in Greece against FYROM's Macedonian claims. This factor reaffirmed the national character of the Eastern Orthodox churches in the Balkans and the fact that nationalism was the dominant force in the charting of national priorities in each Balkan society. Under these circumstances, the common Orthodox faith was not sufficient as a catalyst for the formation of coalitions and alliances in the Balkans and Eastern Europe.

Therefore, the Turkish notion of a Greek-Serbian-Russian, anti-Turkish, Orthodox coalition in the late 1990s was far-fetched, with no basis in fact. By 1997, the Russian economy was in shambles, the Russian Army had been humiliated in Chechnya, and the overall state of affairs in Russia was dismal. As for Serbia, it was completely isolated. It had a very poor economy, was subject to Western economic sanctions, and was under constant pressure from NATO and the United States, first over Bosnia and subsequently over Kosovo.

Ecevit's fear of the Orthodox encirclement of Turkey suffered yet another blow with NATO's air campaign against Yugoslavia over Kosovo from April to June 1999. The myth of the Greek-Serbian-Russian axis collapsed as Greece—notwithstanding popular sentiment—sided with NATO against Serbia. At the same time, Russia played an instrumental role in pressuring Serbian dictator Slobodan Milosevic to capitulate in Kosovo. The fact that, in the late 1990s, Ecevit was still promoting the discredited idea of an Orthodox, anti-Turkish coalition, led by Russia, was the best confirmation of his Russophobia.

Still, as in the past, Ecevit did not allow his fear of Russia to prevent Turkey from benefiting from economic ties between Ankara and Moscow. Indeed, throughout 2000–2001, the Ecevit government entered into a series of commercial agreements with Russia especially in the field of energy. Moreover, Turkey used the "Russian card" to pressure the United States whenever Ankara perceived that Washington was not supportive enough of the Turkish positions regarding the European Union or Greek-Turkish relations. Accordingly, the Ecevit government entered into a series of new economic agreements with Russia in the first part of 2001. This was a period of some uneasiness between the Russian government of Vladimir Putin and the new Republican administration in Washington under President George W. Bush. This was also a time of deep economic crisis in Turkey while at the same time the European Union was pressuring Ankara to introduce a meaningful reform program. By moving seeminlgy closer to Russia, the Ecevit government expected that the George W. Bush administration would be much more forthcoming in accommodating Turkish requests for a more favorable treatment by the international banking community. In addition, Ankara hoped that Washington would pressure the European Union to ease its demands for domestic reform.[13]

It is within the context of Ecevit's fierce nationalism that his earlier rapprochement with Russia should be viewed. He was a leader who would cooperate with Russia but who would not and could not allow Soviet influence to determine Turkey's domestic or foreign policies, even if he desired to do so. In the 1970s, therefore, Washington's fear that Ecevit might lead Turkey away from NATO and into the arms of the Soviets because of the embargo was unfounded. Certainly, serious concern was justified, given the deteriorating domestic situation in Turkey. However, the alarm expressed by General Alexander Haig, Supreme Allied Commander Europe; the Joint Chiefs of Staff;

---

[13]Throughout the 1990s, the Clinton administration took a passive stand on the question of reform in Turkey. While the European Union was asking Turkey to reform its political and economic system so it meets the criteria of western European democracies, the Clinton administration failed, more or less, to support the European Union. The new Bush administration inherited the Turkish policy of the Clinton administration and is still unclear whether Washington will harmonize its policies with the European Union when it comes to the critical issue of reform in Turkey. On the subject of American policies and the question of Turkish reform, see Christos P. Ioannides, "From Bill Clinton to George W. Bush: Greek American Frustrations and Hopes," *The National Herald,* New York, February 17–18, 2001, p. 7.

Clark Clifford, the president's special envoy to Greece, Turkey, and Cyprus; and the National Security Council was not centered on the deteriorating domestic situation in Turkey. Rather, the primary concern was that the American embargo was pushing Turkey into the arms of Russia.

The Carter administration's alarmist view that Turkey was about to fall into the arms of the Soviets or follow a neutralist foreign policy because of the embargo stemmed from a combination of two elements. One represented domestic expediency. It was a pressure tactic to influence Congress but did not reflect Turkish reality. The other element, perhaps more fundamental, was the fact that, by 1978, Carter's idealistic vision of a post-cold war foreign policy had been abandoned for a traditional policy of containing the Soviet Union. National Security Adviser Brzezinski was a strong believer in the return to the containment policy and so was his assistant Paul Henze. They both believed that Turkey was essential to the policy of containment, especially at a time when the pro-American regime of the Shah of Iran, the other pillar of the containment policy along the southern tier of the Soviet Union, was about to collapse.

These were the dynamics behind Turkey's ties and high-level contacts with Moscow from 1976 to 1978. Ecevit had no intention and was in no position to re-orient Turkish foreign policy away from the West and closer to the Soviets. Still, the Turkish-Soviet rapprochement served as a powerful national security argument for the United States, and it was used by the Carter White House to persuade members of Congress to vote in favor of lifting the arms embargo against Turkey. It was precisely this type of alarmist argument, the fear of losing Turkey to the Soviets, that prompted the great majority of Republicans and southern Democrats in Congress to side with the administration and repeal the embargo.

Still, there was a contradiction between the Carter administration's view of Ecevit as a progressive liberal and good friend of the United States, on the one hand, and Ecevit, the leader who was about to lead Turkey out of NATO and into the arms of Russia, on the other. The explanation for this contradiction is rather simple. In the Carter White House, the team that the president had put together to deal with the Eastern Mediterranean did not believe that Ecevit was following a policy of moving closer to the Soviets out of conviction. Brzezinski, Clifford, and Haig believed that Ecevit was being forced by

Washington to move closer to Moscow because of the arms embargo. Neither Ecevit nor his predecessor, Süleyman Demirel, was to blame if Turkey took steps to distance itself from NATO and moved toward Turkish-Soviet rapprochement, the argument went. Ill-advised American actions carried out by Congress and the congressional arms embargo against Turkey were pushing the "proud Turks" away from the West. Therefore, Washington had to view Turkish actions such as the closure of American military bases as understandable.[14] Operating under this logic, the Carter administration embarked on a drive to repeal the embargo as soon as possible, before Turkey moved farther away from the West and closer to Russia.

---

[14]Henze, *Turkey and Ataturk's Legacy*, pp. 84–85.

CHAPTER 10

Turkish Military Might and Critical Developments in the Middle East

The Embargo's Effect on the Turkish Armed Forces

The fundamental argument behind lifting the embargo was counter-ing the weakening of NATO's southeastern flank with regard to the Soviet Union. This weakness was being brought about, the argument went, by the embargo, which had had a devastating effect on the Turk-ish armed forces. However, in addition to the Soviet threat, critical developments in the Middle East dictated that the Turkish armed forces should remain strong and able to project power in the region. Only a militarily strong Turkey could radiate stability in an inherently unstable region. Two developments at work in the Middle East made it more urgent for the United States to resume military aid to Turkey by lifting the embargo. These developments had to do with the revo-lutionary turmoil in Iran and with preparations for the historic Camp David summit between Israel and Egypt.

The administration's thesis was that the embargo had had a debili-tating effect on the Turkish armed forces at a critical juncture, both with regard to the Soviet Union and regional Middle Eastern dynamics. The seriousness of the problem was presented in a White House mem-orandum written by Deputy National Security Adviser David Aaron. The memorandum was written on May 19, 1978, and was classified *Top Secret/Sensitive* at the time. It was addressed to the president and described the status of the Turkish armed forces. The description of their condition was based on an analysis provided to the White House by General Alexander Haig, Supreme Allied Commander Europe.[1] In

---

[1] See Memorandum for the President, by David Aaron—Subject: NSC Weekly Report #59, The White House, May 19, 1978 (hereinafter referred to as *Aaron Memo*, May 19, 1978).

Haig's view, the embargo had had profound effects on the Turkish armed forces. Their command and control system could not effectively communicate on the battlefield. The tank fleet was obsolete. The navy had no air defense capability. The mission capability of the air force was only 50 percent, and its operational readiness rate was only 25 to 30 percent. Turkey's only modern aircraft, the F-4E, had less than 15 percent of its radar and fire control. Only three of the 13 naval anti-submarine and reconnaissance aircraft were in flying condition and even those three were in questionable condition.

The memorandum to the president described a bleak picture of the prospects for the year 1980 if the embargo continued for another two years. According to Haig, the readiness of the Turkish armed forces was bound to decline dramatically because the embargo would not allow the modernization of existing equipment. As a consequence, by the year 1980, Turkish armaments would become unsupportable from U.S. inventories. All tanks and 85 percent of the army aircraft would become insupportable in 1980. Most of the combatant fleet would become insupportable, including 86 percent of the destroyers and 85 percent of the submarines. Forty-four percent of the strike aircraft would be insupportable by 1980. As for on-hand communication equipment, 81 percent was already insupportable. In essence, in May 1978, the president was informed that, in terms of armaments, the Turkish armed forces were semi-paralyzed and that, in less than two years, they would suffer a total collapse unless the embargo were lifted. In addition to briefing the White House on these figures, Haig had also stated publicly that the embargo had caused the Turkish armed forces to lose 80 to 90 percent of their effectiveness.[2] Haig believed that the consequences of continuing the embargo would be "incalculable" in terms of NATO's defense of southeastern Europe.[3]

Mehmet Ali Birand, the author of the most authoritative Turkish study on the embargo question, shared the view that the embargo had a very serious effect on the Turkish armed forces. Birand did not paint as bleak a picture as Haig did, but he agreed that the embargo, com-

---

[2]See General Haig's testimony before the Senate Armed Services Committee, *New York Times*, March 1, 1978. See also General Haig's interview to the *New York Times*, May 23, 1978.

[3]*New York Times*, May 23, 1978.

bined with other factors, drastically reduced the operational capabilities of the Turkish armed forces.[4]

A 1980 Senate Foreign Relations Committee staff study later disputed the argument that the embargo alone had been responsible for the crippling of the Turkish armed forces to the extent that they lost 80 to 90 percent of their effectiveness. There is little doubt that the embargo had a serious impact on the capabilities of the Turkish military machine and that it did represent a form of strong American pressure on Turkey. Still, the Carter administration's claim that the Turkish armed forces were close to losing most of their fighting capabilities only because of the embargo became debatable.

According to the Senate study, the Turkish armed forces had greatly deteriorated. This deterioration, however, had been the result of a longer process that occurred throughout the 1970s. U.S. military aid to Turkey dropped from an average of $165 million annually before 1975 to $130 million during the embargo years, 1975 to 1978, a difference of only $35 million.[5]

In other words, the arms embargo against Turkey was never a total embargo. This was a recurrent argument during the Senate debate that led to the lifting of the embargo. Throughout the debate, advocates of lifting the embargo and supporters of the embargo pointed out that, from 1975 until 1978, Turkey received U.S. arms totaling $600 million or $150 million annually.

According to the Senate study, the embargo, which was partially lifted in 1976, was only one of several factors contributing to the deterioration of the Turkish armed forces.[6] Other factors were: (a) Turkish military equipment dated back to the 1950s and was becoming obsolete *en bloc*. The U.S. logistical system could no longer support such obsolete equipment. (b) The Turkish economy had been deteriorating since the 1974 rise in oil prices, and it was becoming increasingly difficult for the military to gain access to foreign currency, which was needed for higher economic priorities. (c) For several reasons, unrelated to the embargo, fewer foreign credits were made available for the modernization of the Turkish armed forces.

---

[4]Birand, *Pazaremata* (Bargaining), pp. 219–224.

[5]See *Turkey, Greece, and NATO: The Strained Alliance.* A Staff Report to the Committee on Foreign Relations, United States Senate (Washington, D.C.: U.S. Government Printing Office, March 1980), pp. 1, 15–19.

[6]See *Turkey, Greece, and NATO*, pp. 15–19.

The lack of foreign exchange and foreign credit had become a crucial issue for the Turkish government. Turkey's foreign reserves were reaching a critical low by 1977. A variety of reasons, including a downturn in the economy, the dramatic rise in oil prices, and the government's deficit spending for electoral purposes, had made it difficult for Turkey to secure foreign loans. Not only were U.S. banks reluctant to provide Turkey with credit, but European banks were also following suit. As far as the arms embargo was concerned, its partial lifting in 1976 did allow Turkey to buy a limited amount of arms and spare parts directly from U.S. arms manufacturers. The problem was that Turkey did not have the foreign exchange required to buy the larger amount of arms it needed for its defense. That was why Turkey insisted on tying the lifting of the embargo to the signing of a new Defense Cooperation Agreement with the United States, which would allow Turkey to borrow at a low interest rate.[7] In other words, the economic crisis and the lack of foreign exchange had coincided with the embargo and had made it almost impossible for Turkey to secure adequate arms supplies from the arms market.

Whether the 1980 Senate study gave a more accurate picture of the effects of the embargo on the Turkish armed forces becomes immaterial in the sense that the study was conducted after the embargo was lifted. Moreover, by the spring of 1978, the Carter administration had embraced the analysis of the Supreme Allied Commander Europe concerning the status of the Turkish armed forces. General Alexander Haig's alarm over the paralysis of the Turkish armed forces and his prediction that they would collapse because of obsolete and inoperable equipment carried the day and became the official position of the Carter administration.

Under these conditions, the lifting of the embargo had become an extremely urgent matter for the administration. At the same time, the fact that the Turkish armed forces depended completely on the United States for arms and spare parts provided the Carter administration with enormous leverage over the government in Ankara. Only the United States could have prevented Turkey's armed forces from total paralysis. This was consistent with the argument presented by Haig and the Pentagon, namely, that the embargo was undermining the fighting capabilities of the Turkish armed forces and had to be lifted.

---

[7]Birand, *Pazaremata* (Bargaining), pp. 219–223.

Turkey desperately needed U.S. arms as well as economic aid, so the Carter administration had a unique opportunity to exact some concessions on Cyprus in exchange for lifting the embargo.

President Carter failed to recognize that, in his hands, he had enormous American leverage over Turkey, which could have been used to assist Ankara while bringing about a Cyprus settlement. Instead of using this leverage, Carter ignored it and proceeded to lift the embargo without gaining any Turkish concessions on Cyprus whatsoever. It was yet another sign that Jimmy Carter was an erratic leader when it came to the use of U.S. diplomacy in international affairs.

The Iranian Turmoil

In addition to the arguments concerning national security and the Soviet threat, there were two other major factors that made the lifting of the embargo an urgent foreign policy priority for the Carter White House. They had to do with ongoing developments in the Middle East. First, the situation in Iran was deteriorating. Between the time that Carter asked for the lifting of the embargo in April 1978 and the time the embargo was finally lifted in August 1978, Iran entered a state of revolutionary turmoil. It culminated in the overthrow of the Shah's regime less than eight months later, in February 1979. Second, by the summer of 1978, Carter and his advisers were deeply involved with preparations leading up to the Camp David summit of September 1978.

Signs of deterioration in Iran were already evident in 1976. The twelve months of 1977, as James Bill astutely observed, set the stage for the revolution as the Shah's regime faced mounting opposition.[8] Certainly, the Carter administration had inherited the ill-advised policies of earlier administrations, especially those of Nixon and Kissinger. The Nixon-Kissinger policies of unconditional support for the Shah, especially in the area of U.S. arms sales, contributed to the collapse of the Shah's regime.[9] When Carter became president, he had

---

[8]Bill, *The Eagle and the Lion*, pp. 216–218. See also Saikal, *The Rise and Fall*, pp. 187–192; Ioannides, *Injury and Catharsis*, pp. 35–36.

[9]On American policies in Iran prior to the Carter administration, see, Bill, ibid., pp. 15–183; Barry Rubin, *Paved with Good Intentions: The American Experience in*

to deal with the worsening situation in Iran. By April 1978, when Carter made it official that he intended to ask Congress to lift the arms embargo against Turkey, Iran was clearly experiencing revolutionary upheaval. Mass demonstrations and riots were spreading throughout the country while the Shah's security forces attempted to suppress them by force, killing thousands of demonstrators in the process. Under these circumstances, the Carter administration had a keen interest in making certain that Turkey, a key NATO ally and Iran's neighbor, remained strong and stable.

During 1977 and 1978, therefore, the years leading up to the Iranian revolution, Turkey acquired added strategic significance with respect to the U.S. policy of containment of the Soviet Union.[10] For that purpose, a strong Turkish military was essential. This was especially the case given the pivotal role the military had had in Turkish society and politics since the establishment of the Turkish republic in 1923.

While several State Department officials questioned the viability of the Shah's regime, Zbigniew Brzezinski, Carter's national security adviser, became a crusader for a hardline U.S. policy toward the Iranian opposition to the Shah. He was confident that the Shah would prevail if only he took a tougher stance against the demonstrators and unleashed the "iron fist," his powerful military, against them. Brzezinski favored an American-backed military coup to crush the revolution. By the late fall of 1978, Brzezinski was calling for the "use of the iron fist" against the protesters. By that time, over 10,000 demonstrators had been killed by the Shah's security forces.[11] Even the Shah, himself, was shaken by the magnitude of the bloodshed. In essence, Brzezinski followed the path of realpolitik when it came to dealing with the Iranian crisis.

Iran (New York: Oxford University Press, 1980), passim; Ruhollah Ramazani, *The United States and Iran* (New York: Praeger, 1982), passim; Niki Keddie, *Roots of Revolution: An Interpretive History* (New Haven: Yale University Press, 1981), passim; Richard Cottam, *Nationalism in Iran* (Pittsburgh: Pittsburgh University Press, 1979), passim; Kermit Roosevelt, *Countercoup: The Struggle for the Control of Iran* (New York: McGraw Hill, 1979), passim; Ioannides, *America's Iran,* passim.

[10]On Turkey's added strategic significance for the United States due to the Iranian revolution, see Helen Laipson, "U.S. Policy Towards Greece and Turkey Since 1974," in *The Greek-Turkish Conflict in the 1990s,* ed. Dimitri Constas (London: MacMillan, 1991), p. 168. See also Birand, *Pazaremata* (Bargaining), pp. 65–67.

[11]Bill, *The Eagle and the Lion,* p. 251.

Secretary of State Cyrus Vance was staunchly opposed to Brzezinski's recommendation to the president concerning the situation in Iran.[12] The ensuing confusion, with many in the State Department favoring drastic reforms leading to a representative government in Iran and with Brzezinski favoring a tougher policy against the opposition to the Shah's regime, led to indecision. As a consequence, President Carter had to deal with a feud between Vance and Brzezinski over whose view would be preeminent in foreign policy, especially regarding Iran. Carter appeared indecisive or tended to side with his national security adviser. The administration downplayed the importance of the religiously inspired opposition to the Shah's regime at a time when the masses were already solidly in the camp of Ayatollah Khomeini, who was determined to overthrow the Shah. Yet, while Carter followed Brzezinski's advice not to abandon the Shah, the president did not agree that the Shah should unleash the country's military against the demonstrators.[13]

The same foreign policy officials who were agonizing over Iran—President Carter and his top aides in the White House, as well as officials of the Department of State and the Pentagon—had embarked on a campaign to persuade Congress to repeal the arms embargo against Turkey. It is quite revealing that none of the top officials who argued before Congress in favor of lifting the embargo openly linked the situation in Iran with stability in Turkey. It would have been a powerful argument in support of lifting the embargo because Iranian instability had rendered Turkey even more important for the West and for regional stability. This argument, however, was never made, at least in public.

Two factors might account for this omission. First, during the spring and early summer of 1978, most top officials in the Carter administration believed that Iran was experiencing serious turmoil

---

[12]On Brzezinski's support for the adoption of a hardline policy by the Shah, see Bill, *The Eagle and the Lion*, pp. 243–260. See also the comments by William B. Quandt in Rosenbaum and Ugrinsky, eds., *Jimmy Carter*, p. 73. On Brzezinski's own interpretation of events in Iran, see Brzezinski, *Power and Principle*, pp. 353–398.

[13]See Bill, ibid., pp. 243–260. For Vance's view of the dispute with Brzezinski, see Vance, *Hard Choices*, pp. 326–333. On Brzezinski's view of the disagreements within Carter's foreign policy team, see Brzezinski, *Power and Principle*, pp. 353–358. President Carter's perspective of events in Iran from September 1978 to January 1979 appears in Carter, *Keeping Faith*, pp. 438–450.

but did not believe that the turmoil constituted a revolutionary upheaval. Carter and his advisers believed that the Shah was going to prevail, even though the Iranian leader would have to make some concessions and relax his grip on power. Second, even if there had been concern over Iran, it would have been counterproductive to state in public, during the embargo debate, that the Shah's regime was in danger of being overthrown and, therefore, Turkey needed American military aid more than ever. Such an argument would have sent a message to Iran that the United States was abandoning the Shah and would have emboldened the opposition.

For these reasons, the Iranian upheaval never became a salient issue in the eyes of the Carter administration in its drive to lift the embargo. In the back of their minds, however, Carter's foreign policy advisers were gravely concerned about instability in Iran and its repercussions on Turkey when they were asking Congress to repeal the embargo.

The Road to Camp David

In addition to the revolutionary situation in Iran, Turkey's next-door neighbor, there was another reason pushing Carter to seek the lifting of the embargo. The restoration of a normal flow of arms to Turkey would contribute to a more stable environment in the Middle East and the Eastern Mediterranean. By the spring of 1977, Carter had begun his long and successful quest for an Arab-Israeli peace accord. Between March and July 1977, Carter met with Israeli Prime Minister Yitzhak Rabin, Egyptian President Anwar Sadat, Syrian President Hafez al-Assad, and the new Israeli prime minister, Menachem Begin. On November 19, 1977, Sadat made his historic visit to Jerusalem and paved the way for Arab-Israeli rapprochement. The road to Camp David had been opened.

Following 12 days of intense negotiations at Camp David, Israeli Prime Minister Menachem Begin and Egyptian President Anwar Sadat signed the historic Camp David accords on September 17, 1978. President Carter acted as a mediator between Begin and Sadat. At last, Israel was at peace with the most important Arab country.

The road to the Camp David negotiations involved exhaustive preparations by the Carter White House. The key American players in this regard were President Carter, himself, Secretary of State Cyrus Vance, National Security Adviser Zbigniew Brzezinski, and the head of the National Security Council Middle East desk, William B. Quandt.[14] An important role was also played by Alfred Atherton, ambassador at large for the Middle East; Harold Saunders, assistant secretary of state for Near East and South Asian affairs; and Hermann Eilts and Samuel Lewis, U.S. ambassadors to Cairo and Tel Aviv, respectively.

For most of 1977 and up to the time the Camp David accords were signed in September 1978, the White House, the State Department, and other foreign policy agencies were engaged in finding the modalities to bring about an Arab-Israeli diplomatic breakthrough. When this breakthrough came at Camp David, it represented the most important foreign policy achievement of the Carter administration. To a considerable degree, it was the vision and persistence of President Carter that made the Camp David peace accords possible. Throughout 1977 and 1978, Carter was deeply involved in charting the diplomatic path leading to Camp David. Indeed, he exhibited extraordinary commitment and dedication to advancing the cause of Arab-Israeli peace.[15]

Carter's diplomatic approach toward achieving Arab-Israeli peace was rather simple, even though the issues involved were quite complex. Carter believed that he could play the role of an honest broker after having won the trust of both sides in the dispute. In order to play this role, it was not enough to rely on his image as a moral person and a man of character and integrity. He had to proclaim the general principles upon which Arab-Israeli peace would rest. These principles did not have to include any detailed positions or methods of tackling specific issues. Instead, they were meant to illustrate Pres-

---

[14]Quandt was a scholar with exceptional credentials in Middle Eastern affairs and a deep historical understanding of the region. He has given the best account yet of the Camp David accords and the domestic and foreign policy dynamics that led up to them. See William B. Quandt, *Camp David: Peacemaking and Politics* (Washington, D.C.: The Brookings Institution, 1986).

[15]For Carter's own account of the Camp David accords, see Carter, *Keeping Faith*, pp. 267–403. An incisive account of Carter's role in bringing about the Camp David accords is found in Quandt, *Camp David*. Throughout the book, Quandt highlighted Carter's role both in terms of presidential leadership and in terms of style and interaction with various Israeli and Arab leaders.

ident Carter's vision of a just peace in the Middle East for the Israelis and the Arab world. Carter embarked upon that path from the very beginning of his presidency. He realized that time and effort were required to generate domestic and international support for bringing Arabs and Israelis together.

The negative effect of the Arab-Israeli conflict on Western and U.S. prosperity formed the basis for Carter's Middle Eastern diplomacy. The energy crisis, brought about by the Arab oil embargo as a result of the Arab-Israeli war in October 1973, was high on the president's mind when he embarked on his peacemaking mission. He was also aware of the risk of superpower confrontation due to the Arab-Israeli dispute.[16]

Throughout 1977 and up until the Camp David negotiations, Carter found many opportunities to present his vision of peace to the American people and to the leaders and people of Israel and the Arab world. He publicly promulgated the overarching principles upon which Arab-Israeli peace should rest.

In his first State of the Union address to Congress on January 19, 1978, President Carter spelled out these general principles:

> In an effort to break with the rigid approaches of the past and bring about an overall peace settlement [in the Middle East], I have looked into three basic principles: normalization of political, economic and cultural relations through peace treaties; *withdrawal of armed forces from occupied territory* to recognized and secure borders and the establishment of effective security measures; and a resolution of the Palestinian question.[17] (Emphasis added.)

In this way, Carter communicated what he considered to be the foundations of peace in the area both to the world and to all the parties involved in the Middle East peace process.[18] One of the three pillars of a negotiated Arab-Israel peace settlement was the withdrawal of Israel from the occupied Arab territories. The exact amount of ter-

---

[16]These points on the energy crisis and the danger of superpower confrontation were made by Quandt, *Camp David*, p. 58.

[17]"The State of the Union Address: Annual Message to the Congress, January 19, 1978," *Presidential Papers, Carter, 1978*, Book I, p. 121.

[18]On this point, see Quandt, *Camp David*, pp. 58–60.

ritory that Israel would return to the Arabs was to be negotiated, but Carter left no doubt that Israel had to make major territorial concessions in exchange for Arab recognition. The president made this abundantly clear from the very beginning of his presidency. Time and again throughout 1977, Carter stated that Israeli withdrawal from the occupied territories had to be substantial. Barely nine weeks after he entered the White House, Carter declared at a news conference that both the United States and Israel would like to see a termination of belligerence toward Israel by its Arab neighbors, a recognition of Israel's right to exist within secure borders, and a general normalization of relations between Israel and its neighbors. Carter stated how this could be achieved:

> This would involve *substantial withdrawal of Israel's present control over territories.* Now, where that withdrawal might end, I don't know. I would guess it would be some minor adjustments in the 1967 borders. But that still remains to be negotiated.[19] (Emphasis added.)

Carter repeated the three principles for achieving a negotiated settlement in the Middle East on many occasions and at different fora. The withdrawal of Israel from Arab territories always remained a fundamental principle. Israel was being asked publicly to make major territorial concessions, while the Arabs were being asked to recognize Israel and normalize relations with the Jewish state.[20]

Carter followed a very different diplomatic approach with regard to the Cyprus dispute and the Turkish occupation of the northern part of the island republic. As in the case of the Arab-Israeli dispute and movement toward a negotiated settlement—achieved at Camp David—President Carter was personally involved in the efforts

---

[19]"The President's News Conference of March 9, 1977," *Presidential Papers, Carter, 1977*, Book I, p. 342.

[20]For Carter's statements on the three principles for Arab-Israeli peace and the need for Israel to make territorial concessions, see also "The President's Press Conference of May 12, 1977," *Presidential Papers*, Carter, *1977*, Book I, p. 861; "Presidential Address at Commencement Exercises, University of Notre Dame, May 22, 1977," *Presidential Papers, Carter, 1977*, Book I, pp. 959–960; "President Carter's Informal Exchange with Reporters, Plains, Georgia, December 25, 1977," *Presidential Papers, Carter, 1977*, Book II, p. 2173.

toward a Cyprus settlement. Certainly, Carter's personal role in achieving Egyptian-Israeli peace at Camp David was, by far, more intense and much deeper than his involvement with the Cyprus question.

Still, President Carter maintained a personal interest in the Cyprus question, especially since his involvement in Cyprus had become inextricably linked to the arms embargo against Turkey and its eventual repeal. The lifting of the embargo, however, became Carter's primary focus, and Cyprus was viewed by the Carter foreign policy team through the lens of the embargo. This perspective made a Cyprus settlement secondary to the lifting of the embargo. In the case of the Camp David negotiations, a peace settlement, itself, was the objective. In the case of the Cyprus dispute, a settlement was to be pursued only as a means to a higher goal: the lifting of the embargo.

It was for this reason that President Carter never spelled out his vision for peace in Cyprus or the fundamental principles upon which a Cyprus settlement should rest. Had he done so, he might have achieved a just and lasting solution to the Cyprus problem. From the very beginning, the Carter administration adopted a diplomatic approach toward the Cyprus dispute that was deliberately vague and lacked a concrete framework of principles. This approach precluded the taking of a public stand on the question of Turkish-occupied Cyprus. From the time he took office in January 1977 until the embargo was lifted in August 1978, at no point did President Carter— as opposed to candidate Carter—make a public pronouncement to the effect that the withdrawal of the Turkish occupation army from Cyprus, be it substantial, partial, or gradual, was a principle upon which a Cyprus settlement should be built.[21] Such a nebulous approach to negotiations inherently favored the territorial status quo, that is, the power that had the military upper hand in Cyprus by virtue of occupying 38 percent of its territory.

Carter believed that this vague approach facilitated his drive in Congress to persuade its members to lift the embargo. If Carter had publicly talked about the "withdrawal of Turkish troops from the occupied territory" in Cyprus, he might have undermined the chances of lifting the embargo, for he would have justified the reason for its

---

[21]Based on an examination of Carter's Presidential Papers from January 20, 1977, to August 31, 1978.

imposition to begin with. The embargo was imposed because of the illegal use of U.S. arms by Turkey for offensive purposes, namely, the occupation of the northern part of Cyprus. If Carter had announced his support for the withdrawal of Turkish forces from the occupied territory in Cyprus, there is little doubt that Congress would have insisted that the embargo be lifted only if Turkey withdrew its occupation army from the country. After all, this army was enforcing and consolidating its occupation through the illegal use of American arms.

Carter adopted the opposite approach with regard to the Israeli-occupied territories. It was an approach aimed precisely at changing the territorial status quo by asking Israel to put an end to the occupation of Arab lands because this would help achieve the main American objective, a peace settlement.

Carter did not consider his decision to publicly call on Israel to make a major concession by withdrawing from Arab territories to be an impediment to a negotiated Arab-Israeli settlement. On the contrary, it became an essential part of Carter's diplomatic approach to reaching the Camp David peace settlement. His call to Israel to make major territorial concessions was balanced by his call to the Arabs to end their hostility toward Israel, recognize the Jewish state, and establish normal relations with it. It was precisely this *quid pro quo* that enabled Carter to appear fair to all sides and move toward the major accomplishment of his presidency, the September 1978 Camp David accords.

This *quid pro quo* diplomatic approach was clarified further by Secretary of State Cyrus Vance as he was getting ready to visit the Middle East in August 1978 in preparation for the Camp David summit among President Carter, Israeli Prime Minister Menachem Begin, and Egyptian President Anwar Sadat.

On July 28, 1978, Vance appeared on ABC's long-running Sunday television program "Issues and Answers" and discussed the administration's policies concerning the Arab-Israeli dispute and the arms embargo against Turkey. In view of his trip to the region in August 1978 and the prospect of Arab-Israeli peace negotiations, Vance stated in no uncertain terms that these negotiations hinged on Israel's acceptance of the principle of withdrawing its forces from the occupied West Bank. The negotiations would get bogged down unless Israel accepted this principle, Vance declared.[22] Then, the secretary of

---

[22] *Washington Post*, July 24, 1978.

state presented the administration's case for lifting the arms embargo against Turkey and repeated the standard arguments. Unlike the Arab-Israeli negotiations whereby Israel was called upon to accept the principle of withdrawing its occupation forces as a condition for achieving a peace settlement, Vance did not ask that Turkey accept the withdrawal of its occupation forces from Cyprus as a condition for a Cyprus settlement. On the contrary, he asked that the embargo be lifted without securing Turkey's commitment to withdraw its occupation forces from the island republic as part of a peace settlement. Vance's statements clearly contrasted the Carter administration's views on the two disputes and the strategies to be followed for a settlement in each case.

The difference in the Carter administration's approaches to settling the Arab-Israeli dispute and the Greek-Turkish dispute in Cyprus indicated that the pro-Turkish positions of the administration were becoming so entrenched and dogmatic that Israel was being asked to make, relatively speaking, more serious territorial concessions than Turkey. Unlike Israel, Turkey is a huge country, which did not face any threat to its existence. Certainly, Turkey was concerned about the future of the Turkish Cypriot community, which represented 18 percent of the population of Cyprus. Still, territorial concessions by Turkey in Cyprus would be, by any standards, much less painful for Ankara than the concessions demanded of Israel in the occupied Arab territories.

A contributing factor to Carter's divergent diplomatic approaches to the two disputes had to do with critical developments in the Middle East. As stated above, Turkish stability and military strength were more necessary than they had been previously because of the Iranian upheaval. This upheaval was taking place while the Carter team was busy preparing for the Camp David negotiations. In the context of these complex American diplomatic efforts and maneuvers, the Carter administration had a keen interest in ensuring that Syria did not become a spoiler in the game of pursuing an Egyptian-Israeli peace agreement. Turkey was important in this respect because a strong Turkey could keep Syria in check just in case Damascus entertained thoughts of disrupting the negotiations through some kind of military action against Israel.

According to Carter's logic, therefore, it became imperative that the arms embargo against Turkey be repealed unconditionally. By the time the embargo was lifted in August 1978, the preparations for the Camp David talks were in full swing, while the revolution in Iran had entered its final stage.

Thus, the basic thesis for lifting the embargo revolved around cold war geopolitical arguments and two critical developments in the Middle East, the Iranian revolutionary turmoil and the ongoing preparations for the Camp David talks. In addition, the Carter administration argued, with conviction, that the embargo had failed to achieve its stated objective of forcing Turkey to negotiate seriously to end its occupation of Cyprus. In doing so, Carter tilted toward Turkey because his approach to a Cyprus settlement—unlike his approach to an Arab-Israeli settlement—did not rest on the principle that such a settlement had to include the withdrawal of occupation forces. In the end, a Cyprus settlement was not seen as an American diplomatic objective for its own sake. Rather, a Cyprus settlement was seen through the prism of the lifting of the embargo, which dictated the Carter administration's diplomacy in the Eastern Mediterranean.

In the Nixon-Kissinger White House, realpolitik dictated U.S. policies in the Eastern Mediterranean. As a consequence, the United States supported the Greek military junta and condoned the junta's coup against the president of Cyprus, Archbishop Makarios, as well as the Turkish invasion that ensued. The Carter-Brzezinski White House followed a similar realpolitik logic when it came to Cyprus. In the end, the little island republic was expendable in the name of serving what was seen as a more important strategic objective, that of maintaining Turkey's stability and its close ties with NATO.

CHAPTER 11

Revisionism: Inventing a New Discourse for Turkey and Occupied Cyprus

The Fight Begins: Vance's Testimony in Congress

The battle to lift the arms embargo against Turkey was waged on Capitol Hill between April 6 and August 1, 1978. Hearings before the appropriate committees in the Senate and the House of Representatives became the main battleground. The first hearing took place on April 6, 1978, before the House International Relations Committee, chaired by Representative Clement Zablocki, Democrat of Wisconsin. This hearing signaled the opening of Carter's campaign to repeal the embargo. For that purpose, the White House sent the highest foreign policy and defense officials to the Hill for a joint appearance. Testifying before the committee were Secretary of State Cyrus Vance, Secretary of Defense Harold Brown, and General David Jones, chairman-designate of the Joint Chiefs of Staff. Zablocki stated that, to his knowledge, it was the first time that a joint appearance of high foreign policy and defense officials had taken place before the House International Relations Committee.[1] This was an indication of the determination of the Carter White House to exercise maximum pressure on Congress to repeal the embargo.

Secretary of State Vance led the administration's effort to repeal the embargo by presenting its new policy regarding the embargo before Congress. In the process, he set the tone for other administration officials to follow. Before he joined the Carter administration, Vance was a strong supporter of the embargo. As secretary of state, however, he led the drive for its repeal. In his testimony, Vance presented the standard national security arguments as he explained why

---

[1]See *New York Times*, April 7, 1978.

it was imperative that the embargo be repealed. He stated that: "Continued maintenance of the embargo would be harmful to U.S. security concerns, harmful to NATO, harmful to our bilateral relations with Turkey, and harmful to our role as a potential contributor to a Cyprus settlement."[2]

Vance told the committee that the embargo had made it more difficult to achieve a Cyprus settlement and that, by lifting it, the chances for such a settlement would, in fact, improve. The next day, a report in the *New York Times* on Vance's statement appeared under the headline "Vance Says Arms for Turks Will Bring Moves on Bases and Cyprus."[3] The assertion that the lifting of the embargo would facilitate a Cyprus settlement became a pivotal argument of the Carter administration over the next four months in Congress. Turkey was a proud country that would not make concessions under the pressure of the embargo, the argument went. On the other hand, if the embargo were lifted, Ankara would be more conciliatory on Cyprus.

The secretary of state also informed the committee that the repeal of the embargo was to be accompanied by $175 million in FMS (Foreign Military Sales) loan guarantees to Turkey. In addition, the United States would provide a $50 million loan to assist the faltering Turkish economy. No conditions were to be attached to the lifting of the embargo, the FMS loan, or the economic assistance loan.[4]

Occupied Cyprus: Toward a New American Discourse

Throughout his policy statement before Congress, Vance avoided the use of the terms "invasion of Cyprus," "occupation of Cyprus," "withdrawal of foreign forces," or "human rights." The avoidance of the terms "invasion" and "occupation of Cyprus" constituted an indication that the State Department was moving away from viewing the Turkish military presence in Cyprus as an occupation and an illegality pursuant to international law. Avoiding the characterization of the Turkish military presence in Cyprus as an "occupation" or the mention of "foreign military forces" in the country facilitated Vance's

---

[2]For this important testimony by Secretary of State Vance, see Vance, *Administration Policy*. See also, *New York Times*, April 7, 1978.

[3]Ibid.

[4]Ibid.

arguments in seeking the lifting of the embargo since these terms would have raised the issue of upholding the rule of law.

In addition, Vance meticulously avoided stating that the United States supported the U.N. resolutions concerning Cyprus. He did state that the U.S. supported the efforts of the U.N. secretary general regarding Cyprus, but that was not equivalent to supporting the resolutions. The reason for deliberately avoiding mention of the resolutions was that specific resolutions of the U.N. Security Council and the U.N. General Assembly called for the withdrawal of foreign forces from Cyprus.

According to these resolutions, the Turkish forces in Cyprus constituted an illegal occupation army that should "withdraw without delay." The Security Council resolution of July 20, 1974, called for:

> ... all States to respect the sovereignty, independence and territorial integrity of Cyprus; demands an *immediate end to foreign military intervention* in the Republic of Cyprus ... and requests the *withdrawal without delay* from the Republic of Cyprus of *foreign military personnel present otherwise than under the authority of international agreements...*"[5] (Emphasis added.)

In addition, the U.N. General Assembly resolution of November 1, 1974, called for:

> ... all States to respect the sovereignty, independence and territorial integrity of the Republic of Cyprus and for the *speedy withdrawal of all foreign armed forces* and foreign military presence and personnel from the Republic of Cyprus and the cessation of all foreign interference in its affairs."[6] (Emphasis added.)

It was the resolution of November 1, 1974, that candidate Carter cited in his promises to the Greek American community regarding Cyprus. According to these two resolutions, numerous other U.N. resolutions, and U.S. law covering foreign military assistance, the Turkish occupation army was in continuous violation of both inter-

---

[5]U.N. Security Council Resolution 353, July 20, 1974.
[6]U.N. General Assembly Resolution 3212 (XXIX), November 1, 1974.

national law and U.S. law. The U.N. resolutions, which the United
States had voted in favor of, made it clear that the Turkish military
force was in Cyprus illegally. Turkey had used American arms to carry
out the invasion of Cyprus, an act of aggression, which was illegal
under U.S. law. As a result, the terms "occupation army" or "foreign
military forces in Cyprus" carried the meaning of illegality both in
terms of American law—the Foreign Assistance Act of 1961—and in
terms of international law as cited in U.N. resolutions.

Vance, an experienced international lawyer in his own right,
avoided using these terms or referring to the U.N. resolutions on
Cyprus to avoid raising questions of legality when it came to Turkish
military control of occupied Cyprus. After all, Congress had imposed
the arms embargo against Turkey on legal grounds. Vance did state
that the United States supported the position that Cyprus should be
"a sovereign independent nation" and that "partition has been ruled
out as a viable solution" in the country. But his statement left unanswered the question of the legality of the ongoing Turkish military
occupation of Cyprus and whether Turkey was in compliance with
U.N. resolutions. In this way, the Carter administration sidestepped
the rule of law and moved a step closer to the Turkish position that its
invasion and occupation of Cyprus were not actually illegal according to international law. Rather, the Cyprus problem was an internal
dispute to be settled by the two communities in the island republic,
the Greek Cypriots and the Turkish Cypriots.

Again, Vance's avoidance of the term "Turkish occupation" in the
case of Cyprus contrasted with the way the Carter administration and
the State Department viewed the situation in the Israeli-occupied territories—the West Bank and Gaza.[7]

Secretary of Defense Brown and General Jones testified along the
same lines as Vance. They placed more emphasis, however, on the
national security implications of the embargo. They stressed the
strategic importance of Turkey, the deterioration of the Turkish
armed forces, the closure of the U.S. bases in the country, and the serious damage done to the Western alliance in the Eastern Mediterranean as a result. Turkey might even reduce its ties to NATO and
might turn to the Soviet Union, it was argued.[8] Regarding the testi-

---

[7]The policies of the Carter administration toward the Israeli-occupied territories are examined later in this chapter.

[8] *New York Times*, April 7, 1978; *Proini*, April 7, 1978.

mony by the top administration officials before the House committee, the *New York Times* reported the next day that Carter and Vance had been strong supporters of the arms embargo during the 1976 election campaign. As a result, the newspaper pointed out, it had been something of an embarrassment for the administration to change its position and, in effect, accept the arguments used by former secretary of state Henry Kissinger.[9]

Reflecting this thinking, Representative Robert Lagomarsimo, Republican of California, posed the following question to Secretary Vance during the April 6 hearing: "I must say, Mr. Secretary, if I were to close my eyes and carry myself back a couple of years, except for the accent, I think what you're saying sounds very much like what Dr. Kissinger used to say."[10] Vance laughed but did not give an answer. It was uncharacteristic for Cyrus Vance not to respond when he was criticized directly for sounding like Kissinger. Vance was no Kissinger, neither with respect to his worldview nor his demeanor. He was put on the spot, however, by Congressman Lagomarsimo and had no answer. The reason Vance could laugh but could not respond was understandable. His testimony to the House International Relations Committee on April 6, 1978, represented a total reversal of what he had advocated before the same committee on July 10, 1975. At that time, Vance had expressed strong support for maintaining the arms embargo. The famous cartoonist Oliphant did not miss the opportunity to call attention to Vance's apparent contradictions. In a cartoon in the *Washington Star*, Oliphant showed Vance talking out of both sides of his mouth as follows:

> Citizen Vance—1975: We must insist on maintaining our arms embargo against Turkey until we gain some major concessions in the Cyprus situation. . . . How can we otherwise preserve our credibility? . . . Secretary of State Vance—1978: Oh, what the heck! Now is the time to look forward rather than back. Think of our security concerns. Think of NATO. Think of our relations with Turkey—Give'em the arms![11]

Following Vance's April 6, 1978 testimony before Congress,

---

[9]*New York Times*, April 7, 1978.
[10]Ibid.
[11]*Washington Star*, April 21, 1978.

administration officials dropped the use of the terms "invasion" and "occupation" when it came to Cyprus. Instead, they often made use of the terms "Turkish military presence" or "Turkish military troops." The military action of the Turkish Army against Cyprus in July and August 1974 was described by the State Department in the following terms: ". . . [in July] the Turkish government *landed* military forces in the northern coast of Cyprus . . . in August, the Turkish government *landed* additional forces, *taking about 36% of the island.*" (Emphasis added.)[12] In this way, the Turkish invasion was presented as a "landing" of forces and the occupation of 36 percent of Cypriot territory was not qualified as an act of "occupation" but was defined as the "taking" of land. Both terms, the "landing" of troops and the "taking" of land, were legally neutral and, therefore, could not be utilized in Congress as an argument to justify the embargo.

In other instances, when administration officials referred to Cyprus in their addresses to Greek American groups, they avoided altogether the issue of the Turkish military occupation or even "presence." Instead, they referred to a "just and lasting Cyprus solution."[13] President Carter, when asked about the embargo, avoided the terms "invasion" and "occupation" and, instead, described the Turkish action in Cyprus in the following terms: ". . . Turkey has been very greatly disturbed because of the arms embargo, brought about, I think, three years ago by the fact that Turkey did violate the American law in using American-supplied arms *to go into Cyprus.*" (Emphasis added.)[14]

Thus, Carter admitted that Turkey had undertaken military action against Cyprus that violated American law since it had used U.S.-supplied arms for the invasion. In this regard, the congressional embargo was justified, Carter maintained. At the same time, the president described Turkey's aggressive action in the most innocuous terms. The phrase "Turkey did violate the American law . . . *to go into*

---

[12]See the letter by Douglas J. Bennet, Assistant Secretary for Congressional Relations, Department of State, to Senator John Sparkman, Chairman, Senate Foreign Relations Committee, *Congressional Record*, June 28, 1978. The complete text of Bennet's letter appears in the Appendix, Document O.

[13]Letter by Hodding Carter III, Assistant Secretary of State for Public Affairs and Department Spokesman, to Serge Hadji, Member of the Pan-Hellenic Emergency Committee, May, 1, 1978.

[14]*New York Times*, June 15, 1978.

Cyprus" demonstrated that Carter had to use the English language rather awkwardly in order to avoid stating that "Turkey invaded" Cyprus. The phrase "go into Cyprus" is neutral both in legal and political terms. When a foreign army "goes into" another country, a reasonable person can surmise that the action of "going" is not necessarily violent or illegal. The Turkish military action in Cyprus, when described as an act of "going into" another country, could be construed as legitimate. If that were the case, the arms embargo against Turkey would be unjustified, and that was precisely what Carter was attempting to convey through the mixed signals in his statement.

Turkey and Human Rights

In his April 6 statement before the House International Relations Committee, Secretary of State Vance also avoided using the term "human rights." This was particularly important since the Carter administration and the president, personally, had elevated human rights to the top of their foreign policy priorities. Apparently, however, focusing on human rights in a debate regarding Cyprus and Turkey would be counterproductive for the administration as it worked to repeal the embargo. Vance spoke of the Cyprus dispute and the aftermath of the invasion as a "very serious humanitarian issue." He did not refer, however, to the human rights of the people of Cyprus, neither Greek Cypriots nor Turkish Cypriots, especially the refugees. Vance referred to the need for "adequate safeguards respecting the rights of individual Cypriots," thus avoiding the use of the term "human rights" individually or collectively.

While the Carter White House did elevate human rights to the top of its foreign policy agenda, it made exceptions with regard to Iran and Turkey's policies in Cyprus. In both cases, the administration downplayed human rights as realpolitik and strategic concerns carried the day. However, Carter did not hesitate to state publicly that he had discussed the question of human rights with the Shah. With respect to Turkey's policies on Cyprus, the term "human rights" was downplayed by the Carter administration as much as possible.

The State Department submitted its report on human rights practices to Congress on February 3, 1978. It had been exactly four weeks since Bülent Ecevit formed a new government. The administration's retreat on human rights was already evident in the section of the report on Turkey. There was nothing in the section to indicate that, at the time, Turkey was experiencing widespread violence and that political assassinations were almost a daily phenomenon.[15] The report stated that "the new Turkish government which took office in January 1978 has enunciated protection of human rights as one of its primary concerns."[16]

From January 5, 1978, when the Ecevit government took office until February 3, the date the report was submitted to Congress, political violence swept the country and, as a result, 51 people were killed, 444 were wounded, and 129 bombings took place. In 1977, the year covered by the report, 231 people were killed in incidents of political violence. Many of these incidents involved fighting between the political right and the political left, while some incidents involved sectarian fighting. The most important extreme right-wing group carrying out the fighting was the Grey Wolves, the paramilitary organization of the neo-fascist National Action Party (NAP) of Alparslan Türkeş (also known as the Nationalist Movement Party, or MHP). In carrying out many of their attacks, the Grey Wolves were supported by members of some of the state security services in Turkey. Elements of the Turkish police and gendarmerie, and some members of the armed forces, were involved in acts of political violence that included assassinations.[17] Likewise, left-wing terrorists carried out a wave of bombings and political assassinations. Left-wing terror in 1977 matched that of the right wing.

Given the human rights situation in Turkey, it becomes clear that the State Department under Carter made a deliberate decision to exclude Turkey from scrutiny. In fact, the February 1978 report asserted that there was "a competitive political system in Turkey . . . and a vibrant political process." Furthermore, the report refers to Turkey's free press. All this gave the impression that Turkey practiced

---

[15]Political violence in Turkey during this period is discussed at the end of this chapter.

[16]U.S. Department of State, *Country Report on Human Rights Practices: Turkey*, Report Submitted to the Committee on International Relations, U.S. House of Representatives, and the Committee on Foreign Relations, U.S. Senate, Joint Committee Print, 95th Congress, 2nd Session, February 3, 1978, p. 316. For the full text of the 1978 *Country Report on Human Rights Practices: Turkey*, see Appendix, Document E.

[17]Birand, *The Generals' Coup*, pp. 43–44, 48–50, 62–63.

democratic politics, that political dissent was peaceful, and that there was respect for human rights that closely resembled that of countries in the West. In reality, political assassinations, murders of journalists and intellectuals, and armed attacks and bombings were a daily phenomenon in Turkey. By any definition, such actions of political violence, especially political assassinations, constituted an extreme form of human rights violations.

In addition, the State Department human rights report stated that "the small Greek, Christian, and Jewish populations also enjoy freedom of worship . . . there does not appear to be any official discrimination against individuals belonging to minority groups." As far as the Greek Christian minority was concerned, this claim was not rooted in fact. This minority had suffered discrimination and harassment since 1955. About the same time that the report was being submitted to Congress, the Turkish authorities were engaging in the intimidation of the Ecumenical Patriarchate of Constantinople. Turkish security agents had descended upon the Patriarchate, searched every room, and catalogued all the items they found.[18]

In March 1978, Archbishop Iakovos, head of the Greek Orthodox Church of North and South America, sent a letter to Pope Paul VI asking him to express the Vatican's concern with regard to the action against the Patriarchate. The Pope responded diplomatically to Archbishop Iakovos, assuring him that the Holy See was following the events at the Patriarchate with great care.[19] On February 22, 1978, the Commonwealth of Massachusetts issued a resolution asking President Carter and Congress to "strongly protest to the Government of Turkey the renewed persecution of the Ecumenical Patriarchate and the Christians living in Turkey . . ." and "to take steps to ensure the religious freedom of the Christians and Jews in Turkey . . ."[20]

On March 7, the Standing Conference of the Canonical Orthodox Bishops in the Americas (SCOBA) also issued a resolution protesting the persecution of the Ecumenical Patriarchate. The resolution stated: "SCOBA deplores the violation of human rights in any part of the world and is alarmed by recent reports of the persecution of the

---

[18]See *Orthodox Observer*, March 15, 1978.

[19]Ibid., March 29, 1978.

[20]A photocopy of the resolution appeared in the *Orthodox Observer*, March 29, 1978. It was entitled "Resolution Memorializing the President and the Congress to Intervene on Behalf of the Ecumenical Patriarchate of Constantinople."

Ecumenical Patriarchate of Constantinople and the Greek community in Istanbul. SCOBA requests the President of the United States, who has so faithfully advocated human rights in all nations, to empower the Secretary of State to employ a fact-finding apparatus at the disposal of the United States government to investigate these reports and to take whatever action is necessary to remedy this deplorable situation."[21]

These protests, especially the one issued by the religious leaders of SCOBA, constituted direct challenges to the credibility of the February 3 State Department report on human rights practices in Turkey. As a result of the distorted picture it presented of the human rights situation in Turkey, *Washington Post* syndicated columnist Jack Anderson wrote a scathing critique of the report on March 5, 1978, under the headline "A 'Deliberate Whitewash' on Human Rights in Turkey." By that time, Jack Anderson had become a legendary figure in American journalism, primarily because of his critique of the war in Vietnam and his role in exposing the abuses of the Nixon White House.

In his March 5 column, Anderson charged that the Carter administration had ". . . falsified a report on human rights practices in Turkey" and "portrayed the country as a virtual human rights paradise."[22] The reason for this, according to Anderson, was "to avoid irritating a Congress that is already sympathetic to the Greek and Greek Cypriot cause." Anderson also described some of the travails of the Greek Orthodox community in Turkey.[23]

Occupied Territories and Human Rights: Israel and the West Bank, Turkey and the Northern Region of Cyprus

In the February 3, 1978 State Department report on human rights, the Carter administration issued its first assessment of the state of human rights in Cyprus. The State Department had also submitted a human rights report on Cyprus to Congress on April 25, 1977. This earlier report reflected, to an extent, the Ford administration's views since

---

[21] *Orthodox Observer*, March 29, 1978.

[22] *Washington Post*, March 5, 1978. For the complete text of Jack Anderson's column, see Appendix, Document G.

[23] Ibid.

the Carter foreign policy team was barely in place in April 1977. The February 1978 report, however, had the stamp of the Carter administration. A period of one year was adequate for the administration to formulate and begin implementing its human rights policies around the globe.

The February 3, 1978 report constituted a seminal document for understanding Carter's policy on Cyprus.[24] After all, human rights were the guiding principle of Carter's foreign policy. More important was the fact that this report had to deal with the legal status of the territory of a sovereign member of the United Nations, which had been under Turkish military occupation since 1974.

In order to acquire a better understanding of the State Department report on Cyprus and recognize its implications, it is necessary to place the question of human rights in occupied Cyprus in the context of the Carter administration's view of another occupied region, the Israeli-occupied territories. Israel and the occupied territories and Cyprus were in the same geostrategic region. For that matter, the Israeli-occupied West Bank was less than 200 miles from Cyprus.

In the aftermath of the Arab-Israeli War of June 1967, the United States adopted the fundamental position that the Arab areas that came under Israeli rule were "occupied territories," in accordance with U.N. Security Council Resolution 242, adopted on November 22, 1967. This resolution called for the "withdrawal of Israeli armed forces from territories occupied" and for the acknowledgment of the sovereignty, territorial integrity, and political independence of every state in the area and their right to live in peace within secure and recognized boundaries, free from threats or acts of force. Security Council Resolution 242 became the foundation of U.S. policy toward the Arab-Israeli conflict and the basis of future Arab-Israeli negotiations.

The Carter administration adhered to the policy of its predecessors and viewed the Arab areas under Israeli rule as "occupied territories." This was evident in the State Department human rights report of February 1978. The section pertaining to Israel was entitled "Israel

---

[24]U.S. Department of State, *Country Reports on Human Rights Practices: Cyprus,* Report Submitted to the Committee on International Relations, U.S. House of Representatives, and the Committee on Foreign Relations, U.S. Senate, Joint Committee Print, 95th Congress, 2nd Session, February 3, 1978, pp. 285–287 (hereinafter referred to as *Country Reports: Cyprus, 1978*). For a full text of this report, see Appendix, Document C.

and the Occupied Territories," and the opening paragraph read as follows:

> Because of the sharply differing politico-social environments in Israel and in the Arab territories *Israel has occupied since the 1967* war, discussion of this subject must be treated in separate but parallel fashion for the two areas. Therefore, for its first three sections, this report is divided into separate narratives for Israel and the *occupied territories . . .*[25] (Emphasis added.)

In this way, from the outset, the Carter administration made it clear that the areas under Israeli rule were "occupied territories." In the section under the title "Occupied Territories," the State Department defined the areas under occupation as follows:

> Israel's occupied territories consist of the West Bank of the Jordan River, the Gaza Strip, most of the Sinai Peninsula, the Golan Heights, and East Jerusalem. . . . The occupied territories are under military government, and law enforcement and public security are in military rather than civilian hands. Although Israel rejects the view of the United Nations *(including the U.S.)* that the stipulations of the *Fourth Geneva Convention* concerning the protection of civilian population under military occupation apply to its governance of the occupied territories, Israel claims it voluntarily observes most of these stipulations.[26] (Emphasis added.)

The report examined the issues of torture, arbitrary arrest, invasion of home, freedom of the press and religion, freedom of movement, and freedom to participate in the political process in the Israeli-occupied territories.

---

[25] U.S. Department of State, *Country Reports on Human Rights Practices: Israel and the Occupied Territories,* Report Submitted to the Committee on International Relations, U.S. House of Representatives, and the Committee on Foreign Relations, U.S. Senate, Joint Committee Print, 95th Congress, 2nd Session, February 3, 1978, pp. 361–370 (hereinafter referred to as *Country Reports: Israel and the Occupied Territories, 1978*). For the full text of this report, see Appendix, Document D.

[26]Ibid., pp. 364–365.

The designation by the State Department of the areas under Israeli rule as "occupied territories" that were ruled by a "military government" had profound legal and diplomatic implications. From the perspective of international law, the United States government and its agencies considered the Arab territories to be under the foreign military occupation of Israel. As a consequence, the Carter administration held that Israel had an obligation to administer the occupied territories under the rules of the Geneva Convention. Diplomatically, the fact that the Carter administration treated the Arab areas under Israeli control as territories under foreign military occupation enabled the United States to argue that these territories should be returned to their rightful owners, always in the context of a negotiated settlement. In turn, this gave the United States enormous diplomatic leverage over Israel, as Carter sought to promote Arab-Israeli peace. Certainly, this leverage was not applied only in the case of Israel because Carter sought Arab reciprocity and concessions for any Israeli withdrawal from the occupied territories. This was the *quid pro quo* diplomatic approach that led to the historic Camp David accords. There were, of course, other factors at play in the long process toward Arab-Israeli peace. They included Israeli military superiority, along with American support for Israel. This was balanced by Arab control of enormous oil resources and absolute Western need for this oil, and, to a lesser extent, by Soviet support for several Arab regimes and the Palestinian cause.

In contrast to the policy of referring to the Arab areas under Israeli rule as "occupied territories" in the State Department's February 1978 human rights report, the area of the Republic of Cyprus under Turkish military rule was not treated as an "occupied territory" in the report. Under international law, territories under occupation receive special treatment with regard to the way they are ruled by the occupation authority. This authority is subject to certain obligations emanating from the Hague Declaration of 1907. More important in this regard is the Fourth (IV) Geneva Convention of 1949, which provides for the treatment of the civilian population in territories under foreign military occupation.[27] For instance, Article (3) of the Geneva Convention prohibits "violence to life and person, in particular murder of all kinds, mutilation, cruel treatment, and torture."[28] Article (27) states

---

[27]International Committee of the Red Cross, *Convention (IV) Relative to the Protection of Civilian Persons in Times of War*, Geneva, 12 August 1949.

[28]Ibid., Part I, General Provisions, p. 1.

that "protected persons are entitled, in all circumstances, to respect for their persons, their honour, their family rights, their religious convictions and practices, and their manners and customs."[29]

The State Department policy of avoiding references in its official reports to the part of Cyprus under Turkish military rule as "occupied" under the Carter administration continued under successive administrations, including the Clinton administration, and it continues today.[30] As a result, the view of the United States is that Turkey is not under obligation to adhere to the 1949 Geneva Convention with respect to Cyprus. In its annual report on human rights, the State Department under the Clinton administration did not treat Turkey, with respect to Cyprus, as an occupying power that has obligations under the Geneva Convention.[31] Turkey also continues to deny that the occupied part of Cyprus falls under the provisions of the Geneva Convention.

The irresistible logical conclusion leaves little doubt that the role of the Turkish occupation authorities in Cyprus was deliberately left out of the picture in the 1978 State Department human rights report. Instead, the report referred to the "Turkish Cypriot Administration" as if it exercised legitimate as well as actual power. Even if international law and the Geneva Convention were set aside, such a description of the authorities and the exercise of power in the occupied territory would be quite misleading. By any standards, the actual rulers of the occupied territory were Turkish officers, and the army and the security agencies set up and controlled by the army were in charge of domestic security. These security agencies were responsible for the violations of human rights that might have occurred in the occupied territory. Ultimately, therefore, the responsibility for such violations would rest with the Turkish armed forces. That was one of the reasons why the Carter administration did not want to classify the northern part of Cyprus as "occupied territory" because the Turkish armed forces would have been liable for human rights violations. At a time when Carter was seeking to lift the embargo and give more arms to the Turkish military, it would have been counterproductive to

---

[29]Ibid., Part III, Status and Treatment of Protected Persons, p. 8.

[30]See U.S. Department of State, *1999 Country Report on Human Rights Practices: Cyprus*, Bureau of Democracy, Human Rights, and Labor, Washington, D.C., February 25, 2000.

[31]Ibid.

scrutinize the behavior of the Turkish armed forces with respect to human rights violations in Cyprus. It made sense, therefore, for the Carter administration to place all responsibility for the administration of the occupied part of Cyprus on the shoulders of the Turkish Cypriots under the rubric of the "Turkish Cypriot administration." It was a calculated misrepresentation of the power structure in the occupied territory.

The contrast between the treatment of the Arab areas under Israeli rule and the Greek Cypriot area under Turkish rule was quite obvious. The Arab areas were "occupied territories" with all the legal and diplomatic implications emanating from such a designation. The area of northern Cyprus under Turkish rule, the result of the 1974 invasion and military occupation, was not considered by the Carter administration to be a territory under foreign military occupation. This had very significant legal and diplomatic implications.

Under this false argument, therefore, legally, Turkey was not considered an occupier that placed part of the territory of Cyprus, a sovereign member of the United Nations, under illegal control. As a consequence, according to the Carter administration, unlike the case of Israel, Turkey had no obligation under international law to honor the 1949 Geneva Convention governing occupied territories. Likewise, Turkey had no legal obligation to return the occupied part of Cyprus to its rightful owners. Even in the context of a negotiated settlement, the question of territory became a political matter reflecting the power relationship of the parties involved rather than a legal question imposing certain obligations on the occupying power. Diplomatically, this meant that the Carter administration was both unable and unwilling to use the status of northern Cyprus as an "occupied territory" as leverage to pressure Turkey to make territorial concessions, as Israel had been asked to do.

The Issue of Jewish Settlers and the Non-Issue of Turkish Settlers

One of the most critical legal and diplomatic implications of the Carter administration's policy of not categorizing the Turkish-controlled part of Cyprus as "occupied territory" had to do with the question of settlers. According to the Fourth (IV) Geneva Convention, an occupying power is obligated not to change the demography of the territory under its control. Specifically, Section III: Occupied Territories, Article 49 stipulated:

> Individual or mass forcible transfers, as well as deportations of protected persons from *occupied territory* to the territory of the Occupying Power or that of any other country, occupied or not, are prohibited, irrespective of their motive. . . . *The Occupying Power shall not deport or transfer parts of its own civilian population into the territory it occupies.*[32] (Emphasis added.)

The Carter administration did consider the Arab areas under Israeli control to be "occupied territory" and, as a result, Washington held Israel accountable to Article 49 of the Fourth (IV) Geneva Convention. As a result, the State Department human rights report on Israel and the occupied territories dealt with the question of Jewish settlers in the West Bank and Gaza. The February 3, 1978 report stated:

> *In contravention* of the generally accepted interpretation of the [Fourth (IV) Geneva] Convention's Article 49, Israel has established *over 70 nonmilitary settlements* in the occupied territories, with a total population of about 8,000 people. . . . A further problem results from the exploitation of a part of the West Bank's limited resources for the use of *Israeli settlements.*[33] (Emphasis added.)

Clearly, the Carter administration considered Israeli settlements in the occupied West Bank and Gaza to be illegal under international law. The top foreign policy officials of the administration repeatedly and publicly condemned Israel for its policy on settlers.[34] In fact, the Carter administration considered the issue of Jewish settlers in the

---

[32]See International Committee of the Red Cross, Convention (IV) Relative to the Protection of Civilian Persons in Time of War, Geneva, 12 August 1949. See esp. Section III: Occupied Territories, Article 49, p. 13.

[33]*Country Reports: Israel and the Occupied Territories, 1978,* pp. 365, 368.

[34]For the Carter administration's policy of viewing Israeli settlements as illegal under international law, see Vance, *Hard Choices,* p. 185; Brzezinski, *Power and Principle,* p. 104; Quandt, *Camp David,* p. 45, 83.

occupied West Bank and Gaza to be pivotal in any Arab-Israeli negotiations.

President Carter viewed Israel's policy of sending settlers into the West Bank and Gaza as a serious obstacle to peace. During a White House meeting with Israeli Prime Minister Menachem Begin in July 1977, Carter told the Israeli leader "how serious an obstacle to peace were the Israeli settlements being established in the occupied territories."[35] Overall, Carter believed that Israel's policy of establishing settlements in the occupied West Bank and Gaza was "not only irritating, but it endangered the prospects for peace."[36] Carter's opposition to Israeli settlements was a cause of serious friction between his administration and the government of Israel under Begin.

The Carter administration treated the question of Turkish settlers in occupied Cyprus quite differently. The section of the February 3, 1978 State Department human rights report on Cyprus failed to address the critical question of settlers altogether.[37] Yet, the Turkish policy of colonizing occupied Cyprus was a reality, and there is no doubt that such colonization had been taking place during the period covered in the State Department report.[38]

The Cyprus government had been protesting Turkish colonization in occupied Cyprus since 1975. In addition, the Western press, primarily the British, had been reporting that Turkey was engaged in the systematic colonization of Cyprus.[39] In fact, at the time the State Department submitted its human rights report to Congress in February 1978, which covered developments in Cyprus throughout 1977, Turkey was in the process of carrying out a policy of massive colonization of occupied Cyprus.

By the end of 1977, an estimated 37,000 colonists from mainland Turkey had been transferred to the occupied territory as a result of an

---

[35]Carter, *Keeping Faith*, p. 291.

[36]Ibid., p. 304.

[37]See *Country Reports: Cyprus, 1978.*

[38]For documentation of the Turkish colonization of occupied Cyprus, see the official report by the Council of Europe in the *Report on the Demographic Structure of the Cypriot Communities* (Rapporteur, Mr. Alfonse Cuco, Spain), Council of Europe, ADOC 6589, 1403–23/½2-4-E, adopted by the Assembly on October 7, 1992 (hereinafter referred to as *Report on the Demographic Structure of the Cypriot Communities*).

[39]See the *Guardian*, London, October 13 and 15, 1975; "The World Today," *BBC World Service*, October 15, 1975; the *Sunday Times*, London, September 26, 1976.

official policy of the Turkish government.[40] In other words, by the end of 1977, there were almost five times more illegal Turkish settlers in occupied Cyprus than there were Jewish settlers in the occupied West Bank. This limited number of Jewish settlers, compared to the number of Turkish settlers, became a major issue for the Carter administration. On the other hand, the far larger number of Turkish settlers in occupied Cyprus did not appear to be of concern to the Carter White House.

The massive introduction of settlers into occupied Cyprus began causing friction between the settlers and the Turkish Cypriots. In May 1978, barely four months after the State Department report on Cyprus, which omitted the settler issue, a very prominent Turkish Cypriot leader, Dr. Fazil Küçük, wrote a series of articles that were critical of the settlers' presence and their behavior.[41]

By the time Carter left office in January 1981, Turkey had sent 53,564 settlers to the occupied territory. The permanent character of this colonization was indicated by the fact that the Denktash regime gave most of the settlers "citizenship documents." By the end of March 1980, the Turkish Cypriot administration had granted "citizenship" to 31,290 settlers.[42] The right to "citizenship" enabled the settlers to vote in the elections and "constitutional" referenda organized by the Denktash regime. The settlers were also elected members of the "Legislative Assembly" and could become ministers in the Denktash regime. The settlers have been incorporated into the existing struc-

---

[40]For figures on settlers based on Turkish Cypriot ("TRNC") sources, see Ioannides, *In Turkey's Image*, pp. 30–31. These "TRNC" sources included: *The TRNC Statistical Yearbook, 1987*, TRNC Prime Ministry, State Planning Organization, Statistics and Research Department (Nicosia: December 1988); *The Yearly Action Report* (YAR) (Nicosia: Police General Directorate of the TRNC); Records of the Office of the Prime Minister of the TRNC.

[41]For Dr. Küçük's articles, see the Turkish Cypriot newspaper *Halkin Sesi*, May 24 and 25, 1978. On the friction between the settlers and Turkish Cypriots, see also Bahcheli, *Greek-Turkish Relations since 1955*, pp. 111–112.

[42]A report entitled "New Citizens from Turkey," written by Erdoğan Ozbalikki in the Turkish newspaper *Aydinlik*, stated: "According to our finding on 21 March 1980, the number of Cyprus citizenship documents given to Turkish Republic citizens was 17,741; this number exceeded 31,290 on 26 March 1980. That is, within 5 days, 14,149 Turkish Republic citizens were registered as citizens of the Turkish Cypriot Administration." See *Aydinlik*, Istanbul, 18 April 1980. A similar report on the settlers was published in the Turkish Cypriot newspaper *Söz*, 16 April 1980.

tures of the Denktash regime and, from the economic, legal, and political points of view, they are indistinguishable from the Turkish Cypriot population.

Reacting to the widespread reports on the massive introduction of settlers into occupied Cyprus and the continuous protests of the Cyprus government concerning the settlers, the U.N. General Assembly dealt with the settler issue on May 13, 1983, when it approved a resolution which:

> ... deplores the fact that part of the territory of the Republic of Cyprus *is still occupied by foreign forces* . . . and [also] deplores all unilateral actions that *change the demographic structure* of Cyprus . . . and demands the immediate withdrawal of all occupation forces from the Republic of Cyprus."[43] (Emphasis added.)

This resolution not only denounced the illegal transfer of Turkish settlers into occupied Cyprus, but it also made clear that the northern part of Cyprus was an occupied territory. It is noteworthy that the administration of Ronald Reagan did not oppose this resolution, which left no doubt that Turkey was an occupying power in Cyprus.

The continuous colonization of occupied Cyprus by Turkey also compelled the Council of Europe to launch a formal investigation. For this purpose, the Council's Committee on Migration, Refugees, and Demography appointed Alfonse Cuco, a Spaniard, as its rapporteur. Cuco visited Cyprus from November 5 to 9, 1991. He submitted a report to the committee on April 13, 1992, which was approved by 23 votes in favor, 2 against, and 2 abstentions.[44] Cuco's report confirmed that, since the fall of 1974, there had been widespread, systematic colonization of occupied Cyprus by settlers from Turkey. Cuco reported:

> The establishment of Turkish settlers in the northern part of Cyprus is an *undisputed fact*. . . . This influx of settlers has had

---

[43]See U.N. General Assembly Resolution 37/253, UN GAOR, UN Doc. 37/253, May 13, 1983. This resolution was approved by a vote of 103 in favor, 5 against, and 20 abstentions. Voting against the resolution were Turkey, Pakistan, Bangladesh, Malaysia, and Somalia.

[44]See *Report on the Demographic Structure of the Cypriot Communities.*

a real impact on the structure of the population in the northern part of the island. . . . The arrival and establishment of the
Turkish settlers is the most notable demographic occurrence
in Cyprus since 1974.[45]

The adoption of the Cuco report by the Council of Europe meant
that one of the most authoritative European institutions considered
the Turkish colonization of occupied Cyprus to be a matter of serious
concern.

As time went by, the colonization of occupied Cyprus acquired
permanency, which was the Turkish objective from the very beginning.
By the end of 1999, the number of settlers, estimated at 110,000,
exceeded, by far, the number of Turkish Cypriots, which had decreased
to about 65,000.[46] Since the 1974 invasion, about half of the Turkish
Cypriot population has left the occupied territory, emigrating primarily to Britain, Canada, and Australia. They have been replaced by settlers from Turkey and, in this way, the demographic transformation of
Cyprus through Turkish colonization has become a reality.[47]

Just prior to the U.S. presidential election in 1976, Jimmy Carter
proclaimed in his statement on Cyprus that " . . . the widely reported
increase in the colonization of Cyprus by Turkish military and civilians
must cease." (Emphasis added.) As president, however, Carter
dropped the question of settlers altogether. In his bimonthly reports
to Congress on Cyprus, President Carter presented the major developments in the country as they pertained to efforts toward a negotiated settlement. In none of his reports did Carter make reference to
the issue of Turkish settlers.

---

[45]Ibid., pp. 39–40.

[46]Independent estimates of the number of settlers vary from 100,000 to 111,000.
See Gregory R. Copley, "Turkey Falters on the Edge of Ataturk's Dream," *Defense and
Foreign Affairs Strategic Policy: The Journal of the International Strategic Studies Asso-
ciation,* Alexandria, VA, vol. xxviii, no. 3 (March 2000): pp. 7–9; "Hard Line Party
Wins Turkish Cypriot Elections," *Associated Press,* December 8, 1998. On the massive
introduction of settlers into northern Cyprus, see also Niels Kadritzke, "Turkish
Cypriots Dream of Europe," *Le Monde Diplomatique,* August-September 1998.

[47]Turkish Cypriot opposition leader Arif Hasan Tahsin estimated that half of the
Turkish Cypriot population had emigrated since 1974. At that time, the total number of Turkish Cypriots was 116,000. For Tahsin's statement see *BRTK Television Network,* 18:10 hours, April 10, 2000, in *Cyprus PIO: Turkish Cypriot Press and other
Media,* Nicosia, April 13, 2000.

Likewise, the State Department under Carter made no mention of the word "settlers" in its February 1978 human rights report.[48] In this way, the Carter administration removed the settler question from relevancy in the Cyprus dispute. This represented a policy of deliberate deception for two reasons. First, the massive presence of settlers in occupied Cyprus was an internationally recognized fact, and the Carter administration was well informed concerning the illegal presence of Turkish settlers in occupied Cyprus. Second, as the Middle East peace process demonstrated, the question of settlers in the Israeli-occupied territories had been of paramount importance with respect to a negotiated settlement. Likewise, the question of Turkish settlers in occupied Cyprus had a critical bearing on any negotiated settlement.

This policy of deception regarding the colonization of occupied Cyprus by Turkish settlers was necessary if the Carter White House's drive to lift the embargo was going to succeed. If the White House and the State Department had acknowledged that Turkey was following a policy of colonization in the occupied part of Cyprus while Carter was leading the drive to lift the embargo, the admission would have undermined the effort. After all, one of the administration's basic arguments was that Turkey was negotiating in good faith in the effort to reach a Cyprus agreement. The massive, illegal introduction of settlers into occupied Cyprus, while the Carter administration was presenting its argument in Congress against maintaining the embargo, would have contradicted the notion of Turkey's good faith and belied the administration's assertions in this regard. More importantly, the Turkish policy of colonization was in clear violation of Article 49 of the Fourth (IV) Geneva Convention. In order to succeed in lifting the embargo, the question of Turkish settlers and Turkey's violation of Article 49 had to be removed from Carter's Cyprus agenda. The Carter team's failure to address the settler issue in occupied Cyprus, while placing considerable emphasis on Jewish settlers in the occupied West Bank, was a deliberate and successful policy to cover up the settler issue in Cyprus.

In the final analysis, the February 1978 State Department report on human rights in Cyprus represented implicit acceptance by the United States of the Turkish thesis that Turkey had legitimate reasons

---

[48]See *Country Report: Cyprus, 1978.*

to take control of the northern part of Cyprus. Turkey had been arguing that the presence of its army in Cyprus was not illegal but was consistent with the right of intervention accorded to Turkey under the Treaty of Guarantee, which was incorporated into the Zurich-London agreements of 1960. This argument has been rejected by a series of U.N. resolutions that "demanded the immediate withdrawal of all occupation forces from the Republic of Cyprus."[49]

Through a series of statements and reports to Congress by President Carter in 1977 and through the February 1978 State Department human rights report, it became clear that the Carter administration had made a deliberate decision to treat the Israeli occupation of Arab territories and the Turkish occupation of territory in the Republic of Cyprus quite differently. The Israeli-occupied territories were considered illegal under international law. The Turkish-occupied territory in Cyprus was not treated as illegal by Carter, and its status remained deliberately ambiguous. Carter's ambiguity, however, favored the Turkish position on Cyprus since the passage of time consolidated the faits accomplis, which included the transfer of thousands of Turks from the mainland to the occupied territory.

The president of Cyprus, Spyros Kyprianou, viewed the State Department report on human rights as a prelude to lifting the arms embargo against Turkey. He charged that the Carter administration was attempting to create a favorable climate for Turkey in Washington by producing misleading reports on human rights.[50] More important was the reaction of several members of Congress in Washington to the human rights report. Five days after it was submitted to Congress, four members of Congress sent a letter to President Carter. The letter, dated February 8, 1978, was signed by senators Eagleton and Sarbanes and by representatives Brademas and Rosenthal. The four had been the leaders of the congressional drive to impose the embargo, and their views carried a certain weight. They sent the letter to President Carter in order to express their deep concern over the path taken by the administration, which was leading to the lifting of the embargo. Among the several steps the administration had taken, which pointed in that direction, the four members of Congress raised the question of the State Department report on human rights. They wrote:

---

[49]See, for instance, U.N. General Assembly Resolution 37/253 of May 13, 1983.
[50]*Proini*, February 15, 1978.

> In an effort to avoid offending Turkey . . . the Department of State recently submitted a report on human rights in Cyprus which was an *unfair and inaccurate* report of the tragic events on that island.[51] (Emphasis added.)

In this way, the president was informed of congressional concern regarding the accuracy of the State Department report on human rights in Cyprus. The White House ignored the letter from the congressmen because the decision to push for the repeal of the embargo had, more or less, been made. What remained was finding the appropriate time to announce it. This was to happen a few weeks later, at the beginning of April.

When the decision was publicly announced on April 1, 1978, Congressman Brademas, denounced the State Department human rights report again. He proclaimed that " . . . when the United States State Department issued a statement as required by law on human rights with respect to Cyprus, that statement was widely regarded as an inaccurate one, as a false one, not rooted in fact and thereby gave Turkey further reason not to be forthcoming on Cyprus."[52]

Turkey: A "Major Democracy" or a Country in Violent Turmoil?

Secretary of State Cyrus Vance not only avoided characterizing the Turkish-controlled area in Cyprus as "occupied territory," but he also painted a misleading picture of the situation Turkey, itself. He asserted in his April 6, 1978 congressional testimony that Turkey was "a major democracy with a *robust parliamentary system* . . . and has maintained the momentum of development within a strong democratic framework . . ." Vance stated that the signing of a new Defense

---

[51]Senator Paul Sarbanes referred to this letter to the president during the July 25, 1978 Senate debate on the repeal of the embargo. The letter appeared in the *Congressional Record*, 95th Congress, 2nd Session, vol. 124—Part 15, July 21, 1978, to July 31, 1978, p. 22547. The complete text of the letter to President Carter by the four member of Congress appears in the Appendix, Document F.

[52]See Cyprus Press Conference given by congressmen Biaggi, Brademas, and Rosenthal and by senators Eagleton and Sarbanes, Washington, D.C., April 5, 1978. Minutes of the press conference are in the possession of the author.

Cooperation Agreement with Turkey would "reflect the broader interests of our *two democracies*."[53] (Emphasis added.)

While Vance was expressing high praise for Turkish democracy and its "robust parliamentary system," Turkey was going through a profound political and economic crisis. Throughout 1977 and up until September 1980, Turkey experienced serious political turmoil. Violent clashes between rightists and leftists were a daily phenomenon on campuses and in the streets of major cities. By 1978, there were areas in major cities such as Istanbul (Constantinople) and Izmir (Smyra) that were controlled by either leftists or rightists and were off limits to citizens and police alike. From 1977 to 1980, there were days when people did not dare leave their homes for fear of being caught in the crossfire of fighting factions. Even in the capital, Ankara, streets were almost empty after dark, as people stayed home for fear of violence.[54] In 1977, a total of 231 people were killed as a result of political violence. In 1978, there were 832 political killings, while 6,835 people were wounded. That year, there were, on average, 16 violent incidents per day, resulting in 2 dead and 18 wounded.[55]

During Ecevit's first month in office, alone, between January 5 and February 5, 1978, political violence reached epidemic proportions, bringing the country close to civil war. During these four weeks, 51 people were killed, 444 individuals were wounded, and 129 bombings took place.[56] It was during this violent month that Secretary of State Vance paid a visit to Turkey. He was in Ankara on January 20 in order to promote better relations between Washington and Ankara and gain first-hand knowledge of the situation in Turkey.

As far as the economy was concerned, Vance praised Turkey for maintaining its "momentum for development." At the time, however, the economic situation was deteriorating rapidly. By 1978, there were shortages of basic goods throughout Turkey. People had to stand in line for hours to buy sugar, coffee, or butter. Light bulbs and toilet

---

[53]See *Vance Testimony*, April 6, 1978.

[54]Birand, *The Generals' Coup*, p. 36.

[55]On the political violence during this period, see the magazine Tempo, *1923–1993: Türkiye'nin 70 Yılı—Gün, Gün Cumhuriyet Tarihi*, vol. II (1923–1993: 70 Years of Turkey—Day-to-Day History of the Republic) (Istanbul: Tempo Kitapları, no. 9, 1994), pp. 56–65; Birand, *The Generals' Coup*, p. 61; William Hale, *Turkish Politics and the Military* (London: Routledge, 1994), p. 224.

[56]See Paul Henze, *The Turkish Times*, May 15, 1998.

paper were nowhere to be found. Basic pharmaceutical products vanished. The poorer classes in the cities survived on bread, olives, and onions.[57] During the winter months, millions of people in major cities suffered due to bitter cold because there was no fuel to operate the central heating in their apartments. Inflation reached 44 percent in 1978, and it climbed to 68 percent in 1979 and 107 percent in 1980. By 1979, Turkey's foreign debt had reached $14.6 billion. Annual growth experienced a rapid decline, falling 2.9 percent in 1978 and 0.4 percent in 1979.[58] Mehmet Ali Birand described the situation in 1979, stating that ". . . with daily power cuts and bare shelves in shops, Turkey resembled Europe after VE day."[59]

The worsening political and economic conditions in Turkey were reflected in the fact that the country could not maintain a stable government. Between the summer of 1977 and the spring of 1978, there were three changes of government. The rotating coalition governments under prime ministers Bülent Ecevit and Süleyman Demirel were weak and unable to cope with the increasing political violence and the deteriorating economy. Parliamentary politics sank to low level, reflecting the polarization in the streets.[60]

The April 1978 description by Vance asserting that Turkey was a "major democracy with a robust parliamentary system" presented a distorted picture of the country. As the State Department, through Vance, was presenting an image of a country with a solid democracy, Turkey was experiencing "systemic disintegration." Most authoritative observers of Turkey share the view that a disintegrating political system existed in the country during the latter part of the 1970s.[61]

Vance's imaginary picture of a "robust parliamentary democracy" in Turkey was shattered while President Carter was still in office. On September 12, 1980, the Turkish Army, under General Kenan Evren, staged a coup that overthrew the civilian government of Prime Min-

---

[57]This information on the economic hardship in Turkey was provided to the author by a resident of Istanbul at the time. See also Hale, *Turkish Politics*, pp. 222–224. Hale described the situation as "economic collapse."

[58]Ibid.

[59]Birand, *The Generals' Coup*, p. 45.

[60]On the degeneration of parliamentary politics, see ibid., pp. 33–34.

[61]Ahmad, *The Making of Modern Turkey*. See esp. chapter 8, "Military Intervention, Social Democracy, and Political Terror," pp. 148–180. See also Hale, *Turkish Politics*, pp. 222–245; Birand, *The Generals' Coup*, pp. 21–64.

ister Süleyman Demirel, putting an end to the country's slide toward anarchy.

CHAPTER 12

Congressional Minuets

Seesaw in Congress

The April 6, 1978 announcement by Secretary of State Cyrus Vance before the House International Relations Committee, which asserted that the arms embargo against Turkey had to be lifted, did not go unchallenged. Several members of Congress disputed Vance's assertion, pointing out that lifting the embargo would send the wrong message to Turkey. The strongest critic was Representative Benjamin Rosenthal, Democrat of Queens, New York. He warned that lifting the embargo without any previous concessions by Turkey would not only impede a Cyprus settlement, but it would also damage relations with Greece.[1]

Three days after the April 6, 1978 hearing in the House, the *New York Times,* in an editorial, echoed Rosenthal's criticism of the administration's request to lift the embargo. When American pressure is removed, Turkish Prime Minister Bülent Ecevit will have even fewer reasons to make concessions in Cyprus, the *New York Times* wrote.[2] It was a prescient warning that would be borne out with the passage of time.

On May 2, 1978, a month after the Carter administration had presented its arguments before the House of Representatives in favor of lifting the embargo, top administration officials testified before the Senate Foreign Relations Committee to present the arguments. The officials included Secretary of Defense Harold Brown, Deputy Secretary of State Warren Christopher, Chairman of the Joint Chiefs of Staff General David Jones, and Clark Clifford, the president's special envoy to Greece, Turkey, and Cyprus. They all repeated the standard

---

[1] *New York Times,* April 9, 1978; *Proini,* April 7, 1978.
[2] *New York Times,* April 9, 1978.

national security arguments for lifting the embargo. Brown and Jones were more emphatic concerning the threat that Soviet adventurism was posing in the Mediterranean and the Middle East. They also warned of the likelihood that Turkey might turn to the Soviets for armaments if the embargo were not lifted.[3] These dire warnings regarding the increasing Soviet threat in the Eastern Mediterranean came in the immediate aftermath of the visit to Ankara by Soviet Chief of General Staff General Nikolai Organov.

The alarmist arguments concerning the Soviet threat had a certain effect on Congress. This became evident the day after the May 2, 1978 congressional testimony of Brown and other top administration officials. On May 3, 1978, the House International Relations Committee approved, by a vote of 18 to 17, an amendment to the foreign aid bill in favor of the administration's request to lift the embargo.

President Carter had made personal appeals to members of the House International Relations Committee concerning the repeal of the embargo. Former president Gerald Ford and former secretary of state Henry Kissinger had assisted the president by lobbying wavering Republican members of the committee. An influential member of the committee, William Broomfield, Republican of Michigan, had urged other members of the committee to vote in favor of lifting the embargo. After the vote on the amendment, he stated that he had been persuaded to support the administration at the last minute, following telephone calls from Ford and Kissinger.[4] The retired chairman of the Joint Chiefs of Staff, Admiral Thomas Moorer, also aided the Carter administration by lobbying members of the committee. Representative John Buchanan, Republican of Alabama, stated that his decision to vote in favor of lifting the embargo was "one of the most painful decisions" of his legislative life. Buchanan explained that he had decided to support the administration after talking to Admiral Moorer.[5]

The Carter administration suffered a temporary setback in the Senate a week after the favorable vote in the House International Relations Committee. On May 11, 1978, the Senate Foreign Relations Committee decided, by a vote of 8 to 4, to reject an amendment that

---

[3] *Proini*, May 3, 1978.
[4] *New York Times*, May 4, 1978.
[5] Ibid.

would have ended the embargo. Senator Paul Sarbanes, Democrat of Maryland, was instrumental in defeating the amendment in the committee. Still, there was a silver lining in the administration's defeat. Of the four votes cast in support of ending the embargo, two came from liberal Democrats, Senator George McGovern of South Dakota and Senator Frank Church of Idaho. Senator McGovern's role in the debate to end the embargo proved to be critical during the final vote on the issue before the full Senate in August 1978.

Carter's Taste of Victory: Arms to the Middle East

The May 11, 1978 vote on the embargo in the Senate Foreign Relations Committee coincided with another contentious debate also having to do with arms. The Carter administration had proposed a $4.8 billion package deal for the sale of sophisticated fighter planes to Israel, Egypt, and Saudi Arabia. It involved the sale of 60 F-15s to Saudi Arabia, 50 F-5s to Egypt, and 15 F-15s and 75 F-16s to Israel.

Israel's supporters in Congress and the Jewish lobby strongly opposed the deal. On May 11, the Senate Foreign Relations Committee voted 8 to 8 to refer the arms package issue to the full Senate. The motion to refer the matter to the full Senate was made by Senator Sarbanes, a strong supporter of Israel and an opponent of the sale of sophisticated planes to Arab regimes. The Carter administration had hoped to avoid a floor fight in the Senate over the arms deal.

On May 15, 1978, the full Senate voted on the sale of fighter jets to Israel, Egypt, and Saudi Arabia. The Senate debate was intense, with both sides arguing passionately for or against the sale. In the end, the administration carried the day when the Senate voted 54 to 44 to approve the sale. The administration's victory was widely seen as a setback for the Jewish lobby.[6]

Some of the strongest opponents of the Middle East arms sale in the Senate also opposed the lifting of the arms embargo against Turkey. They included Sarbanes; Daniel Patrick Moynihan, Democrat of New York; Joseph Biden, Democrat of Delaware; Edward Kennedy,

---

[6]On the bitter fight in the Senate and the setback for the Jewish lobby, see the reports "Jewish Lobby Loses a Big One" and "F-15 Fight: Who Won What," *Time* (May 29, 1978): pp. 12–17; "Senate 54–44 Backed Sale of Jets" and "The Pressure and More Counter-Pressure," *New York Times*, May 16, 1978.

Democrat of Massachusetts; and Jacob Javits, Republican of New York. By the same token, some of the strongest supporters of the arms sale also supported the lifting of the embargo. They included Senate Majority Leader Robert Byrd, Democrat of West Virginia, one of the strongest supporters of Turkey in Congress; John Sparkman, Democrat of Alabama; and George McGovern, Democrat of South Dakota. There were also senators, such as Thomas Eagleton, Democrat of Missouri, who were staunch supporters of the embargo but also voted for the Middle East arms package.

The voting patterns regarding the arms embargo against Turkey and the Middle East arms sale indicated that, during the 1970s, support for the embargo and support for Israel were compatible policy objectives among members of Congress. Many members of Congress were strong supporters of the embargo, while they were also passionate supporters of Israel.

The congressional delegation from New York offered the best example of the coalition of pro-Israeli and pro-Greek forces in Washington. The leaders of the effort in the House to impose the embargo were Benjamin Rosenthal, a Jewish American, and John Brademas, a Greek American. Rosenthal was elected in Queens, New York. Other Jewish members of Congress from New York emerged as persistent advocates of imposing and maintaining the embargo. They included Representative Ed Koch, who later became mayor of New York City, and representatives Bella Abzug and Elizabeth Holtzman. In other words, the Greek lobby and the Jewish lobby were active along parallel lines and often supported each other in crucial congressional votes. The cooperation of the two lobbies was considered quite effective.[7]

Still, there were several instances in which strong support for Turkey on the Hill coincided with equally strong support for Israel. Representative Steven Solarz, Democrat of New York, who opposed the embargo, was one of the strongest pro-Turkish members of Congress and was also a staunch supporter of Israel. On the other hand, some of the most vocal critics of Israel were determined opponents of the embargo. This was the case with Paul Findley, Republican of Illinois, one of the most outspoken critics of Israel and the Jewish lobby in the 1970s. At the same time, Findley became one of the most active opponents of the embargo of arms to Turkey.

---

[7]See Frank and Weisband, eds., *Foreign Policy by Congress*, p. 193.

During his speech prior to the embargo vote in the House, Findley leveled the following criticism against Greek Americans:

> Greek Americans are prominent in every congressional district of this Nation. . . . The Greek Americans who are vocal on this issue . . . are almost unanimous in supporting the embargo. . . . Indeed, *their feelings here in this country seem to be even more intense than the feelings of Greeks themselves . . .*
>
> . . . A Republican whom I admire very much unburdened himself to me the other day by these words: Why should I vote to lift the embargo? Why should I stick out my neck? Why should I draw the ire, the wrath of Greek Americans in my district? The embargo issue put Jimmy Carter in the White House and denied the White House to Gerald Ford. The election was very close and here I am fighting his [Carter's] arguments . . . Jimmy Carter left the impression . . . that as President he would continue the embargo.[8] (Emphasis added.)

Findley was suggesting that Greek Americans exercised too much power and placed the interests of Greece above the interests of the United States. The congressman from Illinois was casting doubt on the loyalty of Greek Americans to the United States. Findley had employed a similar line of reasoning against American Jews.[9]

Findley's comments elicited a strong response from House Majority Whip John Brademas of Indiana. Brademas, a Greek American, reminded the Illinois congressman that, as an Indiana congressman, he, himself, had been on Nixon's "enemies list" because he believed that "the laws and principles of this country ought to be respected." Brademas also said that his desire to uphold the rule of law was the reason he was supporting the arms embargo against Turkey. The majority whip pointed out to Findley:

> . . . Is the gentleman from Illinois unaware of the fact that I

---

[8]See Findley's statement during the House debate on the embargo, *Congressional Record*, House, 95th Congress, 2nd Session, vol. 124, Part 18, August 1, 1978, to August 8, 1978, pp. 23705–23707.

[9]This was apparent in the controvercial book by John Findley, *They Dare Speak Out* (Chicago: Lawrence Hill Books, 1989).

strongly opposed the executive branch in the sale of U.S. arms
to the Greek military dictatorship several years ago, and I was
very bitterly opposed by some Greek Americans in the United
States . . .[10]

Findley's criticism of Greek Americans elicited an equally strong
response from another leading advocate of the embargo, New York
Representative Benjamin Rosenthal, who was Jewish. Rosenthal proclaimed:

I think, really, let us cut away this subterranean comment that
this is an ethnic-sponsored legislative effort, that some of us
have Greek Americans in our district and some of us do not,
that we are succumbing to their protestations and desires.

Is there something wrong with any group in America
expressing their interests in a part of the world that is important to them? If we eliminated every group like that and permitted the kind of comments that the gentleman from
Illinois suggests, then we leave the making of our policy to
Standard Oil of Indiana, to Esso, to Exxon, to Mobil, and to
the rest of the people who control access to the White House.
. . . I myself find it abominable that anyone, even in the most
cultured phrases that we are able to put together here on the
floor, would suggest that any Member is acting less than his
constitutional oath requires.[11]

Following Rosenthal's caustic comments, addressed at Findley,
another representative from New York, Mario Biaggi, rose and leveled
similar criticism against the Illinois congressman.[12] Brademas, a
Greek American, Rosenthal, a Jewish American, and Biaggi, an Italian
American, were all staunch supporters of Israel, while Findley was,
perhaps, the strongest anti-Israeli member of Congress. In the final
analysis, one could detect a certain trend in Congress. Between 1974
and 1978, members of Congress who were strong supporters of Israel
also tended to be pro-Greek and supported the arms embargo against

---

[10]*Congressional Record*, House, 95th Congress, 2nd Session, vol. 124, Part 18,
August 1, 1978, to August 8, 1978, p. 23706.

[11]Ibid., p. 23707.

[12]Ibid.

Turkey, even though there were several exceptions to this trend.[13]

Overall, what remained a common characteristic of the support that Israel and Greece enjoyed in Congress was that this support helped maintain relations between these countries and several U.S. administrations. This was especially the case when U.S.-Israeli ties or U.S.-Greek ties underwent periods of tension. During these periods, Congress became the intermediary that kept U.S.-Israeli and U.S.-Greek relations on track.[14]

More Pressure on Congress: The Southern Factor

Jimmy Carter's determination to take back some of the president's prerogatives in foreign policy from Congress was made clear in June

---

[13]Two decades later, the picture was to change and become more complex. In February 1996, Turkey and Israel signed agreements on military cooperation, which included the modernization of the Turkish Air Force by Israel, the sale of Israeli arms to Turkey, the training of Israeli pilots in Turkey and Turkish pilots in Israel, and the holding of joint naval exercises. In this way, Israel and Turkey formed a de facto alliance, while Israel became a major arms market for Turkey. Turkey expected to avoid the scrutiny of the U.S. Congress, which often linked arms sales to human rights practices. In addition, Ankara's expectation was that a close military relationship between Turkey and Israel could assist Turkey in neutralizing the "Greek lobby" in Washington. Both Greece and Cyprus viewed the de facto Turkish-Israeli alliance with considerable anxiety. By the fall of 1999, however, Greece and Israel had signed a defense cooperation agreement. The agreement was signed in Tel Aviv on October 14, 1999, by Israeli Prime Minister and Defense Minister Ehud Barak and Greek Defense Minister Akis Tzohatzopoulos. From May 15 to 18, 2000, Greek President Costis Stephanopoulos paid an official, highly successful visit to Israel, becoming the highest Greek official to visit the Jewish state since its establishment in 1948. In addition, relations between Israel and Cyprus improved dramatically throughout the 1990s, despite occasional setbacks. In November 1998, Israeli President Ezer Weizman paid an official visit to Cyprus. Cyprus President Glafcos Clerides reciprocated by visiting Israel in March 2000. Furthermore, the significant improvement in Greek-Turkish relations in the fall of 1999 and early 2000 contributed to easing Greek concerns over the close Turkish-Israeli military cooperation. In the spring of 2000, Turkish-Israeli relations underwent a period of tension because Israeli government officials advocated the teaching of the Armenian genocide to Israeli schoolchildren. See "Turkish-Israeli Relations Sour," *Turkish Daily News*, May 11, 2000; "A Tragedy Offstage No More," *Jerusalem Post*, May 12, 2000; "Israeli Press Insistent Over Alleged Armenian Genocide," *Turkish Daily News*, May 15, 2000.

[14]See Marios Evryviades, "The Umbilical Relationship: Greece and the United States," *Hellenic Studies*, Quebec, Canada, vol. 5., no. 2, 1977, p. 157.

1978. This was the month of maximum mobilization of the White House concerning the lifting of the embargo, when the president became personally involved in a calculated confrontation with Congress over the issue. It was a contest of wills, the presidential will to assert preeminence in the conducting of foreign policy and the congressional will to curb the executive branch's powers in foreign affairs. Since the Democrats not only controlled Congress but also enjoyed comfortable majorities as well, Carter's objective was to persuade enough members of his own party to support the lifting of the embargo. The core support for its repeal came from Republicans in both the Senate and the House of Representatives, as they were more amenable to strategic arguments and more responsive to the Pentagon's requests. Both in the Senate and the House, a large majority of Republicans favored the lifting of the embargo. Their votes, however, fell far short of forming a majority. Carter needed Democratic votes, which were to be provided primarily by southern Democrats. This made sense since Carter was a southerner and a Baptist, and it was easier, relatively speaking, to convince fellow southerners to follow his lead. Moreover, southern Democrats tended to be more conservative and more pro-defense than their northeastern colleagues. Still, neither the southern vote nor the liberal-conservative dichotomy can adequately explain the results of the embargo vote in Congress. In the end, some of the most liberal members of Congress, such as Senator McGovern, played an instrumental role in assisting the administration in its drive to lift the embargo.

On the first day of June 1978, President Carter invited 14 members of the House of Representatives who were supporting the lifting of the embargo to the White House. The president and Deputy Secretary of State Warren Christopher gave them a memorandum describing the administration's plan to win congressional support for its repeal and asked them to canvass uncommitted members of Congress. The president told the 14 representatives that the repeal of the embargo on military aid to Turkey constituted his highest foreign policy priority. He also stated that the embargo had not performed well regarding "peace in the Middle East and Europe."[15] In this way, Carter indirectly linked the embargo to ongoing developments in the Middle East, including the crisis in Iran and his administration's

---

[15] *New York Times*, June 2, 1978.

preparations for the Egyptian-Israeli peace negotiations at Camp David.

Overall, the president left no doubt in the minds of the 14 representatives that he was determined to lead a sustained campaign to repeal the embargo. It was to be an effort not unlike the one he had mounted to secure congressional approval of the Panama Canal Treaties and the sale of fighter planes to Israel, Egypt, and Saudi Arabia.[16] According to a participant in the meeting, "the President made a major commitment of his prestige to get the arms embargo repealed. I think this is an enormously significant development. Without a major presidential commitment, there would have been no chance to get repeal."[17] As the *New York Times* reported the next day, Carter ordered an "all-out drive to lift the ban on arms to Turkey."[18]

The president's personal engagement with Congress was further manifested a few days later when he met with 13 senators. At a working breakfast at the White House on June 8, President Carter, National Security Adviser Brzezinski, Secretary of State Vance, Secretary of Defense Brown, and Chairman of the Joint Chiefs of Staff General David Jones met with members of the Senate Arms Services Committee, nine Democrats and four Republicans. The fact that the president called the top foreign policy officials in his administration to the White House was an indication of how serious the effort to repeal the embargo was.

The Democrats on the committee who attended the White House meeting were Lloyd Bentsen of Texas, Dale Bumpers of Arkansas, Robert Byrd of West Virginia, Robert Morgan of North Carolina, Sam Nunn of Georgia, John Sparkman of Alabama, Frank Church of Idaho, George McGovern of South Dakota, and John Stennis of Mississippi, who was the chairman of the Senate Armed Services Committee. The Republican senators were Howard Baker of Tennessee, Henry Bellmon of Oklahoma, John Tower of Texas, and John Chafee of Rhode Island.

According to the June 1 presidential memorandum, this meeting was aimed at putting together a Senate leadership team. These were the senators who vowed to support the president's effort and led the

---

[16]Ibid.

[17]Ibid.

[18]Ibid.

successful fight on the Senate floor on July 25 that led to the lifting of the embargo. The composition of the team of senators that met with Carter on June 8 was indicative of the strategy to be followed in the weeks to come. These 13 senators shared certain characteristics. They were serving on the Senate Armed Services Committee, which was known to be favoring the lifting of the embargo. In contrast, the Senate Foreign Relations Committee was still opposed to repealing the embargo. In addition, 10 of these 13 senators were from the south. This made it easier for Carter to seek and get their political support. In the end, the great majority of the senators from southern states voted to repeal the embargo. In addition to being southerners, senators Nunn, Sparkman, Stennis, and Tower were widely respected in Congress when it came to defense matters, and their opinion on the subject of military aid to Turkey carried special weight.

McGovern Changes Course

The June 8 White House meeting was important for another reason. Two of the senators who were to lead the Senate fight were well-known liberals, McGovern of South Dakota and Church of Idaho. Senator McGovern's abandonment of the pro-embargo camp had provided significant impetus to the administration's drive to repeal the embargo. This was due to the fact that McGovern's liberal, leftist credentials could, and did, provide a cover for other liberal members of Congress to change their positions and support the lifting of the embargo. After all, no one could charge McGovern of being pro-Pentagon or insensitive to human rights, or a cold warrior for that matter. Quite the opposite was true. To a considerable degree, McGovern had lost the 1972 presidential election to Richard Nixon because he was considered too liberal and too far to the left. Moreover, McGovern was one of the leading political figures in the U.S. who opposed the Greek military junta and was vocal in his condemnation of Nixon and Kissinger for their support of the junta. He was highly critical of the Turkish invasion of Cyprus in 1974 and Kissinger's handling of the affair. As for military aid to Turkey, he had been an ardent supporter of the congressional drive to impose the embargo, especially since its imposition was spearheaded by a core group of liberals, senators Sarbanes and Eagleton, and representatives Brademas and Rosenthal.

With McGovern on its side, the Carter administration could go to Capitol Hill and argue more convincingly that the lifting of the embargo transcended party and ideological lines and was, indeed, in the best interest of the United States. McGovern cited exactly the same reason Carter did as justification for lifting the embargo. The embargo was counterproductive, McGovern argued before the Senate.[19]

McGovern's support for lifting the embargo did not go unnoticed in the American press. The *Christian Science Monitor* reported that the Greek press had commented with irony on the fact that Senator McGovern was leading the campaign to lift the embargo.[20] The *Washington Post* noted that McGovern, who was not known for his militaristic views, supported the lifting of the embargo because, according to the *Washington Post*, the Greek lobby appeared "intransigent" toward the May 20, 1978 Turkish Cypriot proposals for a Cyprus settlement.[21] These proposals revolved around the return of Greek Cypriot refugees to the Turkish-occupied city of Famagusta (Varosha), but only under certain conditions.

The governments of Cyprus and Greece had rejected the Turkish Cypriot proposals because they would have legitimized the Turkish invasion and division of Cyprus. On the other hand, it appeared, according to the *Washington Post*, that McGovern considered the Turkish Cypriot proposals to be reasonable and a basis for a settlement. In turn, this prompted him to support the lifting of the embargo. Whatever the reasoning was behind McGovern's shift from supporter to opponent of the embargo, his siding with the Carter White House greatly increased the chances that the Senate would repeal the embargo. It was ironic that bitter rivals such as Senator McGovern, a former Democratic presidential candidate, and former secretary of state Henry Kissinger had now joined hands and were lobbying for the lifting of the embargo.

Following his retirement from the Senate, McGovern gradually removed himself from issues related to Cyprus, even though it was he who had proposed the amendment that led to the lifting of the

---

[19]See McGovern's statement during the July 25, 1978 Senate debate on the embargo. *Congressional Record,* 95th Congress, 2nd Session, vol. 124, part 15, July 21, 1978, to July 31, 1978, p. 22501.

[20]*Christian Science Monitor,* July 24, 1978.

[21]*Washington Post,* July 24, 1978.

embargo in the Senate. Instead, he concentrated on issues concerning the Arab-Israeli dispute and the Israeli-occupied territories, adopting a rather sympathetic attitude toward the Palestinian position.

Carter's Final Push

By the middle of June 1978, the White House had intensified its efforts to persuade Congress to repeal the embargo. Acting along the lines of the June 1 memorandum, President Carter gave a press conference in which his opening statement pointed out the importance of lifting the embargo. He also continued to invite members of Congress to the White House in order to persuade them to support the administration on the forthcoming vote on the embargo in Congress.

On June 14, 1978, Carter gave a press conference in which he conveyed the urgency of lifting the arms embargo against Turkey. In an opening statement, the president explained the rationale behind the administration's drive to lift the embargo and made a series of assertions. He stated that the embargo had not worked because it had not contributed to a Cyprus settlement. He also said that the embargo had driven a wedge between Greece and Turkey and between Greece and the United States. He asserted that the lifting of the embargo was bound to improve Greek-Turkish relations and that it would "facilitate progress towards a Cyprus settlement."[22] None of these assertions withstood the test of time.

Following the president's press conference, the four members of Congress who were spearheading the effort to maintain the embargo issued a statement that was highly critical of Carter's assertions. They were Representative John Brademas, the House majority whip; Representative Benjamin Rosenthal; and senators Paul Sarbanes and Thomas Eagleton. Along with the statement, these members of Congress made available a package of documents that demonstrated how the Carter administration had undermined the embargo and had "signaled Turkey that it need not take the embargo seriously."[23] The tone taken by these four congressional critics of the administration

---

[22]On Carter's press conference, see *New York Times*, June 15, 1978. For a transcript of Carter's opening statement and his remarks on the embargo during the press conference, see Appendix, Document N.

[23]Ibid.

was quite harsh. They accused the president of breaking his pledge to uphold the embargo and suggested that Carter and other administration officials had been engaged in "devious and misleading" behavior in the effort to lift the embargo. They asserted that "the Administration's request that the embargo be lifted because it hasn't worked stands logic on its head. . . . The embargo has not worked because the Administration has been unwilling or unable to make it work." The four members of Congress also asserted that, at an April 22, 1977 White House meeting, Carter had assured them that a linkage existed between finding a settlement in Cyprus and supplying arms to Turkey. Despite these unequivocal assurances of a linkage, the administration was moving to lift the embargo "without requiring from Turkey either substantive actions or significant proposals regarding Cyprus," the four declared.[24]

The charge that Carter had broken his pledge concerning upholding the embargo and was engaged in "misleading and devious behavior," made by members of his own party, was especially caustic as it was directed against a president who was "a born-again Christian" and had made morality a centerpiece of his presidential campaign. In retrospect, such a strong characterization did not seem unjustified, considering how the administration had engaged in misleading reports to Congress on the Cyprus situation and had distorted the facts on a series of issues. These issues ranged from human rights in Cyprus and Turkey, to the domestic situation in Turkey, to assertions that the embargo was damaging U.S.–Greek relations, to assurances that lifting the embargo would facilitate a Cyprus settlement.

On June 15, 1978, just a day after his press conference that provoked the ire of the embargo supporters, President Carter invited a group of 30 representatives to the White House in order to persuade them to support the repeal of the embargo. In addition to the president, those present at the meeting, along with the members of Congress, were Deputy Secretary of State Warren Christopher; the president's special envoy to Greece, Turkey, and Cyprus, Clark Clifford; and other top national security officials. The representatives heard the standard arguments from the president. Then Clark Clifford, sitting next to the president as if to emphasize his exceptional political stature and his personal relationship with Carter, empha-

---

[24]Ibid.

sized the urgency of lifting the embargo. His argument expressed the familiar view that its continuation threatened Western interests and that "we might wake up one morning and realize that Turkey decided to withdraw from NATO and adopt a neutralist stand."[25] It remained unclear how many members of Congress were convinced by the administration's alarmist arguments during the White House meeting.

---

[25] *Proini,* June 16, 1978.

CHAPTER 13

Greek Americans Face the President

Carter's Personal Appeal in the East Room

During his meeting with members of Congress on June 15, 1978, President Carter told them that he was planning to meet with representatives of the Greek American community on June 22 in order to request their support for his plan to promote the lifting of the embargo. Among the Greek American leaders invited to the White House on June 22 was Archbishop Iakovos, the head of the Greek Orthodox Church of North and South America. He declined to attend and, in a letter to the White House, he said that "as a believing Christian clergyman, I will continue to pray that he [Carter] be given guidance and inspiration from above in his quest for peace." The archbishop also pointed out the following:

> ... Peace cannot be promoted by sending arms to a "well known" ally that has little regard for human rights and certainly less for peace. I therefore must decline the invitation, for I find it inappropriate to attend a discussion and briefing on a matter which has already been crystallized by the Administration and to which I consciously object."[1]

The letter from the Christian Orthodox leader of the Greek American community was meant to be a lesson in ethics for a president who had projected an image of being a leader guided by morality and his Christian beliefs. Having already decided to lift the embargo, and having made it public, Carter was inviting the archbishop for "consultation." Iakovos not only rejected the presidential invitation, but he also clearly implied in his response that Carter was

---

[1] *National Herald,* June 21, 1978.

a hypocrite. The bond that had linked the president and the archbishop appeared to have cracked, but not for long.

On September 18, 1979, a year after the embargo was officially
lifted, the White House announced that Carter would bestow the
Presidential Medal of Freedom upon Archbishop Iakovos in recognition of his service to the United States and its people. The announcement was made by President Carter at a White House ceremony in the
presence of the archbishop. In his speech announcing the prestigious
award, the president first paid tribute to ancient Greek democracy.
Then, he praised Iakovos for his service to the Greek Orthodox
Church, his inspirational leadership of the Greek American community, and his valuable contributions to the cause of racial equality in
the U.S. The president reminded his audience that Archbishop
Iakovos had walked next to Martin Luther King, Jr., at the civil rights
march in Selma, Alabama. Carter also lauded Iakovos for his fight for
human rights around the globe and for his efforts to promote Christian unity among the Orthodox, Catholic, and Protestant churches.
Then President Carter added:

> He [Archbishop Iakovos] has been an advisor for many. He
> has been *an advisor for me*. And I thank God for it. Not too
> long ago, I was at Camp David considering our Nation, some
> of its problems, some possible solutions for it. I needed coun-
> sel on government, politics, energy, taxation, economics, but
> above all I needed counsel on our country's spirit—who we
> are, what we are, what should we be. I asked him to come to
> Camp David and meet with me, and he graciously consented.
> We talked about the need for a rebirth of the American spirit.
> We talked about how we might, as Americans, revitalize the
> basic human values on which our country was founded. . . . *I
> am a great personal admirer of his . . .*[2] (Emphasis added.)

The president made no reference to what had been, by far, the
most important concern of the Greek American community: Cyprus
and human rights in the Turkish-occupied territory of Cyprus. Nor

---

[2]For a complete text of the President's speech, see "Archbishop Iakovos of the
Greek Orthodox Church in North and South America: Remarks at a White House
Reception Honoring the Archbishop, September 18, 1978," *Presidential Papers*,
Carter, 1979, Book II, June 23 to December 31, 1979, pp. 1688–1690.

did the president mention the archbishop's fight for the rights of the Ecumenical Patriarchate in Constantinople. Carter claimed that Iakovos had been an adviser to him, but not on the issues that really mattered to the Greek American community at the time. It remains unclear if, indeed, the president was an admirer of the archbishop. In his memoirs, Carter expressed no such admiration for his "adviser" Archbishop Iakovos. In fact, the name "Iakovos" does not appear in Carter's memoirs.

At the White House ceremony of September 18, 1979, Archbishop Iakovos reciprocated in response to the praise he had received from the president. In his speech, Iakovos had high praise for the president and Mrs. Carter. He thanked Carter for his decision to bestow the Presidential Medal of Freedom upon him. The archbishop's speech was spiritual in content, befitting an archbishop. However, in addition to his role as archbishop, Iakovos also acted as the political leader of the Greek American community and wanted to be recognized as such. Yet, in his speech, he avoided any reference to the issue of human rights in Cyprus. It was, after all, the Cyprus issue that had afforded the archbishop the opportunity to assume the role of political spokesman for the Greek American community and had given him so much publicity in the American media. Still, one could argue that the Cyprus issue had political connotations and that the archbishop was being honored for his spiritual role. In this vein, however, Iakovos failed to refer to the plight of the Ecumenical Patriarchate of Constantinople, which would have been clearly within his spiritual duties. It was ironic that Iakovos was being honored with the Medal of Freedom while the religious freedom of the Patriarchate, for which he had been a champion, had no place in his acceptance speech.[3]

The actual presentation of the Presidential Medal of Freedom to the archbishop took place at a White House ceremony on June 9, 1980. Other recipients of the award included Admiral Hyman Rickover, opera singer Beverly Sills, playwright Tennessee Williams, and photographer Ansel Adams. The next day, the archbishop appeared in a front-page photograph in the *New York Times*, standing near the president at the awards ceremony.[4]

---

[3]For a complete text of Iakovos's speech, see ibid, pp. 1690–1691. See also *Orthodox Observer*, October 10, 1978, pp. 9–10.

[4]See *New York Times*, June 10, 1980.

While Iakovos declined to attend the White House meeting on June 22, 1978, about 150 Greek American community leaders did attend. The meeting took place in the East Room, where the president holds official dinners. It commenced at 11:30 a.m. and ended a little before 1:00 p.m. In addition to the president, those present at the meeting were National Security Adviser Zbigniew Brzezinski, Under Secretary of State Warren Christopher, Air Force Chief of Staff General Allen, State Department Counsel Matthew Nimetz, and Clark Clifford, the president's special envoy to Greece, Turkey, and Cyprus.[5]

The Greek American leaders were first briefed by Warren Christopher and Clark Clifford. The officials employed the alarmist argument that the embargo had damaged NATO and benefited the Soviet Union, which had expansionist designs in the Eastern Mediterranean and the Middle East. To demonstrate the extent of the Soviet threat, the White House exhibited two large maps with red arrows emanating from the Soviet Union and ending at the borders of Greece and Turkey. The president asked General Allen to explain the strategic threat the Soviet Union posed to Greece and Turkey. The general pointed out that the Soviet Union had 25 military divisions near its borders with Turkey, and it was therefore imperative that Ankara receive the military assistance it needed to withstand Soviet pressures.

Then, the president warmly welcomed his Greek American guests, several of whom he had known during his election campaign. He praised ancient Athenian democracy and explained why he was asking Congress to repeal the arms embargo against Turkey. He employed arguments that were similar to the ones he had used at his June 15 press conference, namely, that the embargo had not worked and that it had damaged relations between Greece and Turkey, on the one hand, and between the United States and Turkey, on the other. He also expressed his belief that the lifting of the embargo would help both Greece and Turkey and would also "help bring about a peaceful solution to the Cyprus problem."

Carter cited the proposals on Cyprus submitted to the United Nations by Turkish Cypriot leader Rauf Denktash on May 20, 1978.

---

[5]An account of the White House meeting between President Carter and Greek American leaders appeared in the *New York Times*, June 23, 1978; *New York Post*, June 23, 1978; *Washington Star*, June 23, 1978; *National Herald*, June 23 and 24, 1978; *Proini*, June 23 and 24, 1978; *Proini Update*, June 24, 1978; *Hellenic Times*, June 24, 1978.

These proposals had been rejected outright by both the Cyprus and Greek governments because they were seen as legitimizing the Turkish invasion and occupation. Anticipating the objections of his audience, Carter attempted to deflect any criticism with humor, stating that he would not want his audience to think that he was adopting the Turkish position. He added, "I would not dare do such a thing before this gathering." His audience burst into rather sarcastic laughter upon hearing the statement.

In his speech, the president also emphasized the Soviet threat more than he had at any time in the past and raised the specter of a Greek-Turkish war if Turkey became an ally of the Soviet Union. If Turkey did become a Soviet ally, its greatest enemy would be Greece, Carter stated, echoing an earlier argument by General Alexander Haig, Supreme Allied Commander Europe.[6] It would be better if Turkey stayed in NATO because this would prevent a Greek-Turkish war, the president argued. Carter's premise, that the likelihood of war would increase if Greece and Turkey belonged to opposing camps, is quite debatable. One could argue with a considerable degree of confidence that a pro-Soviet Turkey would not dare attack Greece, a member of NATO. Indeed, none of Greece's northern neighbors that belonged to the Soviet bloc raised any territorial claims against Greece, and at no point during the cold war was there a serious risk of war between Greece and the communist Balkan countries. This was the best proof of the success of the Atlantic alliance in preventing aggression anywhere in Europe by the Soviet bloc. It was far-fetched, therefore, to argue that the likelihood of a Greek-Turkish war would have increased if Turkey had become a Soviet ally. Yet, President Carter did use this argument *in extremis* in his attempt to win support for lifting the embargo.

Evidently, the White House was concerned that Turkey was moving closer to neutrality, a step that would have preceded becoming a Soviet ally. At precisely the time that Carter was uttering his alarming words, Turkish Prime Minister Bülent Ecevit was in Moscow, where he signed a non-aggression pact and trade and cultural agreements with the Soviet Union.[7] It has already been asserted above that this was a tactical move by Turkey to put pressure on the Carter adminis-

---

[6] *New York Times,* May 23, 1978.
[7] Ibid., June 24, 1978.

tration to lift the embargo and that it, by no means, indicated a strategic reorientation of Turkey away from the Western alliance. The Turkish tactic of using the Soviet card to scare the United States was quite effective. Carter and his advisers, Brzezinski and Clifford especially, took the Turkish maneuvering with Russia at face value. This added to the urgency of their attempts to achieve the lifting of the embargo.

Rescinding the Trust: Mr. President, You Broke Your Promise

President Carter's arguments failed to persuade his Greek American audience of the rationale behind the lifting of the embargo or his good intentions. The overwhelming majority of those in attendance were critical of the president in a respectful way, and several of them expressed their opposition to his statements through questions and comments. Throughout the question-and-answer period, Carter was visibly uncomfortable. Nicholas Petris, a widely respected, liberal, Democratic state senator from California, told the president that, although he and most Greek Americans had actively supported him for the presidency, he "was rapidly losing the tremendous moral leadership" he had enjoyed when he was elected. Petris reminded Carter of his pledge to support human rights by holding up a newspaper that contained an article on human rights. Then, Petris, looking Carter straight in the eye, added, ". . . there has been no public criticism of Turkey as an aggressor, as a breaker of the law, and that is very disappointing."[8] Carter said nothing, but he blushed. Mayor Lee Alexander of Syracuse, New York, and Peter Terzis, Supreme President of the American Hellenic Progressive Association (AHEPA), reminded the president of his campaign promises and pointed out that, while he supported human rights around the world, he had forgotten to apply this principle in Cyprus. In the same vein, a friend of Carter's from Georgia, Professor Costas Alexandrides of Georgia State University, reminded the president of the symbolic meaning of the embargo in terms of morality, human rights, and the rule of law.

It was George Christopher, however, the former mayor of San Francisco and a well known Republican, who expressed the pre-

---

[8]Based on the personal communication of the author with California State Senator Nicholas Petris, Sacramento, October 18, 1998.

vailing feeling among Greek Americans. He presented a critique of Carter's speech and his effort to lift the embargo. Looking him straight in the eye, Christopher told Carter:

> I recall my meeting with then candidate Carter in Los Angeles, when you sought our support. . . . As a Republican, I pledged my support, based on your pledge to me that you would rectify the injustice done to Cyprus by supporting U.N. Resolution 3212. With this assurance, I traveled throughout the country (at my own expense) imploring our own communities to support Governor Carter regardless of party. We believe that 95% of our [Greek American] Republican constituents switched to the Carter Camp, and our Democrats were practically unanimous . . .
>
> It is with deep regret that we must now retrace our steps and rescind our prior expressions of trust. You, Mr. President, now tell us that the embargo against Turkey has failed to resolve the Cyprus issue. It should be evident to all that any embargo is doomed to failure when the President openly tells Turkey to be patient, and that, in due time, the embargo would be lifted. Why should Turkey cooperate under such glowing circumstances? Had you honored your electoral pledges, had you manifested some tangible concern about human rights in place of your selective and contradictory rhetoric, then the Cyprus issue might have been solved. You speak of human rights, we all believe in human rights. But the last time I visited Cyprus and saw the elderly and the children of refugees living in misery, I said to myself, "Oh Lord, what human rights are we talking about."
>
> We heard the concern that, if the embargo is not lifted, Turkey may drift towards the Soviet Union. Is this the extent of Turkey's loyalty to the U.S. and NATO? Must the United States submit to blackmail as a price for Turkey's transitory alliance? . . . Already encouraged by the reversal of your campaign promises, Turkey is not satisfied with its illegal adventures in Cyprus, it has expanded its horizons with inordinate claims in the whole Aegean. . . . The solution to these problems is that you must do as President what you promised to do as candidate . . .

> With God's help, we shall persevere and we shall over-
> come until justice and righteousness prevail, and finally we
> will prove that you were right when you were a candidate and
> coveted our support and you were wholly wrong when your
> misdirected advisers steered you from your original course of
> righteousness, justice, and constructive leadership.[9]

The words of San Francisco's former mayor stung President Carter. George Christopher had challenged Carter on certain political grounds. To these challenges, Carter could respond with political arguments, which he did. However, the emphasis of Christopher's remarks was on morality and trust. Such arguments would be rather ineffective under other circumstances because the dictates of foreign policy cannot rest solely on moral grounds. In the case of Carter, however, moral arguments carried extra weight precisely because these kinds of arguments had helped the Georgia governor capture the White House.

What was embarrassing for the president was the fact that, in a face-to-face dialogue, doubt was being cast upon his integrity, his ethics, and his character. The president appeared to be shaken by Christopher's remarks. He blushed and became irate. He responded by saying that it was not pleasant to hear, neither as a human being nor as president, that he had not kept his promises. Carter stated that he had not changed his principles and that his objectives concerning Cyprus were still the same as those he had promised to pursue as a presidential candidate. He said that he had never condoned the Turkish invasion of Cyprus. Our difference is about tactics, the president stated, and he added, "Our objective is the same as George's [George Christopher's]."

The president made an effort to end the meeting on a positive note. While exiting the room, he stopped to chat with Greek American acquaintances, telling them that they represented a dynamic element in American society and that they were indeed devoted to America while also loving Greece. Then, the Greek American guests were invited into the Rose Garden, where they were served baklava and iced tea.

The Greek sweets notwithstanding, the fact remained that the

---

[9] *National Herald*, June 23, 1978; *Proini Update*, June 24, 1978.

meeting had been a disaster for the White House. Those who had argued against such a meeting felt vindicated. Bob Beckel, a Carter aide who was working with Frank Moore, the White House congressional liaison, described the meeting as follows: "We had two hundred Greeks in the East Room, all boiling mad." Beckel recalled this with a shudder.[10] Madeleine Albright, National Security Council congressional liaison, was among those who had advised the president against meeting with Greek Americans. Albright's biographer, Michael Dobbs, described the incident:

> A promise to lift the embargo on arms sales to Turkey had Greek Americans descending to the White House by the coachload. . . . Madeleine [Albright] had an intuitive sense of when to negotiate and when to stand firm. Knowing that the Greek-American vote was largely confined to states like New Jersey, she had argued against providing the Greeks with a forum to vent their grievances in front of the president. "You don't know Greeks, I know Greeks," she told Beckel. She was overruled, but the angry scenes in the State Dining Room proved her right.[11]

It is worth noting that 10 years later, in 1987 and 1988, Albright became the leading member of the foreign policy team of a Greek American, Michael Dukakis, as he sought the presidency. Dukakis, who was the Democratic presidential candidate in the 1988 election, chose Albright to be his chief foreign policy adviser.[12] The fact that Albright had been part of the core team at the Carter White House that worked diligently to defeat the political objectives of the Greek American community by lifting the embargo was not an obstacle to her becoming part of Dukakis's inner circle. Dukakis's choice of Albright as an adviser paved the way for her to join President Bill Clinton's team four years later. In 1997, Clinton appointed Albright secretary of state.

Only one of the 150 Greek American leaders at the June 22, 1978 White House meeting spoke out in support of the president. This

---

[10]Quoted in Dobbs, *Madeleine Albright*, p. 273.

[11]Ibid.

[12]On Albright's role as Dukakis's chief foreign policy adviser, see ibid., pp. 330–337.

almost unanimous opposition to the president was an indirect confirmation that Carter's assertion that the embargo had been damaging to Greece's relations with the United States was misleading. There was an overwhelming belief among Greek Americans that the lifting of the embargo would be a serious setback to U.S.-Greek relations.

In subsequent statements, Greek American leaders stated unequivocally that the meeting with the president came too late. They maintained that the White House meeting should have taken place six months earlier if Carter had really cared about the views of the Greek American community. The fact that he invited Greek American leaders to the White House *ex post facto*, after he had made the decision to lift the embargo, appeared patronizing. Moreover, it was seen as an indication that Carter had not wanted to be placed in a situation where the Greek Americans could ask him to honor his pledges as he was about to make a decision on the embargo. It seemed that Carter could not tolerate circumstances where he thought his moral rectitude could be challenged. The Greek American argument was primarily a matter of morality, and Carter sought to avoid a confrontation on such a subject. He failed, however, because that was precisely what transpired at the White House meeting on June 22, 1978.

The day after the meeting, the Greek American press was full of reports about Carter's failure to persuade the Greek American community that it was a good idea to lift the embargo. In fact, most of the Greek Americans at the meeting ridiculed the arguments made by Carter and his aides.[13] Other American newspapers reported that Carter had become upset at the meeting and that he had failed to win any support among the Greek American community. Instead, several Greek American leaders had warned him that the only thing he would succeed in achieving by lifting the embargo would be to weaken the government of Greek Prime Minister Constantine Karamanlis and reinforce anti-Americanism in Greece.[14] Indeed, Andreas Papandreou's party, PASOK, ran on an anti-American platform in the 1981 parliamentary elections, and he utilized the lifting of the embargo to the maximum extent possible in his successful drive to unseat the pro-American government of Karamanlis.

---

[13] *National Herald,* June 23, 1978; *Proini,* June 23, 1978.

[14] *New York Post,* June 23, 1978; *New York Times,* June 23, 1978; *Washington Star,* June 23, 1978.

Carter's June 22, 1978 meeting with Greek American leaders was an important event in the affairs of the Greek American community. It was also an important event for the Carter presidency. Yet, it was given very little attention. The meeting was important not so much because the president had met with Greek American leaders but because, in the course of this meeting, he had given a significant foreign policy speech. The meeting was even more important due to the fact that the moral foundation of Carter's presidency was challenged inside the White House. If there were to be a legacy for Jimmy Carter, it was believed that he would be, above all, the "moral president." This was now being challenged inside the White House East Room. It was an extraordinary moment of the Carter presidency. It was the first and only time, perhaps, that President Carter was confronted with such a direct, face-to-face challenge to his moral rectitude inside the White House.

In his memoirs, the former president made no mention of his meeting with the Greek American leaders. Even more significant is the fact that his June 22, 1978 speech to the Greek Americans has been omitted from Carter's presidential papers, which include most of his speeches at the White House. In these papers, the only reference to Carter's meeting with the Greek Americans is found in the section entitled "Digest of Other White House Announcements," where the following is listed on the calendar of events: "June 22: The President met at the White House with representatives of the Greek American community."[15]

At the same time, however, the June 22 White House meeting demonstrated the weakening of the Greek lobby. The very fact that Greek American leaders were invited to the White House after the administration had announced the decision to work toward the lifting of the embargo was a clear sign that Carter was not seriously concerned about any political retribution by the Greek American community, retribution that would affect the president's political fortunes. For about a year, since the spring of 1977, the Greek lobby had not reacted effectively to signals indicating that the White House was moving methodically in the direction of lifting the embargo. This demonstrated that the lobby's influence in Washington had peaked in 1975 and 1976.

---

[15]See *Presidential Papers, Carter, 1978*, Book I, p. 1154.

CHAPTER 14

Congress Repeals the Embargo

More Maneuvering as the Vote Approaches

The unanimous Greek American opposition to the lifting of the embargo, as expressed at the June 22, 1978 White House meeting, was of little significance to the Carter administration. It became evident that the president had made up his mind in favor of lifting the embargo, and the invitation to Greek Americans to visit the White House had been a public relations exercise. Carter had no intention of taking the opinions of Greek Americans into account.

On June 28, 1978, the top foreign and defense policy officials of the administration appeared before the Senate Armed Services Committee to argue once more in favor of lifting the embargo. Appearing before the committee were Secretary of State Cyrus Vance, Secretary of Defense Harold Brown, General David Jones, chairman of the Joint Chiefs of Staff, and General Alexander Haig, Supreme Allied Commander Europe. They all repeated the urgency of lifting the embargo and the alarmist view that Turkey would move closer to the Soviet Union if the embargo were not lifted.[1] General Jones asserted that it would be difficult to find any other region of the world that had more significance for U.S. interests than Turkey. His view on the strategic significance of Turkey echoed a similar U.S. attitude toward the Shah's Iran, which had already entered a period of revolutionary turmoil.

What was more controversial, however, was the comment the secretary of defense made about Greece. When Senator Gary Hart of Colorado asked him what would happen if a left-wing government, meaning that of Andreas Papandreou, came to power in Greece as a result of the repeal of the arms embargo against Turkey, Secretary Brown responded by saying that the administration had all sorts of

---

[1] *New York Times*, June 29, 1978.

contingency plans if that were to occur. He could not discuss such plans publicly, Brown stated, but he was willing to "discuss certain matters at a closed session."[2] The secretary of defense's statement caused a firestorm in Greece. It had only been four years since the military junta, which had been supported by the Nixon administration, had collapsed. The overwhelming majority of Greeks blamed the United States for the Turkish invasion of Cyprus since the Greek junta's coup against Makarios had triggered the invasion.

Inevitably, the Greeks were quite sensitive to any suggestion that the United States might intervene again in the internal affairs of the country. Brown's statement, viewed as arrogant by the Greeks, caused Constantine Karamanlis, the pro-American prime minister of Greece, to declare that "the decision of who rules Greece is only for the Greek people to determine and no foreigner can make such a decision."[3] More importantly, Brown's statement gave fresh ammunition to socialist opposition leader Andreas Papandreou for his attack on both the Karamanlis government and the United States. Papandreou declared that the U.S. secretary of defense's statement concerning U.S. contingency plans for Greece clearly demonstrated that the United States was "treating Greece as a satellite. . . . The Greek government should get rid of the corrosive mechanisms of the United States in our country . . ."[4] As for the Greek press, both the pro-Western conservative newspapers and the left-wing press denounced Brown's statement. They saw it as a betrayal of American liberal democratic traditions, a warning that the U.S. could establish a new "fascist dictatorship" in the country, and even more proof of the "incurable" pro-Turkish policies of the Carter administration. The denunciation of Brown's statement by the pro-Papandreou and leftist press was not surprising. What was more indicative of the mood in the country was the strong criticism of the secretary of defense's statement by the pro-Western and pro-Karamanlis press.[5]

This reaction from the entire spectrum of Greece's political forces, from the right to the left, demonstrated the degree to which Greek reality had been distorted by the Carter administration, as it

---

[2] *Proini*, June 30, 1978.

[3] Ibid.

[4] *Proini*, June 30 and July 1, 1978.

[5] See the pro-Karamanlis newspapers *Vradyni*, July 1, 1978; *Apogevmatini*, July 1, 1978. See also the pro-Papandreou newspaper *Ta Nea*, July 1, 1978.

kept insisting that the embargo was creating a "wedge in U.S.-Greek relations." Political reality in Greece pointed in exactly the opposite direction, namely, that it was the lifting of the embargo that was bound to damage Greek-U.S. relations. It was inevitable that Papandreou would exploit the lifting of the embargo in his drive to unseat the pro-Western Karamanlis government. Within three years, in 1981, Papandreou would become the prime minister of Greece by running on an anti-American platform.

In the meantime, the White House effort to woo undecided members of Congress regarding the embargo continued unabated. On July 12, 1978, yet another group of representatives was invited to the White House to meet with the president and several of his top aides. One of them was Tom Corcoran, a Republican representative from Illinois. In the past, Corcoran had supported the lifting of the embargo but, following the meeting with the president, he changed his view and decided to vote against the administration on the issue. The reason for this was that the president was unable to assure Corcoran and his colleagues that Turkey was committed to withdrawing its troops from Cyprus. In a letter to his colleagues, dated July 13, 1978, Representative Corcoran wrote:

> On behalf of those of us concerned about specific, concrete details on the plans to move the Turkish troops from Cyprus, I asked the President whether or not any such details had come to light in any of his discussions with officials of the Turkish government. His [the President's] answer, in effect, was that we have no such concrete details on a timetable for troop withdrawal.[6]

The Illinois Republican, not satisfied with Carter's response concerning troop withdrawal, sent a letter to the president as well. In a letter dated July 13, 1978, Representative Corcoran informed President Carter that:

> I am writing to follow up on yesterday's breakfast meeting with you, your Cabinet officials, the Chairman of the Joint Chiefs of Staff, and our Ambassador to Turkey . . .

---

[6]*Proini*, July 19 and 20, 1978.

I am respectfully saying that unless there is some concrete, specific evidence of a plan for moving Turkish troops
off Cyprus, I am convinced after personal correspondence
and discussions with uncommitted and marginal Republicans on this issue, that we will not support lifting the afore-
said embargo.[7]

Another member of Congress, Representative David Kildee,
Democrat of Michigan, confirmed that the administration had failed
to receive any assurances from Turkey that it planned to withdraw or
even reduce the number of occupation troops in Cyprus if the
embargo were to be lifted. In a speech on the floor of the House of
Representatives on July 19, 1978, Representative Kildee stated:

The Administration is now asking that we totally lift the
embargo on weapons [to Turkey]. In light of the previous
assurances, I have closely scrutinized the language which the
Administration has used. They have said that the lifting of the
embargo may encourage the Turkish government to be more
cooperative. When I directly asked a State Department official if they had *any assurances*, even informal, from the Turkish government that they would be *less intransigent* in
negotiations or make significant reductions in the number of
occupation troops if the embargo were to be lifted, *he
responded negatively.*[8] (Emphasis added.)

Thus, on the one hand, the administration, from the president to
his top aides, was telling members of Congress, Greek American leaders, and the American people in general that the lifting of the embargo
would facilitate a Cyprus settlement. In this respect, it was clearly
understood that such a settlement would include a timetable for the
withdrawal of the Turkish occupation army. On the other hand, the
administration knew very well that Turkey had made no commitment
whatsoever on withdrawing its occupation army.

Indeed, Ankara had refused to make any commitment to withdraw its troops if the embargo were lifted, and the president and top

---

[7] A copy of Congressman Corcoran's letter appeared in *Proini*, July 19, 1978.
[8] Ibid., July 20, 1978.

administration officials admitted that this was the case. Turkish Prime Minister Bülent Ecevit gave no sign that he was in the mood to compromise. This point was stressed in a *New York Times* editorial:

> Administration spokesmen maintain that once [the embargo] is lifted, Ankara will make generous diplomatic proposals. But the Government of Prime Minister Bulent Ecevit has so far given no sign that it is prepared to risk the domestic consequences of offering concessions needed to reach an accommodation.[9]

The charge by top congressional leaders a month earlier, on June 15, 1978, that Carter and other administration officials had indulged in "devious and misleading behavior" had certainly been harsh, but the turn of events had justified such a characterization. The Carter administration had been engaged in politics of deception in its drive to persuade Congress to repeal the embargo.

Six days before the Senate vote on lifting the embargo, President Carter made another effort to win the support of members of Congress. On July 19, 1978, he invited 19 senators, mostly Democrats, to the White House. The majority of the Republicans in the Senate were known to be leaning toward the Carter camp. The White House expected to win the votes of 26 to 28 of the 37 Republican senators. It needed the votes of 25 to 27 Democrats to secure victory in the Senate. This was by no means an easy task. Consequently, Carter made an extra effort to win over as many Republicans as possible. The president used the prestige of his office to solicit the assistance of former president Gerald Ford and former secretary of state Henry Kissinger. Both of them, along with General Alexander Haig, Supreme Allied Commander Europe, launched an intense lobbying campaign on behalf of Carter to convince Republicans to support the lifting of the embargo.

During the July 19 meeting, Carter succeeded in obtaining or solidifying the support of key Republican senators such as Richard Lugar of Indiana and Richard Schweiker of Pennsylvania. He failed, however, to change the minds of Republican senators Pete Domenici of New Mexico and Mark Hattfield of Oregon. Among the Demo-

---

[9]*New York Times*, July 22, 1978.

crats, Carter won the support of two key senators, John Glenn of Ohio and James Culver of Iowa. The president had already won the support of senators Edward Zorinski of Nebraska, Lloyd Bentsen of Texas, and George McGovern of South Dakota, who were also present at the meeting. Three other Democratic senators at the meeting, Kaneaster Hodges of Arkansas, Wendell Ford of Kentucky, and James Sasser of Tennessee were fellow southerners, and Carter was able to count on their support as well. The president failed to persuade Democratic senators Dick Clark of Iowa and Dennis DeConcini of Arizona to support his position. Overall, however, the meeting at the White House was good news for the president because he could now count on the support of even more Republican senators than before, as well as that of some key Democratic senators.

Re-Enter Famagusta

The next day, July 20, 1978, just five days before the Senate vote, Turkish Cypriot leader Rauf Denktash announced some proposals regarding a Cyprus settlement, which modified his earlier proposals of May 20, 1978. The day also marked the fourth anniversary of the Turkish invasion of Cyprus. The May 20 proposals had been submitted to U.N. Secretary General Kurt Waldheim and had been rejected by the Cyprus government. The new modified proposals of July 20 revolved, again, around the city of Famagusta (Varosha). They would allow the return of 35,000 Greek Cypriot refugees to the city, but only under certain conditions. These conditions included the establishment of an interim administration "without any prejudice to the existing plan for the final political status of the area." The refugees could begin resettlement "as soon as feasible with the resumption of inter-communal talks." The administration of the city would be under the aegis of the U.N.[10]

The July 20 proposals were rejected outright by the government of Cyprus President Spyros Kyprianou. The Cyprus government considered them to be a Turkish ploy to influence the forthcoming Senate vote on the embargo. The basis for the Cyprus government's rejection of the Denktash proposals was the assertion that they failed to provide for a comprehensive settlement linking the proposals to

---

[10] *Reuters*, July 20, 1978.

U.N. resolutions and the withdrawal of Turkish troops from the occupied territory. Denktash's proposals on Famagusta (Varosha) were seen by the Greek Cypriots as a step toward legitimizing the partition of Cyprus by dividing the country into pieces, some under the control of the Turkish occupation army, some under Greek control, and some under U.N. control.[11]

The Nicosia government went further and accused the Carter administration of being behind the July 20 Denktash proposals. Addressing a mass protest rally in Nicosia, President Kyprianou stated that Washington had dictated that Denktash make the proposals to facilitate the lifting of the embargo. When the Carter administration came out openly in favor of these proposals, the Cyprus government lodged a strong diplomatic protest accusing the State Department representative who had openly supported the Turkish proposals of behaving in an "undiplomatic manner."[12]

Despite the Cyprus government's outright rejection of the May 20 and July 20, 1978 Turkish proposals on Famagusta, the Carter administration put its full diplomatic weight behind them and carried out a campaign in Congress in favor of the proposals. The Cyprus government had raised legitimate issues in rejecting the Denktash proposals, but the Carter administration brushed aside the concerns of the Cyprus government as if it had no say in a negotiated settlement.

On June 28, 1978, Assistant Secretary for Congressional Relations Douglas J. Bennet, representing the State Department, sent a letter to Senator John Sparkman, chairman of the Senate Foreign Relations Committee, urging the Senate to lift the embargo. One of the main arguments in this letter was the assertion that the Turkish Cypriots had submitted quite reasonable proposals, especially regarding the resettlement of Famagusta (Varosha), a reference to Denktash's May 20 proposals. Bennet indicated in his letter that "these proposals, plus the more favorable environment in Turkey make this an important and hopeful movement in the search for a solution in Cyprus." During the embargo debate on July 25, Bennet's letter was introduced in the Senate and became part of the *Congressional Record*.[13] Senator

---

[11] *Proini*, July 22, 1978.

[12] Ibid.

[13] See *Congressional Record*, 95th Congress, 2nd Session, vol. 124, part 15, July 21, 1978, to July 31, 1978, pp. 22511–22513. The complete text of Assistant Secretary Bennet's letter to Senator Sparkman appears in the Appendix, Document O.

Sparkman and the other supporters of the administration cited the letter and the State Department's support for the Denktash proposals as evidence that Turkey was exhibiting goodwill with regard to reaching a Cyprus settlement.

The Senate Debate and Vote

Texas Senator Lloyd Bentsen: The Embargo is Counterproductive

The Senate vote on lifting the embargo took place on Tuesday, July 25, 1978. Up to the last minute, President Carter had lobbied senators by inviting them to the White House and by making phone calls to wavering lawmakers. The task before the Senate was to consider an amendment to the legislation that had imposed the embargo on October 3, 1974. This was designated as "Amendment No. 1491—Purpose: To repeal the limited embargo on arms sales to Turkey." The sponsors of the amendment were Senate Majority Leader Robert Byrd, a Democrat; Democratic senators George McGovern and Lloyd Bentsen; and Republican Senator John Chafee. The architect of the amendment, however, was Senator George McGovern, and the amendment to repeal the embargo in the Senate became known as the "McGovern amendment."[14]

The fight to lift the embargo was led by Byrd, perhaps the staunchest supporter of Turkey in the Senate, and by Bentsen and McGovern. They were supported by Republican senators Tower and Chafee. In all, 19 senators spoke in favor of lifting the embargo. Eleven of them were from the south, an indication that most of the southern senators supported the lifting of the embargo. Eight of the 10 Democratic senators who spoke in favor of lifting the embargo were southerners who were supporting their fellow southern president. In fact, no senator from the south rose to speak against the repeal of the embargo.

Generally speaking, Bentsen and McGovern, as well as the other senators supporting the lifting of the embargo, employed four basic arguments.[15]

---

[14]The McGovern amendment appears in the *Congressional Record*, Senate, 95th Congress, 2nd Session, Vol. 124 – Part 15, July 21, 1978 to July 31, 1978, p. 22548. For the complete text of the McGovern amendment, see the Appendix, Document P.

[15]The account presented on the Senate debate is based on the *Congressional*

First, Turkey occupied a crucial geopolitical position, was indispensable for NATO's overall defense against the Soviet Union, was the cornerstone of NATO's vital southeastern flank, and was a bulwark against Moscow's attempts to penetrate the Middle East.

Second, Turkey was deeply offended by the embargo, and the wounded Turkish pride might lead the Ankara government away from NATO toward neutrality or even closer to the Soviet Union.

Third, the arms embargo against Turkey had been counterproductive because Ankara had refused to negotiate over Cyprus under pressure. Since its imposition, the embargo had become a stumbling block to a Cyprus settlement. On the other hand, if the embargo were lifted, this would facilitate a Cyprus settlement.

Fourth, Turkey and the Turkish Cypriots had already demonstrated their goodwill by presenting proposals that would allow 35,000 Greek Cypriot refugees to return to Famagusta (Varosha). Turkish Prime Minister Bülent Ecevit was a man of moderation and reason, and the lifting of the embargo would allow him to be much more forthcoming on Cyprus.

In his speech, Senator Bentsen stated these four major reasons for recommending that the embargo be lifted. He also sought to justify the change in his position from a supporter to an opponent of the embargo. The main reason for this change, Bentsen argued, was that after three and one-half years, the embargo had proved to be counterproductive. Instead of bringing about a Cyprus settlement, it had made a settlement more remote. Unless the embargo were lifted, any prospects for a Cyprus settlement were doomed. The best way to thwart progress on Cyprus was "to keep the embargo in place," Bentsen argued.

Senator Bentsen's speech was followed by those of senators Chafee, Stennis, and Church, all in support of the McGovern amendment. By and large, they repeated the four major points in favor of lifting the embargo.

Senator McGovern: Champion of Lifting the Embargo

Then, Senator George McGovern of South Dakota took the podium. His speech acquired special significance, considering the fact that he

---

Record, Senate, 95th Congress, 2nd Session, Vol. 124 – Part 15, July 21, 1978, to July 31, 1978, pp. 22501–22557. Hereinafter *Congressional Record-Senate, July 25, 1978*.

was the architect of the amendment to lift the embargo in the Senate and had worked closely with the Carter administration in the effort to win a Senate majority in favor of its repeal.

Just prior to the commencement of the debate to repeal the embargo, McGovern rose and commended President Carter. McGovern stated that "in recent days, President Carter has experienced some obvious bad breaks." He said that he wanted to praise Carter's performance, especially in foreign policy. The senator from South Dakota cited some of Carter's achievements: the Panama Canal Treaties, "the even-handed policy in the highly volatile Arab-Israeli dispute," and the president's support of majority rule in South Africa. Then McGovern, referring to the embargo issue, told his colleagues:

> ... and now he is calling on us to remove the largely symbolic but self-defeating embargo against Turkey—an embargo which is clearly exacerbating relations involving Greece, Turkey, and Cyprus.[16]

Senator McGovern expressed the hope that his words would "perhaps come to the attention of the President at what we all know is a difficult time for him and for the Nation." This high praise for President Carter by the Democratic senator, as the embargo debate was about to begin, was a clear indication that McGovern identified with Carter's foreign policy goals and was about to play a pivotal role in the fight over the embargo.

It was quite ironic that the stage for repealing the embargo was set by one of the most liberal senators, George McGovern, the icon of the American left and the nemesis of Richard Nixon and Henry Kissinger. From the spring of 1976 to June 1978, McGovern had served as the president of Americans for Democratic Action, the most important political organization of the liberal left in the United States. Thus, when McGovern became the leading advocate of lifting the embargo, he did so as the best-known representative of the left wing of the Democratic Party. McGovern opened his speech as follows:

> Mr. President, few issues in American foreign policy have engendered such passion as the dispute over the proper U.S.

---

[16]Congressional Record-Senate, July 25, 1978, p. 22501.

response to events which began in Cyprus in the summer of 1974. From the outset, the debate was a curious admixture—building from a deep distrust and disappointment of the Kissinger policy in that region, motivated by an urgently felt need to uphold U.S. law at a time when illegality had become a major theme of the American Presidency, and inspired by an earnest desire to provide American support for a just settlement on that small, tragedy-ridden island in the eastern Mediterranean.[17]

Then, Senator McGovern explained why the embargo had not worked and, therefore, had to be repealed. He explained that the imposition of the embargo had led to two contradictory policies that had created an impasse concerning Cyprus. One was the congressional policy in favor of the embargo, and the other was the executive branch's policy opposing it. At the same time, the embargo had been largely symbolic because it had already been partially lifted. "Its principal purpose and effect is not to curtail Turkey's arms supplies but rather to stigmatize that nation for its conduct in Cyprus," McGovern argued.

Congress had made its point on the rule of law by imposing the embargo. But, for over three years, the embargo had failed to produce any progress on Cyprus. Maintaining the embargo would be "a continued imposition of a stigma [on Turkey] and no more than a formula for continued deadlock," McGovern stated. In this way, the liberal senator appeared to be siding with the State Department's human rights report on Cyprus, which had downplayed human rights violations in the Turkish-occupied territory.

The lifting of the embargo would not guarantee progress on Cyprus, but it would make reaching a Cyprus settlement more likely since Turkey had already indicated its willingness to compromise on Cyprus once the embargo was lifted. In this regard, McGovern pointed out the Turkish Cypriot proposals concerning Famagusta (Varosha).

In proposing his amendment repealing the embargo, the liberal senator from South Dakota was quite conscious that he would be criticized by other liberals for putting aside moral principles and human

---

[17] *Congressional Record, Senate,* July 25, 1978, p. 22526.

rights in favor of realpolitik and strategic considerations. He made an effort, therefore, to explain that his amendment included conditions which would ensure that the lifting of the embargo was not meant to reward Turkey. Rather, the conditions for repealing the embargo, McGovern argued, balanced the strategic needs of the United States in the Eastern Mediterranean with moral principles. This balance meant that the president and Congress, acting together, should pursue a policy aiming at a just Cyprus settlement. Senator McGovern declared:

> Such a policy, moreover, must make it clear that, while deleting the embargo provisions from our law, we have not deleted our deep concern for Cyprus from our national conscience and that we will examine, through prescribed executive-legislative procedure, our future policies toward each relevant country with a view to whether it has contributed a good faith effort to the process of bringing justice to the island.[18]

The "just solution on Cyprus" was defined in the McGovern amendment as follows:

1. The continued presence of a major Turkish force is inconsistent with the legitimate status of Cyprus as a sovereign republic.
2. The guidelines for inter-communal talks agreed to in Nicosia in February 1977—setting forth the common goal of an independent, sovereign, nonaligned, bi-communal Federal Republic of Cyprus—continue to provide a sound basis for the negotiation of a just settlement in that region.
3. The United States should actively support efforts to achieve such a just solution, providing full protection for the human rights of all Cypriots.
4. The United States arms transfers to Greece and Turkey shall be made solely for defensive purposes and to sustain their strength as North Atlantic Treaty Organization allies.[19]

---

[18]Ibid.

[19]Ibid., p. 22548. For the complete text of the McGovern amendment, see the Appendix, Document P.

The essence of this definition of a "just Cyprus settlement" was that it would result in the end of the Turkish military occupation and the restoration of the territorial integrity of the Republic of Cyprus. There is no doubt that this is what Senator McGovern had in mind when he proposed his amendment. He genuinely believed that a just Cyprus settlement could only be achieved if Turkey withdrew its occupation forces.

The question was how the United States could promote such a just settlement following the lifting of the embargo. Promoting a settlement was precisely the objective of a key provision of the McGovern amendment. This provision requested that the president submit a report to Congress every 60 days on the status of negotiations concerning Cyprus. In his bimonthly report to Congress, the president had to provide a "fully justified certification that the goal of a just solution on Cyprus has been achieved or that such future [U.S. military and economic] aid would contribute to the achievement of such a goal."[20] In other words, future military aid to Turkey was to be contingent on Ankara's goodwill with regard to reaching a "just solution on Cyprus," as such a settlement was defined in the amendment.

The critical element in this provision was that it was left up to the executive branch, the president, to evaluate the situation on the ground in Cyprus and determine whether Turkey had exhibited goodwill in promoting a settlement. That was precisely the meaning of the provision, which stated:

> The President shall, within 60 days after the enactment of this section and at the end of each succeeding 60-day period, transmit to the Speaker of the House and the chairman of the Committee on Foreign Relations of the Senate a report on progress made during such period toward the conclusion of a negotiated solution of the Cyprus problem.[21]

The senator from South Dakota, who had been the Democratic presidential candidate in 1972, was, more than any other liberal member of Congress, quite conscious of what this provision meant. It was left up to the discretion of the White House to define what "good

---

[20] *Ibid.*, p. 22527.
[21] Ibid., p. 22548.

faith" and "progress toward a settlement" meant in the case of Cyprus. The White House's process of evaluation would deal with developments in a strategic region, the Eastern Mediterranean, which was vital to American interests. Senator McGovern certainly knew very well that cold war considerations could intervene and influence the judgment of the White House when it came to reporting to Congress on developments in this strategically important region. This had been the essence of realpolitik under Nixon and Kissinger, when strategic considerations and the fight against Soviet communism had prevailed over human rights. Cognizant of this tendency, McGovern proclaimed:

> We are all aware, of course, that certification procedures *have in past administrations been abused*. But *I have confidence that President Carter's integrity would preclude abuse in this instance*. Thus, if Turkey does not make a good faith effort in the Cyprus negotiations, *I do not expect the Administration to make a disingenuous false certification*. (Emphasis added.)

In addition to putting his faith in the hands of President Carter with regard to providing a fair and objective picture of developments in Cyprus, McGovern expressed confidence that Turkey was already moving in the direction of good faith negotiations.

The senator from South Dakota stated:

> Mr. President, no policy in any area is foolproof and the approach embodied in this provision [the McGovern amendment] may probably meet the fate of efforts on Cyprus which have gone before. But I trust that this will not be the case. *I am prepared to accept Prime Minister Ecevit's clear indication that he will move constructively on Cyprus once the political straightjacket of 620 (x) [the embargo] is removed.*[22] (Emphasis added.)

Thus, McGovern placed his faith in the efforts of Turkish Prime Minister Bülent Ecevit concerning the achievement of a just Cyprus settlement and the end of the Turkish occupation.

---

[22]Ibid., p. 22527.

The Opposition to Lifting the Embargo: Eagleton vs. McGovern

Senators Thomas Eagleton, Paul Sarbanes, Joseph Biden, and Edward Kennedy, all liberal Democrats, led the opposition to the amendment proposed by McGovern, the Senate's arch liberal. This demonstrated the split in the liberal ranks in Congress, a split confirmed less than two years later when Senator Kennedy challenged Jimmy Carter for the Democratic presidential nomination.

The speeches of these senators focused on five basic points:

First, they all agreed that both Turkey and Greece were important allies of the United States.

Second, they contended that the fundamental argument of the Carter administration asserting that the embargo had not worked was fatally flawed. They argued that the administration had undermined the embargo by informing Turkey that the White House was working to secure its repeal in Congress. In addition, the embargo was limited in scope because, since it had been imposed in 1974, Turkey had received U.S. arms worth an estimated $600 million. This had been occurring at a time when Ankara was giving no tangible sign that it was willing to withdraw its occupation army from Cyprus. Under the circumstances, Turkey had no incentive to make any concessions.

Third, the lifting of the embargo, instead of facilitating a Cyprus settlement, would make it more difficult to achieve and, in the long run, would consolidate the Turkish occupation.

Fourth, the repeal of the embargo would send the wrong message and set a dangerous and immoral precedent. The message would be that a country can act with impunity even if it violates U.S. law and uses U.S.-supplied arms for aggressive purposes. That is exactly what Turkey had done in Cyprus. The rule of law should be reaffirmed by the Senate.

Fifth, the repeal of the embargo would undermine the pro-Western government of Greece under Prime Minister Constantine Karamanlis and would give powerful ammunition to the anti-American platform of opposition leader Andreas Papandreou. Some senators also reminded President Carter of his promises as a presidential candidate to maintain the embargo until Turkey withdrew its occupation army from Cyprus.

The last point, that the lifting of the embargo was bound to undermine the Karamanlis government, was emphasized by Senator

Thomas Eagleton of Missouri. Eagleton and Sarbanes played leading roles in imposing the embargo in 1974. Eagleton had followed developments closely in Greece, Cyprus, and Turkey, and he had paid a visit to Cyprus in December 1975. The senator from Missouri warned his colleagues:

> Another consideration in this vote is the impact lifting the embargo could have on Greece. The last election in Greece was a surprise to many. Not only did Karamanlis not receive the margin anticipated, but the vote also gave a healthy 25 per cent to Andreas Papandreou.... [The lifting of the embargo] could trigger strong anti-American sentiment and play into the hands of Papandreou and his supporters.[23]

In addition, Senator Eagleton strongly defended the principle of the rule of law. He declared:

> If we have learned anything in the aftermath of Watergate, it is that disregard for the law is insidious and habit-forming. Our society is only as strong as the foundation of our law. The decision we make on the arms embargo will be a measure of the strength of that foundation.[24]

Eagleton proceeded to argue that the lifting of the embargo would send the wrong message to other countries that are recipients of American arms. This was particularly the case for countries of the Middle East. He stated:

> If we vote to repeal the embargo, are we not, in fact, sending a message to other countries to whom we supply arms that they need not take U.S. law seriously? ... We are saying to the Shah of Iran, who buys a lot of U.S. weapons and wants a lot more—specifically, the Shah wants a lot of F-14s right now—"Shah, use them any way you want. . . . The same message could be received by Saudi Arabia which has just purchased 60 F-15s from us.[25]

---

[23]Ibid., p. 22523.
[24]Ibid., p. 22522.
[25]Ibid., 22522, 22550.

The senator from Missouri was also highly critical of the Denktash proposals for Famagusta (Varosha), proposals that were lauded by the opponents of the embargo as proof of Turkish goodwill. There was sarcasm in Eagleton's comments on Denktash's proposals:

> Let us examine Mr. Denktash's statement. First, what about the timing coming on the very eve of the embargo debate? I am very suspicious of "death-bed conversions" and "one minute to midnight" changes of heart. The very timing of the statement's release makes suspect of both the intent and the substance of Mr. Denktash's statement. As for the statement itself, I hope my colleagues will read it closely. It does nothing. It says that Mr. Denktash is "prepared to discuss" new [proposals on] Famagusta. Is that not marvelous? Is that not wonderful? I guess we should say, Hallelujah. After four long, tragic years during which 200,000 Greek Cypriots have been homeless, Mr. Denktash is now "prepared to discuss" Famagusta.[26]

Eagleton's sarcastic comments must have resonated in the Senate since the senator from Missouri was criticizing point-by-point the arguments made by the architect of the amendment to lift the embargo, Senator McGovern. As if to leave no doubt that his caustic comments were directed against McGovern, Senator Eagleton declared:

> The truth is, Mr. President, stripped of all *its coquetry and pious words*, the Byrd-McGovern substitute is, pure and simple, a lifting of the embargo. I must disagree with the observation made with respect to the embargo by *one of its principal sponsors, Senator McGovern*. He stated that this embargo, or limitation of sale of arms, was an insult to Turkey and that he was going *to shed deep tears* for this great insult to Turkey. I say, Mr. President, to lift this embargo is an insult to Congress because it is Congress that imposes the restrictions on the transfer of arms to Turkey.[27] (Emphasis added.)

The criticism, indeed sarcasm, that Senator Eagleton directed against Senator McGovern was an indication of the deep feelings that

---

[26]Ibid., 22523.
[27]Ibid., p. 22550.

the embargo had generated in Congress. After all, it was McGovern who had chosen Senator Eagleton in July 1972 as his vice-presidential running mate after he became the Democratic presidential nominee. Eagleton was only briefly on McGovern's ticket because he was forced to withdraw for personal reasons.[28] Six years later, McGovern was coming under the scathing criticism of the man who had been his first choice as a vice-presidential running mate.

Senator Paul Sarbanes of Maryland, who had led the effort to impose the embargo along with Eagleton, also spoke against its repeal. He echoed the basic arguments against lifting it, and he emphasized that the primary reason for its failure to work had been the fact that the Carter administration had undermined it. Sarbanes cited a letter that he had sent to President Carter on February 8, 1978. The letter, signed by senators Sarbanes and Eagleton and congressmen Brademas and Rosenthal, expressed deep concern that the administration was engaged in the process of abandoning the linkage principle. According to this principle, resumption of military aid to Turkey would be linked to tangible progress toward a just Cyprus settlement. The letter cited several examples whereby administration officials had de-linked the embargo from the Cyprus issue and had proceeded to provide military aid to Turkey. In fact, the embargo was not a full embargo since the administration had not only continued to sell arms to Turkey but, in 1977, it had also increased these sales by 40 percent, from $125 million to $175 million.[29]

The senator from Maryland pointed out that, despite the fact that the embargo had been partially lifted and military aid to Turkey had increased, Ankara had made no goodwill gestures on Cyprus whatsoever. In reality, the Carter administration had subverted the embargo. Sarbanes stated:

> The administration has undercut the embargo. . . . Despite the administration's statements in support of the embargo, leading officials have declared their opposition to the embargo. . . . The embargo has not worked because the

---

[28]Eagleton became McGovern's running mate on July 10, 1972, and withdrew on August 1, 1972, following the disclosure that he had undergone psychiatric therapy.

[29]The complete text of the Sarbanes et. al. letter to the president appears in the Appendix, Document F.

administration had been unwilling or unable to make it work. If it is lifted, it will constitute a condoning by the United States of the aggression that took place because it comes in the context of being lifted without a single concrete action to remedy or rectify that aggression.[30]

Sarbanes rejected the Denktash proposals focusing on Famagusta (Varosha), asserting that they were without substance. They were no more than proposals to talk, he maintained, citing a *New York Times* editorial that characterized the Denktash proposals as "vague and scarcely sufficient."[31]

While Eagleton and Sarbanes avoided a direct attack on President Carter for reneging on his pledge to maintain the embargo, Senator Durkin of New Hampshire, a fellow Democrat, engaged in scathing criticism of Jimmy Carter. Durkin stated that, since the Turkish invasion of 1974, little had changed in Cyprus, as Turkey continued its occupation of the island republic. And he continued:

Nothing has changed except the *President has gone back on another campaign promise.* . . . Last week, I submitted for the Record President Carter's numerous campaign statements, in which he told the people of New Hampshire, *he told the people in every primary State, that he was opposed to lifting the embargo.* Now we see a change of heart. . . . I am dismayed and disappointed that he [President Carter] let the State Department talk him into repudiating that [maintaining the embargo]. We talk about human rights a lot in the Senate. Those poor people in Cyprus do not have human rights. They can barely eke out an existence. What is all this hullabaloo for human rights if we are going to turn our backs on the people of Cyprus?[32] (Emphasis added.)

This was the kind of criticism that annoyed the White House because it cast doubt on President Carter's moral rectitude. Carter was the president who would not lie and who would stand up for

---

[30]*Congressional Record*, Senate, July 25, 1978, p. 22548.
[31]Ibid., p. 22536–22537.
[32]Ibid., p. 22524.

human rights around the globe. The supporters of the president in the Senate had no response to Senator Durkin's criticism that Carter had indeed reneged on his promises regarding Cyprus.

Republican Support for the Embargo

The majority of the Republican senators sided with Carter and voted to repeal the embargo. Still, there were several Republican senators who added their voices to the Democrats who opposed lifting the embargo. These senators included Bob Dole of Kansas, Charles Percy of Illinois, Jacob Javits of New York, Edward Brook of Massachusetts, Pete Domenici of New Mexico, and Paul Laxalt of Nevada. Senator Dole, one of the most influential Republican senators of the last 25 years, made three main points:

First, the senator from Kansas told his colleagues that the main reason the Senate was engaged in a debate to lift the embargo was that President Carter had gone back on his word. Dole stated:

> When Mr. Carter was a candidate for President, he expressed the opinion that the restriction on arms sales to Turkey should stand until that government withdrew its occupation forces from Cyprus. Unfortunately, his opinion changed after he had taken office. . . . I agreed with that statement by then-candidate Carter when he was seeking the Presidency. . . . I plan to offer an amendment that would say, in effect, that when the invasion of troops is withdrawn, the embargo be lifted. That seems to this Senator *to be in accord with what was the statement made by candidate Carter, and it is for this reason we are here today debating this issue.*[33] (Emphasis added.)

Through this statement, Robert Dole, a man of stature in the Senate, challenged Jimmy Carter on moral grounds and questioned whether he was a man of his word.

The second point Senator Dole made was that the arms embargo against Turkey was not really a full embargo, but a partial one. Dole stated:

> The embargo has not come near to achieving its initial goal: That of forcing the withdrawal of Turkish troops from

---

[33]Ibid., p. 22534.

Cyprus. In considering why this is so, it is interesting to note that Turkey has actually been receiving military supplies from the United States in the form of annual sales, allowed through a Presidential suspension of the embargo. These sales have totaled some $609.9 million in credits since 1975. This appears to be a substantial amount of aid, when one considers that we are supposed to be prohibiting military assistance to Turkey.[34]

This was a significant statement since it came from a leading Republican senator who had a record of solid support for the Defense Department. No one challenged the accuracy of the figures Dole had presented with regard to the substantial military assistance Turkey had received since the imposition of the embargo. Indeed, the embargo had been a partial embargo. Dole pointed out, however, that the continuation of military assistance to Turkey had found no reciprocity in Ankara when it came to Cyprus, and the complete lifting of the embargo was not likely to make Ankara more forthcoming.

Third, Senator Dole proposed the demilitarization of Cyprus. All Turkish occupation forces and all Greek military forces should be removed from Cyprus as soon as possible, Dole proposed. He also suggested that the United States convene a summit meeting of key NATO countries such as the United States, Britain, France, West Germany, and Canada, as well as Greece and Turkey. Demilitarization should be arranged through such a meeting, he said.[35]

Dole's proposal on demilitarization went nowhere, and no NATO summit was ever convened on the issue. Yet, two decades later, the demilitarization of Cyprus became a key proposal of the government of Cyprus President Glafcos Clerides. In addition, the Cyprus government said it was willing to discuss the stationing of a NATO peacekeeping force in Cyprus in the context of demilitarization.

One of the strongest opponents of the lifting of the embargo was Republican Senator Paul Laxalt of Nevada. Laxalt had a reputation in the Senate of being a gentleman, and he was one of Ronald Reagan's closest friends. Greek Americans only constituted about 5,000 of Nevada's population of 1.4 million, a figure that was too small to have a bearing on politics in the state. Thus, Senator Laxalt's opposition to

---

[34]Ibid.
[35]Ibid., p. 22535.

the repeal of the embargo had little to do with the non-existent "Greek vote" in the state of Nevada.

Laxalt began his speech as follows:

> Mr. President, I am strongly opposed to the lifting of the par-
> tial embargo on security assistance to Turkey because I feel
> that we need to enforce our laws pertaining to unauthorized
> use of U.S. weapons if we are ever to exercise any restraining
> influence over the skyrocketing conventional arms race. Also,
> I see little point in lifting the embargo as an inducement for
> good behavior by the Turks on Cyprus.[36]

In this respect, the senator from Nevada pointed out that, on May 19, 1977, President Carter had criticized the escalating conventional arms trade. Carter had stated that "because of the special responsibil-ity we bear as the largest arms seller, I believe that the United States must take steps to restrain arms transfers."[37] By proposing the lifting of the partial arms embargo against Turkey, the administration wanted to have it both ways, Laxalt argued. This was because, on the one hand, it was seeking to restrain the conventional arms trade and, on the other hand, it was pressing Congress "to lift one of the very few sanctions which we have imposed against unrestricted use of those weapons."[38]

In the same vein, Senator Laxalt reminded his colleagues of Cyrus Vance's support for the embargo before he assumed the post of secre-tary of state. He told the Senate:

> In 1975, Secretary of State Vance made my point. As a private
> citizen, he told the House International Relations Committee
> that lifting the Turkish arms embargo "would create a wide-
> spread impression that no nation that has acquired arms
> from the United States need any longer to pay attention to the
> conditions on which those arms were made available, but
> would be free to use them in pursuit of its own interests in
> local conflicts."[39]

---

[36]Ibid., p. 22555.
[37]Ibid.
[38]Ibid.
[39]Ibid.

Like Senator Dole, Laxalt pointed out that the arms embargo against Turkey was only partial and that, if one included the FMS (Foreign Military Sales) credits requested for 1979, Turkey had received $784.9 million in security assistance since February 1975. Despite all this U.S. military assistance to Turkey, Ankara had showed no willingness to compromise on Cyprus. Under these circumstances, the lifting of the embargo was unlikely to lead to Turkish moderation, Senator Laxalt argued.

Then, the senator from Nevada disputed the Carter administration's primary contention that the lifting of the embargo would enable Turkey to fulfill its role as a major obstacle to Soviet expansionism in the Mediterranean. Laxalt argued that, during the 1973 Middle East War, Ankara had permitted Soviet planes to fly over Turkey and had allowed Soviet land convoys to travel through Turkey to reinforce Syria and Iraq, but Ankara had refused U.S. requests for overflights. Laxalt reminded his colleagues:

> Turkey has allowed passage of the carrier cruiser *Kiev* through the Dardanelles in 1976, despite a clear violation of the Montreux Convention and strong protests from NATO officials.[40]

In this way, the Republican senator brought up the issue of the Soviet aircraft carrier *Kiev*, which the Carter administration had made every effort to avoid in the embargo debate. The embargo's opponents in Congress, who had argued that Turkey played a critical role as a bulwark against Soviet penetration in the Middle East, did not dispute Laxalt's statement that Turkey had facilitated the descent of the *Kiev* into the warm waters of the Eastern Mediterranean. After all, Senator Laxalt was a well-known advocate of strong national defense in order to confront Soviet expansionism.

Finally, like other senators who supported the embargo, Laxalt expressed deep concern over the effects that the lifting of the embargo could have on Greece. He warned that socialist opposition leader Andreas Papandreou was waiting in the wings to exploit the lifting of the embargo because he saw its repeal as a "direct threat to Greece's territorial integrity."

---

[40]Ibid.

The Senate Repeals the Embargo

In the end, the administration was victorious. On July 25, 1978, the Senate voted 57 to 42 to repeal the embargo. The vote was not as close as expected. A major reason for this, in addition to the president's personal lobbying, was that the wavering senators were persuaded to vote for the repeal because Senator McGovern had offered an amendment that appeared to place a condition on the lifting of the embargo. This amendment required that the president submit a report to Congress on progress toward a Cyprus settlement every 60 days. In addition, any new request for military and economic aid by Turkey should be contingent on the president's bimonthly certification that Turkey was acting in good faith to achieve a just Cyprus settlement. Such a settlement should provide for the return of refugees to their homes, for the removal of Turkish troops from Cyprus in the context of a settlement, and for the early resumption of intercommunal talks. The vote on the lifting of the embargo in the Senate was based on this amendment, which defined the parameters of a Cyprus settlement.[41] With his amendment, McGovern contended, it would become possible to reimpose the embargo if Turkey did not make a good faith effort to remove its troops from Cyprus. He stated:

> I, for one, will not hesitate to draw the appropriate conclusions and to join with those who now favor retaining the embargo in seeking appropriate redress through the budgetary authority which Congress will retain even without the continuation of 620 (x) [the law imposing the embargo].[42]

This was a solemn assurance by McGovern that he would support the reinstatement of the embargo if Turkey did not compromise on Cyprus. On the surface, the McGovern amendment appeared to be placing a condition on the lifting of the embargo, and it left open the prospect of restoring the embargo if Turkey did not fulfill the conditions of the amendment. This seemed quite reasonable and provided political cover for several Democratic senators, especially liberals,

---

[41] See *Congressional Record*, Daily Digest, August 1, 1978.

[42] *Congressional Record*, Senate, July 25, 1978, p 22527. On McGovern's statement that he would support the re-imposition of the embargo, see also *Washington Post*, July 26, 1978.

who otherwise would have voted against the lifting of the embargo. By playing a leading role in this effort, McGovern prevented a fight between liberals and conservatives during the debate on the embargo. Instead, the effort to lift the embargo in the Senate became a bipartisan process, carried out in the name of the national interest. Several major newspapers noted McGovern's important role in the Senate vote.[43] The Greek American press put it more bluntly by reporting that liberal senators, who did not want to vote against the president's wishes but still had problems with the lifting of the embargo, were able to hide behind Senator McGovern, the liberal *par excellence* in the Senate.[44]

The breakdown of the Senate vote demonstrated that, without Republican support, President Carter would not have been successful in the Senate. Of the 57 senators who voted for the McGovern amendment repealing the embargo in the Senate, 27 were Republicans and 30 were Democrats. Only 10 Republicans, led by Senator Bob Dole, voted to uphold the embargo. As the *New York Times* put it, "On the Turkish arms question, it was Republican votes that mattered, as they divided 27 to 10 with the Administration while Democrats came down 32 to 30 against it."[45] In other words, the majority of the Democratic senators, 32 in all, voted to maintain the embargo. As the Moore-Beckel memorandum of May 17, 1978, had predicted, the White House needed conservative support to win in the Senate. Focusing on the Soviet threat was the key to winning this support.

The breakdown of the Senate vote on July 25, 1978, to lift the embargo resembled that of the May 15, 1978 vote on arms sales to Israel, Egypt, and Saudi Arabia. On May 15, 33 Democratic senators had opposed the arms package, while 28 supported it. Carter had needed the support of Republicans to win that vote, as 28 Democratic senators joined 26 Republican senators in voting in favor of the arms sales.

On July 25, while President Carter did win a very important foreign policy victory, he failed to win the majority of the Democratic votes in the Senate. This was an indication of the problems he had with the Democratic Congress. These problems grew worse in the

---

[43] *Washington Post*, July 26, 1978; *New York Times*, July 26, 1978; *Wall Street Journal*, July 26, 1978.

[44] *Proini*, July 26, 1978.

[45] *New York Times*, July 28, 1978.

months after that. Before completing only half of his term, there was talk among many Democrats that the standard-bearer of the party in the 1980 presidential election should not be Carter but someone else, preferably Senator Edward Kennedy of Massachusetts. A May 1978 Gallup poll showed that Democrats would prefer Kennedy over Carter as the 1980 presidential nominee by 53 percent to 40 percent.[46] Senator Kennedy was one of the strongest opponents of Carter's drive to lift the embargo and the administration's arms package for Israel, Egypt, and Saudi Arabia.

Another aspect of the Senate vote to repeal the embargo was the fact that the southern senators voted three-to-one to repeal the embargo. Of the 28 southern senators in both parties, 21 voted to lift the embargo, while only 7 voted to maintain it. Of the 30 Democratic senators who voted to support President Carter's request to lift the embargo, 14 came from the south. Apparently, Carter's intense lobbying of fellow southerners had paid off.

The House Cliffhanger Vote

Carter Opposes the Conditional Lifting of the Embargo

Despite Carter's victory in the Senate, the House of Representatives remained a hurdle. The vote on the embargo was set for Tuesday, August 1, 1978, and there was significant uncertainty regarding which way the vote would go. The day of the vote, the *Washington Post*, which had been supportive of the Carter administration's effort to lift the embargo, reported that a "close vote was expected today in lifting the 3-year arms embargo on Turkey."[47] In an effort to avoid a bitter and divisive fight among Democrats in the House, three key Democratic congressional leaders attempted to work out a compromise with the White House. These representatives were House Majority Leader Jim Wright of Texas, House Majority Whip John Brademas of Indiana, and Dante Fascell of Florida.

These three representatives met with the president on July 28, 1978, and tried to work out a compromise. At the meeting, Wright and Brademas, supported by Fascell, proposed that an amendment be

---

[46] *Time*, May 15, 1978, p. 18.
[47] *Washington Post*, August 1, 1978.

added to the Foreign Aid Authorization Act, which was tied to the embargo bill. This amendment would enable a bipartisan vote to be cast and would attract overwhelming support for the bill. The compromise proposed by the Democratic leaders made the lifting of the embargo conditional on the withdrawal of the Turkish occupation troops from Famagusta (Varosha). The embargo would be lifted for one year if Turkish troops withdrew from Famagusta, if the city were placed under U.N. administration and about 35,000 inhabitants were allowed to return to their homes in the city, and if intercommunal talks resumed in 30 days. This compromise proposal took some elements from the plan that Turkish Cypriot leader Rauf Denktash had proposed for Famagusta. However, there were two critical additions to those key elements in the Wright-Brademas-Fascell proposal to the White House. First, the lifting of the embargo had to be linked to the process of a negotiated settlement in Cyprus, starting with Famagusta. Second, a one-year time frame would be imposed to test Turkish good faith. In other words, the embargo was to be lifted conditionally so that the United States could maintain leverage over Turkey.

The moving force behind this compromise was Wright, who persuaded Brademas to accept it.[48] Overall, the compromise proposal appeared reasonable because it reflected, to a degree, Denktash's proposals and also included some important elements of the Greek Cypriot demands.

Wright was a close ally of Carter's and a fellow southerner. He was also an admirer of the president.[49] Moreover, the House majority leader was not known to be a supporter of the embargo. In fact, he had sided with the Ford administration in support of the lifting of the embargo in a critical House vote on July 24, 1975. On that day, the embargo was kept in place by a rather close vote of 223 to 206. In his book, *Balance of Power*, Wright expressed strong opposition to the embargo, seeing it as a bad case of ethnic politics, with Greek Americans, in this case, exercising a disproportionate influence on foreign policy.[50]

---

[48]Ibid.

[49]For Wright's admiration of Carter, see Jim Wright, *Balance of Power: Presidents and Congress from the Era of McCarthy to the Age of Gingrich* (Atlanta: Turner Publishing Inc., 1996), pp. 267–273.

[50]Ibid., pp. 257–258.

According to reports in both the *New York Times* and the *Washington Post*, President Carter rejected the Wright-Brademas-Fascell Cyprus compromise on the grounds that it would not be acceptable to Turkey and that he did not want any conditions attached to the lifting of the embargo. The *New York Times* reported that ". . . White House aides said, however, that the amendment proposed by Mr. Brademas was 'unacceptable' because it would require a modification of the offer made by Mr. Denktash."[51] A similar account appeared in the *Washington Post*: ". . . President Carter, who has made the lifting of the embargo a top foreign policy priority, turned down the compromise. . . . Sources said that the President . . . wanted no preconditions set for the lifting of the embargo."[52]

Reporting on the August 1 vote that lifted the embargo in the House of Representatives, the *Washington Post* wrote on August 2, 1978: "The pro-embargo forces sought unsuccessfully to win approval of an amendment offered by Representative Dante Fascell (D-Fla.) that would have suspended the embargo for one year . . . the Fascell proposal originally was worked out by Wright and offered to the White House last Friday [July 28] as a possible compromise. It was rejected by the administration on the grounds that it would not be acceptable to the Turks."

Carter's rejection of a compromise concerning the lifting of the embargo in the House, one that had been proposed by the House leadership of his own party and linked the lifting of the embargo with tangible goodwill gestures by Turkey in Cyprus, was indicative of how his administration viewed the process of negotiating a settlement concerning the island republic. On the one hand, there were the proposals submitted by Turkish Cypriot leader Rauf Denktash. These proposals were strongly rejected by the Cyprus and Greek governments. The Carter administration had completely ignored the Greek side's deep concerns regarding the Denktash proposals. On the other hand, what was unacceptable to Turkey, such as the Wright-Brademas-Fascell compromise proposal, was also unacceptable to the Carter administration.

Under Carter, U.S. diplomacy was linked to Turkish diplomacy to such a degree that the administration would take no initiative that

---

[51] *New York Times*, July 30, 1978.
[52] *Washington Post*, August 1, 1978

met with the disapproval of the Turkish side. This had already been demonstrated during the April 1977 Vienna negotiations. Unlike the Denktash proposals of July 1978, which were embraced by the Carter administration, the enormous concessions made by the Greek Cypriots in Vienna were brushed aside by Carter because the Turkish side had rejected these concessions. By de-linking the embargo from a Cyprus settlement, Carter had decidedly tilted toward Turkey by relying on Ankara's goodwill to bring about a settlement.

Having rejected the Wright-Brademas-Fascell compromise concerning the embargo, the White House geared up for a fight on the House floor. The president's key ally in the House turned out to be Jim Wright, when the House majority leader abandoned the compromise that he had supported earlier. Instead, he cut a deal with the White House and led the battle in the House to lift the embargo.

The fact that Wright decided to throw his weight behind the president meant that the House majority leader could deliver the 15 to 20 votes Carter needed to win. On the day of the House vote, August 1, the *Washington Post* reported that Wright had decided to "vote with the President." This was a very significant development since Carter did not appear to have changed many votes in the House, despite the personal lobbying of the president and his top foreign policy aides. The president needed "a McGovern" in the House to perform the role that the liberal senator from South Dakota had performed in the Senate a week earlier.

Jim Wright proved to be the House "McGovern." He was not considered a liberal but, nonetheless, he was an influential voice in the Democratic Congress. In fact, at the time, Wright was much more influential than McGovern, and his influence grew in the 1980s. He was known for his ability to cut deals with the White House, and this worked to his advantage. In January 1987, Jim Wright became speaker of the House of Representatives, an office that is third in succession to the president. He was forced to resign at the end of May 1989 in the midst of a scandal that Wright called "an orgy of 'mindless cannibalism,' orchestrated in part by [Republican Representative] Newt Gingrich."[53] The bottom line was that, by having a member of Congress as influential as Wright as his ally, President Carter had edged closer to victory in the embargo vote in the House.

---

[53]Wright, *Balance of Power*, p. 489.

The Fascell Amendment: Lifting the Embargo Conditionally

The debate and the vote on the embargo in the House of Representatives took place on Tuesday, August 1, 1978. The supporters and opponents of the embargo engaged in a heated debated over the issue. The arguments were the same as those used in the Senate. There was one major difference, however. From the outset, the House had to consider two competing amendments. The first one was the Fascell amendment, proposed by Democratic Representative Dante Fascell of Florida, which was cosponsored by two other Democrats, Majority Whip John Brademas of Indiana, and Benjamin Rosenthal of Queens, New York, and Republican Representative Edward Derwinski of Illinois. The Fascell amendment reflected the Wright-Brademas-Fascell compromise proposal that had been rejected by the White House four days earlier, on July 28. The second amendment was proposed by Majority Leader Jim Wright and was similar to the McGovern amendment in the Senate. The Wright amendment was offered as an amendment to the Fascell amendment.

The supporters of the embargo, led by Brademas, Fascell, and Rosenthal, argued that the rule of law should prevail. They contended that the embargo had not worked because the Carter administration had undermined it by assuring Turkey that it would be lifted. As Brademas put it, "If the administration would bring as much pressure on Turkey to settle the Cyprus issue as it is bringing on Congress to lift the embargo, the issue would be settled by now." Massachusetts Representative Paul Tsongas, a rising star in the Democratic Party, presented similar arguments.[54]

Other representatives reminded Carter of his campaign promises. Representative John Rhodes, Republican of Arizona, launched a fierce attack on Carter for being responsible for the creation of the embargo controversy in Congress. Rhodes stated:

> In 1976, the entire Democratic leadership of the Congress supported the embargo. It should be borne in mind that this was an election and the votes of the Greek community were very important.... Thus, the President, during the campaign, played the sleaziest kind of politics with the Cyprus situation.

---

[54] *Washington Post,* August 1, 1978.

He heaped unjustified abuse and blame on the Ford administration. . . . He pledged a solution of the [Cyprus] refugee
problem, a sovereign Cyprus, and a withdrawal of the Turkish troops. . . . These were hollow promises—a pure and simple bamboozling of the Greek community playing on their
desire for peace in Cyprus. . . . The year 1976 was a very close
election, and the nearly unanimous support of the Greek
electorate [for Carter] was undoubtedly decisive.[55]

This criticism of Carter in the House for reneging on his campaign
pledges was even stronger than that heard in the Senate six days earlier. Congressman Rhodes' criticism was particularly harsh since he
accused Carter of practicing the "sleaziest" kind of politics. This charge
must have stung the White House because Carter had won the 1976
presidential election primarily because he had run as the candidate of
honesty, morality, and integrity. The assertion that the Greek American vote was decisive in Carter's victory was an argument often used
by Greek Americans. It is difficult, however, to establish with certainty
that the Greek American vote played a decisive role in this victory.

The advocates of maintaining the embargo threw their weight
behind the Fascell amendment. Congressman Fascell opened the
debate by offering the amendment and explaining to House members
the reasons why they should support it. Fascell's main argument was
that his amendment represented a true compromise between Greek
Cypriots and Turkish Cypriots. Indeed, the Fascell amendment combined elements of the Denktash proposals on Famagusta (Varosha),
while it also addressed some Greek Cypriot concerns.

The Fascell amendment stated that the president could suspend
the embargo for one year and supply arms to Turkey provided that:

. . . the Government of Turkey has removed its troops from
the municipality of Famagusta and allowed the inhabitants of
said city to return to their homes and properties in such
municipalities.[56]

This provision of the Fascell amendment reflected the Denktash
proposals, which provided for:

---

[55] *Congressional Record*, House, August 1, 1978, p. 23710.
[56] *Congressional Record*, House, August 1, 1978, p. 23695.

The opening of Varosha [Famagusta], the major revenue center of tourism, upon resumption of inter-communal talks, to
35,000 Greek Cypriots for re-establishment of homes and
businesses.[57]

Since the provisions on Famagusta in the Fascell amendment and
in the Denktash proposals were similar, Congressman Fascell stated
that his amendment gave the Turkish side the opportunity to demonstrate that it meant what it said.

The Famagusta provision in the Fascell amendment was tied to
the following conditions. The president would suspend the embargo
for one year. At the end of the year, Congress would request that the
president certify that the commencement of intercommunal talks was
being accompanied by the resettlement of Famagusta by Greek Cypriots. This reflected the provisions of the Denktash proposals. At the
same time, these intercommunal negotiations had to be based on
U.N. Resolution 3212, which provided for the withdrawal of all foreign forces from Cyprus. This satisfied the Greek Cypriot demand
that any agreement on Famagusta had to be part of an overall settlement based on U.N. resolutions. In the final analysis, what the Fascell
amendment did was two-fold. First, it put the Denktash proposals on
Famagusta to the test. Second, it provided a test period for the lifting
of the embargo. The embargo was to be lifted for one year provided
that the president certified that the Turkish side was acting in good
faith and moving toward a Cyprus settlement based on U.N. resolutions. The Fascell amendment was a real compromise proposal on
Cyprus for it took into account the concerns of both sides of the dispute. Had it been accepted by the White House, the road for a Cyprus
settlement could have been opened.

The Wright Amendment: Lift the Embargo So Turkey Can Reciprocate

The Carter White House, however, was not interested in a compromise
over Cyprus if the compromise placed certain conditions on Turkey.

---

[57]This provision of the Denktash proposals was included in a letter sent by Melin
Esenbel, Turkish ambassador to the United States, to Senator John Sparkman, chairman of the Senate Foreign Relations Committee. This letter became part of the official record of the debate to repeal the embargo. See *Congressional Record*, Senate, July
25, 1978, pp. 2510–2511.

The Fascell amendment included a timetable for the lifting of the embargo as one of its conditions. This condition was meant to test Turkish goodwill. The embargo had been partially lifted and Turkey had received military assistance amounting to $600 million since the imposition of the embargo on October 3, 1974. Still, the Turkish government did not show any willingness to compromise on Cyprus. In fact, the collapse of the Vienna talks in April 1977 confirmed that Turkey was not interested in a give-and-take settlement. Under these circumstances, the Fascell amendment was quite reasonable. It satisfied some basic demands of each side while it tested Turkish good faith.

The amendments proposed by the representatives were unacceptable to the White House. Carter had taken Turkish goodwill for granted in return for the lifting of the embargo, especially because he considered Turkish Prime Minister Bülent Ecevit to be a man of reason and moderation. Furthermore, since Ecevit had made it clear that Turkey would not consider the conditional lifting of the embargo to be a friendly gesture, President Carter feared that acceptance of the Fascell amendment would be counterproductive for two reasons. It would cause U.S.-Turkish relations to deteriorate further and would push Turkey closer to Moscow. It could also lead to tension in Cyprus and in Greek-Turkish relations, and could eliminate any prospect of Turkish concessions on Cyprus. This White House rationale for opposing the Fascell compromise amendment might have been justified if Turkey were to become more flexible following the lifting of the embargo. But there was no indication that Ankara was in the mood to compromise under any circumstances. Carter based his expectations concerning Turkish goodwill on his own wishful thinking.

With the help of Jim Wright, the White House came up with its own proposal to counter the Fascell amendment since Carter was faced with the prospect of losing the House vote on lifting the embargo. This proposal was the Wright amendment to repeal the embargo. This amendment was similar to the McGovern amendment in the Senate with one notable exception. The Wright amendment made it much clearer that the lifting of the embargo aimed at bringing about a just Cyprus settlement, and it further clarified what a "just Cyprus settlement" involved, defining it as a settlement that brought about the withdrawal of the Turkish occupation army. The president's bimonthly report to Congress was meant to certify that Turkey was acting in good faith toward that end. Thus, the Wright amendment provided that, upon the repeal of the embargo, the president was to report to Congress every 60 days and certify the following:

> ... Turkey is acting in *good faith* to achieve a *just and peaceful settlement* of the Cyprus problem, the *early return of refugees* to their homes and properties and *continued removal of Turkish military troops from Cyprus* and the early serious resumption of inter-communal talks aimed at a just, negotiated settlement. . . . The United States shall use its influence to achieve the withdrawal of Turkish military forces from Cyprus in the context of a solution to the Cyprus problem.[58] (Emphasis added.)

This provision became the law of the land following the approval of the Wright amendment in the House. Before the vote, Wright, the sponsor of the amendment, left no doubt concerning the meaning of the provision. In asking the House to vote for his amendment, he stated:

> The amendment defines what we regard as constituting a *just settlement.* It declares that a just settlement must involve the establishment of a free and independent government on Cyprus and that it must include *the withdrawal of Turkish military forces from Cyprus.* . . . The amendment by no means approves what was done by Turkey in 1974 nor does it permit the repetition of that wrong. . . . President Carter believes that the Government of Turkey wants to redress those wrongs on its own volition, while retaining the dignity and self-respect of its people and that it will do so if given the opportunity. . . . This amendment would provide that opportunity . . .[59] (Emphasis added.)

Thus, the Wright amendment, both in letter and spirit, asserted that a major objective of the lifting of the embargo was the end of the Turkish occupation of Cyprus. Like the Carter White House, Wright entertained the naïve belief that Turkey would reciprocate if the

---

[58] *Congressional Record*, House, August 1, 1978, p. 23697.
[59] Ibid.

embargo were lifted. The amendment left it up to the president, however, to determine whether Turkey was acting in good faith and in compliance with this new American law.

A Close Vote: Southern Democrats and the Liberal Split

The House vote on the lifting of the embargo was a cliffhanger. Several representatives waited to see in which direction the vote was moving before they cast their votes. In the end, the administration prevailed when two representatives switched their votes at the last minute and voted for the Wright amendment, which lifted the embargo in the House. They were Democratic Representative Butler Derrick of South Carolina and Richard Schulze, a Pennsylvania Republican.

The final vote was 208 to 205 in support of repealing the embargo. As in the Senate, President Carter had to rely on Republicans and southern Democrats to win a critical foreign policy vote. The majority of the 142 House Republicans voted to support the administration, 78 to 64. Some of the Republicans who voted in support of the administration complained that Carter had won the election in 1976 by defending the embargo. Thus, it was not just the *New York Times* and Greek Americans that were reminding Carter of his promises. Several Republicans also pointed this out.

Republican complaints reflected the frustration of conservatives who were repeatedly asked to support a Democratic president who could not win the support of a majority of his own party, for example, in the votes on the embargo and the Middle East fighter plane deal. After the embargo vote, Senate Minority Leader Howard Baker of Tennessee complained, "I am tired of doing the right thing," demonstrating Republican exasperation with President Carter.[60]

The Republican frustration concerning Carter was indicated by the fact that 10 Republican representatives who had voted to repeal the embargo in July 1975 switched their positions and voted against the Carter administration's request to lift the embargo in the House vote of August 1, 1978. One of them was a young Republican congressman from Maine, William Cohen. Nineteen years later, in 1997, President Bill Clinton appointed Cohen, who had become a senator, secretary of defense.

---

[60]*New York Times*, July 28, 1978.

In terms of regional distribution, the embargo vote demonstrated that the 14 states of the south had made a disproportionately higher contribution to Carter's victory in the House than other regions of the country. The southern voting power in the House represented only 29 percent of the total vote in the chamber. Still, 90 of the 208 votes in favor of lifting the embargo came from the south. Only 30 southerners voted to uphold the embargo. In other words, the south, which represented less than one-third of the total vote in the House, contributed 43.2 percent of the votes needed to lift the embargo.

The south's overwhelming support for Carter in the House was also indicated by the distribution of the Democratic votes on the repeal of the embargo. The majority of the 271 House Democrats voted against the Democratic president's anti-embargo bill, 141 to 130. Of the 130 Democrats who voted in favor of repealing the embargo, 71, or 54.5 percent, were southern Democrats. Yet, southern Democrats represented only 33.5 percent of the total number of House Democrats. The extent of Carter's hold on southern Democrats was indicated by the fact that only 20 of them defied him and voted to maintain the embargo. Among the southern Democrats who voted to lift the embargo was the newly elected congressman from Tennessee Albert Gore, Jr. Later, Gore was elected to the Senate. In 1992, he became Democratic presidential nominee Bill Clinton's vice-presidential running mate, and he served as vice president for eight years.

Southern Democrats were more inclined to switch their votes and support a Democratic president. On July 23, 1975, the House had voted to uphold the embargo by a 226 to 206 margin. Therefore, in 1978, the White House realized that it needed 15 to 20 more votes in the House in order to achieve the lifting of the embargo. This was pointed out in the May 17, 1978 Moore-Beckel memorandum to the president. To gain these votes, the administration would have to persuade Democratic representatives to switch their votes over to the president's side. Following persistent lobbying by the Carter administration, which included the president's personal persuasion and cajoling, 31 Democrats switched their votes and supported the repeal of the embargo in 1978. Of these 31 Democrats, 13, or 42 percent, were southerners. Southern Democrats were more amenable to Carter's pressure to persuade them to switch their votes than the Democratic members of Congress from the east coast, the mid-west, and the west.

As he did in the Senate, Carter had to rely on fellow southerners, the most conservative wing of the Democratic Party, in order to win the embargo vote in the House. At the same time, it would be an over-simplification to explain the embargo vote simply in terms of a conservative-liberal dichotomy. It is highly unlikely that Carter would have won both the Senate vote and the House vote, the latter especially, had it not been for the "McGovern paradox," which involved the support of several liberal Democrats for a policy that downplayed human rights in favor of realpolitik. In the case of the embargo, realpolitik meant that the strategic significance of Turkey was so paramount that human rights and the rule of law had to give way to the "greater good," NATO's defense against the Soviet Union in the Eastern Mediterranean and the Middle East.

The importance of liberal votes becomes evident if one considers that Carter won the House vote on the embargo by merely three votes, 208 to 205. In other words, two votes would have reversed the result and upheld the embargo. Given the extreme closeness of the embargo vote in the House and, upon examination of the pattern of liberal voting on August 1, 1978, it becomes clear that the votes of southern Democrats would not have been enough to secure victory for Carter. Liberal votes became absolutely necessary to win this slim majority of three votes. A split in the liberal votes enabled Carter to build a winning coalition in the House.

The Carter White House had combined the national security argument and the power of presidential persuasion and cajoling to win over several liberal members of Congress who had voted to uphold the embargo in July 1975 and who had been supportive of human rights and the rule of law. The liberal members of Congress who were persuaded by Carter to switch their votes included representatives Paul Simon of Illinois, Claude Pepper of Florida, James Corman of California, and Augustus Hawkings, also of California. In addition to Simon and Pepper, another key liberal representative who switched sides and supported the lifting of the embargo was the late Barbara Jordan of Texas. It can be argued that, given the extremely close vote, it was these liberal votes that made the difference and enabled Carter to lift the embargo in the House.

The fact that the House vote was extremely close also indicated that almost half of the members of Congress and the majority of Carter's own party, the Democratic Party, did not share his conviction that the lifting of the embargo was the "right thing" to do. While the president scored a political victory in Congress, morally speaking he was rebuffed. If, indeed, the lifting of the embargo had been morally as well as politically right, President Carter would have won at least the majority of the votes of his party in Congress.

The McGovern and Wright Amendments:
Meaningless in the Long Run

The McGovern amendment in the Senate and the Wright amendment in the House, which were the basis for the law that lifted the embargo, were deprived of substance since they gave unlimited discretion to the president to judge Turkey's behavior in Cyprus and the degree to which it was complying with U.S. law. Given the latitude allowed by the amendments, it was inevitable that the White House's bimonthly report to Congress on Cyprus would become a tool that served the administration's policies rather than a report on the actual situation in the occupied region of Cyprus. In 1977 and 1978, President Carter submitted several reports to Congress that did exactly that. They created the false impression that, somehow, there had been some progress concerning Cyprus and that the Turkish side had demonstrated goodwill. Still, one could argue that the amendments that lifted the embargo had set certain criteria that the president was supposed to fulfill in preparing his report for Congress.

Leaving other considerations aside, McGovern and Wright had, in essence, asked Congress to gamble by assuming that both Carter and Ecevit would be in power for some time to come. Given the intractability of the Cyprus dispute, it was not unreasonable to expect that it would take considerable time for a "just Cyprus settlement" to be achieved. President Carter had two and one-half years left in office and was already preoccupied with preparations for the Camp David negotiations. In addition, unpredictable developments in international affairs could divert the attention of the president away from Cyprus. Under any circumstances, Cyprus was not a foreign policy priority for the United States. This became abundantly clear when the Iranian revolution erupted in the fall and winter of 1978, to be followed by the hostage crisis and the Soviet invasion of Afghanistan in November and December 1979. These developments absorbed the attention of the president, while Cyprus became, by necessity, a marginal issue for the Carter administration. Furthermore, McGovern and Wright had not addressed the question of what would happen if Carter failed to get re-elected in 1980. A new president might not necessarily share Carter's commitment to human rights.

Twenty-seven months after the lifting of the embargo, Ronald Reagan scored a landslide victory over Jimmy Carter in the 1980 presidential election. Reagan and his rejuvenated Republican Party had their own foreign policy agenda. The Cyprus issue was at the bottom of this agenda, while there was little desire to pressure Turkey to make any concessions on the issue. At the same time, a new issue emerged in relations between the United States and Greece, that of Middle Eastern terrorism. Reagan and the new Greek prime minister, Andreas Papandreou, elected in 1981, found themselves locked in intense antagonism toward one another over the question of terrorism, with Greece acquiring the image of being "soft on terrorism." The faith of McGovern and Wright in the persona of Jimmy Carter and their hope that he would facilitate a Cyprus settlement following the lifting of the embargo vanished when he lost the White House to Reagan.

As far as the trust that McGovern and Wright had in Ecevit's moderation and goodwill was concerned, the Democratic members of Congress left the question of the Turkish prime minister's political survivability unanswered. The situation in Turkey was extremely volatile, and there was very little certainty that Ecevit could stay in power. Any serious observer of Turkey understood that. Indeed, Ecevit was out of office 14 months after the embargo was lifted. Leaving aside other considerations, such as whether Ecevit was really a moderate and was ready to compromise on Cyprus, his departure a little more than a year after the embargo was lifted dashed the expectations of McGovern and Wright for a speedy Cyprus settlement under the prime minister.

In the final analysis, Senator McGovern and House Majority Leader Wright had asked Congress, through their amendments, to lift the embargo on the basis of the integrity of President Carter and the goodwill and moderation of Turkish Prime Minister Ecevit. Neither of them lasted long, politically speaking.[61]

Following the lifting of the embargo, in accordance with legisla-

---

[61]Ecevit staged a political comeback almost two decades after the embargo was lifted. He became vice premier in 1997 and prime minister in 1999.

tion based on the McGovern and Wright amendments, President Carter submitted his first report to Congress on Cyprus on September 26, 1978.[62] From that time until the end of 1999, three other presidents, Ronald Reagan, George Bush, and Bill Clinton, submitted a total of 128 reports to Congress certifying that, somehow, Turkey was acting in good faith or that both sides were equally to blame for the continuing Cyprus impasse. This was due to the fact that the McGovern and Wright amendments left it up to the discretion of the president to judge Turkey's behavior in Cyprus. The result has been that the bimonthly reports of all presidents since Carter have tended to subordinate Cyprus to broader U.S. interests in the Eastern Mediterranean and to the primacy of American strategic interests in Turkey.

The McGovern and Wright amendments that led to the lifting of the embargo were proved meaningless as the Turkish occupation of Cyprus became more entrenched as time went by. Twenty-three years have passed since the lifting of the embargo, and no Cyprus settlement has been achieved. This fact alone demonstrates that the rationale of the McGovern and Wright amendments, namely, that the lifting of the embargo would facilitate a Cyprus settlement, was utterly flawed from the very beginning.

---

[62]The president's report was in the form of a Presidential Determination (No. 78–18). The president instructed the secretary of state to report this determination to Congress. See *Presidential Papers, Carter, 1978*, Book II, pp. 1636.

CHAPTER 15

Carter's Ephemeral Victory

The lifting of the embargo was hailed by the Carter White House and many in the media as a great foreign policy victory for the administration.[1] President Carter, who had staked his personal prestige on the repeal of the embargo, considered it to be one of the major successes of his administration, of the same magnitude as the approval of the Panama Canal Treaties.[2]

According to Carter, the lifting of the embargo had four policy objectives. First, it would restore the close relationship between the United States and Turkey. Second, it would contribute to the improvement of Greek-Turkish relations. Third, it would contribute to the improvement of U.S.-Greek relations. Fourth, and most importantly, it would promote a Cyprus settlement.

There is no doubt that the lifting of the embargo represented, under the circumstances, a political victory for a president who was perceived as weak by the media and the public at large. However, whether the lifting of the embargo represented an accomplishment for the Carter administration can only be determined if one examines the degree to which the action succeeded in accomplishing its four objectives.

The first objective of lifting the embargo was to remove a serious source of discord between the United States and Turkey and put relations between these two allies back on track. The U.S. renewed military shipments to Turkey, and Turkey re-opened the U.S. military installations in the country that had been closed down. A new U.S.-Turkish Defense Cooperation Agreement was signed, and relations between the United States and Turkey became close once more. From the strictly strategic point of view, the lifting of the embargo did serve American and NATO interests in Turkey quite well. Viewed from this

---

[1] *New York Times*, August 2, 1978; *Washington Post*, August 2, 1978; *Wall Street Journal*, August 2, 1978.

[2] *Washington Post*, August 3, 1978.

perspective, the first objective of the lifting of the embargo was achieved. At the same time, however, the strategic position of Turkey and its contribution to the Western alliance could not be disassociated from the domestic situation in the country. The lifting of the embargo did little to stabilize the political, social, and economic conditions in Turkey. Exactly two years after the resumption of U.S. military assistance to Turkey, the armed forces staged a coup in order to put an end to the chaotic situation in the country.

The second Carter objective was to contribute to the improvement of Greek-Turkish relations because, the argument went, the embargo had contributed to Greek-Turkish tensions. Carter's assertion that the embargo had driven a wedge between Greece and Turkey had been misleading. Indeed, tensions existed in Greek-Turkish relations, but the fundamental reason for these tensions was the Turkish invasion and continuing occupation of Cyprus. In addition, tensions emanated from increasing Turkish claims in the Aegean, including those concerning the continental shelf, and the ongoing repression of the Ecumenical Patriarchate of Constantinople.

From the Greek viewpoint, a Cyprus settlement would go a long way toward normalizing Greek-Turkish relations. In this respect, the second objective was inextricably linked to a Cyprus settlement. As long as the Cyprus dispute remained unresolved, Greek-Turkish tensions were bound to continue. That this was the case has been demonstrated by repeated Greek-Turkish crises since 1978. Turkish claims in the Aegean have exacerbated relations between Greece and Turkey, but Cyprus has remained a permanent source of tensions between the two countries. Under these circumstances, the lifting of the embargo did little to improve Greek-Turkish relations.

Carter's third assertion was that the embargo had driven a wedge between Greece and the United States. The objective, therefore, was to improve U.S.-Greek relations by lifting the embargo. Such a statement implied that U.S.-Greek relations had been suffering because, somehow, Greece had been displeased with the embargo or the United States had been displeased with the government of Greek Prime Minister Constantine Karamanlis due to the embargo. This was not based on fact.[3] Not only had Greece not been displeased with the embargo,

---

[3]For a long time, and up until today, there has been a view in Greece that Karamanlis told Carter that he would not object to the lifting of the embargo because it had run its course. This view was promoted, especially, by Karamanlis's opponents,

but Karamanlis had also told President Carter in very clear terms at a White House meeting that the lifting of the embargo would damage relations between Washington and Athens.[4] Top officials in the conservative, pro-American Karamanlis government had repeatedly warned the Carter administration that the lifting of the embargo would benefit opposition leader Andreas Papandreou and bring him closer to power, and that is exactly what happened three years later. Papandreou had been campaigning on a clearly anti-American platform and utilized the lifting of the embargo to the maximum extent in this regard. Carter's assertion, therefore, that the embargo had been damaging to U.S.-Greek relations and that lifting it would remove a source of friction between Greece and the United States was far removed from reality. In fact, and predictably so, the lifting of the embargo accelerated Papandreou's rise to power.

Papandreou founded the Panhellenic Socialist Movement (PASOK) on September 4, 1974. Less than 10 weeks after being established, PASOK received 14 percent of the vote in parliamentary elections, while Karamanlis's New Democracy Party won the elections with 54 percent. Three years later, in the parliamentary elections of November 20, 1977, PASOK, running on an anti-American platform, almost doubled its electoral strength as it received 25 percent of the vote. Cyrus L. Sultzberger of the *New York Times*, commenting on these election results and the increasing strength of Papandreou, argued that U.S. policies had contributed to stirring anti-Americanism in Greece.[5] In November 1977, New Democracy was able to win again by receiving 42 percent of the vote. After the lifting of the embargo, Papandreou intensified his anti-American campaign and PASOK emerged victorious in the elections of October 19, 1981, receiving 42 percent of the vote. New Democracy came in second with 36 percent.

The precipitous rise to power of a newly formed socialist party such as PASOK is unprecedented in the annals of European politics.

---

the Papandreou camp and the left, who, in the mid-1970s, saw him as "obeying the dictates" of the United States. There is no documented evidence to support such a view.

[4] *New York Times*, June 1, 1978. See also the minutes of the May 31, 1978 meeting between President Carter and Prime Minister Karamanlis in the *Karamanlis Archive*, which is in the Appendix, Document M.

[5] Ibid., November 26, 1977.

Certainly, other factors were at play in Papandreou's rise to power. The majority of the Greek people wanted *allagi* (change) after so many years of conservative rule, and *allagi* became the centerpiece of PASOK's electoral campaign. Still, Carter's decision to lift the arms embargo against Turkey provided Papandreou's anti-American plat- form with a powerful and persuasive weapon. Papandreou not only used the lifting of the embargo to tap into the intense anti-American climate in the country, but the lifting of the embargo also made it politically detrimental for Karamanlis to defend the actions of the United States as he had been able to do in the past. The conservative, pro-American Karamanlis government could not argue that the lift- ing of the embargo had not been damaging to Greek national inter- ests. Few in Greece could argue that its repeal had not rewarded Turkey for its aggression in Cyprus, and even fewer could argue that Carter had not broken his campaign pledges concerning Cyprus. Papandreou capitalized on the lifting of the embargo in a country where the public mood was already anti-American. It was only Kara- manlis's enormous personal prestige that had kept the tides of anti- Americanism in check. The lifting of the embargo undermined Karamanlis's credibility and contributed to bringing Papandreou even closer to power. In April 1978, Greek conservatives and other moderate leaders had expressed grave concern that the lifting of the embargo would facilitate Papandreou's rise to power, and this concern proved to be quite accurate.

Three years later, Papandreou was ruling Greece. It was clear that Carter and his foreign policy team, as well as other decision-makers in Washington, had underestimated the potency of Papandreou's anti-American message. Their policies became Papandreou's best allies as he inched closer to power.[6] During Papandreou's years in

---

[6]The author was in Greece in 1980 and 1981. I spoke to a cross-section of the population as I traveled around the country. Invariably, in every conversation, it was pointed out to me that the lifting of the embargo by Carter was yet more proof that the United States was favoring Turkey and that Carter's action had been damaging to Greece's national interests. Carter was overwhelmingly seen as a leader who did not keep his promises. The majority of the people I spoke to were pleased with Papan- dreou's anti-American stance. Still, about one-third of the people I spoke to thought that Papandreou was becoming too extreme. At the same time, many of those who supported Papandreou were rather sympathetic to Karamanlis, who, by then, had been elected president of Greece. They thought, however, that Papandreou could stand up to the United States in a way that Karamanlis had not. This image of Kara-

office from 1981 to 1989, Greek-U.S. relations were severely tested. Consequently, the effect of the lifting of the embargo on these relations was the opposite of what was intended by the Carter administration.

The fourth critical objective behind the lifting of the embargo was the facilitation of a Cyprus settlement. According to the Carter administration, the embargo had been counterproductive because Turkey had refused to carry out negotiations on Cyprus under pressure. The administration and President Carter put the blame for the Cyprus impasse squarely on the embargo by stating that it "brought into a deadlock or perpetuated the deadlock on Cyprus."[7] Lifting the embargo would open the way for a Cyprus settlement, the argument went.

Carter's belief that this would be the case was a combination of wishful thinking, naïveté, and self-deception. First, as Carter repeatedly acknowledged, the Turkish government had given no assurances that the lifting of the embargo would lead to a more flexible stand on Cyprus and thus facilitate a settlement. Second, any prudent diplomat who is familiar with the negotiating tactics of nations, especially those engaged in bitter historic feuds over issues they consider vital to their interests, understands that governments do not make concessions simply out of magnanimity or goodwill. Carter clearly understood this principle as he embarked on the arduous effort that led to the Camp David accords, one of the former president's monumental accomplishments. But Carter jettisoned this basic diplomatic principle and relied on the goodwill of one of the feuding sides, Turkey, when it came to seeking resolution of the Cyprus dispute and an improvement in Greek-Turkish relations. It is not surprising, therefore, that Carter's assumptions regarding Turkish goodwill in Cyprus, following the lifting of the embargo, were proved utterly wrong. As the embargo's supporters had argued, once the embargo was lifted, Turkey, being the more powerful side in the Cyprus dispute, would have no incentive to negotiate seriously.

---

manlis was cultivated by Papandreou and the left. With the intensification of anti-Americanism because of the lifting of the embargo, it was extremely difficult for Karamanlis and the New Democracy Party to rectify such an image, despite the fact that Karamanlis engaged in a spirited defense of Greek national interests during his meetings with President Carter and other U.S. officials.

[7] *New York Times*, June 15, 1978.

Predictably, the consequences of the lifting of the embargo were the opposite of those intended by Carter. Turkey made no concessions regarding Cyprus. Instead, it consolidated its occupation of the northern part of Cyprus by rendering the occupied territory a de facto province of Turkey. The Denktash regime, acting under the supervision of the occupation authorities, enforced policies that gave permanency to the Turkish occupation. The most tangible example of this was the colonization of the occupied area through the massive, systematic transfer of settlers from Turkey to northern Cyprus. This massive influx of settlers facilitated the Islamization and Turkification of the occupied territory.

Carter's thesis that the lifting of the embargo would facilitate a Cyprus settlement suffered a mortal blow five years after the embargo was repealed. On November 15, 1983, the Denktash regime unilaterally declared its "independence." That day, with Turkey's blessings, the occupied northern part of Cyprus was pronounced the *Kuzey Kıbrıs Türk Cumhuriyeti* ("Turkish Republic of Northern Cyprus," or "TRNC").[8] To this day, the only country in the world that has recognized the Denktash regime has been Turkey. The U.N. Security Council unequivocally condemned this unilateral action by the Turkish side in Cyprus. The Security Council convened on November 18, 1983, and, with American support, issued Resolution 541. This resolution stated that the Security Council:

> Considers the declaration referred to above [the Turkish Republic of Northern Cyprus] *legally invalid and calls for its withdrawal.* . . . It [the unilateral declaration] will contribute to the worsening of the situation in Cyprus."[9]

In this way, the Security Council left no doubt that the "Turkish Republic of Northern Cyprus" was an illegal entity. The November 15,

---

[8]On the developments leading to the declaration of the "TRNC" as well as its organization and activities, see the work of Turkish Cypriot author Halil Fikret Alasya, *Kuzey Kıbrıs Türk Cumhuriyeti Tarihi* (History of the Turkish Republic of Northern Cyprus) (Ankara: Türk Kültürü Araştırma Enstitüsü, Yayınları, 1987).

[9]See *Resolutions Adopted by the United Nations on the Cyprus Problem, 1964–1992,* U.N. Security Council Resolution 541, adopted by the Security Council on November 18, 1983 (Nicosia: Republic of Cyprus, 1992), pp. 87–88. The resolution was adopted by 13 votes to 1 (Pakistan) against, with 1 abstention (Jordan).

1983 unilateral action by the Turkish side in occupied Cyprus made it quite clear that, instead of facilitating a Cyprus settlement, the lifting of the embargo had rendered the dispute even more intractable since the Turkish position as an occupying power had become more entrenched.

The unilateral declaration of independence of the "Turkish Republic of Northern Cyprus" challenged the McGovern and Wright amendments and the law that regulated military assistance to Turkey. This law stipulated that, every 60 days, the president had to certify that Turkey was acting in good faith in order to promote a "just Cyprus settlement." Now, the Security Council had proclaimed that the Turkish action in Cyprus was illegal and would make the situation worse. This was certainly not consistent with a demonstration of good faith by Turkey. Senator McGovern had solemnly declared, when he offered his amendment that lifted the embargo in the Senate, that he would seek to re-impose the embargo if Turkey did not demonstrate goodwill in Cyprus. When Turkey posed a direct challenge to the McGovern amendment and violated its terms through the establishment of the "TRNC," McGovern made no effort to re-impose the embargo. Cyprus was history for the liberal senator from South Dakota.

The actions of the Turkish occupation regime were aimed at creating *faits accomplis* on the ground, which the Greek side could not reverse as time went by. The most visible examples of this policy, the settlement of the occupied area and the unilateral declaration of independence, did not indicate any good faith on the part of Turkey to reach a Cyprus settlement. The colonization and cultural transformation of the occupied territory were in clear violation of the spirit of the stipulation imposed by Congress that the U.S. president would submit a bimonthly report to Congress in order to certify that Turkey was acting in good faith to achieve a negotiated Cyprus settlement. President Carter proceeded to submit his bi-monthly reports to Congress certifying Turkish good faith in Cyprus, which was not borne out by the facts on the ground. In this sense, Carter's reports to Congress were misleading.

In the end, the fourth and most critical objective behind the lifting of the embargo, the advancement of a Cyprus settlement, failed to materialize. The continuation of the Turkish occupation of Cyprus 23 years after the lifting of the embargo demonstrates that Carter's belief that it would facilitate a Cyprus settlement was proved utterly wrong.

Thus, Carter completely failed to achieve three of the four objectives behind his decision to lift the embargo. The fact that he succeeded only in achieving his first stated objective, the restoration of military aid to Turkey and the improvement of U.S.-Turkish relations, demonstrated that, in the end, that was where the priorities of the Carter administration had been all along. Above all, the primary objective of Carter's foreign policy in the Eastern Mediterranean was to see a strong Turkey with a powerful military at a time when the Middle East was undergoing further turmoil. The Turkish military occupation of Cyprus was a secondary concern for the Carter White House. As long as Cyprus did not erupt and cause a confrontation between Greece and Turkey, the status quo on the island republic was acceptable, notwithstanding Carter's lip service to the contrary. Since the lifting of the embargo in 1978, U.S. diplomacy toward Cyprus has been based on tension management. Washington's primary objective has been to make sure that any tension arising from the continuing Cyprus impasse has not gotten out of control.

Overall, Carter's diplomacy concerning Cyprus and Turkey represented realpolitik *par excellence.* That was exactly what the essence of Kissinger's policies were when he had to deal with the Cyprus crisis in 1974. Moral issues, human rights, and the right of the refugees to return to their homes were secondary or marginal concerns. As Kissinger put it:

> ... If success is measured by "solving" every problem, America's Cyprus policy *failed* in restoring a unitary Cypriot state.[10] (Emphasis added.)

On the other hand, Kissinger noted, American policy objectives were achieved because a Greek-Turkish war was prevented and the structure of the Western alliance—the southeastern flank of NATO—was preserved.[11] That was precisely what Carter's diplomacy concerning Cyprus did. It managed tension in the Eastern Mediterranean in a way that did not have a negative effect on U.S. and NATO interests in the region.

---

[10]Kissinger, *Years of Renewal,* pp. 238–239.
[11]Ibid.

Conclusion

In April 1991, 12 years after the embargo was lifted and as the Cyprus impasse continued, there was a hearing in the U.S. Senate on Cyprus. The hearing was before the Subcommittee on European Affairs of the Committee on Foreign Relations, chaired by Senator Joseph Biden of Delaware. A member of this subcommittee was Senator Paul Sarbanes of Maryland, who had led the opposition to Carter's drive to lift the arms embargo against Turkey. During the embargo debate in 1978, Senator Sarbanes had repeatedly warned the Carter administration that Ankara would have no incentive to negotiate seriously over Cyprus and the occupation would be consolidated if the embargo were lifted without any commitment by Turkey to a timetable for the withdrawal of the Turkish occupation army from Cyprus.

Matthew Nimetz testified before the Senate subcommittee in the April 1991 hearing. He had been State Department counsel under Secretary of State Cyrus Vance and had been a key player in the lifting of the embargo and in the formulation of Carter's policies concerning the Eastern Mediterranean. The following exchange took place between Senator Sarbanes and Matthew Nimetz at the hearing:

SENATOR SARBANES: Did you link the return of Varosha (Famagusta) to the more general approach [to a Cyprus solution]?

MR. NIMETZ: I would have to go back, Senator. I really do not remember. As I recall, we had specific—

SENATOR SARBANES: So you, in effect, were in the position of getting nothing for the lifting of the embargo.

MR. NIMETZ: Well, *the lifting of the embargo stood on its own* because we had real security interests in Turkey. And then we negotiated a new base and cooperation agreement which I negotiated, which was very essential.

SENATOR SARBANES: You are here today telling us, you know, people out to put pressure on and take an interest. And you had in your [hands] at the time a tremendously significant weapon [the embargo]. You, in effect, let go of it, and you got absolutely nothing on Cyprus. Now, you may not have gotten the full resolution of Cyprus. I mean, that would have been—if that could have been done, that would have been even better, but you did not get anything.

MR. NIMETZ: *Nope.* Well we—

SENATOR SARBANES: And I thought at the time that you had—you were going to get Varosha—

MR. NIMETZ: We thought so too.

SENATOR SARBANES [continuing]: Just as a starter, unrelated to the ultimate plan. Is that not correct?

MR. NIMETZ: We thought so too. We have to go back in the record on the timing on that. *We got effectively nothing on Cyprus.* No one has gotten anything on Cyprus.

SENATOR SARBANES: Well, but you had the most to get at the time.

MR. NIMETZ: We also, Senator, had the most to lose.

SENATOR SARBANES: Because you had a tremendous weapon in your hands [the embargo] and you let it go and you did not get anything at all. Nothing on this issue. And, you know, we have been wrestling with it ever since.[1] (Emphasis added.)

Thus, 12 years after the lifting of the embargo, one of its architects, Matthew Nimetz, had to admit that the most critical factor in the embargo debate had been preserving American strategic interests in Turkey. That was what Nimetz meant when he said, "Well, the lifting of the embargo stood on its own because we had real security interests in Turkey. And then we negotiated a new base and cooperation agreement which I negotiated, which was very essential." In other

---

[1]U.S. Senate, Committee on Foreign Relations, Subcommittee on European Affairs, *Cyprus: International Law and Prospects for Settlement. Hearings.* 102nd Congress, 1st Session, April 17, 1991, p. 52.

words, Nimetz confirmed that, under the Carter administration, U.S. policies in the Eastern Mediterranean had been guided by realpolitik and not by the principles of idealism, human rights, and democracy that Carter had articulated when he came to office in January 1977.

During the exchange with Senator Sarbanes, Nimetz also confirmed something equally important, namely, that the Carter administration's argument that the embargo had been an obstacle to a Cyprus settlement and that its repeal would facilitate such a settlement had been demolished. When prompted by Senator Sarbanes, who stated that the Carter administration had wasted a tremendous weapon—the embargo—and that Turkey had given up absolutely nothing in exchange for its repeal, Nimetz responded with the proverbial "Nope" and said, "We got effectively nothing on Cyprus."

Yet, this notion, that the lifting of the embargo would facilitate a Cyprus settlement, was at the core of Carter's argument when he pressured Congress to repeal the embargo. Even with the colloquial, yet undiplomatic, "Nope," Nimetz had the courage to admit that one of the pillars of Carter's rationale for lifting the embargo had collapsed. Twenty-three years later, the moralizing former president, Jimmy Carter, had not yet found the strength to admit that the fundamental argument he had used to justify lifting the embargo had failed to achieve its objective.

Carter and his foreign policy team had some explaining to do to justify the fact that the president had reneged on the promises he had made to Greek Americans concerning Cyprus. This was not an easy task, not because it is rare for politicians to break their promises. Many politicians tend to have reputations of being untrustworthy. The Vietnam War, the Watergate scandal, and the abuse of power by the Nixon White House had only increased cynicism among the American public. Jimmy Carter came to Washington as the "White Knight" to restore faith in America's political institutions and their leaders. That was precisely what made it difficult for the Carter administration to explain the about-face of a moralizing president.

The way out of this painful dilemma for the Carter White House was two-fold. First, while Carter was president, his administration engaged in the revision of history by inventing a new discourse on the Cyprus issue and on Turkey. As a consequence, the president and his administration redefined the essence of the Cyprus question from being an issue of an illegal invasion and occupation to being a mere communal dispute. In the process, Carter's own principles and objectives regarding the importance of human rights in U.S. foreign policy were abandoned for the sake of realpolitik.

Second, after he left office, Carter and his top advisers chose the venue of silence when it came to the issue of lifting the arms embargo against Turkey and the unresolved Cyprus dispute. The fact that, in his memoirs, even President Nixon had something to say about the Cyprus dispute, while President Carter had nothing to say about it in his own memoirs, renders Carter's silence on the matter quite remarkable indeed. When Nixon made reference to Cyprus in his memoirs, he was quoting from notes he had made in his diary on July 15, 1974. This had been a time of agony for Nixon, as he struggled for his own political survival. Still, the late president thought it was worth it to include the Cyprus affair in his memoirs, placing the ongoing Cyprus crisis in the context of his struggle for political survival. Jimmy Carter, on the other hand, who had dedicated much more time and effort than Nixon to the Cyprus dispute and its relation to the arms embargo against Turkey, did not mention these matters in his memoirs. Evidently, Carter believed that he had neither a moral nor a political obligation to be held accountable and provide an explanation for the lifting of the embargo, an important decision of his presidency.

A reasonable argument can be made that the embargo affair was not a straightforward matter of morality versus realpolitik. This was the case because a great power, a superpower in fact, such as the United States, has global interests. As a consequence, an effective U.S. foreign policy cannot simply reflect the ethical values of the American people, which include democratic principles and human rights. The vital geopolitical and economic American interests have to be taken into account as well. That is why the challenge every president has faced has been balancing strategic and economic interests with America's moral values. It is precisely the ability to strike this balance that has enabled some presidents to achieve greatness in foreign affairs while others have failed. Indeed, despite several failures in U.S. foreign policy, Vietnam being the best example, it has been the injection of morality and ethical values into foreign policy that has rendered the United States not only an effective great power, but also a force of good in world affairs throughout the twentieth century.

President Carter came to office with the belief that ethical values and human rights should be given more weight on the foreign policy scale. Carter's foreign policy was to be a departure from Kissinger's realpolitik. This new policy, however, was to be tested in several areas by the harsh realities of international politics. In the case of the Eastern Mediterranean, with regard to Greek-Turkish relations and the Cyprus dispute, one could argue that an American policy based on pure morality and human rights was unsustainable in the long run. Eventually, the embargo had to be lifted because it was too rigid an instrument for the implementation of foreign policy under the changing circumstances in the Middle East.

Still, the embargo provided enormous leverage for the United States with regard to its ability to pressure Turkey to exhibit flexibility in Cyprus. The embargo could have been lifted conditionally in a way that nudged Turkey toward a Cyprus compromise. Carter would have had to find the middle ground, that of mutual concessions. That was precisely his tactic as he embarked on the arduous Camp David peace process. When it came to the Cyprus dispute, Carter abandoned the path of compromise. He ignored the enormous concessions that the Greek Cypriots had made, while he overlooked the fact that the Turkish side had failed to reciprocate and remained intransigent. He even rejected a compromise formula for lifting the embargo, the Fascell amendment, which had been proposed by the leaders of his own party. In the final analysis, Carter adopted a policy that was punitive to the Greek side because its end result was to favor the consolidation of the Turkish occupation of Cyprus.

As president, Jimmy Carter certainly had to balance realism—strategic and other interests of the United States—with American moral values and his own high ethical standards. It is tragic for the legacy of an idealist such as Carter that he failed to balance pragmatism and idealism and, instead, chose the path of realpolitik in the case of Cyprus and the arms embargo against Turkey. Yet, it was his own sense of justice, fairness, and morality that served him so well when he led Arabs and Israelis onto the path of compromise and peace through the Camp David accords. President Carter could have achieved the same thing with respect to Greeks and Turks, but he made a deliberate decision not to do so.

On April 6, 1978, President Carter sent an official letter to Greek Prime Minister Constantine Karamanlis informing him of the decision to work toward lifting the embargo. In his April 18 response to Carter's letter, Karamanlis expressed his great disappointment over the decision and warned the president that the lifting of the embargo was bound to make a Cyprus settlement all but impossible and would cause more tension in the Aegean. The Greek prime minister ended his letter by posing a personal, direct challenge to the president of the United States:

> For this reason, I hope that future developments will prove my fears and concerns false and demonstrate that your judgment was more correct than mine.

History has proved the Greek prime minister right and President Carter wrong. The fact that the Greek leader has been vindicated is perhaps one of the reasons why Carter has avoided discussing the lifting of the arms embargo against Turkey, the Cyprus issue, or his meetings with Karamanlis in his memoirs and subsequent writings. It is difficult to say whether the former president has been avoiding the discussion of an important part of his presidency—the embargo affair—out of self-righteousness or because of another unfathomable reason.

In the end, however, after all is said about Jimmy Carter, it will be his four years as president and not his post-presidency, remarkable as it might be, that will shape history's judgment of him. Indeed, it is Carter's political persona as the occupant of the White House from 1977 to 1981 that will ultimately determine his position in the pantheon of American presidents. It was Thucydides, in Pericles' funeral oration, who proclaimed a fundamental characteristic of political leadership that still holds true. As he put it, ἀρχή ἄνδρα δείκνυσι (*arche andra deiknysi*), or the character of a man, is shown in the exercise of power.

Appendix

DOCUMENT A

POLICY STATEMENT TO THE GREEK AMERICAN COMMUNITY BY
DEMOCRATIC PRESIDENTIAL CANDIDATE JIMMY CARTER AND
HIS RUNNING MATE, WALTER MONDALE, SEPTEMBER 17, 1978

SOURCE: Carter-Mondale Campaign Press Release, Washington, D.C.,
September 17, 1977.

Policy Statement by Presidential Candidate Jimmy Carter on Issues Affecting the United States, Greece, and Cyprus

The continuing tensions between Greece and Turkey damage the NATO alliance and endanger stability in the Eastern Mediterranean. If these two allies of the United States are to play a vigorous role in the alliance, there must be a just and rapid settlement of the tragic situation in Cyprus.

The policy of the Ford Administration of tilting away from Greece and Cyprus has proved a disaster for NATO and for American security interests in the Eastern Mediterranean.

Despite repeated warnings, the Administration failed to prevent the 1974 coup against President Makarios engineered by the former military dictatorship in Athens. The Administration failed to prevent or even limit the Turkish invasion that followed. The Administration failed to uphold even the principle of the rule of law in the conduct of our foreign policy. American law requires that arms supplied by the United States be used solely for defensive purposes.

Today, more than two years later, no progress toward a negotiated solution on Cyprus has been made. The lack of progress is disappointing and dangerous. Peace must be based upon the United Nations General Assembly Resolution 3212 of 1 November 1974 endorsed by Cyprus, Greece, and Turkey, calling among other things

413

for the removal of all foreign military forces from Cyprus. The widely reported increase of colonization of Cyprus by Turkish military and civilians should cease. Greek Cypriot refugees should be allowed to return to their homes. Both Greek and Turkish Cypriots should be assured of their rights, both during and after the withdrawal of all foreign troops from Cyprus.

The impasse on Cyprus must be broken. The United States must be prepared to work with others, including the United Nations, to insure the independence, territorial integrity, and sovereignty of Cyprus.

In addition, the dispute over rights in the Aegean must be resolved peacefully, under international law. Provocations must be avoided.

Greece and Turkey are and must remain our allies within NATO and neighbors at peace with each other within the community of nations.

The United States must pursue a foreign policy based on principle and in accord with the rule of law.

DOCUMENT B

MINUTES OF THE MEETING IN ATHENS BETWEEN GREEK PRIME MINISTER CONSTANTINE KARAMANLIS AND CLARK CLIFFORD, PRESIDENT CARTER'S PERSONAL ENVOY, FEBRUARY 18, 1977

SOURCE: Minutes of the meeting as they appear in *The Karamanlis Archive*, vol. 9, pp. 389–395.

Note: President Carter's personal emissary, Clark Clifford, visited Athens in the context of his fact-finding mission to Greece, Turkey, and Cyprus.

On February 18, 1977, Clark Clifford met with Prime Minister Constantine Karamanlis at the prime minister's office. Attending the meeting were Greek Foreign Minister Dimitrios Bitsios, Greece's Ambassador to the United States Menelaos Alexandrakis, and the director of the Prime Minister's Office, Ambassador Petros Molyviatis. On the American side, the meeting was attended by U.S. Ambassador to Greece Jack Kubisch, State Department Counsel Matthew Nimetz, and Nelson Ledsky, the head of the State Department's Office for Southern Europe.

The Minutes of the Meeting:

The meeting opens with Mr. Clifford asking whether we agree not to publish the full text of President Carter's letter to Prime Minister Karamanlis. Instead, we can publish all the main issues covered in the letter. The prime minister agrees.

The American presidential emissary says that his mission is of a fact-finding nature, in order to personally become acquainted with the current situation in the Eastern Mediterranean. Mr. Clifford kindly asks the prime minister to present his views on the serious problems in the region. Mr. Clifford asks the prime minister to present these issues in order of priority, if possible.

The prime minister says that he is going to speak objectively and with sincerity, just as a third, neutral party would speak. Then, the prime minister presents his views as follows:

> All the problems we are currently confronting [Cyprus, the Aegean, the U.S. bases, U.S.-Greek relations] stem from the Greek-Turkish dispute. This dispute is caused by Turkey due to its arbitrary behavior.
>
> U.S.-Greek relations: Let me begin with relations between Greece and the United States. The traditional, heart-felt friendship between our two peoples has been disturbed by the Greek-Turkish dispute as well as by the omissions and mistakes of the American government.
>
> A grave American omission has been the failure to take a timely, official stand in order to refute two criticisms of the United States. One was that the United States encouraged the coup on April 21, 1967. The other was that the U.S. encouraged the coup against Archbishop Makarios [in July 1974]. Yet, the United States suspended military aid to the junta and also warned the archbishop of an impending assassination attempt against him. Therefore, given these facts, refuting these criticisms would not have been difficult. But it was only done recently by Mr. Kubisch [the U.S. ambassador] when it was too late, because the public impressions regarding the American role had already been solidified.
>
> As far as the mistakes are concerned, the most serious one has been the lack of any meaningful reaction in 1974. While

the Geneva negotiations were underway [in August 1974], the Turks launched the second phase of their invasion of Cyprus and occupied about 40 percent of its territory. They did so as Americans [and Britons] watched.

Another mistake: When the Turks provoked Greece in the Aegean through their seismic exploration activities, the United States did nothing to discourage them. This was the case despite the fact that there was a risk of war, which was avoided only because the Greek government exhibited self-restraint.

In any case, the Greek people feel no animosity toward the United States. Rather, there is bitterness because of a sense of disappointment. However, due to the fact that a history of [U.S.-Greek] relations exists, and because the criticism, rightly or wrongly, is directed not against the United States but against a particular official, Mr. Kissinger, U.S.-Greek friendship can be restored. My government not only intends to restore it, but it is also determined to do its utmost in this direction. However, you should also help us accomplish this.

Mr. Karamanlis says the following with regard to specific issues:

1. Greece's Relations with NATO

Mr. Karamanlis says that the Greek government is not against NATO. Given, however, NATO's commonly known and disappointing stand with respect to the Cyprus crisis in 1974, Greece was forced to withdraw from NATO's military command structure. At the time, in August 1974, Greece was in full military mobilization. The people and the armed forces wanted to go to war. Controlling the situation was a severe test for Prime Minister Karamanlis. The prime minister appealed to the Greek people to trust him, and he pulled Greece out of NATO's military command structure. This, however, did not mean that Greece had withdrawn from the alliance. Greece asked that it form a special relationship with NATO as follows:

a. In peacetime, the Greek armed forces would be under Greek command because of the Turkish threat.

b. In wartime, Greece would be a full member of the

alliance, with all of its military forces placed under allied command.

c. A mechanism would be established so that the special relationship with NATO could become operational if necessary.

Mr. Karamanlis says that, as stated in parliament, when the circumstances that forced Greece to withdraw from NATO's military command structure are removed, Greece will re-examine its stand toward NATO. He says it should be noted that, if Greece were to be re-integrated into the military command structure of NATO under the present circumstances, this would be detrimental to the alliance because all the problems created by Turkey would be transferred to the alliance.

2. U.S. Bases

As stated in parliament by Prime Minister Karamanlis, the government supports the position of allowing the American bases to remain in Greece because they serve the common defense. However, Mr. Karamanlis says, the regime of the bases has to be adjusted to present realities. Hence, the present chaotic regime governing the bases needs to be replaced in order to serve the interests of both countries. He says Greece had already started negotiations on the regime of the bases when the issue of the U.S.-Turkish Defense Cooperation Agreement arose [in March 1976]. This agreement was to provide American military assistance to Turkey in the amount of $1 billion over a period of four years. This would have completely overturned the balance of power in the Aegean. It was a mistake for the United States to succumb to Turkish blackmail and thus establish a dangerous precedent. Greece has never asked to be rewarded for [hosting] the U.S. bases. But, under the circumstances, Greece asked for the restoration of the military balance based on two principles:

a. The United States would provide $700 million in military aid to Greece over a four-year period.

b. In some way, the United States should provide a guarantee for peace in the Aegean.

Mr. Kissinger had given Foreign Minister Bitsios a letter [on April 10, 1976] reflecting these requests. But, when the crisis in the Aegean developed in the summer of 1976, he did not keep his promise.

Mr. Karamanlis says that Greece's negotiations concerning the new regime for the bases were not completed because there was a new administration in Washington. Moreover, these negotiations were linked, by necessity, to the U.S.-Turkish Defense Cooperation Agreement. The Greek government would like to see the two agreements disengaged from economic aid provisions. When Greece and Turkey resolve their differences, then the United States can re-examine the issue of military assistance to the two countries. If the two agreements were to be signed now, *this would mean the lifting of the embargo.* (Emphasis added.)

3. Cyprus

The prime minister refers to developments surrounding the Turkish attack on Cyprus in July 1974 and Turkey's position during the Geneva negotiations in August 1974. He refers to the 36-hour Turkish ultimatum and the totally unjustified second phase of the Turkish attack on Cyprus [on August 14], which occurred after the restoration of legitimacy on the island.

The prime minister emphasizes two points:

a. The Greek side agreed to negotiate a new regime in Cyprus, even though Turkey had declared that the purpose of the invasion was to restore legitimacy [restore the constitutional order overthrown by the Athens junta]. In other words, the Greek side could have asked for a return to the regime under the Zurich-London agreements.

b. When the Turks issued their 36-hour ultimatum in Geneva,[1] Britain and the United States were obligated to

---

[1]*Author's note:* The Turkish ultimatum was given to the Greek side in Geneva on August 13, 1974. Turkish Foreign Minister Turan Güneş gave Acting President of Cyprus Glafcos Clerides and Greek Foreign Minister George Mavros 36 hours to accept the following Turkish demand: Cyprus will be divided into cantons and the Turkish side will control cantons amounting to 34 percent of Cypriot territory. The Greek side rejected the Turkish ultimatum on the grounds that it would have legitimized the Turkish invasion. Following this rejection, Turkey launched the second phase of its invasion on the morning of August 14, 1974, and occupied 38 percent of Cypriot territory.

secure the continuation of negotiations. This was the least they could have done, but they did not do it. The Greek people are very bitter about this. That is why the second phase of the attack against Cyprus took place. This Turkish expansionism is the root cause of Greek-Turkish differences, and it makes Greek-Turkish differences very serious and unlike the usual differences between two countries. It is quite obvious that the Turkish invasion plan, known as "Attila," could not have been prepared in five days [between July 15, the day of the coup against Makarios, and July 20, the day of the invasion]. The invasion had been prepared for some time. The Turks were simply looking for an excuse to carry it out. This excuse was given to Turkey by the idiotic colonels [through the coup against Makarios].

Then, the prime minister refers to the tragic consequences of the two phases of the attack on Cyprus. He also talks about the efforts of the United States and the European Community to promote a Cyprus settlement. He points out that Turkey has no intention whatsoever of negotiating seriously, even though Archbishop Makarios had adopted a moderate stand.

Greece's position toward Cyprus is crystal clear, Mr. Karamanlis says. The legitimate government of Cyprus bears responsibility for handling the Cyprus issue. We cannot be a substitute for this government. Even if Greece accepted a certain kind of settlement, it could not impose it on Cyprus. Greece stands in solidarity with Cyprus, gives it advice, and could play a constructive role if there were reasonable and just proposals.

As far as the recent meeting between Archbishop Makarios and Mr. Denktash [on February 12, 1977] is concerned, the optimism expressed by some is not justified. The points that were agreed upon are so vague and so complicated that they are creating more confusion. Makarios told me himself that he does not believe that [agreement on these points] constitutes progress.

What is important, however, is the fact that Makarios, who had been considered "intransigent," is ready to accept a settlement that satisfies the Turkish demands. The Turks demand the abolition of the Zurich-London agreements. The archbishop has agreed to negotiate a new regime. Turkey demands a federal settlement comprised of two territories. This has also been accepted. Turkey wants a weak central government, and this has been accepted as well. The Greek Cypriots are asking—and no one can dispute this—that the territory controlled by the Turkish Cypriots be more or less proportionate to the size of the Turkish Cypriot population. The archbishop agrees that the Turkish Cypriot territory could represent 18 to 22 percent of the total Cypriot territory. He might negotiate a settlement designating up to 25 percent, instead of the 18 percent that represents the actual percentage of the Turkish Cypriot population. But Makarios cannot accept anything beyond 25 percent because the people of Cyprus would never accept it.

Despite the moderation of the Greek side, which is not in doubt, the Turks have not reciprocated. Thus, the problem remains unresolved, and this could lead to a deterioration of the situation. *The prime minister states his firm belief that we will all come to regret it if the embargo is lifted before there is progress on Cyprus as well as the other Greek-Turkish differences. This is the case because the situation will get worse in all areas,* especially in the Aegean. (Emphasis added.) In fact, the Aegean constitutes a more serious problem than Cyprus. [If the embargo is lifted], there will be no means to discipline Turkey.

4. The Aegean

An immediate danger of direct confrontation in the Aegean exists. In this respect, the prime minister states: I am asking Mr. Clifford to believe that I personally averted war two times, first, when the second phase of the Turkish invasion of Cyprus took place and, second, when the *Sismik* [the Turkish oil exploration ship] provocatively went into the Aegean. I was able to control the situation through restraint, but this was done with great difficulty. Neither the Greek people nor I will be able to withstand a third period of tension. Still, the Turks are testing me daily.

The prime minister emphasizes that the territorial regime in the Aegean was defined by the Treaty of Lausanne. A status quo exists. Despite this fact, Greece has agreed to examine the Turkish requests. The prime minister gives a detailed account of how Turkey exhibited bad faith and repeatedly went back on its word.

Specifically, with regard to the question of the continental shelf, Greece proposed that the dispute be submitted to the International Court of Justice in The Hague. This proposal was presented to Turkey in January 1975. Turkey accepted the proposal in February 1975. However, when the Greek and Turkish foreign ministers met in Rome in May 1975, Ankara argued that it was not ready to agree to carry out this proposal. Then, when the two prime ministers met in Brussels on May 31, 1975, they agreed to jointly submit the continental shelf dispute to The Hague, while, at the same time, agreeing to begin negotiations. This agreement was included in the joint communiqué issued after the meeting. Once again, the Turks reneged. At three meetings of experts from the two countries, Ankara refused to even discuss the issue of a preliminary agreement to submit the dispute to The Hague.

Then, in 1976, a U.N. Security Council resolution [August 28, 1976] was followed by an agreement between the two sides to begin negotiations on the continental shelf question in Bern on November 2, 1976. These negotiations were to follow the guidelines of a joint committee that was to study the relevant provisions of international law and custom. Nonetheless, this past January [1977], Turkey demanded at a London meeting that Greece enter into direct negotiations with it on the substance of the dispute. In reality, this meant that international law and custom would have been overlooked. This constituted Turkey's latest reneging on the question of the continental shelf.

Regarding airspace, we had achieved an agreement on civilian air traffic, and the minutes of the agreement had been initialed. In subsequent meetings, however, the Turks again went back on their word. They reneged on the agreement over a fundamental provision regarding airspace. This provision stipulated that any bilateral agreement would not affect the multilateral ICAO Treaty on the Flight Information Region [FIR]. Turkey refuses to acknowledge the multilateral agreement and has not yet responded to a formula proposed by the Greek side.

Finally, on April 17, 1976, Greece proposed that Athens and Ankara sign a non-aggression pact and agree to exchange information on armaments. Initially, Turkey appeared to agree to both of Greece's proposals, but, in reality, it rejected the proposals. In fact, the Turks refused to even receive a draft agreement [on a non-aggression pact].

We are convinced, the prime minister states, that all of these examples reflect the expansionist tendencies of Turkey in the Aegean. Turkish demands regarding the continental shelf more or less coincide with those concerning airspace, and they create a line cutting the Aegean down the middle. East of this line, there are over 500 Greek islands with a total of 320,000 inhabitants. Despite the fact that I have consistently adopted a stand of moderation, I do not have an interlocutor.

The prime minister indicates that there are three ways to resolve Greek-Turkish differences:

1. The first is good-faith dialogue.
2. The second is arbitration.
3. And the third is war.

The United States should help to avert war because the risk of war cannot be underestimated. We are not asking that the United States support the Greek position at the expense of Turkey. What we are asking is this:

1. The Turks must be persuaded to enter into a serious dialogue.
2. During this dialogue, there should be no provocation from either side. A statement by the United States indicating that it will oppose any provocative action could contribute substantially to maintaining peace.
3. If this dialogue is not successful, our differences should be submitted to the International Court of Justice in The Hague.

The prime minister concludes by stating that, in order for such a policy of moderation to be effective, it is important that the U.S.-Turkish Defense Cooperation Agreement be postponed and that *the embargo be maintained.* (Emphasis added.)

Mr. Clifford thanks the prime minister for the eloquence and clarity with which he has presented the Greek positions. We are looking at the situation in the region with a new spirit, as if it were a "new deal," Mr. Clifford states. You should be satisfied by the fact that President Carter, despite the many problems he has to face in a new administration, decided to deal with this problem so quickly. He has not enunciated a new policy as yet, and it might take time for this to happen. What we are interested in at this stage is to become informed. This is why we have taken very good notes during your presentation. Then, Mr. Clifford expresses, as he puts it, a personal opinion as follows:

The way to deal with all of these issues, Mr. Clifford says, is to expand and strengthen the ties between the United States and Greece. At the same time, U.S. responsibilities in NATO dictate a similar relationship between Greece and the alliance. Moreover, the development of the right relationship between the United States and Turkey constitutes additional protection for Greece. If, for instance, the United States severed its ties with Turkey, its ability to help deal with these issues would evaporate.

As far as [U.S.-Turkish] relations are concerned, Mr. Clifford hopes that he will be able to demonstrate to Ankara that the actions of any member of the alliance that create problems among allies are a matter of concern to Washington.

The presidential envoy states that he understands the provocations that Greece had to face. The United States will utilize all of its influence to minimize the differences separating Greece and Turkey. An opportunity exists here, and perhaps the United States is in a unique position to really help. In the past, the United States has evaded its responsibilities with respect to these problems. Mr. Clifford states again that he took careful notes on what the prime minister said with sincerity and that Mr. Karamanlis's views will be taken into account in the charting of a new policy.

Then, Mr. Clifford asks his assistants if they have any comments. Ambassador Kubisch observes that the views expressed by the prime minister represent an expression of Mr. Karamanlis's consistent policy.

State Department Counsel Nimetz asks how the United States and Europe can assist in the promotion of the Cyprus intercommunal talks.

The prime minister responds that the Turks have to be persuaded to be reasonable since the positions of the Greek Cypriots are so moderate. In addition, Mr. Karamanlis states that the United States should not succumb to Turkish blackmail. The Aegean issue is critical, Mr. Karamanlis says, and Turkish provocations might lead to war.

Following this exchange, Mr. Clifford raises the issue of an increasing Soviet military power, while it remains unclear exactly what the Soviet objective is. That is why it is imperative that existing differences among NATO allies be resolved. The presidential envoy states that he will emphasize this in Ankara because the Soviet objective is more important for the Turks. Mr. Clifford notes that he understands the meaning of what Mr. Karamanlis has stated perfectly. He recognizes the danger, and he will recommend that this danger not be underestimated by the United States.

Mr. Karamanlis observes that the mistake of the previous administration in Washington was overestimating the role of Turkey. As a consequence, Greece was being treated unfairly, and the United States kept succumbing to Turkish blackmail. But, when someone succumbs to blackmail once, the blackmail never ends. Turkey has become too audacious. These days, Ankara threatens to leave NATO. Yet, even if it were demanded of Turkey to leave NATO, it would not do so. It would stay in NATO. If Greece had another government, it would be easier to leave NATO and become neutral, or go elsewhere. In this case, the United States would find itself between two blackmailers.

The moderation and prudence of the Greek government should be appreciated, Mr. Karamanlis says. If Turkish expansionism is not confronted effectively, war could be unavoidable in two or three years. Greece is asking nothing from Turkey. Turkey, on the other hand, is continuously raising claims against Greece. If the United States wants to avert the risk of war, it should act in the way I suggested earlier: (a) persuade the Turks to enter into a serious dialogue, (b) ensure that, during this dialogue, there are no provocations from either side, and (c) if this dialogue is not productive, our differences should be submitted to the International Court of Justice. If the United States is not in a position to do this, then what could it do?

Then, Mr. Karamanlis asks Mr. Clifford directly what he would do if he were in the prime minister's position.

Mr. Clifford—following some thinking—evades the question and states that it would not be appropriate to respond because his response might be construed as advice. He notes that the strengthening of relations between Greece and the United States would further Greek security.

The prime minister says that he appreciates this statement by Mr. Clifford and asks him to give the Turks the following advice: Ankara should take advantage of the fact that, in Greece, there is a strong but moderate government, so that an honorable and permanent settlement to the problems can be found. If the Turks do not take advantage of the situation in Greece now, in the future, there is going to be a competition in demagoguery that will have catastrophic results.

Mr. Clifford asks what the effect of a governmental change in Turkey would be?

The prime minister responds that it is difficult to predict what would happen under such circumstances because all the parties in Turkey are competing in demagoguery.

Then, Mr. Karamanlis refers to the issue of fortifying the Greek islands in the Aegean. Any fortification of these islands is at a minimum and is clearly of a defensive character. This fortification was carried out after several crises in Cyprus and especially after the Turkish invasion. These islands have been threatened by Turkish officials including [Turkish Prime Minister Süleyman] Demirel. A special army corps comprised of 120,000 soldiers is based on the Turkish shores opposite these islands. The size of the army corps equals the total strength of the Greek Army. Faced with this situation, it would have been very foolish not to take basic defensive precautions. This defense constitutes the inalienable right of every nation, and Greece has never given up this right.

The prime minister refers to the minority question and the 1923 Treaty of Lausanne. At the time, in 1923, there were 111,000 Greeks in Turkey and 106,000 Muslims in Western Thrace. Today, there are only 15,000 Greeks left in Turkey, while the number of Muslims in Western Thrace has risen to 120,000. Therefore, if a minority question exists, it is Greece that is entitled to raise such a question by demanding that the population balance be restored to that stipulated in the Treaty of Lausanne.

To sum up the situation, if we end up in an adventure, it is not Greece that will bear the responsibility. If there were Greek responsibility, the prime minister would not hesitate to admit it and tell the Greek people about it. Such responsibility, however, does not exist.

In conclusion, the prime minister expresses the hope that Mr. Clifford will be able to play a useful role. Mr. Karamanlis asks Mr. Clifford to convey the prime minister's views and suggestions to President Carter.

The prime minister's discussion with Mr. Clifford continues during lunch.

The next day, February 19, 1977, Mr. Clifford departs for Ankara.

DOCUMENT C

95th Congress, 2nd Session, Joint Committee Print

COUNTRY REPORTS ON HUMAN RIGHTS PRACTICES

REPORT SUBMITTED TO THE COMMITTEE ON
INTERNATIONAL RELATIONS
U.S. HOUSE OF REPRESENTATIVES
and
COMMITTEE ON FOREIGN RELATIONS
U.S. SENATE
by the
DEPARTMENT OF STATE
in accordance with sections 116 (d) and 502 (b) of the
Foreign Assistance Act of 1961, as amended
February 3, 1978

Cyprus

Perhaps more so than elsewhere, human rights questions in Cyprus cannot be treated in isolation from political considerations. As a consequence of past intercommunal troubles and the events of 1974, they constitute an integral element of the Cyprus problem and will no doubt figure largely in any settlement ultimately reached between the two Cypriot communities.

1. Respect for the Integrity of the Person, Including Freedom from:

a. Torture.

There are no indications that torture is currently permitted or practiced by the Government of Cyprus, the Turkish-Cypriot administration, or Turkish forces in northern Cyprus.

b. Cruel, Inhuman, or Degrading Treatment or Punishment

There have been no recent instances of large-scale or politically-inspired cruel or inhuman treatment of persons on Cyprus. It is generally accepted, however, that violations of human rights in the form of cruel and inhuman treatment of civilians and prisoners were committed in the course of the Greek-led coup against President Makarios in July 1974 and during the subsequent Turkish military intervention. These were less a reflection of deliberate governmental policy than a consequence of the scale and intensity of the fighting and of the longstanding antagonisms within and between the two communities on the island. Turkish-Cypriot enclaves not occupied by Turkish troops were reportedly attacked by Greek-Cypriot forces; subsequently, mass graves of executed Turkish-Cypriot villagers were discovered.

For their part, the Greek-Cypriots have charged that the Turkish troops who intervened in 1974 engaged in massive and systematic murder, rape, and inhuman treatment of prisoners. As a consequence of the world-wide attention that these charges attracted, and in response to a Greek-Cypriot petition, the Council of Europe instructed its Commission on Human Rights to undertake an investigation of Turkish actions in 1974. The Commission's report, completed early in 1977, found Turkey responsible for six violations of the European Convention on Human Rights.

The Turks subsequently submitted a lengthy rebuttal that claimed that Greek-Cypriots violated Turkish-Cypriot rights on a massive scale during the 1963–64 period. The Council of Europe has declined to endorse the Commission's findings against Turkey, simply noting in a recent statement that violations of human rights did occur in Cyprus in 1974.

c. Arbitrary Arrest or Imprisonment

Arbitrary arrest or detention is not currently being practiced in Cyprus. Charges that these practices occurred were frequently leveled by both Greek and Turkish-Cypriots during the 1974 crisis and its immediate aftermath.

d. Denial of Fair Public Trial

The authorities in Cyprus respect the right to a fair public trial.

e. Invasion of the Home

Many thousands of Cypriots—both Greek and Turkish—were displaced from their homes during the 1974 fighting. Over the next two years, practically all Turkish-Cypriots remaining in the south moved, whether voluntarily or involuntarily, to the north. Similarly, in the course of 1975 and 1976, all but a few thousand of the Greek-Cypriots remaining in Turkish-controlled northern Cyprus moved to the Greek-administered south. According to the Greek-Cypriots, many of these persons were evicted from their homes as a deliberate act of policy; according to the Turkish-Cypriots, they moved southward voluntarily and subsequently claimed they were forced out in order to qualify for refugee benefits. The report of the European Commission on Human Rights supports the former view. If there was, in fact, a deliberate eviction policy, it appears now to have been dropped. U.N. representatives have verified that those Greek-Cypriots who moved from the north to the Greek-controlled sector in the course of 1977 clearly did so of their own accord.

2. Governmental Policies Relating to the Fulfillment of Such Vital Needs as Food, Shelter, Health Care, and Education

The Government of Cyprus has responded promptly and effectively to the plight of the many thousands displaced as a consequence of the 1974 crisis. Housing, employment, education, and health programs have been designed and implemented—funded in large part by outside (principally U.S.) sources. The Turkish-Cypriots were confronted with substantially less pressing refugee problems after 1974, but they have likewise been attentive to resettlement needs (benefiting also from U.S. assistance).

3. Respect for Civil and Political Liberties, Including:

a. Freedom of Thought, Speech, Press, Religion, and Assembly

Freedom of the press and of assembly exists in both sectors of Cyprus. Minority groups, e.g. Greek-Cypriots in the north and Maronites in the south, practice their religions without hindrance.

b. Freedom of Movement Within the Country, Foreign Travel, and Emigration

Turkish and Greek-Cypriots enjoy normal freedom of movement within their respective sectors. The Turkish-Cypriot authorities continue to impose certain restrictions on the movement of Greek-Cypriots residing in the north. Movement between the two sectors is permitted only under exceptional circumstances.

c. Freedom to Participate in the Political Process

The Government of Cyprus is organized under the 1960 constitution in accordance with Western representative models. Suffrage is universal. Labor unions are free of governmental control. The Turkish-Cypriot regime in the north is democratically elected and controlled.

3. Government Attitude and Record Regarding International and Non-Governmental Investigation of Alleged Violations of Human Rights

The Turkish-Cypriot administration has consistently refused to permit international bodies—including the ICRC and the European Commission on Human Rights—to conduct on-the-spot investigations into cases of persons reported missing and unaccounted for since the events of 1974. Other investigatory bodies, however, have been allowed to work in northern Cyprus without hindrance, and U.N. officials are at present free to pursue humanitarian activities there on behalf of the remaining Greek-Cypriot residents.

DOCUMENT D

95th Congress, 2nd Session, Joint Committee Print

COUNTRY REPORTS ON HUMAN RIGHTS PRACTICES

REPORT SUBMITTED TO THE COMMITTEE ON
INTERNATIONAL RELATIONS
U.S. HOUSE OF REPRESENTATIVES
and
COMMITTEE ON FOREIGN RELATIONS
U.S. SENATE
by the
DEPARTMENT OF STATE
in accordance with sections 116 (d) and 502 (b) of the
Foreign Assistance Act of 1961, as amended
February 3, 1978

Israel and the Occupied Territories

Because of the sharply differing politico-social environments in Israel and in the Arab territories Israel has occupied since the 1967 war, discussion of this subject must be treated in separate but parallel fashion for the two areas. Therefore, for its first three sections, this report is divided into separate narratives for Israel and the occupied territories.

Israel is a full-fledged parliamentary democracy whose standards and administration of justice within Israel proper are comparable to those of the United States and other Western democracies. The Israelis judge themselves in accordance with those standards.

Under the military regime that governs the occupied territories, certain of the normal human rights guarantees that are taken for granted in Israel proper have been superseded on security grounds. This dichotomy poses a dilemma that will probably be resolved only in the context of a final peace settlement with their neighbors.

Israel

1. Respect for the Integrity of the Person, Including Freedom from:

a. Torture

The use of torture in Israel is prohibited by law and is virtually unheard of. Amnesty International has in recent years raised questions with the Israeli Government concerning reports in the Israeli press about two possible instances of the use of torture. We have no information that would corroborate these reports.

b. Cruel, Inhuman, or Degrading Treatment or Punishment

With rare exceptions, this is neither sanctioned nor practiced in Israel, and law enforcement is carried out without the excessive use of force. Exceptions have occurred on two occasions in recent years when force was used to quell violent demonstrations by Israeli Arabs protesting land expropriations and demolition of unauthorized structures, resulting in several deaths and injuries.

c. Arbitrary Arrest or Imprisonment

In Israel proper, this is not practiced. Writs of *habeas corpus* and other guarantees of due process of law are employed, and defendants are considered innocent until proved guilty. Preventive detention is legal during periods of emergency but is not usually practiced.

d. Denial of Fair Public Trial

The right to a fair hearing by an impartial tribunal with representation by counsel is observed. With the exception of security cases, all trials are open. In security cases, Israeli law provides that part or all of a trial may be closed, with the burden of justifying in-camera proceedings falling on the prosecution. Counsel is always present during closed proceedings.

e. Invasion of the Home

There are effective legal safeguards against arbitrary invasion of the home.

2. Government Policies Relating to the Fulfillment of Such Vital Needs as Food, Shelter, Health Care, and Education

Israel is a welfare state whose economy is organized along the general lines of the Western European mixed economies. Income distribution in Israel is relatively egalitarian. All Israelis are guaranteed good health care, and housing for the poor is modestly subsidized. Since 1948, Israel has taken in well over one million largely impoverished Jewish refugees from Europe, the Middle East, and North Africa, and has integrated them into its society and economy. Integration of smaller numbers of immigrants continues at the present time. Because of the wide disparity in educational and cultural backgrounds, there remains a considerable economic and social gap between the Ashkenazi (European) and Sephardi (Middle Eastern) Jewish communities, which the government is committed to narrowing.

All Israelis are guaranteed free public education through the sixth grade and more than half of all secondary students receive full scholarships. There are parallel educational systems for Jews and Arabs, conducted in Hebrew and Arabic, respectively.

Average per capita income among Arabs in Israel is probably higher than in any of the surrounding countries and is, in fact, higher than that of Jewish Israelis of Sephardi origin.

The title to most of the land in Israel is held by state organizations in trust for the Jewish people. Arabs, many of whom are engaged in agriculture, are unable to acquire additional land, except through purchase from other Israeli Arabs. Moreover, there have been frequent complaints that expropriations of Arab land, although subject to logical review as to purpose and amount of compensation, have not been for the benefit of the Arab community, but rather for promoting Jewish settlement in densely Arab-populated areas. The Government has said it plans no more expropriations in the foreseeable future.

3. Respect for Civil and Political Liberties, Including:

a. Freedom of Thought, Speech, Press, Religion, and Assembly

Israelis of all faiths and ethnic groups continue to enjoy freedom of religion, expression, and assembly. An antiproselytizing measure adopted by the Knesset on December 27, 1977, which outlaws the offering of bribes or material benefits as an inducement to religious conversions, has caused unease among some Christian groups in Israel because of its vague wording, but it is too early to judge if there is any valid basis for this concern.

There is full freedom of speech in Israel. Both the Hebrew and Arabic press are free and express a wide variety of political opinions, although all newspapers are subject to censorship on security and military matters.

b. Freedom of Movement Within the Country, Foreign Travel, and Emigration

All Israeli citizens enjoy freedom of movement within the country and are free to travel abroad or emigrate.

c. Freedom to Participate in the Political Process

Israel is a parliamentary democracy, and Israelis enjoy the freedom fully to participate in the political process. The country underwent an orderly major transition with the elections of May 1977, when the party in power since the founding of the state was replaced by its traditional opposition.

The organized labor movement functions without hindrance and, in fact, yields great political and economic power. The right to strike is exercised frequently and effectively. Most workers, Arab as well as Jewish, are members of the *Histadrut*, the general confederation of workers.

Because of the explicitly Jewish character of the state, and the continuing total isolation of Israel by most of its Arab neighbors, the Arab minority tends to feel powerless and largely alienated from Israeli society. Despite some limited governmental and private efforts to bridge the gap, there is very little social interaction between Israeli Arabs and Jews. Nevertheless, the Arab minority has equal rights under the law, and proven instances of discrimination in violation of the law are rare. Although subtler forms of discrimination, in such areas as employment and appointment to government positions, do occur, some Arabs have risen to responsible positions in the civil service, and at least one has served in the position of deputy minister. Unlike Jewish Israelis, Arabs are not subject to the military draft.

Occupied Territories

Israel's occupied territories consist of the West Bank of the Jordan River, the Gaza Strip, most of the Sinai Peninsula, the Golan Heights, and East Jerusalem. The complex human rights situation in the occupied territories, particularly in the West Bank and Gaza, where virtually all of the settled Arab population is located, is largely a result of the tensions between the occupying authorities and the indigenous population, mostly Palestinian Arabs.

The occupied territories are under military government, and law enforcement and public security are in military rather than in civilian hands. Although Israel rejects the view of the United Nations (including the U.S.) that the stipulations of the Fourth Geneva Convention concerning the protection of civilian populations under military occupation apply to its governance of the occupied territories, Israel claims it voluntarily observes most of these stipulations. The major exceptions are with respect to those provisions prohibiting the introduction of civilian settlers from the occupying power into occupied territories and the punitive deportation of individual inhabitants. In contravention of the generally accepted interpretation of the Convention's Article 49, Israel has established over 70 nonmilitary settlements in the occupied territories, with a total population of about 8,000 people.

1. Respect for the Integrity of the Person, Including Freedom from:

a. Torture

Allegations about the use of torture by Israeli officials during interrogation of Arab Security Suspects have been raised frequently. The most widely publicized allegations of this kind were contained in a lengthy report in the June 19, 1977 issue of the Sunday Times of London, which charged that there was a widespread pattern of officially condoned use of torture during interrogations in the occupied territories. This led to a lengthy series of rebuttals and counter-rebuttals, both from official Israeli sources and in the press.

The Government of Israel denied the Sunday Times story, pointing out that use of torture is both contrary to official policy and prohibited by law, and the Sunday Times, itself, later narrowed the scope of its allegations. To reinforce this policy, we understand from press reports that Prime Minister Begin, shortly after returning from the United States in July 1977, reconfirmed existing instructions concerning humane treatment of prisoners. To deter further allegations of mistreatment, Israel recently agreed to allow representatives of the International Committee of the Red Cross (ICRC) resident in Israel to visit detainees during the period of their interrogation, beginning on the fourteenth day after arrest. Previously, ICRC representatives have been allowed access to prisoners only after a longer period of time.

We know of no evidence to support allegations that Israel follows a consistent practice or policy of using torture during interrogations. However, there are documented reports of the use of extreme physical and psychological pressures during interrogation, and instances of brutality by individual interrogators cannot be ruled out.

b. Cruel, Inhuman, or Degrading Treatment or Punishment

There have been instances in which Israeli troops, usually inexperienced reservists, used excessive force in quelling demonstrations and restoring order. These actions did not reflect government policy. The Israeli Government is investigating reports of the recent beating of two Arab students by military authorities, allegedly for having participated in anti-Israeli demonstrations at Bir Zeit University. In several instances, individuals found guilty of such excesses have been disciplined and, in at least one case, sent to jail. Steps have also been taken to provide riot-control training and equipment to special units in an attempt to avoid repetition of such occurrences.

In contravention of the Fourth Geneva Convention, occupation authorities have selectively expelled residents of the West Bank and Gaza suspected of having or known to have engaged in terrorism or anti-Israeli political agitation, although this practice has declined greatly in recent years. Other individuals convicted of or suspected of terrorism have had their homes demolished or sealed up and their families displaced, thereby inflicting a type of collective punishment.

Overcrowding in prisons where security offenders are held, especially at Ashkelon, led to a series of hunger strikes by prisoners in early 1977. The ICRC, which does not normally speak out publicly, issued a statement noting that, while there had been some improvements, some of its recommendations to the Israeli authorities for improvements in medical services, cultural facilities, and family contacts had not yet been implemented. There have been no recent ICRC statements on this subject.

c. Arbitrary Arrest or Imprisonment

As of July 1977, there were about 3,100 non-Israeli-citizen Arabs under arrest or in prison in Israel proper, most of whom were residents of the occupied territories. It is estimated that 75 percent of these were being held for security offenses and, of that number, about 20 are under administrative detention. The remainder of the alleged security offenders have either been tried and convicted by military courts, are awaiting trial, or are being held temporarily for investigation.

Administrative detention is provided for under both Israeli law and the Jordanian and the British mandatory codes that were in force before 1967 in the West Bank and Gaza, respectively, and which continue in force there. Under the Fourth Geneva Convention, this practice is not permissible beyond one year from the "general close of military operations." Israel maintains that administrative detention is necessary in the limited number of cases in which presentation of evidence in a court proceeding would compromise sensitive security information. Such information often includes the nature of the security offense of which the detainee is suspected. Military commanders are authorized to order the administrative detention without trial of any person on security grounds for up to six months. Such detention can be administratively extended indefinitely.

Administrative detainees have three forms of recourse from detention orders:

—All such orders are reviewed by a committee appointed by the regional military commander, which includes the regional legal advisor and which can hold hearings regarding the case.

—They have the right to appeal to an appeals committee, headed by a civilian judge on reserve duty; the committee reviews each case every six months, whether the detainee has appealed or not.

—They also have the right to petition the Supreme Court of Israel for a writ of *habeas corpus.*

In practice, these rights of appeal are rarely exercised and appeals have very rarely resulted in a reversal of the decision of the military authorities.

d. Denial of Fair Public Trial

As required by the Geneva Convention, Jordanian law (with a few Israeli modifications) is still in force in the West Bank in civil and criminal matters. Its adjudication has been left in the hands of the indigenous judiciary, which carries out its duties in an equitable manner. Residents of the occupied territories accused of non-security offenses receive fair public trials by local civilian courts. Alleged security offenders are, with the few exceptions cited in the above section, tried in Israeli military courts by military judges trained in law. There, the proceedings, although not always open to the public, are generally in accord with the standards of fair trials.

e. Invasion of the Home

Under standing emergency regulations, military authorities may enter private homes and institutions in pursuit of security objectives as they see fit. This has occurred frequently, sometimes resulting in damage to property and injury to inhabitants.

2. Governmental Policies Relating to the Fulfillment of Such Vital Needs as Food, Shelter, Health Care, and Education

Residents of the occupied territories have complained that Israelis deliberately restrict economic development on both political and commercial grounds, thereby keeping the West Bank/Gaza as a captive market for Israel. Inhabitants of the occupied territories have also complained about the fact that Israel has applied the value-added tax to their economy, in contravention of the Geneva Convention. A further problem results from the exploitation of a part of the West Bank's limited water resources for the use of Israeli settlements, which has in some cases caused Arab wells to dry up and has had detrimental effects on Arab agriculture. Nevertheless, real per-capita income has more than doubled under the Israeli occupation, largely because of the thousands of jobs now held by Palestinian Arab workers who commute to Israel proper, and the gap between income levels in Israel and the territories has narrowed steadily since 1967. The economy of the occupied areas themselves, however, has remained relatively stagnant, and many individuals, especially those with higher education, feel compelled for economic reasons to migrate to Arab countries where greater economic opportunities exist.

3. Respect for Civil and Political Liberties, Including:

a. Freedom of Thought, Speech, Press, Religion, and Assembly

Implicit in the concept of military occupation is the proposition that observance of civil rights and liberties must be restricted by perceived security requirements. Freedom of religion in the occupied territories is unqualified. Freedom of expression and freedom of assembly are restricted by Israeli interpretation of security requirements. The West Bank press is very outspoken, but is subject to censorship.

b. Freedom of Movement Within the Country, Foreign Travel, and Emigration

Freedom of movement is generally unrestricted in the occupied territories, and thousands of Arabs travel daily to Israel for work. Vehicles owned by inhabitants of the occupied territories are frequently stopped for security inspection, particularly in Israel proper. Inhabitants of the territories, like Israelis, are required to carry identity cards. They are generally free to travel abroad and return, and many thousands cross the "open bridges" to Jordan every year. However, there are restrictions on the travel of individuals for political reasons. Inhabitants of the territories crossing from Jordan into the West Bank, as well as other Arabs or persons of Arab descent (sometimes including U.S. citizens), are subjected to rigorous searches of luggage and person for weapons and contraband.

c. Freedom to Participate in the Political Process

Israel has twice permitted election of mayors and city councils on the West Bank. Political activity other than campaigning for municipal elections is forbidden, and no political parties are permitted. Israel permitted Arab nationalists outspokenly hostile to Israel to run for office in the second West Bank election and honored the results of those elections.

Israel and the Occupied Territories

4. Government Attitude and Record Regarding International and Non-Governmental Investigation of Alleged Violations of Human Rights

The ICRC regularly inspects prison conditions in the occupied territories and has made recommendations for improvement. In 1970, the Israeli Government authorized Amnesty International to conduct an investigation into reports of ill-treatment of prisoners and detainees. Amnesty issued a report which described accounts of several cases of mistreatment it had received. Its recommendation of a formal inquiry with international participation was rejected by Israel. In October 1976, Amnesty renewed its request for an investigation. Since then, it has expressed its concern about the imprisonment or treatment of a number of individual prisoners, Israeli Jews as well as Arabs, in several letters to Israel's Attorney General. According to an AI press release in the summer of 1977, none of these letters had received a reply.

For several years, the U.N. Human Rights Commission and other U.N. bodies have adopted resolutions condemning alleged Israeli human rights violations in the occupied territories. The United States has voted against most of those resolutions, which we regard as one-sided, politically motivated, and based on unsubstantiated allegations. Israel has been generally unresponsive to efforts by U.N. bodies to conduct investigations in territories under its jurisdiction, although it has made efforts to be forthcoming regarding visits by representatives of WHO, ILL, and UNSEEN. In 1976, Israel admitted an informal experts' group from WHO to conduct an investigation of health conditions in the occupied territories. When the group produced a report that reflected favorably on Israel's administration, the report was rejected by the WHO Assembly on political grounds, without reference to the merits of the report.

Because of this and other such incidents, Israel has not been disposed to respond favorably to requests for international investigations. On the other hand, its decision to permit ICRC access to prisoners during the interrogation period is indicative of a willingness to cooperate with international bodies it regards as responsible.

DOCUMENT E

95th Congress, 2nd Session, Joint Committee Print

COUNTRY REPORTS ON HUMAN RIGHTS PRACTICES

REPORT SUBMITTED TO THE COMMITTEE ON
INTERNATIONAL RELATIONS
U.S. HOUSE OF REPRESENTATIVES
and
COMMITTEE ON FOREIGN RELATIONS
U.S. SENATE
by the
DEPARTMENT OF STATE
in accordance with sections 116 (d) and 502 (b) of the
Foreign Assistance Act of 1961, as amended
February 3, 1978

Turkey

Turkey's Constitution, penal code, and administrative regulations provide safeguards which approximate due process as understood in Western European countries and afford protection from arbitrary arrest and detention. Torture or degrading treatment of prisoners is illegal under Turkish law. Turkey's free press and competitive political system have served as additional safeguards. The new Turkish government which took office in January 1978 has enunciated protection of human rights as one of its primary concerns.

1. Respect for the Integrity of the Person, Including Freedom from:

a. Torture

An amnesty in 1974 released all political prisoners, and other legislation restored political rights to all those previously deprived them. In 1976 and 1977, scattered allegations of torture were reported in a few newspapers and in individual witness statements made to Amnesty International; conclusive proof is lacking. While incidents of torture may occur, there clearly is no systematic policy of torture directed by the government.

b. Cruel, Inhuman, or Degrading Treatment or Punishment

There is no verified evidence of cruel, inhuman, or degrading punishment being practiced in Turkey.

c. Arbitrary Arrest or Imprisonment

Occasional allegations that the prescribed detention period has been exceeded are not supported by significant evidence.

d. Denial of Fair Public Trial

Trials in Turkey are open, and defense lawyers are available under all circumstances.

e. Invasion of the Home

Privacy of the home is protected by law, the requirements of which are met.

2. Governmental Policies Relating to the Fulfillment of Such Vital Needs as Food, Shelter, Health Care, and Education

Governmental policies relating to the fulfillment of basic needs for food, shelter, health care, and education are good and limited only by the economic resources of the country.

3. Respect for Civil and Political Liberties, Including:

a. Freedom of Thought, Speech, Press, Religion, and Assembly

Freedom of thought, religion, and assembly are respected in Turkey. Government notification and approval are necessary for large public meetings, but such meetings, including those of a political nature, are freely held.

Freedom of worship is protected under both the Turkish Constitution and the 1923 Treaty of Lausanne. The Armenian Patriarch of Istanbul stated in 1977 that "we enjoy complete freedom of worship."

The small Greek, Christian, and Jewish populations also enjoy freedom of worship.

Charges have been made that various minorities, for example, the Armenians, Greeks, and Kurds, suffer from cultural and economic, although not religious, discrimination. As for the Kurds, the Turkish Government has prohibited publication in, or teaching of, Kurdish since 1925 when a series of Kurdish revolts threatened the stability and unity of Eastern Turkey. However, there does not appear to be any official discrimination against individuals belonging to minority groups, some of whom are prosperous and are leaders in the professions. Minority institutions have encountered problems in such areas as permits to maintain or expand existing churches and other facilities. Such actions appear to be haphazard in nature and do not appear to be the result of deliberate government policy.

b. Freedom of Movement Within the Country, Foreign Travel, and Emigration

There is freedom of movement, foreign travel, and emigration.

c. Freedom to Participate in the Political Process

The ability to participate in the political process is extensively protected in Turkey. Turkey enjoys a vibrant political process, with parties reflecting all parts of the political spectrum. Elections are well contested and honest.

4. Government Attitude and Record Regarding International and Non-Governmental Investigation of Alleged Violations of Human Rights

We are not aware of any obstacles to outside investigation, and members of Amnesty International, for example, operate freely in Turkey.

In light of the Turkish military intervention in 1974 and the continued presence of Turkish armed forces in northern Cyprus, Turkey to some extent shared with the Greek community responsibility for the human rights situation on the island. The report relating to Cyprus takes up charges and counter-charges relating to human rights violations on the island.

DOCUMENT F

LETTER TO U.S. PRESIDENT JIMMY CARTER BY
SENATORS THOMAS EAGLETON AND PAUL SARBANES,
AND REPRESENTATIVES JOHN BRADEMAS AND
BENJAMIN ROSENTHAL, FEBRUARY 8, 1978.

SOURCE: *Congressional Record,* Senate, 95th Congress, Second Session, vol.
124—Part 15, July 21, 1978, to July 31, 1978, p. 22547.

House of Representatives
Washington, D.C.

February 8, 1978

THE PRESIDENT
The White House
Washington, D.C.

Dear Mr. President:

The recent trip by Secretary Vance to Turkey and Greece, following a
visit to those two countries and to Cyprus by United Nations Secretary General Waldheim, underscores the importance of achieving a
just solution to the question of Cyprus. Such a solution is important
for Cyprus itself, for American relations with Cyprus, Greece, and
Turkey, and for the relationships of those countries with one another.

As you know, we have supported your approach to this matter
which, in contrast to the Ford-Kissinger view, recognized that the re-
establishment of the military arms supply relationship between the
United States and Turkey requires a just settlement of the Cyprus
question. That relationship was upset because of Turkey's use of
American arms for aggressive purposes on Cyprus in contravention
of our law.

We believe the linkage you have established between the supply of
arms and a solution on Cyprus is basic to the principled conduct of
American foreign policy which you have urged both before and since
assuming office. We understand that for tactical reasons you have
chosen not to stress this linkage publicly, but we recall, and have
reposed confidence in your direct assurances at our White House
meeting with you, that such a linkage does indeed exist.

In light of our shared objectives, we feel we must bring to your attention our deep concern over what seems to be a pattern of action on the part of members of your Administration in the handling of the Cyprus question. These actions threaten to undermine the principles to which you have committed your Administration. Furthermore, as a practical matter, these actions make it far more difficult to achieve a just settlement on Cyprus.

We trust that the brief summary that follows of some of those actions will enable you to understand better the basis for our apprehension.

The Administration's first arms request for Turkey, submitted by the State Department last March, sought a level of military assistance many times the level supplied by the previous administration. The request, you will recall, engendered strong opposition and was ultimately reduced substantially. Nevertheless, Turkey received a 40 per cent increase in military aid (from $125 to $175 million) although it had taken no positive action on Cyprus. The hope that this significant increase would serve as an inducement for such positive action on the part of Turkey proved empty.

The Department of Defense has used the NATO Maintenance and Supply Agency (NAMSA), located in Luxembourg, to supply Turkey with the weapons beyond the restrictions in American law limiting the amount of military sales. Such circumvention of the military sales limitation makes a mockery of joint Executive-Congressional actions and undermines pressure on Turkey for a Cyprus settlement.

The United States Ambassador to Turkey recently declared in a news interview in Ankara that "the embargo doesn't serve any American interest," that "without changing the law [which prohibits the sending of U.S. arms to aggressor countries] I would like to find some way around it," and that "my only hope is that sanity will prevail and it [the embargo] will be removed." High-ranking U.S. military officers have made similar statements in the past year and have thereby encouraged Turkish intransigence with regard to a just settlement on Cyprus. Obviously, the arms limitation cannot be effective when the Turkish government hears high American officials contradict your own position on the matter.

In an effort to avoid offending Turkey, the United States Mission to the United Nations voted with a very small minority last fall to weaken a General Assembly resolution which called for action on Cyprus. Moreover, the State Department recently submitted a report on human rights in Cyprus which was an unfair and inaccurate report of the tragic events on that island.

The State Department's proposed military aid request for the next fiscal year reduces aid for Cyprus while maintaining the aid level for Turkey and thereby suggests a basic shift in Administration policy. Repeated press reports that Administration officials are preparing to urge Congress to approve the four-year $1 billion Turkish defense agreement without regard to a resolution of the Cyprus question only heighten our concern.

Our restrained comment in the face of each of these developments has largely been due to the assurance we have received from you and your representatives that the Administration is committed to pursuing a policy of linkage. We have, therefore, publicly affirmed the Administration's good faith and urged that you and the Secretary of State be given the time to implement this policy.

Today, we are deeply concerned that actions like those set out above may be placing the Administration on a different path whereby Congress will be asked to approve the Turkish DCA [Defense Cooperation Agreement] without a just settlement on Cyprus or whereby other approaches will be employed to break the linkage that you have expressed to us. Such a changed course would have the most grave consequences for the integrity and principled conduct of our foreign policy and the achievement of a just solution on Cyprus. To reestablish the arms relationship with Turkey without a redress of the aggression on Cyprus would demean the rule of law, contradict your strong commitment to human rights, and weaken your call for proper controls on U.S. arms exports. Such action would also erode the support for democratic, pro-western governments in Greece and Cyprus and make virtually impossible the achievement of normal relationships in the Eastern Mediterranean.

In this crucial period, citizens in this country and throughout the world look to you, Mr. President, for principled leadership to bring justice and peace to Cyprus and to the Eastern Mediterranean.

We stand ready to assist you in this endeavor and would welcome the opportunity to discuss this matter with you at a time convenient to you.

Respectfully,

Thomas Eagleton, United States Senate
Paul Sarbanes, United States Senate
John Brademas, Member of Congress
Benjamin Rosenthal, Member of Congress

DOCUMENT G

THE WASHINTON POST
SUNDAY, MARCH 5, 1978
A "DELIBERATE WHITEWASH" ON HUMAN RIGHTS IN TURKEY
BY JACK ANDERSON

The Carter administration is so worried about declining Turkish military power that it has falsified its report on human rights practices in Turkey and has portrayed the country as a virtual human rights paradise.

The false account, part of the State Department's "Country Reports on Human Rights Practices," was delivered to Congress several weeks ago. The department claimed it had little "conclusive proof" or "significant evidence" to support allegations of human rights abuses in Turkey.

A more enigmatic statement, worthy of master diplomat Henry Kissinger, was issued on Turkish-controlled northern Cyprus. Human rights questions in Cyprus, stated the report, "cannot be treated in isolation from political considerations."

These conclusions are disputed by the State Department's own files, which contain abundant evidence of the harsh treatment of minority groups and political prisoners. Indeed, the Turks have a reputation for brutality, which makes them fierce fighters and cruel jailers.

American citizens, who have had the misfortune of landing in a Turkish lockup, have told of vicious beatings. A favorite Turkish torture is to batter the soles of a prisoner's feet with truncheons, which causes excruciating pain and leaves him unable to walk.

The Greek government, taking exception to the State Department's fairy tale, lodged formal protests both in Athens and Washington. And Cypriot Ambassador Nickos Dimitrios marched into the State Department and indignantly delivered an official letter of protest.

The official view of human rights in Turkey, insiders suspect, is a deliberate whitewash intended to tip-toe around Turkish sensitivities. The Turks are still smarting from an arms embargo imposed by Congress after Turkish troops invaded Cyprus with U.S. weapons.

The Turks retaliated by closing U.S. intelligence installations in their country. These electronic listening posts monitored Soviet missile tests and military maneuvers. At Sinop on the Black Sea, for example, sophisticated radar devices could zoom directly on Soviet missile launch sites.

At the time the bases were closed, intelligence sources claimed they were responsible for about a fourth of the clandestine information gathered about Soviet military activities. American technology and ingenuity, however, have produced substitutes for most of the Turkish installations.

Far more important, in the Pentagon's view, is Turkey's role as the Mediterranean anchor of the NATO alliance. One worried general told us: "The big question is whether they can perform their NATO responsibilities without military aid. We get a real buy with the Turks. Give them a few weapons, and you buy a bunch of divisions. They've got the manpower, and they proved they could use it in the Korean War."

Our sources say that President Carter has adopted the military view. He has been strongly influenced by the joint chiefs, who meet with him frequently. In fact, the president recently boasted to his Cabinet behind closed doors that he "has generated a compatibility among the strategic planners of our government unknown in former administrations."

He reportedly is preparing, therefore, to ask Congress to approve the $1 billion defense agreement that was signed in 1976 between Turkey and the United States. The State Department soft-pedaled Turkish human rights abuses, our sources say, to avoid irritating a Congress that is already sympathetic to the Greek and Cypriot causes.

In any event, the human rights reports on Turkey simply do not reflect the truth. Particularly galling to the Greeks is the statement that "there does not appear to be any official discrimination against individuals belonging to minority groups" and that they enjoy, among other rights, "freedom of worship."

There has been a history of religious discrimination against the Greek Orthodox Church in Turkey. The best evidence can be found in the statistics; the Greek Orthodox population in Turkey has dwindled from 111,700 in 1924 to 13,500 today. A confidential diplomatic document, reporting on the oppression of Greeks in Turkey, cites these flagrant abuses:

• A deliberate campaign of harassment has been reported against Greek Orthodox clerics in Istanbul, the very city where the head of the church traditionally resides. Greek religious leaders have been denied passports to travel abroad, even for pressing personal reasons. Editorials in the Turkish press have railed against the church. Following one series of articles, demonstrators laid a "black wreath on which were pinned slogans asking for the expulsion of the [Greek Orthodox] Patriarchate from Turkey."

• Turkish authorities are cracking down on Greek minority schools. Teaching of the Greek language has been "severely curtailed," and Turkish officials have refused to appoint principals to Greek high schools. All repair requests in excess of $15 were refused last year. And the Turks have begun assessing heavy taxes on Greek schools, though they are owned by charity institutions, which are supposed to be tax-exempt.

Last year, Turkish officials began "the close surveillance of persons who visit the Greek General Consulate in Istanbul" and [they] "systematically ask for [their] identity cards." Leaders in the Greek Orthodox minority have also begun to "receive anonymous letters, threatening the property and lives of the recipients and containing demands for ransom."

There is other evidence, which we lack the space to recount, that the State Department deliberately deceived Congress about human rights in Turkey.

Footnote: A spokesman for the Turkish Embassy said his government would prefer to eschew "polemics" and discuss "issues" instead. Turkish authorities, he said, do not want to expel the Greek Orthodox Church from Istanbul, and they do not tax the church illegally. With respect to passports, the spokesman said that all Turkish citizens are limited to a single trip out of the country every two years, in order to conserve "hard currency." He also claimed that the Turkish minority in Greece is harshly treated.

DOCUMENT H

Meeting Between U.S. Ambassador to Greece Robert McCloskey and Greek Deputy Foreign Minister Evangelos Averof, March 31, 1978

SOURCE: *The Karamanlis Archive*, vol. 10, pp. 173–174.

The intention of President Carter to lift the arms embargo against Turkey was conveyed orally to the Greek side by U.S. Ambassador to Greece Robert McCloskey. This took place on March 31, 1978. As justification for the about-face by Washington, the ambassador pointed out the ineffectiveness—as demonstrated—of the measure [the embargo] and the negative turn in U.S.-Turkish relations. He also pointed out the weakening of the southeastern flank of NATO during a period when there was an increase in Soviet armaments and economic conditions in Turkey were deteriorating. The American ambassador expressed the conviction that the lifting of the embargo would not upset the balance of power. At the same time, the restoration of U.S.-Turkish ties [the lifting of the embargo] would facilitate prospects toward a Cyprus settlement.

Mr. Averof responded instantly, stating that there was bound to be an adverse psychological reaction in Greece as the Turkish threat against the Aegean islands remained intact. The practical consequences of lifting the embargo would upset the military balance in the Aegean and would lead to a new Greek-Turkish arms race. The deputy foreign minister stated that Washington's announcement concerning the lifting of the embargo should be accompanied by a reiteration of a reference to the content of the top-secret letter that Kissinger sent to Greek Foreign Minister Bitsios on April 10, 1976. This letter assured the Greek government of "the unequivocal opposition of the United States to provocative action in the Aegean region."

DOCUMENT I

Minutes of the Meeting Between U.S. Ambassador
to Greece Robert McCloskey and Deputy Foreign
Minister Evangelos Averof, April 2, 1978.

SOURCE: *The Karamanlis Archive*, vol. 10, p. 174.

On April 2, 1978, the day before the official announcement in Washington [of the decision to lift the embargo], the American ambassador held another meeting with Mr. Averof. [Mr. Averof described the
meeting:]

Yesterday, Sunday, April 2, 1978, I asked U.S. Ambassador Robert
McCloskey to visit me at my home in Kifisia [a suburb of Athens]. He
arrived at 10:00 p.m. and stayed about 50 minutes. I told him that I
had some comments to add to my initial reaction— communicated
to him at the Foreign Ministry—to his announcement that President
Carter had decided to ask Congress [to lift the embargo]. I wanted to
convey these comments to him because, in the meantime, I had had
time to think about my personal reaction and I had also had the
opportunity to listen to the reactions of my compatriots. Regarding
the latter, I noted (erroneously) that my office had been flooded with
telephone calls from members of parliament from my own party, representing provinces around the country. They all told me that anti-
Americanism had risen abruptly and was widespread.

Under these circumstances, I, first, had an obligation to brief the
U.S. ambassador. Second, I wanted to ask him to remind the State
Department of what I had recommended with regard to the announcement [on lifting the embargo]. Third, I wondered if, before they made
the decision [to lift the embargo], they had ensured that there would at
least be reasonable proposals [by Turkey] for a Cyprus settlement.

Quite uncomfortably, Mr. McCloskey said that he understood my
reaction. He said that he hoped, in the end, the Greeks would realize
the reasons behind this decision and that it would not harm Greek
interests in any way and would facilitate a Cyprus settlement. He was
even more uncomfortable when he stated that he had received no
promises regarding proposals for a Cyprus settlement. There had
been discussion between U.S. officials and [Turkish Prime Minister]
Ecevit in Ankara about such proposals on Cyprus and, as far as he

knew, it was likely that such proposals would be made. I asked the ambassador if these proposals were going to be satisfactory, and he responded that he did not know.

I told Mr. McCloskey that the damage had already been done. This was the case since those who preached anti-Americanism in Greece appeared to have been vindicated because their moral and political arguments had been strengthened. I also told him that those who followed a pro-Western policy were in retreat, and it had become difficult to find [satisfactory] arguments to present to the public. I stated that the power and prestige of the pro-Western forces in Greece were still substantial, but they were not without limit and could not suffer a series of blows. If this happened [if the pro-Western forces were defeated], it would be a very serious blow to the West and to the United States especially. As we, the pro-Western forces see it, it would also be a blow to Greece. In this case, there was a danger that all the American bases in Greece would be removed immediately. (Emphasis added.)

Still, there was a possibility that the damage could be repaired if developments were favorable. For instance, if we presumed that Ankara had submitted proposals on Cyprus stipulating that 20 percent of the occupied territory would remain under Turkish control, then the people of Cyprus and the Greeks would say that the decision to lift the embargo was the right one. I also repeated my statements about arms supplies, about more or less equal treatment regarding aid, and about the fear we had with respect to the Aegean islands that were threatened.

In conclusion, I asked the ambassador to convey my fears to Washington and ask, on my behalf, if there was a promise [by Turkey] to submit timely and reasonable proposals on Cyprus.

Mr. McCloskey promised to do this and generally exhibited a full understanding of my positions.

Author's note: On April 10, 1978, Ambassador McCloskey responded to the questions raised by Mr. Averof during his April 2 meeting with him. The ambassador informed Mr. Averof that "Mr. [Warren] Christopher [the U.S. assistant secretary of state] did not receive any promises from Turkey regarding Cyprus." (Source: *The Karamanlis Archive*, vol. 10, p. 175.)

DOCUMENT J

SECRETARY OF STATE CYRUS VANCE'S TESTIMONY
BEFORE THE HOUSE COMMITTEE ON INTERNATIONAL
RELATIONS, APRIL 6, 1978.

SOURCE: The Secretary of State, *Administration Policy for the Eastern Mediterranean,* Department of State, Bureau of Public Affairs, Washington, D.C., April 6, 1978.

ADMINISTRATION POLICY FOR THE EASTERN MEDITERRANEAN

SECRETARY VANCE: I am pleased to be here today to review the Administration's security assistance proposals for Greece, Turkey, and Cyprus for fiscal year 1979 and to discuss more generally U.S. relations with the countries of the Eastern Mediterranean. U.S. policy in that sensitive and vital region has several fundamental goals. It is vital that we strengthen our bilateral relationships with two firm and long-standing friends and allies—Greece and Turkey. Further, it is essential to strengthen NATO's southern flank, thus enhancing allied security interests in the Eastern Mediterranean. At the same time, the President and all of us remain fully committed to help in the search for a Cyprus solution that will permit the two Cypriot communities to live peacefully together within one nation.

Let me emphasize that each of these goals is equally important, and great effort and attention must be paid to them if we are to succeed. Their pursuit has been complicated by the way in which history has interwoven the issues at play in the region.

I wish to outline today the Administration's program for dealing with these issues, which we believe will break the present impasse. We urge approval of these proposals. The consequences of failure would be enormous for all of us.

Bilateral Relations

The (Clark) Clifford mission to the region in the first weeks of the new Administration demonstrated the high priority which the

Administration placed and still places on restoring healthy relationships with our Eastern Mediterranean friends.

In Greece, we have watched with admiration and respect as that country returned to its place as a leading member of the family of Western democracies. Greece's democratic institutions have been restored and strengthened under the sound and confident leadership of Prime Minister Karamanlis, who returned in July 1974 to guide Greece out of one of the darkest periods of its history. We have witnessed the economic successes of Greece and the steady progress toward Greek entry into the European Community, an entity whose ideals and aspirations we share.

Because of Prime Minister Karamanlis's international stature and the dynamism of the Greek people, we believe Greece can and will play a vital role in European and world affairs. We value Greece as an old and trusted ally, and we place special emphasis on building an even stronger relationship for the future. In President Carter's discussions with Prime Minister Karamanlis in London last May, and when I visited Athens in January, we were struck by our wide range of common interests.

Our bilateral relations with Turkey are also of great importance. As a result of the Clifford mission, the meeting between President Carter and Prime Minister Demirel during the London Summit in May, my visit to Ankara in January, and that of Deputy Secretary Christopher last week, some progress was made toward working out a revitalized relationship. We believe that the United States must view Turkey from fresh perspectives, for the relationship has many dimensions. Our common security concerns have played in the past and will continue to play an important part in our evolving relationship. Turkey is a major democracy with a robust parliamentary system. It is also an important developing country—one of the few that has maintained the momentum of development within a strong democratic framework. Turkey is both a European and an Asian nation, and it is likely to have a growing role in the region and the world. Our relationship with Turkey has, however, been constrained by the embargo provisions of Section 620(x) of the Foreign Assistance Act (FAA) and the uncertainty concerning our bilateral defense relationship.

Strengthening NATO

The Eastern Mediterranean is the junction point of several critical areas—Western Europe, the Balkans, the Soviet Union, and the Middle East. The continuing strategic significance of this area is clear. To protect our interests and those of our allies, a strong and effective NATO southern flank is essential. Unfortunately, over the last several years, the effectiveness of this flank has been eroded in a manner that is of grave concern to this Administration and to our allies.

The United States has a number of vitally important military installations in Greece which are testimony to the strategic value of that country. These bases are critical to the operations of the 6th Fleet and to a variety of other activities essential to our security interests in the area. The Government of Greece withdrew its military forces from NATO's integrated military structure in 1974, and tied its full reintegration to progress on those issues which it feels forced its decision to withdraw. However, I should note that, in the interim, U.S. military facilities in Greece have continued to operate without interruption. Recently, there have been serious discussions between NATO and Greece offering grounds for optimism that a closer relationship may be developed in the coming months. If this continuing effort is successful, it will be a major step toward a healthy normalization of Greece's participation in NATO.

Turkey, for its part, remains a full NATO member, and its geographic position is critical today—as it has been throughout history. It supplies more ground forces to NATO than any other nation. Yet, the materiel of Turkish forces has deteriorated seriously in recent years. If Turkey is to continue to play its NATO role, our relationship must be revitalized. If we fail to do so, there will be those in Turkey who will question the basis for its continued participation in the Western alliance.

Seeking a Cyprus Solution

This Administration has, from its very first days, placed a high priority on the achievement of a just settlement of the Cyprus problem. We remain committed to that goal.

We are committed to that goal for two reasons: first, so long as

Cyprus is divided and its status uncertain, it constitutes a very serious humanitarian issue; second, so long as the Cyprus problem remains unsolved, it is a substantial impediment to good relations between Greece and Turkey.

In support of our commitment to the achievement of a Cyprus settlement, the Administration has made extensive efforts during the past year to encourage realistic and meaningful negotiations between the parties under the auspices of the Secretary General. Those efforts, which included many high-level visits, meetings, and discussions, have been set forth in detail by the President in his bimonthly reports to the Congress. I will not repeat them here.

Unfortunately, despite these efforts, the inter-communal talks have not to date produced any tangible breakthrough. There has, however, been a growing consensus as to a framework for a solution.

The two communities in Cyprus, as well as the governments of Greece and Turkey and, in fact, the international community as a whole, are in broad agreement with respect to the following: Cyprus must remain a sovereign independent nation—partition has been ruled out as a viable solution. Cyprus should be a federation with two zones. The Turkish zone should provide a viable area for the Turkish Cypriot community but be reduced in size from that now administered by the Turkish side. The Constitution should provide for mutually agreed-upon responsibilities divided between central and local governments with adequate safeguards respecting the rights of individual Cypriots.

The task now is to move from this consensus to a concrete agreement that will be acceptable to the two communities on Cyprus. As a part of this effort, the Greek Cypriot negotiators tabled a map in Vienna in April 1977 and described their constitutional concepts. The Turkish side is now formulating constitutional and territorial proposals which they believe will serve as a basis for the resumption of active inter-communal negotiations. We believe that, with two thoughtful constitutional and territorial proposals on the table, combined with sufficient goodwill and a sense of realism on both sides, there is an opportunity for productive negotiations. We stand ready, if requested, to assist the Secretary General in moving these negotiations forward.

Recommendations

We have mutually agreed with the Government of Turkey to renego-
tiate the matters covered by the Defense Cooperation Agreement so
as to serve our bilateral security interests in a manner that the two
governments can be confident will reflect the broadest interests of our
two democracies. It is not easy to predict when new arrangements will
be concluded, since the issues are complex. However, we have agreed
with the Government of Turkey to give this effort prompt attention
and to act promptly to implement the new agreement after it is concluded. Of course, we will consult closely with the Congress concerning such negotiations. Even as we are working toward this end, we
believe we must deal with issues of immediate concern to us and the
region. We are therefore submitting, in the form of an amendment to
the Security Assistance Act, proposed legislation to deal with this new
situation.

For Turkey, we propose the following with respect to FY 79:

- To provide FMS (foreign military sales) loan guaranties of $175
  million so that we can help meet the most urgent needs of the
  Turkish military. This is the same amount as was provided to
  Turkey last year.

- To lift the embargo contained in Section 620(x) of the FAA so
  that we can fully cooperate with Turkey in a manner consonant
  with the requirements of an alliance important to our mutual
  security. This would facilitate joint and allied defense planning,
  enhance allied support for Turkey's NATO needs via third
  country transfers and improved standardization, and permit
  the delivery of items impounded since the embargo was put in
  force.

- To provide a security supporting assistance loan of $50 million
  to Turkey to assist Turkey in resolving its present economic difficulties. I would note in this connection that a stabilization
  package was recently worked out between Turkey and the IMF
  (International Monetary Fund) staff, and is pending before the
  board.

For Greece, we would likewise continue the level of FMS financ-
ing at last year's level, that is, $140 million. This is somewhat higher

than the Administration requested in its budget submission and reflects our desire to maintain both Greece and Turkey at last year's FMS credit levels. No grant military assistance is being requested for either country at this time.

The lifting of the embargo and the negotiation of new defense arrangements with Turkey will provide a core of stability to our bilateral relations and enable us to establish a renewed sense of trust so that we may work together to resolve important problems. It should be clear that this does not signal any shift in U.S. policy as regards Greek-Turkish differences. They are both friends and valued allies. We support their efforts to resolve all problems between themselves in a peaceful fashion. We strongly believe that our national interests require the restoration of sound, normalized bilateral relationships with Turkey and with Greece, and our proposals today are made for that reason.

They should help restore a stable and peaceful atmosphere in the Eastern Mediterranean, something which will benefit all nations in the region. In that regard, it remains the position of the United States that the disputes which exist in the area must be settled through peaceful procedures, that each side should avoid provocative actions, and that neither side should seek a military solution to these disputes. The United States would actively and unequivocally oppose a military solution and would make a major effort to prevent such a course of action.

It has been suggested that lifting the embargo, or even proposing further military or economic assistance for Turkey, should be delayed until such time as a final Cyprus solution is achieved. The Administration does not share that view and does not, for the important reasons I have outlined, believe U.S. national interests would be served by such a course. The Administration will continue to make every effort to help bring about a just solution to the Cyprus problem. The action we request today is not, in our view, inconsistent with those efforts. We believe it can actually facilitate the negotiation process. With the Cyprus negotiations entering a critical period, the United States can play a more useful role if we are seen by all the parties to be even-handed in our approach. An embargo against one side makes it difficult to play that role.

Let me make another point about the embargo. Section 620(x) was enacted by the Congress to demonstrate that all facets of agreements undertaken with the U.S. Government must be honored or serious consequences faced. This is a point of principle which has had its impact both in Turkey and throughout the world, demonstrating the seriousness with which the American people view any unauthorized use of our military equipment. The point was made dramatically and effectively. Now, the time has come to look forward rather than back. Continued maintenance of the embargo would be harmful to U.S. security concerns, harmful to NATO, harmful to our bilateral relations with Turkey, and harmful to our role as a potential contributor to a Cyprus settlement.

Let me conclude with a brief factual description of our recommendations for assistance to Cyprus for the coming year.

As you will have noted, the Administration is requesting $5 million in FY 78 security supporting assistance for Cyprus as a contribution toward the relief and rehabilitation of displaced persons there. As in the past, these funds will be proportionally distributed to the two ethnic communities on Cyprus and will be earmarked for projects such as housing construction, health care, and vocational education. Since FY 75, the United States has contributed a total of $87.5 million for Cyprus relief and over $9 million annually to support the U.N. peacekeeping forces in Cyprus.

We believe that these new funds will be effectively utilized by Cypriot authorities for worthwhile refugee assistance programs and will underscore our continuing concern for the people of Cyprus and our strong interest in promoting negotiation of a just and lasting settlement on the island.

A settlement of the Cyprus problem and the adoption of a new Constitution with the concomitant creation of two zones will require some significant expenses involving the resettlement of people, the return of refugees, and the creation of new facilities. This Administration wishes to pledge that, when a settlement is achieved, we will reassess the question of economic assistance and are prepared to request from the Congress additional aid to assist both the Greek and Turkish Cypriot communities in making the necessary economic, social, and political readjustment brought about by a solution to this troubling problem.

DOCUMENT K

Minutes of the Meeting Between U.S. Ambassador to
Greece Robert McCloskey and Greek Prime Minister
Constantine Karamanlis, April 11, 1978.

source: *The Karamanlis Archive*, vol. 10, pp. 188–189.

The U.S. ambassador to Greece delivers [on April 11, 1978] a letter
from President Carter to Prime Minister Karamanlis. The letter is
dated April 6, 1978, and refers to the decision to lift the embargo.

Today [April 11, 1978], the prime minister receives at his office
the new American ambassador, Robert McCloskey. Following the
usual pleasantries, the ambassador delivers the letter to the prime
minister.

The prime minister states that, quite often in history, mistakes are
made either because of bad intentions or because of a bad evaluation
of the situation. In the case of Greece and the United States, mistakes
were made not because there were ill intentions on the part of the
American side, but because of a bad evaluation of the situation.

In its drive to regulate its relations with Turkey, the prime minister states, the United States has succumbed to a policy of blackmail by
Turkey. This has been a mistake because the impression has been created that Greece is being treated unfairly or is being ignored altogether. It has also been a mistake because we are afraid that Turkey,
instead of becoming more reasonable, will become more audacious
since Ankara believes that the policy of blackmail is beneficial [for
Turkey]. *Consequently, we believe that neither will a Cyprus settlement
be advanced nor will the bilateral problems with Turkey be resolved. To
the contrary, it is quite likely that we will be confronted with a general
deterioration of the situation.* (Emphasis added.)

The epicenter of our problems in Cyprus: The two Turkish
attacks against Cyprus in 1974 have created not only the current situation in Cyprus, but also the problems in the Aegean, the problems
with NATO, the problems concerning the U.S. bases in Turkey, and the
issue of the embargo. It is really painful to realize that, while a Cyprus
settlement is easy and in the hands of the Turks, they do not want one.
As a consequence, all these other problems remain unresolved as well,
while they could be settled if there were a Cyprus settlement.

Indeed, regarding the Cyprus issue, the Greek side has adopted positions that satisfy almost all of the Turkish demands—a bizonal federal system, a weak central government, and up to 25 percent of Cypriot territory under Turkish Cypriot control. It is impossible to comprehend how the Turkish mind works since they [the Turks] refuse to accept a Cyprus settlement that satisfies them, while such a settlement would rid the Turks, the allies, and us [the Greeks] of all the other problems as well.

Even though there is a [framework] for a Cyprus settlement along these lines, the U.S. government has already decided to lift the embargo, the prime minister states. This decision was made without any progress on Cyprus and without even the submission of any of the proposals that the Turks had promised to submit. This decision is a mistake because we believe that Turkey not only will not become more reasonable, but, on the contrary, the decision will encourage Ankara's intransigence. The consequence is bound to be that no progress will be achieved on Cyprus and no settlement will be reached regarding the Aegean. This creates serious concern for us because the lifting of the embargo could upset the military balance in favor of Turkey at the expense of Greece.

Mr. McCloskey thanks the prime minister for presenting his views. He states that he will not comment on the characterization of Turkish policy as a policy of blackmail, but he wishes to stress that the United States does not succumb to blackmail, whether this comes from Turkey or any other country. President Carter's decision [to lift the embargo] does not constitute succumbing to blackmail. Rather, it is a result of the American desire to break the deadlock in which so many issues have been trapped over the years. Perhaps this decision was not the best possible one, but it does reflect this American desire. Consequently, this initiative [lifting the embargo] should be given the opportunity to prove whether it is going to succeed over time. For this reason, the ambassador hopes that the Turkish Cypriot proposals will not be rejected without due consideration, even though they are not completely satisfying to the Greek Cypriots.

The prime minister also expresses the hope that these proposals will be reasonable so that they can become the foundation upon which the intercommunal talks can resume. Mr. Karamanlis points out that, among the arguments used [by Carter administration officials] during the debate in the International Relations Committee of the U.S. House of Representatives, there was the following: Turkey will distance itself from the West or it will close down the American bases if the embargo is not lifted. Certainly, the prime minister states, this creates the impression that the American government is succumbing to Turkish blackmail. This is the reason the decision [to lift the embargo] has been a mistake. The key to solving all the problems is for Turkey to be convinced that blackmail does not pay. From the moment this happens, it is certain that Turkey will become reasonable and accept solutions to the problems that are acceptable to all parties.

The prime minister concludes by asking the American ambassador to convey his regards to President Carter and thank him for the letter Mr. Carter sent to him [on April 6, 1978].

DOCUMENT L

LETTER FROM GREEK PRIME MINISTER
CONSTANTINE KARAMANLIS TO U.S. PRESIDENT
JIMMY CARTER, APRIL 18, 1978.

SOURCE: *The Karamanlis Archive,* vol. 10, pp. 189–190.

Dear Mr. President,

I would like to express my warm thanks for the letter you have addressed to me through Ambassador McCloskey, as well as for your flattering words.

I appreciate and share your thoughts on the need for solid relations of friendship and cooperation between Greece and the United States. These relations are based on a long tradition of multiple bonds that link our two peoples, and they are also relations of mutual trust. Please be assured that not only do I believe in this need, but I have made a continuous effort to remove the bitterness caused by the mistakes and misunderstandings of the past. I am in a position to state that, during the last two years, there has been considerable progress in this direction.

I do believe, Mr. President, that the trust characterizing our relations demands the sincere exchange of views on the critical issues before us. For this reason, I cannot hide the fact that it is with sorrow that I come to the realization that our views differ with regard to the decision of your Administration to ask Congress to lift the embargo on arms [sales] to Turkey. And I wish, Mr. President, you believed that our stand on this issue is not dictated by any intention to become involved in the internal affairs of the United States or by any animosity towards Turkey. As a matter of fact, we sincerely desire to restore friendly relations with Turkey. This decision, however, could have negative effects on Greek interests.

Judging from public pronouncements as well as from private and confidential briefings by the American government, it becomes apparent that Turkey undertook no obligation whatsoever for the restoration of peace in our region in exchange for the lifting of the embargo. It is inevitable for Turkey, under these circumstances, to conclude that the policy of threats is effective, and, therefore, Ankara will become even more intransigent. This intransigence might also be encouraged by the prospect that the lifting of the embargo could strengthen Turkey militarily at the expense of Greece. If this were to happen, there would be the following consequences:

a. A Cyprus settlement would become more difficult, if not impossible. This is already confirmed by the latest Turkish proposals that seem to lead to a new deadlock.

b. Greek-Turkish differences in the Aegean would become more complicated.

I am sure, Mr. President, that, in managing this whole situation, your Administration would appreciate our fears that are caused by these dangers.

I am afraid, Mr. President, about the prospect that the Greek people might get the impression that the United States is making a choice between Greece and Turkey, and is doing so at the expense of my country. If this happens, my effort to restore relations between our two countries to the traditional warmth will become more problematic. In addition, my effort to stabilize the position of my country in the Alliance will also become more difficult.

I had the opportunity to present in detail my views on the problems of this region to Mr. Vance when he visited Athens [on January 21, 1978]. I have informed the Ambassador, Mr. McCloskey, and I hope that you have been briefed on both meetings.

I ask you to be assured, Mr. President, that I believe deeply not just in the usefulness but also in the necessity of close friendship and cooperation between our two peoples. For this reason, I hope that future developments will prove my fears and concerns false and demonstrate that your judgment was more correct than mine.

Sincerely,

Constantine Karamanlis

DOCUMENT M

Minutes of the Meeting at the White House Between U.S. President Jimmy Carter and Greek Prime Minister Constantine Karamanlis, May 31, 1978.

SOURCE: *The Karamanlis Archive,* vol. 10, pp. 242–246.

On May 31, 1978, Greek Prime Minister Constantine Karamanlis holds a discussion with President Jimmy Carter at the White House, on the sidelines of the NATO summit meeting in Washington. Mr. Carter extended the invitation to Mr. Karamanlis to come to the White House through an official letter on May 11, 1978.

The minutes of the meeting between the two leaders are as follows:

On the Greek side, in addition to Prime Minister Karamanlis, the meeting is attended by Foreign Minister George Rallis, Greece's Ambassador to the U.S. Menelaos Alexandrakis, Director of Political Affairs at the Foreign Ministry Ioannis Tzounis, and Director of the Prime Minister's Office Petros Molyviatis.

On the American side, in addition to President Carter, the meeting is attended by Vice President Walter Mondale, Deputy National Security Adviser David Aaron, State Department Counsel Matthew Nimetz, Assistant Secretary for European Affairs George Vest, and Paul Henze, a member of the National Security Council staff.

[The meeting opens] with President Carter thanking Greece for its constructive stand during the NATO summit meeting in Washington. The president expresses his satisfaction because a way [compromise] was found that allowed a final communiqué to be drafted. Mr. Carter expresses his pleasure in welcoming Prime Minister Karamanlis to the White House and asks him to open the meeting by presenting the issues in the way he sees fit. The president adds that he would like to raise two or three issues.

The prime minister thanks the president and expresses his appreciation for the opportunity he has been given to exchange views with Mr. Carter. Mr. Karamanlis states that he regrets having to add Greece's problems to all the other problems the president is confronted with. But he wants the president to believe that these problems have not been created by the Greeks. They have been created by the neighbors. He does not wish to accuse Turkey, but he wants to emphasize that Greece is not asking for anything. It is Turkey that is raising claims. Not only has Turkey created the problems, but it also refuses to settle them, even though there are solutions. Indeed, there are solutions, but, unfortunately, he finds no understanding from the Turks. He does whatever is possible. The prime minister states that *he adopts positions that work against his popularity* precisely because he believes that the problems should be resolved not just for the sake of the two countries, but also for the sake of the NATO alliance. (Emphasis added.) As he said at the outset, he finds no reciprocity [from the Turkish side].

He wishes to stress that he prevented the outbreak of war on two occasions: The first time was when the Turks invaded Cyprus. Mr. Karamanlis states that he has the second military operation in mind, an inexplicable operation if looked at logically. [This second military operation] is inexplicable because the Turkish invasion took place under the pretext that the Turks wanted to restore [constitutional] legitimacy. Three days after the invasion, legitimacy was restored in Greece by me, and in Cyprus by Mr. Clerides. Logically, Turkey should have withdrawn its forces from Cyprus. Instead, it launched a second attack with results that are known. The issue today is that 18 percent of the population occupies 40 percent of the territory, and there are about 200,000 refugees. In order to form an impression of the severity of the refugee question, by analogy, this would translate into 80 million refugees in the United States.

No reasonable person can accept a continuation of this situation. There should be a settlement. We have been talking for four years to no avail because, until recently, the Turks have refused even to submit proposals. Recently, they submitted some proposals, but these proposals did not lead to a settlement. Those who have studied them, the British, the Germans, and the French, all admit that these proposals cannot lead to a Cyprus settlement.

It is certain that a Cyprus settlement is dependent upon the Turks because they are the occupiers of the island, and it is up to them to provide a settlement. This is especially the case because the positions adopted by the Greek Cypriots satisfy the basic Turkish demands. The Greek Cypriots accept a bizonal federal state with a weak central government. In exchange, they are asking that the territory controlled by the Turks be proportionate to the percentage of the Turkish Cypriot population. The Greek Cypriots could accept designating up to 25 percent of the country to be under Turkish control. These positions satisfy the Turkish demands.

The Cyprus issue and the embargo have been linked together, and they constitute a headache for the United States, Mr. Karamanlis states. Not only did we not impose the embargo, but we also accept the fact that it is an internal affair of the United States and it is up to the Americans to make a decision about it. *However, the United States should keep in mind that any solution to the embargo issue is bound to have political, psychological, military, and other repercussions.* (Emphasis added.) Still, even this issue could be settled by Turkey. If Turkey accepted a reasonable settlement of the Cyprus dispute, the next day the embargo would be lifted, we would return to [the military command structure of] NATO, and everyone else would get rid of the problem, including the U.S. government, the U.S. Congress, and especially Turkey.

The prime minister reiterates that the embargo is an internal American affair, and he cannot put forward any solution to the problem. As he already pointed out in his letter [of April 18] to President Carter, he has an obligation to state that *the lifting of the embargo is going to make matters more difficult, and this has been demonstrated by the Turkish proposals [on Cyprus].* (Emphasis added.)

This is his own assessment of the situation, Mr. Karamanlis says. President Carter might have a different opinion. Since, however, the president was kind enough to ask for his views, he has an obligation to point out what he believes. The lifting of the embargo might lead to the improvement of relations between the United States and Turkey. *In Greece and Cyprus, however, the lifting of the embargo is bound to create bitterness and lead to increased anti-American senti-ment.* (Emphasis added.)

The prime minister refers briefly to the Aegean question. This problem was also created by the Turks. This is the case because it is they who are making claims, not us [the Greeks]. Mr. Karamanlis states that he could have taken the stand that there has been a status quo in the Aegean for 60 years and could have refused any discussion. Nonetheless, he did not do so, and we [the Greeks and the Turks] have been discussing matters for four years. We reach an agreement. Within 10 days, the Turks renege. The prime minister gives an exam-ple. On May 31, 1975, he met with Turkish Prime Minister Demirel in Brussels. They reached an agreement stipulating that Greek-Turkish differences should be resolved peacefully through negotiations. Regarding the Aegean, they agreed that the dispute should be sub-mitted to the International Court of Justice in The Hague. They issued a joint communiqué that covered these agreements. When the time came for the experts to meet in order to draft the legal briefs so that the Aegean dispute could be submitted to The Hague, Mr. Demirel reneged and claimed that he had been deceived because he did not understand the joint communiqué.

The prime minister presents another glaring example. Not long after this incident, Mr. Karamanlis proposed that Turkey and Greece sign a non-aggression pact. He made this proposal because of his desire to promote a better climate between them. The Turks announced that, in principle, they accepted the proposal. But, Mr. Karamanlis says, when we sent them a draft of the pact to study, they refused to receive it. When we asked them why they had done that, they said that we should first resolve our differences, and then we could sign a non-aggression pact. This is totally illogical.

More recently, the prime minister proposed a reasonable proce-dure to Mr. Ecevit. It consisted of the following steps: a dialogue in order to find solutions to the problems [between Greece and Turkey], and avoidance of any provocative acts during this dialogue. If the dia-logue did not produce any results, then we would resort to arbitration or recourse to the International Court of Justice in The Hague. As of today, the Turks have not accepted my proposals. They argue that the dispute has to be resolved on the basis of political criteria. Our side believes, however, that, in resolving the dispute, legal criteria and the practices followed in similar cases should be taken into account. This is the case because, in the final analysis, political criteria mean force, which is unacceptable to us. The prime minister states that he knows three ways to settle disputes: dialogue, arbitration, or war.

Then, Mr. Karamanlis asks President Carter what he would do if he were in the prime minister's position.

President Carter says that he met with Mr. Ecevit in the morning [at the White House] and realizes that his views are different from those of the Greeks. He said they discussed the Aegean issue briefly. The president believes that the Greek positions are quite reasonable and will encourage Turkey to accept dialogue without provocations.

As far as the embargo is concerned, there is a divergence of opinion between the United States and Greece, Mr. Carter says. This is a difficult issue for the American government because it affects relations with Greece, and the United States appreciates Greek friendship. In all of our [the White House's] proposals to Congress, we have kept a balance. We realized that, since the imposition of the embargo, there had been no progress in U.S.-Turkish relations or in U.S.-Greek relations, so we decided to ask for its repeal. We did so with some hesitation because of the concerns raised by Greece. Still, in all of our proposals to Congress, we made sure that the military balance in the Aegean was not upset, and we will continue to maintain this balance.

President Carter adds that he met with Mr. Ecevit for the first time today, and he thought that the Turkish prime minister was more conciliatory on Cyprus than his predecessor, Mr. Demirel. Mr. Carter expresses the hope for a sustained meeting among Mr. Ecevit, Mr. Karamanlis, [Cyprus President] Kyprianou, and [Turkish Cypriot leader] Denktash. He says that, as initial gestures of goodwill, we asked that the Turks agree to reducing the number of occupation forces in Cyprus, opening the Nicosia airport to civilian aircraft, and allowing the return of the residents of Varosha to their homes, under U.N. auspices. The president told Mr. Ecevit that the number of Turkish forces in Cyprus was excessive, and all of the gestures mentioned above should be made before an agreement with the Turkish Cypriots can be reached.

Mr. Ecevit said he considered the recent Turkish Cypriot proposals a reasonable foundation for starting negotiations on the basis of a bizonal federation with a weak central government, Mr. Carter says. Mr. Ecevit believes that, with the passage of time, the central government will assume more powers. Moreover, he believes that there will be no restriction of movement. However, there are bound to be restrictions with regard to the acquisition of land. As far as the territorial question is concerned, the Turkish prime minister points out—without the use of a map—six areas where Turkey is willing to make concessions. The extent of these territorial concessions should be determined during negotiations. The neutral zone, amounting to 3 percent, will be returned, without question, to the Greek Cypriots.

The president asked Mr. Ecevit how negotiations could begin. In Mr. Ecevit's opinion, there should be bilateral talks concerning the Aegean and quatre-partite talks regarding Cyprus. President Carter said he asked Mr. Ecevit whether he would meet with Mr. Kyprianou and Mr. Denktash. After consulting with his advisers, Mr. Ecevit responded that this would be difficult, but he could accept a quatre-partite meeting. The president stated that the United States did not have any specific proposals for a Cyprus settlement. He said the U.S. did believe, however, that the Cyprus question, especially the territorial and refugee issues, should be addressed in a spirit of understanding through negotiations. Mr. Carter stated that, if the embargo were to be lifted, the United States would ensure that the military balance was not disturbed. The president added that the United States was willing to help if it were asked to do so by Greece, Turkey, Cyprus, and Mr. Denktash. But the U.S. would not become involved against the will of the parties.

The prime minister responds by noting that Greece separates the Aegean issue from the Cyprus question. Mr. Carter says that the Turks are doing the same thing. Mr. Karamanlis answers that the Turks would like to deal with Cyprus as a Greek-Turkish dispute, but he has rejected this. He says that he explained the reasons for this to Mr. Ecevit when they met in Montreux [on March 10, 1978]. At the time, the prime minister explained to Mr. Ecevit that: (a) Cyprus is an independent country, and (b) if Greece and Turkey reach a Cyprus settlement, they are not in a position to impose it. Mr. Karamanlis told Mr. Ecevit that, in this respect, he would be able to influence the Greek Cypriots on one condition: if the Turkish Cypriot proposals are reasonable. The proposals submitted by the Turkish Cypriots on April 13, 1978, are not helpful and, therefore, confirm the lack of goodwill on the part of the Turkish side. It was a mistake for Turkey to present these proposals just prior to the lifting of the embargo. The Turks should have submitted reasonable proposals or should not have submitted any proposals at all. They could have declared that they refused to submit proposals under pressure. They did not do this. In this way, the Turkish proposals are leading nowhere. Regarding the territorial question, these proposals stipulate that 18 percent of the population should control 34 percent of Cypriot territory, instead of the 40 percent that Turkey controls today. As far as the refugees are concerned, let us assume for the moment that 30,000 return to their homes' in Famagusta. What is going to happen to the rest of the refugees, 170,000 of them?

There is also the constitutional question, Mr. Karamanlis continues. A state [based on the Turkish Cypriot constitutional proposals] will be dysfunctional. The question is not whether the constitution is good or bad. It simply cannot work. What is attempted is constitutional partition. Each community will have its own army, currency, and international personality, and the president will rotate every two years. Moreover, in all the joint federal agencies, each community will be represented equitably, while there is no provision for the adjudication of disputes. When disputes arise, who is going to resolve them? The constitution provides for a referendum, but this will apply separately for each community.

Given this situation, the prime minister suggests to the president that it is necessary that the Turks be urged to improve their proposals. Otherwise, even if there is a temporary settlement, we are going to have new problems in the future, he states. History teaches us that there are situations in which a settlement generates more problems in the future instead of resolving a dispute. This is bound to be the case if we accept the Turkish Cypriot proposals. They are going to lead to new tension, and the United States will find itself entangled once more in the dispute. The prime minister says that the Greek Cypriot proposals [presented earlier] are reasonable and satisfy what Turkey has been demanding for years. This should not be overlooked, he stresses.

Mr. Carter responds by admitting that the Turkish Cypriot proposals are not satisfactory. It is evident that the proposed constitution will not work. In addition, Mr. Carter states, the rate of Turkish troop reduction [in northern Cyprus] is not satisfactory.

The prime minister points out to the president that the number of troops is not important. [Given Turkey's proximity to Cyprus] even with 10,000 troops, the Turks are in a position to control the whole island. To date, Cyprus has cost Ankara $2 billion, and this is one of the reasons for the economic bankruptcy of Turkey. I told Mr. Ecevit, Mr. Karamanlis adds, that, instead of being a conqueror of Cyprus, Turkey was bound to become its hostage. Unfortunately, Turkey has become hostage to Cyprus because the domestic situation [in Turkey] is very bad, indeed.

Mr. Carter responds by stating that Turkey realizes this. He does not consider the Turkish Cypriot proposals to be final. He expresses the hope that these proposals, with respect to both the territorial and constitutional questions can be combined with the opening of the Nicosia airport and Varosha. He also hopes that these measures might become a basis for a settlement. If negotiations take place and prove fruitless, Greece will have done what it could, the president adds.

In turn, Mr. Karamanlis states that, even if he knows that the Turkish Cypriot proposals will not lead to a settlement, he does wish that the negotiations would resume. But he is afraid that the Cyprus government will not go along with the idea of resuming negotiations because it has experienced eight rounds of talks. Even U.N. Secretary General Waldheim shares this view. He wishes that the Turkish Cypriots would submit more reasonable proposals. If they took this step, Mr. Karamanlis says that he would not hesitate to recommend to the Greek Cypriots that they resume negotiations. However, as these [Turkish Cypriot] proposals stand today, he has no right to recommend the resumption of talks. This is the situation, not because he lacks the courage to do so, but because there is no reasonable basis for negotiations and the Greek Cypriots would be correct in telling him not to become involved. In this way, he would lose his influence over them without bringing about any result.

President Carter notes that Mr. Kyprianou has told Mr. Waldheim that he is not going to agree to resume negotiations. The prime minister responds by saying that he will be meeting with Mr. Waldheim and will see what he can do in this respect. He wants, however, to avoid creating false expectations and states beforehand that he entertains little hope regarding the matter.

Mr. Carter raises the question of who should be the negotiating parties concerning the Cyprus issue. Mr. Karamanlis says that negotiations should be conducted between Mr. Ecevit and Mr. Kyprianou because Mr. Ecevit has complete control over Mr. Denktash.

President Carter responds that this will lead to deadlock because the Turks will deny that they have control over Mr. Denktash. In addition, Mr. Karamanlis might be underestimating his influence over the Greek Cypriots.

Mr. Karamanlis points out that the presence of the Turkish occupation army in Cyprus gives Turkey the means to control Mr. Denktash.

Mr. Carter answers that he does not dispute what the prime minister is saying, but he is trying to find ways to break the deadlock. At the moment, he sees no way out, the president says.

Mr. Karamanlis responds by saying: Only Mr. Ecevit can do that [provide a way out].

President Carter answers: But you can also help.

The prime minister responds to the president: Mr. Ecevit is the conqueror of the island. I do not wish to accuse him because this would not be right, but I believe that the solution to the problem is in his [Ecevit's] hands. The Turkish prime minister might have domestic difficulties. *But I have even bigger difficulties on the domestic front. When I returned to Greece [on July 24, 1974], there was intense anti-Western and anti-American sentiment. Yet, I fought against public opinion in order to convince the Greeks that we belong to the West. But I have paid a price for this. In 1974, I won 54 percent of the popular vote. In the last elections, I received only 42 percent. If the bitterness of the Greek people continues, I am not sure if I can still control the situation. Mr. Karamanlis asks the president to pay close attention to these factors.* (Emphasis added.)

I understand that Turkey must stay in the Western camp, Mr. Karamanlis tells the president. But, in the process, Greece might be lost. Mr. Karamanlis does not utter this statement as a threat. But, if he loses his popularity, there is going to be a chaotic situation. If his policy fails, he will be forced to withdraw [from politics]. The prime minister tells the president that he is not pointing all of this out in order to create impressions. It is in his character to do more than what he says.

The prime minister states that it is conceivable that the situation in Greece and Cyprus is of no interest to the United States. The president assures Mr. Karamanlis that this is not the case. The prime minister makes it clear to the president that the United States has the right to take this viewpoint. But, Mr. Karamanlis says, he has to point out that, if the present confusion continues, we might save Turkey, but we will open new wounds. For this reason, the [American] handling of the situation should be very cautious so that we lose neither Greece nor Turkey.

President Carter tells the prime minister that the discussion has been enlightening, but he does not know whether there has been progress on the Cyprus issue. He assures Mr. Karamanlis of the intense interest of the United States in Greece as well as in Cyprus. His administration is spending a lot of time seeking solutions to these problems, but it does not intervene in a way that could be counterproductive. Mr. Carter says that he will keep up the efforts to persuade Turkey to improve the Turkish Cypriot proposals. He would like all the parties to be open-minded so that negotiations can resume. The Aegean issue is important, but you begin negotiations without knowing what the final settlement will be, Mr. Carter says. Negotiations on Cyprus could begin in a similar fashion. Even though the Turkish Cypriot proposals are unsatisfactory, they constitute an improvement over the existing situation.

The prime minister states that the Aegean and Cyprus issues are different. Greece has been proposing reasonable solutions to the Aegean issue. Instead of mixing up the Aegean and Cyprus issues, let us first try to reach a settlement regarding one of these problems. In this respect, Mr. Karamanlis asks once more that [the United States] advise Mr. Ecevit to accept the Greek proposal on how to proceed on the Aegean issue. This procedure is accepted internationally. Arbitration is in the interest of both countries because it will shield them from internal criticism that each government is making excessive concessions.

In response, Mr. Carter states that he has as much influence over Mr. Ecevit as he does over Mr. Karamanlis.

The prime minister answers that, if there are reasonable proposals, he is personally willing to support them and follow President Carter's advice.

The meeting between President Carter and Prime Minister Karamanlis concludes after one hour and ten minutes.

Later, the Greek prime minister states in an interview that his talks with President Carter were very constructive and took place in a friendly atmosphere. Karamanlis states:

At the end of the meeting, I asked President Carter the following ques-

tion in order to force him to take a position: "I would like to ask you a question as a person seeking advice. If you were in my position, what would you do differently in comparison to my actions?" He remained thoughtful for quite a while, and then he said: "Nothing. I am convinced that you are right."

DOCUMENT N

STATEMENT BY U.S. PRESIDENT JIMMY CARTER ON THE NEED TO LIFT THE EMBARGO ON ARMS SALES TO TURKEY. WHITE HOUSE PRESS CONFERENCE, JUNE 14, 1978.

SOURCE: *Public Papers of the Presidents of the United States,* Jimmy Carter, 1978, Book I, January 1 to June 30, 1978, p. 1091.

The President's Press Conference of June 14, 1978

THE PRESIDENT: Good afternoon, everybody. I have two brief statements to make before I answer questions.

ARMS EMBARGO AGAINST TURKEY: The most immediate and urgent foreign policy decision to be made by the current legislative session is in lifting the arms embargo against Turkey. The points that the Congress intended to underscore 3 years ago, when the embargo was imposed, have all been made, but now the embargo is not contributing to a settlement of the Cyprus dispute, nor is it helping to improve our relationship with our allies, Greece and Turkey. It's driven a wedge between those countries and has weakened the cohesiveness and the readiness of NATO. It's thereby harmed our national security interests in the eastern Mediterranean, an area which is crucial to the defense of the southern flank of Europe, and also to our own access and that of others to the Middle East.

It's important to implement an effective policy in this area of the eastern Mediterranean—Greece, Turkey, Cyprus area. We have three purposes, all of which are equally important: first, to serve U.S. and NATO security interests, as well as the security interests of Greece and Turkey as nations; second, to improve the relationship between Greece and Turkey; and, third, to facilitate progress towards a Cyprus settlement.

I am asking Congress to support me in enacting the full program, which, in addition to removing the embargo against Turkey, provides for military sales credits to both Turkey and to Greece, and provides further funds for relief and rehabilitation of refugees in Cyprus.

Both Greece and Turkey are valuable friends and allies of our own. Lifting the embargo is essential to our hopes for peace and stability in the eastern region of the Mediterranean. And I hope that the American people and the Congress will give me their support in the realization of U.S. interests in this critical area of the world.

(A statement on inflation and federal spending followed.)

DOCUMENT O

THE CARTER ADMINISTRATION'S OFFICIAL REPORT TO CONGRESS EXPLAINING THE REASONS WHY THE EMBARGO ON ARMS SALES TO TURKEY SHOULD BE REPEALED.

SOURCE: Letter by Douglas Bennet, Jr., Assistant Secretary for Congressional Relations, to Senator John Sparkman, Chairman of the Senate Foreign Relations Committee, June 28, 1978, *Congressional Record*, 95th Congress, Second Session, vol. 124, part 15, July 21, 1978, pp. 22511–22513.

This letter to Congress represents the most detailed official position of the Carter administration on the Cyprus dispute and Greek-Turkish relations as the vote on the embargo was approaching.

DEPARTMENT OF STATE
Washington, D.C., June 28, 1978

Dear Senator Sparkman:

You will be voting soon after the July 4 recess on the International Security Assistance Bill (S. 2846) which includes the Administration's programs for Greece, Turkey, and Cyprus. The central element in this program is a proposal to lift the arms embargo on Turkey.

The central questions are these: (a) will lifting the embargo improve prospects for a just, lasting settlement on Cyprus, and (b) will perpetuating the embargo damage U.S. security interests?

We have put together some materials on both these questions, which may be helpful to you in considering the embargo issue and in answering questions from your constituents during the recess.

Attached are brief papers on the following subjects:

Turkey: An Important Partner in NATO
U.S. Military Facilities in Turkey
The Cyprus Problem: New Hope for a Solution
The Return of Greek Cypriot Refugees to Varosha
Lifting the Turkish Arms Embargo

We would welcome an opportunity to review with you personally the complex issues involved in the Eastern Mediterranean prior to this important vote. Please call me or my Deputy, Nelson Ledsky (632–4768), if we may arrange a further briefing or answer any questions you may have.

Sincerely,

Douglas J. Bennet, Jr.,
Assistant Secretary for Congressional Relations

Enclosures: as stated

(The papers appear below:)

TURKEY: AN IMPORTANT PARTNER IN NATO

Turkey contributes to NATO's strength through its strategic geographical location, its forces, and its Western orientation.

Turkey's geographical location is a key element in discouraging Warsaw Pact and Soviet aspirations toward the Mediterranean and Middle East. Major land, sea, and air routes from the Soviet and Bulgarian Black Sea areas to the Mediterranean lead across Turkey.

Turkey has the largest standing army in NATO—approximately 480,000. Along with the Greek Armed Forces, Turkey ties down approximately 26 Warsaw Pact divisions plus associated air and naval units in the Caucasus, Balkans, and Black Sea areas. Without having to contend with credible Greek and Turkish defenses, a significant portion of these Warsaw Pact forces could be reoriented toward other areas of NATO where significant money and manpower would be required to balance them.

Turkey provides important facilities for U.S. and NATO requirements for peacetime training, forward basing of tactical fighter aircraft, support of the Sixth Fleet, and intelligence collection.

Unlike Greece, which withdrew its forces from the NATO integrated military command structure in 1974, Turkey remains fully integrated within NATO.

A combination of severe economic problems and the U.S. arms embargo has resulted in a significant reduction in the capability of the Turkish Armed Forces. Most equipment in the Turkish Armed Forces is of U.S. origin and most is quite old. The effect of the U.S. arms embargo in 1975 and continuing restrictions has been to stop almost completely a modest modernization program with the Turkish Armed Forces and to prevent the Turks from maintaining aging equipment in working order. Cannibalization to keep some major weapon systems in operation has become widespread, particularly in the Turkish Air Force. Maintenance difficulties have become massive, and crew training has suffered.

U.S. MILITARY FACILITIES IN TURKEY

In reaction to the 1975 arms embargo, Turkey suspended U.S. operations at five of seven major installations in July 1975. Four were used for intelligence collection (Sinop, Karamursel, Belbasi, Diyarbikir) and the fifth is a long-range navigation station (Kargaburum).

The three-year suspension of U.S. operations in Turkey has degraded our capability to collect information on Soviet weapon systems technology, research, training and operations. Specifically:

Valuable data has been lost on Soviet space, missile, and military systems development and strategic nuclear activities, thereby reducing our level of confidence in our knowledge of these subjects.

Continued loss of information which can be collected from sites now in Turkey hampers our ability to develop countermeasures to

Soviet weapon systems under development and could allow these systems to reach an advanced stage without our having a complete understanding of their potential threat.

Certain needed information can be collected only from Turkey. Therefore, all present losses could not be recovered simply by relocating the facilities elsewhere. In any event, relocation to recover partially the capability represented by U.S. intelligence installations in Turkey involves a significant amount of time and money.

The Government of Turkey has informed us that the lifting of the embargo would lead to the reopening of these installations. We intend to work out shortly an interim arrangement followed by negotiations for a permanent basis for operation of these facilities. If necessary, we will also explore with the Government of Turkey immediate reopening upon repeal of the embargo on an interim basis even if new arrangements have not yet fully been worked out.

Two major installations (Incirlik Air Base and Ankara Air Station) are in full operation in direct support of the NATO mission. They provide:

Forward basing of USAF tactical fighter aircraft in support of NATO defense plans. Accommodations are also maintained for wartime augmentation by reinforcement aircraft and NATO strategic reserve forces.

Peacetime training. Konya Range is one of the very few air-to-ground firing ranges east of Spain which is available and adequate for regular use by theater tactical air forces.

Terminal support for inter-theater staging of strategic airlift aircraft, including the only U.S. owned and controlled major aircraft refueling facility in the eastern Mediterranean area.

Naval depot services and stocks for the replenishment, refueling, and aviation POL resupply for units of the U.S. Sixth Fleet. Twenty percent of Fleet fuel assets in the Mediterranean are stored in Turkey.

Major contingency storage of war reserve materials, munitions, and petroleum supplies for use by the U.S. Forces.

Communications in support of logistics requirements, intelligence, and command and control of U.S. and other NATO forces in Southern Europe and the Mediterranean.

THE CYPRUS PROBLEM: NEW HOPE FOR A SOLUTION

Introduction

When Cyprus gained independence from Britain in 1960, a centralized government was established with checks and balances to protect the Greek-Cypriot majority and the Turkish-Cypriot minority. Cypriot Archbishop Makarios was elected President, and the leader of the Turkish-Cypriot community was chosen as Vice President. Greece, Turkey, and the United Kingdom guaranteed the maintenance of this arrangement.

Strains between the Greek and Turkish communities developed immediately after independence. Violence erupted in 1963–64, 1967, and again in 1974. A U.N. peacekeeping force was introduced on Cyprus in 1964, and, under U.N. auspices, talks between Greek-Cypriot and Turkish-Cypriot community leaders were undertaken.

In 1977, the two communities agreed, for the first time, on principles under which a new government might be organized. Both the Greek-Cypriots and the Turkish-Cypriots accepted the idea of two ethnic zones on the island with some kind of central government uniting them. Specific details as to which activities were to be handled in the zones and which at the federal level were not resolved.

The United States played an important role in encouraging the two sides to reach this agreement in principle. It remains an important objective of U.S. policy to insure that follow-on negotiations successfully resolve these fundamental constitutional issues as well as the territorial question of where the dividing line between the two zones shall be established.

The 1974 Crisis and the Arms Embargo

The present U.S. arms embargo on Turkey stems from the 1974 crisis. In July 1974, elements of the Greek-Cypriot National Guard, supported by the Greek military junta in Athens, deposed President Makarios. In his place, they installed a Greek-Cypriot extremist known to be fiercely anti-Turkish and anxious to unite Cyprus with Greece. Five days later the Turkish Government, claiming it was acting under the 1960 guarantees, landed military forces on the northern coast of Cyprus to protect the Turkish-Cypriot population and prevent union with Greece.

Shortly thereafter, the coup on Cyprus collapsed, a cease-fire was achieved, and the legitimate government was restored. The Turkish troops did not leave Cyprus, however, and, in August, the Turkish Government landed additional forces, taking about 36% of the island. These events resulted in bloodshed and displaced a large number of persons. In 1975, a separate Turkish-Cypriot administration was established in the northern part of Cyprus. In succeeding months, Turkish-Cypriots moved north and Greek-Cypriots moved south to join their ethnic communities. It was in reaction to the second Turkish invasion that the U.S. arms embargo was imposed.

Negotiations Begin

As a result of diplomatic pressure by the U.S. and other nations, inter-communal negotiations were resumed in 1975 under the aegis of U.N. Secretary General Waldheim. Some progress was made towards resolving humanitarian problems resulting from the 1974 fighting, but, through 1976, the two sides remained deadlocked on the fundamental problems of the structure and functions of a future government and the future geographic division of the island.

Early in 1977, however, President Makarios and Turkish-Cypriot leader Denktash met personally under the aegis of Secretary General Waldheim and agreed on a set of principles that would constitute a framework for a comprehensive Cyprus settlement. Cyprus was to be a sovereign, independent, bi-zonal, bi-communal federal republic; the Turkish-Cypriots would withdraw from an unspecified portion of the territory they occupy; and the basic rights of freedom of movement, settlement, and property ownership would be respected with certain conditions.

Turkish-Cypriot Proposals

When Turkish Prime Minister Ecevit assumed office in January 1978, chances for a settlement improved. Ecevit's predecessors had all ruled with a coalition which made concessions politically difficult, whereas Ecevit commands an actual majority. Ecevit has declared that a Cyprus settlement is in Turkey's own best interest, and a matter of high priority for his government. Turkish-Cypriots, with Ecevit's encouragement, submitted fresh constitutional and territorial proposals.

The Turkish-Cypriots have amplified the latest proposals to include offers:

That the Turkish Government would make further troop reductions as the inter-communal negotiations progress;

That some 30–35,000 Greek-Cypriots could commence returning to their homes and businesses in the city of Varosha as the negotiations progress:

That the Turkish-Cypriots are prepared to discuss the reopening of Nicosia airport for civilian traffic, and to explore the possibility of joint economic ventures between Greek and Turkish-Cypriots.

The Greek-Cypriots have stated that these proposals are unacceptable as a basis for resuming negotiations, and they have maintained this position despite subsequent assurances that the Turkish-Cypriot side is prepared to be flexible and forthcoming as soon as the two parties are back at the table.

The Turkish-Cypriot proposals appear to represent a real advance over the positions assumed by Turkish-Cypriot negotiators in previous rounds of talks. The constitutional proposal is substantially more developed and the Turkish-Cypriots have, for the first time, clearly agreed to discuss territorial changes. These proposals plus the more favorable political environment in Turkey make this an important and hopeful movement in the search for a solution in Cyprus.

THE RETURN OF GREEK-CYPRIOT REFUGEES TO VAROSHA

Recent declarations by the Turkish-Cypriots have moved the problem of resettling a sizable number of Greek-Cypriots in the important seaside town of Varosha closer to solution.

Prior to the 1974 hostilities in Cyprus, Varosha (New Famagusta) was a flourishing and prosperous Greek-Cypriot resort center of some 40,000 full-time inhabitants, not unlike a small-scale Miami Beach. In August 1974, the population of Varosha fled to the south to escape advancing Turkish forces. Rather than being opened to Turkish or Turkish-Cypriot settlement, as were other abandoned Greek-Cypriot communities, Varosha remained sealed off under the direct control of the Turkish Army.

Varosha is now a ghost town. Yet, it is perhaps the single most significant piece of territory in dispute between the Greek and Turkish-

Cypriots. For the former, the regaining of a major Greek-Cypriot town of substantial economic importance has become a sine qua non of a settlement. For the latter, Varosha is of crucial significance because of its value to the Greek side and on account of its proximity to Famagusta Harbor, the only deep-water port in the Turkish-Cypriot zone.

Varosha has now become a key element in efforts to resume the Cyprus inter-communal negotiations. The proposals submitted by the Turkish-Cypriots to Secretary General Waldheim on April 13 include a separate section on Varosha, which provided for the return of some Greek-Cypriot inhabitants subject to the laws and regulations of the Turkish-Cypriot administration. This latter condition was rejected by the Greek-Cypriots. The Turkish-Cypriots have now clarified and elaborated on their proposal: They have specified that up to 35,000 Greek-Cypriots will be able to return to Varosha; they have conceded that this return need not await conclusion of a settlement but can commence as soon as negotiations are resumed; and they have given assurances that the future political framework of Varosha is open to negotiation, thereby admitting the possibility of a reversion to Greek-Cypriot control.

These are welcome clarifications. Nevertheless, we understand why Greek-Cypriots may well be reluctant to return to Varosha while negotiations are underway, should this mean they will be subject to Turkish-Cypriot jurisdiction.

A practical solution would be for the United Nations to assume an interim role in the administration of Varosha, pending arrangements to be worked out in a final settlement. Secretary General Waldheim has tentatively endorsed this approach, noting in his May 31 report on the Cyprus question that, with reference to the status of Varosha, "it would seem natural to envisage United Nations assistance in this connection." Furthermore, the Turkish side has indicated that, in the context of a resumption of inter-communal talks, it would accept an interim United Nations role in Varosha to facilitate the return of the Greek-Cypriot inhabitants.

Progress on the Varosha issue now seems possible. Such progress will be important not only for itself but also because it could be instrumental in moving towards a resumption of full negotiations.

LIFTING THE TURKISH ARMS EMBARGO

Jimmy Carter was right on the mark when he said the forthcoming Senate vote to lift the Turkish arms embargo is the most important piece of foreign-affairs business the Congress has left in this session. It is really quite simple. If the embargo is lifted, diplomacy gets a chance to start healing the wounds in Cyprus, the rent in Turkish-Greek relations, the strain in Turkish-American and Greek-American relations, and NATO's whole sorry disarray in the eastern Mediterranean. If the embargo stays on, everything gets worse.

The argument has been cast in pro-Turkish and pro-Greek terms, but that is misleading. There is a great deal in it for both Turkey and Greece, and for both the Turkish and Greek communities in Cyprus if the stalemate signified by the embargo is broken. The United States had gone to considerable lengths to make that case, explaining the vista that a lifting of the embargo would open, removing the previous administrations' pro-Turkish tilt in military aid, and supporting Greece's wish not to be muscled by Turkey in their Aegean Sea dispute. The Administration has also labored, successfully, to induce the Turks to offer a new Cyprus position conducive to negotiations. Ankara's position is not yet what Athens and the Greek Cypriots want it to be. The way to improve it is by talks that would surely follow the lifting of the embargo.

The Greek lobby is hanging tough. That has led Sen. George McGovern (D-S.D.) to offer an imaginative way out. Mr. McGovern can hardly be regarded as someone dominated by the strategic concerns that, for good reason, guide the views of many others who wish to end the embargo. He is sympathetic to the division and hardship on Cyprus. McGovern suggests lifting the embargo, while linking future Turkish-aid requests (including arms sales) to a presidential certification of good-faith diplomacy. His amendment is designed to eliminate the stigma that the embargo is for Turkey, but to retain a non-humiliating form of encouragement to the Turks to continue moderating their policy. The Administration supports this approach.

Let us underline the essential point. The embargo was at its outset a well-meant, legally mandated protest against the use of American arms for the occupation of almost half of Cyprus. But experience has proven it to be destructive of the purpose it was meant to serve—reducing the occupation—and of much else. The embargo stands now simply as a hostile act against an ally, and one not in the slightest endorsed by any other NATO ally—except Greece. The Senate should end it in the manner suggested by Mr. McGovern.

DOCUMENT P

THE AMENDMENT BY SENATOR GEORGE McGOVERN THAT WAS ADOPTED BY THE SENATE ON JULY 25, 1978, AND LED TO THE LIFTING OF THE EMBARGO ON ARMS SALES TO TURKEY

SOURCE: *Congressional Record*, Senate, 95th Congress, Second Session, vol. 124 – Part 15, July 21, 1978, to July 31, 1978, p. 22548.

The amendment is as follows:

At the end of the language proposed to be inserted by the Senator from Alabama (Mr. Sparkman) (UP-1491), insert the following:

(b) The Foreign Assistance Act of 1961 to be amended by inserting, after section 620B, the following new section:

Sec. 620C U.S. Policy and Procedure Regarding Cyprus, Greece and Turkey.

(a) Congress finds that:

(1) events in Cyprus in 1974, precipitated by a coup sponsored by the Greek military dictatorship and resulting in an intervention by Turkish military forces, created an international problem within the authority and responsibility of the United Nations;

(2) given the presence in Cyprus of a United Nations peacekeeping force mandated to prevent further inter-communal violence, and given the inter-communal negotiating process established under the aegis of the United Nations Secretary General, the continuing presence of a major Turkish force is inconsistent with the legitimate status of Cyprus as a sovereign republic;

(3) the United States policy with respect to this problem should continue to accord high priority to supporting implementation of United Nations resolutions regarding Cyprus and United Nations efforts to restore full Cypriot sovereignty through the negotiation of a just settlement;

(4) U.S. limitations on arms transfers to Turkey enacted in 1975

represented a strong American desire to support such efforts and affirm basic U.S. foreign assistance statutes;

(5) although events in Cyprus have caused bitterness among the people of Cyprus, Turkey and Greece, the United States continues to have a strong interest in maintaining stable and sound relations with each of these nations;

(6) the maintenance of such positive relations will inevitably depend on the achievement of a just solution on Cyprus;

(b) Regarding such a solution, Congress finds that—

(1) the guidelines for inter-communal talks agreed to in Nicosia in February 1977—setting forth the common goal of an independent, sovereign, nonaligned, bicommunal Federal Republic of Cyprus— continue to provide a sound basis for the negotiation of a just settlement in that nation;

(2) serious negotiations, under United Nations auspices, will be necessary to achieve detailed agreement on, and implementation of, constitutional and territorial terms within such guidelines;

(3) the United States should actively support efforts to achieve such a just solution, providing full protection for the human rights of all Cypriots;

(c) United States policy regarding Cyprus, Greece and Turkey shall be directed toward the restoration of a stable and peaceful atmosphere in the Eastern Mediterranean region and shall therefore be governed by the following principles:

(1) The United States should actively support the resolution of differences through internationally established peaceful procedures, shall encourage all parties to avoid provocative actions, and shall strongly oppose any attempt to resolve disputes through force or the threat of force;

(2) The United States arms transfers to Greece and Turkey shall be made solely for defensive purposes and to sustain their strength as North Atlantic Treaty Organization allies, shall be designed to insure that the present balance of military strength among countries in the region is preserved, and shall not signify a lessening of the United States commitment to a just solution on Cyprus;

(3) The achievement of such a solution shall remain a central concern of United States policy in the region, and

(4) Because future United States relations with the nations con-

cerned must be shaped according to progress toward such a solution, the President and Congress shall continually review such progress and shall determine United States policy in the region including United States economic and military assistance, accordingly.

(d) To facilitate such review, the President shall, within 60 days after the enactment of this section and at the end of each succeeding 60-day period, transmit to the Speaker of the House of Representatives and the chairman of the Committee on Foreign Relations of the Senate, a report on progress made during such period toward the conclusion of a negotiated solution of the Cyprus problem. Such transmission shall include any relevant reports prepared by the Secretary General of the United Nations for the Security Council.

(e) Upon enactment of the Act, the President, with any request for funds for military or economic assistance under this Act, or credits or guarantees under the Arms Export Control Act, for countries named in this section, transmits to the Speaker of the House of Representatives and the chairman of the Committee on Foreign Relations of the Senate his certification (with a full explanation thereof) that the goals set in this section have been substantially achieved or that such assistance would contribute to their achievement. Such certification shall accompany any notification of anticipated arms sales to such countries submitted for Congressional consideration under the provisions of section 36 (b) of the Arms Control Export Act.

Bibliography

U.S. OFFICIAL DOCUMENTS

The White House. Memorandum to the President, from Zbigniew Brzezinski—Subject: NSC Weekly Report #53, April 7, 1978.

_____. Memorandum to the President, from Zbigniew Brzezinski—Subject: NSC Weekly Report #57, May 5, 1978.

_____. Memorandum to the President, from Frank Moore and Bob Beckel—Subject: Turkish Arms Embargo, Status Report, May 17, 1978.

_____. Memorandum for the President, by David Aaron—Subject: NSC Weekly Report #59, May 19, 1978.

Jimmy Carter, 1977. *Public Papers of the Presidents of the United States.* Washington: U.S. Government Printing Office, Book I, January 20 to June 24, 1977.

_____. "Inaugural Address of President Jimmy Carter." January 20, 1977, pp. 1–4.

_____. "President's Personal Emissary to Greece, Turkey, and Cyprus: Designation Clark M. Clifford." February 3, 1977, pp. 77–78.

_____. "The Cyprus Conflict: Message to the Congress Reporting on Progress Made Toward a Negotiated Settlement." February 11, 1977, pp. 143–144.

_____. "The President's News Conference of March 9, 1977," pp. 341–345.

_____. "Clinton, Massachusetts: Remarks and a Question-and-Answer Session at the Clinton Town Meeting." March 16, 1977, pp. 382–388.

_____. "The Cyprus Conflict: Message to the Congress Reporting on Progress Made Toward a Negotiated Settlement." April 15, 1977, pp. 638–639.

_____. "Meeting with Prime Minister Suleyman Demirel of Turkey: Remarks to Reporters Following the Meeting." [London] May 10, 1977, pp. 847–848.

_____. "The President's Press Conference of May 12, 1977," pp. 860–870.

_____. "Presidential Address at Commencement Exercises, University of Notre Dame, May 22, 1977," pp. 954–962.

_____. "The Cyprus Conflict: Message to the Congress Reporting on Progress Made Toward a Negotiated Settlement." June 22, 1977, pp. 1137–1138.

Jimmy Carter, 1977. *Public Papers of the Presidents of the United States.* Washington: U.S. Government Printing Office, Book II, June 25 to December 31, 1977.

_____. "The Cyprus Conflict: Message to the Congress Reporting on Progress Made Toward a Negotiated Settlement." August 25, 1977, pp. 1550–1501.

_____. "The Cyprus Conflict: Message to the Congress Reporting on Progress Made Toward a Negotiated Settlement." October 28, 1977, pp. 1928–1929.

_____. "President Carter's Informal Exchange with Reporters, Plains, Georgia, December 25, 1977," p. 2172–2174.

Jimmy Carter, 1978. *Public Papers of the Presidents of the United States.* Washington:

U.S. Government Printing Office, Book I, January 1 to June 30, 1978.

————. "The State of the Union Address: Annual Message to the Congress, January 19, 1978," pp. 98–122.

————. "The Cyprus Conflict: Message to the Congress Reporting on Progress Made Toward a Negotiated Settlement." January 20, 1978, pp. 127–128.

————. "Reception Honoring Polish Americans: Remarks at White House Reception." February 6, 1978, pp. 281–284.

————. "The Cyprus Conflict: Message to the Congress Reporting on Progress Made Toward a Negotiated Settlement." March 23, 1978, pp. 555–556.

————. "Interview with the President: Remarks and a Question-and-Answer Session with a Group of Editors and News Directors." May 19, 178, pp. 937–941.

————. "North Atlantic Summit: Toast of the President at the Dinner Honoring the Heads of Delegation." May 30, 1978, pp. 1016–1018.

————. "Meeting with Prime Minister Constantine Karamanlis of Greece: White House Statement." May 31, 1978.

————. "North Atlantic Alliance Summit: Remarks Following the Conclusion of the Final Session." May 31, 1978, pp. 1024–1025.

————. "The President's News Conference of June 14, 1978," pp. 1091–1099.

————. "Atlanta, Georgia: Remarks to Members of the Southern Baptist Brotherhood Commission." June 16, 1978, pp. 1113–1117.

————. "The Cyprus Conflict: Message to the Congress Reporting on Progress Made Toward a Negotiated Settlement." June 23, 1978, pp. 1151–1153.

Jimmy Carter, 1978. *Public Papers of the Presidents of the United States.* Washington: U.S. Government Printing Office, Book II, June 30 to December 31, 1978.

————. "The President's News Conference of July 20, 1978," pp. 1322–1329.

————. "The Situation in Cyprus: White House Statement, July 21, 1978," p. 1331.

————. "Arms Embargo Against Turkey: Statement by the White House Press Secretary Following Senate Action." July 25, 1978, p. 1137.

————. "Arms Embargo Against Turkey: Statement on House of Representatives Action to End the Embargo." August 1, 1978, p. 1357–1358.

————. "The Cyprus Conflict: Message to the Congress Reporting on Progress Made Toward a Negotiated Settlement." September 1, 1978, pp. 1481–1482.

————. "Interview with the President: Remarks and a Question-and-Answer Session with Editors and News Directors." September 22, 1978, pp. 1588–1592.

————. "International Security Assistance Act of 1978: Statement on Signing S. 3075 Into Law." September 26, 1978, pp. 1636.

————. "United States-Turkey Military Cooperation: Memorandum from the President—Presidential Determination No. 78–18." September 26, 1978.

————. "Interview with the President: Remarks and a Question-and-Answer Session with Editors and News Directors." November 17, 1978, pp. 2061–2068.

————. "The Cyprus Conflict: Message to the Congress Reporting on Progress Made Toward a Negotiated Settlement." November 30, 1978, pp. 2103–2104.

————. "Memphis, Tennessee: Remarks at the Democratic National Committee's National Finance Council Breakfast." December 9, 1978, pp. 2195–2198.

————. "The President's News Conference of December 12, 1978," pp. 2219–2224.

————. "Interview with the President and Mrs. Carter: Question-and-Answer Session with Barbara Walters of the American Broadcasting Company." December 15, 1978.

U.S. Department of State. "Secretary Kissinger Discusses Cyprus, Greece, and Turkey in Informal News Conference." July 22, 1974. *Department of State Bulletin* 71, no. 1833, August 12, 1974, pp. 257–261.

————. "Letter by Hodding Carter III, Assistant Secretary of State for Public Affairs and Department Spokesman, to Serge Hadji, Member of the Pan-Hellenic Emergency Committee," May, 1, 1978.

————. "Secretary Kissinger's News Conference of August 19, 1974." *Department of State Bulletin* 71, no. 1837, September 9, 1974, pp. 353–358.

————. Secretary of State Vance. "Administration Policy in the Eastern Mediterranean." Statement before the House Committee on International Relations. The Department of State, Bureau of Public Affairs, Washington, D.C., April 6, 1978.

————. *1978 Country Report on Human Rights Practices: Cyprus.* Report Submitted to the Committee on International Relations, U.S. House of Representatives, and the Committee on Foreign Relations, U.S. Senate. Joint Committee Print, 95th Congress, Second Session, Washington, D.C., February 3, 1978.

————. *1978 Country Report on Human Rights Practices: Israel and the Occupied Territories.* Report Submitted to the Committee on International Relations, U.S. House of Representatives, and the Committee on Foreign Relations, U.S. Senate. Joint Committee Print, 95th Congress, Second Session, Washington, D.C., February 3, 1978.

————. *1978 Country Report on Human Rights Practices: Turkey.* Report Submitted to the Committee on International Relations, U.S. House of Representatives, and the Committee on Foreign Relations, U.S. Senate. Joint Committee Print, 95th Congress, Second Session, Washington, D.C., February 3, 1978.

————. *1999 Country Report on Human Rights Practices: Cyprus.* Bureau of Democracy, Human Rights and Labor, Washington, D.C., February 25, 2000.

U.S. Congress. Senate. "The Embargo Debate and Vote." *Congressional Record*, 95th Congress, Second Session, vol. 124, part 15, July 21, 1978, to July 31, 1978, pp. 22501–22557.

————. Senate. "Letter by Douglas J. Bennet, Assistant Secretary for Congressional Relations, to Senator John Sparkman, Chairman of the Senate Foreign Relations Committee," June 28, 1978. *Congressional Record*, 95th Congress, Second Session, vol. 124, part 15, July 25, 1978, pp. 22511–22513.

————. Senate. *Turkey, Greece, and NATO: The Strained Alliance.* A Staff Report to the Committee on Foreign Relations. Washington, D.C.: U.S. Government Printing Office, March 1980.

————. Senate. *New Opportunities for U.S. Policy in the Eastern Mediterranean.* A Staff Report to the Committee on Foreign Relations. Washington, D.C.: U.S. Government Printing Office, April 1989.

————. Senate. Committee on Foreign Relations. Subcommittee on European Affairs. *Cyprus: International Law and Prospects for Settlement.* Hearings. 102nd Congress, 1st Session, April 17, 1991.

U.S. Congress. House. Subcommittee on Europe and Subcommittee on the Middle

East. *The Decision to Homeport in Greece. Report.* Washington, D.C.: December 31, 1972, U.S. Government Printing Office, 1972.

————. House. *Cyprus-1974: Hearings before the Committee on Foreign Affairs and the Subcommittee on Europe,* August 19 and 20, 1974. 93rd Congress, Second Session, Washington, D.C.: U.S. Government Printing Office, 1974.

————. House. *Cyprus-1974: Statement of Hon. George Ball, Former Under Secretary of State. Hearing before the Committee on Foreign Affairs, Subcommittee on Europe,* August 19 and 20, 1974. 93rd Congress, Second Session, Washington, D.C.: U.S. Government Printing Office, 1974, pp. 33–51.

————. House. Extension of Remarks. "Statement by George W. Ball and Cyrus Vance," July 10, 1975. *Congressional Record,* 94th Congress, 1st Session, vol. 121, part 17, July 8, 1975, to July 14, 1975, pp. 22258–22259.

————. House. "The Embargo Debate and Vote." *Congressional Record,* 95th Congress, Second Session, vol. 124, part 18, August 1, 1978, to August 8, 1978, pp. 23694–23729.

————. House. Committee on Foreign Affairs. Subcommittee on Europe and the Middle East. *U.S. Interests in the Eastern Mediterranean: Turkey, Greece, and Cyprus.* 98th Congress, 1st Session, June 13, 1983. Report Prepared by the Library of Congress, Congressional Research Service, Foreign Affairs and National Defense Division. Washington, D.C.: U.S. Government Printing Office, 1983.

————. House. Committee on Foreign Affairs. Hearings before the Subcommittee on Europe and the Middle East. *Status and Negotiations in the Cyprus Dispute and Recent Developments in Cyprus.* 98th Congress, 1st Session, November 2, 1983. Washington, D.C.: U.S. Government Printing Office, 1983.

OTHER OFFICIAL DOCUMENTS

Council of Europe. *Report on the Demographic Structure of the Cypriot Communities* (Rapporteur, Mr. Alfonse Cuco, Spain), ADOC 6589, 1403–23/4/92-4-E, adopted by the Assembly on October 7, 1992.

Great Britain. *Conference on Cyprus, Documents Signed and Initialed at Lancaster House on February 19, 1959.* Cmnd. 979. London: HMSO, 1959.

International Committee of the Red Cross, *Convention (IV) Relative to the Protection of Civilian Persons in Time of War,* Geneva, 12 August 1949. See, especially, Section III: Occupied Territories, Article 49, p. 13.

Republic of Cyprus. Government of Cyprus Public Information Office. *Colonization of Occupied Cyprus.* Nicosia, December 1979.

The Montreux Convention (in French and Greek). *Official Gazette of the Kingdom of Greece,* no. 333, August 7, 1936, pp. 1695–1710.

Turkey. Ministry of Foreign Affairs. *Turkey and Cyprus: A Survey of the Cyprus Question with Official Statements of the Turkish Viewpoint.* London: Embassy of Turkey, 1956.

BOOKS AND MONOGRAPHS

Memoirs

Brzezinski, Zbigniew. *Power and Principle: Memoirs of the National Security Adviser, 1977–1981.* New York: Farrar, Straus, Giroux, 1983.

Carter, Jimmy. *Keeping Faith: Memoirs of a President.* Toronto and New York: Bantam Books, 1982.

Christopher, Warren. *In the Stream of History: Shaping Foreign Policy for a New Era.* Stanford: Stanford University Press, 1998.

Clerides, Glafcos. *My Deposition.* Nicosia: Alithia Publishing. In four volumes, 1989–1992.

Dean, John. *Blind Ambition: The White House Years.* New York: Simon and Schuster, 1976.

Eden, Anthony. *The Memoirs of Anthony Eden: Full Circle.* Cambridge: Riverside Press; London: Cassell; and Boston: Houghton Mifflin, 1960.

Ford, Gerald. *A Time to Heal.* New York: Harper and Row, 1979.

Grivas, George. *The Memoirs of General Grivas,* edited by Charles Foley. New York: Frederick Praeger, 1965.

Jordan, Hamilton. *Crises.* New York: G.P. Putman's and Sons, 1982.

Kissinger, Henry. *Years of Renewal.* New York: Simon and Schuster, 1999.

————. *Years of Upheaval.* Boston and Toronto: Little Brown and Co., 1982.

Liddy, G. Gordon. *Will: The Autobiography of G. Gordon Liddy.* 3rd ed. New York: St. Martin's Press, 1977.

Nixon, Richard. *The Memoirs of Richard Nixon.* New York: A Touchstone Book, The Richard Nixon Library Edition, 1990.

Rallis, George. *Politikes Ekmystirevseis, 1950–1989: Apokalyptikes Martyries gia Krisimes Stigmes tes Sychronis Ellinikis Politikis Zoes* (Political Confessions, 1950–1989: Anecdotal Evidence Concerning Critical Moments in Contemporary Greek Political Life). Athens: Proskenio Publishing, 1990.

Vance, Cyrus. *Hard Choices: Critical Years in America's Foreign Policy.* New York: Simon and Schuster, 1983.

Vidalis, Orestis. *Istoriko Imerologio: Chronia Ekpatrismou, 1968–1975* (A Historical Diary: Years of Exile, 1968–1975). 2 vols. Athens: Libro, 1997.

Wright, Jim. *Balance of Power: Presidents and Congress from the Era of McCarthy to the Age of Gingrich.* Atlanta: Turner Publishing Inc.: 1996.

Other Selected Books

Adams, Thomas, and Alvin Cottrell. *Cyprus: Between East and West.* Baltimore: The Johns Hopkins University Press, 1968.

AHI Conference Proceedings. *United States Foreign Policy Regarding Greece, Turkey, and Cyprus: The Rule of Law and American Interests.* Washington, D.C.: American Hellenic Institute, 1989.

Ahmad, Feroz. *The Making of Modern Turkey.* London: Routledge, 1993.

Alasya, Halil Fikret. *Kuzey Kıbrıs Türk Cumhuriyeti Tarihi* (History of the Turkish Republic of Northern Cyprus). Ankara: Türk Kültürü Araştırma Enstitüsü, Yayınları, 1987.

Albright, Joseph. *What Makes Spiro Run: The Life and Times of Spiro Agnew.* New York: Dodd, Mead, and Co., 1972.

Alexandris, Alexis. *The Greek Minority in Istanbul and Greek-Turkish Relations, 1918–1974.* Athens: Center for Asia Minor Studies, 1983.

————, et al., eds. *He Ellino-Tourkikes Scheseis, 1923–1987* (Greek-Turkish Relations, 1923–1987). Athens: Gnose, 1988.

Alford, Jonathan, ed. *Greece and Turkey: Adversity in Alliance.* New York: St. Martin's Press, 1984.

American Psychiatric Association. *Diagnostic and Statistical Manual of Mental Disorders.* 2nd ed. Washington, D.C.: APA, 1968.

————. *Diagnostic and Statistical Manual of Mental Disorders.* 3rd ed. Washington, D.C.: 1980.

Arapakis, Petros. *To Telos tes Siopis* (The End of Silence). Athens: Nea Synora, 2000.

Aristotelous, Aristos. *Greece, Turkey, Cyprus: The Military Balance, 1995–1996.* Nicosia: Cyprus Center for Strategic Studies, 1995.

Attalides, Michael. *Cyprus: Nationalism and International Politics.* New York: St. Martin's Press, 1982.

————, ed. *Cyprus Reviewed.* Nicosia: The Juris Cypri Association, 1977.

Ayman, Gülden, and Nurşin Ateşoğlu Güney, "Değişen Uluslararası Koşullarda Strateji, Türkiye Ve Komşuları" (Turkey and Its Neighbors, Strategy in a Changing International Environment). In Faruk Sönmezoğlu, Derleyen, *Türk Dış Politikasının Analizi* (Analysis of Turkish Foreign Policy). Istanbul: Der Yayınları, 1994.

Bahcheli, Tozun. *Greek-Turkish Relations Since 1955.* Boulder: Westview Press, 1990.

Ball, George. *The Past Has Another Pattern.* New York: W.W. Norton and Co., 1982.

Beschloss, Michael. *Taking Charge: The White House Tapes, 1963–1964.* New York: Touchstone, Simon and Schuster, 1997.

Bill, James. *The Eagle and the Lion: The Tragedy of American-Iranian Relations.* New Haven and London: Yale University Press, 1988.

————. *George Ball: Behind the Scenes in U.S. Foreign Policy.* New Haven: Yale University Press, 1997.

Birand, Mehmet Ali. *Pazaremata (Bargaining).* Greek translation of Birand's book *Diyet.* Athens: Floros Publishers, 1985.

————. *The Generals' Coup in Turkey: An Inside Story of 12 September 1980.* London: Brassey's Defense Publishers, 1987.

————. *Thirty Hot Days.* London, Nicosia, and Istanbul: K. Rustem and Brother, 1985.

Bitsios, Dimitrios. *Cyprus: The Vulnerable Republic.* Thessaloniki: Institute for Balkan Studies, 1975.

Blinkhorn, Martin, and Thanos Veremis, eds. *Modern Greek Nationalism and Nationality.* Athens: Sage-ELIAMEP, 1990.

Brinkley, Douglas. *The Unfinished Presidency: Jimmy Carter's Journey Beyond the White House.* New York: Viking Penguin, 1998.

Brzezinski, Zbigniew. *The Grand Chessboard: American Primacy and Its Geostrategic Imperatives.* New York: Basic Books, 1997.

_____. *The Soviet Bloc: Unity and Conflict.* Cambridge: Harvard University Press, 1967.

Burne, Peter. *Jimmy Carter: A Comprehensive Biography from Plains to Postpresidency.* New York: Scribner, 1997.

Callaghan, James. *Time and Chance.* London: William Collins and Sons, 1987.

Campany, Richard. *Turkey and the United States: The Arms Embargo Period.* New York: Praeger, 1986.

Carter, Jimmy. *Talking Peace: A Vision for a New Generation.* New York: Puffin Books, 1993.

_____. *Why Not the Best? Jimmy Carter, the First Fifty Years.* Fayetteville: The University of Arkansas Press, 1996. (Originally published: Nashville: Broadman Press, 1975.)

Central Intelligence Agency. *The World Factbook: 1997–98.* Washington and London: Brassey's, 1997.

Christodoulou, Miltiades. *He Poreia ton Ellino-Tourkikon Scheseon ke e Kypros* (The Course of Greek-Turkish Relations and Cyprus). 2 vols. Nicosia: Proodos Publishers, 1995.

Clifford, Clark, with Richard Holbrooke. *Counsel to the President: A Memoir.* New York: Random House, 1991.

Clogg, Richard, and George Yannopoulos, eds. *Greece Under Military Rule.* New York: Basic Books, 1972.

Compton, R.J. *A Concise History of Bulgaria.* Cambridge: Cambridge University Press, 1997.

Confino, Michael, and Shimon Shamir, eds. *The U.S.S.R. and the Middle East.* Jerusalem: Israel Universities Press, 1973.

Cottam, Richard. *Nationalism in Iran.* Pittsburgh: Pittsburgh University Press, 1979.

Coufoudakis, Van, ed. *Essays on the Cyprus Conflict.* New York: Pella Publishing Co., 1976.

Couloumbis, Theodore. *Kypriako: Lathi, Didagmata, Prooptikes* (The Cyprus Issue: Mistakes, Lessons, Prospects). Athens: Sideris Publishing, 1996.

_____. *The United States, Greece, and Turkey: The Troubled Triangle.* New York: Praeger, 1983.

Couloumbis, Theodore, and Sally Hicks, eds. *U.S. Foreign Policy Toward Greece and Cyprus: The Clash of Principle and Pragmatism.* Washington, D.C.: The Center for Mediterranean Studies, American University and the American Hellenic Institute, 1975.

Couloumbis, Theodore, and John Iatrides, eds. *Greek-American Relations: A Critical Review.* New York: Pella Publishing Co., 1980.

Couloumbis, Theodore, John Petropoulos, and Harry Psomiades, eds. *Foreign Interference in Greek Politics: A Historical Perspective.* New York: Pella Publishing Co., 1976.

Cranshaw, Nancy. *The Cyprus Revolt: An Account of the Struggle for Union with Greece.* London: George Allen, 1978.

Cronin, Thomas, and Rexford Turgwell, eds. *The Presidency Reappraised.* 2nd ed. New

York: Praeger, 1977.

Dallek, Robert. *Flawed Giant: Lyndon Johnson and His Times.* New York: Oxford University Press, 1998.

Danopoulos, Constantine. *Warriors and Politicians in Modern Greece.* Chapel Hill: Documentary Publications, 1984.

Denktash, Rauf. *The Cyprus Triangle.* London: K. Rustem and Brother, 1988.

Dobbs, Michael. *Madeleine Albright: A Twentieth-Century Odyssey.* Henry Holt and Co.: New York, 1999.

Dodd, Clement, ed. *Turkish Foreign Policy: New Prospects.* Cambridgeshire: Eothen Press, 1992.

Donovan, Hendley. *Roosevelt to Reagan.* New York: Harper and Row, 1985.

Engin, Anın. *Atatürkçülük Savaşımızda Kıbrıs Barış Destanımız* (Our Cyprus Peace Epic in our Fight for Atatürkism). Istanbul: Gün Matbaası, 1975.

Erksan, Metin. *Mare Nostrum.* Istanbul: Hil Yayın, 1997.

Ertekün, Necati. *The Cyprus Dispute and the Birth of the Turkish Republic of Northern Cyprus.* 2nd ed. Nicosia: K. Rustem and Brother, 1984.

Findley, Paul. *They Dare Speak Out.* Chicago: Lawrence Hill Books, 1989.

Foley, Charles. *Legacy of Strife: Cyprus: From Rebellion to Civil War.* Baltimore: Penguin, 1964.

Foley, Charles, and W. I. Scobie. *The Struggle for Cyprus.* Stanford: Hoover Institution Press, 1975.

Foot, Michael, and Mervyn Jones. *Guilty Men, 1957: Suez and Cyprus.* New York: Rinehart, 1957.

Frank, Thomas, and Edward Weisband, *Foreign Policy by Congress.* New York: Oxford University Press, 1979.

Fuller, Graham, and Ian O. Lesser, eds. *Turkey's New Geopolitics: From the Balkans to Western China.* Boulder, Colorado: Westview Press, A Rand Study, 1993.

Gregoriades, Solon. *Istoria tes Diktatorias* (History of the Dictatorship). Athens: K. Kapopoulos Publications, 1975.

Hale, William. *Turkish Politics and the Military.* London: Routledge, 1994.

Halley, Laurence. *Ancient Affections: Ethnic Groups and Foreign Policy.* New York: Praeger, 1985.

Harris, George. *Troubled Alliance: Turkish-American Problems in Historical Perspective, 1945–1971.* Washington, D.C.: American Enterprise Institute and Hoover Institution, 1972.

————. *Turkey: Coping with Crisis.* Boulder, Colorado: Westview Press, 1985.

Hart, Parker. *Two NATO Allies at the Threshold of War: Cyprus—A First Hand Account of Crisis Management, 1965–1968.* Durham, N.C., and London: Duke University Press, 1990.

Henze, Paul. *Turkey and Ataturk's Legacy: Turkey's Political Evolution, Turkish-U.S. Relations and Prospects for the 21st Century.* Haarlem, Netherlands: Research Center for Turkestan and Azerbaijan, Turquoise Series, no. 2, 1998.

Hersch, Seymour. *The Price of Power: Kissinger and the Nixon White House.* New York: Summit Books, 1983.

Hitchens, Christopher. *Hostage to History: Cyprus, from the Ottomans to Kissinger.* London, New York: Verso, 1977.

Holland, Robert. *Britain and the Revolt in Cyprus, 1954–1959.* Oxford: Oxford University Press, 1998.

Howard, Harry. *Turkey, the Straits, and U.S. Policy.* Baltimore: Johns Hopkins University Press, 1974.

Hunter, Robert. *Presidential Control of Foreign Policy.* New York: Praeger, 1980.

Iatrides, John. *Revolt in Athens: The Greek Communist "Second Round," 1944–1945.* Princeton: Princeton University Press, 1972.

Ierodiakonou, Leontios. *To Kypriako Problema* (The Cyprus Question). Athens: Papazisis, 1975.

Ilhan, Suat. *Türk Askeri Kültürünün Tarihi Gelişmesi: Kutsal Ocak* (The Historical Evolution of Turkish Military Culture: Sacred Heart). Istanbul: Ötüken, 1999.

International Institute of Strategic Studies. *The Military Balance: 1998/9.* London: Oxford University Press, 1998.

Ioannides, Christos P. *America's Iran: Injury and Catharsis.* Lanham, New York, and London: University Press of America, 1984.

————. *In Turkey's Image: The Transformation of Occupied Cyprus into a Turkish Province.* New Rochelle, New York: Aristide D. Caratzas, Publisher, 1991.

————, ed. *Cyprus: Domestic Dynamics and External Constraints.* New Rochelle, New York: Aristide D. Caratzas, Publisher, 1992.

Isaacson, Walter. *Kissinger: A Biography.* New York: A Touchstone Book, 1992.

Ismail, Sabahattin. *Kıbrıs Sorunu* (The Cyprus Problem). Istanbul: K.K.T.C. Turizm ve Kültür Bakanlığı Yayınları, 1986.

Joseph, Joseph S. *Cyprus: Ethnic Conflict and International Politics.* New York: St. Martin's Press, 1997.

Kalb, Marvin, and Bernard Kalb. *Kissinger: The Virtuoso of Diplomacy, the Legend, the Dazzle, the Man Within.* New York: Dell Publishing, 1975.

Karpat, Kemal. *Turkey's Foreign Policy in Transition: 1950–1974.* Leiden: E.J. Brill, 1975.

Keddie, Niki. *Roots of Revolution: An Interpretive History.* New Haven: Yale University Press, 1981.

Koumoulides, John. *Cyprus in Transition, 1960–1985.* London: Trigraph, 1986.

Kutler, Stanley I. *Abuse of Power: The New Nixon Tapes.* New York: The Free Press, 1997.

————. *The Wars of Watergate: The Last Crisis of Richard Nixon.* New York: W.W. Norton and Co., 1992.

Kyriakides, Stanley. *Constitutionalism and Crisis Government.* Philadelphia: University of Pennsylvania Press, 1968.

Kyrris, Costas. *History of Cyprus.* Nicosia: Nicocles Publishing, 1985.

Landau, Jacob. *Pan-Turkism in Turkey: A Study of Irredentism.* Hamden, Conn.: Archon Books, 1981.

Llewellyn-Smith, Michael. *Ionian Vision: Greece in Asia Minor, 1919–1922.* London: Allen Lane, 1973.

Mackenzie, Kenneth. *Greece and Turkey: Disarray on NATO's Southern Flank.* Study No. 154. London: The Institute for the Study of Conflict, 1983.

Mango, Andrew. *Turkey: A Delicately Poised Ally.* Washington Paper Series, no. 28. London: Sage Publications, 1975.

Manizade, Derviş. *Kıbrıs: Dün, Bugün, Yarın* (Cyprus: Yesterday, Today, Tomorrow). Istanbul: Kıbrıs Türk Kültür Derneği, Yaylacık Matbaası, 1975.

Markides, Kyriacos. *The Rise and Fall of the Cyprus Republic.* New Haven: Yale University Press, 1977.

Meininger, Thomas. *The Formation of a Nationalist Bulgarian Intelligentsia, 1835–1878.* New York: Garland Publishing, 1987.

Mirbagheri, Farid. *Cyprus and International Peacekeeping.* London: Hurst and Co., 1998.

Moens, Alexander. *Foreign Policy Under Carter: Testing Multiple Advocacy Decision Making.* Boulder, Colorado: Westview Press, 1990.

Morris, Kenneth. *Jimmy Carter: American Moralist.* Athens, Georgia: University of Georgia Press, 1996.

Moskos, Charles. *Greek Americans: Struggle and Success.* 2nd ed. New Brunswick: Transaction, 1989.

Necatigil, Zaim. *The Cyprus Question and the Turkish Position in International Law.* Oxford: Oxford University Press, 1989.

Nikolaou, Ioannis. *O Diaplous ton Tourkikon Stenon kata teis Diethneis Synthykes kai Praktiki* (Passage Through the Turkish Straits According to International Treaties and Practice). Athens: Sideris Publishers, 1995.

Nicoloff, Assen. *The Bulgarian Resurgence.* Cleveland: Published by the author, 1987.

O'Malley, Brendan, and Ian Craig. *The Cyprus Conspiracy: America, Espionage, and the Turkish Invasion.* London: I.B.Tauris Publishers, 1999.

Öznur, Hakkı. *Ülkücü Hareket* (The Idealist Movement), vol. 1. Ankara: Alternatif Yayınları, 1999.

Pallis, Alexandros. *Greece's Anatolian Venture and After: 1915–1922.* London: Methuen and Co. Ltd., 1937.

Papachelas, Alexis. *O Viasmos tes Demokratias: O Amerikanikos Paragon, 1947–1967* (The Rape of Democracy: The American Factor, 1947–1967). Athens: Estia, 1977.

Papadopoulos, George. *To Pistevo Mas: Logoi ke Synentevxeis* (Our Creed: Speeches and Interviews). 8 vols. Athens: Press General Directorate, 1968–1972.

Papandreou, Andreas. *Democracy at Gunpoint.* New York: Doubleday and Co., 1970.

————. *He Ellada stous Ellines* (Greece for the Greeks). Athens: Karathanasi Publications, 1976.

Papandreou, Margaret. *Nightmare in Athens.* Engelwood Cliffs, N.J.: Prentice Hall, 1970.

Patrick, Richard. *Political Geography and the Cyprus Conflict: 1963–1971.* Department of Geography, Publication Series no. 4. University of Waterloo, 1976.

Psomiades, Harry J. *The Eastern Question, the Last Phase: A Study in Greek-Turkish Diplomacy.* Thessaloniki: Institute for Balkan Studies, 1968.

Psomiades, Harry, and Alice Scourby, eds. *The Greek American Community in Transition.* New York: Pella Publishing Company, 1982.

Psomiades, Harry, and Stavros Thomadakis, eds. *Greece, the New Europe, and the Changing International Order.* New York: Pella Publishing Company, 1993.

Quandt, William. *Camp David: Peacemaking and Politics.* Washington, D.C.: The Brookings Institution, 1986.

Ramazani, Ruhollah. *The United States and Iran.* New York: Praeger, 1982.

Reddaway, John. *Burdened with Cyprus: The British Connection.* London and Nicosia: Rustem and Weidenfeld and Nicholson, 1986.

Roosevelt, Kermit. *Countercoup: The Struggle for the Control of Iran.* New York: McGraw Hill, 1979.

Rosenbaum, Herbert D., and Alexej Ugrinsky, eds. *Jimmy Carter: Foreign Policy and Post Presidential Years.* Westport, Connecticut: Greenwood Press, 1994.

Rossides, Eugene, ed. *The Truman Doctrine of Aid to Greece: A Fifty-Year Retrospective.* New York and Washington, D.C: The Academy of Political Science and the American Hellenic Institute, 1998.

Rousseas, Stephen. *The Death of Democracy: Greece and the American Conscience.* New York: Grove Press, 1967.

Rozakis, Christos, and Petros Stangos. *The Turkish Straits.* Dortrecht: Martinus Nijhoff, 1987.

Rubin, Barry. *Paved with Good Intentions: The American Experience in Iran.* New York: Oxford University Press, 1980.

Rubinstein, Alvin. *Soviet Policy Toward Turkey, Iran, and Afghanistan.* New York: Praeger, 1982.

————. *The Foreign Policy of the Soviet Union.* New York: Random House, 1972.

Saikal, Amin. *The Rise and Fall of the Shah.* Princeton: Princeton University Press, 1980.

Salih, Halil Ibrahim. *Cyprus: The Impact of Diverse Nationalism on a State.* University of Alabama Press, 1978.

Saloutos, Theodore. *The Greeks in the United States.* Cambridge: Harvard University Press, 1964.

Sarris, Neoklis. *E Alli Plevra. Politiki Chronographia tes Tourkikes Eisvolis sten Kypro me Vasi Tourkikes Piges* (The Other Side: A Political Chronicle of the Turkish Invasion of Cyprus Based on Turkish Sources). Athens: Gramme Publishers, 1977.

Scourby, Alice. *The Greek Americans.* Boston: Twayne, 1984.

Sergis, George. *E Mache tes Kyprou: Ioulios-Avgoustos 1974* (The Battle of Cyprus: July-August 1974). Athens: Vlassis Bros., 1996.

Servas, Ploutis. *Kypriako: Evthines* (The Cyprus Issue: Responsibilities). Athens: Gramme Publishers, 1980.

Sheffer, Gabriel. *Modern Diasporas in International Politics.* New York: St. Martin's Press, 1986.

Sherer, John. *Blocking the Sun: The Cyprus Conflict.* Minneapolis, Minn.: A Modern Greek Studies Yearbook Supplement, University of Minnesota, 1997.

Stavrou, Nicolaos, ed. *Greece Under Socialism: A NATO Ally Adrift.* New Rochelle, New York: Aristide D. Caratzas, Publisher, 1988.

Stearns, Monteagle. *Entangled Allies: U.S. Policy Toward Greece, Turkey, and Cyprus.* New York: Council on Foreign Relations Press, 1992.

Stephens, Robert. *Cyprus, A Place of Arms: Power Politics and Ethnic Conflict in the Eastern Mediterranean.* London: Pall Mall Press, 1966.

Stern, Lawrence. *The Wrong Horse: The Politics of Intervention and the Failure of American Policy.* New York: New York Times Books, 1977.

Strategou, Xenofontos. *He Ellada sten Mikra Asia: Istoriki Episkopese* (Greece in Asia Minor: A Historical Overview). Athens: Demiourgia Publishers, 5th ed., 1994, 1st ed., 1925.

Strout, Kandy. *How Jimmy Won: The Victory Campaign from Plains to the White House.* New York: Morrow, 1977.

Summers, Anthony. *The Arrogance of Power: The Secret World of Richard Nixon.* New York: Viking, 2000.

Tempo, *1923–1993: Türkiye'nin 70 Yılı—Gün, Gün Cumhuriyet Tarihi* (1923–1993: 70 Years of Turkey—Day to Day History of the Republic), vol. II. Istanbul: Tempo Kitapları, no. 9, 1994.

Tsoukalas, Constantine. *The Greek Tragedy.* London: Penguin, 1969.

Türkeş, Alparslan. *Dış Politikamiz ve Kıbrıs* (Our Foreign Policy and Cyprus). Istanbul: Kıbrıs Türk Kültür Derneği, 1966.

Tzortzis, Costas. *To Chroniko tes Kypriakes Tragodias: Dokumenta gia to Praxikopima ke ten Eisvoli* (The Chronicle of the Cyprus Tragedy: Documents on the Coup and the Invasion). Nicosia: Lithopress, 1991.

Vali, Ferenc. *Bridge Across the Bosporus: The Foreign Policy of Turkey.* Baltimore: The Johns Hopkins University Press, 1971.

Vatikiotis, P.J. *Greece: A Political Essay.* Beverly Hills, California: Sage Publications, 1974.

Veremis, Thanos. *The Military in Greek Politics: From Independence to Democracy.* Montreal: Black Rose Books, 1997.

Vlahos, Helen. *House Arrest.* Boston: Gambit, Inc., 1970.

Volkan, Vamik. *Cyprus: War and Adaptation.* Charlottesville, Virginia: University of Virginia Press, 1979.

Vryonis, Speros, Jr. *The Turkish State and History: Cleo Meets the Grey Wolf.* Thessaloniki: Institute for Balkan Studies, 1982.

————, ed. *Cyprus Between East and West.* Herakleion, Crete: Published for the Alexander S. Onassis Center at New York University by Crete University Press, 1994.

————, ed. *Greece on the Road to Democracy: From the Junta to PASOK.* New Rochelle, New York: Aristide D. Caratzas, Publisher, 1991.

Watanabe, Paul. *Ethnic Groups, Congress, and American Foreign Policy: The Politics of the Turkish Arms Embargo.* Westport, Connecticut, and London: Greenwood Press, 1984.

Watson, Bruce, and Susan M. Watson, eds. *The Soviet Navy: Strengths and Liabilities.* Boulder: Westview Press, 1986.

Weber, Frank. *The Evasive Neutral: Germany, Britain, and the Quest for a Turkish Alliance in the Second World War.* Columbia, Missouri, and London: University of Missouri Press, 1979.

Woodhouse, C.M. *The Rise and Fall of the Colonels.* New York: Franklin Watts, 1985.

Woodward, Bob, and Carl Bernstein. *All the President's Men.* New York: Simon and Schuster, 1974.

Xydis, Stephen. *Cyprus: Reluctant Republic.* The Hague: Mouton, 1974.

ARTICLES

Adams, T.W. "The First Republic of Cyprus: A Review of an Unworkable Constitution." *Western Political Science Quarterly*, vol. 19, no. 3 (September 1966): pp. 475–490.

Ağaoguları, Mehmet Ali. "The Ultra-Nationalist Right." In *Turkey in Transition: New Perspectives*, edited by Irvin Cemil Schick and Ertuğrul Ahmed Tonak. New York: Oxford University Press, 1987.

"Albright at War: Behind the Scenes with Secretary of State as She Pushes for Victory in Kosovo." *Time* (May 17, 1999).

"All About the MHP." *Turkish Daily News*, April 27, 1999.

Allen, Keith. "The Black Sea Fleet and Mediterranean Naval Operations." In *The Soviet Navy: Strengths and Liabilities*, edited by Bruce Watson and Susan M. Watson. Boulder, Colorado: Westview Press, 1986.

"An Unproductive Embargo." *Washington Star*, July 22, 1975.

Arikan, Buran. "The Programme of the Nationalist Action Party: An Iron Hand in a Velvet Glove?" In *Turkey Before and After Ataturk: Internal and External Affairs*, edited by Sylvia Kedourie. London: Frank Cass, 1999.

Barry, Brian. "Political Accommodation and Consociational Democracy." *British Journal of Political Science* 5 (October 1975): pp. 477–505.

Bilge, Suat. "The Cyprus Conflict and Turkey." In *Turkish Foreign Policy in Transition: 1950–1974*, edited by Kemal Karpat. Leiden: E.J. Brill, 1975.

Birand, Mehmet Ali. "Agca Foresaw His Return." *Turkish Daily News*, June 15, 2000.

Broder, David. "Halos and Hardball from the White House: Carter is an Example of Good Character, but Bad Political Skills." *Washington Post*, September 23, 1998.

Burns, Nicholas (U.S. Ambassador to Greece). Interview in the magazine *Greek America*, vol. 4, issue 6 (September 1998).

Buzan, Barry. "The Status and Future of the Montreux Convention." *Survival*, vol. 18, no. 6 (November-December 1976): p. 243.

Campbell, John. "The United States and the Cyprus Question, 1974–75." In *Essays on the Cyprus Question*, edited by Van Coufoudakis. New York: Pella Publishing Company, 1976.

Cevik, Ilnur. "Agca Back Home, Eyes on MHP." *Turkish Daily News*, June 15, 2000.

"Congress and Turkey." *Chicago Tribune*, July 16, 1975.

Copley, Gregory R. "Turkey Falters on the Edge of Ataturk's Dream." *Defense and Foreign Affairs Strategic Policy: The Journal of the International Strategic Studies Association, Alexandria, VA*, vol. xxviii, no. 3 (March 2000): p. 8.

Coufoudakis, Van. "Cyprus and the European Convention of Human Rights: The Law and Politics of Cyprus vs. Turkey, Applications 6780/74 and 6950/75." *Human Rights Quarterly*, vol. 4 (1982): pp. 450–473.

———. "The Dynamics of Political Partition and Division in Multiethnic and Multireligious Societies—The Cyprus Case." In *Essays on the Cyprus Conflict*, edited by Van Coufoudakis. New York: Pella Publishing Company, 1976, pp. 27–490.

———. "The Greek-American Lobby and Its Influence on Greek Foreign Policy." *Mediterranean Quarterly*, vol. 2. no. 4 (Fall 1991): pp. 70–82.

———. "The Reverse Influence Phenomenon: The Impact of the Greek-American

Lobby on the Foreign Policy of Greece." In *Diasporas in World Politics: The Greeks in Comparative Perspective*, edited by Dimitris Constas and Athanasios Platias. London: The Macmillan Press, 1993, pp. 51–75.

———. "To Kypriako, he Ellino-Tourkikes Scheseis, ke he Yperdynameis." (The Cyprus Issue, Greek-Turkish Relations, and the Superpowers). In *He Ellino-Tourkikes Scheseis, 1923–1987* (Greek-Turkish Relations, 1923–1987), edited by Alexis Alexandris et al. Athens: Gnose, 1988, pp. 215–268.

———. "U.S. Foreign Policy and the Cyprus Question: An Interpretation." *Millennium, Journal of International Studies* 5, no. 3 (Winter 1976–1977): 245–268.

"Critics Say Greece Gaining Time not to Solve Major Issues." *Turkish Daily News*, April 6, 2001.

Ecevit, Bulent. "A Speech on Turkish Foreign Policy." *Turkish Review of Balkan Studies, Istanbul* (Annual 1998/1999): pp. 9–19.

Elekdağ, Şükrü. "The Greek Base in Paphos and the S-300s." *Milliyet*, September 22, 1997.

Evryviades, Marios. "The Problem of Cyprus." *Current History*, vol. 70, no. 412 (January 1976): pp. 18–21, 38–42.

———. "The Umbilical Relationship: Greece and the United States." *Hellenic Studies*, Quebec, Canada, vol. 5, no. 2 (Autumn 1997): pp. 153–167.

———. "The U.S. and the Search for a Negotiated Solution in Cyprus." Athens University of Economics and Business, July 1994.

———. "Turkey's Role in the United States Strategy During and After the Cold War." *Mediterranean Quarterly*, vol. 9, no. 2 (Spring 1998): pp. 30–51.

Gelb, Leslie. "Inside the Cyprus Crisis: How U.S. Policy Appeared to Change Course." *New York Times*, September 9, 1974.

"Getting the Turks to Move on Cyprus." *Newsday*, July 11, 1975.

Goldbloom, Maurice. "United States Policy in Post-War Greece." In *Greece Under Military Rule*, edited by Richard Clogg and George Yannopoulos. New York: Basic Books, 1972, pp. 228–254.

Grunwald, Harry. "Are We 'Destroying' Jimmy Carter?" *Time* (May 15, 1978): pp. 97–98.

Hackett, Clifford. "The Role of Congress and Greek-American Relations." In *Greek-American Relations: A Critical Review*, edited by Theodore Couloumbis and John Iatrides. New York: Pella Publishing Co., 1980, pp. 131–147.

"Hard Line Party Wins Turkish Cypriot Elections." *Associated Press*, December 8, 1998.

Harrington, Joseph F. "American-Romanian Relations: A Case Study in Carter's Human Rights Policy." In *Jimmy Carter: Foreign Policy and Post Presidential Years*, edited by Herbert D. Rosenbaum and Alexej Ugrinsky. Westport, Connecticut: Greenwood Press, 1994, pp. 89–101.

Henn, Francis. "The Nicosia Airport Incident of 1974—A Peacekeeping Gamble." *International Peacekeeping*, vol. I, no. 1 (Spring 1994): pp. 80–98.

Henze, Paul. "Out of Kilter—Greeks, Turks, and U.S. Policy." *The National Interest*, no. 8 (Summer 1987): pp. 71–82.

———. "Turkey: Toward the Twenty-First Century." In *Turkey's New Geopolitics: From the Balkans to Western China*, edited by Graham Fuller and Ian O. Lesser.

Boulder, Colorado: Westview Press, A Rand Study, 1993, pp. 1–35.

Hunt, Sir David. "The Use of Force in the Middle East: The Case of Cyprus." *Mediterranean Quarterly*, vol. 2, no. 1 (Winter 1991): pp. 66–70.

"Insulted, Far-Right Party Snubs Coalition Talks in Turkey." *Associated Press*, May 16, 1999.

Ioannides, Christos P. "Greek Americans and the Cyprus Issue: 1980–1992." In Hellenic Studies Forum, ed., *Greeks in English Speaking Countries*. Melbourne: Ellikon Fine Printers, 1993, pp. 239–257.

———. "The Truman Doctrine: Has it Benefited Greece?" *The Greek American* (March 15, 1997): p. 8.

———. "The Turkish Occupation of Northern Cyprus: Demographic and Political Consequences." In *Cyprus Between East and West*, edited by Speros Vryonis, Jr. Herakleion, Crete: Published for the Alexander S. Onassis Center at New York University by Crete University Press, 1994, pp. 108–131.

———. "From Bill Clinton to George W. Bush: Greek American Frustrations and Hopes." *The National Herald*, New York (February 17–18, 2001): p. 7.

"Israeli Press Insistent Over Alleged Armenian Genocide." *Turkish Daily News*, May 15, 2000.

"Jewish Lobby Loses a Big One." *Time* (May 29, 1978): pp. 14–15.

Kadritzke, Niels. "Turkish Cypriots Dream of Europe." *Le Monde Diplomatique*, August-September 1998.

Kamm, Henry. "Papandreou: The Politics of Anti-Americanism." *New York Times Magazine*, April 7, 1985.

Karpat, Kemal. "Turkish-Soviet Relations." In *Turkish Foreign Policy in Transition, 1950–1974*, edited by Kemal Karpat. Leiden: E.J. Brill, 1975, pp. 73–107.

Kinzer, Steven. "Results in Turkish Election Reflect Kurdish War's Fault Line: The Two Parties That Did Best [DSP and MHP] Insist There is No Kurdish Problem." *New York Times*, April 20, 1999.

———. "Will Turk Tell Secrets on Shooting of the Pope?" *New York Times*, June 15, 2000.

Kitroeff, Alexander. "Greek American Lobbying, 1974–1978: Myth and Realities." *The Greek American*, New York, January 27, 1980, pp. 12–14.

Kitromilides, Paschalis. "From Coexistence to Confrontation: The Dynamics of Ethnic Conflict in Cyprus." In *Cyprus Reviewed*, edited by Michael Attalides. Nicosia: Juris Cypri Association, 1977, pp. 35–70.

Kondrake, Morton. "The Greek Lobby." *The New Republic* (April 29, 1978): pp. 14–16.

Kuniholm, Bruce. "Turkey and the West Since World War II." In *Turkey Between East and West*, edited by Vojtech Mastny and R. Craig Nation. Boulder, Colorado: Westview Press, 1996.

Kut, Sule. "On Challenge, Threat, and Violation in Turkish-Greek Relations." *Turkish Review of Balkan Studies*, Istanbul (Annual 1988/1999): pp. 95–102.

Laipson, Helen. "Cyprus: A Quarter Century of U.S. Diplomacy." In *Cyprus in Transition, 1960–1985*, edited by John Koumoulides. London: Trigraph, 1986, pp. 54–81.

———. "U.S. Policy Towards Greece and Turkey Since 1974." In *The Greek-Turkish Conflict in the 1990s*, edited by Dimitris Constas. London: MacMillan, 1991.

Landau, Jacob. "Johnson's 1964 Letter to Inonu and the Greek Lobbying of the White House." *Jerusalem Papers on Peace Problems.* Jerusalem: Hebrew University, 1979.

Leigh, Monroe. "The Cypriot Communities and International Law." *Turkish Review Quarterly Digest* 22 (Winter 1990): pp. 47–60.

Lesser, Ian O. "Bridge or Barrier? Turkey and the West After the Cold War." In *Turkey's New Geopolitics: From the Balkans to Western China*, edited by Graham Fuller and Ian O. Lesser. Boulder, Colorado: Westview Press, A Rand Study, 1993, pp. 99–140.

"Lift the Embargo Now." *Pittsburgh Press*, September 20, 1975.

"Lift the Turkish Arms Embargo." *Christian Science Monitor*, July 28, 1975.

Maroudas, Peter. "Greek American Involvement in Contemporary Politics." In *The Greek American Community in Transition*, edited by Harry Psomiades and Alice Scourby. New York: Pella Publishing Company, 1982, pp. 93–109.

McCaskill, Charles. "The United States and Cyprus from 1974 to 1991." In *Cyprus: Domestic Dynamics, External Constraints*, edited by Christos P. Ioannides. New Rochelle, New York: Aristide D. Caratzas, Publisher, pp. 105–131.

McDonald, R.St.J. "International Law and the Conflict in Cyprus." *The Canadian Yearbook of International Law*, vol. 19 (1981): pp. 3–49.

"Military Aid Bill: Turkey Arms Ban Lifted." *1978 Congressional Quarterly Almanac.* 95th Congress, Second Session, vol. xxxxiv, Washington, D.C., 1978.

Nimetz, Matthew. "The Cyprus Problem Revisited." *Mediterranean Quarterly*, vol. 2, no. 1 (Winter 1991): pp. 58–65.

Olgun, Mustafa Ergun. "Turkey's Tough Neighborhood: Security Dimensions of the Cyprus Conflict." In *Cyprus: The Need for New Perspectives*, edited by Clement Dodd. Huntington, Cambridgeshire: Eothen Press, 1999, pp. 232–233.

Pappas, Peter. "The Junta in America." *The Greek American* (April 18, 1987): pp. 20–21.

Pyrros, James. "PASOK and the Greek Americans: Origins and Development." In *Greece Under Socialism: A NATO Ally Adrift*, edited by Nicolaos Stavrou. New Rochelle, New York: Aristide D. Caratzas, Publisher, 1988, pp. 211–250.

Risen, James. "Secrets of History: The CIA in Iran." *New York Times*, April 16, 2000.

Rosati, Jerel. "The Rise and Fall of America's First Post-Cold War Foreign Policy." In *Jimmy Carter: Foreign Policy and Post Presidential Years*, edited by Herbert D. Rosenbaum and Alexej Ugrinsky. Westport, Connecticut: Greenwood Press, 1994, pp. 35–52.

Rossides, Eugene. "Cyprus and the Rule of Law." *Syracuse Journal of International Law and Commerce*, co. 17, no. 1 (Spring 1991): pp. 21–90.

"Senate 54–44 Backed Sale of Jets." *New York Times*, May 16, 1978.

Smith, Hedrick. "A Changed Man, a Changed Office, Not Yet in Step." *New York Times*, May 21, 1978.

Smith, Terence. "A Changed Man." *New York Times*, May 21, 1978.

_____. "Why Carter Admitted the Shah." *New York Times Magazine*, May 17, 1981.

Stavrou, Nicolaos. "The Hellenic-American Community in Foreign Policy Considerations of the Motherland." In *Diasporas in World Politics: The Greeks in Comparative Perspective*, edited by Dimitris Constas and Athanasios Platias. London:

Macmillan Press, 1993, pp. 76–87.

Tachau, Frank. "Republic of Turkey." In *The Middle East: Its Government and Politics*, edited by Abdi Al-Marayati. Belmont, California, Duxbury Press, 1972.

————. "Turkish Foreign Policy and Cyprus." In *Cyprus Between East and West*, edited by Speros Vryonis, Jr. Herakleion, Crete: Published for the Alexander S. Onassis Center at New York University by Crete University Press, 1994, pp. 75–83.

Taubman, Philip, and Leslie Gelb. "U.S. Aides Cautious in Pope Shooting." *New York Times*, January 27, 1983, p. A12.

"A Tragedy Offstage No More." *Jerusalem Post*, May 12, 2000.

Tsilas, Loucas. "Greek-Turkish Relations in the Post-Cold War Era." *Fordham International Law Journal*, vol. 20, no. 5 (June 1997): pp. 1589–1605.

"The Turkish Aid Knot." *Indianapolis Star*, July 19, 1975.

"Turkish-Israeli Relations Sour." *Turkish Daily News*, May 11, 2000.

Vatikiotis, P.J. "Greece and the Crisis in the Eastern Mediterranean." *Millennium: Journal of International Studies*, vol. 4, no. 1 (Spring 1975): pp. 75–81.

Vavrina, Vernon. "The Carter Human Rights Policy: Political Idealism and Realpolitik." In *Jimmy Carter: Foreign Policy and Post Presidential Years*, edited by Herbert D. Rosenbaum and Alexej Ugrinsky. Westport, Connecticut: Greenwood Press, 1994, pp. 103–117.

"Victory at a Price." *Newsweek*, June 14, 1999, pp. 27–29.

Vlanton, Elias, and Diana Alicia. "The 1959 Cyprus Agreement: Oracle of Disaster." *The Journal of the Hellenic Diaspora*, vol. xi, no. 4 (Winter 1984): pp. 5–31.

Warren, James, Jr. "Origins of the 'Greek Economic Miracle': The Truman Doctrine and the Marshall Plan Development and Stabilization Program." In *The Truman Doctrine of Aid to Greece: A Fifty-Year Retrospective*, edited by Eugene Rossides. New York and Washington D.C.: The Academy of Political Science and the American Hellenic Institute, 1998, pp. 77–105.

NEWSPAPERS AND PERIODICALS

United States

Chicago Tribune (Chicago)
Indianapolis Star (Indianapolis)
Newsday (New York)
New York Times (New York)
Newsweek (New York)
Pittsburgh Press (Pittsburgh)
Time (New York)
Wall Street Journal (New York)
Washington Post (Washington, D.C.)
Washington Star (Washington, D.C.)

Greek American Press

Ahepan (New York)

Ethnikos Kyrex (National Herald) (New York)
Greek America (Burlington, Massachusetts)
The Greek American (New York)
Proini (New York)

Britain

Guardian (Manchester)
Observer (London)
The Times (London)
Sunday Times (London)

Greece

Apogevmatini
Eleftherotypia
Kathimerini
To Vima
Vradini

ARCHIVES

Archeio, Gegonota, Keimena: Konstantinos Karamanlis, 50 Chronia Politikis Istorias
    (Archive, Events, Records: Constantine Karamanlis, 50 Years of Political His-
    tory). Constantinos Svolopoulos, General Editor. Athens, Ekdotiki Athinon, 11
    vols., 1992–1996.
The Archives on the Greek American Mobilization in the Aftermath of the Turkish
    Invasion: *Serge Hadji Archives of the Pan-Hellenic Emergency Committee,*
    1974–1978, New York. These archives are at the Speros Basil Vryonis Center for
    the Study of Hellenism, Rancho Cordova, California.

Index

505